2014 NHL DRAFT BLACK BOOK
PROSPECT SCOUTING REPORTS AND DRAFT RANKINGS

by HockeyProspect.com

© 2014 by The Hockey Press

ALL RIGHTS RESERVED.

ISBN-13: 978-0991677559 (The Hockey Press)

ISBN-10: 0991677552

TABLE OF CONTENTS — 3

2014 NHL DRAFT RANKINGS 9
2014 NHL DRAFT PROSPECTS 14

- Aho, Sebastian 15
- Amadio, Michael 15
- Angello, Anthony 16
- Aronsson, Emil 16
- Atwal, Arvin 17
- Aubé-Kubel, Nicolas 17
- Audette, Daniel 18
- Bahl, Julien 18
- Baillie, Tyson 19
- Baltisberger, Phil 19
- Barbashev, Ivan 20
- Bayreuther, Gavin 21
- Beaudoin, Guillaume 21
- Bennett, Sam 21
- Bergman, Julius 22
- Bratina, Zach 28
- Brown, Graeme 29
- Brown, Chris 30
- Bukarts, Rihards 30
- Bunting, Michael 30
- Cave, Colby 31
- Centorame, Santino 31
- Chapman, Joshua 31
- Chartier, Rourke 32
- Chatham, Connor 32
- Collins, Ryan 33
- Connolly, Josh 33
- Cook, Dawson 34
- Core, Zachary 34
- Cornel, Eric 35
- Cramarossa, Michael 35
- Cummins, Conor 36
- Dal Colle, Michael 36
- Darcy, Cam 37
- De Leo, Chase 37
- De Sousa, Daniel 38
- DeAngelo, Anthony 38
- DeLuca, Anthony 39
- Demko, Thatcher 39
- Descheneau, Jaedon 40
- DiGiacinto, Cristiano 40
- DiPerna, Dylan 41
- Donaghey, Cody 41
- Donato, Ryan 42
- Dougherty, Jack 42
- Draisaitl, leon 43
- Duchesne, Jonathan 44
- Duke, Reid 44
- Dulong, Trevor 45
- Dvorak, Christian 45
- Ehlers, Nikolaj 45
- Eiserman, Shane 47
- Ekblad, Aaron 47
- Elie, Tristen 48
- Englund, Andreas 48
- Evans, Jake 48
- Fabbri, Robby 49
- Fazleev, Radel 50
- Fiala, Kevin 50
- Fidler, Miguel 51
- Fiegl, Jared 51
- Fleury, Haydn 51
- Flinn, Jack 52
- Ford, Keegan 53
- Forsling, Gustav 53
- Fortunato, Brandon 54
- Foss, Ryan 54
- Franklin, C.J. 55
- Fram, Jason 55
- Friedman, Mark 55
- Gadoury, Philippe 56
- Gagnon, Ryan 57
- Gambrell, Dylan 57
- Garcia, C.J. 58
- Gardiner, Reid 58
- Garland, Conor 58
- Gavrikov, Vladislav 59
- Gendron, Miles 59
- Gersich, Shane 59
- Gilligan, Jeffrey 60
- Glover, Jack 60
- Goetz, Keigan 61
- Goldobin, Nikolay 61
- Goulet, Alexandre 62
- Graham, Charlie 62
- Grasskamp, Charley 63
- Gutierrez, Justin 63
- Halbert, Nathanael 63
- Halladay, Logan 64
- Halverson, Brandon 64
- Hargrave, Brett 65
- Harlacher, Edson 65
- Hawkey, Hayden 65
- Hawryluk, Jayce 66
- Haydon, Aaron 67
- Helewka, Adam 67
- Herbst, Liam 68
- Hicketts, Joe 68
- Highmore, Matthew 69
- Hillman, Blake 69
- Hitchcock, Ryan 70
- Ho-Sang, Joshua 70
- Hodge, Kris 71
- Hodgson, Hayden 72
- Holmstrom, Axel 73
- Honka, Julius 73
- Hopponen, Waltteri 74

- Hora, Frank 74
- Hore, Tyler 75
- Hunt, Dryden 76
- Husso, Ville 76
- Iacopelli, Matheson 76
- Irving, Aaron 77
- Iverson, Keegan 78
- Jacobs, Joshua 78
- James, Cordell 79
- Jamieson, Aiden 79
- Jenkins, Kyle 79
- Jenys, Pavel 80
- Jevpalovs, Nikita 80
- Johansson, Emil 81
- Joly, Michael 81
- Jones, Nicholas 81
- Joshua, Dakota 82
- Kähkönen, Kaapo 82
- Kamenev, Vladislav 83
- Kapanen, Kasperi 83
- Karabacek, Vaclav 84
- Karlsson, Anton 85
- Kase, Ondrej 85
- Kempe, Adrian 85
- Keskitalo, Miro 86
- King, Jeff 86
- Kirkland, Justin 87
- Kiviranta, Joel 87
- Kraskovsky, Pavel 87
- Kuhlman, Karson 88
- Kulda, Edgars 88
- LaBanc, Kevin 89
- Lagesson, William 89
- Laliberté, Kevin 90
- Lammikko, Juho 90
- Larkin, Dylan 91
- Lazarev, Maxim 91
- Leblanc, Olivier 92
- Leblanc, Stefan 92
- Lee, Michael 93
- Leedahl, Dawson 93
- Lemieux, Brendan 93
- Lernout, Brett 94
- Lindblom, Oskar 95
- Lindo, Jaden 96
- Lintuniemi, Alex 96
- Lipsbergs, Roberts 97
- Llewellyn, Darby 97
- Lorentz, Steven 97
- Lyamkin, Nikita 98
- MacDonald, Owen 98
- MacInnis, Ryan 99
- MacIntyre, Bobby 99
- MacIntyre, Duncan 100
- MacLeod, Johnathan 100
- MacMaster, Tanner 100
- Maguire, Josh 101
- Magyar, Nick 101
- Mallette, Trent 102
- Malone, Seamus 102
- Manchurek, Joe 103
- Mancina, Matthew 103
- Mangiapane, Andrew 104
- Mantha, Ryan 104
- Martin, Brycen 105
- Masin, Dominik 106
- Mayo, Dysin 106
- McDade, Owen 107
- McDonald, Mason 107
- McKeown, Roland 108
- Middleton, Jacob 109
- Mikulovich, Aleksandar 110
- Milano, Sonny 110
- Minney, Edwin 111
- Mistele, Matt 111
- Montour, Brandon 111
- Moody, Zachery 112
- Moran, Brent 112
- Crevier-Morin, Marc-Olivier 113
- Morrison, Tyler 113
- Moynihan, Danny 114
- Mpofu, Vukie 114
- Murphy, Matt 114
- Nanne, Tyler 115
- Nantel, Julien 115
- Nedeljkovic, Alex 116
- Neill, Carl 116
- Nejezchleb, Richard 117
- Nekolenko, Arkhip 117
- Nikolishin, Ivan 118
- Nogier, Nelson 118
- Nylander, William 119
- Okulov, Konstantin 120
- Ollas Mattsson, Adam 120
- Olofsson, Fredrik 120
- Orlovich-Grudkov, Denis 121
- Owre, Steven 122
- Pastrnak, David 122
- Pelletier, Julien 123
- Pépin, Alexis 123
- Perlini, Brendan 124
- Perron, Francis 125
- Peters, Alex 125
- Pettersson, Marcus 126
- Petti, Niki 126
- Pettit, Kyle 126
- Phelps, Chase 127
- Philp, Luke 127
- Piccinich, J.J. 128
- Pilut, Lawrence 128
- Pionk, Neal 128

- Poganski, Austin 129
- Point, Brayden 130
- Pollock, Brett 130
- Prapavessis, Michael 131
- Prophet, Brandon 132
- Protapovich, Alexander 132
- Quenneville, John 132
- Raddysh, Darren 133
- Ratelle, Joey 133
- Rehill, Ryan 134
- Reich, Kevin 134
- Reinhart, Sam 134
- Renaud, Alexandre 135
- Revel, Matt 136
- Ritchie, Nick 136
- Robinson, Brandon 137
- Rod, Noah 137
- Rosdahl, Kim 138
- Sadowy, Dylan 138
- Sandhu, Tyler 138
- Sanheim, Travis 139
- Sanvido, Patrick 140
- Scherbak, Nikita 140
- Schierhorn, Eric 141
- Schmaltz, Nick 141
- Schmalz, Matt 142
- Schmidt, Logan 143
- Schoenborn, Alex 143
- Serebryakov, Nikita 144
- Sergeev, Dmitrii 144
- Sharipzyanov, Damir 145
- Sharov, Alexander 145
- Sheehy, Tyler 146
- Sherwood, Kiefer 146
- Shestyorkin, Igor 147
- Shirley, Collin 147
- Siebenaler, Blake 147
- Sleptsov, Alexey 148
- Smith, Hunter 148
- Smith, Jake 149
- Sodestrom, Linus 149
- Spinner, Steven 149
- Spinozzi, Kevin 150
- Stadel, Riley 150
- Stefano, Anthony 151
- Suter, Pius 151
- Sweeney, Jacob 151
- Sweezey, Billy 152
- Tait, Ryan 152
- Thomas, Ben 153
- Thomas, Jared 153
- Thrower, Josh 154
- Tkachev, Vladimir 154
- Tornqvist, Henrik 155
- Tryamkin, Nikita 155
- Tuch, Alex 156
- Turgeon, Dominic 156
- Ustaski, Matt 157
- Valentine, Dallas 157
- Vanier, Alexis 157
- Vanko, Alec 158
- Verbeek, Ryan 158
- Virtanen, Jake 159
- Vrana, Jacub 160
- Walcott, Daniel 161
- Wallmark, Lucas 162
- Walman, Jake 162
- Walsh, Jared 163
- Watson, Matthew 163
- Watson, Spencer – 164
- Wegwerth, Joe 164
- Wesley, Josh 164
- Weyrick, Blake 165
- White, Patrick 165
- Wilkie, Chris 165
- Williams, Devin 166
- Willman, Max 166
- Wolanin, Christian 167
- Wolff, Nick 167
- Wong, Tyler 168
- Wood, Kyle 168
- Yakimowicz, Chandler 168
- Yazkov, Nikita 169
- Zwerger, Dominic 170

2015 NHL DRAFT TOP 30 172
2015 NHL DRAFT PROSPECTS 174

- Addison, Jeremiah 175
- Ahl, Filip 175
- Aho, Sebastian 175
- Andersson, Rasmus 175
- Artemov, Artem 175
- Askew, Cam 176
- Bachman, Karch 176
- Baker, Tarek 177
- Barwell, Jesse 177
- Barzal, Matthew 177
- Beauvillier, Anthony 177
- Bear, Ethan 178
- Bell, Jason 178
- Birdsall, Chris 178
- Bittner, Paul 179
- Blackwood, MacKenzie 179
- Blaisdell, Doug 179
- Boka, Nick 179
- Bondra, Radonovan 180
- Booth, Callum 180
- Bouchard, Jérémy 180
- Bourque, Simon 181
- Bracco, Jeremy 181
- Bricknell, Jake 181
- Brisebois, Guillaume 181
- Burke, Cal 182

- Burns, Andrew 182
- Bushnell, Noah 182
- Capobianco, Kyle 183
- Carignan-Labbe, Julien 183
- Carlo, Brandon 183
- Carlsson, Lucas 183
- Cascagnette, Jacob 184
- Joseph Cecconi 184
- Cernak, Erik 184
- Ciccarelli, Matteo 185
- Chabot, Thomas 185
- Connor, Kyle 185
- Craievich, Adam 186
- Crawley, Brandon 186
- Crouse, Lawson 186
- Dahlström, John 186
- Davies, Jeremy 187
- Davidsson, Jonathan 187
- Davies, Mike 187
- Davis, Kevin 188
- De Farias, Joshua 188
- Dergachyov, Alexander 188
- Dermott, Travis 189
- Deschênes, Luc 189
- Dhooghe, Jason 189
- Dostie, Alex 189
- Dove-McFalls, Samuel 190
- Dunda, Liam LW 190
- Dunn, Vince 190
- Eichel, Jack 191
- Estephan, Giorgio 191
- Evers, Christian 191
- Fitzgerald, Casey 191
- Fortin, Alexandre 192
- Fournier, Jordan Ty 192
- Franzen, Gustaf 192
- Gabriel Gagné 193
- Gabrielle, Jesse 193
- Galipeau, Olivier 193
- Gicewicz, Carson 194
- Gignac, Brandon 194
- Goberis, Zach 195
- Greenway, Jordan 195
- Greer, A.J 195
- Guryanov, Denis 195
- Gropp, Ryan 195
- Guhle, Brendan 196
- Hanifin, Noah 196
- Harkins, Jansen 196
- Harding, Sam 197
- Heid, Nick 197
- Henley, David 197
- Henderson, Jacob 197
- Henley, Troy 198
- Hughes, Cameron 198
- Jackson, Robby 198
- Jones, Caleb 199
- Joseph, Mathieu 199
- Juulsen, Noah 200
- Karrer, Roger 200
- Kase, David 200
- Karlsson, Gabriel 200
- Kashtanov, Ivan 201
- Kolesar, Keegan 201
- Kolias, Vasili 201
- Knott, Graham 201
- Kodola, Vladislav 202
- Kohn, Mason 202
- Konecny, Travis 202
- Korostelev, Nikita 203
- Kotsovos, Anthony 203
- Kovacs, Robin 203
- Kreis, Matthew 203
- Kylington, Oliver 204
- Laczynski, Tanner 204
- Larsson, Jacob 204
- Lazarev, Leo 205
- Lemcke, Justin 205
- Lalonde, Bradley 205
- Lanoue, Vincent 206
- Lauzon, Jeremy 206
- Léveillé, Loik 206
- Lindberg, Brandon 207
- Lizotte, Cameron 207
- Malgin, Denis 207
- Marner, Mitchell 208
- McAvoy, Charles 208
- McBride, Nick 208
- McCool, Hayden 208
- McDavid, Connor 209
- McFadden, Garrett 209
- McKenzie, Brett 209
- Miller, David 209
- Meier, Timo 210
- Meloche, Nicolas 210
- Merkley, Nick 210
- Samuel Montembeault 211
- Moore, Ryan 211
- Morrison, Brad 211
- Morrison, Lochlan 212
- Moynihan, Connor 212
- Murray, Troy 212
- Musil, Adam 213
- Myers, Philippe 213
- Nättinen, Julius 213
- Newhouse, Ben 214
- Noël, Nathan 214
- Niku, Sami 214
- Norman, Ryan 215
- Novak, Thomas 215
- Osburn, Zach 215
- Ott, Donovan 215
- Pawlenchuk, Grayson 215
- Pernsteiner, Frank 216
- Pilipenko , Kirill 216
- Phelan, James 216
- Picco, Andrew 216
- Pilon, Ryan 217
- Platonov, Alexei 217
- Price, Ethan 217
- Provorov, Ivan 218
- Rantanen, Mikko 218
- Reddekopp, Chaz 218

- Richard, Anthony 218
- Rook, Austin 219
- Roslovic, Jack 219
- Roy, Jeremy 219
- Roy, Nicolas 220
- Ruggiero, Steve 220
- Saarela, Aleksi 221
- Salituro, Dante 221
- Sandström, Felix 221
- Seagraves, Bailey 221
- Schemitsch, Thomas 222
- Schlichting, Connor 222
- Siegenthaler, Jonas 222
- Spacek, Michael 223
- Speers, Blake 223
- Spencer, Matt 223
- Soy, Tyler 223
- Sprong, Daniel 224
- Stephens, Mitchell 224
- Strome, Dylan 224
- Svechnikov, Yevgeni 225
- Svoboda, Martin 225
- Szypula, Ethan 225
- Texeira, Keoni 226
- Thompson, Will 226
- Tkachuk, Matthew 226
- Tremblay, Olivier 226
- Tretiak, Maxim 227
- Trottier, Brenden 227
- Tweten, Tanner 227
- Tyanulin, Artur 227
- Vande Sompel, Mitchell 227
- Vladar, Daniel 228
- Wahlin, Jake 228
- Warren, Brendan 228
- Webb, Mitchell 228
- Welsh, Nick 228
- Werenski, Zach 229
- White, Colin 229
- White, Colton 229
- Wilkie, Zach 229
- Wotherspoon, Parker 230
- Yan, Dennis 230
- Young, Spencer 230
- Zacha, Pavel 230
- Zeppieri, David 231
- Zhukenov, Dmitri 231

2016 NHL DRAFT PROSPECTS 232

- Allard, Frédéric 233
- Allen, Sean 233
- Anderson, Joey 233
- Ang, Jonathan 233
- Balmas, Mitchell 234
- Bastian, Nathan 234
- Barron, Travis 234
- Belisle, Brad 235
- Bellows, Kieffer 235
- Bitten, William 235
- Bourque, Trent 235
- Brown, Logan 236
- Brown, William 236
- Brushett, Ryan 236
- Bunnaman, Connor 237
- Campoli, Michael 237
- Candella, Cole 237
- Chychrun, Jakob 238
- Crossley, Brett 238
- Day, Sean 238
- Dineen, Cam 239
- Dubois, Pierre-Luc 239
- Dhillon, Stephen 239
- Dorval, Zack 239
- Felhaber, Tye 240
- Fitzpatrick, Evan 240
- Fortier, Maxime 241
- Fox, Adam 241
- Garin, Will 241
- Gauthier, Julien 241
- Getson, Keith 242
- Girard, Samuel 242
- Gleason, Ben 243
- Green, Luke 243
- Greenway, JD 244
- Hellickson, Mat 244
- Jones, Max 244
- Hanley, Jack 244
- Henderson, Eric 244
- Katchouk. Boris 245
- Keller, Clayton 245
- Khodorenko, Patrick 246
- Kirwan, Luke 246
- Knierim, William 246
- Kutkevicius, Luke 246
- Kyrou, Jordan 247
- Krys, Chad 247
- Kunin, Luke 247
- Laberge, Pascal 248
- Lawr, Jake 248
- Lauzon, Félix 248
- Lindgren, Ryan 249
- Luce, Griffin 249
- Maher, Jordan 249
- Mascherin, Adam 249
- Matthews, Auston 250
- McAvoy, Charles 250
- McInnis, Luke 250
- McPhee, Graham 250
- McLeod, Michael 250
- Mete, Victor 251
- Middleton, Keaton 251
- Neveu, Jacob 251
- O'Leary, Michael 252
- Paquette, Christopher 252
- Pastujov, Nick 253
- Pezzetta, Michael 253
- Picard, Miguel 253
- Pu, Cliff 254
- Raaymakers, Joseph 254
- Raddysh, Taylor 254
- Reynolds, Keenan 255
- Rossini, Sam 255
- Saigeon, Brandon 255

- Salinitri, Anthony 256
- Sanchez, James 256
- Stanley, Logan 256
- Stillman, Riley 257
- Sylvestre, Gabriel 257
- Thom, Matthew 257
- Timms, Matthew 257
- Wells, Dylan 258
- Zimmer, Max 258

SCOUTS GAME REPORTS *260*

CREDITS   452

2014 NHL DRAFT RANKINGS

HP	PLAYER	TEAM	LEAGUE	POS	HEIGHT	WEIGHT
1	BENNETT, SAMUEL	KINGSTON	OHL	C	6' 0.25"	178
2	REINHART, SAM	KOOTENAY	WHL	C	6' 0.75"	185
3	EKBLAD, AARON	BARRIE	OHL	D	6' 3.5"	216
4	EHLERS, NIKOLAJ	HALIFAX	QMJHL	LW	5' 11.0"	162
5	RITCHIE, NICHOLAS	PETERBOROUGH	OHL	LW	6' 2.25"	226
6	DRAISAITL, LEON	PRINCE ALBERT	WHL	C	6' 1.5"	204
7	DAL COLLE, MICHAEL	OSHAWA	OHL	LW	6' 1.5"	182
8	NYLANDER, WILLIAM	MODO	SWEDEN	C/RW	5' 11.0"	169
9	LARKIN, DYLAN	USA U-18	USHL	C	6' 0.75"	190
10	FLEURY, HAYDN	RED DEER	WHL	D	6' 2.5"	203
11	TUCH, ALEX	USA U-18	USHL	RW	6' 3.5"	213
12	MILANO, SONNY	USA U-18	USHL	LW	5' 11.5"	183
13	BARBASHEV, IVAN	MONCTON	QMJHL	C/LW	6' 0.0"	180
14	SCHERBAK, NIKITA	SASKATOON	WHL	RW	6' 1.0"	175
15	FIALA, KEVIN	HV 71	SWEDEN	LW	5' 10.0"	180
16	SANHEIM, TRAVIS	CALGARY	WHL	D	6' 3.0"	181
17	PASTRNAK, DAVID	SODERTALJE	SWEDEN-2	RW	6' 0.0"	167
18	VIRTANEN, JAKE	CALGARY	WHL	RW	6' 0.75"	208
19	KAPANEN, KASPERI	KALPA	FINLAND	RW	6' 0.0"	180
20	PERLINI, BRENDAN	NIAGARA	OHL	LW	6' 2.75"	205
21	KEMPE, ADRIAN	MODO	SWEDEN	LW	6' 1.5"	187
22	BLEACKLEY, CONNER	RED DEER	WHL	C	6' 0.25"	192
23	HONKA, JULIUS	SWIFT CURRENT	WHL	D	5' 10.75"	180
24	FABBRI, ROBERT	GUELPH	OHL	C	5' 10.25"	170
25	MCCANN, JARED	SAULT STE. MARIE	OHL	C	6' 0.25"	179
26	LEMIEUX, BRENDAN	BARRIE	OHL	LW	6' 0.25"	206
27	DOUGHERTY, JACK	USA U-18	USHL	D	6' 1.0"	186
28	SCHMALTZ, NICK	GREEN BAY	USHL	C	5' 11.5"	172
29	GOLDOBIN, NIKOLAY	SARNIA	OHL	RW	5' 11.75"	178
30	VRANA, JAKUB	LINKOPING	SWEDEN	LW/RW	5' 11.0"	185
31	MCDONALD, MASON	CHARLOTTETOWN	QMJHL	G	6' 4.0"	178
32	DEMKO, THATCHER	BOSTON COLLEGE	H-EAST	G	6' 3.75"	192
33	PETTERSSON, MARCUS	SKELLEFTEA JR.	SWEDEN-JR.	D	6' 4.0"	167
34	DEANGELO, ANTHONY	SARNIA	OHL	D	5' 10.5"	175
35	KAMENEV, VLADISLAV	MAGNITOGORSK 2	RUSSIA-JR.	LW	6' 2.0"	203
36	MASIN, DOMINIK	SLAVIA JR.	CZREP-JR.	D	6' 2.0"	189
37	MACINNIS, RYAN	KITCHENER	OHL	C	6' 3.25"	183
38	DVORAK, CHRISTIAN	LONDON	OHL	LW	6' 0.25"	178
39	ROD, NOAH	GENEVE JR.	SWISS-JR.	RW	6' 0.0"	188
40	AHO, SEBASTIAN	SKELLEFTEA	SWEDEN	D	5' 9.25"	165
41	SADOWY, DYLAN	SAGINAW	OHL	LW	5' 11.75"	183
42	ENGLUND, ANDREAS	DJURGARDEN	SWEDEN-2	D	6' 3.25"	189
43	OLLAS MATTSSON, ADAM	DJURGARDEN JR.	SWEDEN-JR.	D	6' 4.0"	209
44	POLLOCK, BRETT	EDMONTON	WHL	LW	6' 2.0"	182
45	POINT, BRAYDEN	MOOSE JAW	WHL	C	5' 9.75"	160
46	AUBE-KUBEL, NICOLAS	VAL-D'OR	QMJHL	RW	5' 11.0"	187
47	BUNTING, MICHAEL	SAULT STE. MARIE	OHL	LW	5' 11.0"	174
48	FORSLING, GUSTAV	LINKOPING JR.	SWEDEN-JR.	D	5' 11.25"	176
49	NEDELJKOVIC, ALEX	PLYMOUTH	OHL	G	5' 11.75"	190
50	MACLEOD, JOHNATHAN	USA U-18	USHL	D	6' 1.5"	200
51	LETUNOV, MAXIM	YOUNGSTOWN	USHL	C	6' 2.25"	155
52	LAMMIKKO, JUHO	ASSAT JR.	FINLAND-JR.	RW	6' 2.5"	189
53	DONATO, RYAN	DEXTER SCHOOL	HIGH-MA	C	6' 0.25"	174
54	SMITH, HUNTER	OSHAWA	OHL	RW	6' 6.5"	208
55	WALMAN, JAKE	TORONTO JC	OJHL	D	6' 0.5"	170
56	HICKEY, BRANDON	SPRUCE GROVE	AJHL	D	6' 1.5"	177
57	MONTOUR, BRANDON	WATERLOO	USHL	D	5' 11.5"	172
58	JOHANSSON, EMIL	HV 71 JR.	SWEDEN-JR.	D	5' 11.75"	194
59	HALLADAY, LOGAN	JANESVILLE	NAHL	G	6' 0.5"	188
60	LINDBLOM, OSKAR	BRYNAS JR.	SWEDEN-JR.	LW	6' 1.25"	191

2014 NHL DRAFT RANKINGS — 11

HP	PLAYER	TEAM	LEAGUE	POS	HEIGHT	WEIGHT
61	HO-SANG, JOSHUA	WINDSOR	OHL	C/RW	5' 11.0"	175
62	DUKE, REID	LETHBRIDGE	WHL	C	5' 11.5"	189
63	NANTEL, JULIEN	ROUYN-NORANDA	QMJHL	C/LW	6' 0.0"	193
64	HAWRYLUK, JAYCE	BRANDON	WHL	C	5' 10.25"	190
65	MAGYAR, NICHOLAS	KITCHENER	OHL	RW	6' 1.75"	194
66	GLOVER, JACK	USA U-18	USHL	D	6' 3.25"	190
67	KARLSSON, ANTON	FROLUNDA JR.	SWEDEN-JR.	RW	6' 1.25"	187
68	KIRKLAND, JUSTIN	KELOWNA	WHL	LW	6' 2.25"	175
69	JACOBS, JOSHUA	INDIANA	USHL	D	6' 1.75"	193
70	KESKITALO, MIRO	JOKERIT JR.	FINLAND-JR.	D	6' 2.0"	176
71	FRANKLIN C.J	SIOUX FALLS	USHL	F	5' 11.0"	190
72	TKACHEV, VLADIMIR	MONCTON	QMJHL	LW	5' 9.0"	141
73	GENDRON, MILES	RIVERS ACADEMY	HIGH-MA	D	6' 1.5"	181
74	HILLMAN, BLAKE	DUBUQUE	USHL	D	6' 1.0"	170
75	VANIER, ALEXIS	BAIE-COMEAU	QMJHL	D	6' 4.5"	215
76	JOSHUA, DAKOTA	SIOUX FALLS	USHL	C	6' 1.5"	182
77	CHATHAM, CONNOR	PLYMOUTH	OHL	RW	6' 2.0"	222
78	KULDA, EDGARS	EDMONTON	WHL	LW	5' 11.25"	177
79	KARABACEK, VACLAV	GATINEAU	QMJHL	RW	5' 11.75"	196
80	KASE, ONDREJ	CHOMUTOV	CZREP	RW	6' 0.0"	165
81	QUENNEVILLE, JOHN	BRANDON	WHL	C	6' 0.5"	182
82	PRAPAVESSIS, MICHAEL	TORONTO LAKESHORE	OJHL	D	6' 0.75"	173
83	MCKEOWN, ROLAND	KINGSTON	OHL	D	6' 0.75"	195
84	COLLINS, RYAN	USA U-18	USHL	D	6' 5.0"	202
85	SIEBENALER, BLAKE	NIAGARA	OHL	D	6' 0.5"	192
86	PERRON, FRANCIS	ROUYN-NORANDA	QMJHL	LW	5' 11.5"	166
87	THOMAS, BEN	CALGARY	WHL	D	6' 1.0"	190
88	SCHOENBORN, ALEX	PORTLAND	WHL	RW	6' 0.5"	196
89	CORNEL, ERIC	PETERBOROUGH	OHL	C	6' 1.5"	186
90	DE LEO, CHASE	PORTLAND	WHL	C	5' 9.0"	178
91	WALCOTT, DANIEL	BLAINVILLE-BOISBRIAND	QMJHL	D	5' 11.0"	161
92	MORAN, BRENT	NIAGARA	OHL	L	6' 3.5"	186
93	HODGSON, HAYDEN	SARNIA	OHL	RW	6' 2.0"	204
94	HUSSO, VILLE	HIFK	FINLAND	G	6' 3.0"	205
95	PETERS, ALEXANDER	PLYMOUTH	OHL	D	6' 3.25"	207
96	LLEWELLYN, DARBY	KITCHENER	OHL	LW	6' 0.5"	176
97	EISERMAN, SHANE	DUBUQUE	USHL	C/LW	6' 1.5"	200
98	CHARTIER, ROURKE	KELOWNA	WHL	C	5' 10.25"	173
99	NOGIER, NELSON	SASKATOON	WHL	D	6' 2.25"	191
100	IACOPELLI, MATHESON	MUSKEGON	USHL	RW	6' 1.5"	192
101	BISHOP, CLARK	CAPE BRETON	QMJHL	C	5' 11.5"	182
102	HOLMSTROM, AXEL	SKELLEFTEA JR.	SWEDEN-JR.	C	6' 0.0"	198
103	LAGESSON, WILLIAM	FROLUNDA JR.	SWEDEN-JR.	D	6' 2.0"	196
104	BERKOVITZ, MATTHEW	ASHWAUBENON	HIGH-WI	D	6' 1.0"	180
105	POGANSKI, AUSTIN	TRI-CITY	USHL	RW	6' 1.25"	198
106	JENKINS, KYLE	SAULT STE. MARIE	OHL	D	6' 0.0"	166
107	MAYO, DYSIN	EDMONTON	WHL	D	5' 11.75"	181
108	GARDINER, REID	PRINCE ALBERT	WHL	C/RW	5' 10.5"	183
109	FRIEDMAN, MARK	WATERLOO	USHL	D	5' 10.5"	185
110	AMADIO, MICHAEL	NORTH BAY	OHL	C	6' 1.0"	190
111	AUDETTE, DANIEL	SHERBROOKE	QMJHL	C	5' 8.0"	175
112	BRISTEDT, LEON	LINKOPING JR.	SWEDEN-JR.	C	5' 8.0"	180
113	TURGEON, DOMINIC	PORTLAND	WHL	C	6' 1.75"	198
114	FAZLEEV, RADEL	CALGARY	WHL	C	6' 0.75"	176
115	GOULET, ALEXANDRE	CHARLOTTETOWN	QMJHL	C	5' 11.0"	191
116	VERBEEK, RYAN	KINGSTON	OHL	LW	5' 11.5"	190
117	PELLETIER, JULIEN	CAPE BRETON	QMJHL	LW	5' 11.0"	177
118	YAKIMOWICZ, CHANDLER	LONDON	OHL	RW	6' 2.0"	198
119	SHAROV, ALEXANDER	CSKA 2	RUSSIA-JR.	LW	6' 2.0"	187
120	MANGIAPANE, ANDREW	BARRIE	OHL	LW	5' 10.0"	160

HP	PLAYER	TEAM	LEAGUE	POS	HEIGHT	WEIGHT
121	KRASKOVSKY, PAVEL	YAROSLAVL 2	RUSSIA-JR.	C	6' 4.0"	187
122	GAVRIKOV, VLADISLAV	YAROSLAVL 2	RUSSIA-JR.	D	6' 2.0"	191
123	NEJEZCHLEB, RICHARD	BRANDON	WHL	LW	6' 2.0"	203
124	IVERSON, KEEGAN	PORTLAND	WHL	C/RW	6' 0.75"	219
125	WALLMARK, LUCAS	LULEA	SWEDEN	C	6' 0.0"	176
126	LAVIGNE, HAYDEN	TRI-CITY	USHL	G	6' 2.75"	182
127	GERSICH, SHANE	USA U-18	USHL	C/LW	5' 11.0"	175
128	LABANC, KEVIN	BARRIE	OHL	RW	5' 10.5"	186
129	LERNOUT, BRETT	SWIFT CURRENT	WHL	D	6' 4.0"	206
130	WILLMAN, MAXWELL	WILLISTON-NORTHAMPTON	HIGH-MA	C	5' 11.5"	181
131	WATSON, SPENCER	KINGSTON	OHL	RW	5' 9.75"	170
132	MARTIN, BRYCEN	SWIFT CURRENT	WHL	D	6' 1.75"	195
133	BAILLIE, TYSON	KELOWNA	WHL	C	5' 9.5"	188
134	SUMMERS, KELLY	CARLETON PLACE	CCHL	D	6' 1.75"	191
135	REHILL, RYAN	KAMLOOPS	WHL	D	6' 2.0"	210
136	SHESTERKIN, IGOR	SPARTAK 2	RUSSIA-JR.	G	6' 1.0"	187
137	BOUCHARD, KEVEN	VAL-D'OR	QMJHL	G	6' 2.0"	205
138	BIRD, TYLER	KIMBALL UNION	HIGH-NH	RW	6' 0.0"	200
139	EVANS, JAKE	ST. MICHAELS	OJHL	C/RW	6' 0.25"	172
140	PHILP, LUKE	KOOTENAY	WHL	C	5' 9.5"	178
141	PEPIN, ALEXIS	GATINEAU	QMJHL	LW	6' 2.5"	218
142	BAYREUTHER, GAVIN	ST. LAWRENCE	ECAC	D	6' 0.5"	195
143	LEBLANC, OLIVIER	SAINT JOHN	QMJHL	D	5' 11.5"	157
144	KUHLMAN, KARSON	DUBUQUE	USHL	C/RW	5' 10.0"	175
145	DONAGHEY, CODY	QUEBEC	QMJHL	D	6' 0.5"	184
146	HALVERSON, BRANDON	SAULT STE. MARIE	OHL	G	6' 3.5"	176
147	BRADFORD, ERIK	OTTAWA	OHL	C	6' 0.0"	192
148	MANCINA, MATTHEW	GUELPH	OHL	G	6' 2.25"	178
149	ROSDAHL, KIM	MALMO JR.	SWEDEN-JR.	LW	6' 2.0"	187
150	MISTELE, MATTHEW	PLYMOUTH	OHL	LW	6' 1.5"	190
151	IRVING, AARON	EDMONTON	WHL	D	6' 0.5"	185
152	TORNQVIST, HENRIK	LINKOPING JR.	SWEDEN-JR.	RW	6' 1.0"	165
153	LINDO, JADEN	OWEN SOUND	OHL	RW	6' 1.0"	201
154	BUKARTS, RIHARDS	BRANDON	WHL	LW	5' 8.5"	183
155	GUTIERREZ, JUSTIN	TRI-CITY	WHL	LC	6' 4.0"	185
156	HAYDON, AARON	NIAGARA	OHL	D	6' 2.5"	197
157	FOSS, RYAN	WINDSOR	OHL	C/LW	6' 3.0"	183
158	KORSHKOV, YEGOR	YAROSLAVL 2	RUSSIA-JR.	RW	6' 3.0"	170
159	GAMBRELL, DYLAN	DUBUQUE	USHL	C	5' 11.0"	179
160	BRATINA, ZACHARY	NORTH BAY	OHL	LW	6' 1.0"	181
161	STADEL, RILEY	KELOWNA	WHL	D	5' 9.5"	166
162	ANGELLO, ANTHONY	OMAHA	USHL	C	6' 3.75"	190
163	MIKULOVICH, ALEKSANDR	NIAGARA	OHL	D	6' 2.5"	206
164	HITCHCOCK, RYAN	USA U-18	USHL	LW	5' 10.0"	170
165	LAZAREV, MAXIME	CAPE BRETON	QMJHL	LW	5' 10.0"	170
166	PROPHET, BRANDON	SAGINAW	OHL	D	6' 2.0"	202
167	KALAPUDAS, ANTTI	KARPAT JR.	FINLAND-JR.	C	6' 0.0"	161
168	BROWN, CHRISTOPHER	CRANBROOK KINGSWOOD	HIGH-MI	C	6' 0.0"	179
169	DESROCHER, STEPHEN	OSHAWA	OHL	D	6' 3.5"	187
170	WESLEY, JOSH	PLYMOUTH	OHL	D	6' 2.5"	194
171	LYAMKIN, NIKITA	CHICOUTIMI	QMJHL	D	6' 0.0"	165
172	BJORK, ANDERS	USA U-18	USHL	LW	5' 11.75"	182
173	USTASKI, MATT	LANGLEY	BCHL	LW	6' 6.0"	225
174	STARRETT, BEAU	SOUTH SHORE	USPHL PRE.	C/LW	6' 4.75"	197
175	SPINNER, STEVEN	EDEN PRAIRIE	HIGH-MN	RW	5' 11.5"	196
176	KIVIRANTA, JOEL	JOKERIT JR.	FINLAND-JR.	RW	5' 10.0"	167
177	DESCHENEAU, JAEDON	KOOTENAY	WHL	RW	5' 8.75"	186
178	BILLIA, JULIO	CHICOUTIMI	QMJHL	G	5' 11.0"	164
179	SNUGGERUD, LUC	EDEN PRAIRIE	HIGH-MN	D	6' 0.25"	180
180	BELPEDIO, LOUIS	USA U-18	USHL	D	5' 10.5"	193

HP	PLAYER	TEAM	LEAGUE	POS	HEIGHT	WEIGHT
181	WOLFF, NICK	EAGAN	HIGH-MN	D	6' 3.5"	200
182	YON, ZACH	ROSEAU	HIGH-MN	LW	5' 11.5"	190
183	SLATTERY, MITCHEL	HILL-MURRAY	HIGH-MN	LW	5' 11.5"	185
184	ENGVALL, PIERRE	FROLUNDA JR.	SWEDEN-JR.	LW	6' 4.0"	191
185	BARRY, JONATHAN	THAYER ACADEMY	HIGH-MA	D	6' 1.0"	192
186	LOTZ, AUSTIN	EVERETT	WHL	G	6' 1.0"	200
187	DUDEK, JOEY	KIMBALL UNION	HIGH-NH	C	5' 11.25"	180
188	TUULOLA, JONI	HPK JR.	FINLAND-JR.	D	6' 2.5"	180
189	KAHKONEN, KAAPO	BLUES JR.	FINLAND-JR.	G	6' 1.5"	209
190	NEKOLENKO, ARKHIP	SPARTAK 2	RUSSIA-JR.	LW	6' 2.0"	176
191	FIDLER, MIGUEL	EDINA HIGH	HIGH-MN	LW	5' 11.75"	186
192	JONES, NICHOLAS	SHERWOOD PARK	AJHL	C/RW	5' 10.0"	173
193	HELEWKA, ADAM	SPOKANE	WHL	LW	6' 1.0"	194
194	VALENTINE, DALLAS	MOOSE JAW	WHL	D	6' 3.5"	195
195	RUOPP, SAM	PRINCE GEORGE	WHL	D	6' 3.25"	174
196	OLOFSSON, FREDRIK	CHICAGO	USHL	LW	6' 1.0"	185
197	LEE, MICHAEL	THE GUNNERY	HIGH-CT	D	5' 11.25"	167
198	BOBYK, COLTON	SPOKANE	WHL	D	6' 1.25"	190
199	DESCLOUX, GAUTHIER	GENEVE JR	SUI	G	5' 11.0"	161
200	MALONE, SEAMUS	DUBUQUE	USHL	C	5' 9.25"	165
201	SHUKIN, KIRILL	KUZNETSKIE	RUS	D	6' 3.0"	192
202	BRESSER, JAKE	EAU CLAIRE MEMORIAL	HIGH-WI	RW	6' 1.75"	195
203	BEAUDOIN, GUILLAUME	BLAINVILLE-BOISBRIAND	QMJHL	D	6' 0.0"	182
204	WOLANIN, CHRISTIAN	MUSKEGON	USHL	D	5' 11.0"	179
205	PHELPS, CHASE	SHATTUCK-ST.MARYS PREP	HIGH-MN	LW	6' 0.25"	180
206	REICH, KEVIN	DUBUQUE	USHL	G	6' 1.25"	208
207	PICCINICH, JOHN	YOUNGSTOWN	USHL	RW	5' 11.5"	190
208	SODERSTROM, LINUS	DJURGARDEN JR.	SWEDEN-JR.	G	6' 3.5"	187
209	WOOD, KYLE	NORTH BAY	OHL	D	6' 3.75"	195
210	DIGIACINTO, CRISTIANO	WINDSOR	OHL	LW	5' 10.75"	186

2014 NHL DRAFT PROSPECTS

Aho, Sebastian
LD - Skelleftea (SWE) – 5'9.25"

Aho is a smallish offensive minded defenseman who played so well this year he played his way into a surprise call-up to the SHL. Sebastian is very mobile and uses quick feet and agility to buy himself time and space to make plays. He moves the puck smartly seeing multiple offensive options in which he chooses the best option more times than not. He can skate the puck but knows when it's better to move it than carry it himself.

Aho is a smart hockey player who is more active than reactive as he anticipates the play very well in all three zones. Aho plays well defensively especially considering his size constraints. He is smart with his stick and plays as physical as he can, He uses smart positioning to improve his effectiveness defensively.

He is very good on the powerplay using his great feet to give himself both shooting and passing options. He possesses a good shot from the point that find it target and creates rebounds. He is very adept at making himself available for the puck.

Quotable:" Might be best served remaining in Sweden and playing in the SHL. - NHL Scout

Quotable:" Thought he played good hockey the first time I saw him at the U17 last season. Really liked him this season as he improved his ability to make quick decisions and move the puck. Has smarts on the PP. I spoke to him at the combine and he gave me an accurate self assessment of his game, which is something I like to hear from players." - Mark Edwards

Quotable:" He's right there with Honka as far as I'm concerned." - NHL Scout

SEASON	LEAGUE	GAMES	GOALS	ASSISTS	PPG	PIM	HP RANKING
2013/14	U20 S.Elit	27	7	16	0.85	18	40
2013/14	SHL	21	1	4	0.24	2	

Amadio, Michael
RC – North Bay Battalion (OHL) – 6'1" 192

Amadio isn't flashy and won't wow you, but he's a very good two-way forward. He's very smart, and has a high hockey IQ. He makes simple, smart plays with the puck, and doesn't force anything. He knows where to be on the ice, and always backchecks hard. Amadio takes care of his responsibilities in the defensive zone, and can play in any situation.

Offensively, he sees the ice well, and is very smart, changing angles or waiting for a lane to open up to exploit. He protects the puck well, has a good, accurate shot, and will take a hit to make a play. He's a very good penalty killer, can skate, and wins more than his fair share of battles along the wall. Simply put, Amadio is a 200-foot player.

Quotable: "We liked Michael when he was up for the OHL Draft, yet every time I see him he keeps getting better. Great skater who can create offense but is always on top of his defensive responsibilities. I really like his two-way potential as a pro." - Ryan Yessie

SEASON	LEAGUE	GAMES	GOALS	ASSISTS	PPG	PIM	HP RANKING
2012/13	OHL	63	6	13	0.3	8	110
2013/14	OHL	64	12	26	0.59	14	

Angello, Anthony
RC – Omaha Lancers (USHL) – 6'04" 190

Left wanting more; that's the thought that comes to mind when viewing Anthony Angello. Some nights you see exactly what you wanted to see, and others you see nothing at all and he is hardly noticeable. Finding consistency is key to Angello's development going forward, but the tools are all there for him to one day become an NHL player. Angello is a big, fast moving body and is a bear to stop and defend when he's bearing down on you at full speed. Excellent speed, great length and stride, quick, mobile feet and slick, crafty hands to top it all off, Angello has everything necessary physically to be a dominating power forward. Good offensive instincts and awareness. Finds the holes and soft spots on the ice in coverage. He has a very good shot and a nose for the net when motivated, but therein lies part of the rub. For someone with the size and skills he has, one would expect much better, more consistent offensive production than was the case this season. Needs to learn how to use line mates better and not try to do so much solo. Defensively, he uses that speed and frame to deliver punishing checks. He is a big hitter, and has a knack for lining players up in open ice and dropping them. Has elements of a mean streak and never passes up an opportunity to plant someone. Good on faceoffs and decent defensively, however, can get caught being passive at times in the defensive zone. Questionable decision making on occasion on both sides of the puck.

For someone so big and skilled, it is hard to wrap your head around someone like that being capable of completely disappearing on some nights. There were some games this season where he was extremely noticeable, but others where you wouldn't know he was even taking shifts and everything in between. He needs to find consistency to his game not only on a night in, night out basis, but even shift to shift within a game. If he can put it all together the sky is the limit for him. He is expected to return to Omaha for one more season before heading to Cornell University in 2015.

SEASON	LEAGUE	GAMES	GOALS	ASSISTS	PPG	PIM	HP RANKING
2012/13	EmJHL	40	31	29	1.5	60	162
2013/14	USHL	58	11	10	0.36	85	

Aronsson, Emil
LC – Blainville-Boisbriand Armada (QMJHL) – 6'0" 185

Aronsson was selected 45th overall in last year's CHL import draft by the Armada. The Swedish prospect is a rare breed in the QMJHL, as the league has not had many Swedish members throughout its history. The Stockholm native has a good hockey IQ, understands the game well and has a strong positional game defensively. He is always first to come back to help his defensemen out in his zone, his play without the puck is excellent and he understands when to cover for one of his defensemen who's pinching in the offensive zone. He's been used in key defensive situations late in periods or games by the Armada coaching staff, a staff that trusts him in key defensive situations.

While he may not be a speedster, Aronsson gets around quickly enough at this level but would need some improvement in his starts and overall quickness. An underrated playmaker that sees the ice well, is good on the cycle and works hard on the forecheck. Not a flashy offensive player, as most of his offense comes from cycling the puck and working the plays behind the net. His shot is average, and he needs to get it on net quickly. Doesn't have a goal-scorer shot, many times he will simply shoot it in the goalie's crest. An honest player that works hard and does all the little things well, that coaches will appreciate. His offensive production cooled off after a hot start and there were also some concerns with his health over the course of the year with a shoulder, ankle and concussion issues.

SEASON	LEAGUE	GAMES	GOALS	ASSISTS	PPG	PIM	HP RANKING
2012/13	S.Elit U20	35	11	7	0.51	12	NR
2013/14	QMJHL	47	11	17	0.60	12	

Atwal, Arvin
RD – Vancouver Giants (WHL) – 6'01" 195

In his first full season in the WHL, Atwal has done a good job asserting himself providing a strong physical game and two-way mentality. His strongest asset is his physical mindset. He never looks up a chance to finish his checks and does so very effectively. He is tough along the wall and can use his strength to win battles. He isn't afraid to jump up in the rush and has better hands than your average physical defender. He received some time on the power play for the Giants and possesses a decent shot that he keeps low and deflectable. Arvin has a chance at being picked up late. He provides a lot of different assets but will likely be looked at in the future as a potential shutdown defender who plays a physical game and can chip in offensively.

SEASON	LEAGUE	GAMES	GOALS	ASSISTS	PPG	PIM	HP RANKING
2012/13	WHL	30	3	8	0.37	50	NR
2013/14	WHL	58	5	17	0.38	83	

Aubé-Kubel, Nicolas
RW – Val-d'Or Foreurs (QMJHL) – 5'11" 190

A former first-round draft pick by the Val-d'Or Foreurs in the 2012 QMJHL Draft, Aubé-Kubel was the guy anchoring the second line of his team this season. Playing along Anthony Richard (2015) and 18 year old Anthony Beauregard most of the season, he averaged nearly a point per game. He is a great explosive skater, possessing blazing top-speed and tremendous agility on his skates. He can turn on a dime pretty easily and get rid of opponents with quick changes in direction. He creates a lot of space for himself that way. He extends his legs properly while skating, which makes his stride powerful. He is also a tremendous dangler and he uses his body properly to protect his puck while being in the offensive zone. It's pretty tough for defenders to get the puck away from him. He can dangle through sticks and opponents without much difficulty. He has great balance as well. One of his main qualities is his ability to always get open for his teammates. He knows where he has to go in order to create scoring chances. Aubé-Kubel can also find space in the offensive zone, then open up to take passes and put one-timers on net. He can be really effective off the rush as he now uses his accurate wrist shot more than last year. That's one of the reasons his goal totals went up this season. Aubé-Kubel can be especially deadly on the powerplay where he can set up his teammates pretty well, as he has great vision. He works hard on both ends and he is not prone to turnovers at all when he needs to clear the puck out of his zone. He makes the right decisions in the neutral zone and he cuts through the ice pretty well while on the forecheck. His positioning without the puck is great and he will use an active stick to block the passing lanes. While not a menacing physical player, the Sorel native can lay the body on occasion and he will engage a physical battle on the wall. Although he adjusted nicely his play on the wings as the season progressed, it won't be a surprise for us to see him moving back at his natural position (center) next year. We would have liked him to be a tad more involved physically, but we see him as a complete player with great vision. We fully expect him to be drafted in the 2nd round, possibly quite early.

Quotable: "Not much worthy of making trips to the Q this year but this kid is a solid player." – NHL Scout

Quotable: "I really enjoyed what Aube-Kubel can do on the ice. Every time I saw him, he was very good, and took his game to another level when he had to. He's a player that has the potential to surprise a lot of people in the next couple of years." – HP Scout Jean Francois Dore

SEASON	LEAGUE	GAMES	GOALS	ASSISTS	PPG	PIM	HP RANKING
2012/13	QMJHL	64	10	17	0.42	26	46
2013/14	QMJHL	65	22	31	0.82	61	

Audette, Daniel
LC - Sherbrooke Phoenix (QMJHL) - 5'09" 176

Selected 1st overall in the 2012 QMJHL Draft by the Sherbrooke Phoenix, Audette has lived up to expectations this season, as he leads his team in scoring with 76 points in 68 games. He was one of the few draft eligible players to get named to Team QMJHL for Canada-Russia Super Series. He also competed for Team Canada Under-18 team at the 2013 Memorial of Ivan Hlinka tournament. Son of former NHL'er Donald Audette, he is already one of best stick-handlers in the QMJHL at 17 years old. He is lightning-quick with the puck and can beat defenders on one-on-one without much difficulty. A pretty explosive skater, Audette is easy to recognize on the ice, as he never stops skating and is in control of the puck more often than not. He is a great playmaker as he can dish out some nice saucer passes through traffic rather easily at top speed. Offensively, it's pretty tough to find a weakness in his game with the puck. He has great offensive hockey sense as he always gets in a good position to accept a pass or to take a shot at the net. When he will rush the puck, which happens a lot in a game, he is able to find open ice easily to get good scoring opportunities.

Compared to last year, he has improved his play in his own end, supporting defensemen pretty well. He played in all situations this season. In our viewings, he was fairly good on the PK as he anticipated plays on a regular basis, making him a threat offensively even in those situations. On the other hand, Audette will shy away from physical contact. He will lose puck possession rather easily when he is engaged in a battle in the corners and he seemed to disappear when the game gets physical or once he receives a solid hit. He really needs to work on his lower body as it was very easy for almost any experienced QMJHL defenseman to push him off of the puck.

Quotable: "Our scouts are pretty mixed on Audette. Let's face it, he's not a big kid, so it's only logical that there are going to be some mixed reviews on him out there. He's got skill, no doubt about that." - NHL Scout

Quotable: "This combination of skill and speed doesn't go unnoticed in the QMJHL. He progressed a lot this season and has the potential to be a dominant player in this league next season." - HP Scout Jean Francois Dore

SEASON	LEAGUE	GAMES	GOALS	ASSISTS	PPG	PIM	HP RANKING
2012/13	QMJHL	54	10	19	0.54	65	111
2013/14	QMJHL	68	21	55	1.12	79	

Bahl, Julien
RD - Sherbrooke Phoenix (QMJHL) - 5'11" 177

Julien Bahl played the first half of the season in the Blainville-Boisbriand, but he was traded at the trade deadline to Sherbrooke for 19 year old defenseman Dominic Talbot-Tassi and Sherbrooke's first round draft pick in 2015, joining his former midget teammate Jérémy Roy (2015). He earned his share of ice time with the Phoenix and that helped him gain confidence in his abilities. He played smartly in all three zones. He plays steady defense and simple hockey. He plays the body on one-on-one confrontations and he has the smarts to have good gap control. Defensively, he positions himself properly, uses his reach and is more of a passive defender. He moves the puck adequately and even though he is neither super fast nor quick, he can move fairly well on the ice. He keeps his play simple and rarely pushes the play offensively because of his limited abilities with the puck. He has satisfying speed as a skater but is not very explosive.

He was used on Sherbrooke's first pairing in our viewings and often let Roy start the breakouts. We saw him on power plays as well and he wasn't taking shots at all, he was just cycling the puck. On the other hand, Bahl never takes a night off. He clearly lacks a good toolbox (size, skating, skills), but his smarts and work ethic makes him a candidate to get drafted in late rounds.

SEASON	LEAGUE	GAMES	GOALS	ASSISTS	PPG	PIM	HP RANKING
2012/13	QMJHL	62	0	14	0.23	30	NR
2013/14	QMJHL	54	2	8	0.19	22	

Baillie, Tyson
RC – Kelowna Rockets (WHL) – 5'10" 187

Tyson has excellent vision and an innate ability to read the play that allows him to quickly react and put himself in good position to either force a turnover or create a scoring chance before the play fully develops. He also possesses as a nice blend of soft hands and slick puck moves that let him thread passes through defenders or unleash his plus-rated shot with a quick release. Tyson seems to hang around the slot or behind the net often, which has made him very dangerous because he finds ways to disappear and reappear in a position where he can either score, or set up a scoring chance. Tyson's offensive instincts allow him to score from many angles and set up good scoring chances.

Baillie has good skating abilities and combined with his quickness and agility has made him a very dangerous offensive threat off the rush, his quickness and shifty moves have made it tough for the opposing defenders to control. His ability to read and react to the play defensively has made him a strong asset in his own zone. Positionally, he seems to know where he needs to be on the ice in all 3 zones, and he brings an aggressive style to his play without the puck. Tyson can be very elusive at times on the forecheck because he plays fast and anticipates well. Combined with his strong pressure on his opponents, he doesn't require much time to make the correct decision in the play. As a result, he has been able to force an enormous amount of turnovers. It has also allowed him to flourish as a two-way player when combined with his offensive acumen. He's a competitive player who has shown a good willingness to fight along the walls. One thing we identified as an area of improvement for Tyson is his consistency. He can create a lot of offense and contribute in all three zones, but can also go quiet for long stretches of time. He is on the smaller size and despite his big heart, he'll have to show that he can overcome the size and increased speed against bigger and stronger players at the next level. If he can round out his game, he has the potential to be a checking line forward in the pro ranks.

SEASON	LEAGUE	GAMES	GOALS	ASSISTS	PPG	PIM	HP RANKING
2012/13	WHL	67	26	30	0.84	53	133
2013/14	WHL	56	22	33	0.98	53	

Baltisberger, Phil
LD – Guelph Storm (OHL) – 6'1" 214

Baltisberger is a Swiss import defender from the Guelph Storm. He was the defender the Storm would rely on in key defensive situations and was usually matched up against the opponent's top 6 forwards in primarily a shutdown role. Although Phil is a pretty thick guy he moves well north and south but would benefit from improving his foot speed in transition and lateral movement situations. He is very steady with the puck in the defensive zone and shows excellent poise under pressure making the right decision with puck movement. He uses his size well in the corners and looks for opportunities to knock opponents off the puck at all times.

Baltisberger did not show much offensive flash in the regular season finishing with 1 goal and 15 assists although he did show flashes of potential in the playoffs including a 2 goal game versus the London Knights. He sometimes allows attacking forwards to back him deep into the defensive zone and would benefit from having a more active stick and closing gaps at the blue line. Overall Baltisberger had a very steady season and showed improved confidence and development as the season progressed.

He may be worthy of a mid-to-late round selection as he has a high ceiling if his development can continue to progress to the North American style.

SEASON	LEAGUE	GAMES	GOALS	ASSISTS	PPG	PIM	HP RANKING
2012/13	NLB	39	3	12	0.38	48	NR
2013/14	OHL	57	1	14	0.26	36	

Barbashev, Ivan
LC – Moncton Wildcats (QMJHL) – 6'01" 190

The top pick in the 2012 CHL Import Draft, Barbashev really exploded in his second year with the Moncton Wildcats. He registered 68 points in only 48 games on a team where he was clearly identified as their main offensive weapon. He has a complete package of speed, skills and physical abilities. He is able to carry the puck effectively into the offensive zone quite easily. He's a strong skater with a low center of gravity, explosive enough to get past defenders who get caught flat-footed. It's really tough to get the puck out of his stick as he protects his puck pretty well and he can drive the net hard. His strength is great, which gives him solid balance on his skates.

He will find soft areas quickly and always keeps his feet moving in the offensive zone. The Moncton Wildcats' product is not exceptionally dynamic, but he can get to that extra gear very quickly. He has the ability to create plays from the hash marks and he proved to us that he can be an effective in the cycle game. When he was able to control the puck down low, which happened quite often this year, his great vision provided multiple scoring opportunities for his teammates. In that regard, we see him more as a playmaker than as a pure finisher, although he has a quick release on his deadly wrist shot off the rush. Barbashev has also displayed his great offensive hockey sense, reading and reacting well to find open ice or to create plays. His quick hands allow him to create room for himself in the offensive zone. On top of that, he is not afraid to get his nose dirty in the traffic in order to deflect pucks or to crash the opposing net.

One of the biggest things that we really liked about his game is the fact that he is a complete player. He was often the first man back in his zone and we liked his hustle in both ends of the ice. He covers the point effectively when he needs to and he's willing to support his defensemen down low. Overall, he is quite reliable in his own end. Although he will not be labelled as a grinder, he finishes his checks on a regular basis. We noticed that when he gets involved physically, his overall game is better. Barbashev can simplify the skills and speed game to a chippy North-South game and be as effective. He was outstanding in the QMJHL playoffs where he registered 10 points in six games facing a strong Blainville-Boisbriand Armada team. He took his game to another level. Our scouts saw him on multiple occasions this season and all agreed that Barbashev is hard-working and will rarely take a night off. We feel his high-end attributes and attitude on the ice make him a first round talent for the 2014 NHL Draft.

Quotable: "The first time I saw Barbashev play was three years ago and he was the laziest player on the ice. He must have been feeling sick or something that day because I have never seen a trace of that since. He competes hard, is a smart player, has skill and plays well in all three zones. He could make an NHL team earlier than some may expect." - Mark Edwards

Quotable: "He doesn't play like your average player from Russia" - NHL Scout

Quotable: "We are careful drafting Russians but in Barbashev's case we would probably be a lot quicker to pull the trigger on draft day." - NHL Scout

SEASON	LEAGUE	GAMES	GOALS	ASSISTS	PPG	PIM	HP RANKING
2012/13	QMJHL	68	18	44	0.91	36	13
2013/14	QMJHL	48	25	43	1.42	27	

Bayreuther, Gavin
LD - St. Lawrence University (NCAA) - 6'01" 195

Gavin is a re-entry player who had an outstanding freshman year with St. Lawrence University. He is a smooth puck moving defender who consistently finds the right lanes. He handles the puck well under pressure and rarely makes a bad play with the puck.

In addition to his puck moving ability he has a powerful shot from the point and is capable of getting it through screens. He displayed excellent power play quarterback potential this season. He needs to improve on his skating, especially since he is an offensive defenseman. He will also need to improve on his defensive zone coverage over the next few years before going professional.

SEASON	LEAGUE	GAMES	GOALS	ASSISTS	PPG	PIM	HP RANKING
2012/13	USHL	60	9	24	0.55	43	142
2013/14	NCAA	38	9	27	0.95	20	

Beaudoin, Guillaume
LD – Blainville-Boisbriand Armada (QMJHL) –6'0" 182

Beaudoin just completed his rookie season with the Armada, and the team's 3rd round pick in the 2012 QMJHL draft made some good improvements in the first half of the season that made the other 17 year old defenseman on the team, Julien Bahl, expendable. Bahl was sent to Sherbrooke during the QMJHL trade period. Meanwhile, the former Trois-Rivieres Estacades player didn't get the same quality ice time as other top 17 year old defensemen this season, although his ice time saw an increase after the Bahl trade. One of the most impressive things about his game that we like is his decision-making. He knows when to pinch in the offensive zone and when to play it safe, as he rarely gets caught out of position. He moves the puck well and can really help his team's transition game with either passing or rushing game. Beaudoin is a good skater with a nice top speed who likes to rush the puck in the offensive zone. If he sees an opportunity to rush the puck, he will take it. An area we would like to see improvement in is his footwork, as improving his quickness would also help him improve his gap control—he would give opposing forwards in the offensive zone less time and space to work with. With that, he could also become more aggressive on the puck-carrier in defensive situations.

One area where we saw some improvement during the season was in his physical game, as he was much more confident in the 2nd half with and even got into some good scraps. We feel Beaudoin is a player that didn't get the exposure that other players in the league had, but with some added ice time and responsibility next season, he could end up being a nice steal for a team at the NHL Draft.

SEASON	LEAGUE	GAMES	GOALS	ASSISTS	PPG	PIM	HP RANKING
2012/13	QMAAA	35	10	23	0.94	42	203
2013/14	QMJHL	57	3	13	0.28	37	

Bennett, Sam
LC – Kingston Frontenacs (OHL) – 6'00" 181

Sam had an outstanding second season in the OHL leading to him becoming one of the top prospects for the entire 2014 NHL Entry Draft. Sam is a smooth effortless skater who has decent size, and provides a strong forecheck. He brings a little bit of a physical element and pressures opponents into mistakes. While his work ethic is a key to his success, his offensive instincts are what make him such an excellent prospect. He has a precise shot that packs a lot of power. He also possesses outstanding playmaking ability, which can sometimes go under the radar because he will sometimes try to force his shot from bad angles.

He displays good vision in the offensive zone, and quick decision-making. He constantly threads the needle, and makes difficult passes look easy. When he's moving the puck as much as he's shooting it, he is extremely difficult for goaltenders, and defenders to read.

Despite his offensive abilities, Sam has developed into a strong defensive player who has made an impact on the Frontenacs penalty kill. He does an effective job of getting into passing lanes, and really pressures the point effectively. When the puck leaves the zone he utilizes his skating ability to chase down the puck, and take away time and space from the puck carrier. This causes mistakes to be made, and results in a few short handed scoring opportunities. In a draft that isn't overly strong at the top, Bennett has a chance to be one of the top 3 picks in the draft. Sam is an offensive skilled forward who is capable of playing a 200-foot game, and providing a good work ethic without the puck on his stick.

Quotable: "I was so impressed with the season he had this year. He played hard with a will to win." - Mark Edwards

Quotable: "I'm not totally sold on him as a top five prospect." - NHL Scout

Quotable: "He's my number one." - NHL Scout

Quotable: "I take him over Ekblad without thinking about it." - NHL Scout

Quotable: "It's close for me between Reinhart and Bennett but I'd take Reinhart." - NHL Scout

SEASON	LEAGUE	GAMES	GOALS	ASSISTS	PPG	PIM	HP RANKING
2012/13	OHL	60	18	22	0.67	87	1
2013/14	OHL	57	36	55	1.6	118	

Bergman, Julius
RD - Frolunda Jr. (SWE) 6'1" 187

There is no doubt that Bergman brings skill to the table but he lacks some basic grit in his game and we think he played too soft. He is a skilled guy with good hands who posted some numbers in junior, skating is above average. Bergman looks fantastic in open ice when he has lots of room but as soon space gets a bit tighter or he gets in the hard areas of the ice he just didn't show us that he could be a player we could project as a future NHL'er.

SEASON	LEAGUE	GAMES	GOALS	ASSISTS	PPG	PIM	HP RANKING
2012/13	U20 S.Elit	15	1	5	0.4	6	NR
2013/14	U20 S.Elit	45	13	21	0.76	54	

Berkovitz, Matthew
LD - Ashwaubenon High (HS-WI) - 6'01" 180

Matthew is a slick skating offensive defenseman who moves the puck well and can carry the puck end to end seemingly at will. It was this puck rushing ability along with his hockey sense and quick shot that helped him put up big numbers this year as a defenseman. He has a strong skillset but needs to gets stronger and use his frame a little more effectively as he can be a little too soft at times. Matthew is slated to join the University of Wisconsin in September 2014.

SEASON	LEAGUE	GAMES	GOALS	ASSISTS	PPG	PIM	HP RANKING
2012/13	USHS	23	11	14	1.09	14	140
2013/14	USHS	45	14	36	1.11	12	

Billia, Julio
G - Chicoutimi Saguenéens (QMJHL) - 5'11" 168

Billia saw plenty of action this season with the Saguenéens in his second year in the QMJHL. As the season went on, he has progressed nicely. Billia played for Canada's gold medal-winning U18 team at the 2013 Ivan Hlinka Memorial Tournament last August, posting some solid numbers all tournament long and he was also named to BMO Top Prospects Game. He's one of the fastest and athletic goalies in the league, which allows him to be very aggressive in front of the crease and to confront shooters. Because of his stature, he knows he must defy shooters in order to be successful and he does that pretty well. When he doesn't, bad things happen. His defense was porous this year and he had to make a difference to help his team win. He has sharp reflexes and his coverage of the top part of the net with his glove and his blocker is above average.

He's very strong mentally and does not get affected when he lets in a bad goal. We believe that is his main quality. He keeps working to make saves and it is difficult to shake his confidence. He constantly communicates with his teammates and we clearly can hear him from everywhere in the rink. Billia jumps on loose pucks quickly and is extremely quick in his lateral movements. Billia's legs are quick and powerful, enabling him to make great lateral movements and be in position quickly on crisp passing plays. His major weakness is his size, as pucks will get through him and he is often forced to make tough saves when they would be routine saves for a bigger goalies. He really improved his rebound control as he now absorbs the puck better compared to last year.

Quotable: "I liked his season, even if he could have been better in the playoffs. I like his attitude in his crease as he battles for every puck." - HP Scout Jean Francois Dore

SEASON	LEAGUE	GAMES	GAA	SV%	W	L	SO	HP RANKING
2012/13	QMJHL	22	3.18	0.888	9	5	1	178
2013/14	QMJHL	41	3.52	0.894	10	27	0	

Bird, Tyler
RW – Kimball Union (HS-NH) – 6'02" 200

Tyler is a big strong winger who put up excellent numbers this year. He competes hard very consistently. He is almost impossible to move from the front of the net and got a number of his goals in the slot area using his size and strength to create rebounds and finish. He wins a lot of battles in the corner utilizing his great strength but isn't an overly physical player and we'd really like to see him develop more of a mean streak. While he is capable of putting up points at the High School level and should post effective numbers in junior and college he projects to be a third line forward if he can pick up the physical area of his game. Tyler is expected to join Brown University in September 2015 and has a few options next year as he was selected by the Tri-City Storm of the USHL and Rimouski Oceanic of the QMJHL last season.

SEASON	LEAGUE	GAMES	GOALS	ASSISTS	PPG	PIM	HP RANKING
2012/13	USHS	19	10	12	1.16	NA	138
2013/14	USHS	37	33	27	1.62	NA	

Bishop, Clark
LC – Cape-Breton Screaming Eagles (QMJHL) – 5'11" 173

Bishop, who hails from Newfoundland, is a speedy gritty forward with a great work ethic. He was chosen 3rd overall by the Screaming Eagles in the 2012 QMJHL Draft.

A terrific skater who can reach his top speed very quickly, he excels on the forecheck by always keeping his feet moving. A very tenacious forward with the puck, one that drives the net hard all the time. A very capable puck-carrier, he can rush the puck from his zone to the offensive zone with no problems thanks to his great speed. Controls the puck really well at top speed. Plays a physical game, loves to hit, and can make some good open-ice hits, too. Once he is able to add more mass to his frame, we feel he will be more effective in this area of the game.

Bishop is good in all three zones; he is always first to come back to support his defensemen. Makes good decisions with or without the puck, and won't get his team into trouble. Not an overly creative playmaker, as he possesses limited vision and a shoot-first mentality could make him more effective on the wing at the pro level. Not a natural scorer either, as he will score by getting his nose dirty in front of the net and jumping on rebounds. Clark brings a lot of energy and enthusiasm to his team; he is always working hard and his motor never stops.

Cape-Breton is starting to emerge from the bottom of the league and the St-John's native will be a big part of this club for the next two seasons.

Bishop has played in different international competitions over the last two years, such as Team Atlantic at the 2013 U-17 in Drummondville/Victoriaville and for Canada at this year's Ivan Hlinka tournament. He also played for Canada at the recent U18 world championship in Finland. Both times while representing his country this year, Bishop was used in an energy and defensive role. With his smarts, speed and work ethic, he is a perfect candidate for a defensive and penalty-killing role in one of those teams, a possible future role as an NHL player.

Quotable: "I liked his work ethic in Finland but he made some plays decision wise that had me questioning his hockey sense." Mark Edwards

Quotable: "The fact that Bishop could be a possible top 90 selection says a lot about the draft this season. He works hard but he's just a guy in my opinion." NHL Scout

SEASON	LEAGUE	GAMES	GOALS	ASSISTS	PPG	PIM	HP RANKING
2012/13	QMJHL	58	8	14	0.38	33	101
2013/14	QMJHL	56	14	19	0.59	55	

Bjork, Anders
LW/C – USNTDP (USHL) – 5'11" 181

Bjork seems to get less attention than many of his teammates, and perhaps that's because he plays a more understated, intelligent, mistake-free game than most. That's not to say he can't be flashy; he has excellent hands, speed, and is a crafty playmaker, but he isn't on the same level as some of his teammates. Bjork plays a strong game in his own zone, very smart. He carries the puck through the neutral zone really well, ebbing and flowing through traffic with ease. He plays a really strong game on the boards, wins a lot of battles. Excellent vision and passing ability, finds his point men across ice from the half board in the offensive zone. Has the vision, accuracy, and zip on his passes to hit them in those areas and create quality open shots for them. Displays patience with the puck, has confidence and poise and allows plays to develop while creating space for himself and teammates with a tight curl or a subtle move to evade defenders. Trustworthy, intelligent, sound player who can play in all situations with better offensive skill than he probably gets credit for. Committed to the University of Notre Dame.

SEASON	LEAGUE	GAMES	GOALS	ASSISTS	PPG	PIM	HP RANKING
2013/14	USHL	26	9	12	0.81	0	172
2013/14	(U18)USDP	61	21	21	0.69	10	

Bleackley, Conner
RC – Red Deer Rebels (WHL) – 6'01" 195

Bleackley is a workhorse who consistently puts forward an excellent effort. Named captain of Brent Sutter's young Rebels squad at 17, Bleackley is a coach's dream as he is able to do whatever is needed for his team to win. He'll score key goals, win key faceoffs and kill off penalties. His versatility will allow a coach to insert him anywhere in the lineup. He has excellent awareness and ability away from the puck. While he impressed us with his tremendously responsible play as a 16 year-old, Bleackley has since been able to utilize his heavy wrist shot and good vision to develop a more complete offensive game. A selfless and fluid puck distributor, Bleackley is able to make plays in tight, but can sometimes be subject to tunnel vision when he's overly focused on taking a shot. With limited support on his team, Bleackley was able to generate much of his own scoring chances using his one-on-one skills and with the aforementioned underrated playmaking ability. He has scored the vast majority of his points at even strength against 1st line players. While Bleackley did much of his damage coming up the ice with power, he also showed good strength along the walls and a strong work effort that allowed him to generate chances off the cycle. While he doesn't always position himself correctly along the walls, he is able to read the play well enough that he is able anticipate the play and ready himself. Bleackley plays with high energy and is able to force turnovers with his good anticipation skiils and his high hockey IQ. He tested among the best of those competing at the Top Prospects game in leg strength and jumping exercises and he is able to translate that into a powerful stride. His skating continues to improve each and every month. His own zone reads are generally good, although like many young players, he is subject to losing his man in his own end from time to time. Bleackley has been a workhorse for the Rebels this season and while he is a solid two-way player, where he goes in the draft will be dependent on a team's assessment of his offensive upside.

Quotable: "Connor was one of my favorite draft-eligible players this year. He competes hard, is a strong skater and has developed some offensive skill after being better known for his play away from the puck last season. He can be used anywhere in the lineup and will do anything to win." – Scott McDougall

Quotable: "I'm a big fan of this player. I really enjoyed my talk with him at the NHL Combine and NHL scouts I spoke to raved about his combine interviews with them as well. I see him as a great third line NHL contributor and I suspect he will become one of the leaders on his NHL team down the road." – Mark Edwards

SEASON	LEAGUE	GAMES	GOALS	ASSISTS	PPG	PIM	HP RANKING
2012/13	WHL	66	9	9	0.27	28	22
2013/14	WHL	71	29	39	0.96	48	

Bobyk, Colton
LD – Spokane Chiefs (WHL) – 6'02" 190

Colton is a big defender who has plenty of room to add size in the coming years. He's played a solid defensive game and always seems to be in the right defensive position to shut down the play. He is strong along the wall - winning puck battles and moving the puck out of the zone effectively. He is able to move the puck with good decision-making ability. His one-on-one game is good and he seems to handle the oncoming forwards well. Colton is not an elite skater by any means, but has good quickness and mobility. He moves laterally well and can cover his defensive zone quickly. He is able to force the puck carrier outside fairly well and uses his stick to shut down lanes. He can play with an edge and does not mind engaging in the physical play.

At times he seems to panic with the puck under pressure or gets caught watching the play. This can lead to him losing track of his man and blown defensive zone coverage. Colton has shown a little offensive potential from the back end. He has a good slap shot with a quick release. He needs to show a little patience and not rush his shot and find a good shooting lane as his hard shot puts out good rebounds for his forwards. Colton has a good mix of skills and has the potential to be a solid defender in the coming years if he can continue to show improvements.

SEASON	LEAGUE	GAMES	GOALS	ASSISTS	PPG	PIM	HP RANKING
2012/13	AMHL	31	8	24	1.03	61	198
2013/14	WHL	56	5	7	0.21	62	

Boikov, Sergei
LD- Drummondville Voltigeurs (QMJHL) – 6'2" 195

Boikov was selected by Drummondville 90th overall in the 2013 CHL Import Draft. The Russian defenseman was an important part of the Voltigeurs' defense corps this season. Started the year on the third pairing, but finished with a top-4 role. More of a defensive-minded defenseman, Boikov has good size and moves decently around the ice. Doesn't mind playing a physical game and got much more comfortable playing a rugged game as the year went on. Needs to be more aware of his surroundings, as he got hit hard many times this year while having his head down in his own zone or being caught in a position where he was not ready to get hit. But Boikov is a tough kid, and didn't miss any games in the regular season, despite the hits he received having mostly been big-time hits. His puck skills are average, he's at his best when he keeps things simple and doesn't try anything fancy with the puck. When he gets the puck in the offensive zone, he won't wow you with his vision or passing game, he will usually just get the puck on net for a tip or possible rebounds in front of the net. Doesn't own a powerful shot from the point, and will need to add some zip to it. Needs to make better reads defensively, often he will get attracted by the puck and will get caught out of position. Does a decent job on the penalty killing unit, gets his stick in passing lanes and became a good shot blocker as the year went on.

SEASON	LEAGUE	GAMES	GOALS	ASSISTS	PPG	PIM	HP RANKING
2012/13	MHL	3	0	0	0	6	NR
2013/14	QMJHL	68	2	10	0.18	89	

Bouchard, Keven
G - Val-d'Or Foreurs (QMJHL) - 6'03" 205

In his first season in the QMJHL, Bouchard has been riding the bench a lot. Being a backup on a powerhouse doesn't help you get significant attention from scouts, but we believe the Metabetchouan native has some interesting tools that may get him drafted. His physique matured a lot during the offseason and he showed that he gained confidence this year in front of his net. He's a butterfly goalie with very good legs who's efficient on the ground and when there's a lot of movement around him. He uses his size to his advantage by standing tall and keeps his legs under his shoulders to give himself maximum power as he pushes off on his skates. He tracks the puck well and looks through traffic quite easily. Bouchard will usually battles for loose pucks to the end. He has quick hands and although he is quick on knees sometimes, his reactions are accurate and quick with the glove. However, he doesn't anticipate very well and can get caught out of position at times. He knows he has a large frame, so he does not get out of his crease often to defy shooters. He needs to improve on his rebound control as well. When he was playing Midget AAA, we had doubts regarding his mental strength as one bad goal often changed the outcome of his night's work and the way he played. We still have those doubts in the QMJHL.

SEASON	LEAGUE	GAMES	GAA	SV%	W	L	SO	HP RANKING
2012/13	QMAAA	25	3.76	0.884	NA	NA	NA	137
2013/14	QMJHL	27	2.95	0.887	17	6	2	

Bourne, Damian
LW – Mississauga Steelheads (OHL) – 6'04" 209

Damian is in his second season with the Mississauga Steelheads after being selected in the first round of the 2012 OHL Priority Selection Draft. Damian has asserted himself very well in the physical department. He is very strong and built very solid. He will finish his check every chance he gets.

He's also willing to drop the gloves and is moderately effective in doing so. Using his huge frame he is able to shield the puck from opponents effectively. In addition to his physicality Damian is willing to compete hard on the backcheck and works hard in the defensive zone providing a 200 foot game. The major concern around his game is his skating which is far below average and while he has the willingness to play a 200 foot game, he drastically struggles with the pace of games, constantly being late to the play because he is so far behind it do to a lack of explosiveness, a lack of top speed and lack of mobility. He also has decent power in his shot but commonly shoots at the goaltenders chest. Damian's upside projects as a big physical two-way forward but his major skating deficiencies could potentially knock him right out of the 2014 NHL Entry Draft.

SEASON	LEAGUE	GAMES	GOALS	ASSISTS	PPG	PIM	HP RANKING
2012/13	OHL	50	2	10	0.24	30	NR
2013/14	OHL	49	5	9	0.29	74	

Brack, Justin
LW – Owen Sound Attack (OHL) – 5'10" 187

Playing in his rookie season in the OHL, Justin really impressed us in his viewings playing his role perfectly. Brack played bottom-six all season for the Attack, and provided an excellent 200-foot effort every single shift. He provides great forecheck pressure, and is all over the puck carrier. He goes 100 mph every shift, and utilizes his great skating ability to take away time and space. He also uses this speed on the backcheck. He is regularly going full speed back to the defensive zone, and almost acts as a third defender when the opposition takes the puck up ice. Despite not having great size, Brack follows through on every opportunity to hit. He showed a few flashes of offensive ability, and a powerful wrist shot. However, if he were to make the NHL, it would likely be as a role player if he can grow, and continue to get stronger.

SEASON	LEAGUE	GAMES	GOALS	ASSISTS	PPG	PIM	HP RANKING
2012/13	OJHL	1	0	0	0	0	NR
2013/14	OHL	67	2	2	0.06	55	

Bradford, Erik
LC – Ottawa 67's (OHL) – 6'00" 192

Despite being passed over at the 2013 NHL Entry Draft, Bradford has continued to work extremely hard, and has put himself in a position to be picked up as a re-entry pick at the 2014 NHL Entry Draft. Bradford is a smart two-way player who provides a tireless forecheck, and finishes his checks with authority. He has gotten much stronger over the past 12 months, which has really enabled him to be even more devastating on the forecheck.

We mentioned in last years Black Book that, due to the depth the 2013 Eastern Conference Champion Barrie Colts had up front, Erik was stuck on the third line, and his offensive potential remained untapped. Well with increased ice in Barrie, followed by top line minutes in Ottawa that offense was tapped in a hurry. In addition to being the Colts/67's best penalty killer this season, Bradford has also received top powerplay minutes in Ottawa, which has really established his intelligence with the puck as well as his patience, and vision to read plays, and create scoring chances. He protects the puck effectively, and does a good job on the cycle. Defensively he's excellent on the backcheck. He does a great job providing support to defensemen picking up the man in the slot, checking sticks, and forcing turnovers. He is also willing to sacrifice his body, and block shots. Bradford is the kind of player you can put on the ice in the final minute of the game up a goal, or down a goal, and he will contribute. We believe some team will take a shot at Bradford at the 2014 NHL Entry Draft, and see his potential as a two-way forward at the highest level, who can provide a little offense as well.

Quotable: "We always loved Bradford's defensive abilities in Barrie but the trade to Ottawa sure put his offensive potential on full display. He's gotten bigger, stronger and much more dangerous on the offensive side while remaining a solid defensive forward." - Ryan Yessie

SEASON	LEAGUE	GAMES	GOALS	ASSISTS	PPG	PIM	HP RANKING
2012/13	OHL	68	18	15	0.49	46	147
2013/14	OHL	66	25	43	1.03	50	

Bratina, Zach
LW – North Bay Battalion (OHL) – 6'1" 183

Bratina started the season with the Saginaw Spirit. He received limited action and was ultimately dealt to the North Bay Battalion just after Christmas time. This move really helped Bratina find his game. However a concussion in the playoffs stunted his development a bit. He's a mobile forward who gets around the ice well for his size and when on his game he can distribute the puck well. Bratina sees the ice well, and can not only create plays for teammates, but also score himself when given the chance. He's effective at both ends of the ice and could develop into a solid two-way forward. He also brings a physical element as he's willing to finish his checks, but lacks a major mean streak. If he can stay healthy, and improve on his consistency, he could turn into a real good player. He's a good sleeper.

SEASON	LEAGUE	GAMES	GOALS	ASSISTS	PPG	PIM	HP RANKING
2012/13	OHL	50	6	8	0.28	27	160
2013/14	OHL	58	12	18	0.52	75	

Bristedt, Leon
LC- Linkoping Jr. (SWE) - 5'8" 180

Bristedt is a kid who is just a pleasure to watch play the game. He never gives up on a play. Leon is an undersized but is very creative offensively with the puck. He has patience with the puck that allows him to create plays for his teammates. He is built like a block and he will drive the net. He has a powerful shot and uses it smartly. Defensively he gets all over opposing players forcing turnovers. Last year we told you that Leon is the type of player NHL teams would love to have, but wish was much bigger. We ranked him 156 last season and he slipped through the draft. There's concern about his 5'8" frame but he should get picked this year.

Quotable: "I love this kid. He's loaded with skill and his compete level is off the charts, has some Brendan Gallagher in him but his skating is average at best.

He has a high motor, never say die - relentless type player. He's heading to the NCAA at the U of Minnesota." - Mark Edwards

SEASON	LEAGUE	GAMES	GOALS	ASSISTS	PPG	PIM	HP RANKING
2012/13	U20 S.Elit	31	9	13	0.71	49	112
2013/14	U20 S.Elit	43	32	28	1.4	91	

Brouillard, Nikolas
LD- Drummondville Voltigeurs (QMJHL) – 5'10" 160

Brouillard completed his third season with the Voltigeurs, and showed again why he's one of the premier power play quarterbacks in the QMJHL. He was once again part of the point-leaders among defensemen in the league this season. He has great offensive abilities, is a great puck rusher who often acts as a 4th forward on the ice for his team. Not an explosive skater, but generates good speed when carrying the puck. His good footwork makes him look everywhere on the ice.

A strong passer who distributes the puck very well on the power play, and key to the Voltigeurs' transition game at even-strength. Often you will see Brouillard follow a rush all the way to the opposing net, creating havoc in front. He does take chances offensively and tries to make things happen for his team, but has enough speed to get back defensively in case of a turnover. On the power play, rarely you will see Brouillard stay immobile on the blueline, he's always in movement, trying to generate things. Compared to last year, we saw some improvement with his shot and he can score more regularly from the blueline now. Defensively, Brouillard is a good enough defender at this level due to his smarts and skating abilities, as he is quick to retrieve loose pucks and won't be outskated by anyone. He gets into trouble when playing versus bigger forwards in the corners or in front of the net. Gets outmuscled for positions in front of the net and loses puck battles in corners. Overall, his defensive game has gotten better each year in his QMJHL career. His lack of size will still hurt him when he turns pro, as he might not grow much anymore but still needs to add mass to his tiny frame. Has the smarts and hockey sense to play at a higher level.

SEASON	LEAGUE	GAMES	GOALS	ASSISTS	PPG	PIM	HP RANKING
2012/13	QMJHL	68	14	43	0.84	49	NR
2013/14	QMJHL	68	12	49	0.9	86	

Brown, Graeme
LD – Windsor Spitfires (OHL) – 6'01" 184

Graeme played a regular role on the Spitfires blueline, commonly slotting in as a third pairing defenseman. When injuries struck his team, he was moved up to top four minutes.

Graeme is a good overall skater with decent starts, and good speed, but is lacking a little bit in the mobility department. This affected him at times in one-on-one match-ups, as he would get beat wide pivoting too late, and also beat by shifty, skilled forwards. He had some success catching some opponents off guard with his aggressive mindset in these situations, but it is an area he will need to improve. Graeme usually makes the smart decision with the puck, but will have some mental lapses. and toss up some unnecessary turnovers. Overall Graeme shows some upside but is still very raw, and will need to gain more experience at the OHL level before he can be considered a prospect for the NHL Entry Draft.

SEASON	LEAGUE	GAMES	GOALS	ASSISTS	PPG	PIM	HP RANKING
2012/13	GOJHL	42	6	7	0.31	67	NR
2013/14	OHL	53	0	4	0.08	35	

Brown, Chris
RC – Cranbrook Kingswood (HS-MI) – 6'00" 179

Chris posted outstanding numbers this season on a dominant line at Cranbrook Kingswood. He displays good skill and skating ability and can both create and finish scoring opportunities. The biggest question is whether or not he can do this on a bigger stage. He will get the opportunity to do this as he is slated to join Boston College in September 2015 and in the mean time has his rights held by the Green Bay Gamblers of the USHL.

SEASON	LEAGUE	GAMES	GOALS	ASSISTS	PPG	PIM	HP RANKING
2012/13	USHS	31	23	27	1.61	6	168
2013/14	USHS	28	26	58	3	21	

Bukarts, Rihards
LW – Brandon Wheat Kings (WHL) – 5'09" 189

Rihards is small, gritty forward who ended up putting up good offensive numbers in his first year playing in North America after needing a bit of an adjustment period over the first couple months in the league. Rihards possesses good speed and skating abilities and can use those abilities to generate offense chances from multiple areas of the ice. He has smooth hands and can handle the puck at a high pace. His wrist shot is strong and he combines it with a quick release. His hands around the crease are strong and he can deftly lift the puck on both the forehand and backhand. Rihards can be very elusive for defenders to handle because of his speed and strength. He plays a fearless game and always seems to be on the attack, not shying away from the physical play. While he will attempt the gain inside position, he can be kept outside at times due to his size. Rihards is still learning the defensive side of the game which he will need to improve over time. A long term project with good potential.

SEASON	LEAGUE	GAMES	GOALS	ASSISTS	PPG	PIM	HP RANKING
2012/13	MHL	62	18	17	0.56	44	154
2013/14	WHL	65	28	26	0.83	50	

Bunting, Michael
LW – SOO Greyhounds (OHL) – 6'00" 178

Michael is a player who seemingly worked his way out of nowhere to sign with the Sault Ste. Marie Greyhounds after one year of AAA hockey with the Don Mills Flyers Major Midgets. Michael had an excellent rookie season and is really capable of doing a little bit of everything. He plays a 200 foot game and will compete in all three zones and every possible game situation. His work ethic is very consistent and will compete shift after shift. He finishes his checks hard although could benefit from some added muscle. He has good evasiveness when bringing the puck into the offensive zone and can beat defenders. He also has a powerful shot and is generally very intelligent around his decision making. Michael projects to be a player who can really fill into any role but is safe because he is willing to work for his ice time, play a physical 200 foot game and shows very strong hockey sense.

Quotable: "Impressed with him right from my very first viewing." - Mark Edwards

SEASON	LEAGUE	GAMES	GOALS	ASSISTS	PPG	PIM	HP RANKING
2012/13	GTHL	28	27	12	1.39	NA	47
2013/14	OHL	48	15	27	0.88	34	

Cave, Colby
LC – Swift Current Broncos (WHL) – 6'00" 185

As a '94-birth year player, Colby has been overlooked in previous drafts but had a breakout season this past year. He has developed into a capable two-way player with strong leadership skills and a high work ethic. He showed he was capable of holding his own against some of the best players in the CHL Subway Super Series. Colby is strong on his skates and has above average skating abilities. He is a player who can contribute in all three zones. He has shown an ability to produce offensively, but has only average hands. He likely won't score much in the pros and the production he will have will stem from his ability to get himself in good scoring position. He's not afraid to go hard to the net and battle for rebounds or makes plays around the dirty areas on the ice. While he is strong on the back check, Cave is still refining the defensive aspects of his game. Colby could develop into a bottom six contributor with continued improvements.

SEASON	LEAGUE	GAMES	GOALS	ASSISTS	PPG	PIM	HP RANKING
2012/13	WHL	72	21	20	0.57	39	NR
2013/14	WHL	72	33	37	0.97	30	

Centorame, Santino
RD – Owen Sound Attack (OHL) – 5'10" 178

Centorame was dealt from the London Knights to the Owen Sound Attack at the OHL's trade deadline. Centorame provided depth for the Memorial Cup hosts, but went through a great deal of growing pains. His skating is effective but his puck decisions are not good. He has a decent shot, but doesn't always choose the right times in which to utilize it. Defensively he was a bit of an adventure. There was absolutely no shortage of competitiveness from Centorame, but he would lose positioning, and was unpredictable one-on-one sometimes making effective plays, other times getting beat pretty bad. Since coming to Owen Sound, he has gained an increased role, and got a little trial by fire with the Attack. Santino is still growing and learning in the OHL, and could become a solid junior defenseman. As far as NHL potential goes he's facing an uphill battle.

SEASON	LEAGUE	GAMES	GOALS	ASSISTS	PPG	PIM	HP RANKING
2012/13	OJHL	48	0	13	0.27	54	NR
2013/14	OHL	61	3	15	0.3	50	

Chapman, Joshua
RD – Sarnia Sting (OHL) – 6'04" 208

Due to his late birthdate, this is Chapman's second year of eligibility. Chapman has displayed a huge gap in improvement over the past two seasons which has given him a possibility to be considered as a re-entry player for the 2014 NHL Entry Draft. Chapman is a huge defenseman who plays an imposing physical game. He handles some of the biggest forwards in the league along the wall and in the slot and wins a ton of battles. He rarely passes off a chance to finish a check and is very effective when dropping the gloves. His play with the puck has come miles and while he may only be capable of making the smart simple play with it, it's something he struggled with in the past. His skating also shows room for improvement but has also improved over the past two seasons. Josh projects as a bottom pair defenseman who plays a mean physical game and intimidates opponents by playing right on the edge without crossing the line. He will still occasionally mail it in on a few plays at times where he needs to remain focused, loses positioning at times and makes puck mistakes, but at the rate in which he's improved he's certainly going to have to gain some consideration on draft day.

SEASON	LEAGUE	GAMES	GOALS	ASSISTS	PPG	PIM	HP RANKING
2012/13	OHL	64	1	3	0.06	72	NR
2013/14	OHL	56	1	11	0.21	154	

Chartier, Rourke
LC – Kelowna Rockets (WHL) – 5'11" 180

Rourke brings a special blend of speed, poise, and raw undeveloped skill. While not the biggest player, Chartier shows great determination and heart with every shift he plays. His mobility and speed make him a very shifty player who's hard to hit open ice or along the boards.

As the son of Saskatoon Contacts Midget AAA coach Marc Chartier, Rourke has an appreciation for the little details and tactical approaches to the game. Rourke is both relentless and tenacious on the forecheck and does not mind engaging the dirty areas of the ice to create scoring opportunities. He plays with a high compete level and wins the small puck battles all over the ice.

Rourke possesses an uncanny ability to sneak into the scoring areas untouched and combined with his smooth hands and offensive abilities he can score from the tops of the circles or finish in tight. He has an above average shot with a decent release and at times the puck seems to be glued to his tape. Rourke brings speed, raw skill, and a high compete level night in and night out. Rourke has a good understanding of his defensive responsibilities. He plays aggressive in his own zone using his stick to shut down passing lanes or taking good defensive angles to force the puck carrier to turn over the puck. This resulted in Rourke playing a big role on his team's penalty kill. He does a great job in this situation showing good positional awareness and knows when to pressure the point and when to maintain positioning all while keeping his stick in the passing lanes. He shows a great willingness to do the small things that win hockey games. Over the next few years with continuous development, Rourke could become a complete all-around player.

SEASON	LEAGUE	GAMES	GOALS	ASSISTS	PPG	PIM	HP RANKING
2012/13	WHL	72	21	20	0.57	39	98
2013/14	WHL	72	33	37	0.97	30	

Chatham, Connor
RW – Plymouth Whalers (OHL) – 6'3" 225

Chatham is a big winger for the Plymouth Whalers. He fits the mold of the classic north/south winger and shows a willingness to drive the net when entering the zone down the wing. He possesses a good size for a winger and is not afraid to mix things up in the corners or along the half wall while battling for pucks in the offensive zone. Connor gets to the front of the net and is not afraid to take a beating in order to maintain position.

He moves relatively well for a big man but would benefit from improving his stride in order to maximize his output. He is reliable in the defensive zone along the wall and succeeds by using his size to shield opponents from the puck and work it out into the neutral zone. He does need to improve at picking up a man when defensive systems break down as he sometimes gets caught in no man's land which results in puck watching and scoring chances against.

Chatham lacks much vision in the offensive zone and generally looks to drive the net with his head down instead of looking to make a play. He was able to score a few goals in the playoffs but benefitted by facing a weaker defensive pairing than some of his more skilled teammates. He also has a tendency to hold onto the puck too long which causes missed opportunities to move the puck up ice to linemates in better offensive positions. His size is obviously attractive and with an improved vision and work ethic he could have the potential to take the next step next season.

SEASON	LEAGUE	GAMES	GOALS	ASSISTS	PPG	PIM	HP RANKING
2012/13	USHL	63	18	17	0.56	71	77
2013/14	OHL	54	13	18	0.57	51	

Clarke, Blake
LW – Saginaw Spirit (OHL) – 6'01" 190

Going into this season after an extremely successful rookie campaign, Clarke had very high expectations placed upon him. However, what occurred this season could best be described as enigmatic. After scoring two goals in his first 5 games in the OHL last season, it took the entire season for Clarke to put up the same total this season. Blake isn't an energetic, physically engaging player as he more relies on positional play in the offensive zone. He gets himself open for passes, and also distributes the puck moderately well, and will cycle the puck if there isn't an intelligent available lane. With that said he isn't much of a playmaker, and more so gets the puck to teammates who can make something happen rather than doing it himself. Watching Clarke on the powerplay there is a real appreciation for his positional awareness. He continuously gets himself open, and available for passes. He plays a real 200-foot game, and works hard on the backcheck. Clarke was able to contribute on a consistent basis with his ability to force turnovers, and send the puck going the other way. Blake is a tough player to predict because he has shown potential in both the offensive and defensive zone but his major decline in offensive contribution can't be ignored.

Quotable: "Biggest faller from last season." – NHL Scout

SEASON	LEAGUE	GAMES	GOALS	ASSISTS	PPG	PIM	HP RANKING
2012/13	OHL	68	19	32	0.75	42	NR
2013/14	OHL	54	2	10	0.22	26	

Collins, Ryan
RD – USNTDP (USHL) – 6'05" 202

A tower of a player at 6'5", Collins has very good control of his body and shows no signs of awkwardness or lack of control in his body on the ice. A very mobile skater for his size, I came away impressed with how well he moves and the quickness of his feet. He has a smooth stride and gets around very well. Collins plays a smart, simple game in his own zone. He always looks to make the good first pass out of his zone and head-man the puck, and if he has no options he'll wisely put it off the glass or flip it out. He plays the body well and uses his size to be a physical presence.

Collins has decent offensive skill, but we don't foresee him being an overly offensive defenseman. He's much a stay-at-home type that can chip in occasional offense. He plays a strong game on the offensive blue line, however, making smart passes and dump-ins, taking his shots when they're there, and doing a solid job of keeping the puck in the zone on clearing attempts. He does need to work on his defensive zone awareness. There's a tendency there for him to lose track of forwards and allow them to get in behind him in coverage. He also has moments of indecisiveness with the puck and needs to improve on that, but those were fewer and farther between by the end of the season. He will join fellow defenseman Jack Glover at the University of Minnesota next season.

Quotable: "Got better late in the season, huge kid who can really skate, he's tough to get around and became harder to play against." – Mark Edwards

SEASON	LEAGUE	GAMES	GOALS	ASSISTS	PPG	PIM	HP RANKING
2013/14	USHL	26	0	2	0.08	10	84
2013/14	(U18)USDP	59	1	6	0.12	26	

Connolly, Josh
RD – Kamloops Blazers (WHL) – 5'11" 173

Josh is a high risk, high reward defenseman for the Blazers. The '95-born defenseman was passed over in last year's draft, before having a breakout 11 goal, 45 point season this year.

Offensively, his ability to handle the puck and skate it out of trouble and then lead the rush is among the best of all defensemen in the WHL. His skating abilities are really quite good and he is able to both accelerate quickly away from opponents as well as use his good agility to dodge checks. That being said, Connolly is very raw and he doesn't always pick his spots well. While he seems to be able to defend the rush well, at times he is a complete mess in his own end as his positioning, size, and strength all need improvement if he is going to be able to contain opponents with regular frequency. He struggles along the walls and he desperately needs to add weight and strength to compensate for that. Josh has shown tremendous improvements year over year and the younger brother of Brett may be worth a late pick to see how he develops as there has been exceptional growth since he was first eligible last season and the high impact offensive skill he possesses.

SEASON	LEAGUE	GAMES	GOALS	ASSISTS	PPG	PIM	HP RANKING
2012/13	WHL	53	1	5	0.11	12	NR
2013/14	WHL	72	11	34	0.63	34	

Cook, Dawson
LW – Green Bay Gamblers (USHL) – 6'01" 196

Cook is a re-entry player who played on a line with Nich Schmaltz this past season in Green Bay. Dawson isn't flashy but he's a very versatile forward who can play in any situation, including being slotted in the Center position. He plays a strong two-way game, and while not flashy offensively, has decent offensive skill and can produce some. He's an exceptionally hard worker and never takes a shift off. High motor type who never stops moving. Plays real physical with a beat of mean streak and is very sound defensively. Excellent penalty killer.

Cook was skipped over in his first year of eligibility but he can be worth a late-round flier or remain on the radar for a free agent look whenever he completes his college career. He is committed to Notre Dame starting this Fall.

SEASON	LEAGUE	GAMES	GOALS	ASSISTS	PPG	PIM	HP RANKING
2012/13	(U18)USDP	59	7	7	0.24	14	NR
2013/14	USHL	59	15	18	0.56	38	

Core, Zachary
LD – Sarnia Sting (OHL) – 6'02" 185

Zachary made a very brief appearance for the Sting during the 2012-2013 OHL Season, but has played regularly for the Sting this season logging a fair amount of ice time for a rookie. Zachary has developed well over the course of the season clearly growing as a player in his first season and has learned from some of his mistakes. He has great size and is willing to use it at times completing a few strong hits. He generates good speed but needs to improve his first few steps. He is not afraid to carry the puck a little when given a lane and has a decent shot when he gets it off from the point.

Our biggest concern about his game has been his decision making with the puck. He has turned the puck over several times, particularly in his own zone which has resulted in consistent scoring chances for the opposition. He has received some ice on the penalty kill and has decent positioning, but needs to use his size more effectively and build a little more of a mean streak against opposing players. With his size and the flashes of ability he shows, along with the development he has shown over the course of this season, he has the potential to be a late bloomer. However at this point in time we don't consider him a prospect for the 2014 NHL Entry Draft.

SEASON	LEAGUE	GAMES	GOALS	ASSISTS	PPG	PIM	HP RANKING
2012/13	AHMMPL	26	2	6	0.31	48	NR
2013/14	OHL	55	1	5	0.11	33	

Cornel, Eric
RW – Peterborough Petes (OHL) – 6'02" 184

There are a lot of things to like about Cornel as a prospect but there are consistent glaring concerns as well. On the positive, Cornel is an excellent skater for a 6'2" forward. He rushes the puck up ice with great speed and can take it end to end at times. He will also use this skating ability on the backcheck too. He showed flashes of puck skills and puck handling ability but lost control of the puck at times as well. He is more of a playmaker than a scorer and has good vision in the offensive zone to make creative, smart passes. He doesn't have a lot of power in his shot but gets it off with pretty good accuracy. Despite lacking any physical element in his game, Cornel is capable of protecting the puck well and will drive the net.

One of the biggest concerns about Cornel is his lack of willingness to go to the dirty areas and battle for pucks. While he has good skill to be an offensive contributor at the junior level, we don't see him being able to produce enough to play a role in the NHL. Combined with a lack of physicality or strong forechecking ability he isn't really suited for a bottom six role. He has talent but our draft ranking for him incorporates his very soft play.

Quotable: "We ranked him high in his OHL Draft year so I kept keeping an open mind hoping Eric would come around, but he's never come close to living up to our ranking. No pleasant way to say it, he looks scared on the ice. At the NHL Combine, he even told multiple teams himself that his weakness is that he is timid. I'll give him high marks for an accurate self-assessment and honesty. Apart from playing 'timid', I thought he really struggled moving pucks on time, especially when he played down the middle. I counted one game where he missed five obvious chances to get the puck to Ritchie. Hopefully Eric improves on his main weakness and makes me look dumb." - Mark Edwards

SEASON	LEAGUE	GAMES	GOALS	ASSISTS	PPG	PIM	HP RANKING
2012/13	OHL	63	4	12	0.25	13	89
2013/14	OHL	68	25	37	0.91	25	

Cramarossa, Michael
LW – Belleville Bulls (OHL) – 6'00" 180

Michael, the brother of current Anaheim Ducks prospect Joseph saw a slight increase in his role with the Bulls this season and did his best to contribute when he could. He displays a good work ethic consistently in our viewings. He is a good skater who has above average quickness and a good top speed which he uses to provide a strong forecheck for his team. He competes hard along the boards and although he needs to improve his strength he is effective with good body positioning and a relentless effort on the puck carrier. He shows basic offensive ability knowing how to make the smart pass, going hard to the net and getting pucks deep. He has shown a few flashes of puck handling ability but nothing that suggests he will be an offensive player at the NHL level.

Michael is a very simple hard working player who has the potential to hear his name called late in the NHL Draft by a team who loves his work ethic and sees a few similarities in the development of Michael in comparison to his brother but he doesn't possess the same kind of upside and would likely be an energy role player if he makes the NHL.

SEASON	LEAGUE	GAMES	GOALS	ASSISTS	PPG	PIM	HP RANKING
2012/13	OHL	45	1	1	0.04	12	NR
2013/14	OHL	66	7	10	0.26	24	

Cummins, Conor
LD – Sudbury Wolves (OHL) – 6'02" 214

After two seasons with the Wolves, Conor hasn't progressed quite as expected, but was a consistent contributor on the Wolves blueline this season. Despite his size, and weight, he is a deceptively strong skater with good mobility, and top speed. He was very hit or miss in multiple areas of the game. Cummins has done well in more than half of the one-on-one situations he's been involved in during our viewings. He does a good job of taking the body, and can utilize his stick. He also sticks with opponents well, but has got walked pretty bad on a few occasions. His puck playing ability is another big hit or miss, as he can make sole good reliable plays with the puck, but on other times he simply misreads the play, and they result in some pretty risky turnovers; primarily in the defensive zone. He also has a bad habit of icing the puck when pressured.

Conor shows good potential with his size, and flashes of good defensive ability, but needs to improve his puck handling ability in a big way. If he can correct his deficiencies he projects to be a big shutdown defender with good skating ability.

SEASON	LEAGUE	GAMES	GOALS	ASSISTS	PPG	PIM	HP RANKING
2012/13	OHL	51	0	3	0.06	14	NR
2013/14	OHL	51	2	1	0.06	24	

Dal Colle, Michael
LW – Oshawa Generals (OHL) – 6'02" 171

Michael was a top performer for the Oshawa Generals and a key part in the Generals being the top team in the OHL's Eastern Conference during the regular season. Michael controls the puck very well in traffic and is most effective in the offensive zone. He is capable of evading multiple checkers with good calm and patience and really doesn't seem to panic regardless of the pressure that is around him. He has a laser release on his shot but can sometimes miss the net point blank. He is also a smooth passer with strong vision and generally picks the right times to shoot and pass while leaning slightly towards the shot.

On the power play he is very positionally sound, always knowing where to go. Michael is a dangerous offensive talent but our concerns generally surround the lack of physicality and lack of defensive ability in his game. He was moderately effective on the penalty kill getting into passing lanes, but five on five he struggled to find the effort to provide consistently energy on the backcheck and would sometimes take his time on the defensive side of the red line. He will also need to get stronger and lacks a mean streak. Michael Dal Colle is one of the top offensive prospects available for the 2014 NHL Entry Draft, but has a little work ahead of him before making the jump to the next level because he lacks in one main area every NHL teams cares about - defensive responsibility.

Quotable: "He excels in the offensive zone both playmaking and scoring. Despite some weaknesses in his game playing without the puck, Dal Colle is a high-end prospect because he excels at putting up crooked numbers on the scoreboard. If you're going to be great at something, that's a good thing to be great at." - Mark Edwards

SEASON	LEAGUE	GAMES	GOALS	ASSISTS	PPG	PIM	HP RANKING
2012/13	OHL	63	15	33	0.76	18	7
2013/14	OHL	67	39	56	1.42	34	

Darcy, Cam
RC – Cape Breton Screaming Eagles (QMJHL) – 6'0" 185

Darcy finally joined the Screaming Eagles two years after being drafted in the 10th round of the 2011 QMJHL Draft. The South Boston native played two seasons with the US National Team's development program and then split last season between Northeastern University and Muskegon of the USHL. Still undrafted in the NHL, the 19 year old American took his game to the QMJHL with the Cape Breton Screaming Eagles this season and had a great year.

Without a doubt, he was the offensive leader of this team, finishing the year with 82 points in 67 games, playing a ton and in every situation of the game. Darcy is a strong player who uses his size well, although he won't ever be known as a physical guy. He still protects the puck well along the boards, however. He will need to keep working on getting quicker; he has heavy feet and doesn't generate a lot of speed, as his top speed is just average. Has a strong and heavy slap shot and likes to use it from anywhere in the offensive zone. Has a good on-ice vision and shows good patience with the puck to make plays. Darcy is a smart player who works hard in all three zones and doesn't cheat in the defensive zone. Darcy is an underrated playmaker with good passing skills, and we also like his patience with the puck in the offensive zone, as he can hold on to the puck an extra second to make a play or let a teammate to get open to receive his pass.

SEASON	LEAGUE	GAMES	GOALS	ASSISTS	PPG	PIM	HP RANKING
2012/13	USHL	45	12	19	0.69	40	NR
2013/14	QMJHL	65	35	47	1.26	51	

De Leo, Chase
LC – Portland Winterhawks (WHL) – 5'10" 175

Chase is a real competitor. He lacks in the size department but that has not stopped his tenacious style of game. Chase is involved in every aspect of the game. He possesses a compete level that is second to very few and has shown that night in and night out, he will be the hardest working player on the ice. He is always moving at top speed through all 3 zones. His skating abilities are excellent - he possesses both lateral quickness and breakaway speed. He is very shifty and agile and can be hard to deter for defenders when trying to play him 1-on-1. Chase is very good at puck protection and combined with his quick hands, he can easily slip checks and use his quickness to gain space to create excellent scoring chances. He will go to the dirty areas of the ice to scores goals or set up offensive chances. Chase complements his quickness and competitive nature with a nice blend of hockey awareness, vision and playmaking capabilities. Chase has a 3 shot arsenal and can put the puck on net quickly, but needs to add some strength to his shot. Chase is very dangerous offensively with or without the puck. He uses his strong instincts to compete in all areas and plays much bigger than his size.

Without the puck, Chase shows a good understanding of how the play is developing and will make good choices to force his opponent into making a play. He is tenacious on the backcheck where he has developed good instincts in stripping opponents off the puck. He will outwork any player on the ice and is not afraid to play physical. His defensive instincts are excellent and his quickness allows him to pounce on loose puck. Chase has skill along with a willingness (and capability) to do the little things that go often go unnoticed, but are very critical to winning hockey games. Chase uses his stick to shut down the passing lane and will lay down to block shots. His defensive positioning and hardworking attitude have had very positive effects each game. Size will be a concern for a team selecting, but there is no questioning the skill and compete level.

SEASON	LEAGUE	GAMES	GOALS	ASSISTS	PPG	PIM	HP RANKING
2012/13	WHL	71	18	38	0.79	24	90
2013/14	WHL	72	39	42	1.13	36	

De Sousa, Daniel
RD – Saginaw Spirit (OHL) – 5'11" 175

De Sousa went into the OHL with very high expectations after a great Minor Midget run with the Toronto Marlboros being drafted in the 2nd round of the 2012 OHL Priority Selection Draft by the Belleville Bulls. After not living up to expectations in his rookie season, and early into this season De Sousa was dealt to the Saginaw Spirit. He was slightly more successful with the Spirit after the deal, but is a work in progress in terms of getting his game back to where it needs to be. Daniel possesses quick hands, and he controls the puck rather well. He was utilized on the powerplay, and displays solid effective puck movement. He is willing to engage physically, but lacks the size or strength to make an impact in this area. He generates decent speed, but has an uncomfortable skating stride, and doesn't do well in transition. De Sousa will need to improve his defensive zone positioning in order to play as big of an impact as he has the potential to. Daniel has the potential to eventually turn into a solid OHL defenseman who contributes offensively, and hopefully improves defensively. However, we don't expect him to be selected at the 2014 NHL Entry Draft.

SEASON	LEAGUE	GAMES	GOALS	ASSISTS	PPG	PIM	HP RANKING
2012/13	OHL	40	0	1	0.03	22	NR
2013/14	OHL	43	2	12	0.33	32	

DeAngelo, Anthony
RD – Sarnia Sting (OHL) – 5'11" 167

Due to his late birthdate, Anthony is now in his third OHL season, and is among the highest producing offensive defensemen over the past two seasons in all of junior hockey let alone the OHL. Anthony is a very speedy, slightly undersized defenseman who can change directions on a dime. He is very tough to contain and provides good elusive moves which over time he's learned to use more appropriately. Despite his size he packs a lot of power in his slap shot from the point, but when he has a lane he also utilizes a quick and silent wrist shot, which has created several goals for him this season. He runs the power play for the Sting and shows a good mix of creativity and intelligence moving the puck, making quick decisions and has done a better job of limiting high risk decisions that result in short handed opportunities. His defensive game has improved as he has played top minutes and penalty kill all year and has shown better understanding of his positioning, but his defensive play is still largely a work in progress and not an asset in his game at this point.

DeAngelo plays a fearless style and will engage physically and generally gives pushback when bigger opponents impose on him. He can be a little reactive and has dropped the gloves a few times after being hit hard. Anthony's biggest concern over his three seasons in the OHL has been his conduct on the ice. He has received numerous penalties, misconducts and even suspensions for the way he conducts himself on the ice, towards officials and towards opponents and even on occasion teammates. This issue, while a concern over his first two and a half seasons really escalated in the final months of this season which included an increase in misconducts and suspensions due to abuse of officials and also included Anthony making a derogatory slur towards a teammate which included a major suspension under the OHL's harassment, abuse and diversity policy. While he plays with a ton of passion and drive, agitators have been effectively capable of turning this strength into a liability as Anthony has made some decisions that have played a negative impact on his team in return for instant gratification for a situation that is bothering him. There is no questioning the fact DeAngelo has top end talent for the 2014 NHL Entry Draft, but he may find his name being called much later than his skills suggest due to a combination of size, defensive play and behavior that may scare a few teams away from where he could potentially be selected.

SEASON	LEAGUE	GAMES	GOALS	ASSISTS	PPG	PIM	HP RANKING
2012/13	OHL	62	9	49	0.94	60	34
2013/14	OHL	51	15	56	1.39	90	

DeLuca, Anthony
LW – Rimouski Océanic (QMJHL) – 5'8" 198

After a sub-par rookie season in the 2012-2013 season, DeLuca came into this season with things to prove. In the first half of the season his overall effort was much better, and he became a player that the Oceanic coaching staff could trust on the ice in any situation. Won't ever become a defensive player or shot-blocking specialist, but DeLuca was used on the Rimouski penalty killing units, as he has good anticipation and is a threat to score anytime he has the puck.

Skating was another area where we saw some improvement. Last year he looked slow, even at this level. An improved conditioning level might be a reason behind this improved speed, but he still will not be known as a speedster--his speed is only good enough for this level. He will need to keep improving his starts to achieve more success at a higher level, as he's not an explosive skater but his top speed is above-average. He needs to keep his feet moving at all times, not just in the offensive zone.

The best asset of DeLuca's game is his hands. They are magic and can beat any defenseman in this league with some impressive dekes. He's incredible in the shootout one on one versus a goaltender as well. His hands are very quick, and he has a great arsenal of moves that can make look every goalie look foolish. Then you add this to his great wrister and it becomes a dangerous combination. He loves to have the puck on his stick, and if he doesn't have it, he will ask for it in the offensive zone. He can fire his shot from anywhere in the offensive zone, as he can score at will. He possesses a lethal release on this wrist shot, which allows little time to goaltenders to react. He has great goal-scoring instincts, always trying to get open in the offensive zone to take a shot.

When the puck doesn't go in as well it did in the 2nd half of the season for him this season, he needs to stay focused even more, as the rest of his game tends to suffer and he gets impatient and selfish on the ice. At times, he needs to simplify his game, as he cannot try to beat every player on the ice. He can be too fancy with the puck. When he wants he can play a decent physical game, but it needs more regularity. He is not tall, but has a wide frame, and is tough to knock off his feet. His work ethic will need to be addressed if he wants any success at higher level.

SEASON	LEAGUE	GAMES	GOALS	ASSISTS	PPG	PIM	HP RANKING
2012/13	QMJHL	67	22	18	0.6	33	NR
2013/14	QMJHL	67	35	43	1.16	60	

Demko, Thatcher
G – Boston College – (NCAA) 6'4" 192

His game has improved a lot over the past 16 months or so. He is sound technique wise as he limits rebounds game after game. Demko tracks pucks well from the outside, and stays in good position, showing quickness for a big goalie. He has made numerous big-time saves off odd-man rushes and clear-cut scoring chances during our viewings. He performs well as shots go through traffic, or on passing plays. He stays mentally sharp for the entire game on a consistent basis. Demko uses his size and big equipment to his advantage. He positions himself well to make the save in multiple situations by reading the play very well.

Thatcher seems to be gaining more confidence with every start. He is not an overly athletic goaltender but is so good with positioning, knowing shooting angles and playing a composed mental game, that it adds up to great success.

SEASON	LEAGUE	GAMES	GAA	SV%	W	L	SO	HP RANKING
2012/13	USHL	19	2.21	0.902	15	3	1	32
2013/14	H-East	24	2.24	0.919	16	5	2	

Descheneau, Jaedon
RW – Kootenay Ice (WHL) – 5'09" 186

After being passed over in last year's draft despite scoring 78 points, Descheneau came back this year stronger, grittier and more dangerous than ever before. Jaedon is a fireplug winger who plays the game at high level and competes every night. Jaedon is not overly big but has a solid frame. He's strong for his size but will need to add some muscle in the coming years. An above average skater with quick feet and good speed allows him to pull away from defenders and win races to the loose pucks. Jaedon never stops moving. He uses his quickness to pressure the puck carrier and force turnovers. He can find the open ice to make himself a scoring option. Jaedon has a set of soft hands and tremendous puck control which has allowed him to move the puck through traffic or develop a play in close. Descheneau's hockey IQ is above average and he is equal parts scorer and playmaker with his ability to watch the play develop. His uncanny ability to thread a tape-to-tape pass through traffic or find an open player in the scoring areas has been a huge aspect to his offensive production. Jaedon doesn't have the hardest shot, but he has both good accuracy and a quick release allowing him to surprise goaltenders more than overwhelm them with power. Jaedon is not afraid to battle for rebounds or play in the dirty areas on the ice. His quickness makes him elusive, but he is not a perimeter player and is very willing to engage in one-on-one battles. He often wins puck battles due to grittiness and positioning. When he is occasionally caught with a big hit, he is very quick to collect himself and get back in the play. He has shown over and over again that he is willing to take a hit to make a play. He has a very strong awareness for both sides of the puck and has shown to play a responsible defensive game.

SEASON	LEAGUE	GAMES	GOALS	ASSISTS	PPG	PIM	HP RANKING
2012/13	WHL	69	30	48	1.13	22	177
2013/14	WHL	70	44	54	1.4	54	

DiGiacinto, Cristiano
LW – Windsor Spitfires (OHL) – 5'11" 185

DiGiancinto plays the energetic, pesky style of game that frustrates opponents, playing right on the edge. Christiano plays with a ton of energy forechecking hard, and is a quick battler with high energy, and never gives up on a play. He works hard beating quicker, and bigger opponents out of pure work ethic and compete. He is a physical player who finishes his checks whenever possible. He also utilizes smart body positioning in relevance to the play to win battles in all three zones. He plays a full 200-foot game battling hard defensively, hurrying on the back check, and is like a third defenseman when his team is under sustained pressure in the defensive zone. He is also willing to sacrifice the body, and block shots on a consistent basis. With all of his positives he does have some concerns. One major concern in particular is his skating. His skating may be best described as looking like he's running on ice. There's no fluidity in his stride, and he simply looks like he's running with skates on. This has affected him in all areas of the game because he is unable to build up very good speed. He wastes a great deal of energy to get his feet moving, get up and down the ice, and simply needs a ton of work in order to get to an acceptable point. Whether or not Chrstiano gets drafted could come down to whether or not a team feels his skating is correctable. He has somewhat limited offensive upside. He has shown flashes of good passing ability, and loves to shoot the puck whenever possible with a decent shot, but he projects more so as a pesky third liner who shows a tremendous work ethic every shift, and is a player opponents hate to play against.

Quotable: "Skating is very weak and hurts his draft chances but plenty to like about his game. He has some Andrew Shaw in him." - Mark Edwards

SEASON	LEAGUE	GAMES	GOALS	ASSISTS	PPG	PIM	HP RANKING
2012/13	AHMPL	29	22	19	1.41	52	210
2013/14	OHL	50	17	11	0.56	101	

DiPerna, Dylan
RD – Kitchener Rangers (OHL) – 6'01" 187

Dylan started out his OHL career with the Kingston Frontenacs. However he was dealt to the rebuilding Kitchener Rangers as a key part of a deal that sent Vancouver Canucks prospect Evan McEneny the other way. Dylan immediately got a fair amount of ice in Kitchener being given a chance to produce. Unfortunately he hasn't quite had the impact that we, and surely the Rangers', expected of him. He has good size, but is very hit or miss when it comes to physical contact. There were times he finished every check he could, and asserted himself. Others he refused to use anything but his stick against opponents. His strongest asset may very well be his shot. He packs a lot of power in his shot, and when he gets it through the screens, he's a threat to not only score, but also send a deflectable shot on goal. He does, however, have a tendency to shoot the puck into opponents' shin pads. His skating isn't great. He has ok top speed, but his first few steps are a struggle. Dylan needs to work on his one-on-one play, as he was beat far too often for a legitimate NHL prospect in these situations. He needs to be quicker on the pivot, and read the play more effectively. Dylan has size, and some potential, which we saw, especially during his time with the Mississauga Rebels Minor Midget team. However, he hasn't translated this potential into results at the OHL level. If DiPerna were selected, we would imagine it would be in the late rounds by a team who has the patience to allow Dylan to develop, and the confidence in him becoming the player he could be.

SEASON	LEAGUE	GAMES	GOALS	ASSISTS	PPG	PIM	HP RANKING
2012/13	OHL	46	2	5	0.15	17	NR
2013/14	OHL	57	1	3	0.07	47	

Donaghey, Cody
RD - Quebec Remparts (QMJHL) - 6'01" 182

As the season progressed, Donaghey became a fixture on Quebec's defense squad, playing in all situations. Donaghey is an offensive defenseman who likes to join the rush and has tools to play on the power play. He has an above-average shot from the point and moves fairly well on the ice. He can thread passes through small seams and be mobile to create some space and time to make a play. He has slick hands, which he displays time and time again when he carries the puck up the ice through defenders. He saw some quality ice time on the power plays all year long as he constantly played on the first unit. He can make some nice long, crisp passes to start the transition. In fact, his puck play has been more hit than miss, as he shows good patience, allowing lanes to open up for him and making the smart, accurate pass. He still has some growing to do in his play in his own end as he can get caught being too aggressive in his coverage at times. He is good around tight areas to make quick starts and stops to stick to his man in coverage.

Donaghey is physical and battles hard in the corners, which is a good sign for a defenseman like him. On the other hand, he handles one-on-one situations moderately well. He is not always in the right position, and he could do a better job with his stick to knock away passes and shots and to take away lanes. He needs to stay more patient and let the play come to him when he is in the slot. However, we clearly saw signs of improvement in his play over the season and he has become a good prospect of his own.

Quotable: "He was one of the key players of the Quebec Remparts' powerplay this season. He possesses an NHL shot and will be a key player next season, with Quebec hosting the Memorial Cup." - HP Scout Jean Francois Dore

SEASON	LEAGUE	GAMES	GOALS	ASSISTS	PPG	PIM	HP RANKING
2012/13	QMJHL	38	3	4	0.18	8	145
2013/14	QMJHL	67	9	29	0.57	24	

Donato, Ryan
RC -Dexter School (High-MA) 6'2.5" 174

Donato should be a lock to be the first High School player selected in this years draft. Ryan has excellent hockey sense and is one of those players who seems to have the puck on his stick a lot more often than other players on the ice. He seemingly makes some sort of play almost every single shift. He's a smart responsible player who continues to improve. His skating is just ok. He needs to improve his foot speed to get quicker and faster.

Whoever drafts Donato is going to land a highly skilled forward with great hands. He has great touch, can score and make plays, and protect the puck. NHL bloodlines won't hurt him any on draft day but this kid won't be a favor pick. He's a legit top 60 talent in our opinion.

Quotable: "Liked him going back to the All American Prospects Game back in September. He had a couple points that day, won some faceoffs and kick started his draft year off on a good note." – Mark Edwards

SEASON	LEAGUE	GAMES	GOALS	ASSISTS	PPG	PIM	HP RANKING
2012/13	USHS	28	29	31	2.14	60	53
2013/14	USHS	30	37	41	2.6	78	

Dougherty, Jack
RD – USNTDP (USHL) – 6'02" 185

Dougherty has a good blend of offensive skill, hockey smarts, positioning, and physicality. He is a good skater. Dougherty plays a calm, cool, and collected style game.

He has excellent poise with the puck in all situations. He is dependable and smart in his own zone, capable of moving the puck up ice through the neutral zone, and ups the ante in the offensive zone. His mobility is solid enough to allow him good lateral movement along the blue line, and he's really creative with the puck in that area. He opens up the lanes really well and does a good job creating options for himself. Pressure doesn't faze him, he excels under it. He possesses a heavy slap shot and equally effective wrist shot. Has excellent offensive instincts.

Physicality is certainly in his recipe. He finishes his checks and is a heavy hitter. Passing up a hit isn't in his vocabulary. Defensive zone awareness is a strong suit, as Dougherty is always in position and doesn't drift or get caught day dreaming. He always makes a good first pass and protects the puck well in the defensive zone. Dependable, smart, simple hockey in the defensive zone is his game. He will have time to develop further under Mike Eaves at the University of Wisconsin next season.

Quotable: "Hard nosed tough kid, very soft spoken when I spoke to him. He was bigger than I expected. He moves the puck but is not very dynamic. He logs a ton of minutes and he doesn't make a lot of mistakes." – Mark Edwards

Quotable: "Big physically strong, NHL size, NHL skating, hockey sense is lacking a bit." – NHL Scout

SEASON	LEAGUE	GAMES	GOALS	ASSISTS	PPG	PIM	HP RANKING
2013/14	USHL	23	4	8	0.52	34	27
2013/14	(U18)USDP	55	6	16	0.4	65	

Draisaitl, leon
LC – Prince Albert Raiders (WHL) – 6'01" 209

With pro size and tremendous strength, Draisaitl play brings a consistent effort and his compete level is tremendous every night. Leon can dazzle you with his hands, crisp passes or his serious determination to make a difference in the defensive zone - Leon is a rare player that can impact the game in multiple ways. Leon possesses an excellent set of hands and is always a threat offensively. Leon tends to be more of a playmaker than a prolific goal scorer as he is able to make dazzling sauce passes through traffic. That being said, he does have a plus shot and soft hands in tight when given a path to the net.

His powerful skill set derives from his proven hockey sense and his excellent ability to make plays happen in all situations. Leon has this uncanny ability to recognize the play unfolding and reads and reacts before his opposition knew what hit them. Around the net Leon has tremendous hands combined with his quick release which caused havoc all year for goaltenders. He will use his power to drive the net and bang home a garbage goal or fend off a defender using his powerful size to control and protect the puck then unleash a quick snapper in the back of the net. His first few strides are sub-par, but when the train gets moving look out, there is no one in this year's draft class who can use his size and strength to protect the puck like Leon does. The kid is a horse and defenders struggled to knock him off the puck all year. Leon has proven night in, night out, that he can be a consistent offensive contributor and possesses and great opportunity to make the jump to the NHL next year.

He loves to slow the pace of the game and work his magic down low. His exceptional strength and reach make it difficult to take the puck from him. Draisaitl likes to bait players into thinking they can strip him of the puck so that he can force a player out of position before he makes a tape to tape pass while being checked. The problem with this is that Draisaitl has had so much success at the Major Junior level by slowing things down, using the walls and physically dominating opponents that he doesn't often show the ability to switch gears and generate offense with speed. He'll have a much harder time physically overmatching defenders if he can't do it at a higher pace of play. Leon brings a unique blend of skill and power to his game both offensively and defensively. Draisaitl enjoys the offensive zone time, but is quite apt and comfortable when defending. The skating is a definite concern, but if he's able to improve his pace, he could end up as the best player in the entire draft class.

Quotable: "Skating is obviously the biggest concern but this kid can buy time with the puck to make plays." – NHL Scout

Quotable: "Leon is a tremendous talent. He has great vision, skill and size. Not overly physical, but tough to knock off the puck. If he can increase his pace of play, he has all the talent to be the best player in the draft." – Scott McDougall

Quotable: "He's the trailer of all the big guns at the top of the draft for me." – NHL Scout

Quotable: "Our staff is a bit split on him." NHL Scout

SEASON	LEAGUE	GAMES	GOALS	ASSISTS	PPG	PIM	HP RANKING
2012/13	WHL	64	21	37	0.91	22	6
2013/14	WHL	64	38	67	1.64	24	

Duchesne, Jonathan
LD – Ottawa 67's (OHL) – 6'00" 204

Jonathan has received a large amount of ice in his first two years with the 67's on a rebuilding team. He has good size, and is very physically strong. He loves to play physical, and finishes his checks consistently along the wall. Very rarely does he pass up a chance to impose his strength on the wall. He wins his fair share of battles, but has trouble containing some of the higher skilled forwards in the OHL. Duchesne was used on the penalty kill, and did an effective job battling hard, and clearing bodies from the slot area. Unfortunately his skating is a major concern, and while it has shown some mild improvements, it hasn't come nearly as far as we had hoped by this point. He is clumsy off the start, and doesn't generate a good top speed due to not getting enough power in his strides. His puck movement ability is minimal at best. He struggles visualizing appropriate lanes to pass through, and can serve up some big turnovers in his own zone. When pressured with the puck he will rely on the glass and out concept, which limits the number of turnovers when pressured hard. Overall we see some positives in Jonathan's game, but not enough to consider him a prospect for the 2014 NHL Entry Draft.

SEASON	LEAGUE	GAMES	GOALS	ASSISTS	PPG	PIM	HP RANKING
2012/13	OHL	52	0	4	0.08	63	NR
2013/14	OHL	64	6	8	0.22	83	

Duke, Reid
RC – Lethbridge Hurricanes (WHL) – 6'00" 188

Reid is a strong skater with good speed and agility. He is strong on his feet and his improved core strength allows him to bounce off checks where he previously was knocked off the puck. He is able to handle the puck without losing his overall speed and quickness. Playing for a terrible Hurricanes team this year, Reid was relied upon to play big minutes and help carry the team along with a select few veterans. Reid centered Lethbridge's 2nd line this season and often played the point on the team's 1st powerplay unit where he was able to utilize his strong passing abilities. Almost exactly half of his offensive contributions came with the man advantage. He does well to find space in the offensive zone and he is able to create his own scoring chances. This is of importance as when he distributes the puck, he often didn't get it back it back as few of his linemates were able to play at his pace. While he may have been able to produce a bit more offensively had he played on a better team, he also left us wanting more. His effort level varied from time to time as did that of many of his teammates throughout some lopsided scores. Reid is willing to go to the tough areas of the ice and has a bit of a mean streak. He finishes his checks and does not tolerate opponents taking any liberties. Defensively he has an active stick, but he can be prone to give up too much space to opponents. In addition to his contributions Duke was one of the best draft eligible players in the face-off circle in the entire 2014 NHL Entry Draft. He commonly won 75-90% of draws in our viewings and was relied upon to win some big draws in some of the closer games for his team. This is certainly an underrated asset within his game. Duke shows good projection at the next level if he can play to his capabilities on a regular basis. He has good offensive skills, he has an edge and a mean streak to his game and he's willing to compete defensively.

Quotable: "Duke is a player I've been able to see in international competition/camps and I was very impressed by his ability to play so many different roles providing energy, finishing checks, winning face-offs and chipping in offensively." - HP Scout Ryan Yessie

SEASON	LEAGUE	GAMES	GOALS	ASSISTS	PPG	PIM	HP RANKING
2012/13	WHL	57	8	16	0.42	30	62
2013/14	WHL	62	15	25	0.65	91	

Dulong, Trevor
LC – Ottawa 67's (OHL) – 5'11" 193

Trevor is a simplistic two-way forward who has accomplished everything he has to this point because of his work ethic. He provides a lot of energy, finishes his checks hard, and pressures the puck carrier hard. He plays a full 200-foot game, and competes well in the defensive zone, working for pucks. He is a very responsible forward, who can almost chip in as a third defenseman when his line is pinned deep. He possesses very limited offensive ability, but is smart with getting the puck deep, and competing on the cycle. He also skates well, which is a real boost to his forecheck. We don't expect Dulong to be selected at the 2014 NHL Entry Draft.

SEASON	LEAGUE	GAMES	GOALS	ASSISTS	PPG	PIM	HP RANKING
2013/14	CCHL	19	4	14	0.95	17	NR
2013/14	OHL	18	0	2	0.11	6	

Dvorak, Christian
LW – London Knights (OHL) – 6'00" 178

Christian signed with the London Knights over the summer, and made an impression on our scouts right from training camp with his skillset. Dvorak turned into an excellent two-way forward for the Knights after getting his feet wet in the OHL. He filled in primarily in the bottom six showing great defensive awareness, and responsibility. He is generally the first forward back in the defensive zone, and battles down low forcing turnovers. He excelled in five-on-five situations. Dvorak was utilized regularly on the penalty kill, despite several veteran forwards on the roster. He gets into passing lanes well, and pressures the point effectively. He is also a threat to score short handed. He possesses speed, and hands to create offense. When the Knights' were short a few forwards, Christian filled into the scoring lines, and did an impressive job with less than half an OHL season under his belt. He is creative with the puck, and a dangerous playmaker that both possesses the puck, and can create a scoring chance for himself, but also his linemates. Unfortunately a knee injury caused Dvorak to miss the entire second half of his draft year. However, he was able to show not only skills in all three zones, but the ability to quickly learn, and improve on a very sharp curve making him an appealing option, and a virtual lock to be selected at the 2014 NHL Entry Draft, regardless of injury.

"Christian's knee injury was very disappointing as he was just hitting his stride. But he showed before the injury and at the MasterCard Memorial Cup he is capable of playing in every situation and is very reliable both offensively and defensively." - Ryan Yessie

Quotable: "Saw enough him before his injury to see his skill. He's made an impressive comeback from injury and will show his stuff next season." - Mark Edwards

SEASON	LEAGUE	GAMES	GOALS	ASSISTS	PPG	PIM	HP RANKING
2012/13	Midget	58	35	57	1.59	8	38
2013/14	OHL	33	6	8	0.42	0	

Ehlers, Nikolaj
RW – Halifax Mooseheads (QMJHL) – 5'11" 163

The Danish forward was selected 6th overall by the Mooseheads in the 2013 CHL Import Draft after playing in Switzerland, where his father coached for several years. Ehlers had an amazing year, one of the best rookie seasons by a European player ever in the league. He reached the 100-point plateau, and came one goal short of hitting the 50-goal mark.

In the first half of the season, Ehlers was great, adapting in little time to a new league and a new culture. He established himself as the top draft-eligible player from the QMJHL in our view, but it was in the second half of the season that he took his game to a higher level. Ehlers speed was too much for defensemen in the QMJHL. He is a fantastic skater, he has an effortless stride and can gain his top speed in two or three strides. He has explosive skating abilities and is able to accelerate exceptionally well, always keeping his feet moving which helps him create space for himself and openings for his linemates. Ehlers possesses tremendous puck control and has made magnificent plays in tight spaces. He changes direction abruptly, twisting and turning on a dime, and has shown tremendous control with the puck, executing complex manoeuvres quickly and effectively through and around players. One of the aspects that we appreciate out of Ehlers a lot is that he likes to use his backhand shot when he's one-on-one with a goaltender. Backhand shots are tough for goaltenders to read, and have become a lost art in today's hockey.

Ehlers might be the best skater in the entire draft, but he's also very good at slowing down the play in the offensive zone and creating plays as the playmaker as well. He's also very adept at making plays at top speed, which is what separates him from other great skaters. He has a goal-scorer's wrist shot, with a lightning-quick release which gives no time for goaltenders to react. His slapshot might not be as good as his wrist shot, but it is still very dangerous and Ehlers can score from just about anywhere in the offensive zone. Ehlers' season was remarkable because of the fact that in the majority of the games he played on a different line than Jonathan Drouin.

The biggest question mark with Ehlers this year has been his size. He does lack strength, and there's a reason why we would be very surprised to see him make the jump to the NHL next season. He needs to physically mature, which he would be able to do in the next two years. Although he's not overly big, Ehlers doesn't back down from physical play or from playing in the tough areas. He has a great compete level and can throw some good hits here and there. At the moment, when facing bigger players, he can struggle to win those puck battles in the corners, but with an added mass to his frame, he should be fine. Another area of Ehlers' game that is underrated is his play without the puck. He is one of the league's plus/minus leaders if you put weight in such stats. He competes hard in the defensive zone and he has become an excellent penalty killer during the year. He has great anticipation and, with his great speed, that makes him a constant threat to score shorthanded.

Quotable: "Our pre-season rank was a bit cautious as a late first rounder. He quickly showed us he could be worthy of a much higher selection. In my own live viewings he had four periods I would consider average, he was dynamite the rest of the time. Amongst other things, I love his intelligence and his quick feet. He is fantastic at moving laterally with great speed, even while carrying the puck. We moved him into the top 5 and he went on a hot streak, many others soon had him moving up their boards." - Mark Edwards

Quotable: "I saw you moved Ehlers all the way up to number three overall, I don't think he will make you look dumb." - NHL Scout

Quotable: "Our staff loves him." NHL Scout

Quotable: "I saw him play poorly twice, tonight and at the Top Prospects Game." - NHL Scout

Quotable: "I think we may have him ranked higher than some teams but obviously that's just an educated guess." NHL Scout

Quotable: "So you can take Ehlers on a wing or a big kid like Perlini, why wouldn't you take the six foot four kid?" - NHL Scout

SEASON	LEAGUE	GAMES	GOALS	ASSISTS	PPG	PIM	HP RANKING
2012/13	SWI Jr. A	32	26	23	1.53	34	4
2013/14	QMJHL	63	49	55	1.65	51	

Eiserman, Shane
LC – Dubuque Fighting Saints (USHL) – 6'02" 200

The QMJHL draftee opted for the USNTDP for a season before leaving the national program for Dubuque after the 2012-2013 season. While with the national program he also represented Team USA at the 2013 U18's, where he recorded one assist in six games during the tournament.

Eiserman is a big, strong, physical power forward with the skill and skating ability to match. He is a heavy hitter, and is always looking to put a body on someone whenever given the chance. Some of the biggest hits viewed all season long came courtesy of Shane. High compete level at both ends of the ice, responsible defensively. He backchecks hard, always covers his assignment in the defensive zone, has good support, and is responsible with the puck in his own end. He always plays it safe and smart outleting the puck, and is very largely mistake-free in his own end. He's a big body, and that combined with his high effort level leads to him winning most board battles. There are times where the effort level was in question, however, and was less consistent than you would like.

Offensively, Shane has the skating ability, strength, and hands to bull his way through traffic. When he's not bulldozing, he's drawing defenders to him and dishing the puck off to teammates. He uses his line mates well and creates a lot of space for them and himself to operate. He often just simply overpowers defenders, plain and simple. He has decent foot speed and mobility, but it could be improved. Once at full speed, though, he's tough to stop.

His offensive play did tail off a bit toward the end of the season, and he had a disappointing Clark Cup Playoff, registering only two assists in seven games. The dip was a bit concerning, as were the periods where it seemed like he could work harder, so it will be interesting to see how he responds at the University of New Hampshire next season. If he works hard and the effort is there, he could be a real good power forward at the NHL level, but the effort has to become much more consistent.

SEASON	LEAGUE	GAMES	GOALS	ASSISTS	PPG	PIM	HP RANKING
2012/13	(U18)USDP	56	10	11	0.38	37	97
2013/14	USHL	53	16	24	0.75	71	

Ekblad, Aaron
RD – Barrie Colts (OHL) – 6'4" 217

Ekblad is a big, strong defenseman who can skate well for his size. His strides aren't always pretty, but they're powerful, and he gets around the ice pretty well. Defensively, he uses his long reach, and an active stick to get in passing lanes, and knock the puck off of sticks. Ekblad isn't as physical as you'd like to see given his size advantage over almost every player, but every now and then he shows signs of a mean streak that helps him dominate games. We would like to see it a lot more. Typically he uses his solid positioning to keep players to the outside before rubbing them off the puck along the wall. At times he chases the play, and gets caught out of position, which burned him on occasion in the playoffs. He already has a pro shot, and is effective with both his slapper, and wrist shot. On the powerplay he's a huge threat, and is definitely more of a shooter than playmaker. Ekblad's backhand passing is pretty good, and he's typically good passing in a straight line or cross-ice on the powerplay. Ekblad is a good stationary passer, and his outlet passes are OK, but at times he throws it in his teammates feet or flat out misses them. That's something that should be automatic at this point of his OHL career. He likes to carry the puck out of the zone whenever he can, and is confident with the puck on his stick. Ekblad's a good stickhandler, and is able to step around defenders more often than not.

On the penalty kill, Ekblad is good. He uses his long reach to disrupt the passing lanes, which helps him a lot. He usually can clear the front of the net as well, though if he had more of a mean streak he could do it more effectively. His backwards skating is OK, but he seems to struggle with pivots at times, which allows opposing players to get around him.

It also can lead to some shots from the outside, that probably could be prevented. Ekblad loves one-on-one battles with top players, but at times he struggled with physical opponents like Nick Ritchie and Ben Thomson.

SEASON	LEAGUE	GAMES	GOALS	ASSISTS	PPG	PIM	HP RANKING
2012/13	OHL	54	7	27	0.63	64	3
2013/14	OHL	58	23	30	0.91	91	

Elie, Tristen
LW – London Knights (OHL) – 5'10" 175

Tristen is the brother of current Dallas Stars' prospect Remi Elie, and spent the majority of the season playing for the London Jr. B Nationals team, but was one of the first call-ups. Tristen was very effective during his stints with the Knights. While he lacks the power forward size that big brother Remi possesses, Tristen plays with the same mindset trying to hit everything that moves. He battles hard for pucks, and displays no shortage of effort on a shift-by-shift basis. While Tristen lacks the size of his brother, he does possess the speed that his brother lacks, allowing him to provide relentless pressure on the forecheck. He didn't create much offense, but displays a shoot first mentality with an above average shot. Being on a team that boasts 7 NHL prospects at the forward position, Tristen was unable to display his potential on a wide spectrum. He is a player who may receive late round consideration, but ultimately is not a player we expect to see selected in this year's draft. When several Knights' forwards graduate, Tristen is expected to take on a regular role with the team, where he should be able to show his true potential at the OHL level.

SEASON	LEAGUE	GAMES	GOALS	ASSISTS	PPG	PIM	HP RANKING
2013/14	GOJHL	34	21	19	1.18	30	NR
2013/14	OHL	11	0	0	0	0	

Englund, Andreas
LD - Djurgarden (SWE 2) – 6'3.25" 189

Englund is really big kid who competes hard. He didn't show us a huge amount of hockey sense but he can really skate. He was in a group of the 'big three' we needed to see more of coming into the season. He's the best skater by far over Lagesson and Olas-Mattsson. The size, skating ability and compete level make it easy to rank him as a draftable player. He plays with heart and wants to make a difference every game. He could have a wide range of rankings amongst the NHL teams.

SEASON	LEAGUE	GAMES	GOALS	ASSISTS	PPG	PIM	HP RANKING
2013/14	U20 S.Elit	33	5	5	0.3	26	42
2013/14	SHL 2	19	1	1	0.11	14	

Evans, Jake
RW – St. Michael's Buzzers (OJHL) – 6'0" 180

Evans is a skilled offensive winger for the St. Michael's Buzzers. Jake is currently committed to play NCAA hockey at the University of Notre Dame. Evans displays a strong offensive skill set and has continuously improved his offensive numbers at the Junior A level. He is an elite finisher in the league and has the ability to take over games with his offence. Jake is a strong smooth skater and has the ability to beat defenders wide with a quick burst. He displays good hands and elite puck skills in the offensive zone and is good at finding openings in coverage.

Evans has a strong wrist shot with a quick release coming off the half wall on the powerplay that is very effective. Jake is also a good playmaker and uses his vision well to set up teammates with crisp cross ice passes or threads the needle through traffic for backdoor opportunities. He stands up for himself after whistles and is not afraid to use his stick for cross checks or slashes when pushed. Jake can disappear at times when games get to physical and needs to work at bringing a consistent effort every shift. There are some games when he is an absolute game changer while others he looks like he does not even want to be on the ice.

SEASON	LEAGUE	GAMES	GOALS	ASSISTS	PPG	PIM	HP RANKING
2012/13	OJHL	50	12	32	0.88	45	139
2013/14	OJHL	49	16	47	1.29	79	

Fabbri, Robby
LC – Guelph Storm (OHL) – 5'11" 170

Fabbri is an elite offensive center from the Guelph Storm. He is constantly displaying a high level of offensive instincts, providing a threat to score whenever he is on the ice. Robby was an offensive dynamo this season falling just short of 50 goals after having to sit out a 10 game suspension mid-way through the season. Although he scored a lot of highlight reel goals, he was also a very effective playmaker putting up similar assist numbers as well. He showed great chemistry with Kerby Rychel and Zach Mitchell centering one of the top offensive lines in the league. Robby is also strong in the faceoff circle taking numerous key draws late in games of all situations. One underrated aspect of his game is his skating ability, he is deceptively fast and shows good burst entering the offensive zone allowing him to beat defenders wide or up the middle depending on the situation. He has one of the best sets of hands in tight in the draft class this season leaving both opponents and teammates in awe on numerous occasions. Fabbri is also lethal on the power play utilizing a heavy shot with a quick release coming down off the high wall or finding teammates back door. While his offensive accolades jump off the page he is also a very reliable defender and is constantly helping out down low in the defensive zone and picking up forwards in key scoring positions. He is very good at not playing where the puck is instead playing where it is going to be which allows him to find holes and openings in all areas of the ice. Although considered to be undersized for the center role at the National League level, Fabbri consistently plays much larger than he is, initiating contact all over the ice including a number of big body checks one of which resulted in the aforementioned suspension. Fabbri also shows a very high compete level and a willingness to play through injury. He does have a tendency to put himself into tough areas of the ice where opponents are able to finish him with big checks but he works hard to get up every time and shows no fear taking a hit to make a play for his teammates but will have to work on this in order to stay healthy at the next level. Fabbri is such a clutch big game player and one whom the Storm would lean on to get the offence rolling or to make a play on many key goals throughout the season. He had an exceptional playoff run in the Ontario Hockey League capped off by winning the Wayne Gretzky trophy as MVP of the playoffs. Robby continues to improve each season and has proved doubters wrong at each level he has reached. He is expected to be a first round pick this year. He needs to work at putting weight onto his frame this offseason in order to be better prepared for the next level.

Quotable: "Not a huge kid but he did get slightly bigger and he did everything in his power this season to play himself into being selected in the first round." - Mark Edwards

Quotable: "Maybe a late first but more likely a 2nd rounder." - NHL Scout

SEASON	LEAGUE	GAMES	GOALS	ASSISTS	PPG	PIM	HP RANKING
2012/13	OHL	59	10	23	0.56	38	24
2013/14	OHL	58	45	42	1.5	55	

Fazleev, Radel
LW – Calgary Hitmen (WHL) – 6'00" 178

Radel translated some strong international play into the Hitmen selecting him in the 1st round of the 2013 CHL Import draft. While his skill was apparent early on, Fazleev struggled to adjust to the WHL style of play at first. He lacks high-end top speed and quickly found out he wasn't able to dangle through entire teams. After making some strides, Fazleev suffered a wrist injury that kept him out of the second half of the season. He returned from injury in the playoffs where he was among Calgary's best players in a first round loss to the Kootenay Ice. Fazleev's strengths are his strong puck possession skills, his ability to control the puck while on his edges and ability to distribute the puck. That being said, he can sometimes be his own worst enemy when he isn't firm enough with cross ice passes allowing them to be picked off by opponents. He has shown good character is standing up for his teammates. He also earned the praise of team trainers with his solid work ethic in trying to rehabilitate his wrist and hitting the gym to get stronger and faster. Especially considering his late season play, Fazleev remains an intriguing option for teams trying to infuse some skill into their prospect pool.

SEASON	LEAGUE	GAMES	GOALS	ASSISTS	PPG	PIM	HP RANKING
2012/13	MHL B	23	7	10	0.74	8	114
2013/14	WHL	38	5	20	0.66	12	

Fiala, Kevin
LW – HV71 (SWE) – 5'10" 180

We first saw Fiala at the Four Nations tournament last fall. While he made an impression, he has certainly made big strides in his game since then. Kevin blends speed and skill in a smallish package. He possess good speed and impressive agility, especially when he has the puck. His first few steps are strong, allowing him to dance off walls or breakout quickly from the offensive zone. In order for us to rank players measuring in the 5'10" range we like to see them possess some high end skills and skating ability amongst other traits. Fiala has shown us some of those abilities in our viewings.

Kevin is a competitive player who doesn't back down from battling for pucks. He can be relentless in his puck pursuit at times. He brings that compete level along with a high hockey IQ to the offensive zone where he really shines. He's adept at buying himself time and space using quick feet and great puck handling skills. His hands are soft- they are high-end. He has a great shot with a quick release, again like some of his other skills, it's high end. He has great poise in the offensive zone and reads the play well. Fiala can also beat defenders off the rush using a combination of his speed, agility, puck skills and smarts. He can tend to try to do too much at times, a common trait amongst some highly skilled players, this leads to needless turnovers. He needs to work on playing a simple game at times, pucks in, pucks out. Dangles in your own zone leading to turnovers won't help your career.

Fiala is not a star in the defensive zone but he's not a complete disaster either. He uses his smarts to be in position and read plays but can be timid at times along the wall. He is generally solid providing back pressure and does a fair job getting pucks out of the zone. His size will limit his effectiveness in all three zones in the NHL as far as winning pucks consistently but that's a tradeoff teams make for players with his type of skillset. He can be seen flying the zone a bit early, cheating offensively at times.

Fiala is a good example of a player who continued to get better in his draft year. Offensively he shows the ability to project as a top 6 player at the next level because of his scoring abilities. Speed and scoring skills without being a liability in his own zone make it easier to look past his 5'10" (generous?) frame. He is a first round talent.

Quotable: "Wasn't impressed with him in his interview using the number of games he played this year to opt out of testing at the combine. Fabbri played a few games this year didn't he?" - NHL Scout

Quotable: "Fiala showed me improvement in many areas at the U18 in Finland as compared to seeing him last season at the Four Nations. I loved his blend of speed and skill combined with smarts and the ability to beat players off the rush. To draft smaller players in the first round, I like them to have the ability to make plays at high speed. Fiala showed me that ability." - Mark Edwards

SEASON	LEAGUE	GAMES	GOALS	ASSISTS	PPG	PIM	HP RANKING
2013/14	U20 S.Elit	27	10	15	0.93	40	15
2013/14	SHL	17	3	8	0.65	10	

Fidler, Miguel
LW – Edina High (HS-MN) – 6'00" 186

Miguel displays some good natural athletic ability. He is a decent skater and effective size and really improved offensively this year but what he's most noticeable for is the edge he plays with. Miguel can border on dirty at times delivering questionable hits from behind, taking the extra shot whenever he can and is a very difficult and agitating player to play against. He is the type of player you hate to play against and will likely wind up a little bruised if you're matched up against his line.

SEASON	LEAGUE	GAMES	GOALS	ASSISTS	PPG	PIM	HP RANKING
2012/13	USHS	23	5	6	0.48	28	191
2013/14	USHS	45	21	29	1.11	56	

Fiegl, Jared
LW/C – USNTDP (USHL) – 6'01" 198

Big-bodied, physical forward is a crasher and a banger. Relishes the physical side of the game. Decent puck handler but not a lot of offensive skill. He protects the puck well with his body and is pretty good with it in tight areas and along the boards, drives the net hard. Fiegl is smart and responsible in his own end, and is an aggressive forechecker and backchecker. He is likely best suited in a bottom six role at the NHL level. Cornell University commit.

SEASON	LEAGUE	GAMES	GOALS	ASSISTS	PPG	PIM	HP RANKING
2012/13	(U17)USDP	56	7	9	0.29	37	NR
2013/14	(U18)USDP	45	2	4	0.13	26	

Fleury, Haydn
LD – Red Deer Rebels (WHL) – 6'03" 198

Haydn is a solid two-way defender with excellent speed and agility for a player of his size. He plays a mature defensive zone game where his speed, mobility, and reach allow him to be able to maintain a tight gap when defending. His footwork in tight areas is very good. He can be very difficult to beat one-on-one and he is able to effectively challenge zone entries. Haydn prefers to tactically obtain the puck with a stick check rather than to go for a crushing hit. Not overly physical, but is willing and capable of finishing his checks when presented the opportunity. He is not shy of physical contact and while he could be described as composed and a calculated individual, he has developed a bit of a mean streak when defending his goalie. Haydn is calm under pressure and is as equally comfortable skating the puck out of his zone as he is making accurate stretch passes to move the play up ice. His play in front of the net combined with his size and physicality is excellent. He has no issues moving out unwanted players from the paint but still could add strength to his frame. He seems to understand that he is more valuable to his team when he is out on the ice and not in the penalty box. Haydn possesses a high compete level. Offensively, Haydn can be dangerous when leading the rush and his pivoting is strong enough to keep defenders honest. While he improved his offensive totals considerably from the prior season in going from 19 to 46 points, he can still develop this part of his game. He realized that the strength of his game is in taking care of his end first. As a result, he likes to simplify things and conserve energy by simply making an accurate outlet pass rather than challenge defenders with his good stick-handling abilities off the rush. He will be relied upon to take charge of the rush on a more consistent basis going forwards. Haydn needs to improve his shot. Currently he has put more pucks on net this season through traffic, but he needs to improve his release on his wrist shot as well as add some velocity to his clapper. His offensive vision is still limited but has shown huge improvements in this area of this game and has been able to produce more offensive number consistently because of it. Although Fleury uses his size and speed to shut down the rush he can still learn to take better angles on opposing forwards to take away any sort of offensive opportunities and be a very dominate defender in this department. Haydn will also need to improve his decisions regarding pinching to keep the puck in the offensive zone as he doesn't always pick his spots well. This is something he often gets away with at the WHL level as he is able to recover with his strong skating skills, but is something he'll definitely need to clean up as he graduates to the pro ranks. The team picking Fleury will be getting a shutdown defenseman that is able to log huge minutes due to his reliability and the way he is able to conserve energy so that he can selectively choose his spots offensively. Fleury has shown great improvement year over year and the team that picks him will also have to be patient with his offensive game as it will require time to mature. Fleury likely won't be a powerplay guy at the next level, but will be able to log considerable time at even strength and on the penalty kill.

Quotable: "I don't understand the hype on this kid. He's a solid player but this top 12 stuff baffles me. He's a future third pairing guy." – NHL Scout

Quotable: "It's a lock that he is the 2nd defenseman taken in this draft. He's got very few weaknesses in his game." – NHL Scout

Quotable: "I really liked him going back to last season. He impressed me with his improvement in the Dzone, especially his battles along walls. He knew it was a weakness and he's not all the way there yet, but he became harder to play against this year." – Mark Edwards

SEASON	LEAGUE	GAMES	GOALS	ASSISTS	PPG	PIM	HP RANKING
2012/13	WHL	66	4	15	0.29	21	10
2013/14	WHL	70	8	38	0.66	46	

Flinn, Jack
G – Owen Sound Attack (OHL) – 6'07" 205

Jack is a huge 6'7" goaltender who spent last season with the Sherbrooke Phoenix. After being claimed off waivers by the Owen Sound Attack in the first week of this season, he served as the backup for Brandon Hope. He does a good job keeping calm under pressure. He handles sustained pressure in his zone well, and maintains focus effectively. He consistently made the first save, but was sometimes out of position on second chance opportunities.

His rebound control isn't horrible, but it is below average, and can get him into trouble. His side-to-side is the biggest area of concern. His reflexes aren't excellent, and he generally gets beat on cross-ice one-timers, and struggled on a regular basis in all of our viewings with side-to-side movement. His lower body in general is not very quick.

SEASON	LEAGUE	GAMES	GAA	SV%	W	L	SO	HP RANKING
2012/13	QMJHL	18	4.49	0.870	1	13	0	NR
2013/14	OHL	21	4.01	0.894	3	10	0	

Ford, Keegan
LD – Dubuque Fighting Saints (USHL) – 5'09" 180

Keegan had a strong 2013-2014 campaign, further developing and improving his game from the previous season despite no major changes to his stat line. Slated to become a Wisconsin Badger this Fall, Keegan had a fine USHL final season and will be a great addition to Mike Eaves' lineup next season.

Scrappy describes Keegan's game mildly, and 87 PIM this season attests to that. While not an imposing figure physically, Keegan is extremely strong, and combined with his speed has the ability to put players into the fourth row with his hits. Relishing the physical side of the game, Keegan takes his opportunities to lay a body on players any chance he gets. He backs down from no one, and is capable of dropping players much bigger than him and did so numerous times this season. He's no stranger to taking a shot after the whistle and sucking players into taking retaliatory penalties. He gets under your skin and is just an abrasive player to play against.

Aside from the snarl, Keegan plays a smart defensive game. He is always in position, supports his partner well, and makes smart, safe decisions with the puck in his own zone. He takes good angles on attacking players and is very good at stepping up and forcing their hand at his defensive blue line. Especially for a smaller player with less length, he's extremely difficult to get around. He does a great job at jumping the passing lanes and anticipates the play very well. He's a smooth skater and is very mobile with his quick feet. Moves very well laterally, and has a very quick first step, which aides in his abilities to move the puck up out of his own zone as well as making plays in the neutral and offensive zones. Excellent in transition. Size is a concern.

SEASON	LEAGUE	GAMES	GOALS	ASSISTS	PPG	PIM	HP RANKING
2012/13	USHL	43	4	12	0.37	94	NR
2013/14	USHL	60	1	16	0.28	87	

Forsling, Gustav
LD – Linkoping (SWE Jr) -5'11.25"

Gustav measures in slightly under the ideal height threshold that NHL teams seek when it comes to drafting defensemen but it's not like their aren't some quality 5'11" D-Men in the NHL. Forsling has some impressive offensive attributes to his game.. He is a good puck mover, making good smart passes out of his zone. He loves the offensive side of the game and will jump into the rush when the opportunity presents itself. He really likes to skate the puck as well and he is effective doing so. He is able to gain the offensive zone with his feet. His skating is very good, he has quickness and shows off good agility. Once in the offensive zone he shines, he has impressed us with smart accurate passes and a fantastic shot, including an effective one-timer, we used the word "cannon" more than once in our notes. We liked him on the powerplay. He's a smart player and made good decisions with the puck but he shines by blasting his one-timer on net.

Forsling looked timid at times under duress during potential physical plays. He is smart enough that we think he will grow out of it. While he's not what we would describe as a shutdown guy, he was effective in his positioning and understands team defense. If not for his timid play at times, Forsling would be ranked higher.

Quotable: "Looking back at my game report notes, most of what I wrote was positive going all the way back to the U17 in Victoriaville. Love the cannon shot and he is a smart player. The difference between him and guys like Aho & Honka, is that Forsling is more tentative retrieving pucks versus a heavy forecheck. He also tends to try to skate out of trouble rather than use his head to explore options. Tough to skate it all the time." - Mark Edwards

SEASON	LEAGUE	GAMES	GOALS	ASSISTS	PPG	PIM	HP RANKING
2012/13	U20 S.Elit	14	0	1	0.07	8	48
2013/14	U20 S.Elit	44	6	12	0.41	36	

Fortunato, Brandon
LD – USNTDP (USHL) – 5'11" 148

There is a lot to like about Fortunato's game. The first thing is obviously his size. He's definitely light at 5'11. You can't teach Fortunato's hockey IQ, vision, or skating ability. He is an excellent skater, silky smooth in transition and extremely nimble and mobile. With his vision and skating prowess, he evades opposing players very well and is rarely hit, especially in open ice. With that said, he doesn't shy away from contact and will always take a hit to make a play. He doesn't lay people out, but he will put a body on puck carriers and have enough impact to remove them from the puck and disrupt their path. He's smart enough and good enough with his stick that he successfully defends without contact often. He has a really good offensive skill set, and puts himself in position for quality looks on net often. His vision and IQ enable a really strong playmaking ability, and he's a dangerous player in the offensive zone. His size is a concern but there's room for him to fill out and the rest of his skill set is solid. He has value later on in the draft and should take his time developing and getting stronger at the NCAA level. He will have plenty of time to do that at Boston University, where he will be attending this Fall along with teammate and roommate, Jack Eichel.

Quotable: "He probably goes later in the draft, I like everything but his size, smooth skater, smart player. - Mark Edwards

SEASON	LEAGUE	GAMES	GOALS	ASSISTS	PPG	PIM	HP RANKING
2013/14	USHL	26	1	16	0.65	6	NR
2013/14	(U18)USDP	61	3	34	0.61	14	

Foss, Ryan
LC – Windsor Spitfires (OHL) – 6'02" 170

In his rookie season Ryan posted great numbers for a young player, and got a lot of ice time on the top line for the Spitfires, being on the top two lines for the majority of the season. He plays a very systematic game, and does a lot of the simplistic basic things that helps a team succeed. Foss has good size, and protects the puck well down low. He is an expert at the cycle game, and loves to control the puck around the corners, up the walls, and behind the net. When he has the puck in the neutral zone he will get pucks deep regardless of the situation, and has decent speed for his size to have moderate success in the dump and chase game. His game is like clockwork, and was very consistent in these areas. He plays a full 200-foot game, and competes in the defensive zone.

He also shows physicality but isn't overly aggressive or mean. Despite getting top minutes along with powerplay ice, he is very limited in the offensive department, and his point totals can be deceptive. He isn't a natural goal scorer, and gets a lot of his points from playing with skilled players, and doing the little things right to help his line develop scoring chances. His upside is very limited, but he shows positive signs of being a solid role player at the NHL level. He has good size, and is an effective skater. Foss simply needs to add muscle, and hopefully develop a bit more of a mean, aggressive edge to him.

SEASON	LEAGUE	GAMES	GOALS	ASSISTS	PPG	PIM	HP RANKING
2012/13	CAHS	68	39	63	1.5	NA	157
2013/14	OHL	58	13	19	0.55	10	

Franklin, C.J.
LW – Sioux Falls (USHL) 5'11" 190

Franlin is a big strong heavy player who bulls through people out on the ice. He's a tough kid who goes hard to the net and wins battles. He's got good speed and is a high character player. When it comes to shooting, he's got that covered with great shooting fundamentals and a heavy shot with a quick release that will translate and still be effective at higher levels.

Franklin gets 'after it' and is hard to play against. He is going run people over and generally piss the other team off. He's not afraid to do the things like blocking shots. In our opinion, this kid could be a steal if he's available in the middle rounds. He was really good at the Jr. A Challenge. Had over 30 goals last year to show some consistency.

SEASON	LEAGUE	GAMES	GOALS	ASSISTS	PPG	PIM	HP RANKING
2012/13	USHL	63	32	27	0.94	60	71
2013/14	USHL	53	22	29	0.96	43	

Fram, Jason
RD – Spokane Chiefs (WHL) – 6'00" 195

A '95 birth-year player that was passed over in last year's draft, Jason has shown tremendous improvement is his game this season. Jason complied 57 points from the back end this season compared to only 15 points the previous year. Defensively Fram is very reliable as he has good body positioning and decent foot work. He has the ability to play with (and shut down) all type of forwards. His one-on-one play is probably the most impressive part of his defensive game as he is very difficult to beat. He is very aware of every situation on the ice and rarely makes mistakes. He has been the anchor on the penalty kill. Offensively, Fram has quarterbacked the power play very successfully this season. He chooses his options very well and makes quick decisions. He constantly uses a combination of shots from the point and is very effective at getting his point shot on net. Between his positional play and offensive ability, he is a two-way defender.

SEASON	LEAGUE	GAMES	GOALS	ASSISTS	PPG	PIM	HP RANKING
2012/13	WHL	60	1	14	0.25	20	NR
2013/14	WHL	72	6	51	0.79	34	

Friedman, Mark
RD – Waterloo Black Hawks (USHL) – 5'11" 185

Posting 75 points in 115 USHL games over two seasons, Friedman's offensive output and capability speaks for itself. That doesn't include his 12 points in 17 USHL playoff games.

Excellent speed and highly mobile, Friedman is a superb puck mover. Great stride, low, wide base, he packs a ton of power with each stride and has an explosive burst. His first few steps are excellent and he can reach top speed almost immediately. Moves the puck up ice through the neutral zone extremely well and is well suited for the power play. He is great at moving the puck back and forth along the blue line, creating passing and shooting lanes and keeping the puck moving in rotation for a quality open look on net. Pinches and keeps the puck in well, and does a great job reading the play and dropping low in the offensive half boards and corners to keep a puck in and maintain possession. Solid slap shot and a very quick, efficient wrist shot. Pucks find the net off of his stick. Very calm and comfortable with the puck. Great passer, especially on the stretch pass. Always tape to tape. High end offensive weapon on defense.

Mark is much more reliable defensively than the average offensive defenseman. Good hockey sense, smart, reads the play really well. Excellent anticipation. A cross ice pass in the neutral zone is virtually impossible when Friedman's on the ice. Between his ability anticipate and read the play and his mobility, he's able to jump the lane and disrupt the pass with ease, and that's not even taking into account how often he's able to take that puck right back the other and start a rush into the offensive zone. Shot blocking machine. All around, just a great influence to have in your defensive zone. He has the ability to slow the game down and calm things down, never panicked or looking rushed. Friedman obviously isn't a big body on defense, but his size is okay and his speed, strength, and hockey sense make up for a lot of things his smaller size may take away. He will need to continue to overcome his size at the next level in order to really show his true NHL upside.

Quotable: "Very competitive, good puck mover, offensive D but also competes defensively, size is only question." - HP Scout Sean White

SEASON	LEAGUE	GAMES	GOALS	ASSISTS	PPG	PIM	HP RANKING
2012/13	USHL	64	8	27	0.55	44	109
2013/14	USHL	51	10	30	0.78	30	

Gadoury, Philippe
LC – Halifax Mooseheads (QMJHL) – 5'11" 172

Gadoury was signed as a free agent by the Mooseheads last January while playing for the Nepean Raiders of the CCHL. He was originally committed to play with Northeastern University in the NCAA, but his chance to play major junior hockey with Jonathan Drouin was a great opportunity he couldn't pass up. Gadoury played at different levels these last couple of years; after playing two years in Midget AAA with College Charles Lemoyne, he went to play one prep school season with Hosaac School. The year after, he came back to Quebec and played one season with Cegep Andre-Laurendeau in the Quebec Collegial league before making the jump to the CCHL. Once with Halifax, he was an instant fit on Drouin's wing, and averaged a goal per game in 19 regular season games to finish the year showing a great scoring touch around the net. Gadoury has great positioning in the offensive zone, and knows how to get open, as he knows if he's open he's very likely to get a pass from Drouin. His hockey IQ is the best quality of his skillset. He's a decent skater with good straightaway speed, but not an overly physical player who can disappear when he gets hit. Possesses quick hands around the net, is known as a goal scorer but has above average vision, as he can make some good passes. The fact that Gadoury played with Jonathan Drouin in the second half of the year clearly helped him with his stats and also helps showcase himself for scouts. Drouin was a major reason for Gadoury's success with the Mooseheads, as Drouin makes players around him so much better. Gadoury is expected to be one of the Mooseheads overagers next season and should rack up tons of points.

SEASON	LEAGUE	GAMES	GOALS	ASSISTS	PPG	PIM	HP RANKING
2012/13	QCHL	31	20	15	1.13	24	NR
2013/14	QMJHL	19	20	6	1.37	12	

Gagnon, Ryan
D – Victoria Royals (WHL) – 6'01" 190

Ryan has good size and plays with a strong mean streak. Gagnon is a physical player who focuses on the defensive side of the game first. Although he has room to add size to his frame, he's already fairly strong and possesses good core strength. He has delivered some devastating checks over our viewings this season. However does have a tendency to get into penalty trouble with overaggressive play.

He is at his best with the puck when he makes the simple smart play. His puck skills are very limited and can get into trouble when making a play beyond the simple basic option. Ryan projects as a very physical shutdown defenseman who doesn't have a lot of upside, but could develop into a solid bottom pairing defender.

SEASON	LEAGUE	GAMES	GOALS	ASSISTS	PPG	PIM	HP RANKING
2012/13	WHL	48	0	3	0.06	24	NR
2013/14	WHL	66	2	6	0.12	55	

Gambrell, Dylan
RC – Dubuque Fighting Saints (USHL) – 5'11" 179

The Colorado Thunderbirds U16 product completed his second season with Dubuque this season after being drafted by the club 11th Overall in the 2012 Futures Draft. The slick-skating forward finished third in scoring for Dubuque this season.

Dylan is a strong two-way forward who can play both Right Wing and Center and was on both the power play and penalty kill units this season. Dylan has decent size but plays a big game. He likes to drive the net, with or without the puck, and picked up a lot of goals doing just that this season, be it tipping in one-timers on the rush or putting home rebounds.

Often on the power play you could find him planted right in the front of the net, giving the opposing goaltender fits. He's not afraid of the tough areas of the ice. He has good length and handles the puck really well in traffic. Dubuque, as a team, was very good at gaining zone entry with control of the puck, and Dylan was part of that group. He has an above average shot and decent release, and combined with his work ethic and nose for the net he can score goals in all fashions.

Dylan plays a responsible defensive game, though he can take some bad penalties from time to time. There were a couple of games this season in which he had third periods where he took more than one penalty, one time doing so within seconds of getting out of the box for his first penalty. He didn't have a large PIM amount this season, but untimely, unnecessary penalties are among those he did record. There were also some consistency issues, as witnessed by his 0 points in this year's Clark Cup Playoffs. Dylan can be a solid two-way forward at the next level, but he'll need to find some consistency to his game and have better in-game awareness with regard to taking penalties. Offensive zone penalties are never desired. He will have a chance to work on those things back in Dubuque next year for one more season before heading to the University of Denver in 2015.

Quotable: "Smart player, with good hockey sense and a responsible two-way center. He needs to battle more." – HP Scout Sean White

SEASON	LEAGUE	GAMES	GOALS	ASSISTS	PPG	PIM	HP RANKING
2012/13	USHL	58	9	18	0.47	14	159
2013/14	USHL	60	14	29	0.72	29	

Garcia, C.J.
D – Barrie Colts (OHL) – 6'0" 187

After a slow start to the season where he was inconsistent at the best of times, Garcia seemed to get better as the year went on, and played well on a pairing with Liam Maaskant in the playoffs. Garcia is a smooth skating defenseman who can move the puck or skate with it, and has a lot of offensive potential. He's sort of a work in progress in the defensive zone, but he did improve in that aspect this season. He's not afraid to be physical, and will fight on occasion. At times he will go for a big hit, and overcommit defensively, but that happened less frequently down the stretch. He'll probably be a late pick if he's drafted, but for a team looking for a mobile defenseman with potential, he certainly fits the bill.

SEASON	LEAGUE	GAMES	GOALS	ASSISTS	PPG	PIM	HP RANKING
2012/13	OHL	29	0	1	0.03	22	NR
2013/14	OHL	52	1	8	0.17	27	

Gardiner, Reid
RC – Prince Albert Raiders (WHL) – 5'11" 185

Reid is a versatile forward who has played all the different forward positions. Reid is at his best when he is winning puck battles along the boards, coming off the corners and driving to the net in order to create scoring chances for himself and teammates. Reid is a ball of energy, relentlessly forechecking and finishing his checks. He always seems to be in the right position to take the puck from his opposition. Reid put up decent offensive numbers this year mainly due to the fact that he'll go to the dirty areas and he's aware of the developing play enough to get into position to be a scoring option. He seems to find the open spaces unnoticed and attacks the net looking for rebounds. Reid has a good shot with a fairly good release. Reid is not a high-end puck carrier and will need to improve on his stick skills. His decision-making with the puck has improved and he has cut down on his turnovers, but he can still be panicky with the puck under duress. This is unfortunate as Reid works so hard to create turnovers, but then doesn't make good puck-possession decisions resulting in him having to chase the puck again. He has the general understanding of his defensive role but will need to improve his overall game and skating. As he possesses average skating abilities and is not very explosive, he may be best suited as a winger at the pro level. His skating has improved throughout the year but he will need to continue his foot work and speed.

SEASON	LEAGUE	GAMES	GOALS	ASSISTS	PPG	PIM	HP RANKING
2012/13	WHL	54	7	13	0.37	28	108
2013/14	WHL	70	22	22	0.63	39	

Garland, Conor
RW – Moncton Wildcats (QMJHL) – 5'08" 165

In his second season with the Moncton Wildcats. Garland established himself as a highly talented little player. Playing alongside Ivan Barbashev, he displayed his quickness and his footspeed in all of our viewings as he got rid of the opposition quite easily with quick changes in direction. He likes to control the play around the corners and he showed his ability to distribute the puck all season long. This young American really can control the puck at high speed and his hands are fast, allowing him to keep control of the puck in high traffic areas.

Garland has a great wrist shot with terrific accuracy and he unleashes it at will. We really liked his decision making with the puck as well. He clearly can anticipate plays in the offensive zone. It's easy for him to get open for scoring chances.

On the other hand, he needs to improve in physical games as he doesn't win many battles. His small frame is clearly a major knock as it's pretty easy to separate him from the puck when he gets hit. While in control of the puck, his feet never stop moving. This isn't the case when he doesn't have the puck. He needs to improve his play without the puck, especially in his own end, even though we saw some improvement as the season progressed. His game is all about speed and skills. Now averaging a point-per-game production, Garland will no doubt have a successful Q career, but we're not sure if his offensive skills will translate that well to the professional level.

SEASON	LEAGUE	GAMES	GOALS	ASSISTS	PPG	PIM	HP RANKING
2012/13	QMJHL	26	6	11	0.65	16	NR
2013/14	QMJHL	51	24	30	1.06	39	

Gavrikov, Vladislav
LD – Yaroslav 2 (RUS Jr.) – 6'2" 191

Gavrikov had a solid showing at last year U18 in Sochi, but as a late '95 he wasn't eligible for this year's tourny. He possesses a real nice combo of long reach and mobility, and he is hard to beat on the outside as he skates well laterally and backwards; these qualities give him very good potential defensively. He can also be physical on the boards, but that part of his game doesn't always show up. Vladislav would probably need to start carrying the puck a bit more to further develop the offensive part of his game.

SEASON	LEAGUE	GAMES	GOALS	ASSISTS	PPG	PIM	HP RANKING
2012/13	MHL	47	3	3	0.13	18	122
2013/14	MHL	45	3	9	0.27	28	

Gendron, Miles
LD – The Rivers (HS-MA) – 6'02" 181

Miles is an outstanding skater, especially for his size and he utilizes his size and speed to take the puck end to end. He has strong puck handling ability but likes to utilize his skating to his advantage. Miles is a bit of a project as he needs to get stronger and needs to improve defensively but he has the skating to recover when he goes out of position. He has signed on to join the Penticton Vees of the BCHL for one year before heading to the University of Connecticut in September 2015.

He will be a long term project but could really pay off in the end to a team that remains patient.

SEASON	LEAGUE	GAMES	GOALS	ASSISTS	PPG	PIM	HP RANKING
2012/13	USHS	28	12	16	1	NA	73
2013/14	USHS	22	6	13	0.86	NA	

Gersich, Shane
LW/C – USNTDP (USHL) – 5'11" 174

Gersich has elite speed and agility, and gets to top speed quickly. He has decent but not spectacular hands, and generates much of his offense with his speed and positioning. You can often find him camped out in front of the net creating traffic and tucking home tips and rebounds. He has an active stick and creates a lot of turnovers, forechecks hard.

There's definitely an inconsistency to his game. A lot of times he can be fairly pedestrian, and it's not really a lack of effort but more just a matter of not accomplishing much or standing out.

It would be good to see more consistency to his game, that became more noticeable as the season wore on and was definitely the case the last couple of months. Gersich is slated to attend the University of North Dakota starting in 2015.

SEASON	LEAGUE	GAMES	GOALS	ASSISTS	PPG	PIM	HP RANKING
2013/14	USHL	26	8	8	0.62	4	127
2013/14	(U18)USDP	61	16	16	0.52	18	

Gilligan, Jeffrey
RC – Owen Sound Attack (OHL) – 5'11" 159

Jeffrey combined skating; skill, and a strong compete level to make an impression in his rookie OHL season. Gilligan is average height, but very slender in frame. He skates well, and can rush the puck end-to-end with good puck protection, and speed. He handles the puck well, and is an effective passer earning some ice on the second powerplay unit. He is also evasive along the wall with the puck. Without the puck Gilligan shows good energy, and even battles along the wall. He competes hard, and finishes his checks despite a lack of strength. Jeffrey always keeps his feet moving, and while we don't expect him to be selected at the 2014 NHL Entry Draft, he's doing a lot of things that will help him develop as a hockey player.

SEASON	LEAGUE	GAMES	GOALS	ASSISTS	PPG	PIM	HP RANKING
2012/13	Midget	31	11	12	0.74	NA	NR
2013/14	OHL	63	3	12	0.24	40	

Glover, Jack
RD – USNTDP (USHL) – 6'03" 192

Being a big bodied defenseman with a solid set of wheels and good offensive skill, it is understandable why Glover gets a lot of the attention he gets. He does possess those skills and have those things going for him, but he had some largely unimpressive performances this season. He lacks hockey sense and his decision making ability needs a lot of work. He often freezes and hesitates to make plays, only further opening to the door to turnovers and mistakes. Losing track of players in the defensive zone and getting caught drifting is a common occurrence, and there is no defenseman on the US roster who I have seen get completely walked as often as Glover does.

He has a habit of looking down at the puck and only playing the puck, and the puck carrier will skirt right past him and in for a quality scoring chance. He is turnover prone and doesn't protect the puck well in his own zone.

Glover does have some offensive skill. He handles the puck better in the offensive zone and is pretty good at making adjustments to open up shooting and passing lanes. There is some offensive upside there but I am not sure if it's worth the price of all the other negatives. Glover skates well and has size, so hopefully with further development at the University of Minnesota, Glover can begin to experience his true potential.

SEASON	LEAGUE	GAMES	GOALS	ASSISTS	PPG	PIM	HP RANKING
2013/14	USHL	24	1	9	0.42	12	66
2013/14	(U18)USDP	59	2	26	0.47	30	

Goetz, Keigan
RW – SOO Greyhounds (OHL) – 6'01" 190

Keigan plays a very simple but noticeable game. He has good size and plays with a tremendous amount of energy. He finishes his checks very hard and shows a real love for the physical game producing some of the biggest hits we've seen this season. In addition to his physical play he forechecks hard and will force turnovers. He plays a 200 foot game and will backcheck hard every time. He really shows very limited offensive ability but seems aware of this keeping his puck decisions simple while maximizing it's effectiveness by getting pucks deep or getting them to players who can create a little more offense. Despite the lack of offense Keigan has a realistic shot at hearing his name called at the 2014 NHL Entry Draft simply because he plays such an ideal role projected for the bottom six at the NHL level and has the size to accomplish it.

"Keigan won't put up many points for his team, but he will go through a wall for them. He plays with an outstanding amount of heart and a really big physical edge that got him noticed. Very well suited as a role player next level." – Ryan Yessie

SEASON	LEAGUE	GAMES	GOALS	ASSISTS	PPG	PIM	HP RANKING
2013/14	OJHL	22	3	5	0.36	82	NR
2013/14	OHL	26	0	3	0.12	27	

Goldobin, Nikolay
LW – Sarnia Sting (OHL) – 6'00" 185

Nikolay is in his second season with the Sarnia Sting after joining the team at the 2012 CHL Import Draft. Goldobin has come miles since first arriving in Sarnia and is one of the most dangerous offensive threats in the Ontario Hockey League. Nikolay utilizes a combination of speed and shiftiness with the puck to acquire the offensive zone and is capable of beating opposing team's top defensive defensemen one on one on a regular basis. He has the ability to score highlight reel goals and scores from angles that seem near impossible. He has soft hands and a laser quick release on his shot. While his goal scoring ability seems to gain him the most attention, what's most impressive about Nikolay is his passing ability. He makes high difficulty passes look easy and has an exceptional level of vision which allows him to see things that few players can see. He is extremely creative and regularly chooses smart options with the puck. If you base purely off of offensive talent, Nikolay is one of the most pure skilled players in the entire 2014 NHL Entry Draft. What causes Nikolay to drop is his play without the puck. He is uninterested in physical play and generally isn't willing to engage in anything that involves physical play unless he has the puck and is capable of evading the contact with skill. He can put pressure on the forecheck but will pull up and try to get his stick in the lanes and poke at the puck. He also does this along the wall as he is non-existent along the wall and in the corners. His defensive play is very hit or miss. He has shown urgency at some necessary times to get back defensively and get his stick in passing lanes, but he has also lagged behind at times as well. While his skill set is undeniable, his play without the puck makes him a real wildcard in the first round of this draft. There is a wide range where he could be selected because his potential is through the roof, but his timid style around contact without the puck gives him a concerning bust factor.

Quotable: "Goldobin is a very exciting player to watch. He is a smooth skater who can create scoring chances out of nothing for both himself and his teammates. If Nikolay goes into the right situation he could be one of the most successful players from this draft class." – Ryan Yessie

Quotable: "*Amazing skill but he needs to shoot more and be willing to play less on the perimeter. I expect he will slide a bit due to his soft play and the Russian KHL fear factor.*" – Mark Edwards

Quotable: "*Buy the time we would be willing to pull the trigger he will be long gone.*" NHL Scout

SEASON	LEAGUE	GAMES	GOALS	ASSISTS	PPG	PIM	HP RANKING
2012/13	OHL	68	30	38	1	12	29
2013/14	OHL	67	38	56	1.4	21	

Goulet, Alexandre
LC – Charlottetown Islanders (QMJHL) – 5'11" 182

Goulet was the Islanders' second first-round pick in last year's midget draft, after being passed over in his first year of eligibility in 2012. He played two seasons in Midget AAA with Levis and exploded last season, becoming one of the best players in the league. This year, Goulet played regularly on the Islanders' top two lines and produced a decent amount offensively. He quickly became a core player on the rebuilding Islanders with the likes of Sprong and McDonald. He's a goal-scoring center and possesses great bursts of speed, able to beat any defensemen on the outside. His speed makes opposing defensemen back down, which gives him and his linemates more room to make plays in the offensive zone. He has a shoot-first mentality and likes to shoot the puck at every opportunity; we would like to see him improve his release so that he can get it on net quickly and not leave the opposing defense or goaltender time to react. He also has a good wrist shot, but lacks velocity on it. Not a natural playmaker, Goulet doesn't have a good on-ice vision. He can be too predictable offensively at times, and his decision-making is lacking as well. He handles the puck well, and can make plays at high speed. There are some concerns with his physical game and character, as he has a tendency of leaving his zone too quickly to jump into offensive mode.

SEASON	LEAGUE	GAMES	GOALS	ASSISTS	PPG	PIM	HP RANKING
2012/13	QMAAA	42	29	30	1.4	32	115
2013/14	QMJHL	66	26	22	0.73	26	

Graham, Charlie
G – Belleville Bulls (OHL) – 6'00" 173

Charlie is a re-entry goaltender for the 2014 NHL Entry Draft. After being passed over in last year's draft, Charlie played the vast majority of the action this season with former starting goaltender Malcolm Subban graduating to the professional ranks. Charlie appeared in all but 15 games for the Bulls and really did an outstanding job keeping the Bulls in some games that could have been much, much worse otherwise. He has an excellent glove hand and is lightning quick in goal. His reflexes are outstanding and he displays exceptional quickness. Charlie is capable of making some highlight reel goals and in our viewings of the Bulls, a lot of the goals scored on Charlie would have been very difficult for any goaltender to stop. If he played on a more veteran team with a little more offensive support, Graham would be a lot more talked about for this draft, but could still end up being a solid late round steal in this draft. He lacks size and plays a bit of an athletic style but has grown a bit since last season and does a good job getting to the top of his crease to compensate for his size.

SEASON	LEAGUE	GAMES	GAA	SV%	W	L	SO	HP RANKING
2012/13	OHL	25	2.59	0.922	15	5	3	NR
2013/14	OHL	53	3.70	0.902	17	24	0	

Grasskamp, Charley
RC – SOO Greyhounds (OHL) – 6'01" 190

In a surprising move Eau Claire Memorial High School Senior and team leader Grasskamp chose to make a late season move to the Sault Ste. Marie Greyhounds of the Ontario Hockey League. Grasskamp played a limited bottom six role with the Greyhounds before becoming a healthy scratch when a few forwards began returning from injury. Grasskamp filled his role effectively getting pucks deep and chasing them down. He is a good skater for his size and wasn't hesitant in competing for pucks. With that said he was dominated for the most part in puck battles especially along the wall. Despite playing an energy role Charley displayed flashes of good puck handling ability and a fairly strong shot. He also distributes the puck well in transition but struggles with his decision making while under pressure. He had a modest debut in the OHL and while there are flashes of potential in Grasskamp we don't expect him to be selected for the 2014 NHL Entry Draft. However he does show the potential to be a late bloomer.

SEASON	LEAGUE	GAMES	GOALS	ASSISTS	PPG	PIM	HP RANKING
2013/14	WPH	23	18	29	2.04	48	NR
2013/14	OHL	11	1	5	0.55	8	

Gutierrez, Justin
LC – Tri-City Americans (WHL) – 6'04" 185

Justin is a late 1995 birthdate who has excellent size and really emerged as an intriguing prospect this year. Justin made an impact in a depth role for the Americans this season providing a much needed physical element to his team. He loves to finish his checks and can deliver them with solid power. On the forecheck when he bares down on the puck carrier can force his opponent to make puck playing mistakes. His speed is good considering his size but the first few steps will need some improvement as he is still a bit heavy on his feet. He works hard playing a 200 foot game and will compete in all three zones. He doesn't have many offensive tools but he does protect the puck well and make basic intelligent passes to feed more skilled players. He has very good core strength but still has a lot of room on his frame to bulk up. While he may be a bit of a longer term project he projects the potential of a player you'd find on the bottom six of an NHL team.

SEASON	LEAGUE	GAMES	GOALS	ASSISTS	PPG	PIM	HP RANKING
2012/13	WHL	48	4	5	0.19	35	155
2013/14	WHL	70	3	18	0.3	103	

Halbert, Nathanael
LD – Blainville-Boisbriand Armada (QMJHL) – 5'11" 172

Halbert was in his rookie season with the Armada, making the jump from the OJHL in Ontario after being passed over in the OHL Draft. The Armada sent him an invitation for their training camp and he made the team, playing his way into a top-4 role on the Armada defense corps this season. He's a stay-at-home defenseman who takes care of things in his own zone first, has a good gap control in his coverage defensively but can find himself in trouble when facing a speedy forward off the rush, as he doesn't own the quickest feet. He uses his stick very well to keep opposing forwards in check and break up passes. Keeps his play simple with the puck, will make the easy outlet pass, but won't try to rush the puck too often unless there's an open lane in front of him. Knows his limits as a hockey player, and plays well within those limits. During the year, he saw some time on the 2nd power play unit but I wouldn't describe him as a natural puck-mover. One of the most underrated defensive defensemen in the league, he should get more recognition next season in his 2nd year.

His physical game is decent, he's not overly physical but will finish his hits if he has to. He uses his smarts to check the opposing players. Halbert likes to be matched up against the opposing top line. He played part of the year with Daniel Walcott and they were both used in this role, night in and night out.

SEASON	LEAGUE	GAMES	GOALS	ASSISTS	PPG	PIM	HP RANKING
2012/13	OJHL	48	3	10	0.27	59	NR
2013/14	QMJHL	64	7	10	0.27	41	

Halladay, Logan
G - Janesville (NAHL) – 6'2" 180

A few years ago Anthony Stolarz was drafted in the 2nd round by the Philadelphia Flyers and went on to play with the London Knights. We think Halladay is better than Stolarz. He is one of the most athletic goalies in the draft. Logan has good size, is physically strong and makes himself big in the net, his positioning is also good. His rebound control is good, he understands how to direct pucks towards an area where his own player will reach the puck first. One of the things we like most about him is his ability to read the play, he makes saves easier for himself by anticipating where he needs to be and what options are available to the puck carrier. If he needs to get across his net he excels at it with quick lateral ability. He's a great skater and has fantastic quickness. His puck playing ability is high end and he never seems to let a goal against affect is play.

Halladay has a chance to be one of the first few goaltenders selected in this draft.

SEASON	LEAGUE	GAMES	GAA	SV%	W	L	SO	HP RANKING
2012/13	HPHL	17	3.07	0.893	NA	NA	NA	59
2013/14	NAHL	31	2.26	0.932	18	8	2	

Halverson, Brandon
G – SOO Greyhounds (OHL) – 6'04" 179

Brandon was well liked by HockeyProspect during his time with the Little Caesars U16 program and after a year with the Oakland Grizzlies U18 program Halverson was ready to join the SOO Greyhounds of the OHL. Halverson received ice behind veteran OHL netminder Matt Murray and while he didn't have a great deal of appearances, he made a positive impression in the ones he did play in. Brandon has excellent size for a netminder and moves side to side extremely well. In fact his direction changes in general are very strong, especially for such a big goaltender. His size allowed him to see through traffic effectively and setting himself properly for incoming shots. He struggles a little with rebounds and handling shots as he drops some of them right into the slot which can get him into trouble.

Despite being a rookie goaltender, Halverson may handle the puck better than an goaltender in the OHL and several defensemen. He is poised when pressured and makes smart decisions. He keeps his head on a swivel and identifies the proper option on a consistent basis. Halverson is one of the best goaltending prospects to come out of the OHL this year and should be selected at some point of the 2014 NHL Entry Draft.

SEASON	LEAGUE	GAMES	GAA	SV%	W	L	SO	HP RANKING
2012/13	MWEHL	21	2.88	0.906	NA	NA	NA	146
2013/14	OHL	19	2.96	0.904	12	6	2	

Hargrave, Brett
RW – Owen Sound Attack (OHL) – 6'04" 206

After being selected in the first round of the 2013 OHL Priority Selection Draft by the Sarnia Sting, Hargrave didn't quite live up to expectations, and was dealt to the Owen Sound Attack early this season. Hargrave showed great potential putting on a couple electrifying performances in camp, and during the pre-season. However, when the regular season began he wasn't able to produce much offensively, despite playing on the team's second line. Hargrave displays good positional play without the puck. This applies in all game situations, and all zones as he has gained some power-play time in addition to playing on the second penalty killing unit. Where he was dominant along the walls in Minor Midget, he simply hasn't been able to translate this to the OHL, as he loses far more battles than someone of his size and strength should. With the puck Brett is at his best when using his size to drive the net. He struggles with the pace of the game at times. The potential is there for Hargrave, but because he lacks top end offensive ability, he would need to make the NHL as a hard working physical two-way player. While his defensive side of the game was strong this season, he needs to up the physicality before he gets seriously considered as an NHL prospect.

SEASON	LEAGUE	GAMES	GOALS	ASSISTS	PPG	PIM	HP RANKING
2012/13	OHL	63	6	5	0.17	24	NR
2013/14	OHL	59	5	9	0.24	51	

Harlacher, Edson
LD – Kamloops Blazers (WHL) – 6'03" 185

Edson has shown improvement throughout the season after a tough start. He showed a high pedigree of skill at times but seemed very underwhelming at other times. Consistency is a problem as is his need to work on his skating. He tends to have heavy feet and doesn't own a very powerful stride. He can't be paired up against opponents' top players as he struggled to skate and compete with them. He lacks a sense of urgency and seemed to struggle with his decision-making for most of the season. As the season went on, he improved slightly, but never showed much of an offensive game. Edson will need to play with more consistency. He also needs to improve his defensive game and ability to make plays with the puck under pressure.

SEASON	LEAGUE	GAMES	GOALS	ASSISTS	PPG	PIM	HP RANKING
2012/13	SWI Jr.A	34	1	5	0.18	22	NR
2013/14	WHL	71	0	9	0.13	44	

Hawkey, Hayden
G – Omaha Lancers (USHL) – 6'02" 180

The Providence College commit and USHL Goaltender of the Year clearly is coming off of a strong season in Omaha. Hawkey lead all USHL goaltenders in goals against average and save percentage.

Hawkey's a big, athletic body in net. He might be the quickest and most athletic of any goaltender in the USHL this season. For a team as solid as the Lancers were, their goaltender got hung out to dry more often than you would figure. Hawkey had more breakaway stops and odd-man break stops than anyone else viewed this season, stopping the likes of Jack Eichel, Dylan Larkin, and other top notch offensive players in those situations on numerous occasions. In a game against Green Bay in late February he had three breakaway saves within that one, single game. His lateral, post-to-post ability is phenomenal, and is a major reason why he is so effective on breakaway and odd-man breaks. He made saves going post to post this season that were seemingly impossible to stop, but he stopped them.

The rare time he does give up a rebound that leads to a quality second chance, he shuts the door much more often than not. He's able to make adjustments and move in order to make a rebound save as good as anyone. Exceptionally difficult to beat down low. He's quick with his legs, and has both a strong blocker and glove. All in all, his USHL Goaltender of the Year honor was well, well earned.

SEASON	LEAGUE	GAMES	GAA	SV%	W	L	SO	HP RANKING
2012/13	MWEHL	26	1.94	0.927	NA	NA	NA	NR
2013/14	USHL	33	1.99	0.926	22	6	3	

Hawryluk, Jayce
RW – Brandon Wheat Kings (WHL) – 5'10" 190

Listed 37th on NHL Central Scouting's final draft ranking. Jayce is a smallish forward with tremendous offense of abilities and a strong work ethic. He possesses impressive vision and strong skating skills. His first couple of steps are quick and he has shown both good top speed and agility. He is also very tough to contain along the walls due to his slippery skating. He has good lower body strength and plays much bigger than his size. A fearless player who is very relentless on the forecheck and isn't afraid to engage in puck battles along the boards. He loves to throw the body and hits hard. Combined with his good stick and ability to spin off checks, he's able to gain puck possession and quickly turn the play into a quality scoring opportunity.

His speed and puck control make it hard for opposing defenders to deter when trying to control him during one-on-one situations. Defenders at this level have a hard time knocking him off the puck because he so elusive and quick, but he will need to learn new ways to create offense against more mobile defenders in the pros. He makes smart decisions with the puck on his stick and has strong passing skills. He possesses a good set of hands and a great touch down low. Combined with his above average shot with good release, Jayce is a very dangerous player in the offensive zone. From the top of the circles in, Hawryluk is among the best pure scorers out of the WHL this year. Jayce will go to the tough areas in pursuit to find opportunities to score. When he's on his game, he is able to score quickly and frequently and dominate at the offensive end.

He has shown at times that he can be a responsible defensive player. However it is this part of his game that is particularly inconsistent. At times, he is agitating to play against as his quickness allows him to close the gap quickly or pester his opposition to force turnovers or get to the shooting lanes to shut down passes or shots on net. Other times, he doesn't seem to give enough effort along the wall. As of now, Hawryluk can be described as mainly a one-dimensional player, but he is very good at what he does. Once he is able to add a little muscle to his frame and improve the consistency of his defensive play, he'll be a very challenging player to compete against.

Quotable: "Skating is too big an issue for us, I doubt he will stay on our list." – NHL Scout

Quotable: "Love his compete level, he plays bigger than he is." NHL Scout

Quotable: "I didn't like him as much at the U18 as I did in previous viewings." – Mark Edwards

SEASON	LEAGUE	GAMES	GOALS	ASSISTS	PPG	PIM	HP RANKING
2012/13	WHL	61	18	25	0.7	46	64
2013/14	WHL	59	24	40	1.08	44	

Haydon, Aaron
RD – Niagara Ice Dogs (OHL) – 6'04" 200

Haydon came to the Ice Dogs as a first round pick in the 2012 OHL Priority Selection Draft. While he battled injuries a little bit this year he was able to maintain a physical presence on the blue line. Aaron is a hulking defenseman who loves to take the body and assert himself along the wall. He fights for pucks and uses his upper body strength to his full advantage in these situations. He never passes up an opportunity to hit and has delivered some crushing hits this year. His skating is OK in general and has shown clear improvements from last season. He played in all game situations and was a consistent part of the Ice Dogs' penalty kill. Despite being a defensive first defenseman he actually moved the puck moderately well considering his style of play. Defensively he uses his size well but his decision making ability has come into question a few times and has ultimately cost his team scoring chances and goals by making the wrong decision or taking too long to make a decision. He will need to focus on being quicker mentally in the defensive zone and making the safe play if there is not option to limit turnovers. He will also need to improve one on one situations, because while he was effective in some of these situations he did get beat a fair amount as well. We expect Haydon to get picked and see some good potential as a big physical shutdown defenseman but has some work to do before he can start to reach his potential.

Quotable: "Doesn't play a smart game." – NHL Scout

SEASON	LEAGUE	GAMES	GOALS	ASSISTS	PPG	PIM	HP RANKING
2012/13	OHL	42	4	6	0.24	39	156
2013/14	OHL	61	5	11	0.26	112	

Helewka, Adam
LW – Spokane Chiefs (WHL) – 6'01" 190

The '95-born re-entry Helewka was the most improved forward from the Chiefs roster this past season as he more than doubled his goals and points. It's not just Adam's offensive skills that makes him attractive, he also possess incredible hockey sense and has played a pretty simple game with limited mistakes most of the year. He has shown a good willingness to battle for loose pucks and brings a good compete level every shift. His offensive positioning has improved and he is constantly putting himself in good scoring positions or making himself an outlet for his teammates from pressure. He has the awareness to get the puck deep in the offensive zone when he is under pressure. He makes smart decisions with the puck and has utilized the cycle down low very effectively. He can play a physical game when needed and is very good on the forecheck forcing the puck carrier into making mistakes. Adam is a slightly above average skater with decent speed, but will need to improve on his foot work. He has decent hands and uses his big frame to protect the puck or drive the net. He's not afraid to play in the corners or fight for space in the dirty areas of the ice. His passing is above average and makes good tape to tape passes. Adam has some untapped offensive potential that he shows glimpses of when he's moving his feet and making himself big. He has a good understanding of his defensive role and has sacrificed his body blocking shots and winning battles along the boards in the defensive zone. He's shown a good ability to chip the puck out of the zone to create offensive rushes. Adam is definitely a long-term prospect, but the level of improvement he's shown in addition to the untapped potential make him worth the investment of a mid-to-late round selection.

SEASON	LEAGUE	GAMES	GOALS	ASSISTS	PPG	PIM	HP RANKING
2012/13	WHL	60	10	17	0.45	12	193
2013/14	WHL	62	23	27	0.81	32	

Herbst, Liam
G – Ottawa 67's (OHL) – 6'03" 181

Two years ago Herbst was considered by our scouts to be the best goaltender in Ontario, and possessed some intriguing NHL potential due to his size and bright future. Unfortunately two separate hip surgeries, and knee surgery caused Liam to start all over from the very bottom. This season Herbst was finally able to get back into the net, and make his junior hockey debut after missing the entire season last year. He was able to get his feet wet with the London Jr. B Nationals, and started to put together a string of solid performances before making his debut with the Knights. He was then subsequently dealt to the Ottawa 67's. Herbst is a big goaltender that prefers the butterfly style. He is effective getting in front of the initial shot very well, as he gets to the top of the crease, and calmly takes away angles. His glove hand is a bit of a work in progress, as he has let in a few in our viewings he should have had, but he also flashed some great saves with the glove on other occasions. His biggest area of concern is his side-to-side movement. He struggles with the ability to push off quickly, and comfortably due to his surgeries, which has left him open to get scored on, sometimes in streaks by more talented players. Liam still has a lot of potential in him, but he has a very long way to go before he can get back to the goaltender he showed the potential to be. After being a top prospect two years ago, he would ultimately need to be a late bloomer as far as the NHL Draft goes with three seasons left in his junior career.

SEASON	LEAGUE	GAMES	GAA	SV%	W	L	SO	HP RANKING
2013/14	GOJHL	15	2.86	0.892	NA	NA	NA	NR
2013/14	OHL	10	6.18	0.853	1	4	0	

Hicketts, Joe
LD – Victoria Royals (WHL) – 5'08" 186

The diminutive defender played a strong season for the Royals this year despite missing a large chunk of the season due to injury. When Hicketts is operating at the top of his game, he is dangerous in the offensive zone. He combines quick, agile skating with strong puck skills and a good awareness of the developing play. As a result of these skills, Hicketts is adapt to running his team's powerplay. He has a good shot and a strong base of which to derive power from. He has good leadership abilities and displays a willingness to play the body. He defends the rush well, keeps good gap control and holds the defensive blueline. He is generally pretty good positionally. While he is a pretty complete player, the unfortunate attribute that he can't control is his size. Teams interested in selecting Hicketts will obtain a highly-skilled, intelligent player, but they'll have to project whether they think he'll grow and whether he'll be able to defend in the pros against big, strong forwards that drive to the net and cycle the puck with high efficiency. We are fans of Hicketts' talent and ability and wish he was bigger but the lack of size as a defender is too much to ignore and will cause him to be ranked much lower than we feel his ability alone would warrant.

SEASON	LEAGUE	GAMES	GOALS	ASSISTS	PPG	PIM	HP RANKING
2012/13	WHL	67	6	18	0.36	45	NR
2013/14	WHL	36	6	18	0.67	12	

Hickey, Brandon
RD – Spruce Grove Saints (AJHL) - 6'2" 180

Brandon is an excellent skating defender that shows good poise with the puck. Brandon makes a good first pass and is able to identify when to make a pass or when to skate it out of trouble. Brandon has very good size, yet is still quick on his feet with very good mobility.

His footwork is good and he's able to adjust well in transition and to force opponents outside against the rush. He is good on his edges and is able to walk the blueline on the point. He has above average vision and makes a strong pass. He has a strong shot from the point, although he could stand to unload it quicker. While he's been successful in his own end, he shows the ability to carry the play and should develop into more of a two-way threat.

Quotable: "I love his combination of size, smarts and skating ability. He's good in his end and his smooth skating and smarts should allow for continued development offensively. He looks like he'll be a two-way player with good upside." - Scott McDougall

SEASON	LEAGUE	GAMES	GOALS	ASSISTS	PPG	PIM	HP RANKING
2012/13	AJHL	55	1	6	0.13	11	56
2013/14	AJHL	37	4	12	0.43	22	

Highmore, Matthew
C - Saint John Sea Dogs (QMJHL) - 5'11" 174

Highmore was the 8th overall pick in the 2012 QMJHL draft and we can clearly assess that he has progressed quite well this season. Now centering Saint John's first line, he has been getting more offensive responsibilities and he has delivered. He suffered a minor injury in the middle of the season, but it was the first time in the last three years that he almost played a full season of hockey. A two-way player, he works hard at both ends of the ice. Highmore displays very good awareness out on the ice without the puck. He has good hockey sense and he has been a constant threat around the net. He is fairly strong on his skates and protects his puck nicely on his way to the offensive zone. His wrist shot is decent but accurate, and he doesn't mind using it at all, as he took more than 200 shots this season. He has decent hands, but he's clearly not the kind of guy that will beat the same defender twice. Highmore gets most of his points from close range. In our viewings, we saw him blocking shots when the game was on the line and being a "shit-disturber" as well. He's a gritty center with good vision that is good at installing the play down low. He forechecks hard with good contact and an active stick, pressing the defense aggressively. However, his skating lacks quickness and explosiveness, and that's a major knock on his game. Nevertheless, he has played the right way to get his name in the mix in this year's draft.

SEASON	LEAGUE	GAMES	GOALS	ASSISTS	PPG	PIM	HP RANKING
2012/13	QMJHL	30	4	5	0.3	26	NR
2013/14	QMJHL	68	19	31	0.74	62	

Hillman, Blake
LD – Dubuque Fighting Saints (USHL) – 6'01" 170

The future University of Denver commit really impressed our staff this season. Drafted 240th Overall in the 2013 USHL Entry Draft out of Elk River High School in Minnesota, Hillman proved to be an steal at that pick.

Blake has great hockey sense and has as good of anticipation of the play as just about anyone viewed this season. He is great at picking off passes, but especially in the neutral zone where he keeps tight gaps with his excellent skating ability. His anticipation combined with his active stick make neutral zone play tough, let alone offensive zone entry. He steps up very well on attacking players and space is at a major premium at his defensive blue line. He is quick in transition and wins most races to dump-ins.

His decision making is strong, and he has a lot of confidence in his vision and passing ability. He isn't afraid to make short little chip passes to his centers in the middle of the ice or make the long stretch pass.

Blake has a rocket for a slap shot and gets it off quick. He's just as willing and able to make a move at the blue line with pressure to open up a shooting lane and let a good wrister go. He likes to jump up into the play and into rushes coming up ice. He only had 13 points this season but there is higher offensive upside there as he gets more confident and that is also an attribute to his defense-first mentality. He displays great poise with the puck and loses no speed when carrying it. There is definitely higher offensive output there going forward in his career.

Quotable: "Extremely smart player who defends with his feet and stick. He's a good puck mover with possible offensive upside. Downside is lack of physical game." - Mark Edwards

SEASON	LEAGUE	GAMES	GOALS	ASSISTS	PPG	PIM	HP RANKING
2012/13	USHS	24	2	12	0.58	8	74
2013/14	USHL	57	3	10	0.23	24	

Hitchcock, Ryan
LW – USNTDP (USHL) – 5'09" 172

Ryan really brought it the final month or so of the season this year. His game was solid previous to that but he seemed to turn a corner that final month and really turned the heat up to his game, especially offensively. Highly speedy and equally shifty, Hitchcock keeps defensemen on their heels guessing. He can change directions so quickly, it makes him tough to defend. Aside from his ability to evade, he is equally open to driving hard through people and to the net. Despite his size, he plays a powerful game with the puck. Shifty hands and underrated scoring touch, Hitchcock is a dangerous weapon on offense. His awareness and vision are excellent, and he's got great playmaking ability. He plays fearless, and will drive the net and the tough areas without hesitation and more than holds his own. Scrappy, speedy, with underrated skill, Hitchcock has the make up to be a successful NHL player despite his smaller stature. He is strong on his feet, has a nice wide base, and is smart enough and quick enough to avoid the bigger bodies roaming around the ice. When push comes to shove, he still takes his lumps to make a play and backs down from no one. He will have time to further develop at Yale, where he'll be attending starting this Fall.

SEASON	LEAGUE	GAMES	GOALS	ASSISTS	PPG	PIM	HP RANKING
2013/14	USHL	20	5	18	1.15	6	164
2013/14	(U18)USDP	53	12	37	0.92	10	

Ho-Sang, Joshua
RW – Windsor Spitfires (OHL) – 5'11" 166

Ho-Sang went on to have a very successful season statistically for the Spitfires, leading the team in scoring after the departure of Kerby Rychel. Joshua displays exceptional level of skating ability, and loves to carry the puck. He rarely passes off in the neutral zone, and will use his explosive speed to rush the puck into the offensive zone. He also possesses a laser release on his shot, and is dangerous whenever he has the puck in the offensive zone. If he gets the puck, and the defenders are caught flat-footed even for a second, Ho-Sang will take the puck in alone on the breakaway. He has excellent hands, and combined with his speed make for some highlight reel type of goals.

Ho-Sang really seems to live for the highlight reel style of goals, as he constantly looks for that perfect play, and will sometimes try to beat 3 or 4 defenders at once on his own instead of utilizing his teammates. To his credit, when he does choose to pass he displays good vision, and finishes some slick, creative passes. His play with the puck is extremely effective, and his level of talent is unquestionable.

Our concerns are with his play without the puck. When he doesn't have the puck on his stick he's very complacent, sometimes even wandering around seemingly waiting for his next chance to possess the puck, instead of competing for the puck or assisting his team defensively. With that said, he has made strides over the course of this season in regards to back checking, and helping his team defensively. However, he still remains inconsistent in that area. He has a habit of slashing opposing players every opportunity he gets, which seems to frustrate opponents.

Looking at the total package, Ho-Sang is very much a boom or bust prospect. If he makes it, it will be as an offensive forward in the top-six of an NHL team, and he will utilize his speed and hands to create offense. However, if he isn't able to crack the top six, he will likely be a player who spends his career in the AHL or Europe. There is a lot to like within Joshua's package of skills, which makes him so highly regarded, but mentality, and play without the puck remain our biggest concerns.

Quotable: "I'll be shocked if he goes in the first round." - NHL Scout

Quotable: "If he goes in the 1st round, that team gets what they deserve." - NHL Scout

Quotable: "I had a lot of conversations about Ho-Sang (with NHL scouts) this season. He made for interesting conversation. I'm looking forward to seeing who takes him and what round." - Mark Edwards

Quotable: "First time I saw him he reminded me of a better skating Rob Schremp. He still does. I wouldn't take him in the first round, he'd probably be selected before I'd be willing to pull the trigger." - Mark Edwards

Quotable: "I don't think we are interviewing him at the combine." - NHL Scout

SEASON	LEAGUE	GAMES	GOALS	ASSISTS	PPG	PIM	HP RANKING
2012/13	OHL	63	14	30	0.7	22	61
2013/14	OHL	67	32	53	1.27	44	

Hodge, Kris
LW - Shawinigan Cataractes (QMJHL) - 6'01" 192

Hodge is a hard nosed winger who has been able to provide a lot of energy for the Shawinigan Cataractes with his speed and defensive play. On a better team, the Newfoundland native would probably have played a bottom 6 role, but with the Cataractes, he had the opportunity to play a key role in their offense and was able to put up some decent numbers. He is good on the forecheck and he causes a lot of havoc as he hustles hard to get to the puck carrier. This late birthday forward makes sure to finish all his hits along the boards. His skating has improved significantly over the season which has helped him play his role with more energy and effectiveness. He doesn't have an astonishing top speed, but it's fairly good for major junior. He provides a good net front presence and is willing to drive the net with authority when he is controlling the puck. When he is rushing the puck, he likes to dump it in before entering the offensive zone.

Hodge is good along the boards, as he is able to use his body effectively to protect the puck, but does not have much skill to do anything after. He shows somewhat limited offensive upside providing a decent shot and efficient passing, but he has the mentality and attitude of a player who could go very far in the "grinder" role. Much of his offensive production comes from hard work as he scores goals off the rebound in front of the net and working hard off the cycle. He is most effective in his own zone with his tenacity and speed. He plays hard without the puck and is quite responsible in his own end. He is good at chasing down loose pucks and quickly getting it out of the defensive zone along the walls. He is not afraid to block shots, and does an above average job of taking away shooting lanes.

SEASON	LEAGUE	GAMES	GOALS	ASSISTS	PPG	PIM	HP RANKING
2012/13	QMJHL	42	6	8	0.33	36	NR
2013/14	QMJHL	67	9	22	0.46	68	

Hodgson, Hayden
RW – Sarnia Sting (OHL) – 6'02" 204

Hayden opened the season with the Erie Otters player a limited role the fourth line due to the Otters possessing a ton of offensive talent. Hodgson was sent over to the Sarnia Sting and immediately made an impact on the team. Due to his early performances he was eventually promoted to the top line for a few weeks during Korestelev's injury. Hayden is a big power forward who is built solid with a great frame and hits like a truck. He lost 10 games this season for delivering what was realistically a clean hit. Hayden didn't shy away from the physical side of the game when he returned and played a big role for the Sting down the stretch creating space for Sarnia's more skilled players. Hayden finishes hits hard and punishes opponents who are willing to go into the corners to the extent that some would concede to him on a race into the corner or rush a play to avoid being hit. He displays a good work ethic and pressures effectively on the forecheck. His skating is just OK but he is able to generate good speed over long stretches. He has a bit of a shoot first mentality but will distribute the puck when it is the clear option. He possesses good power in his shot but his accuracy is questionable at times. He will also at times take perimeter, low percentage shots.

He is effective driving to the net and causing a disruption in the slot. He also does a lot of smart simple things right like reading the play and using his big frame as an obsticale for opponents to skate around when smaller skilled players possess the puck. While he doesn't show many signs of having high end offensive ability, Hodgson has the upside and the mindset of an NHL power forward and could be one of the most underrated players in the draft as his season consistent of a questionable suspension, limited ice on a top team, then top ice on the last place team in the OHL.

"Hayden really turned the corner when he joined the Sting. Playing a more prominent role really allowed him to show his power forward attributes and was one of the hardest hitters I've seen all year among draft eligible players. Very under the radar prospect." - Ryan Yessie

Quotable: "He was already on our radar when I made a trip to Sarnia late in the year to get a last viewing of Goldobin. Hodgson played so well that I went back to Sarnia the next week to get an extra viewing of him. He's not a first rounder but I like his game." - Mark Edwards

SEASON	LEAGUE	GAMES	GOALS	ASSISTS	PPG	PIM	HP RANKING
2012/13	OHL	60	8	4	0.2	60	93
2013/14	OHL	52	9	9	0.35	64	

Holmstrom, Axel
LC/LW – Skelleftea Jr. (SWE) – 6'0" 198

Works his tail off but isn't blessed with a whole lot of skill. Always seems to be in the middle of all the action. He plays a smart responsible game. An effective player for his team. Played on a line with Nylander and Lindblom vs Canada at the 2014 World U18 and had an effective game helping those two more skilled players. Smart player but skating is weak, makes him an ugly looking player to watch for lack of a better word. In the end he is just a responsible, gritty hard working typo forward. Nothing wrong with those players but not all of them translate to the next level.

Quotable: "Works his tail off." – NHL Scout

SEASON	LEAGUE	GAMES	GOALS	ASSISTS	PPG	PIM	HP RANKING
2012/13	U20 S.Elit	10	2	1	0.3	0	102
2013/14	U20 S.Elit	33	15	23	1.15	12	

Honka, Julius
RD – Swift Current Broncos (WHL) – 5'11" 175

Honka is a very productive and athletic offensive-minded defenseman. He's a two-way type player with an excellent understanding of both sides of the puck. Combined with his tremendous skating ability and elite hockey sense, Honka is able to utilize his ability to read the play quickly and control the tempo of the game. Honka is a gifted skater who possesses dynamic mobility and footwork. When he combines all his skating dynamics together, Honka is able to efficiently move up and down the ice quicker than just about any other defender in the league. He's able to read the ice well with his good vision and he can move the puck swiftly out of the defensive zone with a hard, crisp outlet pass or by rushing the puck up the ice. He is able to pounce on turnovers and quickly turn the play up the ice for scoring opportunities. He knows when to take the play deep into the offensive zone and it isn't uncommon to see him at the opposing team's goal line looking to create scoring chances or simply to kill time until a teammate is available to cycle the puck down low.

Honka is very poised and calm with the puck he doesn't panic when under pressure. He uses his excellent mobility and agility to get out of tight situations. His ability to analyze and read the play allows him to know when to join the offensive rush or stay back in a more defensive role. He's very dangerous player offensively when controlling the puck. Honka's ability to score from the top of the point or down low makes him a unique among defensemen. He possesses a solid shot with a quick release and is able put the puck on net quick and efficiently from all angles of the ice. He just has a great ability to do so many things with the puck on his stick. Defensively, Honka relies on his intelligence and skating to contain his opponents defensively. With exceptional lateral movement, he can close the gap quickly when he identifies the need to (which isn't always the case). In one-on-one situations, he will engage anyone physically to gain possession of the puck although his lack of strength can prevent him from collecting the puck. He actively forces opponents to the outside and is difficult to beat off the rush. The biggest issue for him is related to his small build and stature. He knows what needs to be done, but he can be easily knocked off the puck by larger players. He struggles to defend against the cycle against those larger players and can be left pinned in his own end for long periods of time when he's unable to gain possession of the puck. Honka has a very exceptional blend of skills that will translate well to the pro ranks. His dynamic skating and hockey awareness can make him a very dangerous offensive-minded defender who will be hard to contain. Honka projects as a powerplay specialist that can handle softer offensive minutes at the pro level. As the sky is the limit for him offensively, his ability to hold a top 4 role is going to be largely dependent on his gains in the defensive aspect of his game.

Quotable: "I take him over DeAngelo. It's not close for me." NHL Scout

Quotable: "The thing I like about Honka and a guy like Aho as well, is their ability to make plays under heavy forecheck. Both of them are able to suck forecheckers in and make an evasive move. They are able to use their brain and not have to rely on their feet all the time to get them out of trouble." — Mark Edwards

SEASON	LEAGUE	GAMES	GOALS	ASSISTS	PPG	PIM	HP RANKING
2012/13	Jr.A SM-liiga	42	4	11	0.36	47	23
2013/14	WHL	62	16	40	0.9	52	

Hopponen, Waltteri
LW – Sioux City Musketeers (USHL) – 6'01" 190

Hopponen played one game to start this season with the Everett Silvertips of the Western Hockey League before leaving for Sioux City for the remainder of the season. In addition, he has represented his native Finland internationally in a number of tournaments, most recently at the World U18's, and has played well in those big games. Hopponen plays with a lot of grit to his game and thrives in the tough areas of the ice. He is willing to pay the price in front of the net and takes hits to make plays. Does not shy away from contact and likes to throw his own weight around. He has a good size and likes to use it on both sides of the puck. Highly intelligent Hopponen has a good awareness of his surroundings. Subtle things like being along the offensive half board and allowing a pass directed at him go through him and to his point-man behind him, all while drawing that defender to him thinking he's the one that's going to accept the pass.

In addition to his smarts, he has a good skill level. He's a good finisher and has a solid, but unspectacular, wrist shot. Good speed allows him to drive wide on defensemen and he's often able to beat them and drive to the net, which he has no fear of doing it. He crashes the net hard, but has the hands to operate in tight finesse the puck where it needs to go. While he can drive wide, he has the agility and control of his feet at top speed to shift laterally and cut to the middle, and even cut back again. Great lateral movement. Excellent work on the power play, and collected a lot of points there this season. He is a dangerous player in those situations where he more time and space to work with. He excels at finding the open man and can thread passes with the best of them.

Hopponen is equally as effective on the defensive side of the puck. He does a great job at disrupting the passing lanes through the neutral and causes a lot of turnovers. His quickness allows him to take those turnovers and get into transition at the snap of a finger and has led to many odd-man breaks. Positionally sound in his defensive zone, he plays a hard defensive game. Battles hard, wins the board battles, blocks shots, creates good outlet options for his Center and defensemen, always makes the safe, smart play but has the vision and skill to spring someone on a breakaway with stretch pass or utilize a saucer pass to create a higher-risk but higher-reward opportunity. He knows when to pick his spots. Hopponen is a solid two-way forward and an attractive player to pick, as he can play in any situation and has some offensive upside.

SEASON	LEAGUE	GAMES	GOALS	ASSISTS	PPG	PIM	HP RANKING
2012/13	Jr.A SM-liiga	18	5	3	0.44	14	NR
2013/14	USHL	54	17	14	0.57	36	

Hora, Frank
RD – Kitchener Rangers (OHL) – 6'01" 189

In his rookie season in the OHL, Frank received a ton of ice for the rebuilding Kitchener Rangers. While never looking spectacular, he was consistently one of their most frequently used defender for the Rangers. Frank was a tough player to get a consistent read on because he was never consistent in any one area of his game. He generates good speed, but his footwork isn't particularly ideal.

He is capable of quickly finding good initial positioning, and is good at tying up sticks, and neutralizing them in scoring areas. However, he constantly drifted out of position, some occasions subsequently lead to goals against his team. Hora uses his size well down low sticking with his man well along the wall, but can get beat, and take penalties when a stronger forward is controlling the puck, and beats him. His one-on-one play was very hit or miss.

Generally when he's at his best it's due to utilizing his stick, and negating the play by knocking the puck away from the oncoming forward. When he is unsuccessful it's usually due to a late pivot caused by a speedy forward, or a skilled forward with quick hands. He is inconsistent with the puck in his own zone. We have watched him make some excellent passes to a forward in the neutral zone to initiate the rush. However, when pressured he tends to rush puck plays resulting in turnovers, passes to dangerous areas of the defensive zone, or flipping the puck over the glass for a penalty.

In the offensive zone he displays limited offensive tools, but is capable of making basic puck distribution plays. He also possesses a good shot, which he can get on net about half the time. When it's on goal it's not overly powerful, but it is easily deflectable, and has been beneficial to his team on the powerplay on a few occasions that we've witnessed. Frank has good size, and has shown flashes of potential, but if he is selected at the 2014 NHL Entry Draft we expect it to be a late selection.

SEASON	LEAGUE	GAMES	GOALS	ASSISTS	PPG	PIM	HP RANKING
2012/13	MWEHL	36	2	10	0.33	16	NR
2013/14	OHL	65	1	19	0.31	53	

Hore, Tyler
RD – SOO Greyhounds (OHL) – 6'03" 182

Tyler is a big defenseman who was delt to the Greyhounds from the Sarnia Sting at the trade deadline. Hore's ice time declined a bit after the deal but he maintained the same style of game.

Tyler is most noticeable along the wall where he is able to use his strength and dominate battles. He wins the vast majority of battles along the boards in which he engages in. He also finishes his hits along the wall effectively.

He proved to be a tough player to scout this season because he would show such wide ranges in so many different areas. He would at times rush the puck up ice very effectively for a defender his size using his body extremely well to shield the puck. However there were occasions when he tried to do this and it resulted in a turnovers and an odd man rush. He can sometimes be forced to rush puck decisions which he will sometimes react well to, but other times will try to force a pass that isn't there or ice the puck when he has available options. His one on one situations have also been wide ranged. He handles size very well and won the majority of match-up's against bigger forwards and would drive them outside and into the wall. Smaller speedy defenders had a little more success getting inside at times or evading the check when being driven wide.

Ultimately Tyler is a big physical defenseman who does well in battles and would be a project if selected at the 2014 NHL Entry Draft. A defender who already possesses physical tools but will need to become more consistent in the other areas of the game to reach his potential.

SEASON	LEAGUE	GAMES	GOALS	ASSISTS	PPG	PIM	HP RANKING
2012/13	OHL	57	1	12	0.23	14	NR
2013/14	OHL	63	7	13	0.32	40	

Hunt, Dryden
LC – Regina Pats (WHL) – 5'11" 195

Hunt had to overcome a wealth of concussion issues to put forward a pretty solid performance this season. Dryden combines work ethic and skill to put himself on the radar. Despite missing almost a full year of development last season, Dryden shows a tenacious work ethic and competes hard for pucks. He battles down low and provides an excellent forecheck. He is consistently effective pressuring the opposing puck carrier. He wins races to pucks and is able to show flashes of creativity to set up teammates but is ultimately a very shoot first type of player who has a hard, quick and accurate release on his shot leading to a 20 goal season and four goals in four playoff games.

Dryden is a bit of a risky pick which could see him fall later in the draft due to suffering three concussions over the last 18 months. However a team could land a steal in the late rounds if Dryden can overcome his concerns and continue to develop the way he has this season.

SEASON	LEAGUE	GAMES	GOALS	ASSISTS	PPG	PIM	HP RANKING
2012/13	WHL	2	0	0	0	0	NR
2013/14	WHL	62	21	19	0.65	64	

Husso, Ville
G – HIFK (FIN) 6'3" 205

Husso was undrafted in last year NHL draft had a great year playing in finland top men's league with HIFK where he he played 41 games and had 1, 76 goals against average and a 923sv%. He also played for his national team at the world junior hockey championship as a backup to Jusse Jaros.

Husso is a big size goaltender who covers his net very well due to his size but also because of his quickness. He's very calm in his crease and doesn't make unnecessary movement in his crease. He can tracks the puck very well even with traffics in front of him, has a strong glove. He control his rebound well using the classic butterfly technique.

Needs to be little more patient in his net and let the shooter make the first move instead of committing earlier. There were concern with him last year and that cause him to go undrafted but fair to say he respond well with a big season playing against men in Finland.

SEASON	LEAGUE	GAMES	GAA	SV%	W	L	SO	HP RANKING
2012/13	Jr.A SM-liiga	41	2.63	0.909	NA	NA	NA	94
2013/14	SM-liiga	41	1.99	0.923	NA	NA	NA	

Iacopelli, Matheson
LW – Muskegon Lumberjacks (USHL) – 6'02" 185

Iacopelli is blessed with what may be one of the best wrist shot in the entire USHL. He has a quick release, tons of zip, and great accuracy. He picks corners with the best of them, and his arsenal also includes an absolute laser of a slap shot. These skills were utilized by Muskegon this year by employing Iacopelli on the point on power plays and it paid off numerous times, as Iacopelli netted goal after goal from the point, many coming on one-timer slap shots that opposing goaltenders simply had no chance at. Other times he would be able sneak into the slot or make a move to open up the shooting lane and fire that rocket of a wrister, many times with the goaltender hardly moving in response. Iacopelli's a big body, but he moves really well. He has good top speed, a nice long, fluid stride, and his mobility is above average.

Excellent hands, combined with a big body and speed make him extremely difficult to defend. He's incredibly tough to stop when coming down the ice at full speed, and he's not afraid to initiate contact even when he's the one carrying the puck. He bounces off opposing checks as much as anybody I have seen this season. He also uses his body really well to protect the puck in tight and is a beast around the net and below the goal line in the offensive zone.

His playmaking and passing are average. He is much more a pure goal scorer. The aforementioned average passing and playmaking skills can be on account of his overall lack of hockey sense, awareness, and vision. His decision making is flawed and he often can be found loafing around the ice and can get caught wandering out of position. His effort and compete level are generally high on the offensive end, but away from the puck and on the defensive side he is much less engaged and involved. Even in the offensive zone at times he can be lackadaisical and sit back in the open areas just waiting for someone to get him the puck as opposed to making things happen and supporting line mates.

At the end of the day, Iacopelli is a real boom or bust prospect, with little to any in-between. He has the shot and skating ability to be a pure goal scorer at the NHL level, but if he doesn't cut as a goal scorer he may have a tough time sticking at that level. He doesn't seem to have the hockey smarts nor the work ethic to evolve his style of play to adapt to a different role in order to stick in the NHL like other high-scoring junior players have prior to him. He has the physical abilities that give him huge potential, but at the moment he is very one-dimensional.

Quotable: "He has home run ability, an NHL shot and he can fly. He lacks courage, doesn't play aggressive or go into dirty areas and lacks hockey sense." - Mark Edwards

SEASON	LEAGUE	GAMES	GOALS	ASSISTS	PPG	PIM	HP RANKING
2012/13	MWEHL	39	26	20	1.18	65	100
2013/14	USHL	58	41	23	1.1	47	

Irving, Aaron
RD – Edmonton Oil Kings (WHL) – 6'01" 190

Aaron is a good-sized defender that makes a good first pass. He started the season well and was able to lead his forwards with good passes in transition as well as to jump into the play and help contribute at the offensive end. As a result, Irving had 27 points by Christmas. For whatever reason as the season progressed, his passes weren't as crisp and he seemed to struggle with his confidence at times. His offense effectively dried up in the 2nd half of the season as he only managed a combined 5 points in 47 games between the 2nd half of the regular season and Oil Kings' WHL Championship run. While Aaron hasn't been putting up points, he was still able to contribute to the team by displaying good physicality, sprinkled in with some leadership and a willingness to block shots and fight. As the Oil Kings are such a veteran-laden team, he hasn't always needed to be that type of leader for the Oil Kings, but he has stepped up when needed. Irving has a big shot from the point that he likes to use. His skating is just average and we'd like to see him increase the explosiveness of his first few strides as well as his top speed. Defensively, Irving can be difficult to play against as he will punish players for entering his coverage areas. However, his positioning and decision-making have both been suspect at times.

SEASON	LEAGUE	GAMES	GOALS	ASSISTS	PPG	PIM	HP RANKING
2012/13	AJHL	43	1	6	0.16	57	151
2013/14	WHL	63	9	21	0.48	88	

Iverson, Keegan
LW – Portland Winterhawks (WHL) – 6'00" 215

A big, thick power winger who is physical and punishing. Iverson plays a very rugged style of game and seems to thrive in the tough areas of the ice. Keegan loves to throw his weight around and hits very hard. Keegan is at his best when fighting for loose pucks and battling for space in front of the opposing teams net. He does not possess the highest skill level, but brings a very intimidating presence when he steps on the ice. He can be depended on to do some heavy lifting on a scoring line in order to create time and space for linemates. Keegan has surprisingly decent hands for his size and style of play. He is able to control the puck while maneuvering through high traffic areas. Keegan uses his size and strength well and his hands allow him to release the puck quickly in close. Keegan has a heavy shot and is able to get the puck off his stick quickly though his shot accuracy can be a bit inconsistent at times. His overall skating abilities will need to improve. His first couple steps are not very quick but once he's moving he does have good top speed. His defensive play is above average. Keegan has a good understanding of how to box out his man and keeping the puck carrier to the outside. Keegan is not afraid to block shots and moves the puck out of the zone with confidence. Keegan never gives up on the play and has been rewarded with that effort by making some key defensive zone plays through hard work. Keegan is a big power forward who possess good offensive potential but will need to improve other facets of his game.

SEASON	LEAGUE	GAMES	GOALS	ASSISTS	PPG	PIM	HP RANKING
2012/13	WHL	47	6	4	0.21	69	124
2013/14	WHL	67	22	20	0.63	70	

Jacobs, Joshua
RD – Indiana Ice (USHL) – 6'02" 194

Fluid-skating defenseman with high end offensive skill, Jacobs will be playing either for the Sarnia Sting of the OHL or the Green Bay Gamblers of the USHL after being picked up in the dispersal draft with the Indiana Ice going dormant next season. If he goes Green Bay, Jacobs is committed to Michigan State University starting in 2015.

Jacobs has a lot of offensive skill and is as good a skating defenseman as you will see in the USHL. While he could put more power behind it, he has an excellent slap shot and really good, quick-release wrist shot as well. He has good offensive instincts, is very poised and patient with the puck in all three zones, and can move the puck up ice exceptionally well. He likes to rush the puck up ice and does so with ease, and any time he can join a rush he looks to do so. He has a knack for getting pucks on net, and part of the is attributed to his confidence with the puck along the blue line and his ability to be mobile, nimble, and makes moves around defenders to open up space and lanes. His stride is explosive and his speed is high end.

Defensively, Jacobs plays with a bit of a mean streak. He is a physical presence, and will plant you any chance he gets. His aforementioned explosive stride is well utilized when throwing hits. He explodes into his hits. His positioning and awareness could be improved, but his skating ability allows him to recover from those errors. He will need to improve that at the next level, however, because the game will be too fast for him to recover. Good shot blocker.

Jacobs, all around, is a bit raw as a young defenseman. The tools are all there, he just has to learn to put it all together and develop a better awareness of the ice when he's out there. His decision-making can freeze at times, and when this happens he's apt to try and force a pass that isn't there or just lose the puck altogether for a turnover. He has high upside, and is a high-end offensive defenseman talent. If he can put together the defensive and decision-making side to even an average level, his offensive prowess, skating ability, and size can take over the rest and he could become a solid offensive defenseman at the NHL level one day.

Quotable: "Struggles with decision making and overall awareness. If you just watched him once you might think he has 1st round in him. Has some upside because of the tools." – Mark Edwards

SEASON	LEAGUE	GAMES	GOALS	ASSISTS	PPG	PIM	HP RANKING
2012/13	USHL	48	2	13	0.31	52	69
2013/14	USHL	56	5	18	0.41	46	

James, Cordell
LC – Barrie Colts (OHL) – 6'1" 190

James knows his role, and never strays from it. He's always in position defensively, and shadows his man well in the defensive zone. He was one of the Colts' top penalty killers, and was used a lot in defensive situations – especially after Erik Bradford was traded. James gets in on the forechecks, causes havoc behind the net, and isn't afraid to go to the dirty areas. He's willing to stand up for teammates and drop the gloves as well. I think he has a little bit of untapped offensive potential that we'll see as he continues to develop and see more ice, but he projects to be a good bottom-6 forward who is responsible defensively, and can kill penalties.

SEASON	LEAGUE	GAMES	GOALS	ASSISTS	PPG	PIM	HP RANKING
2012/13	GOJHL	49	12	20	0.65	26	NR
2013/14	OHL	66	5	8	0.2	22	

Jamieson, Aiden
LD – London Knights (OHL) – 6'2" 185

Jamieson has split time between the London Knights and St. Thomas Jr. B Stars. Aidan has a good combination of size, and speed that makes him an effective player, and gives him some strong long-term potential. He has been hit or miss with his decisions with the puck, and needs to get some experience under his belt in regards to his positional play, as he is in his rookie season of the OHL. With multiple injuries/sickness on the Knights blueline during the playoffs Jamieson got a second opportunity to show his improvements. Most notably was his ability to compete in battles against veteran forwards. His decision-making was still very hit or miss, but showed promising signs that his development is headed in the right direction. We don't expect Aidan to be selected at the 2014 NHL Entry Draft, but he certainly combines skills that should make him a player to watch as a late bloomer as he continues to develop.

SEASON	LEAGUE	GAMES	GOALS	ASSISTS	PPG	PIM	HP RANKING
2013/14	GOJHL	30	1	7	0.27	22	NR
2013/14	OHL	24	0	5	0.21	4	

Jenkins, Kyle
LD – SOO Greyhounds (OHL) – 6'01" 166

Jenkins is a defender who we really liked going back to his Minor Midget days with Mississauga Rebels. Kyle has adjusted well to the OHL game and plays an offensive role for the Greyhounds from the blueline. Kyle is a smooth skater who displays good mobility in all directions. He is very capable of rushing the puck identifying options and knowing when to pass, when to carry into the offensive zone and when to get pucks deep.

His passing while on the rush needs to become more consistently accurate as he can miss his target from time to time. In the offensive zone Kyle moves the puck accurately and efficiently around the point. He will pinch in from time to time and try to get involved in the offense. He also possesses a decent shot which he doesn't force or rush to get off. He struggles a little defensively with puck battles and at times, positioning. Getting stronger is part of the issue which he needs to address in the summer. Jenkins has good size for a puck rushing defender and shows a lot of promise in the middle rounds of the 2014 NHL Entry Draft.

SEASON	LEAGUE	GAMES	GOALS	ASSISTS	PPG	PIM	HP RANKING
2012/13	OJHL	46	9	20	0.63	47	106
2013/14	OHL	63	7	18	0.4	28	

Jenys, Pavel
LC – Brno – (CZE) – 6'2.5" 192

One of those guys that the more we saw him the more slid down our list. He's a big kid who played way too much on the perimeter, not a good combination for us. Not much offensive ability, if any at all combined with soft play in our viewings equals sliding in the rankings.

Quotable: "He's great in the warm-up, a big guy who can skate and you can't wait to see him play. He just doesn't get involved in the play when the game starts." – Mark Edwards

SEASON	LEAGUE	GAMES	GOALS	ASSISTS	PPG	PIM	HP RANKING
2012/13	CZE U20	26	13	6	0.73	35	NR
2013/14	CZE	29	2	0	0.07	4	

Jevpalovs, Nikita
C/W – Blainville-Boisbriand Armada (QMJHL) – 6'1" 198

The Latvian forward, in his 2nd year with the Armada, had a strong year for them. His game has been better from the get-go, compared to last year where he had a slow start.

Jevpalovs averaged just under a point per game and played a big role offensively for the Armada, night in and night out. A threat on the power play, he loves to shoot the puck and has a great one-timer playing the point on the power play. He and Daniel Walcott had great chemistry on the man advantage and Walcott loved to set up Jevpalovs for those one-timers from the left face-off circle. He's not afraid of anyone, will hit, get hit and get his nose dirty in front of the net. A popular team-mate, he has good hands in close, but his game still goes through inconsistency periods.

Jevpalovs, who was the 40th selection overall in the CHL Import Draft in 2012, is a shoot-first type of player. His game lacks creativity at times and is one reason why I believed his game is better suited for the wing at the pro level. With the Armada, he has played all three forward positions. He is a decent skater with an average top speed that likes to take the puck to the net. He still has things to learn in the defensive end, as sometimes he can get carried away and run a little bit too much in his own zone, but he has made some nice progress since last season. As a late 1994-born player, Jevpalovs isn't expected back next season, unless the Armada wants to have an overage Euro on their squad. It should be interesting to see where Jevpalovs plays next year. If he gets drafted, you could see him in the AHL or ECHL and if not, he will be looking for a place in Europe to play.

SEASON	LEAGUE	GAMES	GOALS	ASSISTS	PPG	PIM	HP RANKING
2012/13	QMJHL	60	18	21	0.65	36	NR
2013/14	QMJHL	61	28	26	0.89	32	

Johansson, Emil
LD – HV 71 Jr. (SWE) – 5'11.75" 194

There is a lot to like about Emil including the fact that he is one of the best skating players in this draft class. Where it comes crashing down for us is the fact that we question his ability to think the game at a level that would allow us to rank him higher. Emil plays well along the walls and understands defensive positioning. He uses his fantastic skating to his advantage, keeping good gaps and pivots when forwards attempt to go wide. Not a huge offensive threat, it's an area he could get better. He struggles to make quality decisions with the puck when the game speed picks up.

SEASON	LEAGUE	GAMES	GOALS	ASSISTS	PPG	PIM	HP RANKING
2012/13	J18 Allsv.	17	4	7	0.65	8	58
2013/14	U20 S.Elit	42	2	7	0.21	28	

Joly, Michael
RW – Rimouski Oceanic (QMJHL) – 5'10" 172

Joly went undrafted last year after finishing his rookie year with the Rimouski Oceanic. It took him a while to adjust to the QMJHL, but he has made some great strides in the second half and was only starting to scratch the surface of his talent. This year the Gatineau native has been one of the most pleasant surprises in the league, finishing among the top scorers in the league and a constant threat on the penalty killing unit. Joly's number one quality is his stick-handling prowess; he could literally stickhandle in a phone booth. One of the best pairs of hands in the QMJHL, he can make defensemen look silly with his great arsenal of dekes.

He has great anticipation, which makes him a threat on the penalty killing unit. Over the last two years, he has become one of the most dangerous players shorthanded in the QMJHL. He started to play there last year when he didn't get to play in an offensive role and really learned his craft. Although he's undersized, Joly will play in tough areas of the ice and will score goals in front of the net, battling hard all over the ice. That can lead to injuries as it did the last two seasons, both interrupted with his shoulder problems.

He has a good, quick shot and during the course of the year, as his confidence grew, it felt like everything he touched ended up in the back of the net. He's a smart player who makes players around him better, a great passer who sees things on the ice that others don't. Skating might be Joly's biggest weakness, as he just doesn't generate enough speed and his starts are average at best. That won't cost him at the junior level but could eventually catch up with him at a higher level. He needs to keep his feet moving all the time and needs to find a way to be more explosive as well. Tough for any smallish forwards to have success at the pro level if they're not quick enough.

SEASON	LEAGUE	GAMES	GOALS	ASSISTS	PPG	PIM	HP RANKING
2012/13	QMJHL	50	11	18	0.58	25	NR
2013/14	QMJHL	64	44	30	1.16	29	

Jones, Nicholas
RC – Sherwood Park (AJHL) – 5'10" 173

We loved the compete level Nicholas showed on a nightly basis. He battles hard for pucks and competes at both ends of the ice. He wins more than his share of battles not out of strength or size but out of pure determination. When he wins battles in the offensive zone he can be very dangerous with the puck. He has a quick release on his shot which is very accurate.

Our biggest concern for Nicholas is his combination of size and skating, or lack there of. For a player of his size it simply has to improve and is a glaring concern for us going into the 2014 NHL Entry Draft. He is slated to join Ohio State University in September 2014.

SEASON	LEAGUE	GAMES	GOALS	ASSISTS	PPG	PIM	HP RANKING
2012/13	AJHL	48	11	13	0.5	36	192
2013/14	AJHL	16	12	10	1.38	8	

Joshua, Dakota
LW/C – Sioux Falls Stampede (USHL) – 6'02" 182

The little talked about power forward out of Dearborn, Michigan is an intriguing prospect. Hailing from the well-esteemed Detroit Honeybaked Midget program, this was Joshua's first full season in the USHL. Joshua puts his 6'2" 182 pound frame to good use, punishing opposing puck carriers and making his presence known. He is a heavy hitter, and conversely he more times than not bounces off of attempted checks on him. Rock solid on his feet and very strong, Joshua is a physical force to be reckoned with and a perfect, prototypical player for the power forward mold. Aside from his physicality, Joshua has no shortage of finesse and smarts to his game. Soft, quick hands and a boatload of patience and poise allow for him to create offensive opportunities in all sorts of ways. His high-end speed doesn't hurt, either. Has the ability to beat defensemen wide in the offensive zone with his speed, but also has the hands to be able to toe-drag and power around them to the inside.

Defensively responsible, solid on the penalty kill and a willing shot blocker. Uses a smart active stick. Hard and aggressive on the puck and good, quick decision making in his own zone. Doesn't drift or get caught out of position. Uses his patience with the puck to allow for the play to develop in order to get a clean exit from the zone as opposed to just throwing it up the boards or off the glass. Able to bounce of an evade attacking players and maintain puck possession.

All in all, Joshua is a very nice two-way player. He will have another season in Sioux Falls to further develop before heading to Ohio State University in 2015. The Plymouth Whalers own his OHL rights after drafting him 156th Overall in the 2013 OHL Priority Selection Draft.

Quotable: "Dakota needs to improve his pace of play at times but could turn out to be a mid round home run. He has great potential with size smarts and skill." – Mark Edwards

SEASON	LEAGUE	GAMES	GOALS	ASSISTS	PPG	PIM	HP RANKING
2012/13	(U16)HPHL	18	12	10	1.22	18	76
2013/14	USHL	55	17	21	0.69	58	

Kähkönen, Kaapo
G – Blues U20 (Jr.A SM-liiga) – 6'2" 201

Kähkönen is an intriguing goaltending prospect because he has already pro size and moves well laterally in his crease. Already at the 2013 U17 hockey challenge in the province of Quebec he showed sign of a strong goaltending prospect with his size and quickness. He's above average in most areas as he has a strong active blocker, not weak glove side and covers the lower part of the net very well. Biggest issue has been with his mental game, can lose focus and give weak goals. Can lose positioning in his crease due to his lack of focus. He's aggressive when he challenge shooters and that's given his size doesn't give much to shoot at for shooters. He's a strong puck handling goaltender and can act as a 3rd defenseman out there for his team.

This season internationally, Kähkönen played at the Ivan Hlinka and the April world under-18 hockey championship and played in the 38 games with his club team in the Finland junior league.

SEASON	LEAGUE	GAMES	GAA	SV%	W	L	SO	HP RANKING
2012/13	Jr.A SM-liiga	28	2.43	0.917	NA	NA	NA	189
2013/14	Jr.A SM-liiga	38	NA	0.912	NA	NA	NA	

Kamenev, Vladislav
LW - Magnitogorsk (RUS) – 6'2" 203

Our first viewings of Kamenev were at the World Under 17 in Victoriaville. He didn't get a whole lot of icetime. He played on a line with Yazkov and Kraskovsky and Svechnikov subbed in as well. Kamenov showed off his skill when we got to see him.

Kamenev is a big skilled forward with good natural offensive instincts. He showed to be an intelligent player in our viewings. He posted good numbers up at the World Junior A Challenge back in November, finishing the tourney 4th in scoring with 1 goal and 6 assists. Kamenev has a good shot, including a solid one-timer. He passed up on some good opportunities to shoot the puck at times by choosing to look for the perfect play. He did show off great playmaking ability as for the most part, he distributed the puck to teammates very well. He has good feet, especially when you consider his size, skating was solid with good balance and speed.

Effort level impressed us, he worked hard in all three zones in our viewings. He has good hands, he bought himself time and space by utilizing his puck control skills.

Quotable: "In general I liked him, he did have some real brain cramps in his game that along with the Russian factor might make me back off him a bit at rankings time." - Mark Edwards

Quotable: "I liked him less with each viewing." - NHL Scout

SEASON	LEAGUE	GAMES	GOALS	ASSISTS	PPG	PIM	HP RANKING
2013/14	MHL	15	4	6	0.67	12	35
2013/14	KHL	16	1	0	0.06	2	

Kapanen, Kasperi
RW – KalPa (SM-liiga) – 6'0" 180

Last year's scouting report holds pretty true for Kasperi as he completed his NHL Draft eligible season at home in the U18 in Finland. While Kapanen didn't put too many crooked numbers up on the scoreboard at the 2014 World U18, he did flash some of the aspects we saw him his game last season.

Kasperi plays an aggressive game and the fact that he has grown this season isn't hurting him any. He's a force on the forecheck, he uses his speed well taking away time and space from opposing players. While he still needs to get stronger, he is effective along walls winning battles for pucks. He's not afraid to lay the lumber sort of speak, he is willing and capable of laying solid body checks. He's shown us the ability to be creative and shows off good puck skills. He can control the play in the offensive zone and can also beat defenders one on one both coming off the boards or off the rush. When rushing the puck he has displayed good vision and decision making skills. He showed us he can pass the puck but he is very comfortable shooting the puck. His shot is very good. It is accurate with a quick release. He sports a solid one-timer as well.

Kapanen is a very good skater. He has explosive speed and he is very elusive because he possesses fantastic lateral skating abilities. He competes hard and has shown to be a good penalty killer where he's willing to block shots.

Our concern for Kaspanen is that he continues have some issues with consistency. We saw him play quite a bit the past two seasons and he has shifts where he is not very visible. It's frustrating because when he is on his game he is a productive player in all three zones. It's not that he drops his effort level, he just seems to go through stretches where he doesn't achieve much on the ice.

Quotable: "He's a top 15 pick." NHL Scout

Quotable: "He reminds me of Alex Steen." NHL Scout

Quotable: "My opinion on Kapanen hasn't changed much over the past 16 months. He flashed his package of tools in one of the first shifts I saw him in Finland at the U18. He went end to end displaying his speed and explosiveness. He also had shifts where I had trouble finding him. In general, I like his blend of skill combined with some high end skills." - Mark Edwards

SEASON	LEAGUE	GAMES	GOALS	ASSISTS	PPG	PIM	HP RANKING
2012/13	SM-liiga	13	4	0	0.31	2	19
2013/14	SM-liiga	47	7	7	0.3	10	

Karabacek, Vaclav
RW – Gatineau Olympiques (QMJHL) – 5'11" 185

Karabáček was the 18th overall pick in last year's CHL Import Draft. The Czech forward played one season in Austria with the EC Red Bull Salzburg before joining the Olympiques. In his first season in the QMJHL, the Prague native was able to make a considerable impact with his team and also played for his country at the recent U-18 World Championships in Finland. Karabáček finished the season with 21 goals and 47 points, also finding a lot of success in the first round of the playoffs against Cape-Breton with 12 points in 9 games.

He's a strong skater with great explosion and bursts of speed, which makes him tough to handle off the rush and he's dangerous when he tries to beat defensemen wide. He has great top speed that he can reach quickly. We saw great amounts of improvement with his skating since the beginning of the year. Overall, his agility is decent, but he's more of a North-South skater than East-West.

Karabáček is a very streaky player. When he's on, he can be dominant, using his speed and quick release on his wrist shot, getting his nose dirty as well in front of the net. When his game is off, you don't see a lot out of him, he can be invisible on the ice, lacks involvement and plays a soft game. Likes his puck protection along the wall and has a good reach; this helps him to shield defenders away and he's effective cycling the puck with his line. He's good at finding space in the offensive zone to get open or make room for himself. Without the puck, Karabáček won't put his team in trouble. He's smart and gets involved in the defensive zone.

Quotable: "I have time for him because of his skill level. He scored a goal at a game I was at late in the season versus Halifax with a ridiculously quick release. He had flashes of strong play in Finland at the U18 as well." - Mark Edwards

SEASON	LEAGUE	GAMES	GOALS	ASSISTS	PPG	PIM	HP RANKING
2012/13	RBHRC U18	21	26	19	2.14	55	79
2013/14	QMJHL	65	21	26	0.72	40	

Karlsson, Anton
RW – Frolunda Jr (SWE Jr.) – 6'1.25" 187

Anton is hard working winger that we have referred to a few times as a 'worker ant'. He is not blessed with a ton of skill but he competes very hard all over the ice. He's a good skater, including a solid first few steps. He plays a simple game but is effective doing so. He plays hard along the walls and is a gritty player. He is a decent player in the defensive zone and uses his stick wisely, taking away lanes. Karlsson is not blessed with an overly hard or accurate shot.

Quotable: "He's a player that slid in my personal rankings with each viewing. Early on I thought he had more skill than I think he has now. While he brings valuable assets to the table, I don't value his skill-set enough to draft him up amongst the big boys." - Mark Edwards

Quotable: "Not one of our better interviews." NHL Scout

SEASON	LEAGUE	GAMES	GOALS	ASSISTS	PPG	PIM	HP RANKING
2013/14	U20 S.Elit	28	12	10	0.79	88	67
2013/14	SHL 2	9	0	0	0	2	

Kase, Ondrej
RW – Chomutov (CZE) – 6'0" 165

Kase has shown us flashes of having great skills and excellent speed. Liked his ability to change speeds quickly, delaying and doing turn-ups. We have seen him burn defenders with his quick bursts. Skated some pucks into trouble causing needless turnovers when he had options. Showed some faceoff prowess in our viewings winning some draws clean. Flashed a good wrister and some stick handling abilities.

SEASON	LEAGUE	GAMES	GOALS	ASSISTS	PPG	PIM	HP RANKING
2012/13	CZE U20	22	9	7	0.73	18	80
2013/14	CZE	37	4	3	0.19	10	

Kempe, Adrian
LW – MODO (SWE) – 6'1" 187

Kempe is a player our staff has been fans of going back to last season. He's a smart player who competes hard in all three zones playing a responsible game. Kempe has some Sean Monahan like traits in his game in that he is committed to playing solid defense from the forward position.

Kempe is stromg kid and a good skater with a powerful stride. He has a decent shot but can struggle with consistency at times as far as turning scoring chances into goals. His strength is winning battles by playing hard down low and playing smart positional hockey. He's a player coaches will give ice to because of his hockey IQ and ability to do things like block shots and play smart low risk hockey when the situation calls for it. He protects the puck well and is able to create plays with decent creativity and special awareness. He reads the play well and takes advantage of what defenders give him. He will seldom turn pucks over trying high risk plays, he plays a pro style game already. Going back to last season his penalty killing stood out to us and he has continued playing great hockey on the PK.

The drawback on Kempe is his lack of high-end skills, mainly scoring ability. We don't project him to be a big points guy at the next level. We have seen him score but too often we saw solid scoring chances not get converted. There are not many holes in his game but elite scoring ability is not something Kempe flashes.

Quotable: "Love his game." NHL Scout

Quotable: "A smart player but he lacks top six skill." NHL Scout

Quotable: "I just love watching him play and just got to see him again in Finland. He's the same reliable player I grew to respect last season. I can tell you this, Team Canada brass noticed him. To me Kempe projects to be a trusted player that some NHL Coach will rely on in key situations because he does all the little things coaches preach." - Mark Edwards

SEASON	LEAGUE	GAMES	GOALS	ASSISTS	PPG	PIM	HP RANKING
2013/14	U20 S.Elit	20	3	16	0.95	32	21
2013/14	SHL	45	5	6	0.24	12	

Keskitalo, Miro
D - Jokerit Jr. (FIN Jr.) – 6'2" 176

Supports his partner well all over the ice. Showed us good D Zone awareness and positioning plus a willingness to block shots, in fact, he is a shot blocking machine. showing a willingness to take the body whenever the chance arose. Uses head fakes to effectively move the puck, flashed us a numerous impressive simple little 10 foot passes, showing the understanding of making smart, high percentage puck movement plays. Feet looked great considering his size, showed an ability to skate the puck a little bit but seemed to prefer to pump out the smart passes to his forwards. His gap awareness was good and read the play well in all three zones.

A heart and soul player who played big minutes for the national team. Could see him potentially working his into a 5/6 Dman in the NHL with some future development.

SEASON	LEAGUE	GAMES	GOALS	ASSISTS	PPG	PIM	HP RANKING
2012/13	Jr.B U18	33	6	14	0.61	40	70
2013/14	Jr.A SM-liiga	39	2	8	0.26	36	

King, Jeff
RD – Sarnia Sting (OHL) – 5'10" 160

Jeff joined the Sting for his OHL rookie season this year after playing top minutes as a 16 year old with the Sarnia Legionnaires (GOJHL). He has been effective for the Sting utilizing his speed and puck rushing ability to take the puck up ice. His speed is above average and he displays good mobility. He received some power play ice and has had some strong moments moving the puck but also some mistakes that come with adjusting to the speed at the OHL level. His mistakes generally occur in the defensive zone as he can get pressured into mistakes and lose his defensive positioning. He also needs to get stronger in battles. He seemed to improve a bit playing forward near the end of the season getting a little more involved in the offensive zone and playing more so as a third defenseman when the play is in his zone, which helped limit the amount of puck decisions he needed to make behind his own blue line. While Jeff has some strengths that make him an effective player at the junior level, we do not believe he will be selected at the 2014 NHL Entry Draft.

SEASON	LEAGUE	GAMES	GOALS	ASSISTS	PPG	PIM	HP RANKING
2012/13	GOJHL	51	7	18	0.49	27	NR
2013/14	OHL	61	4	15	0.31	32	

Kirkland, Justin
LW – Kelowna Rockets (WHL) – 6'03" 189

Justin is a long term prospect, but brings a unique blend of size, skill, offensive instincts, and skating ability to develop into a very dominant power forward. When Justin's game is firing on all cylinders, he can be a hard player to contain. He can drive to the net and fend off the opposing defenders seemingly at will. While he doesn't always do it consistently, Justin can bring a strong, physical aspect to his game which makes him very difficult to contain. He has shown good aggression during the small puck battles along the boards for most of the year. Much like his offensive game, he suffers from inconsistent play in his own end. At times it looks like Justin has a good understanding of his defensive responsibilities and other times he has looked like he was lost. Justin's footwork needs some improvement, but there is some power in his stride. While his stride is a little clunky at times, he is capable of generating good speed with it. He has shown on several occasions to be capable of forcing many turnovers and doesn't give up on the rare occasion that his team got down. Like many big players, he could stand to improve his acceleration. Justin possesses a lot of raw undeveloped talent and over the course of the next few years he should round out all facets of his game and develop into a very dominating player.

Quotable: "Kirkland is still very raw, but has great potential. He has the frame that NHL teams love and uses his reach well. He plays a North-South game and he's not afraid to go to the dirty areas. He knows his role as a puck-fetching, big-bodied winger, but his good IQ has helped him identify how best to make his mark in a particular situation and his offensive game has grown as a result." – Scott McDougall

SEASON	LEAGUE	GAMES	GOALS	ASSISTS	PPG	PIM	HP RANKING
2012/13	SMHL	44	25	24	1.11	42	**68**
2013/14	WHL	68	17	31	0.71	40	

Kiviranta, Joel
RW – Jokerit Jr. (FIN) – 5'10" 167

Really liked this him, especially as a potential CHL Import Draft prospect. Kiviranta is a smallish skilled forward who possesses great quickness, a good shot with a quick release. He's not afraid to let it rip. He is an effective forechecker, getting on top of opposing players quickly. He's slightly undersized and needs to get stronger, but he has a lot of skill and plays in all game situations. He showed us good defensive awareness as well.

Biggest concern is he looked like he might not even be as tall as his listed 5'10". He's a very safe prospect for the CHL Import Draft.

SEASON	LEAGUE	GAMES	GOALS	ASSISTS	PPG	PIM	HP RANKING
2012/13	Jr.A SM-liiga	40	7	13	0.5	35	**176**
2013/14	Jr.A SM-liiga	38	18	19	0.97	40	

Kraskovsky, Pavel
LC - Yaroslav (RUS) – 6'4" 187

Barely eligible for this year draft, Pavel is a battler who works as hard defensively as he does on offense. It's hard to think of other legit Russian prospects that could match the intensity level that he brings with his game.

Albeit not overly skilled, Kraskovsky is not without any offense in his game; he can pass the puck and a nice reach paired with his strong skating may help him to create scoring chances on the smaller North American rinks by forcing turnovers.

He projects as a 3rd line center who kills penalties, the type of forward that can be used in 3 vs 5 situations, something that already happened this year in MHL despite being one of the youngest players on the Loko jr. team.

SEASON	LEAGUE	GAMES	GOALS	ASSISTS	PPG	PIM	HP RANKING
2013/14	MHL	39	10	17	0.69	16	121
2013/14	KHL	8	1	0	0.13	14	

Kuhlman, Karson
RC – Dubuque Fighting Saints (USHL) – 5'10" 175

Kuhlman is an excellent skater. He has a smooth, strong, effortless stride and handles the puck with similar effortlessness. He zig-zags through the neutral zone with the puck with ease, and has excellent zone entry ability, yet he has the intelligence and sense to know when it is better to chip the puck in and go after as opposed to coughing it up at the blue line and causing a break the other way. His speed is breakaway caliber. He takes defensemen wide and beats them to the net often. In a couple of cases, one in particular, he stole the puck from an opposing player near his own blue line on the backcheck, drove wide on the defenseman on his strong side, completely beat him and cut to the net and toe-dragged along with his body to the middle of crease, getting the goaltender to commit to a pad-stack and he placed the puck right between the pads as they raised. It was a beautiful play all around, and was all done at top speed. It was truly one of the best goals viewed all season long. He's great on his edges and can cut and turn at top speed and loses no speed at all when handling the puck. He uses his body well to protect, be it along the boards spinning and turning to shake off defenders, or in anticipation of receiving a pass, turning his body in directions so as to receive the pass in stride but also block out the defender coming at him. Very good hockey sense and overall awareness of the ice both with and without the puck.

Defensively he plays a pretty strong game, rarely doesn't hustle. He was viewed saving icings a number of times this season simply outskating the backpedaling defenseman. He has a very active stick and causes a lot of turnovers and he backchecks hard. His defensive game allows for him to play the point on the power play, being trusted to be the last man back. His only real issue is consistency. There are nights when he's simply just not on his game and doesn't appear to have the complete effort level in all facets of his game, and his game suffers as a result. Sometimes it's not even a full game but just shifts within the same game. When he brings his full game, he's a force to be reckoned with, but he needs to consistently bring that effort level every night. He isn't the ideal power forward size, but when he is on, he plays that style of game successfully.

Quotable:" Coaches love him." NHL Scout

SEASON	LEAGUE	GAMES	GOALS	ASSISTS	PPG	PIM	HP RANKING
2012/13	USHL	16	1	8	0.56	0	144
2013/14	USHL	56	25	19	0.79	12	

Kulda, Edgars
LW – Edmonton Oil Kings (WHL) – 6'00" 178

After being passed over at the 2013 NHL Entry Draft, Edgars showed some things we really liked about him last season but ultimately felt his offensive game needed to pick up before he would receive a chance to be selected.

Kulda went above and beyond in that department more than tripling his offensive numbers and scoring 32 more goals this season than last between regular season and playoffs combined. It goes without saying his shot has come miles and is among the more dangerous shots in the draft as he has a lot of power, it flies off his stick but it's also accurate.

His physical game also saw a wealth of improvement. While his weight didn't change much he slimmed down a little and got a little more solid which helped when he applied himself along the wall and delivered some solid checks. He was able to accomplish all of this, all while remaining the defensively responsible/reliable forward that we liked last season. Edgars thinks the game at a high level and is often able to make quick decisions that create space for his linemates. He is able to make plays at high speed and in traffic. He has a good wrist shot and is an above average passer. His skating is pretty good and he is definitely quicker than last season. Kulda has good awareness and with continued improvements he's expected to be one of the first re-entry players off the board at the 2014 NHL Entry Draft.

Quotable: "I liked Kulda's all-around game last year, but had been left wanting more offensively. This season, Kulda has polished his offensive game and the growth of his game had been pretty well under the radar before being exposed big-time with his MVP performance at the Memorial Cup. Still has a ways to go, but he's a smart player that's not afraid to get dirty." – Scott McDougall

SEASON	LEAGUE	GAMES	GOALS	ASSISTS	PPG	PIM	HP RANKING
2012/13	WHL	64	6	11	0.27	34	78
2013/14	WHL	66	30	30	0.91	57	

LaBanc, Kevin
LW – Barrie Colts (OHL) – 5'11" 185

Kevin doesn't have a real stand out skill but he's a very well rounded player who is solid at both ends of the rink. He's a quick skater, and has a good first few steps. He'll battle for loose pucks, and he has a non-stop motor that keeps on running. LaBanc will drive the net, and crash for rebounds. He has good vision, and is a pretty good passer, especially when he has time to create, and find open ice on the powerplay. There were a couple times this year where he stood in the slot, Lemieux stood in front of the net and LaBanc was used in a double screen, which seemed to be effective.

LaBanc owns a pretty good shot, can handle the puck effectively, and is confident with it on his stick. He'll skate with the puck, and is patient enough to wait for plays to develop before passing or shooting. He took a regular shift on the penalty kill, and was good there, as he always seemed to get pucks out, and was willing to sacrifice his body to block shots. He continued to get better all year, and there's no reason to believe he won't continue to improve.

SEASON	LEAGUE	GAMES	GOALS	ASSISTS	PPG	PIM	HP RANKING
2012/13	(U18)USDP	62	9	12	0.34	28	128
2013/14	OHL	65	11	24	0.54	30	

Lagesson, William
LD – Frolunda Jr. (SWE Jr.) – 6'2" 196

Reminds us of Ollas-Mattsson as they share some similar traits. Not overly skilled and somehow limited offensively. He plays a tough rugged game. He's physical and makes himself tough to play against. His feet are average, skating is not a strength.

He lacks a bit in reading the play and joining the play, reading situations overall. While he lacks in many areas he's a player we still see in a positive light and think is worthwhile selecting. He competes hard and is a tough kid who plays a lunch pail blue collar game.

SEASON	LEAGUE	GAMES	GOALS	ASSISTS	PPG	PIM	HP RANKING
2012/13	J18 Elit	20	1	12	0.65	60	103
2013/14	U20 S.Elit	44	8	12	0.45	30	

Laliberté, Kevin
LD – Charlottetown Islanders (QMJHL) – 6'01" 182

Laliberté is a fine young defenseman used mostly at even strength with the Charlottetown Islanders. His biggest strength is his hockey sense. He thinks the game really well. He positions himself properly in the defensive zone depending on the situation he is facing and is rarely getting caught out of position. While we want to see him get stronger, he did relatively well against the boards using the strength he has to contain forwards and win battles on some occasions. He usually plays one-on-one and 2-on-1 situations very well and utilizes his stick moderately well. Laliberté is also a solid backwards skater and is good at pushing opponents to the outside and not allowing them to back him deep into the zone. He has good footwork and overall speed in his game, but lacks a bit of explosiveness. His breakouts passes are fairly good. In fact, he shows good patience allowing lanes to open up for him and making the smart accurate pass. He is a hard worker and generally makes strong simple crisp breakout passes and moves the puck quickly when pressured. When he is pressured, he will rarely turn the puck over. His awareness is very good, always showing maturity and intelligence on the ice. His play with the puck is controlled in tight spaces. He is able to maintain puck possession by carrying the puck through traffic. He joins the rush at the right times and makes safe decisions at the offensive blue line, rarely exposing his team to risk, while skating well to hold the blue line and maintain puck possession. He doesn't have elite skills, but we feel he's a sound underrated defenseman.

SEASON	LEAGUE	GAMES	GOALS	ASSISTS	PPG	PIM	HP RANKING
2012/13	QMJHL	36	0	0	0	10	NR
2013/14	QMJHL	67	0	13	0.19	37	

Lammikko, Juho
RW – Assat Jr. (Finland Jr.) – 6'2.5" 189

Juho is another player who impressed us going back to last season at the U17 in Victoriaviille. Lammikko also impressed us at the recent U18 in Finland. He plays big and is smart player who seems to understand exactly what role to play depending on where is in the lineup. He's a simple player but we use that term in a positive light. He scored a ton of points in Jr. He showed us some skill with some solid rushes and great shots of the rush. Scored a beauty goal going to the top shelf in April at the U18. We like that he has transferable skills to play in the bottom six in the NHL if his scoring skills come up short. He goes to the net hard, plays with fire, can open up space and doesn't try to dangle all over the ice.

Quotable: "Not sure if he is a sleeper or not with Euro based scouts, but I'll call him one of my sleepers anyway. I had nothing but positive notes on him." - Mark Edwards

SEASON	LEAGUE	GAMES	GOALS	ASSISTS	PPG	PIM	HP RANKING
2013/14	Jr.A SM-liiga	37	17	25	1.14	32	52
2013/14	SM-liiga	20	0	1	0.05	0	

Larkin, Dylan
LC – USNTDP (USHL) – 6'00" 192

There really is nothing not to like about Dylan Larkin's game. An elite-level, well-rounded power forward, Larkin can do it all. His game has improved over the course of the season, as he's learned some of the subtleties to the center position and the game overall. Larkin possesses high-end skating ability with excellent speed and quick feet. He has a great first step and breakaway speed that comes with a burst. Great closing speed on the forecheck and is able to catch players on the backcheck. He never takes a shift off and his compete level is as good as anyone's. Larkin possesses high-end offensive skill. He is a great puck handler and has superb vision, which enables him to be equally dangerous as a playmaker and goal scorer. He can finesse the puck, or he can use his speed, size, and determination and bulldoze the puck to the net. Larkin drives the net hard and isn't afraid to stick his nose in there and mix it up. More than willing to take a hit to make a play, he plays a very unselfish, team-first game. His defensive game is equally impressive and mature. He always supports his defensemen and wingers. Plays a smart game in his own zone and is solid as a rock defensively. Larkin's game is very mature for his age and stage of development. He is a natural leader and plays equally hard at both ends of the ice, and has the makeup of a future captain. He's off to the University of Michigan in the Fall.

Quotable: "I liked him going back to last season and every time I saw him this year I liked him a bit more. His play at the U18 in Finland sealed the deal for me. I think he has enough skill to play 2nd line, combine that with everything else he brings and you get a great NHL player." – Mark Edwards

SEASON	LEAGUE	GAMES	GOALS	ASSISTS	PPG	PIM	HP RANKING
2013/14	USHL	26	17	9	1	24	9
2013/14	(U18)USDP	60	31	25	0.93	56	

Lazarev, Maxim
LW – Cape Breton Screaming Eagles (QMJHL) – 5'10" 170

Lazarev was selected 3rd overall by the Screaming Eagles in last year's CHL Import Draft, and it took a while to get him out of his contract with his Russian club. He was also hurt at the beginning of his season. Lazarev, who shone for Russia at the 2013 U-17 Hockey Challenge in Drummondville and Victoriaville (where Russia lost in the final vs Sweden), recorded 10 points in 6 games.

Maxim loves to have the puck on his stick, he's a good stickhandler that sees the ice well and a smooth passer with an accurate passing game. Loves to challenge defensemen one-on-one when rushing the puck, a situation where he can showcase his quick hands and creativity. Also owns some quick feet and a good burst of speed. He possesses a good shot that he showed well at the U-17, but this year with the Screaming Eagles, we saw him more as a playmaker and pass-first guy. But don't get fooled by this, as the young Russian forward can be a dangerous sniper and can beat a goalie from anywhere in the offensive zone. It gets tough for Lazarev when he's battling for the puck in corners or along the boards. A clear lack of strength prevents him from being more effective as an offensive player. He has a tendency to disappear when the opposing teams start to play physical on him. When he's playing at his best, he can be a decent two-way forward, but often tends to be lazy with his defensive-zone assignments. He needs to pick up his work ethic without the puck. Lazarev was hurt in Team Russia's training camp just before the U-18 World Championship in April, which was not the first injury Maxim had this year, only playing 43 regular season games with the Screaming Eagles.

SEASON	LEAGUE	GAMES	GOALS	ASSISTS	PPG	PIM	HP RANKING
2012/13	MHL	32	9	10	0.59	6	165
2013/14	QMJHL	43	13	18	0.72	12	

Leblanc, Olivier
LD – Saint John Sea Dogs (QMJHL) – 5'11" 161

The 11th overall pick in the 2012 QMJHL draft, Leblanc has been the best defenseman on his squad all season long. On a rebuilding Sea Dogs squad, he had the opportunity to prove himself and didn't disappoint. Before the QMJHL season started, he was at the Ivan Hlinka tryout camp last August in Toronto and was eventually cut. Leblanc can contribute at both ends of the ice. He has a good hockey IQ that has been showcased by his ability to rush the puck on some occasions and by the quality of his breakouts. His main attribute is his footwork. His feet are always in movement and that helps him a lot when he's facing explosive skaters on one-on-one situations. He is not caught off-guard very often and his mobility helps him to cover more ice on his side. Leblanc also uses his mobility to maintain his sound positioning between opposing players and the net with a good gap. He stays aggressive between the blue lines with his gap control, and gives opponents very little room to try to go wide on him. Even though he is still undersized, Leblanc is tough as nails. He even has developed a mean streak, distributing some great open-ice hits.

Playing in all kinds of situations, Leblanc brings a solid all-around game. When he is used on the power play, he's bright enough to use either his slap shot or his wrister to take good shots at net, depending on the situation and he can set up his teammates nicely. His one-timer needs some improvement, though. Defensively, he's been steady and aggressive at the right times. He attacks the puck carrier properly along the boards and is strong enough to maintain most of the forwards he is facing. He also likes to talk a lot after the whistle, which is a big part of his game. We really like the consistency of his compete level. He's a hard worker and rarely takes a shift off. Assuming he still has growing to do, he has the upside to be chosen at the next NHL Draft.

SEASON	LEAGUE	GAMES	GOALS	ASSISTS	PPG	PIM	HP RANKING
2012/13	QMJHL	60	4	14	0.3	41	143
2013/14	QMJHL	56	7	26	0.59	58	

Leblanc, Stefan
LD – Mississauga Steelheads (OHL) – 6'00" 183

Stefan provided us with a very wide range of looks in his rookie season. Early on this season he showed a ton of promise as a two-way defenseman. He rushed the puck up ice, made smart decisions in regards on when to rush and when to pass. He showed good intelligence with the puck and was very effective on the power play. Sometimes, players run out of gas when they are in their first OHL season and immediately play huge minutes, especially at the defensive position and this may have been the case for LeBlanc who played top pairing minutes almost the entire season as a rookie. In later viewings he began struggling with his decision making with the puck in his own zone, resulting in several scoring chances for the opposition off his stick. He would get caught trying to do too much with the puck at times which also resulted in turnovers. He also lost his defensive positioning more often than earlier viewings.

Stefan has good potential as an offensive puck rushing defenseman and was consistent in that department. He will be a bit of a wildcard for the 2014 NHL Entry Draft but should be selected and hopefully the earlier version of LeBlanc prevails in his sophomore OHL season. It goes without saying that consistency will be his biggest area of improvement. When he's on his game he is better in his own zone than the average offensive defenseman.

SEASON	LEAGUE	GAMES	GOALS	ASSISTS	PPG	PIM	HP RANKING
2012/13	OJHL	49	4	29	0.67	48	NR
2013/14	OHL	64	5	23	0.44	26	

Lee, Michael
LD – The Gunnery (HS-CT) – 5'11" 167

Michael is an undersized defenseman for The Gunnery Prep School in Connecticut. He provides a very smart and steady game from the back end for his team which allowed him to put up a point per game this season. He displays good hockey sense and can move the puck effectively. He makes smart accurate passes under pressure and is very consistent with his decision making. He is also very effective without the puck understanding the positional game and always seems to be exactly where he is supposed to be. He doesn't show a lot of flash in his puck rush but he is capable of bringing the puck up ice and knowing when to carry and when to pass off. Michael is slated to join the University of Vermont in September 2015.

SEASON	LEAGUE	GAMES	GOALS	ASSISTS	PPG	PIM	HP RANKING
2012/13	USHS	31	1	11	0.39	NA	197
2013/14	USHS	28	7	21	1	NA	

Leedahl, Dawson
LW – Everett Silvertips (WHL) – 6'01" 200

Dawson is an energy-type forward who plays a very consistent game night in and night out. His pursuit of the puck on the forecheck is relentless and he seems to enjoy engaging in the one-on-one puck battles. He plays with a high compete level and strong work ethic. Dawson has shown a small offensive upside to his game this year as he is willing to go to the scoring areas and sacrifice his body to create scoring chances for himself or his teammates. He possesses both average hands and shot and will need to improve on these aspects. He is very much a one-dimensional North and South type player who seems to thrive on the physical parts of the game. As the season progressed his coaches gained enough confidence in his play where he started to see significant time on both the power play and penalty kill. His defensive game pretty much mirrors his offense game where he brings physicality and energy every shift. Dawson shows a willingness to do the little things such as blocking shots to help his team win. Dawson possesses a lot of raw undeveloped talent but will need to develop more of an offensive game and skill set if he wants to become impact type player.

SEASON	LEAGUE	GAMES	GOALS	ASSISTS	PPG	PIM	HP RANKING
2012/13	WHL	56	3	6	0.16	34	NR
2013/14	WHL	70	8	24	0.46	66	

Lemieux, Brendan
LW – Barrie Colts (OHL) – 6'1" 210

Lemieux is definitely his father's son. He's the type of player that every team needs, and opponents hate to play against. He'll take a hit to make a play, and will dish out more than his fair share of punishment. He always finishes his checks, and more often than not he'll give a little more after the whistle. Almost every game he seems to get under his opponent's skin. He's more than a super pest, though. He's excellent around the net.

Lemieux has a good pair of hands, and can not only finish in tight, but he can deflect pucks, and score that way, too. He has a nose for the net, and is effective when he sets up shop there, especially on the powerplay. He also has a pro shot, which makes him dangerous from a distance as well. He's a smart player, and can make decisions quickly. Lemieux's skating has improved a ton over the last year or so. He can now outskate opposing players to loose pucks, etc. His skating ability allows him to take defenders wide with speed before making a power move towards the net. He wins a lot of puck battles, and is good cycling the puck as well as grinding along the boards.

He plays on the top powerplay unit, and was used killing penalties as well. There's room for improvement in the defensive zone, but for the most part he's pretty responsible in his own end.

Quotable: "He will go in the first round." – Mark Edwards

SEASON	LEAGUE	GAMES	GOALS	ASSISTS	PPG	PIM	HP RANKING
2012/13	OHL	42	6	8	0.33	52	26
2013/14	OHL	65	27	26	0.82	145	

Lernout, Brett
RD – Swift Current Broncos (WHL) – 6'04" 205

Lernout has quietly gone about his business this season without much, if any, attention. The late '95-born Swift Current defenseman has shown very good improvement over the course of the season and has worked his way into becoming a mainstay on the Broncos defense corps. Lernout has tremendous size at 6'4 and a nasty mean streak to match. He is a mobile skater with both good acceleration and top speed. While his edge work needs some refining, he is an impressive skater for his stature. Lernout is an intimidating presence on the ice as he's not afraid to get in the face of opponents and his 11 fights this season attest to both his willingness to fight and his fighting prowess.

Lernout makes an average first pass. His passes are very firm, but accuracy seems to come and go at times. His ability to make defensive reads is improving as well. While Lernout is still quite raw, he has a lot of tools at his disposal and has shown tremendous improvements over the course of the season. As a result, Lernout may be worth a pick as a long-term project with good upside.

Quotable: "Brett showed good improvement through the course of the season. A toolsy player with great size, strength, and skating abilities. He's still raw, but if given time to develop, he should become the type of physical defenseman that teams love to have and hate to play against." – Scott McDougall

SEASON	LEAGUE	GAMES	GOALS	ASSISTS	PPG	PIM	HP RANKING
2012/13	WHL	59	1	1	0.03	43	129
2013/14	WHL	72	8	14	0.31	103	

Letunov, Maxim
C – Youngstown Phantoms (USHL) – 6' 2" 150

Drafted by Youngstown in the second round of the 2013 USHL Entry Draft out of the Dallas Stars U16 program, the Russian-born centerman is committed to Boston University but is slated to return to Youngstown this fall after an excellent rookie USHL season.

After putting up 43 points in 60 games during his rookie campaign, offensive skill is an obvious observation when watching Maxim play. He has slick hands and an excellent wrist shot to match. It's released quick, high velocity, and accurate. Equally impressive is his passing ability. His passes are always crisp, on the money, and he makes some many others are simply not capable of as a result of his excellent vision and awareness of his surroundings. Maxim seems to always know where everyone on the ice is at all times when he is out there and that combined with his high offensive skill make him a bear to defend. He is surprisingly adept at using his body to protect the puck given his slight build, but he still does get pushed around at times by defenders. The effort is always there, he never shies away from a hit or a battle for the puck, and he has some grit to his game but sometimes he simply is overmatched physically. He is tall but is very thin and lanky, and will need to improve his size and strength going forward.

Also resulting from his lanky build is a need to improve his mobility. He could stand to improve his foot speed and overall mobility. With all of that said, he still has the ability to be flashy offensively and he has good speed despite it not looking overly pretty. His stride is deceptive, it makes him look slower than he is, and many times this lulls defenders into false angle and approaches and while his foot speed could use some improving, he has enough there to turn it on in those moments and go right around those defenders. His ability to gain offensive zone entry is excellent, and comes in handy on the power play in which he is a major fixture. Conversely, he is an excellent defensive forward. You can lose count how many times he pick-pockets a player from behind and starts a rush going back the other way. That doesn't happen without hard backchecking, which he does all of the time. Maxim never takes a shift off, and his defensive effort and awareness are every bit as a good as his offensive abilities.

High end offensive skill, high hockey IQ, strong defensively, high compete level, and a frame to improve and build; Maxim has a lot of tools that can make him an excellent NHL'er, but will need some time at the college level to further develop.

SEASON	LEAGUE	GAMES	GOALS	ASSISTS	PPG	PIM	HP RANKING
2012/13	Midget	40	29	37	1.65	6	51
2013/14	USHL	60	19	24	0.72	42	

Lindblom, Oskar
LW – Brynas (SWE Jr) – 6'1.25" 191

It's all about the skating for Lindblom. He's a smart skilled forward with the ability to make plays, but he lacks in the skating department. The good news is it appears his skating is improving. He still lacks some quickness in his first few steps but once he gets rolling is where we saw some signs of improvement.

Oskar is a true offensive talent. You might recall his performance at the 2013 World U-17 Challenge where he posted 13 points including 8 goals in 6 games. Oskar displays excellent hands and makes plays with the puck that show off his level of skill. He has shown us the ability to beat goaltenders on a regular basis.

While he has really impressed us with his offensive skill, he has lacked to overly impress us in some other areas of his game. He sometimes lacked effort along walls in attempting to win battles for pucks, being a little slow a foot didn't help his cause. He also had shifts where we have liked to see more effort on the backcheck. We will note that he was better in these areas this year than he was last year. His positioning is good all over the ice.

Lindblom excels with the puck on his stick. He has great puck handling skills and has above average skill both scoring and playmaking.

Quotable: "Lindblom impressed me in my viewings with some of the fantastic plays he made in the offensive zone. I just saw him at the U18 in Finland and thought his skating showed signs of improvement. He looks much better on the smaller ice though." – Mark Edwards

Quotable: "I was told he's working hard with a skating coach." – NHL Scout

SEASON	LEAGUE	GAMES	GOALS	ASSISTS	PPG	PIM	HP RANKING
2012/13	J18 Elit	22	20	21	1.86	4	60
2013/14	U20 S.Elit	43	13	20	0.77	28	

Lindo, Jaden
RW – Owen Sound Attack (OHL) – 6'01" 202

Jaden is in his second season in the OHL, but was built like a man going into juniors. Lindo has an excellent frame for his power forward style of game, and has excellent strength. He is physical, and capable of winning a large amount of the battles he engages in. He is also relentless along the wall fighting for the puck, and using his strength to pin opponents effectively. He does a good job going to the slot, battles hard creating a disruption, and making things difficult for opposing players. He is also very effective at the cycle protecting the puck, and making it very difficult for opponents to get him off the puck. Without the puck in the offensive zone he does a good job opening himself up in scoring areas, and displays a shoot first mentality. Fortunately he is able to get a good amount of power in his release. Lindo chips in defensively as well working hard to get the opposition off the puck, and will sacrifice the body to block shots. While he has the potential to develop into an offensive threat in the OHL it's unlikely he will become an offensive threat at the NHL level. Instead he would be utilized as a third liner who hits hard, wins battles, and cycles the puck while working hard in all three zones. Physically he is about as mature as you'll find for his age, he simply needs to improve his skating. Lindo missed the end of the season with a "lower body injury" which limited viewings down the stretch.

SEASON	LEAGUE	GAMES	GOALS	ASSISTS	PPG	PIM	HP RANKING
2012/13	OHL	63	5	17	0.35	55	153
2013/14	OHL	40	9	9	0.45	41	

Lintuniemi, Alex
LD – Ottawa 67's (OHL) – 6'03" 227

Alex was the 2nd Overall pick at the 2013 CHL Import Draft by the Ottawa 67's. Alex made the jump to North America, and had high expectations placed upon him. Lintuniemi has excellent size for a defenseman, and a very big frame to work with. He does a good job of getting pucks deep, and is capable of intercepting passes up the middle. He played in all game situations, and with the puck in the offensive zone he was able to make good hard passes. He also does a good job holding the line. Despite his size, he isn't overly physical, but is capable of making an impact when he does choose to impose his size on opponents. He was moderately effective in battles along the wall, but did lose some battles against smaller forwards, which he should have won. He also struggled to contain bigger forwards in the slot. He struggled in one-on-one match-ups between giving up too much space due to his lack of mobility, and holding his stick the wrong way on multiple occasions. With his lack of mobility, and large gap he has a small window to shutdown oncoming forwards, and was generally beat easily by the higher skilled forwards in the OHL. He had moments where he was capable with the puck, but also had many occasions, especially in his own zone, where he served up some huge turnovers into high percentage scoring areas.

Lintuniemi has some hype behind him along with great size, which could end up hearing his name called in the draft. Though, we would not be surprised to see Alex go into next season as a re-entry player. He has a lot of potential if he improves his areas of concern, but has a long way to go before he reaches that potential.

Quotable: "Nothing to see in Ottawa this year. I'll wait until next year for Travis Konecny." - NHL Scout

SEASON	LEAGUE	GAMES	GOALS	ASSISTS	PPG	PIM	HP RANKING
2012/13	Jr.A SM-liiga	38	4	10	0.37	76	NR
2013/14	OHL	68	4	17	0.31	26	

Lipsbergs, Roberts
LW – Seattle Thunderbirds (WHL) – 5'11" 195

Roberts is a 1994 born re-entry player. He is a smaller forward who possess excellent speed and quickness. He has very good hands and can protect the puck through traffic. He often operates as a perimeter player. He seldom drives the net looking for rebounds or engages in the battle areas. He has a strong scoring ability, often using a good wrist shot. As it will be difficult to have success in that type of role going forwards, he needs to improve his tenacity and compete level. He would also benefit by engaging in more puck battles. He is offensively gifted and could be a top-end finisher. If Roberts would like to play pro hockey, he will need to bring more of a work ethic and spend some time learning how to play a defensive game.

SEASON	LEAGUE	GAMES	GOALS	ASSISTS	PPG	PIM	HP RANKING
2012/13	WHL	64	30	28	0.91	24	NR
2013/14	WHL	68	33	19	0.76	37	

Llewellyn, Darby
LW – Kitchener Rangers (OHL) – 6'01" 179

Darby enjoyed a successful sophomore season for the Rangers playing an assortment of roles from first line to fourth line, from powerplay to penalty kill. Darby is a good skater with good acceleration, speed, and he displays awareness in all three zones. He really developed his defensive game well this season, and was commonly the first forward to get back on the back check. He has good defensive positioning, gets into shooting/passing lanes, and battles for pucks on the wall despite losing some of them due to a lack of strength while 5-on-5, which translated to good penalty kill ice where he pressured the point effectively.

Despite leading the Rangers in goals, Llewellyn doesn't own any standout offensive skills. He does have a good shot, but is a bit of an opportunist jumping on opportunities or catching the opposition off guard. He also showed flashes of strong puck handling ability, which allow him to beat defenders, and goaltenders one-on-one. He is capable of setting up linemates, but will sometimes throw the puck blindly towards a crowd when he doesn't have a shooting option.

Darby provides a solid forecheck using his speed to take away time, and space, but needs to improve his strength. If he plays with a bit more edge, it will add a valuable element to his game, since he doesn't project as an offensive first player at the top level rather a jack-of-all-trades type of guy whom can penalty kill, play a 200-foot game, and chip in offensively.

SEASON	LEAGUE	GAMES	GOALS	ASSISTS	PPG	PIM	HP RANKING
2012/13	OHL	40	7	6	0.33	15	96
2013/14	OHL	66	25	11	0.55	43	

Lorentz, Steven
LC – Peterborough Petes (OHL) – 6'02" 177

Steven made the Petes to open the season after being a 12th round pick just 18 months prior. He put forward some promising performances early on, but seemed to drop off a bit as the season went on. He has great size and provides a moderately effective work ethic. He is willing to hit but doesn't possess a mean streak and needs to get stronger. He provided a strong two-way presense and was rewarded with time on the penalty kill. He doesn't possess much skill and generally creates his scoring chances out of hard work and determination. He does protect the puck well using his frame to shield off defenders.

Steven was in only his first year and his improvement over the past two seasons has been impressive. However we don't expect him to be selected at the 2014 NHL Entry Draft and will look to continue his improvement if he would like to be selected as a re-entry player.

SEASON	LEAGUE	GAMES	GOALS	ASSISTS	PPG	PIM	HP RANKING
2012/13	AHMPL	31	17	17	1.1	24	NR
2013/14	OHL	64	7	11	0.28	18	

Lyamkin, Nikita
LD - Chicoutimi Sagueneens (QMJHL) - 6'04" 180

Nikita Lyamkin arrived in Chicoutimi with a good resume and high expectations after a great showing at the U17 in Victoriaville and some hit and miss games at the Ivan Hlinka with Team Russia. For some reason, he didn't deliver this season. At the beginning of the year, he played with confidence and we all thought he was going to be used on Chicoutimi's second pairing, at the very least. That didn't happen.

Nikita is a strong skater with great mobility. He is clearly one of the most fluid skaters in this year's draft. Lyamkin can rush the puck and his overall game is better when he has the freedom to do so. Even though he is tall, he still has to fill out in order to be good in one-on-one battles along the wall. He lost many battles for loose pucks. In short, he has the size but not the strength. He gets mesmerized by the puck far too often, thus getting caught out of position. His lack of concentration with the puck clearly affects his game and leads to many turnovers. Even without pressure, he anticipates plays that even his teammates don't understand. The language barrier didn't help at all to understand his team's system. His defensive zone coverage has been atrocious at times, but he was a bit better at it as the season has progressed. At the end of the season, he had quality ice time and he showed some progression in his play. We still think there might be something there.

Quotable: "One of the biggest surprises of the season for me was how far this kid has fallen. I'll give him some credit, he actually played better in a Russia jersey in Finland at the U18, albeit it was in a game versus Slovakia. In a game vs Canada he once again showed the glaring weakness in one on one battles. The kid is not without talent though." - Mark Edwards

Quotable: "What a miss by me. I had him as an easy first rounder as recently as after the Hlinka tournament." - NHL Scout

Quotable: "He ended the season on a good note, and I'm expecting good things from him next season in Chicoutimi. A role on the top four awaits him." - HP Scout Jean Francois Dore

SEASON	LEAGUE	GAMES	GOALS	ASSISTS	PPG	PIM	HP RANKING
2012/13	MHL	13	0	0	0	8	171
2013/14	QMJHL	65	3	9	0.18	41	

MacDonald, Owen
RW – London Knights (OHL) – 5'8" 151

Owen is a player we really wish was about 4 or 5 inches taller. He plays every shift with a high compete level, isn't afraid of engaging, and even on rare occasion dropping the gloves against a player much bigger than him. This has allowed him to play a strong role for the Knights with minimal ice providing energy on their fourth line.

Owen is a strong skater with quick acceleration, and can handle the puck at high speed. However, he doesn't receive passes very well at top speed. He handles the puck, and will challenge defenders, occasionally winning one-on-one match-ups. He has shown creative passing ability, and completed some difficult passes resulting in a few scoring chances. Owen would project very well as a role player at the next level if he were bigger. His lack of size should however push him out of the 2014 NHL Entry Draft, but should make him a very good player at the junior level.

SEASON	LEAGUE	GAMES	GOALS	ASSISTS	PPG	PIM	HP RANKING
2012/13	GOJHL	50	20	20	0.8	100	NR
2013/14	OHL	47	7	7	0.3	31	

MacInnis, Ryan
LC – Kitchener Rangers (OHL) – 6'04" 185

Ryan made the transition from the USNTDP, and the USHL to the Kitchener Rangers this season. It was a bit of a rough transition at first as MacInnis struggled to keep up with the pace constantly chasing the play, but over time he was able to adjust, and get stronger with his pace, which still has a ways to go. Ryan is a two-way centre who is very effective in the face-off circle winning the majority of the draws he factors in on, and plays a true 200-foot game. He seems to be at his best when relying on his instincts. He has good positional, and situational awareness, and reads plays effectively. Sometimes it comes down to getting his big body there in time. His top speed is effective for a big forward, but his mobility, and first few steps are still a long way off. He has a powerful shot, and gets into good scoring positioning, but wasn't able to finish at times he was expected to. He uses his size effectively to protect the puck, but really doesn't play with much of an edge or assert himself nearly as much as he should for his size. He is more of a shooter than a passer, and can be pressured into rushing his passes when his shooting lanes are unavailable. Ryan is very competitive in the neutral, and defensive zones displaying good positioning, and an effective stick to intercept passes and take away lanes. He forces turnovers, and uses his long reach to frustrate opposing players. MacInnis projects to be a very solid, reliable third line centre at the NHL level one day. He should go to a team who has the patience to let him develop, refine his game, and build his skating and strength in order to take his game to the next level.

Quotable: "After a very slow start he got much better this year." – NHL Scout

SEASON	LEAGUE	GAMES	GOALS	ASSISTS	PPG	PIM	HP RANKING
2012/13	USHL	41	8	6	0.34	6	37
2013/14	OHL	66	16	21	0.56	18	

MacIntyre, Bobby
LW – Mississauga Steelheads (OHL) – 5'09" 178

Bobby is a speedy, undersized forward who was caught behind some of the depth on the Steelheads this season. He is an excellent skater and can drive the wing effectively with the puck. He showed a few flashes this season of the offense he displayed with Whitby Wildcats in Minor Midget but wasn't a consistent offensive threat. He provides an energetic forecheck and can be a pesky player to play against. He works hard and attacks the puck carrier. Unfortunately he is fairly small and isn't strong enough yet. Bobby could be a late bloomer but isn't a player we expect to be selected for the 2014 NHL Entry Draft.

SEASON	LEAGUE	GAMES	GOALS	ASSISTS	PPG	PIM	HP RANKING
2012/13	OHL	61	4	7	0.18	28	NR
2013/14	OHL	61	12	8	0.33	38	

MacIntyre, Duncan
LD - Quebec Remparts (QMJHL) - 6'00" 195

MacIntyre was drafted by the Quebec Remparts in the 2nd round of the 2012 QMJHL draft. This Nova Scotian is a good two-way defenseman that has played a lot on a young Remparts' squad this season. He has good hockey sense and is rarely out of position in his zone. When he is caught off position, he can recover nicely because of his footwork. He makes a good first pass and chooses the right option most of the time in transition. He can take a hit to make a play and move the puck up the boards to get it out of his own end. The Remparts' product is another player that likes to join the rush and has some good abilities with the puck. MacIntyre can move the puck all right in the offensive zone and could be an option to help out on the power play, but he saw limited time in those situations. He can hold the offensive line pretty well and protect the puck from the op- position's pressure and tries to keep his shot down low to generate rebound opportunities for teammates in front of the net. He's a smart defensive player that rarely gets beaten wide by opposing players, keeping a great positioning at all times. He relies on intelligence to handle faster players coming at him. He has a good stick that he uses to pick off passes and to stir opponents to the outside. However, MacIntyre has to use his body more to block shots and be tougher to play against along the walls and win more puck battles. In fact, he doesn't excel in any area of his game as he's a bit of a jack-of-all-trades. He does not possess elite vision or a heavy shot from the point, but he has the smarts to get him drafted. He had problem staying healthy missing good chunk of his first 2 major junior seasons.

SEASON	LEAGUE	GAMES	GOALS	ASSISTS	PPG	PIM	HP RANKING
2012/13	QMJHL	43	1	11	0.28	12	NR
2013/14	QMJHL	54	2	9	0.2	26	

MacLeod, Johnathan
RD – USNTDP – 6'01" 179

MacLeod plays a safe, sound defensive game with physicality and a good mean streak. He is an adequate skater with average hands but is an effective player on account of his intelligent play and sound decision making. He is a very good passer, and has a knack for springing his forwards on breaks with stretch passes. There is no panic to his game, and he handles the puck well under pressure. Solid, physical, stay at home defenseman. Committed to Boston University.

Quotable: "Better late in year after trying to do too much earlier in the season. He figured out who he is, a physical shutdown defender who blocks shots. Enjoyed chatting with him. – Mark Edwards

SEASON	LEAGUE	GAMES	GOALS	ASSISTS	PPG	PIM	HP RANKING
2013/14	USHL	19	1	4	0.26	36	50
2013/14	(U18)USDP	51	5	6	0.22	70	

MacMaster, Tanner
LC – Camrose Kodiaks (AJHL) – 5'09" 156

Tanner is an undersized but very skilled forward who uses his speed and skill to create scoring chances. He reads plays fairly well and has a strong shot for someone his size. He is capable of evading checkers in neutral ice and finishes well on breakaways. In addition to that he has good vision and is capable of completing difficult passes. He will need to improve upon his consistency and get stronger as well as hopefully bigger.

Tanner has shown both at the World Under 17 Challenge and in the AJHL what he is capable of doing offensively. He is a bit of a risk due to his size but can prove his doubters wrong at a higher level joining Quinnipiac in September 2014. He is also a former first round selection of the Spokane Chiefs of the WHL.

SEASON	LEAGUE	GAMES	GOALS	ASSISTS	PPG	PIM	HP RANKING
2012/13	AJHL	54	24	24	0.89	66	NR
2013/14	AJHL	48	11	29	0.83	62	

Maguire, Josh
LW – Peterborough Petes (OHL) – 5'11" 190

After being selected early in the second round of the 2012 OHL Priority Selection Draft, Josh hasn't quite lived up to the expectations of a player selected that high. However, he has provided a consistent and effective work ethic to the Petes' bottom six forward group. Maguire uses his stick to force turnovers in the offensive zone and pressures opponents hard. While he isn't an overly physical player, Maguire will take the body from time to time. He provides a good work ethic and will compete in all three zones. He has a good backcheck due, in part to good skating ability. He is willing to sacrifice the body and block shots for his team. He has shown a few flashes of puck skills beating a defender one on one here and there and making intelligent passes. When contributing offensively Maguire is more of a passer than a shooter and only possesses an average shot. Josh has an outside chance of being selected and projects as a bottom six role player.

SEASON	LEAGUE	GAMES	GOALS	ASSISTS	PPG	PIM	HP RANKING
2012/13	OHL	49	1	7	0.16	30	NR
2013/14	OHL	59	4	9	0.22	44	

Magyar, Nick
RW – Kitchener Rangers (OHL) – 6'02" 191

Magyar joined the rebuilding Rangers, and ended up leading his new team in scoring in just his first season in the OHL. Nick made a relatively smooth transition to the league thanks to his excellent positional awareness. He always seems to find the right spot in the slot, and gets himself open for passes, and in great positioning for rebounds. He scored several goals in our viewings being able to bang home pucks in the slot area. He also does a great job creating a disruption in the slot. Nick possesses a shoot first mentality, and a very powerful release on his shot. He is a capable passer, and makes effective plays when moving it, but is much more of a scorer than a playmaker. He is also smart in the offensive zone without the puck, always seems to read the play well, and get himself where he needs to be. This is also beneficial for the Rangers in the cycle game, as Nick protects the puck well with his big body, and cycles the puck effectively. Although he isn't very quick, he did a fairly good job in one-on-one situations beating defenders with hands, and puck control ability. He backchecks hard, but his skating partially negates his effort at times. He struggles when the pace of the game really picks up due to a lack of mobility, and speed. Nick's game was extremely consistent throughout this season, and regularly displayed the same strengths, and flaws in a game-by-game basis. He has good hockey sense, and good offensive tools, but really needs to improve his skating in order to truly maximize his potential.

Quotable: "Noticed him often and he got better as the season progressed." - Mark Edwards

SEASON	LEAGUE	GAMES	GOALS	ASSISTS	PPG	PIM	HP RANKING
2012/13	USHL	27	1	5	0.22	6	65
2013/14	OHL	66	20	26	0.7	20	

Mallette, Trent
RW – SOO Greyhounds (OHL) – 5'10" 169

Trent is a role player for the Greyhounds and has done an excellent job in his role. He is a little undersized but compensates for this by being a pest on the forecheck using his excellent speed and good stick to create turnovers. He isn't afraid to take the body and will still need to add muscle, but makes some solid hits for a smallish forward. He plays a full 200 foot game and was a key contributor on the Greyhounds penalty kill applying pressure to the point and getting his stick and body in front of passes and shots. Mallette has a bit of an outside shot of a selection for the 2014 NHL Entry Draft with the bloodlines and the work ethic, but his lack of size along with a lack of high end offensive ability poses as a bit of a risk for NHL teams.

SEASON	LEAGUE	GAMES	GOALS	ASSISTS	PPG	PIM	HP RANKING
2012/13	OHL	58	5	0	0.09	32	NR
2013/14	OHL	51	3	8	0.22	32	

Malone, Seamus
LC – Dubuque Fighting Saints (USHL) – 5'10" 165

Originally with the USNTDP to start the 2012-2013 season, Malone left the program and came over to Dubuque and never looked back. Malone's season early on included a couple of International tournaments between his Dubuque Fighting Saints heading to Russia to start the season at the World Junior Club Cup, where he had two goals and two assists in five games. He then represented Team USA at the World Junior A Challenge where he netted one goal in four games.

On US soil this season, he lead his team with 46 points in 55 regular season games. A highly dynamic offensive player, Malone brings almost as much pest as he does offense. Yet another of many "get under your skin" types on Dubuque's roster, the 165 pounder has no idea he is only 165 pounds. While he's often able to avoid contact with his evasive quickness and shiftiness, he has shown a willingness to take the hit to make the play when necessary.

No stranger to after the whistle shenanigans, Malone is fearless, both after the whistle and between them. He drives the net hard, with and without the puck, and isn't afraid to be go to the tough areas of the ice. He has excellent awareness and vision. He is, by far, one of the best passers in the USHL and he is extremely crafty with the puck. He often gains zone entry at full speed, forcing the defenseman back, and he tightly curls just around the top of the circle, creating a world of space for himself and allowing trailing line mates and defensemen time to come into the zone with open space and creating all kinds of options. He is deadly in space with time, and is great at making players miss when attacking him. His size and quickness make him extremely slippery with the puck, but he is stronger than his size would suggest, and is rarely knocked off of the puck. He's an absolutely excellent playmaker, sometimes to a fault. Occasionally he will pass up a good shot opportunity for a cute pass attempt. Other times, his own teammates find themselves stunned the puck has found them and often flub opportunities as a result. Malone finds his teammates even if they aren't aware they're open at all. Highly dynamic playmaker with exceptional vision.

Defensively he plays a solid game. He is a hard backchecker and has a great compete level in his own zone. He always supports his defensemen and never shies away from getting dirty in the corners and along the boards in his own zone. He is great on the penalty kill and ultimately very dangerous there for opposing teams, as he had a high number of shorthanded goals and opportunities this season. With his quick feet and quick stick, he's adept it poke-checking the puck away or picking off passes in open space and once he is off to the races there is no catching him.

Despite his elite speed and offensive skill, his size is a legitimate concern at the NHL level. He will definitely need to fill out and add some muscle to his frame, all the while having to be sure not to lose any of his speed or quickness.

He has the willingness to engage and adapt to the physical part of the game, but doing that against men in the NHL is a whole different world. It will be interesting to see how he develops physically at the college level, as he is committed to the University of Wisconsin starting in 2015, but is expected back in Dubuque next season.

Quotable: " Always had a soft spot for this kid." - HP Scout Sean White

SEASON	LEAGUE	GAMES	GOALS	ASSISTS	PPG	PIM	HP RANKING
2012/13	USHL	50	6	21	0.54	44	200
2013/14	USHL	55	23	23	0.84	93	

Manchurek, Joe
RW – Oshawa Generals (OHL) – 6'01" 195

Manchurek had to adjust from playing without his triplet brothers as they went on to play prep school and Jr. C while Manchurek went on to make the LaSalle Jr. B Vipers team as a 16 year old. After one year under his belt there, Joe made the Generals out of camp and played a limited but effective role for them. With good size he does a little bit of everything. He is capable of delivering punishing body checks but isn't overly aggressive. He works hard in all three zones providing a strong forecheck and backcheck. He has decent speed but needs to improve in the skating department slightly. He was willing to sell out for his team and block shots and really played whichever role that was needed. In addition to his defensive play, Manchurek was able to contribute modest offensive numbers for a rookie playing bottom six minutes. He has a bit of a shoot first mentality and gets good power in his shots. Manchurek has an outside chance of being selected and could be a late bloomer with the graduation of so many forwards out of Oshawa.

SEASON	LEAGUE	GAMES	GOALS	ASSISTS	PPG	PIM	HP RANKING
2012/13	GOJHL	40	11	17	0.7	18	NR
2013/14	OHL	64	8	10	0.28	8	

Mancina, Matthew
G – Guelph Storm (OHL) – 6'1" 172

Mancina was the backup goalie for the Guelph Storm this season. Although backing up Justin Nichols, Mancina was able to show good promise in the games that he did start this season. He finished with a record of 17-5-1 with a 2.43 GAA and a 0.919 SV%. Matt is a tall athletic goaltender that is good at cutting down angles by getting to the top of his crease. He uses his size well and is positionally sound resulting in a better chance of making stops through screens. He is relatively light for his frame and thus is more athletic than heavier goaltenders allowing him to get back to a standing position easier. He has solid legs and is good at sliding across to eliminate back door and cross crease opportunities. Mancina battles for rebounds and excels when having to face first and second opportunity shots. He shows a good glove and works to take away the top half of the net. Matthew needs to improve on his puck handling behind the net and needs to work at maintaining confidence and composure when giving up a goal. Mancina did not get much playing time down the stretch but showed enough during the season to gain the possibility of being drafted as a backup. At this point he is a project with a high ceiling and getting the opportunity to be a starter next season will go a long way to determining his future success and give him the chance to develop into an elite level goaltender.

SEASON	LEAGUE	GAMES	GAA	SV%	W	L	SO	HP RANKING
2012/13	GOJHL	29	2.77	0.904	19	8	0	148
2013/14	OHL	28	2.43	0.919	17	5	3	

Mangiapane, Andrew
LW – Barrie Colts (OHL) – 5'10" 160

Mangiapane is a sleeper who has won over our whole staff this season. After being ranked in the 6th round of the 2012 OHL Priority Selection Draft by HockeyProspect.com, Mangiapane was passed over both in 2012 and 2013. The Barrie Colts invited Mangiapane to their camp as a free agent and he made the team. He was able to build off of strong performances on the fourth line and by the end of the season he was a critical part of the Colts top six forward group. He's an undersized winger but plays much bigger than his size. He's not at all afraid to engage in the physical game and has delivered some huge hits on much bigger opponents. Andrew has great hands and is extremely elusive. He is tough to contain one on one and has beaten some of the best defenders in the OHL in a few different ways. He has very high level hockey sense and is capable of both passing and shooting to create offensive opportunities. While he is a strong offensive player he appreciates the cycle game and moves the puck well around the corners. He sees the ice well and regularly displayed his good playmaking abilities. He's not afraid to crash the net for rebounds, either, and played regularly on the power play, but also the penalty kill with Andreas Athanasiou this season. He's pretty responsible defensively, and usually backchecks well. He is also willing to block shots and sacrifice his body for the team. Mangiapane's performance this season was nothing short of impressive. What made it more impressive is this was Andrew's first season of junior hockey. He adjusted well and shows a lot of heart, grit, determination and skill that should give him a great chance at overcoming his size and becoming a legitimate NHL prospect.

Quotable: "Andrew did an outstanding job adjusting to his first year of junior hockey. He is fearless, plays with an edge but has a great deal of skill and creativity. Really enjoyed watching him develop this year and I see him as a potential steal in this draft." - Ryan Yessie

Quotable: "Speedy player who has relentless work ethic. Undersized but this kid has some intangibles." - Mark Edwards

SEASON	LEAGUE	GAMES	GOALS	ASSISTS	PPG	PIM	HP RANKING
2012/13	GTHL	32	14	22	1.13	22	120
2013/14	OHL	68	24	27	0.75	28	

Mantha, Ryan
RD – Indiana Ice (USHL) – 6'05" 225

The son of Moe Mantha Jr. and grandson of Moe Mantha Sr., Ryan had the bloodlines many covet in a prospect. Ryan spent the entire 2012-2013 season and about half of this past season with Sioux City before being traded to Indiana. He was drafted by the Soo Greyhounds 97th Overall in the 2012 OHL Priority Selection Draft. As of the time of this writing, Mantha remains uncommitted to an NCAA program.

A lot of people like Ryan on account of his enormous size but at least at this point in his development, his size works against him. He needs a lot of improvement in his mobility. He is slow in transition and is slow in tight situations. His lack of foot speed allows him to get beat in tight in his own zone, especially going from a stand-still position. His first step is very slow and loses a lot of races and battles for pucks as a result of it. In addition, despite his size, he does not play an overly physical game. Further, he often gets outmuscled and leveraged against by smaller players.

He does handle the puck decently and makes the good first pass out of his zone. He tends to keep things simple and doesn't make a lot of mistakes in that regard. His shot is decent but he is slow to get it off and his lack of mobility makes it difficult for him to get open looks and open lanes.

All in all, Mantha will get attention on account of his bloodlines size, and may get taken based on the "you can't teach size" mantra. Unfortunately, he's going to have to be taught and learn just about everything else. He can be characterized as awkward, simply put, and while he will be taken higher than he should be on account of his size and pedigree, he is a long-term project as an NHL prospect. If Ryan remains in the USHL next season, it will be as a member of the Muskegon Lumberjacks, as they drafted him in the recent dispersal draft on account of the Indiana Ice franchise going dormant for next season.

Quotable: "He really struggles in a lot of areas, he could be worthy of a late 7th round pick based on his size but that's debatable." – Mark Edwards

SEASON	LEAGUE	GAMES	GOALS	ASSISTS	PPG	PIM	HP RANKING
2012/13	USHL	50	6	21	0.54	44	NR
2013/14	USHL	55	23	23	0.84	93	

Martin, Brycen
LD – Swift Current Broncos (WHL) – 6'2" 185

Listed 26th on NHL Central Scouting's final draft ranking. Martin is not a flashy player, he's content to play a two-way game by focusing on his own end and springing teammates on odd-man rushes with tape-to-tape passes when he has the puck. Martin is a smooth-skating defender with overall good mobility. For being such a smooth skater, he doesn't generate as much power as hoped with his stride. As he matures, he'll develop that portion of his skating.

Offensively, Martin has made most of his contributions by using good vision and passing skills to set up teammates. He has also been able to put pucks on net with his above average shot. Defensively, he's had success when he's able to close gaps quickly when playing one-on-one situations. Unfortunately, he doesn't always recognize quickly enough of when to press and close gaps until it is sometimes too late.

When Martin is at his best, he uses an active stick to cause turnovers and then he quickly transitions the puck forward with hard, efficient passes. Martin moves well laterally and this allows him to keep the play to the outside. Very rarely does Martin give the forward the middle of the ice. He places himself in good defensive positions along the boards and in the corners and uses his size and stick to gain possession of the puck. When handling the puck in his defensive zone Martin is usually calm and relaxed.

While Martin has good size, he needs to gain much more strength, as he actually plays smaller than his size due to his inability to push opponents off the puck. While there are things to like about Martin, he's drifted a bit into a becoming a bit of a jack of all trades, master of none type player. How does he project at the next level? As a pro, he lacks the awareness to be a powerplay guy and he's not good enough to be a shutdown defender. He's also not overly physical. At this time, Martin is likely a bottom-pairing player as he looks to round out his game, but could develop into something more if he can clean up the defensive aspect of his game. His biggest area of concern is his inconsistent play where he can look like a top 10 first round prospect one shift then struggle to make any positive contributions the next.

SEASON	LEAGUE	GAMES	GOALS	ASSISTS	PPG	PIM	HP RANKING
2012/13	WHL	67	2	17	0.28	32	132
2013/14	WHL	72	6	31	0.51	42	

Masin, Dominik
LD - Slavia Jr. (CZE Jr.) – 6'2" 189

We love the fact that Masin plays with a ton of passion. He's a big kid who plays hard along the walls. He makes himself difficult to play against and wins most of his one on one battles. Skating is good, he is a mobile big defender, plays with a good gap and challenges forwards. Q.B on PP and made good decisions with the puck on it. He used quick puck movement but still didn't show us enough on the PP to project him as an offensive guy in the NHL. Shot impressed though. He used his feet well to buy himself time but also had moments where he seemed to panic under pressure and make very poor plays with the puck. Masin is a player that the more we watched the more we saw flaws. There is a lot to like but the panic he showed in his game forced some stray passes and absolute giveaways that sent us warning signals.

Quotable: "I like a lot about him but he reminded me of Kingston's McKeown with some of the decision making blunders." - Mark Edwards

SEASON	LEAGUE	GAMES	GOALS	ASSISTS	PPG	PIM	HP RANKING
2012/13	CZE U20	25	1	2	0.12	16	**36**
2013/14	CZE U20	39	2	19	0.54	102	

Mayo, Dysin
RD – Edmonton Oil Kings (WHL) – 6'1" 180

Mayo is a smooth-skating defenseman that has shown good progression this year after a surprisingly stellar 16 year-old season. Dysin is able to read and anticipate the play well. He is comfortable in his own end and his awareness and active stick make it tough to get pucks past him. He pinches at the right times and his good skating allows him to funnel forwards to the outside. He hits for purpose and is improving on the physical side of his game and has improved his strength. As a result, his heady play is being helped out by improving physical traits that make him very effective in his own end. There is still room for improvement on his ability to defend down low. Additional strength is required to be able to push opponents off the puck instead of chasing around after it. Dysin makes a very good first pass, even under pressure and his good speed allows him to jump into the play whenever possible. He is a strong puck rusher who is capable of skating the puck out of trouble. He is a good stickhandler and can make players miss while skating with the puck. He doesn't have a strong shot, but puts pucks in scoring areas whether that's a shot through traffic or a pass to a teammate in better scoring position. After a slow start to the season point-wise, Mayo has seen continual progress all season to the point where he is a legitimate two-way player. Mayo has some very good upside and really just needs to become more consistent in the defensive zone.

Quotable: "Had both flashes of brilliance at the Memorial Cup and a few plays he would probably like to forget." - Mark Edwards

SEASON	LEAGUE	GAMES	GOALS	ASSISTS	PPG	PIM	HP RANKING
2012/13	WHL	42	1	4	0.12	12	**107**
2013/14	WHL	63	7	28	0.56	50	

McCann, Jared
LC – SOO Greyhounds (OHL) – 6'01" 175

Jared has been one of the most polarizing players for us over the past few seasons. We loved his potential in Minor Midget and his rookie season with the Greyhounds. He was really developing into a potential star player with a powerful shot, intelligent positioning and 200 foot game.

He struggled at Ivan Hlinka Camp and while he had some solid early season performances his play regressed a little throughout the season. For example his face-off ability was around 80-90 percent in regards to face-offs won by the centreman. In games late in the season it was closer to 20 percent. His backcheck was another key area that diminished. He looked good in sustained zone situations, however in transition he lacked urgency. He has the ability to coast through several shifts then turn it on and make a highlight reel play to create a goal.

While his shot is powerful and effective, he has attempted to pass the puck more often. However in several of these situations he will just throw the puck up the middle and hope for the best. This commonly resulted in the puck going the other way. One of his best abilities is his positional awareness and is capable of finding the right place in the offensive zone to score.

McCann has the potential to be an impact player and while he has shown this season there is more risk in his long term potential than previously indicated, Jared still has a lot of upside as an NHL prospect and if he can regain his focus and once again become as consistent as he's capable of being he will be an excellent selection.

Quotable: "A big faller for me." - NHL Scout

Quotable: "Liked him a lot in his OHL Draft year but this season I left the rink thinking he was just ok too often." Mark Edwards

SEASON	LEAGUE	GAMES	GOALS	ASSISTS	PPG	PIM	HP RANKING
2012/13	OHL	64	21	23	0.69	35	25
2013/14	OHL	64	27	35	0.97	51	

McDade, Owen
LC – Oshawa Generals (OHL) – 5'11" 190

McDade is a speedy forward who contributed a minimal role to the high powered Oshawa Generals this year. McDade's strongest asset is his skating ability. He has explosive speed and can rush the puck up ice when taking it from his own zone. He will commonly drive wide on defenders and displays a shoot first mentality. He has a decent shot and is capable of deking out goaltenders one on one. McDade did moderately well in a limited checking role this season, but is much more comfortable in offensive roles. We didn't feel that he showed enough this season to warrant being drafted at the 2014 NHL Entry Draft. However showed signs of very intruging talent in Minor Midget and it would not be a surprise to see him take off next season with the departure of several key Generals.

SEASON	LEAGUE	GAMES	GOALS	ASSISTS	PPG	PIM	HP RANKING
2012/13	CCHL	53	12	13	0.47	6	NR
2013/14	OHL	44	1	3	0.09	22	

McDonald, Mason
G - Charlottetown Islanders (QMJHL) - 6'04" 186

Traded during the midseason to the Charlottetown Islanders for a first round pick and two fourth round picks at the 2014 QMJHL Entry Draft, MacDonald has posted some solid stats for a young goaltender and finally seized the opportunity to shine in the QMJHL. MacDonald was Julio Billia's backup at the 2013 Memorial of Ivan Hlinka tournament and he was also named to BMO Top Prospects Game. He has great size and plays a dynamic butterfly style very well.

Like many butterfly goalies, his lower-net coverage is great, as he possesses quick legs and his pushes are powerful, enabling him to cover a lot of space in a short amount of time with accurate lateral movements. He follows the play very well and he possesses good reaction time.

The 1996 born goaltender never seems to lose eye-contact with the puck, even in traffic. The Halifax native rarely makes the first move and waits for the right moment to get on his knees. He displays great quickness and recovery for such a big goaltender. On the other hand, he seemed to have trouble dealing with shots coming off his blocker in some of our viewings, but we saw him getting better as the season progressed. He has a very good glove and sets up with it properly in the butterfly.

MacDonald keeps fighting to make saves and it is difficult to shake his confidence, which is a good thing when you are playing for a young team like Charlottetown. He doesn't go out to handle the puck a lot and seems to prefer to stay in his crease. MacDonald needs to improve his rebound control, as his technique doesn't always seem controlled, which sometimes results in him putting himself out of position. Otherwise, in a world where tall goaltenders are hot commodities, MacDonald truly has the physical package to be taken quite high in this year's draft.

Quotable: "I thought he struggled and looked really raw at the Hlinka camp back in August but he really progressed this season and made a strong impression on me in Finland. I like the fact that he doesn't play like many of the other big goalies who just play a style that gives them the best chance to have a puck hit them. Mason has some old school goalie in him. I like the way he challenges shooters and doesn't play a guessing game. He reacts. I had a brief chat with Fred Brathwaite in Finland, I told him I thought Mason has big upside because he's already stopping lots of pucks and he hasn't even scratched the surface as far as refining his skills go. Fred seemed to agree."

Quotable: "One of the most impressive players at the U18 in Finland as far as I'm concerned." NHL Scout

Quotable: "In a tournament that left me generally unimpressed and wanting more, MacDonald was a very pleasant surprise." - NHL Scout

Quotable: "I'm not a fan, I think he's got too much work to do just to master the most basic of goaltending skills." - NHL Scout

SEASON	LEAGUE	GAMES	GAA	SV%	W	L	SO	HP RANKING
2012/13	QMJHL	13	3.57	0.887	3	7	0	31
2013/14	QMJHL	16	3.35	0.907	5	8	0	

McKeown, Roland
RD – Kingston Frontenacs (OHL) – 6'01" 195

Roland was a very talented Minor Midget defender who was capable of skating around opponents, and was an impact player at both ends of the ice. After two seasons in the OHL, he really hasn't turned the corner for us. He displays good skating for a defender of his size, but lacks that top gear to win puck races or beat good defenders wide on the rush.

In the defensive zone he is usually effective in the slot checking his opponents stick using his body to make sure the defender can see, but sometimes is a little late in regards to his reaction time. He has decent size, but lacks the mean streak you'd hope to see out of a big defender.

He was very hit or miss with his first pass, sometimes landing a perfect accurate pass, then on other occasions tried to force passes that simply weren't there. He does rush the puck and evades checkers carrying the puck up ice.

Sometimes he doesn't identify passing options skating through the neutral zone, and will live or die on that play based on whether or not he can beat the opponent.

In the offensive zone his questionable puck play continued where once again he would make some impressive passes to create scoring chances, but then would not be able to identify simple passing options that sent the puck down the ice. He has a good shot from the point when he gets it through, but will sometimes try to force his shot into screens he won't be able to get it through. He plays in all game situations, and the extra spotlight on him has really brought us to question his hockey sense. Roland needs to refine his consistency, and decision making concerns in order to start to progress into the player he once showed the potential to be.

Quotable: "Liked his potential entering the season. I saw him early in the season and he struggled and I saw him a ton late, including in Finland at the U18. I didn't see him play a smart game all season. I saw a lack of hockey sense. One example is still fresh in my mind, watch the last few seconds of the Slovakia game in Finland. He almost allowed the Slovaks to tie the game with a mental blunder." - Mark Edwards

SEASON	LEAGUE	GAMES	GOALS	ASSISTS	PPG	PIM	HP RANKING
2012/13		61	7	22	0.48	33	20	**83**
2013/14		62	11	32	0.69	61	16	

Middleton, Jacob
LD – Ottawa 67's (OHL) – 6'02" 208

Middleton has excellent size, and a huge frame. He received top minutes in his second OHL season with the Ottawa 67's, and asserted himself very well in the physical department. He finishes his checks, and utilizes his big size to punish opponents along the wall. When even the biggest of opponents attempt to hit him it doesn't affect him.

Jacob was beat badly by speed. His footwork, and mobility are very weak and need to improve before he can be more successful in these situations. His skating in general isn't great, as he can generate OK speed in a straight line, but lacks explosiveness in his stride, and is slow when moving side-to-side. When the pace of the game ramps up, Jacob has struggled to keep up with the increase. He is capable of moving the puck in the offensive zone, making the smart simple play. However, sometimes he can hold onto the puck, take too long to make a decision, and get stripped of the puck. He does possess a powerful, effective shot from the point.

In his own zone there have been many scenarios where he has struggled mightily with the puck. Between not choosing the right options when multiple options present itself, throwing the puck through the slot, and in dangerous lower percentage areas, and taking too long to make decisions, his puck play in his own end needs to improve. While we like the size, and the physical element to his game, he has a long way to go before he can become the defenseman he once showed the potential to be with the Huron-Perth Lakers. Jacob could be selected later in the draft by a team who feels they can work with his deficiencies, but it isn't out of the question for him to slide right out of the draft.

Quotable: "I had conversations with NHL Scouts to ask them if I was crazy for thinking his skating got worse this year. He is one of our biggest fallers this season. I personally wouldn't draft him." - Mark Edwards

SEASON	LEAGUE	GAMES	GOALS	ASSISTS	PPG	PIM	HP RANKING
2012/13	OHL	29	1	4	0.17	25	**NR**
2013/14	OHL	65	2	21	0.35	64	

Mikulovich, Aleksandar
LD – Niagara Ice Dogs (OHL) – 6'03" 200

After posting a strong performance at the 2013 World Under 17 Challenge, Mikulovich was selected by the Niagara Ice Dogs at the 2013 CHL Import Draft. Mikulovich made a pretty steady transition to the OHL in part thanks to his size. He is capable of playing a physical game and is really built for the North American style of game. He is also a pretty effective skater for his size. His stride looks rather uncomfortable, but he gets the job done. He also improved his backwards skating and did well in transition. He was a little hit and miss in one on one situations with skilled player but he handles big forwards well in these situations. He showed the ability to jump up on the rush and pinch from the point at intelligent times despite being a more defensive first defenseman. He has a strong shot from the point and although he didn't play much in offensive situations he found a way to contribute throughout the year. For the most part he was capable of maintaining good defensive positioning but would have the occasional mental lapse. A minor concern we had with Mikulovich was the frequency in which he would dive or embellish plays. Many didn't result in penalties and some ended up becoming scoring chances against his team. He's at his best when playing a physical safe defensive role and picking his spots. He needs to work on becoming more consistent in the defensive zone as he can have mental lapses in his own zone which have turned costly on a young team. We would not be surprised if an NHL team takes a shot at Aleksandar later on in the draft due to his size and potential.

SEASON	LEAGUE	GAMES	GOALS	ASSISTS	PPG	PIM	HP RANKING
2012/13	Ural-Sib. 1996	24	1	9	0.42	40	163
2013/14	OHL	57	7	7	0.25	57	

Milano, Sonny
LW – USNTDP (USHL) – 5'11" 185

Skill, speed, and creativity in abundance, Milano is one of the most dynamic offensive players in this draft. Milano loves to have the puck on his stick and be in control. His playmaking skills are superb, aided by his excellent vision and awareness. He is a very intelligent player and reads the play in front of him exceptionally well. His complete control of his feet and edges is very impressive, and the result his ability to shift and change directions on a dime. He is extremely difficult to defend; it's hard to defend what you can't catch. Highly elusive and incredibly crafty, Milano is a magician on skates when handling the puck. His elusiveness draws a lot of penalties. Add to all of that an elite shot with pinpoint accuracy and what you have is a deadly offensive weapon.

On the other side of the puck, Milano also excels. He's an aggressive defender, and desperately wants that puck back from you so he can have it. He engages physically, finishes his checks, and is a bit of an antagonist in his own right. He gets under opponents' skin and is somewhat of a pest. Defensively responsible and smart, he's solid in his own zone and is a fast, aggressive forechecker. His stick is active and with his speed and quickness he creates a lot of turnovers.

Milano has shown to be capable of overcoming size at the junior level and will look to do so when he advances to the NCAA joining Boston College in September 2014 and again when he goes professional.

Quotable: "He has some flaws and I think he might drive coaches crazy once in a while but at the end of the day he's one of the most skilled players in the draft." – Mark Edwards

SEASON	LEAGUE	GAMES	GOALS	ASSISTS	PPG	PIM	HP RANKING
2013/14	USHL	25	14	25	1.56	21	12
2013/14	(U18)USDP	58	29	57	1.48	23	

Minney, Edwin
G – USNTDP (USHL) – 6'04" 201

Highly athletic and mobile, the 6'4" goaltender makes you earn it. With his size, athleticism, aggressiveness, and sound positioning, open space in the net is at a premium. Minney plays with extreme poise and never gets rattled. As good of rebound control as any goaltender in the USHL, he swallows everything up and gives few second chances. Highly focused and unshakeable, Minney will take his abilities to Michigan State University in the Fall.

Quotable: " I just don't see him as an NHL prospect." – NHL Scout

SEASON	LEAGUE	GAMES	GAA	SV%	W	L	SO	HP RANKING
2013/14	USHL	17	2.63	0.905	12	3	1	NR
2013/14	(U18)USDP	38	2.63	0.899	22	9	4	

Mistele, Matt
LW – Plymouth Whalers (OHL) – 6'2" 190

Mistele is a big skilled winger from the Plymouth Whalers. After having a very strong sophomore campaign in the Ontario Hockey League, Mistele struggled this season with consistency. While dealing with some injuries throughout the season he never looked quite right for long stretches of the year. He would play stiff at points which would result in pucks bouncing off his stick or losing races for loose pucks. When playing more of a relaxed style he showed strong puck movement and decision making in the offensive zone. He reads the play well and is good at finding teammates in open ice. Matt shows bursts of speed and quickness but needed to work at bringing the same energy throughout the shift. He displays a very heavy wrist shot with excellent accuracy making him a deadly shooter when the puck finds him in the slot. Mistele also had moments of creativity and puck skill when facing defenders in 1-on-1 situations. Loose pucks seem to find him in front of the net. After much hype last season, Mistele failed to live up to his potential this year. If nagging injuries were the problem then Matt would certainly be a solid mid-to-late round pick that could turn out to be a steal if he can get back the offensive production of his sophomore season.

SEASON	LEAGUE	GAMES	GOALS	ASSISTS	PPG	PIM	HP RANKING
2012/13	OHL	68	34	26	0.88	69	150
2013/14	OHL	56	18	19	0.66	59	

Montour, Brandon
RD – Waterloo Black Hawks (USHL) – 6'00" 172

Montour made the most of his lone USHL season after coming over from the Caledonia Jr. B Corvairs of the GOJHL. Slick feet and hands with a laser beam slap shot and superb vision make him about as dangerous as they come on the point. He has good speed, quick feet, very mobile in all directions. He moves the puck along the offensive blue line well and confidently, great at opening up the shooting and passing lanes and creating space for himself to get good look on net. He's slick and smooth carrying the puck up ice through the neutral zone, extremely comfortable and poised with the puck. Sound defensively, always in position, plays the body well and smothers the defensive zone at the blue when opposing players are attempting to enter. Steps up well. Can play in all situations but is especially strong on the power play. Can be placed with any kind of partner and will be able to carry them and cover for them. His performance this season make him a virtual lock at being selected at the 2014 NHL Entry Draft.

Quotable: "If he was younger he might just be a first rounder. He's still way up there for me. He had 10 or 11 interviews at the combine. Montour plays aggressive hockey and makes things difficult for the opposing team." – Mark Edwards

SEASON	LEAGUE	GAMES	GOALS	ASSISTS	PPG	PIM	HP RANKING
2012/13	GOJHL	49	18	49	1.37	94	57
2013/14	USHL	60	14	48	1.03	36	

Moody, Zachery
LW - Quebec Remparts (QMJHL) - 6'02" 162

Moody was a second-round draft pick by the Cape Breton Screaming Eagles at the 2012 QMJHL draft and has since been traded at the beginning of this season to the Quebec Remparts for a 4th round draft pick. He played sparingly early on, but he has climbed up the depth chart, even earning quality ice time on the second line alongside Mikhail Grigorenko. An average skater at best, Moody really works hard on both ends and uses his smarts effectively to make plays with the puck. He's good around the corners, as he uses his body properly in order to protect the puck. He is an adept forechecker as well, putting effective pressure on the puck carrier and cutting down the space on the ice. He can find space to work within the offensive zone and opens up well to take passes and put some good shots on net. When he does get chances offensively he shows good moves, he's capable of beating defenders one on one but can get caught trying to over handle the puck. Unlike many forwards on his squad, he never takes a night off. He has to fill out a bit in order to be more successful at the next level, though. Otherwise, he's been exceeding expectations and is now considered to be one of Philippe Boucher's favourite players.

SEASON	LEAGUE	GAMES	GOALS	ASSISTS	PPG	PIM	HP RANKING
2012/13	QMJHL	52	5	2	0.13	22	NR
2013/14	QMJHL	62	10	7	0.27	35	

Moran, Brent
G – Niagara Ice Dogs (OHL) – 6'04" 190

Brent was one of the highest goaltenders selected in the 2012 OHL Priority Selection Draft. He had to wait for his opportunity to take the starting role but did eventually accomplished this early on this season allowing him to get viewed regularly by scouts. Brent's size in goal is about as ideal as you could possibly ask for. He does a good job getting into position to make the initial save but looked shaky at times and would sometimes fight pucks, even on strong nights when he was having a good game.

Moran's glove hand is our biggest concern as he would not only get beat there, but he would struggle catching the puck. When this occurred it would result in a rebound dropped right into the slot and resulted in some goals against. At times he fought the puck and created some rebounds that otherwise should not have occurred. He also had some struggles with balance and would wind up on his back in big scrambles when he should be getting onto his knees or back on his feet. His puck playing ability was solid and he is capable of making the intelligent play with the puck. Moran has a lot of upside but also has a lot of work. We love the frame he has to work with and his ability to get into position to make the initial save but will need to improve multiple areas of his game to reach his potential. A team with some time to develop Brent properly would be the best destination for him and his upside.

Quotable: "I saw him play some games where he made a ton of saves but I didn't leave the rink thinking he just played his way up our rankings. He struggled with his glove hand in all my viewings. For what it's worth I'm told he's a great kid and I really liked him in his OHL Draft year." - Mark Edwards

SEASON	LEAGUE	GAMES	GAA	SV%	W	L	SO	HP RANKING
2012/13	OHL	19	4.26	0.872	7	10	0	92
2013/14	OHL	40	3.85	0.891	14	19	0	

Crevier-Morin, Marc-Olivier
LD - Gatineau Olympiques (QMJHL) - 6'01" 197

Crevier-Morin has been a pleasant surprise for the Gatineau Olympiques. An healthy scratch early in the season, he paved his way up into the depth chart and is now playing regularly on his team's third pairing. He is stay at home defenseman with surprising puck skills.

The Châteauguay native skates well going forward, however his backward skating could still improve and become more fluid and natural. He has below average footwork and overall speed, but his compete level and his tenacity overcome this a bit. He plays with a chip on his shoulder and plays a tough, physical game. He is excellent stepping up at the blueline when appropriate and he makes good contacts. He protects the front of his crease nicely. His defensive zone coverage is good overall as he is aggressive and likes to pressure the opposition, but it can leave some zone openings for the other team and can get his team into trouble. He makes a few good surprising plays off the transition, but he mostly uses the windows to clear the puck out of his zone. He keeps things simple and will not try to force any plays or take any major risks. When things get out of control for him offensively, he is prone to some nasty turnovers.

SEASON	LEAGUE	GAMES	GOALS	ASSISTS	PPG	PIM	HP RANKING
2012/13	QMAAA	37	2	3	0.14	81	NR
2013/14	QMJHL	48	1	13	0.29	29	

Morrison, Tyler
LD – Vancouver Giants (WHL) – 6'00" 191

Tyler is a smooth skating defenseman who is capable of rushing the puck up ice effectively. He made smart decisions on the rush in regards to when he should pass and when he should possess the puck. He received secondary ice in all game situations contributing on the power play with a smart accurate shot. He also moved the puck adequately well and finished behind only Brett Kulak and Dalton Thrower for defenseman points on the Giants.

Morrison leans a little towards the offensive side of the game but does a good job battling for pucks down low in the defensive zone. He needs to continue to get stronger and really elevate his game next season with a few graduates butt he late 1995 birthdate could get some attention late in the 2014 NHL Entry Draft.

SEASON	LEAGUE	GAMES	GOALS	ASSISTS	PPG	PIM	HP RANKING
2012/13	WHL	64	2	19	0.33	18	NR
2013/14	WHL	65	6	17	0.35	23	

Moynihan, Danny
C - Halifax Mooseheads (QMJHL) - 6'00" 178

Signed at the beginning of the season by the Halifax Mooseheads, Danny has been a pleasant surprise for Dominique Ducharme's staff. He is a quick skater who accelerates well, and has a good top speed. He is not recognized as an offensive threat in the QMJHL, but Moynihan plays a sound two-way game and he likes to pay attention to little details in his zone. Defensively, he covers his point man quite well, and does not make any huge mistakes without the puck, and as a result he can be relied upon on the penalty kill regularly. He makes the most impact on the forecheck when he quickly closes the gap between him and the opposing defensemen and lands a solid hit and create a turnover. He brings a consistent effort out on the ice at all times, and coaches trust him and know what they are getting from him at all times. Not a highly skilled player by any means, he still has above average puck control and fairly quick hands. He plays a high energy dump-and-chase, North-South game very well creating opportunities coming off the cycle. He shows good hockey sense and is smart with the puck. While he can be caught making the odd mistake, he usually makes the right choice with the puck and showed the ability to shoot and pass well. We don't think he has the potential to be a top 6 forward in professional hockey by any means, but he could settle into a defensive role.

SEASON	LEAGUE	GAMES	GOALS	ASSISTS	PPG	PIM	HP RANKING
2012/13	EmJHL	21	11	8	0.9	16	NR
2013/14	QMJHL	68	9	17	0.38	66	

Mpofu, Vukie
LW – Red Deer Rebels (WHL) – 5'09" 170

Vukie is a little ball of energy. He plays the game much larger than his listed size, he skates well and is able to turn speed into substantial momentum for heavy checks. He hits at all opportunities and will engage larger players in fights. Mpofu is a converted defenseman and you can see some offensive defenseman tendencies like how he is comfortable leading the rush out of his zone.

SEASON	LEAGUE	GAMES	GOALS	ASSISTS	PPG	PIM	HP RANKING
2012/13	SMHL	43	31	40	1.65	36	NR
2013/14	WHL	65	9	6	0.23	46	

Murphy, Matt
LD – Halifax Mooseheads (QMJHL) – 6'2" 200

Murphy went undrafted in the 2013 NHL Entry Draft after an up-and-down 2012-2013 season which saw him traded out of Val-d'Or to eventually get dealt to the future Memorial Cup Champions, the Halifax Mooseheads. This season, Murphy made some nice strides in his game with an expanded role with his team. Murphy is at his best when he keeps his game simple and doesn't try too many fancy things with the puck or try to rush it end to end. This is when he gets into trouble, when he rushes things and his less effective decision-making can be really exposed. He possesses good footwork that helps him keep up with opposing forwards, but can struggle versus quick forwards that can beat him wide, due to his lack of explosiveness. He's a strong player who can log tons of ice time. He can play a physical game as well, but has been inconsistent in that area in his three seasons in the QMJHL. He can play on the power play at the junior level, as he has a decent shot from the point, but we would like to see him get his shot on net quicker. His passing game is also inconsistent; he can make some real good, crisp, tape-to-tape passes at times and in the same game you will see miss an easy, short outlet pass that can leave you scratching your head.

His play in his zone has improved, but he still has a tendency to get attracted by the puck carrier and lose his positioning.

Quotable: "Murphy has flashes of brilliance but in two years worth of my own viewings, I think he simply makes too many mistakes by way of brain cramps for me to consider him draft worthy. Last season he had one of the single worst games I have seen by a draft eligible player." - Mark Edwards

Quotable: "The kid is a tease, just when you think there might be something there he does something to remind you why you didn't draft him last year." NHL Scout

SEASON	LEAGUE	GAMES	GOALS	ASSISTS	PPG	PIM	HP RANKING
2012/13	QMJHL	69	2	31	0.48	36	NR
2013/14	QMJHL	64	10	26	0.56	63	

Nanne, Tyler
RD – Edina High (HS-MN) – 5'10" 174

Tyler is a speedy undersized defenseman with great bloodlines. He displays strong puck rushing ability and likes to get involved in the offense. He will jump up in the offensive zone and will sometimes neglect his defensive responsibilities in order to try and create something offensively. Despite his lack of size he shows no fear in regards to the physical game and can deliver some solid hits along the wall. He needs to improve his defensive game and be a little more reliable. He sometimes doesn't read the situation which gets him in trouble despite having the skating ability to recover. Tyler is slated to join Ohio State University in September 2015.

SEASON	LEAGUE	GAMES	GOALS	ASSISTS	PPG	PIM	HP RANKING
2012/13	USHS	25	9	10	0.76	6	NR
2013/14	USHS	45	9	26	0.78	59	

Nantel, Julien
C/LW – Rouyn-Noranda Huskies (QMJHL) – 6'0" 193

Nantel was the Huskies' second round pick in the 2012 QMJHL Draft. He played two years of midget hockey with the Laval-Montreal Rousseau Royal before making the jump this year to major junior. Enjoyed a lot of success in his last midget year, leading his team to a third place finish at the Telus Cup. The Laval product is a strong skater with a smooth skating stride, whose great first steps can give opposing defensemen issues off the rush. Protects the puck well and uses his size well, continuing to get stronger on the puck and tougher to knock off his skates. Not shy to play a physical game along the wall. He battles hard for pucks and will drive the net with authority. Nantel is a versatile forward; he can play either on the wing or at center as he did this season with the Huskies. He mostly held a third line role for the Huskies with limited power play time. He played a dump-and-chase role as well, but he's capable of playing a puck-control game as he showed in Midget. This year, he was not able to find a consistent scoring touch, which cost him a spot on the Huskies' top six. We still feel he could surprise people with his offensive output down the line. He has a good, quick release on his wrist shot and will hit the net most of the time, though he could work on his velocity, as it's only average now. He does lack some creativity in his game in the offensive zone and is a shoot first type of player. Represented the province of Quebec at the 2013 U-17 Hockey Challenge and was one of the better forwards for his team. He was also at the Ivan Hlinka tryout camp last August in Toronto and was eventually cut, but left a real good impression in camp for a guy coming from the midget level.

A strong player without the puck, Nantel is always first to come back in his zone to support his defensemen and has a good active stick. He has a strong positional game in his zone and with his speed and anticipation, he is also a good penalty killer. We like his competitiveness and work ethic. Nantel is one of the youngest players available for the 2014 NHL Entry Draft with a September birthdate, and was only playing in his first QMJHL season. Didn't have the offensive output we were expecting, but it wouldn't be surprising for us if he has a breakthrough year in 2014-2015, there's too many things we like about this player.

SEASON	LEAGUE	GAMES	GOALS	ASSISTS	PPG	PIM	HP RANKING
2012/13	QMAAA	36	19	21	1.11	18	63
2013/14	QMJHL	68	14	20	0.5	18	

Nedeljkovic, Alex
G – Plymouth Whalers (OHL) – 6'0" 182

Nedeljkovic is an elite athletic goaltender from the Plymouth Whalers. He finished the regular season with a record of 26-27-0-7 with a 2.88 GAA and a 0.925 SV%. Alex is very agile and is able to slide from side to side with ease stopping a number of high quality cross ice scoring chances. Alex seems to have strong legs and is exceptional at taking away the bottom half of the net. He is good at finding pucks through traffic and does not seem fazed by having traffic in front of him. Nedeljkovic shows good rebound control and is very effective at deflecting pucks away from danger areas. He is not afraid to come out of his crease and play the puck and generally shows a good pass when pressured by aggressive forwards. Alex displays a strong glove hand and is quick to flash the leather when tested on the glove hand. He also shows a good compete level for loose pucks and is not afraid to use his stick on opponents standing in front of the net. He also shows good poise in the net and does not let one or two goals against faze him. When Nedeljkovic is locked in he possesses the ability to steal games for his teammates including game three of the first round playoff series against eventual league champion Guelph Storm facing 53 shots in a 2-1 victory. He can be susceptible to quick shots upstairs and would benefit from standing up longer and utilizing his size rather than getting down quick so early. He needs to add some bulk in the offseason and look to cut down angles better by using his size and getting out to the top of the crease quicker. Nedeljkovic carried a heavy load in the Whaler net this season and certainly looked to be up to the task. If the development level continues he could soon find himself as the top goaltender in the Ontario Hockey League.

SEASON	LEAGUE	GAMES	GAA	SV%	W	L	SO	HP RANKING
2012/13	OHL	26	2.28	0.923	19	2	2	49
2013/14	OHL	61	2.88	0.925	26	27	1	

Neill, Carl
RD - Sherbrooke Phoenix (QMJHL) - 6'03" 215

Neill was picked 9th overall in the 2012 QMJHL draft by the Val d'Or Foreurs but didn't report, and was then traded to the expansion Sherbrooke Phoenix in August 2012. At the beginning of the season, he competed for Team Canada Under-18 team at the 2013 Memorial of Ivan Hlinka tournament. He is a strong puck distributor from the point and can quarterback a powerplay, as he did this season with the Phoenix alongside Jérémy Roy. When he is patrolling the opposing blueline, Neill can unleash a booming shot that is well known by goaltenders across the league. His breakouts are pretty good when he plays within his limits. He likes to join the rush and has good passing skills. He has the vision to try some astonishing cross-ice passes through the neutral zone that can be successful against weaker teams.

However, we question his decision-making as he is forcing the play when he is overconfident. That can lead to many turnovers. He also pinches aggressively in the offensive zone. Defensively, he positions himself properly, uses his reach and is more of a passive defender, as he is conscious that his biggest weakness is definitely his mobility. We haven't seen much improvement in that area since last year, though. He still has trouble dealing with players with quick feet on one-on-one confrontations, letting his defensive partner down more often than not in order to deal with them, especially on a bigger ice surface. His defensive zone coverage has been a bit better than last season, but he's still getting attracted by the puck, losing his man while doing so. He loves to be aggressive along the walls and on the blue line, and there are times when he gets caught in a terrible position, and he has a difficult time recovering.

SEASON	LEAGUE	GAMES	GOALS	ASSISTS	PPG	PIM	HP RANKING
2012/13	QMJHL	61	3	17	0.33	30	NR
2013/14	QMJHL	65	4	18	0.34	58	

Nejezchleb, Richard
RW – Brandon Wheat Kings (WHL) – 6'02" 210

Richard is a second year import from the Czech Republic playing for the Wheat Kings. Twice passed over for the draft, Richard had a strong season this year potting 32 goals in a comeback season. He is a big, strong forward that is hard to knock off the puck. He has good core strength and protects the puck well. He is an upright skater and he has a powerful stride, however his first few steps do need some help. He drives hard to the net and can be tough to contain when he wants to go to the dirty areas of the ice. He has a heavy wrist shot that he has used with continued success. He is responsible in picking up the trailer on a play and typically displays tight coverage when defending. While he is more advanced at this time than many of the other prospect eligible for this year's draft, he is also a couple years older. As a result, teams will have to decide how much of his success has been a result of his maturing and experience advantage over fellow prospects and how much more he'll develop. He's likely a player that can play a checking role by being generally difficult to play against while also being able to contribute a little offense along the way. Richard is a player we were very high on in international play but struggled when he came over to North America. Not only has he adjusted to the game on this side of the pond, but he's excelling.

SEASON	LEAGUE	GAMES	GOALS	ASSISTS	PPG	PIM	HP RANKING
2012/13	WHL	35	11	13	0.69	3	123
2013/14	WHL	66	32	25	0.86	75	

Nekolenko, Arkhip
RW – Spartak 2 (RUS Jr.) – 6'2" 189

Akhip looked very promising at the start of the 2012/13 season as a 16yrs old and put together a good rookie year in the MHL. This season he was sidelined for the first four months, had his first game only after Christmas and struggled to find his game, completing a disappointing campaign with only 2 goals while registering an average of one shot per game, which is basically half the pace he sustained as a rookie. Even if he did better in the playoffs, helping his low scoring team to win the Kharlamov Cup, his lack of progress from last year is of concern.

That however can't make you forget the qualities he possesses. Gifted with nice size and skills, the right-shooting left winger can dangle, challenge defensemen one on one off the rush, beat them wide both sides and manage to get into scoring positions.

For the type of player he is supposed to develop into (a dynamic one), he needs to improve his straight ahead acceleration. Once he gets going, skating becomes a strength.

Without the puck, Nekolenko effectively attacks the slot with his stick down, always making himself available to one time the puck to the net. He can get in troubles when he gets the puck in the defensive zone, but he shows better promptness in the offensive zone and a willingness to pay the price to stay in front of the net.

While his weak goals scoring production becomes even more baffling when thinking of it, his capability of bringing the puck into scoring positions to shoot off a better angle, along with his size and potential, makes him worth of a draft pick.

SEASON	LEAGUE	GAMES	GOALS	ASSISTS	PPG	PIM	HP RANKING
2012/13	MHL	41	11	11	0.54	18	190
2013/14	MHL	19	2	5	0.37	16	

Nikolishin, Ivan
LC – Everett Silvertips (WHL) – 5'9" 160

Ivan is a shifty playmaking forward. He's a decent skater who possesses tremendous passing abilities. Combined with his vision and hockey sense, he is a continuous offensive threat. Ivan had a solid rookie campaign and finished second in scoring this season for Everett. Every time Ivan steps on the ice he is making something happen whether it be offensive or defensive. His passing abilities allow him to find his teammates tape through traffic or in tight areas. He has shown good poise and patience when controlling the puck although sometimes he gets excited and tries to force the pass when the window of opportunity has passed. Ivan is a magician with the puck when given time and space to work with. He can be hard to contain when he's utilizing his strong puck protection skills. He is a very talented individual and can dazzle with his stick skills or by feeding a saucer pass cross ice to set up a backdoor goal. He's very creative offensively and possesses a unique blend of skill. Ivan is not an overly physical player, but does not mind engaging in the puck battles or going to the dirty areas of the ice. He has a good above average shot. Often he needs to be more selfish and shoot the puck as he often looks to distribute despite being in a good shooting lane. Ivan's defensive play has improved over the course of the year. He has a decent stick and has shown he can be effective shutting down both the passing and shooting lanes. One of our concerns with Nikolishin is he can sometimes embellish a play too much, especially in international play which has not only taken him out of the play, but resulted in penalties as well. Ivan is a playmaking forward who has a tremendous skill set but will need to work on getting quicker and adding foot speed to his game along with smoothing out other aspects of his skill set.

SEASON	LEAGUE	GAMES	GOALS	ASSISTS	PPG	PIM	HP RANKING
2012/13	MHL	53	11	12	0.43	6	NR
2013/14	WHL	72	18	41	0.82	16	

Nogier, Nelson
RD – Saskatoon Blades (WHL) – 6'02" 193

Nelson is a big shutdown defender who is consistently playing a physical game and has excellent defensive awareness. Nelson is a strong, balanced skater with great mobility who can cover a lot of ice very quickly. His ability to move laterally allows him to close down the offensive rush and get to loose pucks and turn the play back up the ice. He has shown good maturity and poise in his own end of the ice when controlling the puck carrier in tight/close situations. Nelson has shown good gap control during one-on-one battles and also takes good angles and closes off the puck carrier well.

He uses a very active stick to shut down the lanes and breaks up many offense chances with his good defensive positioning. Nelson makes good defensive checks and is very smart defender who reads and reacts to the play with a very calm demeanor. He's a tough in front of his crease and has shown he can punish you with a crushing body check or just be a pest to play against. He has many tools to be a solid shut down defender. He has a solid outlet pass and makes good puck moving decisions out of his own zone. He will need to develop his offensive game but has all the tools to put up offensive numbers.

SEASON	LEAGUE	GAMES	GOALS	ASSISTS	PPG	PIM	HP RANKING
2012/13	WHL	55	0	4	0.07	8	99
2013/14	WHL	37	1	5	0.16	25	

Nylander, William
C/RW – MODO (SWE) – 5'11" 179

William is a dynamic player, in fact he is probably the most creative and flashy player in the 2014 NHL Entry Draft. He seems to thrive when he has the puck in the offensive zone with some space. Nylander will circle the zone with the puck on a string inspecting his options. He has fantastic puck skills and combines them with his great skating ability - which includes amazing quickness, acceleration and balance to be an absolute menace for opposing teams. Whether it's using his speed off the rush or his agility and ability to move laterally with speed, Nylander puts himself in position to be a scoring threat multiple times per game. He uses weapons that include a laser of a shot and filthy quick hands. He's a smart player who understands how to create offense. It's easier with his skills.

Going back to last season, our hang-up with Nylander was his knack of playing a solo game too often. William would too often forget that he had four other players to move the puck too. He's improved in that regard. While he will still make the odd ill advised solo effort attempting to beat multiple defenders, they are fewer and far between. There is talk of Nylander not being willing to buy into playing a team game. Regardless if it's true or not, it's difficult to ignore this much talent in a player. Something else that might concern NHL teams is his smallish frame. He isn't a physical player. It's not like anyone expects him to play a power forwards game but you want him to have the strength to win puck battles. His defensive play is hit and miss as well. If he posts big points in the NHL it won't matter as much, it's not like he needs to be a Selke award winner, but in the NHL you can't be a complete liability. He does use his speed to his advantage on the defensive side of the puck.

Nylander might wind up being a boom or bust player. We are bigger fans of him this year as opposed to last season, but he's still a player who has lacked consistency.

Quotable: "He's a top 10 pick. Period." - NHL Scout

Quotable: "He's better than Kapanen. It's not close." - NHL Scout

Quotable: "I've had a bit of a love hate with Nylander. Last season at the U17 he would wow me with highlight reel plays on some shifts and then make me shake my head with Sunday men's league type plays on others. He was great in Finland this year though, he flashed his complete arsenal of skills, shot, release, explosive skating, speed, agility, great vision, it went on and on." - Mark Edwards

Quotable: "I don't think it (puck distribution) has ever been a problem for me." - William Nylander

SEASON	LEAGUE	GAMES	GOALS	ASSISTS	PPG	PIM	HP RANKING
2013/14	SHL 2	35	15	12	0.77	16	8
2013/14	SHL	22	1	6	0.32	6	

Okulov, Konstantin
LC – Sibirskie Novosibirks (RUS Jr.) – 6'00" 160

Okulov came out of nowhere in 2011/2012 to dominate his age group in his region competition and as a result appeared on the Russian national team at the 2012 World Junior A Challenge. He turned 18 few months later in his first full MHL season and ended up undrafted. In his second year of eligibility for the NHL Draft, the Siberian enjoyed a breakthrough season, registering the best PPG ratio among his MHL peers despite a limited supporting cast and even gaining a brief stint with the Novosibirsk KHL team.

An artful two-way center at the junior level, Okulov as of now still appears to lack intensity in his game and to be too soft on the puck to succeed at the pro level. Even if he shows good positioning and predisposition to protect the puck along the walls , he simply seems to be lacking the strength in his forearms and hands to hold onto the puck through battles and traffic. He plays a finesse game and probably is not the kind of guy who would feel comfortable outside of a top six role even if he can play a two-way game and is used to kill penalties.

This underdeveloped and skinny Russian is however very talented. Needs to become stronger on his skates, but he has agile feet and showcases good speed through the neutral zone. He can make good use of his stick both offensively and defensively, his puck skills are obvious and he is a terrific passer, a creative one who knows where his linemates are and who can open up passing lanes by making use of his good backhand.

The main question is if moving forward he will show the drive and the capability to get as strong as he needs to succeed at the next level.

SEASON	LEAGUE	GAMES	GOALS	ASSISTS	PPG	PIM	HP RANKING
2012/13	MHL	51	15	7	0.43	24	NR
2013/14	MHL	46	24	39	1.37	35	

Ollas Mattsson, Adam
LD – Djurgarden Jr. (SWE) – 6'4" 209

Adam is a big defenseman and uses his size to his advantage making hits all over the ice. Adam plays a simple stay at home game but did jump up into the play more this season. It's not going to make him an offensive prospect at the next level though. He makes smart decisions with the puck and plays a poised game. He is solid on the penalty kill and his positional play is good.

Adam is not a very good skater at all. He struggles a lot matching up to better skaters. Small ice is his friend. He shows a lot of potential but needs to improve his skating because his intelligence and physical game are very solid.

SEASON	LEAGUE	GAMES	GOALS	ASSISTS	PPG	PIM	HP RANKING
2012/13	J18 Elit	22	0	7	0.32	28	43
2013/14	U20 S.Elit	33	1	8	0.27	42	

Olofsson, Fredrik
LW – Chicago Steel (USHL) – 6'01" 185

Fredrik, whose older brother Gustav signed his ELC with the Minnesota Wild this past April after one season at Colorado College, is also a Colorado College commit, himself. Drafted by the Green Bay Gamblers in the fifth round of the 2012 USHL Futures Draft, Fredrik played a handful of games with the Gamblers during the 2012-2013 season while a member of the Colorado Thunderbirds U16 program.

After representing his native Sweden at the 2013 Ivan Hlinka Memorial Tournament where he had one point in four games, he joined the Gamblers full time until his trade to Chicago in late January.

Fredrik's play this season while in Green Bay could be described as maddeningly inconsistent. Fredrik has all the tools in the world, but he struggled to put it all together game in and game out, as shown by his six points in 28 games with Green Bay. There were moments where effort and compete level were in question, but those moments were muted by others of tenacity and aggressiveness. You really were not sure which player you would see when you showed up to the rink that particular day.

After being traded to Chicago, this all changed. You saw a much, much different player on a nightly basis and while it did not show up on the score sheet right away, Fredrik proved to be a much different player post-trade. Compete level remained high on a nightly basis, and his offensive game began to shine and he never looked back. Fredrik plays a strong, two-way game that might not have been anticipated earlier on this season. A fixture on the penalty kill, not only is he responsible defensively but his skating ability, hands, and ability to read and anticipate plays make him a threat to score while shorthanded. Five-on-five he is equally responsible, always being in position, active with his stick, intelligent, and aggressive. He is strong along the boards and always supports his line mates. His play and awareness away from the puck are exceptional. Also speaking to his defensive acumen is the fact that he was always on the point on the power play and trusted by the coaching staff to potentially be the last man back in a transition situation going the other way.

Spinning off of that, Fredrik's offensive game shines even brighter than his solid defensive game. He is one of the more intelligent players in the USHL all season long. He sees the ice exceptionally well and with that vision is an excellent playmaker. Despite his own abilities to stickhandle and finish, he uses his line mates very well, be it finding them when they're open or using his intelligence and effort away from the puck to get himself open, support them, and give them options. He is an excellent skater, has a really smooth, pro-caliber stride, quick feet, and uses his feet exceptionally well to catch the puck all without missing a step. He is solid and strong on his feet, uses his size well in all situations, and has great length. Everything he does is just so smooth and effortless looking. An above-average release and excellent finish along with a heavy slap shot make him a dangerous player in the offensive zone. Whatever the situation, there is never even a hint of panic; always cool and poised. Fredrik is just a very polished player who very much plays a pro-style game already, especially with the compete level up where it was after his arrival to Chicago.

Quotable: "Our Chicago based scout really likes him and Fredrik got much better as the season went on. I just think he needs to step it up a bit physically, he can have an occasional soft shift." – Mark Edwards

SEASON	LEAGUE	GAMES	GOALS	ASSISTS	PPG	PIM	HP RANKING
2012/13	MWMMEHL	31	26	43	2.23	8	196
2013/14	USHL	52	6	15	0.4	45	

Orlovich-Grudkov, Denis
RW – SKA 1946 (RUS Jr.) – 5'11" 170

A left shooting right winger, in his second MHL season Orlovich-Grudkov easily led the SKA junior team in scoring, but as a late '95 born was not eligible for the U18 in Finland. Not as dynamic as you might expect from a Russian winger, but still a pretty good skater with good balance. Denis plays a smart game, displaying good vision and an excellent passing game. Hard to read when he has the puck on his stick, he is a solid stickhandler with very good puck control. Quick in reading and processing the play, he is an underrated player even if his upside appears to be questionable.

SEASON	LEAGUE	GAMES	GOALS	ASSISTS	PPG	PIM	HP RANKING
2012/13	MHL	59	7	6	0.22	18	NR
2013/14	MHL	51	20	32	1.02	60	

Owre, Steven
RC – Medicine Hat Tigers (WHL) – 5'11" 165

It can be tough sometimes for hard working players to find ice on a team loaded with veterans, but Steven was able to gain more than his share of ice playing primiarily on the third line plus plenty of penalty kill action and a little bit of power play here and there. While he doesn't have great size or strength, Owre is a pretty solid checker who always finishes his checks along the wall. He has a great work ethic which he applies to the forecheck to break up plays and create offense with it. He has limited offensive skills but when he has the opportunity he can do some damage from time to time. Steven plays a full 200 foot game and backchecks hard. He competes for pucks in all three zones and is always engaging along the wall. He has also shown the willingness to take the hit for his team. He has limited upside and if he was to make it, it would be as a bottom six forward, but he has the work ethic and the determination to potentially receive late round consideration.

SEASON	LEAGUE	GAMES	GOALS	ASSISTS	PPG	PIM	HP RANKING
2012/13	WHL	37	0	2	0.05	6	NR
2013/14	WHL	70	12	20	0.46	42	

Pastrnak, David
RW- Sodertalje (SWE 2) – 6'0" 167

A player we really liked going back to last season when we saw him a lot. David is blessed with excellent skills. He has fantastic hands and his stickhandling is up with the best in the draft class. At times he can try a few too many dangles, which leads to turnovers, but there is no denying his ability to control the puck on his stick. He shows good body control on his skates and is able to beat defenders one on one. He's not a physical player and tries to avoid contact and seldom initiates it.

Pastrnak has impressed us in the past by being the most creative player and main offensive catalyst for his team on multiple occasions. He's a good passer with good vision and he makes players around him better with his playmaking ability. Along with the playmaking ability he adds the ability to shoot the puck. He combines a hard shot with a quick release to beat goaltenders.

Defensively Pastrnak needs to get better. He has flashes of showing he is a capable player in his own half of the rink, but too many times he is a non factor defending. We have seen him cheat at times and pull the chute in puck races against bigger defenders. He struggles with defensive zone awareness at times and gets caught chasing.

Pastrnak projects to be a top six forward at the next level who will need to commit more effort on his own side of centre ice. He needs to get stronger to help him along the walls. He can live off his sneaky wrister and hard one-timer on the powerplay.

Quotable: "One of our best interviews" (at the combine). - NHL Scout

Quotable: "That kid (Pastrnak) was really good in our interview." - NHL Scout

Quotable: "He gave great answers in our interview and added some insightful information." - NHL Scout

Quotable: "I saw him a lot last season and late this season at the U18 in Finland where he had a poor showing coming off an injury. He played down the middle in Finland and I didn't like him there at all. I see him as a winger." - Mark Edwards

SEASON	LEAGUE	GAMES	GOALS	ASSISTS	PPG	PIM	HP RANKING
2012/13	U20 S.Elit	36	12	17	0.81	67	17
2013/14	SHL 2	36	8	16	0.67	24	

Pelletier, Julien
LW – Cape Breton Screaming Eagles (QMJHL) – 5'11" 178

Pelletier, who played his first season in the QMJHL this season after playing two seasons with the Gatineau Intrepides in the Quebec Midget AAA league, had a successful but relatively quiet first season with the Screaming Eagles. Not a lot of noise was made of Pelletier's rookie season, but Julien became the highest-scoring rookie player in Screaming Eagles' history with his 25 goals and 50-point season. He's a shoot-first type of player who possesses a good wrist shot with a quick release. From the start of the regular season, Pelletier's offensive contribution was steady, with no real long lethargy during the year. Like all good goal scorers, he knows how to escape defensive-zone coverage and get open to score his goals, as he has very good positioning in the offensive zone. Pelletier's premier qualities are his shots and goal scoring prowess. His passing game is average and I would like to see him pass the puck quicker. The Gatineau native is a decent skater but he's not overly explosive. He has a good top speed and likes to beat defensemen on the outside. He can play a physical game on the forecheck, and along the wall he has good puck protection, but is still inconsistent with his physical game and doesn't like to get hit.

SEASON	LEAGUE	GAMES	GOALS	ASSISTS	PPG	PIM	HP RANKING
2012/13	QMAAA	34	23	20	1.26	44	117
2013/14	QMJHL	67	25	25	0.75	28	

Pépin, Alexis
LW – Gatineau Olympiques (QMJHL) – 6'2" 224

Pepin was the 2nd overall pick in the 2012 QMJHL draft. Despite having a good rookie season with the PEI Rocket, he was traded to Gatineau during this season's trade period in the QMJHL following a rough first half of 2013-2014. He only scored five times in the first three months of the season leading up to January. The Candiac native enjoyed a lot more success after his trade to Gatineau, with 17 points in 23 games. Pepin is a big kid who uses his size well in front of the net and along the wall. Likes to finish his hits and can really hit hard when he wants to. Does a good job protecting the puck and is tough to move from the front of the net with that big frame. For a big guy, he has some real soft, quick hands and is a natural scorer. Pepin can play either on the left wing or at center, but due to his lack of foot-speed, we feel his future will be on wing. He has played mostly on the wing since joining Gatineau. Skating has been an issue for him since he joined the Quebec Major Junior Hockey league, and we didn't see any improvements in his strides and footwork since last year. Once again this year, one of the biggest flaws in Pepin's game was his intensity. He was very inconsistent in his compete level from game to game. Pepin made Team Canada for the Ivan Hlinka tournament last August but had limited ice time and there were numerous reports that Pepin was out of shape coming into camp. Pepin's stock took a big fall this season, once touted as first rounder last year and now he's a wildcard in this draft. Who knows where he could go, though he still has some great tools that could make him an NHLer but also has some red flags that appeared this year. It was announced after the season that Pepin will need shoulder surgery that would require 4-6 months of rehabilitation.

Quotable: " The first time I saw him this season was in Toronto for the Hlinka camp. I had liked him quite a bit last season at the U17 but was not impressed in the August camp. He was overweight and IMO never should have made the team. He barely got ice overseas. My more recent viewing this spring was more positive." - Mark Edwards

SEASON	LEAGUE	GAMES	GOALS	ASSISTS	PPG	PIM	HP RANKING
2012/13	QMJHL	64	18	12	0.47	78	141
2013/14	QMJHL	60	17	17	0.57	69	

Perlini, Brendan
LW – Niagara Ice Dogs (OHL) – 6'03" 205

Perlini came flying out of the gate after a strong Ivan Hlinka tryout and caught NHL scouts a little bit off guard based on his previous season where he had a fairly quiet season. We saw NHL scouts scrambling to see him, including many out of province scouts who made trips into Ontario to get an early look. Our first viewing was the Hlinka camp and he made us do a 360 on our initial opinion of him. He had a good camp. Flash forward to December, we had several viewings under our belt and it was hard to ignore his size and speed combined with the points he was posting game after game. The only thing that still bothered us was how soft he played game after game. Brendan, much like his older brother before him tends to play much smaller than his listed size.

It's a pleasure to watch Brendan skate, he has an effortless stride and closes ground on defenders with ease. He takes away time and space and is effective in causing turnovers with his legs. He is able to beat defenders off the rush using his speed to his advantage. He has puck skills and was adept at protecting the puck. He word well with leafs pick Carter Verhaeghe. His shot is hard and accurate. He has a quick release. Niagara liked to have him setup on the right side on the PP and let him unload his one-timer, he made plenty of teams pay.

We saw Perlini in Finland where he played for Team Canada after a poor playoff performance. While scored some nice goals, we felt overall he was average at best in the tournament.

Quotable: "He's what I call a scout killer. He can either extend your contract or possibly make it your last one." - NHL Scout

Quotable: "I hope he's off the board when we pick." (laughs) - NHL Scout

Quotable: "Does it really matter if you are a bit soft these days? He has a shitload of talent." - NHL Scout

Quotable: "Probably a faller based on his poor play late in the season, could make him a steal if he pans out." - NHL Scout

Quotable: "We have him ranked in the twenty range." - NHL Scout

Quotable: "Who do you take on the wing Ehlers at 5'10" or Perlini at 6'3" - It's not close for me." (Would take Perlini) - NHL Scout

Quotable: "Brendan provided me with one of my favorite post-game interviews all season. Very laid back kid who loves the game and understands who he is as a player and was very honest and direct. I've got nothing but great things to say about his character" - Ryan Yessie

Quotable: "Struggled evaluating this kid all season. Wasn't a big fan in Minor Midget and didn't see him a ton in his rookie year, then liked him at Hlinka camp. I saw good games and bad games this year but saw more good ones. Love the size speed combo. I had as many conversations with NHL scouts about him as any player in this draft. Opinions were all over the map." - Mark Edwards

Quotable: "I was given mixed reviews by NHL scouts on his interviews at the Combine, some really liked him, some thought he was just OK." - Mark Edwards

SEASON	LEAGUE	GAMES	GOALS	ASSISTS	PPG	PIM	HP RANKING
2012/13	OHL	59	8	4	0.2	8	20
2013/14	OHL	58	34	37	1.22	36	

Perron, Francis
LW – Rouyn-Noranda Huskies (QMJHL) – 6'0" 163

The Huskies selected Perron with the 6th overall pick in the 2012 QMJHL Draft out of the St-Eustache Vikings' Midget AAA program. The Rosemere native has one of the best visions of any players available from this year's draft class in the QMJHL. He plays on the wing but almost acts as a centerman, the way he can set up plays. Perron is very creative with the puck; his linemates have to be alert all the time as they can get the puck back when they don't expect it. When in possession of the puck, you can see him wait an extra second to find open teammates, making him tough to predict for the defense. Because of this creativity and playmaking ability, the Huskies used Perron on the point on the power play all year long, a rare case for a 17 year old in the QMJHL. Another advantage of using him on the point is they don't have him battling in front of the net or in the corners, helping Perron keep his energy, as he's not the strongest physically. He will need to add a lot strength to his frame, and the toughest part of projecting Perron's future in 3-4 years is to guess how much stronger he will get in those next couple of years. He's a great stickhandler with good puck control and he loves to challenge opposing defensemen one-on-one with his great arsenal of dekes. His hands are very soft and agile. Perron is a decent skater with a good top speed; he's shifty on his skates and can change direction very quickly. He's a first and foremost a playmaker, but he has a decent touch around the net, though he lacks velocity on his shot. However, he can get his shot on net very quickly with his quick, soft hands. Perron's biggest weakness is his physical play, though he won't back down and has a good compete level. Still, at this point his lack of strength is a concern.

Quotable: "The more the season progressed, the more I became a fan of Perron, whose size is a major concern, but you can't deny his puck skills and vision. If he ever could put some weight on, he could become a real good sleeper pick." - HP Scout Jerome Berube

SEASON	LEAGUE	GAMES	GOALS	ASSISTS	PPG	PIM	HP RANKING
2012/13	QMJHL	57	7	11	0.32	28	86
2013/14	QMJHL	68	16	39	0.81	32	

Peters, Alex
LD – Plymouth Whalers (OHL) – 6'4" 205

Peters is a big two-way defender from the Plymouth Whalers. He uses his size well in the defensive zone to gain body position against smaller forwards. Alex also shows good moments of physicality but should strive to bring this on a more consistent basis. He has an active stick and uses it to keep rushers to the outside before finishing them off along the boards. Peters is not afraid to mix things up after the whistle and does not back down when battling for loose pucks in front of the net. His stride is a little choppy and he would benefit from improving his mechanics and foot movement. He generally holds the offensive blue line well and shows good transition speed when forced to change quickly. Alex shows a tendency to jump into the offensive rush on occasion and displays a strong wrist shot when given space to get it off. He does not show much offensive upside but can contribute in ways such as drawing defenders and opening lanes when coming in back door. Peters is at his best when he keeps things simple in the defensive zone. He gets himself into trouble by trying to make fancy plays or forcing tight passes through traffic. Alex would benefit from improving his vision and understanding of when to push things and when to keep them simple.

SEASON	LEAGUE	GAMES	GOALS	ASSISTS	PPG	PIM	HP RANKING
2012/13	OHL	58	0	12	0.21	31	95
2013/14	OHL	50	3	6	0.18	44	

Pettersson, Marcus
LD - Skelleftea Jr. (SWE Jr) – 6'4" 167

We first saw Pettersson jumping back and forth between forward and defense. We liked him at both positions but he's on the back-end to stay now. There are parts of Petterson's game that remind us of Travis Sanheim. He skates well with really good mobility (especially considering his size) and has offensive upside. Our knock on Pettersson is he doesn't play physical at all. He has so much upside so we kept on watching him closely. He makes good decisions with the puck in all three zones. He can use his feet to skate the puck out of trouble but also moves the puck well. His shot is good and he uses it wisely.

When you consider that he is new to playing defense it makes what you see on the ice all the more impressive. If not for the lack of any sort of physical play in his game we would have him ranked even higher.

Quotable: "The first time I ever saw him I wrote a note 'was physical' I don't recall writing that note again. I still really like this kid and think he has a lot of upside. He reminds me of Sanheim in that he has so much room to get even better." - Mark Edwards

SEASON	LEAGUE	GAMES	GOALS	ASSISTS	PPG	PIM	HP RANKING
2012/13	U20 S.Elit	37	4	8	0.32	16	**33**
2013/14	U20 S.Elit	38	4	14	0.47	38	

Petti, Niki
LC – Belleville Bulls (OHL) – 6'00" 184

Niki was a former first round pick of the Belleville Bulls and saw a boost in his offensive numbers playing in his sophomore season with the Bulls primarily on the third line with a little action on the second line and power play. His strongest asset without question is his skating ability. He has a great top speed and is explosive after just one step. He utilizes his speed to fly up the ice and get involved offensively. He has a shoot first mentality but possesses good power in his shot. He also provides an excellent compete level in the offensive zone. He is capable of cycling the puck effectively and protects it moderately well for his size. Unfortunately while Niki is always the first forward to jump up in the offense, he's consistently the last forward to get back defensively and consistently lacks urgency to get back in the defensive zone. Looking at his skill set there is some intrigue in Petti but the concern is his lack of top six offensive ability combined with a lack of defensive urgency which makes a projection for the NHL level tough and could ultimately scare some teams off in this draft.

SEASON	LEAGUE	GAMES	GOALS	ASSISTS	PPG	PIM	HP RANKING
2012/13	OHL	50	4	9	0.26	19	**NR**
2013/14	OHL	59	12	11	0.39	17	

Pettit, Kyle
LC – Erie Otters (OHL) – 6'04" 190

In his second season with the Otters, Kyle played a limited role behind many veteran, and skilled forwards. He did a very good job in his role as a two-way centre on the fourth line, and gained our attention on a few occasions. He provides a strong forecheck presence, and uses his stick well adding in the occasional hit. His first few steps still need some work, but his top speed is pretty good for a 6'4" forward, and he keeps his feet moving.

He is good at the cycle game, and uses his body well to protect pucks down low. He has some offensive upside that is currently untapped because of the role he plays, and has a powerful shot. Kyle is almost like a third defenseman when the puck is deep in his own end, and will battle hard on the walls, and do what it takes to get the puck out of the zone showing strong work ethic regardless of the zone he's playing in. He has also done moderately well in the face-off circle in our viewings. Kyle projects to be a two-way player at the next level, and should receive increased ice time. Despite his lack of ice time, he is a legitimate prospect in the mold of a defensive forward with size.

SEASON	LEAGUE	GAMES	GOALS	ASSISTS	PPG	PIM	HP RANKING
2012/13	OHL	67	3	3	0.09	21	NR
2013/14	OHL	53	5	5	0.19	24	

Phelps, Chase
LW – Shattuck St. Mary's (HS-MN) – 6'00" 180

Chase is a hard working player who battles hard consistently in all three zones. He doesn't put up a ton of offense but does possess a strong shot. His best asset is his consistency in the work ethic department. Chase will need to improve his skating ability as his first few steps are a struggle and he doesn't possesses a very good top speed. Chase is slated to join Boston University in September 2014.

SEASON	LEAGUE	GAMES	GOALS	ASSISTS	PPG	PIM	HP RANKING
2012/13	USHS	51	22	32	1.06	22	205
2013/14	USHS	53	24	42	1.25	46	

Philp, Luke
RC – Kootenay Ice (WHL) – 5'10" 177

The late-born '95 is a skilled forward who really started to break out after the Christmas break and started to show his full potential. He always keeps his feet moving. He has shown an ability to control the puck well and can be tough to knock off his feet. He seems to take his play to the net and create scoring chances this way. He has good shot and decent release. His hands and vision are average and he tends to not panic with the puck under pressure. His offensive game is sound and he has put up good offensive number this season. He makes good decisions with the puck and seems to know when to make a pass or rush up ice. Luke was often utilized on the point during Kootenay powerplays in order to take advantage of his passing skills.

Luke will sacrifice his body to help his team win games. He seems to lead by example and blocks shots. He battles hard along the boards and has been effective in his defensive zone. He backchecks hard and seems to be able to identify the open man and provide coverage. He does seem to play with a head on a swivel and is always watching the play and his man on defensive coverage staying in good position. While he has some offensive skill, we would like to see Luke operate at a higher pace in order for his offense to translate. This goes for the defensive aspect of this game as well. Things happen a lot quicker at the pro level and in order for Luke to make the jump, he'll have to get used to having less time and space. This is especially important considering Luke isn't the biggest player. Pace and the ability to operate in limited space will have huge implications for Philp.

SEASON	LEAGUE	GAMES	GOALS	ASSISTS	PPG	PIM	HP RANKING
2012/13	WHL	66	20	25	0.68	24	140
2013/14	WHL	71	31	46	1.08	31	

Piccinich, J.J.
RW – Youngstown Phantoms (USHL) – 5' 11" 174

Piccinich is a playmaker with good vision and hockey sense. High motor, high energy guy who's always moving his feet but skating is an issue. Piccinich is aggressive on the forecheck and backcheck and plays a really good defensive game. Strong in his own zone, always in position, always covering his proper assignment. Creative with the puck, solid shot. Two-way player who can play on the power play and penalty kill. Could find a role as a bottom-six, penalty kill type player at the NHL level. Not dynamic enough offensively to make up for smallish size. He is planning to attend Boston University in September 2014. Skating is the issue.

SEASON	LEAGUE	GAMES	GOALS	ASSISTS	PPG	PIM	HP RANKING
2012/13	USHL	63	3	12	0.24	4	**207**
2013/14	USHL	60	27	31	0.97	31	

Pilut, Lawrence
LD - HV 71 Jr. (SWE) 5'11' 175

Not to sound too negative but we just don't see him as a player we would add to our fictitious HockeyProspect.com team. Skating isn't there and we saw enough that we knew we didn't need to pay attention anymore.

SEASON	LEAGUE	GAMES	GOALS	ASSISTS	PPG	PIM	HP RANKING
2013/14	U20 S.Elit	30	3	15	0.6	26	**NR**
2013/14	SHL	22	0	4	0.18	18	

Pionk, Neal
RD – Sioux City Musketeers (USHL) – 5' 11" 170

Pionk is the style of defenseman every team would love to have. He can play in every situation, play any style of game, reliable defensively, offensively skilled, all with a nasty edge to his game.

Drafted 66th Overall by Sioux City in the 2012 USHL Entry Draft, Pionk got in 12 games with the Musketeers in the 2012-2013 season, notching one goal and five assists in that stint. He began the 2013-2014 season representing Team USA at the World Junior A Challenge, collecting two assists in four games before beginning his first full season in Sioux City.

Pionk is tough as nails. He's not a big body, but you know when he's on the ice. He plays nasty, and isn't above giving you a little extra shot after putting a body on you just for good measure. He plays with a major edge, but usually stays on that edge and avoids taking bad penalties. Despite being on the smallish side for a defenseman, he can lay people out. He had a number of highlight reel open ice hits this season, and always finishes his checks in all situations. Pionk is very aggressive on the puck in the defensive zone and refuses to lose board battles. Very active stick, causes a lot of turnovers and with his speed and quick feet, he's able to translate turnovers into instant defensive zone exits. He's really good at skating the puck up through his defensive zone on his own, very shifty and exceptionally calm and collected with the puck. Always looks to make the good first pass first and head-man the puck. He keeps tight gaps on attacking players coming through the neutral zone and causes way more dump-and-chase situations than allowing a controlled entry. Smart player, with and without the puck. Never out of position. Excellent penalty killer. You can pair him with any defenseman and the pair will work. Has the intelligence, anticipation, and skating ability to bail out partners and even forwards' mistakes. Reads and reacts to the game very well. Constantly mucks up passing lanes and is great in transition. He lead odd-man breaks going back the other way after picking off passes numerous times this season.

Pionk has some offensive skill and is a crafty, heads up passer, who sees the ice well. He has a solid slap shot but not overwhelming velocity. Good wrist shot. He's really strong on the offensive blue line. He doesn't bail and back off until absolutely necessary, and is aggressive pinching the puck and holding in clearing attempts. Rarely gets caught when pinching and even when he does, he usually is able to get back and cover on account of his speed.

There's a lot to love about Pionk's game, but he may run into trouble at the NHL level. While solid, his offensive game is not dynamic and may not be enough to counter his lack of size. He's a mean, nasty, physical player, but at his size will have a more difficult time executing that style of play at the pro level. His wheels, hockey sense, tenacity, compete level, and attitude all are there and make him draft worthy, but his upside isn't as great as you would like when considering his lack of size and lack of dynamic offensively ability. Pionk is currently uncommitted as of the time of this writing.

Quotable: "He's a tough kid who is hard to play against." – Mark Edwards

SEASON	LEAGUE	GAMES	GOALS	ASSISTS	PPG	PIM	HP RANKING
2012/13	USHS	45	15	25	0.89	57	NR
2013/14	USHL	54	2	21	0.43	93	

Poganski, Austin
RW – Tri-City Storm (USHL) – 6'01" 198

Poganski has a ton of tools, it's just a matter of him putting them all together. He's a big, big body and with his speed he's extremely difficult to defend against when having a full head of steam with the puck. If he has a full head of steam without the puck, it's bad news for you, because that means that full head of steam is coming to put you through the glass. Poganski's hits are never subtle, he flat out crushes people. He has a thick, solid frame and excellent wheels and that's just a bad combination if you're on the other team.

Very much a north-south type player, Poganski runs at full speed the majority of the time he is on the ice. There is no let up from him, and effort level is never in question. 100% all the time. If he ever struggles, it's never for a lack of effort. High motor is an understatement. He has a strong, explosive, powerful stride and is akin to a runaway locomotive when he's a top gear. There are other players who have the same physical stats, but something about his frame and the way he skates just gives the impression he's even bigger than he's listed.

He's a beast along the boards and rarely loses a board battle to anyone. His physicality causes a lot of turnovers, and Poganski created a lot of quality scoring chances on those turnovers this season in the offensive zone, whether it's during a board battle or going full speed on the forecheck and forcing an error directly or indirectly in causing the opposing player to panic or feel forced to make a play that simply isn't there and turn the puck over.

For a big, bruising type player, Poganski has a fairly soft set of hands and can handle the puck well. He has a decent shot but he gets it off quicker than the average player, so it's very effective. Thrives on driving the net with the puck. He's hard to stop and he knows it, and exploits that in opposing defensemen. He has solid hockey sense, though his decision making, especially in the offensive zone, could improve and should improve over time. Sometimes he'll force things that aren't there or just throw the puck to an area blindly in hopes of a teammate being there but they aren't. Could stand to improve his awareness in that regard.

As for his skating, as previously stated, he's fast in a straight line but his agility could be improved. He isn't great laterally and in tight situations his feet can be a little slow, especially in start-stop scenarios. First step needs to be quicker and overall foot speed and agility need to be improved upon. He can disappear for stretches offensively, but overall his production was solid this season.

There's more there in the tank, however, and if he can improve in those previously listed areas, his production will increase.

Poganski's played well in big games, as his track record in international play shows, so he should do well next season at the University of North Dakota. He has the attitude and work ethic to improve in the areas he needs to, and he'll have time work on those things and develop further at a strong North Dakota program that has no shortage on developing NHL players.

SEASON	LEAGUE	GAMES	GOALS	ASSISTS	PPG	PIM	HP RANKING
2012/13	USHS	28	21	20	1.46	14	105
2013/14	USHL	55	19	12	0.56	57	

Point, Brayden
RC – Moose Jaw Warriors (WHL) – 5'09" 160

Brayden has tremendous skill and a matching work ethic. He is a spark plug center with the elite hockey sense and top-notch scoring ability. Those attributes combined with his skating and keen offensive instincts have made him a high impact player. He has a strong work ethic and a motor that just keeps going. He plays a two hundred foot game and has shown a lot of grit throughout the year. Point lacks fear and will engage in all puck battles along the boards regardless of the defenders size. He goes to the tough areas of the ice and isn't afraid to sacrifice his body to make a play. Point's offensive instincts and quick feet put him in good scoring positions, he just seems to dart out of nowhere to receive passes and get to the scoring lanes. He can be very elusive at times and combined with his tremendous stickhandling ability and great touch down low, he is a continuous scoring threat. He is a very hard player to control when he has possession of the puck below the circles. He possesses an average shot with a decent release and once he adds some weight to his frame, his shooting skills should improve. Although his +/- stats aren't flattering, he is a complete all-around player who is a responsible when playing the defensive side of the puck. He's very relentless in his pursuit to shut down scoring lanes and cause his opposition to turn over the puck. Although he falls in the small player category, Point's only real fault is his lack of size. Point's size is sure to scare away some teams, but his non-stop motor, high compete level, and excellent skill make him an attractive value pick with high-end skill.

Quotable: "I can't recall him having a bad game in one of my viewings. I was saddened to see him get hurt in Finland." – Mark Edwards

SEASON	LEAGUE	GAMES	GOALS	ASSISTS	PPG	PIM	HP RANKING
2012/13	WHL	67	24	33	0.85	26	45
2013/14	WHL	72	36	55	1.26	53	

Pollock, Brett
LC – Edmonton Oil Kings (WHL) – 6'02" 183

Pollock is a big, rangy forward with good skills. He plays up and down the ice and can be used in a variety of situations. He worked his way onto the top line this year and has found success despite being matched up against the league's best players on a regular basis. He works hard away from the puck and is able to create space for his linemates. He has a powerful, accurate wrist shot, but could use some work on the quickness of his release. He has pretty good hands in tight and uses his long reach to protect the puck extremely well. He is able to distribute the puck effectively and likes to get the puck into the hands of his teammates. He has a good compete level and can be tough to play against when he's on his game. That being said, while he uses his body to protect the puck ideally for a big forward, he really doesn't use his size to provide a physical game what so ever in our viewings of him all season long. He doesn't use his size to punish opponents, in fact it is rare to see Brett deliver a check. Pollock seems to get where he's going with above average speed for his size, but his skating stride is very uncomfortable and clunky. That stride, while it needs work, shouldn't be too much of a concern as it seems to be correctable. All in all, Pollock is A project pick, but with his size, two-way play and soft hands, Pollock could one day develop into a great forward for whoever selects him down the road.

Quotable: "Spoke to him at the Memorial Cup and he told me that he thought he made big strides in his physical play this year. He has a ways to go still in my opinion. It just doesn't come natural to him and he spends a lot of time on his rear end because his balance is so poor. I really liked the kid though." – Mark Edwards

Quotable: "Great interview with us (at the combine) he knew what he was good at and what he needs to work on. His interview helped him." – NHL Scout

Quotable: "He was one of our best interviews." – NHL Scout

SEASON	LEAGUE	GAMES	GOALS	ASSISTS	PPG	PIM	HP RANKING
2012/13	WHL	40	2	2	0.1	2	44
2013/14	WHL	71	25	30	0.77	36	

Prapavessis, Michael
LD – Toronto Lakeshore Patriots (OJHL) – 6'1" 180

Prapavessis is an elite skilled offensive defender from the Toronto Lakeshore Patriots. Michael is currently committed to play NCAA hockey at RPI, his OHL rights are owned by the London Knights. The most impressive aspect of his game is his high hockey IQ and vision. He is constantly finding teammates in quality scoring positions and is able to thread the needle through traffic almost with ease. Prapavessis is constantly aware of his surroundings and where opponents are on the ice which allows him to slow things down to his pace and make passing plays look easy. He shows excellent poise with the puck and never appears rushed even when faced with aggressive fore-checkers. Michael was the powerplay quarterback for the Patriots this season which was one of the top units in the league in powerplay percentage. He is without a doubt a pass first player and sometimes passes up clear shooting opportunities in order to make the one extra pass. He does not display a very strong shot and needs to work at adding strength in the offseason to improve the height and speed of his slap shot. Michael is more of a precision shooter and succeeds by fgetting pucks on target through screens or to look for a tip. Prapavessis is a strong skater and while his stride may sometimes appear choppy he always is able to keep opponents in front of him with quick transitions and long strides. He does not display much aggression and is not a physical player. He wins puck battles with smarts rather than physicality. While not afraid to take a hit to make a play, this is the biggest area that Prapavessis must improve on. He makes up for the lack of physical game with his smarts and an excellent stick.

Quotable: "I'm a fan. I think he is one of the smartest players in the draft which allows him to play through his lack of physical play. He is fantastic with his stick, he uses good positioning and his reach to his advantage. –Mark Edwards

SEASON	LEAGUE	GAMES	GOALS	ASSISTS	PPG	PIM	HP RANKING
2012/13	OJHL	25	2	9	0.44	2	82
2013/14	OJHL	47	5	49	1.15	2	

Prophet, Brandon
LD – Saginaw Spirit (OHL) – 6'02" 202

Brandon remained buried in Saginaw's depth on the blueline, but had an overall successful second season for playing primarily on the third pairing. He is a tough, physical defenseman who hits hard, delivers powerful checks, and brings a mean streak at times. He punishes opponents who get in his space. He is very strong, and works really hard along the boards winning his share of battles. He is also aggressive in front of his own net making opponents who venture into the slot area pay for it. He shows an occasional willingness to drop the gloves. He fares moderately well in these situations, but doesn't do it often, and doesn't dominate when it occurs. Brandon doesn't project to be an offensive defenseman long term, but made some smart plays in the offensive zone. He keeps his feet moving on the point regularly opening himself up as a passing option on the blueline. He also pinches occasionally, which resulted in a few goals for his team. From the defensive zone he likes to go after long distance passes, and lands them fairly often but doesn't always choose the correct options with the puck. He can also panic at times under pressure resulting in turnovers. His skating needs improvement, as his first few steps are as well as his lateral movement area little slow. Brandon shows one of the best mean streaks you'll find out of any 2014 NHL Draft Eligible defenseman in the draft. He has a low risk, low reward label as he projects as a big physical shutdown defenseman, and simply needs to improve his footwork, and become more consistent in one-on-one match-ups in order to fulfill that projection. He won't become an impact player, but a reliable defender who shows that he enjoys engaging in the rough stuff.

SEASON	LEAGUE	GAMES	GOALS	ASSISTS	PPG	PIM	HP RANKING
2012/13	OHL	54	3	8	0.2	53	166
2013/14	OHL	65	2	17	0.29	72	

Protapovich, Alexander
RC – Niagara Ice Dogs (OHL) – 6'03" 195

Protapovich came over to the Niagara Ice Dogs from Kazan's MHL program. Alexander has good size and is strong on the forecheck. He does a good job of getting into passing lanes and is capable of forcing turnovers. He's considered a two-way forward as he lacks a real dynamic element to his game. He is however capable of moving the puck to his teammates making simple passes and possesses a hard shot. While he has good size and is capable of providing a steady two-way game at the OHL level we do not expect Alexander to be selected at the 2014 NHL Entry Draft.

SEASON	LEAGUE	GAMES	GOALS	ASSISTS	PPG	PIM	HP RANKING
2012/13	MHL B	30	9	6	0.5	36	NR
2013/14	OHL	47	4	9	0.28	16	

Quenneville, John
LC – Brandon Wheat Kings (WHL) – 6'01" 186

Listed on NHL Central Scouting's final draft ranking. John is a skilled center who posted solid offensive numbers this season. He has good size and possesses good transition skills and a long stride. John always seems to be moving his feet allowing him to find open ice and make himself a scoring option. He has the makeup of a pro player and seems to play with a restless work ethic. Quenneville is a hard worker who plays a quick game. He's strong at moving the puck up the ice and seldom gets knocked off the puck due to his good puck protection. He finds the open spaces and has the ability to make plays with a combination of passes that are very effective. He has shown good poise and maturity with the puck and seems to be a very patient puck distributor. John does not seem to engage in high traffic areas, but has shown a willingness to battle along the boards.

John has shown flashes of his defensive game, but will need to improve this part of his game as he's struggled with consistency issues in this aspect of his game. John has developed nicely this year and is still very raw. He is a long-term project, but one with good potential.

SEASON	LEAGUE	GAMES	GOALS	ASSISTS	PPG	PIM	HP RANKING
2012/13	WHL	47	8	11	0.4	14	81
2013/14	WHL	61	25	33	0.95	71	

Raddysh, Darren
RD – Erie Otters (OHL) – 6'00" 180

Darren played a big role for the Otters despite playing in his first full season of OHL action. Darren got top pairing minutes most games with World Junior Team Canada defender Adam Pelech, and played in all game situations. Darren skates well in all directions, and maintains ideal positioning, even against speedy skilled forwards. He keeps his game very safe, simple, and doesn't get ahead of himself. He can go stretches being unnoticeable because of his defensive first mindset, and ability to consistently, and quietly get the job done. He is very vocal on the ice communicating well with his teammates. His positional play is consistently intelligent, and relevant to the play around him. On occasion he will pick his spots and jump up offensively. He is capable of skating the puck out of trouble with smooth footwork, and can rush the puck up ice. He was able to create scoring chances on the occasions he does choose to jump up, and also does a good job of opening himself up on the point as a passing option. Darren isn't a top prospect for the draft, and doesn't have ideal size for a defenseman, but his size is adequate enough to play the role of a shutdown defender. He missed the majority of the Erie Otters playoff run, which could hurt his stock a little, but he showed during the regular season to be a very reliable defensive first defenseman.

SEASON	LEAGUE	GAMES	GOALS	ASSISTS	PPG	PIM	HP RANKING
2012/13	OHL	24	0	2	0.08	2	NR
2013/14	OHL	60	3	10	0.22	27	

Ratelle, Joey
LW – Drummondville Voltigeurs (QMJHL) – 5'10" 170

In his second year in the league, Ratelle saw his role and ice time increase with the Voltigeurs. Started the year on a 3rd line, but finished on their top two lines with a regular shift on the power play. Ratelle always finds a way to get noticed, whether it's scoring a key goal or getting under the skin of the opposing team. Plays the pest role very well, as he can agitate the opposing team well while remaining disciplined. An average skater that still needs work with his starts, but we saw a nice progression from last year skatingwise. Not the most skilled player with the puck, but he's very tenacious and will take the puck to the net as much as he can. Loves to get his nose dirty, whether it's in the corners or in front of the net. On the power play, he plays likes a Brendan Gallagher in front of the net, making life harder for the opposing goaltender. Knows his role well on the power play and he's willing to take the beating that comes with it. A good forechecker who love to finish his checks. Ratelle's vision is lacking a bit, as he doesn't find his teammates quickly enough and has tunnel vision, only seeing what is in front of him. To continue to play this type of game in the pro ranks, he will need to keep getting quicker and a lot stronger. Doesn't have the ideal size to play this game at the pro level but he has a big heart. Ratelle played his midget hockey with College Antoine-Girouard and was a second-round pick by Drummondville (31st overall) in the 2012 QMJHL Draft.

SEASON	LEAGUE	GAMES	GOALS	ASSISTS	PPG	PIM	HP RANKING
2012/13	QMJHL	63	7	13	0.32	63	NR
2013/14	QMJHL	67	21	14	0.52	87	

Rehill, Ryan
RD – Kamloops Blazers (WHL) – 6'03" 213

Ryan is a physical defender that plays a very simple game. Ryan has pro size and knows how to use it. Throughout the year he has been punishing his opposition with crushing hits and tenacious defensive play. He has a good stick and rarely seems to lose a one-on-one battle. Ryan makes a good first pass, but can be overly keen to use the glass instead of making finding an outlet. Ryan is a decent skater who has shown good foot work, his skating has allowed him to rush the puck and jump into the play. That being said, he could use some help with his first few strides along with his skating in transition. You cannot teach size and toughness and Ryan has both. He's a tough kid who is not afraid to drop the gloves or come to the aid of his teammates. At times, his aggressive play can lead to penalties and he will need to learn when to engage the play or when to let the play develop. Rehill's strong, physical style makes him a player of interest as a later round pick as teams crave the game he plays.

SEASON	LEAGUE	GAMES	GOALS	ASSISTS	PPG	PIM	HP RANKING
2012/13	WHL	46	0	3	0.07	104	135
2013/14	WHL	72	4	15	0.26	182	

Reich, Kevin
G – Dubuque Fighting Saints (USHL) – 6'01" 198

Coming over from Germany, Kevin played 28 games with the Saints, including seven playoff games. Previously, he has represented Germany at the U17, U18, and most recently at the 2014 World Junior Championships.

He is a decent sized body at 6'1" and almost 200 pounds, and he has really good athleticism. He has a habit of letting in a softie here and there, but came up big for the Saints numerous times in his starts. Kevin's really strong in tight at point blank range and when he's down on the ice he doesn't move, he holds his ground well and doesn't give up his net. He maintains good positioning and likes to challenge shooters. Many times he was Dubuque's best penalty killer.

Quotable: "He struggles to get across his net, lateral movement struggles would kill him in the NHL." – Mark Edwards

SEASON	LEAGUE	GAMES	GAA	SV%	W	L	SO	HP RANKING
2012/13	DNL	14	1.63	NA	NA	NA	NA	206
2013/14	USHL	21	3.02	0.897	10	7	0	

Reinhart, Sam
RC – Kootenay Ice (WHL) – 6'01" 183

Sam is an excellent two-way player and has shown he can play a complete game at both ends of the ice. Sam seems to do everything well and makes it looks effortless at times. He has a very powerful release on his shot and has ideal positioning in the offensive zone, always finding some open ice and utilizing it to his advantage. He is capable of beating defenders one on one but isn't an overly flashy player. He can sometimes very quietly start producing points simply out of his calm, poised demeanor and hockey sense with and without the puck. He is also effective dishing the puck to the streaking forward of threading the needle in tight for a back door goal. Both offensively and defensively Sam can be very dangerous every shift. Sam has proven to be the guy you always want on the ice in critical situations and has shown he can play consistent every night at the junior level.

He has adopted the mindset of playing the 200ft game and he has shown to be extremely responsible in all areas of the ice. What makes Reinhart stand out from most prospects is his exceptional anticipation, he reads the play so well and seems to be a very good opportunist as well, with his uncanny ability to make something happen when there is no play to be made. His intelligence stands out and he is always seems to be steps ahead of the play.

Sam has good leadership abilities and a very high compete level. He also possesses a nice blend of poise, maturity, and a high hockey IQ. He will tenaciously battle for the puck in all situations and is not afraid to work the corners and fight for space in the dirty scoring areas. Reinhart needs work on the strength and speed aspects of his game. While he is highly intelligent, he doesn't possess top notch speed. He also needs to add weight and strength. His lack of strength impacts his ability to battle along the walls and his ability to win faceoffs.

Sam presents a lot of attributes that would be intriguing and desired by many NHL teams coming into this year draft. Sam has the ability to step into pro hockey as soon as next season, and start making an impact which is a great convenience for whoever selects him.

Quotable: "He would scare me a bit to take at the top. He plays a bit too much of a perimeter game for me." NHL Scout

Quotable: "Sam is so smart in the offensive zone. He is able to read the play two steps ahead of his opponents and as a result, the puck seemingly follows him around. He shows good maturity and leadership and will become a focal piece for the team that drafts him." – Scott McDougall

Quotable: "He is easily my number one overall." – NHL Scout

SEASON	LEAGUE	GAMES	GOALS	ASSISTS	PPG	PIM	HP RANKING
2012/13	WHL	72	35	50	1.18	22	2
2013/14	WHL	60	36	69	1.75	11	

Renaud, Alexandre
LW – Sarnia Sting (OHL) – 6'04" 214

Alex is a former 2nd round selection of the Sarnia Sting and now has two seasons under his belt in the OHL. He hasn't developed quite the way he was expected to, but he has massive size on the wing. He has been very up and down in the past season. He is most effective when using his size and finishing his checks. He hits opponents hard and is capable of over powering some opponents along the wall. He has also faired moderately well when choosing to drop the gloves and is capable of getting his team going.

His skating has shown some improvement in regards to top speed but his acceleration and overall skating ability is not very strong at the moment. He also lacks effective offensive ability and has his best opportunities to produce offensively when cycling the puck and going to the net creating a disruption in the slot. While his size and physical play makes him a potential prospect that projects as a bottom six forward, his play has been drastically inconsistent and can go multiple games without playing a physical style of hockey which at this point of his career is the only way he has been able to be effective for his team.

SEASON	LEAGUE	GAMES	GOALS	ASSISTS	PPG	PIM	HP RANKING
2012/13	OHL	63	1	3	0.06	22	NR
2013/14	OHL	46	2	3	0.11	30	

Revel, Matt
RC – Kamloops Blazers (WHL) – 5'11" 177

Revel split time between Saskatoon and Kamloops this season after being traded midway through the year. Matt is an average size forward who has good speed but is not an elite skater. He possesses a decent combination of skill and awareness. He moves the puck very well with a pass first mentality and accurate passing ability. He's not overly physical and does not seem to play with any type edge. His play was inconsistent at times and didn't play with any type of urgency or compete level. He would battle for loose pucks but seemed uninterested in winning the battles although at times he would outwork his opposition. His defensive game was okay, not overly impressed with his defensive positioning. Matt has some potential but needs to improve many aspects of his game and play with more of a compete level.

SEASON	LEAGUE	GAMES	GOALS	ASSISTS	PPG	PIM	HP RANKING
2012/13	WHL	61	7	12	0.31	18	NR
2013/14	WHL	73	15	30	0.62	18	

Ritchie, Nick
LW – Peterborough Petes (OHL) – 6'03" 229

Nick Ritchie is a very large power forward who just completed his 3rd OHL season. Ritchie is a player we ranked 7th overall in our pre-season rankings based mostly on potential and on what we saw when he was at his best. Nick played some his best hockey ever this season. While he still had some bouts with consistency issues at times, they were fewer and farther between than in his previous two seasons.

Ritchie was a dominant force at times this season. He played a power forward game but mixed in his skill. Nick is blessed with a huge frame, his skating could be considered excellent given he weighs in at 230 pounds. He is far more than just a big forward though. He has one of the best wrist shots in the draft, it's hard and accurate with a quick release. He is also a smart hockey player. He reads plays all over the ice, has great hockey sense and anticipates developing plays quickly. He doesn't get enough credit for his playmaking ability, probably because he has had so little talent playing with him during his career in Peterborough.

While he probably isn't a future Selke award winner, he is far from a liability in his own zone. He wins battles and is adept at starting the breakout. He took away lanes and used his anticipation skills to take away opponents options. His biggest weakness might be some laziness at times applying back pressure coming back into his own zone. He played a ton of minutes every single game, if he was going to glide, that's probably when he would choose to do it.

Ritchie also impressed us by intimidating his opponents. He ran over players like Ekblad and won fights versus some of the leagues best. He hits hard, he hit to hurt opponents and he was successful on many occasions. He caused turnovers by being productive with his physical game. He separated his man from the puck in the true sense of the word.

Nick projects as a top six power forward in the NHL. He is one of the most NHL ready prospects in this draft. He blends size, strength, scoring ability and a mean streak into his game. We expect him to be off the board by pick number 8.

Quotable: "What happens if you put Dal Colle on the Petes and Ritchie on Oshawa this season?" – NHL Scout

Quotable: "He is a beast, did you see that fight in the Oshawa game?" – NHL Scout

Quotable: "Dal Colle or Ritchie? Who do you take? I go Ritchie." – NHL Scout

Quotable: "I take Ritchie over Reinhart." NHL Scout

Quotable: "Ritchie finally got some talent down the middle (Garlent) to play with and he showed a little bit of what he could do. Can you imagine what he could do on a wing in the NHL with a top-flight center? He can score, he hits a ton, gets in opponents faces and gets under their skin and I love that he can play downright nasty at times. He enjoys contact, you can't teach that." - Mark Edwards

SEASON	LEAGUE	GAMES	GOALS	ASSISTS	PPG	PIM	HP RANKING
2012/13	OHL	41	18	17	0.85	50	5
2013/14	OHL	61	39	35	1.21	136	

Robinson, Brandon
LW – Kitchener Rangers (OHL) – 6'03" 216

Brandon is a big power forward for the Rangers who spent the past two and a half seasons with the Brampton/North Bay Battalion before being dealt to the Rangers early this season. The change of scenery appeared to go well for Brandon before missing six weeks due to a severed tendon in his wrist. Over the last three seasons in the OHL Brandon's play has been very much inconsistent for us. He shows flashes of puck protection ability, and a very powerful shot, which has been without question his best asset. However, he doesn't always use his size to his advantage, and can sometimes shoot from low percentage areas or at the chest of the goaltender. He has a very shoot first mentality, and can get his shot off quickly. Brandon's physical game is also highly inconsistent. He has lowered some solid checks, but generally when the physicality picks up in a game Robinson does not apply himself nearly enough. A team could select Brandon later in the draft based off of size, shot, and potential, but he would be considered a project that has a long way to go before reaching his potential. The potential to be a late bloomer is certainly in Robinson, but the compete level simply has to improve on a game-by-game, and shift-by-shift basis for this to happen.

SEASON	LEAGUE	GAMES	GOALS	ASSISTS	PPG	PIM	HP RANKING
2012/13	OHL	62	17	17	0.55	29	NR
2013/14	OHL	40	7	9	0.4	28	

Rod, Noah
RW – Geneve Jr. (SUI) – 6'0" 188

We really like Rod. He was fantastic in Finland at the U18 playing with Fiala and Malgin, he was the perfect compliment to their skill. He's big and knows what he is. He created space and was very effective shift after shift. Destroyed Glover with a hit right through his chest in the USA game to start the tourney. Our evaluation is pretty basic but that's just what Rod is, a simple player who played great on the PK, competes hard all over the ice and plays big. He's very good at his job.

Quotable: "Rod is the type a player that scouts would've noticed very quickly with the way he played at the U18 this year. He was impressive in every viewing." - Mark Edwards

SEASON	LEAGUE	GAMES	GOALS	ASSISTS	PPG	PIM	HP RANKING
2013/14	SWI Jr,A	31	16	21	1.19	58	39
2013/14	NLA	28	1	2	0.11	8	

Rosdahl, Kim
LW - Malmo Jr. (SWE JR.) – 6'2" 187

He impressed us with his gritty game, he mixes it up taking the body any chance he gets. First note we wrote on him was 'hits a ton'. Skating isn't pretty, takes a short stride but he still seems to manage to 'get there'. Big kid who plays big but skating will hold him back a bit. Reminded us a little bit of a weaker skating poor man Jacob de la Rose.

Quotable: "Saw him recently at the U18 and he was hard to miss because of his high compete level and the sheer volume of hits he made." - Mark Edwards

SEASON	LEAGUE	GAMES	GOALS	ASSISTS	PPG	PIM	HP RANKING
2013/14	U20 S.Elit	42	10	10	0.48	48	149
2013/14	SHL 2	12	0	0	0	0	

Sadowy, Dylan
LW – Saginaw Spirit (OHL) – 6'01" 180

Sadowy has improved miles in his second season in the OHL with Saginaw. He possesses a good combination of size, and speed. He is a powerful skater who is smooth, and will use this ability in both directions. He is a true 200-foot player who does a great job in all three zones. Dylan backchecks very hard every time. He pressures for turnovers skating back, and gains decent positioning in the defensive zone to get his stick in lanes. He will need to react a little quicker in regards to gaining his positioning, as he can start out a little out of place in relevance to where he needs to be. He isn't afraid to block shots, and we have witnessed a wealth of shots that Dylan didn't hesitate to get in front of. Because of his defensive zone prowess he was a key contributor to the Spirit penalty kill. Offensively is where Dylan's game saw its biggest improvement. He uses his speed to beat defenders wide, but also has the ability to win some one-on-one match-ups on the rush. He is willing to drive towards the net, and has a very shoot first mentality. He gets plenty of pucks on net, and due to his huge improvement in the shooting department, he was able to pick his spots, and fire a powerful and accurate shot on goal. When he doesn't have the option to take the puck in he is comfortable getting pucks deep, and going into the corner. His forecheck pressure is relentless, and can take away time, and space. Dylan doesn't project to be a top line player at the NHL level, but he brings a lot of things to the table, which teams value highly, especially during NHL playoffs. His game projects very well at the next level in a few areas, which makes him a valuable selection for the 2014 NHL Entry Draft.

Quotable: "Dylan really emerged as one of the best two-way forwards in the 2014 NHL Draft class. He has the speed and skill to chip in offensively but always takes care of his own end. Very projectable for the pro game." - Ryan Yessie

SEASON	LEAGUE	GAMES	GOALS	ASSISTS	PPG	PIM	HP RANKING
2012/13	OHL	61	2	6	0.13	45	41
2013/14	OHL	68	27	9	0.53	69	

Sandhu, Tyler
RC – Everett Silvertips (WHL) – 5'10" 170

Tyler is a small forward who possesses good speed and quick feet, he is shown to have some offense aspects to his game. His style of play is typical to a grinder and is willing to get physical and aggressive around the corners or along the boards to gain possession of the puck.

He is another player willing to play in the dirty areas of the ice to create scoring chances for himself or his teammates. His skill set is average and will need the round out his passing and shooting to be a more affective offensive player. Throughout the first half of the season he has shown he can be very dangerous off the rush when using his speed to create scoring chances. His defensive game is average and he uses his speed to close the gap quickly to cause turnovers and possesses a decent stick when defending his passing lanes. Tyler has a good understanding of both sides of the puck but needs the round out his skill set to become a complete player.

SEASON	LEAGUE	GAMES	GOALS	ASSISTS	PPG	PIM	HP RANKING
2012/13	WHL	62	19	14	0.53	12	NR
2013/14	WHL	49	13	17	0.61	10	

Sanheim, Travis
LD – Calgary Hitmen (WHL) – 6'03" 189

Sanheim has been on an accelerated upward trend all season. Sanheim made the Hitmen as a bottom-pairing defenseman that struggled with consistency early on. He has shown flashes of apparent upside, but was thought of as a long-term prospect requiring much development time. While he will still require some time to adjust to the pro ranks, Sanheim's progress this season has been staggering and he was able to move from being a fringe roster player into roles where he was able to contribute as an impact player for both the Hitmen and for Team Canada at the U18s.

Despite only managing 3 points through the end of November, Sanheim showed the ability to jump into the play and create offensively. With the assurance that his partner (fellow 2014-eligible player Ben Thomas) was there to back him up, Sanheim grew more confident in his abilities and was consistently making good reads in support of the offensive zone play. He picked his spots well on when to pinch, when to carry the play up ice, when to support the rush and by the end of the season, he was almost automatic to making the right play. To complement Sanheim's great offensive zone reads were his excellent rangy size and good skating. While he needs to fill out, Sanheim uses his length to his advantage in protecting the puck, and his good mobility makes him a threat on the powerplay. He often was able to walk the puck along the blue line looking for an opening to put a wrist shot in on net.

Defensively, Sanheim still has his challenges in front of him. While he has the right tools to make plays, he struggles with consistency and those decision-making skills that are so good with the puck on his stick, can fail him at times when he is on the defence. At times his stick isn't always as active as you'd like to see, and he can be prone to losing his man in front of the net. He generally does well in the corners as far as winning puck battles, but his positioning can leave him vulnerable to giving up a lane to the net. Travis' strong play late in the season has really allowed him to showcase his talents at the right time and that could result in him vaulting into a potential first round selection at the 2014 NHL Entry Draft.

Quotable: " I think he's a top 30 pick." NHL Scout

Quotable: " Great interview at the Combine." NHL Scout

Quotable: " One of our best interviews (at the Combine) NHL Scout

Quotable: " I had a long discussion with our Calgary based scout about Sanheim when I got home from Finland. Basically I told him that I won't be surprised if Travis becomes the better player in the long term than Fleury. It's not a slight on Fleury because I like him. I just think Sanheim has a ton of room to get even better whereas Fleury is already closer to his ceiling. - Mark Edwards

Quotable: "Travis came out of nowhere this year to become one the top players available for the upcoming draft. He showed constant improvement throughout the season. By the end of the year, he was picking his spots wisely and really driving the play offensively. I really like his high-end potential." - HP Scout Scott McDougall

SEASON	LEAGUE	GAMES	GOALS	ASSISTS	PPG	PIM	HP RANKING
2012/13	MMHL	43	12	23	0.81	44	16
2013/14	WHL	67	5	24	0.43	14	

Sanvido, Patrick
LD – Windsor Spitfires (OHL) – 6'05" 219

Sanvido has always been a giant, going back to his Bantam, and Minor Midget AAA days. Sanvido has seen moderate improvements in his skating ability, but really hasn't made the progression we were hoping he would over the past few seasons. He is uncoordinated, but seems aware of it, and will make the safest play with the puck when he's under consistent forecheck pressure. Overall, he is a below average puck mover, and will pass up smarter puck plays in favour of the safest play. He is strong, and moderately physical with effective board play, but doesn't own much of a mean streak. He can, however, intimidate some opponents due to his massive size.

Sanvido's defensive zone coverage improved. He has particularly done a great job in the slot making sure he clears opponents from the area, but also allows his goaltender to see the play on the penalty kill. He does a good job getting his long reach into passing lanes, and was pretty effective in the shot blocking department. Patrick still has a long way to go, but possesses the potential of a big shutdown defenseman. Big defenders can sometimes go higher in drafts than expected in hopes that he will pan out. This could be the case with Sanvido, but he could also end up going unselected. He has good upside, but has a lot of work to put forward before reaching this upside.

SEASON	LEAGUE	GAMES	GOALS	ASSISTS	PPG	PIM	HP RANKING
2012/13	OHL	60	0	6	0.1	40	NR
2013/14	OHL	64	1	7	0.13	82	

Scherbak, Nikita
RW – Saskatoon Blades (WHL) – 6'02" 174

Nikita's game is built around his strong skating ability, creative vision, slick hands, and his offensive creativity. A left-shooting RW for the Blades, Nikita is offensively savvy and possesses a good hockey IQ. Scherbak skates very upright and uses his body exceptionally well to protect the puck. His lower-body strength and posture make him look quite large despite the fact that he is actually smaller than listed. Nikita is an excellent skater who is very mobile with good agility.

While Nikita is a skilled Russian-import, he had no trouble accounting for the gritty WHL style of play. He is not easily deterred and isn't afraid to play in the dirty areas of the ice. He shows an exceptional willingness to engage in physical play with a high compete level when battling for pucks at both ends of the ice. Nikita will use his quick agility to evade body contact along the boards combined with the slick hands and vision he is able to set up good scoring chances from all angles of the ice. He's very calm and poised with the puck and does not falter under pressure. He possesses a strong shot with a quick release that drives netminders crazy.

Nikita has shown he can be very relentless on the forecheck when he wants to be. Nikita is a strong offensive player who'll need the round out his defensive responsibilities and start to develop a defensive aspect to his game and play with a more consistent effort in the coming years.

The ability to operate in traffic using smarts, size and skill make Nikita very valuable and should result in him being a first round pick at the 2014 NHL Entry Draft.

Quotable: "I love the kid but we won't draft him...if that makes any sense." NHL Scout

Quotable: "He's going to be anywhere from 10th to 2nd rounder, he's a top 10 talent though." NHL Scout

Quotable: "I doubt we take him. I heard all the he's not the average Russian stuff but he's still a Russian." - NHL Scout

Quotable: "I really like this kid and he was difficult to rank. We acted as if we were an NHL team and the Russian factor dropped him a bit for us. I wouldn't be totally shocked if he slipped to the 2nd round but I think he's too good and will hang on." - Mark Edwards

Quotable: "Is he a one year wonder?" - NHL Scout

SEASON	LEAGUE	GAMES	GOALS	ASSISTS	PPG	PIM	HP RANKING
2012/13	MHL	50	7	7	0.28	14	14
2013/14	WHL	54	26	43	1.28	28	

Schierhorn, Eric
G – Muskegon Lumberjacks (USHL) – 6'00" 183

The Anchorage, Alaska native started his USHL career with the USNTDP, playing in limited action last season and after three games this season, left the program for Muskegon and had a strong season with the Lumberjacks.

With decent size, Schierhorn looks big in net. He is an aggressive goaltender, liking to come out and challenge shooters often and cutting down the angles. His angles are always solid and he always seems to be in the right position in his net. Really athletic, quick glove. His reaction time and quickness are impressive. Adept at making the second and third save, which on the one hand is a positive attribute, but on the other it speaks to his occasional issues with rebound control. Really good on breakaways and point-blank chances in tight. Aggressive poke-checker. He came up large for the Lumberjacks this season and was a big reason they were within one point of a playoff spot at the end of the season. He makes the big saves at the big times. As of this writing, Schierhorn remains uncommitted and is slated to return to Muskegon next season.

SEASON	LEAGUE	GAMES	GAA	SV%	W	L	SO	HP RANKING
2012/13	MWEHL	17	3.01	0.893	NA	NA	NA	NR
2013/14	USHL	40	3.21	0.905	20	17	1	

Schmaltz, Nick
RC – Green Bay Gamblers (USHL) – 6'00" 172

The younger brother of Jordan, drafted by the St. Louis Blues 25th overall in the 2012, Nick very well might be one of the most talented player in the entire draft.

It seems the bigger the games, the better Nick plays. He represented Team USA at both the Ivan Hlinka Memorial Tournament and the World Junior A Challenge this season, netting eight points in five games and 12 points in four games, respectively.

Nick's skill level is truly elite. He does everything at top speed, and his top speed is every bit as fast as anyone in this draft, if not faster. He is extremely agile, can shift and change directions on a dime, and none of these feats are slowed or hindered when he has a puck on his stick. He keeps defenders off balance and trying to guess or anticipate what he is going to do with the puck, and with his vision, intelligence, playmaking ability, and elite shot, it's simply impossible to do that. It's as if the puck is on a string attached to his stick blade. He has so much control of the puck when handling it, and has the skill to literally do anything with it. To top it off, he's cool as ice. He's never panicked, never rattled, he just always smooth and collected and seemingly is always able to do whatever it is he wants to do with the puck. Patience in spades.

As eluded to earlier, Nick has truly elite and little-matched vision. One play in particular sticks out this season where he was needling his way through the neutral zone with the puck on his strong side. He crossed the offensive blue line and slowed his pace and drew the defenseman and trailing forward to him, and the opposite defenseman had started to drift toward him as well. He made a tight little curl, drifted a few feet, gave a couple of stick handles and then threw a perfect backhanded saucer pass over all of their sticks to a streaking line mate of his who went in all alone on a breakaway and scored. The play perfectly encapsulated what Nick is capable of all in one play; speed, hands, control, vision, skill. Defenders are constantly guessing and his ability to skate all over the ice with the puck often leads to mass confusion in coverage and he either exploits that himself and takes advantage of the empty space for a quality scoring chance or finds a teammate wide open and sets them up. He also draws more penalties than any player I have viewed. Players have no choice but to hook, trip, hold him, or just cross-check him out of frustration. There is nothing he can't do offensively with the puck on his stick.

On the defensive side of the puck he also excels; when he wants to. He causes a lot of turnovers with his quickness and positioning and ability to sneak up on opposing puck carriers. He doesn't shy away from the physical game and will finish checks and stay on assignments, and generally is good away from the puck with his positioning and willingness to help out and support his defensemen and wingers. The downside to his game is that these things don't always happen. He has moments where he will loaf a bit and not get as involved in the dirty work as he should. There will be a board battle and instead of supporting and trying to dig in and help, he will sit back and wait for the puck to come and let someone else do all the hard work. He can get lazy and lackadaisical with the puck in his own end, and often times it's lead to turnovers and the puck winding up in the back of his own net. His International play is dominant, so it goes to show how much more he could be capable of at this level if that effort level was always there.

Nick is a high end talent who will likely go in the first round. He has the potential to boom or bust based on his style of game. While he's not huge, he has a really strong, wide based stride and skates low to the ice. In addition, he's so agile and nimble that he can elude most anything that comes his way, and he will likely fill out his frame a bit over time. He is one of the more interesting prospects in this draft and one of the harder ones to project just given the aforementioned unknowns. He is slated to attend the University of North Dakota this Fall, but it's worth remembering that the Windsor Spitfires own his OHL rights

SEASON	LEAGUE	GAMES	GOALS	ASSISTS	PPG	PIM	HP RANKING
2012/13	USHL	64	18	34	0.81	15	28
2013/14	USHL	55	18	45	1.15	16	

Schmalz, Matt
RC – Sudbury Wolves (OHL) – 6'06" 210

Despite being selected in the first round of the 2012 OHL Priority Selection Draft, Schmalz has never really lived up to the seemingly unfair hype of a first round selection. While he had great size, he wasn't a big impact player in Minor Midget, and struggled to make the adjustment to the OHL.

Now with a second year under his belt he has improved, but again not at the rate in which we were hoping. First and foremost, Schmalz has tremendous size at the centre position. He is capable of generating speed but his footwork is a major struggle, and affects him in battles at times due to a lack of balance. When he is able to maintain balance he is effective in battles on the wall. It appears his mind hasn't caught up with his body just yet, as there were plays where he seemed to read it correctly, but didn't react quickly enough to be effective. Matt was very effective on the second unit powerplay going to the front of the net creating traffic, and becoming a practically unmovable object out front. He isn't overly physical, but he does finish his checks. Matt has been above average in the face-off circle. While he has some potential long-term, he has a lot of work ahead of him before being considered an NHL Draft Eligible prospect.

SEASON	LEAGUE	GAMES	GOALS	ASSISTS	PPG	PIM	HP RANKING
2012/13	OHL	49	4	6	0.2	13	NR
2013/14	OHL	66	3	5	0.12	60	

Schmidt, Logan
RD – Kitchener Rangers (OHL) – 5'11" 169

Logan joined the Rangers after going undrafted two seasons in a row. He started the season going back and forth from Kitchener Jr. B Dutchmen, and the OHL Rangers before sticking full time with Kitchener. By the end of the season Schmidt was their most reliable offensive threat from the blueline. Logan was a consistent presence in our viewings with great skating, and puck rushing abilities. He is capable of skating the puck out of trouble, and taking it end-to-end when necessary. He makes quick, intelligent passes in all three zones, and despite his rookie status, he handled pressure fairly well on most occasions. He was susceptible to getting too casual or over confident with the puck at times, which resulted in some risky, and avoidable turnovers. From the blueline Schmidt showed a good low deflectable shot. Defensively he did a much better job than expected due to an excellent stick. He is very tough to beat one-on-one because he is consistently effective knocking the puck off sticks, and handles speed very well in one-on-one battles. He does, however, struggle containing big power forwards who are able to protect the puck and drive the net. His lack of size and strength is Logan's biggest concern moving forward. While 5'11" isn't that small, it is still a concern at the NHL level for a defenseman who doesn't possess high-end talent. He also needs to add a fair amount of muscle onto his frame in order to be successful against bigger, and stronger opponents. He is a hard worker defensively while possessing strong skating ability, and good offensive talent. He could hear his name called later on at the 2014 NHL Entry Draft.

SEASON	LEAGUE	GAMES	GOALS	ASSISTS	PPG	PIM	HP RANKING
2012/13	GOJHL	30	2	8	0.33	0	NR
2013/14	OHL	58	2	23	0.43	12	

Schoenborn, Alex
RW – Portland Winterhawks (WHL) – 6'01" 195

Alex is a power forward who possesses good size and a strong mix of skill. Despite limited production, there is good offensive potential with Alex's game, which should be exposed as he gets more ice time on a deep Winterhawks team next season. Combined with his size and strength, he is able to develop time and open up space to create scoring chances for himself and teammates. Alex tends to find himself in the dirty areas of the ice looking to pounce on a rebound then scoring flashy highlight goals. His hands in tight are good and he's strong on the puck with good protection. Alex has a strong three shot combination and is able to release a quick, hard accurate shot on net from most scoring angles.

Has good abilities to make plays under pressure and delivers clean passes in all three zones. Important aspects for a guy that is a complimentary offensive player is that he needs to create space, help out defensively, and not turn over the puck – all things of which Alex does well. Alex does well to use his body to aid him in protecting the puck and he realizes that the game is more easily played when your team has the puck than when chasing it. He plays a physical game and has a strong compete level battling for puck possession along the boards. His defensive game and awareness is good. He has a strong ability to box out the player and take the play to the boards. Alex has shown an active stick to shut down the passing lanes and uses his body to block shots. He is calm with the puck in the defensive zone and will use the boards to chip the puck out then force an unwanted play that leads to puck turnovers. His overall skating is decent, has shown to possesses some speed to his game, but his overall quickness will need to improve. There is a lot to like in Alex's game and he looks to be a Top 9 forward with versatile enough skills to allow him to be plugged in all over the lineup.

SEASON	LEAGUE	GAMES	GOALS	ASSISTS	PPG	PIM	HP RANKING
2012/13	WHL	20	1	1	0.1	22	88
2013/14	WHL	72	18	18	0.5	121	

Serebryakov, Nikita
G – Saginaw Spirit (OHL) – 6'00" 170

Nikita is playing his second season in North America after coming over from Russia in the 2012 CHL Import Draft. Serebryakov was effective in a backup role for the Spirit, and saw a lot of action this year despite backing up one of the best goaltenders in the OHL in Jake Paterson. Nikita does a very good job of cutting down shooting angles, and challenging oncoming forwards. He possesses good reflexes, and gets in front of shots. However, he gives up more rebounds than usual, and many of them wind up in the slot, which is where he gets into trouble. Many of the goals he has scored against him come off of rebounds, and he can sometimes let one bad goal turn into two bad goals by overcompensating after a costly mistake. Nikita has provided some big game performances in our viewings, most notably the Gold Medal Game at the 2012 World U17 Challenge where he stood on his head, and stole the Gold Medal for his country. We have also seen him really struggle to get into his rhythm some games. For Nikita to reach his potential he will need to become more consistent, and be able to forget the bad goals immediately. Also, while he is quick side-to-side, he can leave his five-hole wide open which shooters have exploited on rushes. He will need to close that up while maintaining his quickness.

SEASON	LEAGUE	GAMES	GAA	SV%	W	L	SO	HP RANKING
2012/13	OHL	22	4.19	0.876	6	11	0	NR
2013/14	OHL	28	3.53	0.897	9	12	0	

Sergeev, Dmitrii
LD – Kitchener Rangers (OHL) – 6'02" 195

After a strong performance for Team Russia at the World Under 17 Challenge, the Kitchener Rangers selected Sergeev at the 2013 CHL Import Draft. His performance this season wasn't quite as effective as expected, as at times he was a healthy scratch or reduced to a limited role. The early part of the season was a struggle for Dmitrii consumed by mistakes, and lack of positional play. He did improve throughout the season but still showed he has a long way to go. He is a decent forward skater for his size, and was willing to jump up in the rush, and carry the puck. Despite his good forward skating, backwards is another story, and is an area of improvement for Sergeev along with his pivot. He is capable of making strong passes on the rush to set up offensive chances. He has good positioning at the blue line in the offensive zone, and would get back defensively with plenty of time occasionally pinching. He has some good power in his shot, but will try to force it sometimes into shin pads. Defensively he did a good job getting into passing lanes, and breaking up passes, but struggled in physical battles for the puck despite his size, some of which result in scoring chances in his own end. Dmitrii is not a player we expect to be selected at the 2014 NHL Entry Draft.

SEASON	LEAGUE	GAMES	GOALS	ASSISTS	PPG	PIM	HP RANKING
2012/13	Ural-Sib. 1996	28	4	12	0.57	30	NR
2013/14	OHL	49	2	7	0.18	22	

Sharipzyanov, Damir
LD – Owen Sound Attack (OHL) – 6'01" 208

Sharipzyanov came over to the Attack after being selected in the 2013 CHL Import Draft, and made a surprisingly quick transition to the North American game. His adjustment was facilitated by his willingness to get involved in the physical play. He finishes his checks, and is very aggressive in the slot, sometimes a little too much. He is hit or miss in battles, and can lose them, which has resulted in goals. He has good reaction time in the defensive zone, and does a fairly good job of breaking up potential chances. He is very consistent with his positioning, and regularly makes the simple play to advance the puck up ice. He also shows the ability and knowledge to use the boards to advance the puck.

Offensively he rarely pinches, but when he does he chooses smart times in which to do so. He consistently made the right play with the puck in the offensive zone. While not playing a huge role offensively he was steady in helping his team maintain puck control, and finding the open man. He played in all game situations gaining secondary roles on the penalty kill and powerplay. His skating is OK, but his balance isn't great, and even leans on his stick a little too much at times. Damir showed the potential to be selected at the 2014 NHL Entry Draft. It likely won't be until later if he is selected, but needs to improve his skating ability. He is nothing flashy, and won't be a game breaker; he is just extremely steady from the blueline.

SEASON	LEAGUE	GAMES	GOALS	ASSISTS	PPG	PIM	HP RANKING
2012/13	MHL	54	0	7	0.13	24	NR
2013/14	OHL	67	5	11	0.24	65	

Sharov, Alexander
LC – CSKA 2 (RUS Jr.) – 6'2" 187

A two-way center with legit size, after the first break of the MHL season in November Sharov produced at a point per game ratio throughout the rest of the season, playoff run included.

He is a good stickhandler who doesn't shy away from traffic, likes going to the net and getting involved. His skating may not appear to be a strength at first glance, but he will surprise you with nice acceleration through the neutral zone when the opportunity arises. The Moscow native doesn't mind the physical play, even if he could do a better job avoiding checks; reads the play well offensively to get open without the puck and is responsible defensively.

SEASON	LEAGUE	GAMES	GOALS	ASSISTS	PPG	PIM	HP RANKING
2013/14	MHL	39	8	11	0.49	42	119
2013/14	MHL	41	17	17	0.83	38	

Sheehy, Tyler
RC – Waterloo Black Hawks (USHL) – 5'09" 172

High energy sparkplug would put mildly what Sheehy brings to the lineup on a nightly basis for the Waterloo Black Hawks. After spending a brief period of time with the USNTDP to start the season, the Black Hawks were happy to have Sheehy back for the remainder of the season, which included a run all the way to the Clark Cup Final. During that run, Sheehy posted eight goals and seven assists in 12 games, having himself a fantastic playoff showing.

While not a big body, Sheehy plays with a lot of spunk and intensity, and is still rarely outmatched or outmuscled despite his smaller size. He has a stocky build and is strong in the legs, strong base. He frequently wins board battles and the body positioning battle in front of the net. High speed, high motor, just a pesky player to play against.

He isn't just work ethic, he has offensive skill to go along with his excellent workman like approach to the game. He is sneaky and excels at finding the holes in coverage and getting himself open looks at the net. He handles the puck with ease in traffic, and is slippery to defend in and around the net. He scores a lot of his goals from inside just outside the crease, but he has the ability to pick corners from further out and does that plenty, as well.

Sheehy is in his element when on the power play and having the extra time and space to work with. He generally is down low around the goal line setting up shop and is highly unpredictable and hard to defend there. His shiftiness allows him to open up passing lanes to his point-men for one-timers, or fakes to them and is able to drive the net himself. He has great patience with the puck, and never tries to force anything on the power play or otherwise.

There may not be a forward in the entire league who causes more turnovers than him. He always has his stick in the passing lanes, has great anticipation, and is always moving at top speed and limiting opposing players' options and often forcing them to make a play out of desperation which ultimately always winds up being a mistake. While sneaky offensively, he's even more sneaky defensively. One particular play that stands out is one against Green Bay in March. Nick Schmaltz was carrying the puck behind his own net, albeit casually and without much regard for his surroundings, and Sheehy made darted from the corner after him, picked Schmaltz's pocket and put it through Cam Hackett's legs on a wrap-around, all in one quick, fluid motion. It was a thing of beauty, and just one example of what Sheehy is capable of.

Sheehy obviously has things going against him as far as his NHL prospects go. Clearly, he is undersized and while he has some positive offensive attributes, he's not dynamic enough to make it on sheer offensive skill alone.

Quotable: "Skating is a big issue, so is size. Two big strikes against." – Mark Edwards

SEASON	LEAGUE	GAMES	GOALS	ASSISTS	PPG	PIM	HP RANKING
2012/13	USHS	45	28	39	1.49	8	NR
2013/14	USHL	49	21	28	1	4	

Sherwood, Kiefer
LW – Youngstown Phantoms (USHL) – 5'10" 168

Smooth skating, shifty forward plays a very similar style game as his teammate, J.J. Piccinich.. He has a really quick, accurate wrist shot, and is capable of picking corners. He plays a smart, simple game but has flashes of offensive creativity. Sherwood plays the point on the power play and does an excellent job on the back end. He has great poise with the puck, being the last man back and a forward, and has an above average slap shot.

Solid two-way player but his size can be an issue at the NHL level. His speed is an asset and while he has some offensive skill and creativity, it may not be dynamic enough at that size at that level. Sherwood is heading to Miami University in the Fall.

SEASON	LEAGUE	GAMES	GOALS	ASSISTS	PPG	PIM	HP RANKING
2012/13	MWEHL	34	28	19	1.38	10	NR
2013/14	USHL	55	13	19	0.58	31	

Shestyorkin, Igor
G – Spartak 2 (RUS Jr.) – 6'00" 183

After a forgettable appearance at the Super Series, Shestyorkin went on leading his low scoring junior team to the final for the 2nd straight year and this time ended up taking home the big prize. Whippy and competitive, he can be a whiner and often dramatizes the goals he allows, but that seems to be a posture that doesn't affect his game afterwards. Igor covers the lower part of the net very well, but goes down early and often leaves some room open in the higher part where it's usually a bit easier to beat him.

SEASON	LEAGUE	GAMES	GAA	SV%	W	L	SO	HP RANKING
2012/13	MHL	15	2.10	0.920	9	1	2	136
2013/14	MHL	23	1.42	0.947	14	5	5	

Shirley, Collin
LW – Kamloops Blazers (WHL) – 6'02" 180

Collin is a big-bodied center that possesses some raw, undeveloped skill. If given time to develop, he could become a physical two-way player. Despite his size, he does not yet always use it and he should be stronger for his size. He loves to drive the puck to the net and he has shown that he is able to with a good top speed and ability to carry the puck. He won't likely ever be a big-time scorer as his creativity is lacking. Once he adds some strength to his frame he will be a force along the boards battling for loose pucks. He has a nice shot and release. Despite this kid having a bit of a disappointing season Shirley's potential makes him a diamond in the rough for the 2014 NHL Entry Draft.

SEASON	LEAGUE	GAMES	GOALS	ASSISTS	PPG	PIM	HP RANKING
2012/13	WHL	60	9	14	0.38	20	NR
2013/14	WHL	70	14	13	0.39	26	

Siebenaler, Blake
RD – Niagara Ice Dogs (OHL) – 6'01" 190

Blake joined the Ice Dogs for his rookie season in 2013-2014 and made a very strong impression in his rookie year. On a team with pretty solid depth at the defensive position, Blake earned every second of ice he got and worked his way up to being a regular in five on five situations and the power play. His strongest ability is his speed and at 6'1" it is a huge asset to his game. He is capable of rushing the puck up ice and is generally more effective in the neutral zone as he can try to do too much in regards to skating with the puck in his own zone. He has good offensive instincts and is capable of moving the puck effectively. He also has a big shot from the point which he utilizes intelligently in different situations.

His defensive game needs to show some improvement and consistency, but didn't have too many moments where he struggled defensively. Blake is an average sized defenseman with high level skating and projects to be an offensive defenseman at the next level.

SEASON	LEAGUE	GAMES	GOALS	ASSISTS	PPG	PIM	HP RANKING
2012/13	Midget	39	9	9	0.46	22	85
2013/14	OHL	68	6	24	0.44	24	

Sleptsov, Alexey
RD – Moose Jaw Warriors (WHL) – 6'00" 165

Alexey is a good skating, two-way defenseman. He has good body positioning and while he isn't the biggest defender, he has shown good strength and defensive positioning to force his opposition outside. He often eliminates the puck-possessing forward from creating any scoring opportunities during one-on-ones. He can be very effective in shutting down the passing lanes and taking away time and space. His skating ability allows him to create the time and space to move the puck out of the zone intelligently, if there is no pass option he can be found skating the puck until a passing outlet opens up.

While the tools are present with Alexey, he doesn't always have the best awareness and can be caught flat-footed at times. He is underrated offensively and has shown a good ability to join the rush on occasion. He possesses an average shot and is able to put the puck on net through traffic. He needs to work on his release and when to shoot the puck. Alexey has a good all-around skill set and an understanding of both sides of the puck but will need to smooth out other facets of his game.

SEASON	LEAGUE	GAMES	GOALS	ASSISTS	PPG	PIM	HP RANKING
2012/13	MHL	45	0	3	0.07	26	NR
2013/14	WHL	66	4	21	0.38	44	

Smith, Hunter
RW – Oshawa Generals (OHL) – 6'06" 210

Hunter was the definition of a project in the Minor Midget ranks. While he's taken a while to develop he's turned into a true legitimate NHL prospect and while he goes from being a project at the OHL level to a project at the NHL level, the rewards could pay off for one team who takes a chance on Hunter. Battling through an array of injuries and development issues, Smith took his time over the first two years improving his areas of concerns. He always had massive size, much bigger than the opposition and he showed good puck smarts and puck handling ability but the skating was so detrimental to his game it really made him a risk. This season Hunter has broken out and really shown that potential we saw at the 2011 OHL Priority Selection Draft. His skating has come miles over the past three years, but he still has a very long way to go before getting to the point it needs to be at, just to give an idea of how far off his skating was and still is. He is big and physical and absolutely crushes opponents along the wall. He has delivered some devastating checks and strikes fear in opponents who see him coming at them. In addition to this he handles the puck fairly well for a big guy and also protects it when driving the net as a nearly unstoppable object. He is more of a shooter than a passer and doesn't really possess much in terms of passing skills. Hunter competes in all three zones but needs to continue putting a ton of effort into the improvement of his skating because it will in all likelihood be the determining factor in whether or not Smith has an NHL career ahead of him.

Quotable: "Multiple teams told me he was their best interview at the combine." - Mark Edwards

SEASON	LEAGUE	GAMES	GOALS	ASSISTS	PPG	PIM	HP RANKING
2012/13	OHL	30	0	1	0.03	22	54
2013/14	OHL	64	16	24	0.63	100	

Smith, Jake
G – North Bay Battalion (OHL) – 5'11" 183

Smith is by no means a big goaltender, but what he lacks in size he makes up for in agility, and athleticism. Playing in North Bay he rarely had to steal games, but he stole a couple in the Battalion's 4-2 series win over the Barrie Colts. At times he's vulnerable high in the net when in the butterfly because his lack of size, but thanks to his speed, and athleticism he's often able to recover before he can be taken advantage of. He's really flexible, and does a good job taking away the bottom half of the net. His rebound control is good for the most part, and he has a good, quick glove. He is vulnerable high blocker at times.

Smith is a confident goaltender, and can handle the puck when he needs to, as well. He likely won't be selected in the 2014 NHL Draft, but if he could grow another inch or two, and continue to improve his positioning, he could make an NHL team look good for giving him a chance.

SEASON	LEAGUE	GAMES	GAA	SV%	W	L	SO	HP RANKING
2012/13	OHL	20	2.57	0.891	9	6	0	NR
2013/14	OHL	42	2.52	0.904	23	12	4	

Sodestrom, Linus
G - Djurgarden Jr. (SWE Jr.) - 6'3.5" 187

As time progressed and we got more viewings, we began to sour on Sodestrom. Too many soft goals just starts to affect our faith in him as a potential NHL goaltender. While we don't see this as an exceptionally strong goalie class, it would still be a stretch for us to pull the trigger on him in the draft. In the end, it seems to us that mental toughness, including concentration issues will plague him. Not someone we would draft.

SEASON	LEAGUE	GAMES	GAA	SV%	W	L	SO	HP RANKING
2012/13	J18 Allsv	11	1.90	0.933	NA	NA	NA	208
2013/14	U20 S.Elit	23	2.61	0.915	NA	NA	NA	

Spinner, Steven
RW – Eden Prairie (HS-MN) – 6'00" 196

Steven has decent size and combines it with good speed. He plays with a ton of energy and is willing to compete shift in and shift out. He can however get caught running around a little too much. He is a threat to score every time he jumps on the ice at the high school level but will need to prove this ability at the next level. His hockey sense is a bit of a concern for us as he doesn't read and react quickly enough to the play going on around him. Steven is slated to join the University of Omaha-Nebraska in September 2014.

SEASON	LEAGUE	GAMES	GOALS	ASSISTS	PPG	PIM	HP RANKING
2013/14	USHS	45	24	35	1.31	66	175
2013/14	USHL	11	2	3	0.45	14	

Spinozzi, Kevin
LD – Sarnia Sting (OHL) – 6'02" 201

Kevin joined the Sting around the trade deadline in a move that sent him from the Sault Ste. Marie Greyhounds to the Sting. He is a big physical defenseman who plays with a bit of an edge and regularly finishes his checks. He consistently makes the intelligent first pass up ice and while he displays very little offensive ability he is capable of regularly making the safe smart play whether that entails protecting the puck and skating up ice then getting it deep or finding an open teammate under pressure to advance the play. His board play is good and he displays good strength and is able to contain on a regular basis. His skating is a concern as he can generate average speed but his stops and starts along with his direction changes drastically need improvement as this is generally the way forwards are able to beat him the majority of the time. Increased quickness will make a huge difference in how difficult he is for opposing forwards to beat. His one on one play has been drastically hit or miss as he is capable of taking the body and is effective using his stick but can get caught trying to force a physical play one on one. Some very skilled forwards are able to get inside on him too easily. He displays good initial positioning in the defensive zone and is usually in the right place, but can sometimes chase a hit slip out of position over time. He shows some promise in lesser credited areas like staggering behind his defensive partner and always making sure he is open as the safe option for a pass, always having defense on his mind and playing well over thirty minutes in his third game in three nights. Kevin is not a defenseman who will put up great points likely at any level of hockey, but if he can improve his skating, pivoting and general footwork, this should help him in all the areas he has concerns as he has pretty close to a pro ready frame already.

SEASON	LEAGUE	GAMES	GOALS	ASSISTS	PPG	PIM	HP RANKING
2012/13	OHL	22	0	2	0.09	31	NR
2013/14	OHL	69	5	17	0.32	60	

Stadel, Riley
LD – Kelowna Rockets (WHL) – 5'10" 162

Riley is two-way defenseman who will jump into the rush and create scoring chances. Riley tends to make decisions quickly, and seems to make the right plays with the puck. The first thing you will notice about Stadel is his first pass out of the zone - he moves the puck with purpose and his first pass is flat and crisp most of the time. He tends to get the attack going quickly for his team, handles the puck well under pressure, and has the ability to make a stretch pass. Outside of moving the puck, much of Riley's game needs work. He is an above average skater who is decent in the transition. His first few steps however will need to improve – especially considering he is already an undersized defender that will need quickness to compensate for lack of reach. Riley has decent top speed, but takes him some time to reach it. His footwork around the corners is good, but his lateral movement needs to improve so he can control the shifty players. Defensively, Riley's game in his own zone is okay. He stays patient and seems to adjust to the flow of the play - he is rarely ever caught out of position due to a poor read. As mentioned above, he can improve with his quickness, as he tend to get beat off the wall to the slot and scoring areas from time to time. At the WHL level, Riley has shown an ability to recover with his good defensive positioning and skating, however he will be challenged to handle NHL forwards in the same manner. He has a good stick to knock away passes and shots. Riley definitely needs to work on getting size to compete with bigger players. While he does have a good compete level and won't back down from opponents, it will be critical for him to continue to develop his offensive game, explosiveness and strength in order for him to play at the next level.

SEASON	LEAGUE	GAMES	GOALS	ASSISTS	PPG	PIM	HP RANKING
2012/13	WHL	49	2	9	0.22	21	161
2013/14	WHL	63	10	25	0.56	62	

Stefano, Anthony
LC – Peterborough Petes (OHL) – 5'10" 177

Despite being a little undersized, Anthony showed great energy and fearlessness when it came to competing against bigger players. He wanted to be the first guy into the corner and was willing to take the hit to make the play. He competes and battles regardless of the opposition and won more than his share of battles. He skates well and provides a great top speed which really helps him in puck races. He also showed some solid offensive upside at very least for the junior level putting up good stats on the third line. He has excellent power in his shot and can get the puck top shelf in a hurry. He also showed flashes of good puck handling ability which should be intriguing as he develops further.

SEASON	LEAGUE	GAMES	GOALS	ASSISTS	PPG	PIM	HP RANKING
2012/13	GNML	33	36	63	3	40	NR
2013/14	OHL	65	15	20	0.54	22	

Suter, Pius
LC – Guelph Storm (OHL) – 5'10" 151

Suter is a Swiss imported center from the Guelph Storm. Used primarily in a depth forward role, Suter showed considerable improvement and development as the season progressed. Starting in a 4th line role, he eventually played himself into the 3rd line center role while filling in admirably in injury situations. Pius was extremely effective on the penalty kill using a combination of speed and relentlessness to force turnovers and bad decisions even getting rewarded with a few short-handed goals throughout the season. Standing at about 5'10" Suter keeps himself out of trouble with a combination of speed and excellent vision. While not afraid to get hit or go to the dirty areas Pius generally does not go out of his way to initiate contact although he has shown that he is willing to stand in front of the net to capitalize on garbage goal opportunities. In the offseason Pius would benefit from adding some strength to his frame. He is very shifty and showed improved offensive instincts as the season progressed, filling in for Fabbri at one point on the first line due to injury. He is excellent at puck pursuit and has very quick feet catching opposing defenders off guard with an unexpected burst through the neutral zone.

SEASON	LEAGUE	GAMES	GOALS	ASSISTS	PPG	PIM	HP RANKING
2012/13	SWI Elite Jr.A	33	12	9	0.64	14	NR
2013/14	OHL	66	9	15	0.36	16	

Sweeney, Jacob
LD - Moncton Wildcats (QMJHL) - 6'04" 212

A late bloomer this year, Jacob Sweeney has been one of the few bright spots on the Wildcats defensive squad. He shows some pretty decent physicality in his own end along the boards and in front of his net, but we would like him to be meaner in his coverage. He sometimes loses battles because of his lack of toughness. Sweeney uses his stick really well to knock the puck off the opposition on their rush and held the offensive zone nicely to get a cycle going in the offensive zone. He has improved on his footwork, which now allows him to have more time to move the puck up out of his zone and to be better on one-one-one confrontations. However, it's still a work in progress if he want to succeed at the next level. He can skate pretty decently going forward and backward for a big guy and his play with the puck has been improved as well. Sweeney is calm and patient with the puck and can get his shots through to the net from the point. His breakout pass can occasionally be all over the place, but it was on tape most of the time on most of our viewings.

The 1995 born defenseman is strong on the puck, protects it well from the opposition's pressure and moves it around pretty nicely in the offensive zone. He faced opposing top lines on a regular basis this season and he did a good job while doing so. He is smart enough to play within his limits this season on both ends. His smarts and his size made him attractive enough to get significant attention from our scouts. He is on the verge of becoming one of the best defenders in the QMJHL next season.

SEASON	LEAGUE	GAMES	GOALS	ASSISTS	PPG	PIM	HP RANKING
2012/13	QMJHL	63	2	5	0.11	14	NR
2013/14	QMJHL	68	3	25	0.41	57	

Sweezey, Billy
RD – Noble & Greenough (HS-MA) – 6'00" 192

Billy is a strong physical defenseman who split time this year Noble & Greenough School and Cape Cod Whalers U18 team. Billy shows limited offensive upside but plays with a real mean streak. He is physically strong and loves to finish his checks. He hits hard and displays a lot of strength along the wall winning more than his share of battles. He is at his best when he sticks to his role as a shutdown defender and takes care of his own end. He cean get into trouble when he tries to make plays with the puck and generally needs to make the smart simple play in order to limit his mistakes. Billy is slated to join Yale University in September 2015.

SEASON	LEAGUE	GAMES	GOALS	ASSISTS	PPG	PIM	HP RANKING
2012/13	USHS	27	1	8	0.33	NA	NR
2013/14	USHS	28	8	20	1	NA	

Tait, Ryan
RC – Omaha Lancers (USHL) – 5'10" 181

The speedy southern California forward was drafted 192nd Overall by the Tri-City Americans in the 2011 WHL Bantam Draft, but opted to go the USHL route and will be joining teammate Hayden Hawkey at Providence College next season.

Tait is an absolute burner. World class speed, and he loses none of that speed with the puck on his stick. Super shifty, can make moves on the dime, with hands equally as crafty, combined with this speed and excellent hockey sense, Tait has the potential to be a dangerous sniper going forward as he continues to develop.

Not a big player but has decent size and plays a big game. Very strong, packs a lot of power and with his speed carries a lot of force which he uses on opposing puck carriers. He likes to hit and likes the physical game. Good shot blocker, always in position in the defensive zone. Tenacious on the puck, causes turnovers often. Intelligent player, good decision maker and always gets the puck out of his own zone. Hard on the fore check and pesky to play against.

Offensively gifted with speed and hands, he also possesses an above average wrist shot. He's really good at taking the wrister while in full stride, and if often fools goaltenders because they aren't expecting it and don't see it coming. I recall a game specifically against the USNTDP U18's, Tait was burning to the outside along the boards and beat the US defenseman wide, and while his quick feet were striding and crossing over, just as he approached the faceoff dot he just rifled a lightning quick wrister and completely fooled Minney in goal. It actually wasn't a great goal to give up, but is a prime example of Tait's ability to have goaltenders caught on their heels. Very elusive and deceptive, he can lull defenders into him and then explode with his first step and turn the burners on, passing them right up. Despite not being an overly big body, he plays with no fear.

He's not afraid to camp out in front of the net and get dirty, and collected a lot of goals and assists chipping away at rebound and tips on shots. Really heads up player, excellent vision and awareness. Really smart and just all around crafty. He's able to find line mates and set them up well, gets himself open to support them. He has excellent feet, not only in foot speed but he's really adept at using his feet to catch the puck if a pass is thrown there and kicking it up to himself. Many at this level can do that, but not many can do it in stride without a missing step like Tait. Just a really fun, spark plug type player that's a lot of fun to watch.

SEASON	LEAGUE	GAMES	GOALS	ASSISTS	PPG	PIM	HP RANKING
2012/13	USHL	56	3	15	0.32	2	NR
2013/14	USHL	59	16	13	0.49	28	

Thomas, Ben
RD – Calgary Hitmen (WHL) - 6'02" 193

Ben is a steady shutdown defender that has started to develop a knack for opportunistic goals throughout the season. Ben shows good gap control and uses his body well to shield opponents away from rebounds. He has good size and he uses his reach and weight well both along the boards and in forcing opponents to the outside. He is a good skater with good agility and top speed. He has just an average first few steps and could stand to improve in that area.

While he makes his mark in his reliable own zone play, Ben moves the puck very well. He also started learning to read the offensive play well enough that he knows when to sneak in from the far end of the play sniffing for rebounds and loose pucks near the far side hashmarks. For Ben to be a defense-first defender at the next level, he needs to develop more of a mean streak. He does not always stand up for himself or teammates as much as you'd like and can be outright disinterested in physical play at times.

SEASON	LEAGUE	GAMES	GOALS	ASSISTS	PPG	PIM	HP RANKING
2012/13	AJHL	44	5	3	0.18	37	87
2013/14	WHL	72	7	24	0.43	39	

Thomas, Jared
LC – Sioux City Musketeers (USHL) – 6'01" 190

Committed to the University of Minnesota-Duluth next season, Thomas potted 60 points on 19 goals and 41 assists in his final USHL season. Thomas was also named as an Alternate Captain this season. A bit of a late-bloomer, Jared came on strong this season after having a solid 2012-2013 campaign. Really good offensive instincts, finds the soft spots in the offensive zone well; really sneaky. Excellent wrist shot, very accurate, gets it off quick. Really creative with the puck, good at backing defenders off and creating space, protects the puck well with his body and has good, quick bursts in tight. Crafty passer, finds the holes really well. Has a lot of "seeing eye" passes. Manages to find team mates open in situations where you wonder how he managed to know they were there at ice level. Great playmaking ability. Good length, strong hands. His size and skill combo make him a potentially potent goal scorer as his career progresses.

Plays a sound defensive game. Backchecks hard, responsible in his own zone. He has a few too many blue line-area turnovers for my liking. Has a habit of trying to beat defensemen one on one instead of chipping the puck out of the zone and going after it, but all in all, not a liability defensively and effort is usually there.

Thomas does have moments within a game where he can be kind of loaf and coast around. Compete level is in question at times. Happens more on a game by game basis than in-game.

When he's on, he's on, and the effort is there for the whole game. When he's off, the effort is off the whole game and it leaves you wanting more.

Jared's size and skill set make him worthy of a later round pick, but he just as easily could be a guy to keep an eye on as a free agent option when his college career comes to a close. I like his offensive upside, would just like to see more consistency in his game.

Quotable: "Very good speed, very good puck skills." HP Scout Sean White

SEASON	LEAGUE	GAMES	GOALS	ASSISTS	PPG	PIM	HP RANKING
2012/13	USHL	59	18	23	0.69	39	NR
2013/14	USHL	58	19	41	1.03	70	

Thrower, Josh
RD – Tri-City Americans (WHL) – 6'01" 200

Listed on NHL Central Scouting's final draft ranking. Josh is an average-sized defender who tends to play a gritty physical game. Josh does not make good decisions when handling the puck. He takes unnecessary chances with the puck in his own zone which can be either very effective or caused turnovers. He's a decent skater but will need to improve his speed and transitioning game. He's slow to transition when playing the forward one-on-one and has shown he can be beat wide by players with speed. He always seems to be patrolling the ice looking for that big open ice hit, to the point it is a fault as he'll go way out of his way to make contact. He does not shy from the physical play and will engage the battles along the boards. He needs to play with a more active stick and take away the passing and shooting lanes. Thrower's offensive game has stalled. The pitbull mentality and physical play are both highly coveted traits and Josh has the potential and raw talent to be a physical shutdown defender if he can show some all-around improvements along with more consistent play.

SEASON	LEAGUE	GAMES	GOALS	ASSISTS	PPG	PIM	HP RANKING
2012/13	WHL	37	1	3	0.11	46	NR
2013/14	WHL	62	2	4	0.1	89	

Tkachev, Vladimir
LW- Moncton Wildcats (QMJHL) – 5'8" 163

Tkachev only joined the Moncton Wildcats in January after a long negotiation between the Wildcats and his Russian team. He was chosen 39th overall in the 2013 CHL Import Draft after a strong showing at the 2013 U-18 World Championship, where he racked up 11 points in 7 games. Tkachev can play both wing positions and can really do some special things with the puck on his stick, as he did during the Subway Super Series, scoring a highlight-reel goal against Team QMJHL. A little wizard with the puck that loves to have the puck on his stick and has eyes around his head. Loves to go back deep in his zone to take control of the puck and start the rush from there. He does that often on the power play, as Moncton didn't have a lot of good puck movement coming from the back end this year. His vision and smarts are top notch, he sees things on the ice that not many players can see and can make some incredible passes on the power play.

The Russian winger his physically immature and will need time to get stronger before making the jump to professional hockey. After joining the Wildcats in January, he really brought another dimension to the team and was dynamic playing alongside Ivan Barbashev. In the first half of the season, it was tough offensively for Barbashev as he didn't have anyone who could play at the same level as him.

Tkachev had an immediate impact for Barbashev and the Wildcats. Both Russians have great on-ice chemistry dating back to the 2013 U-18 World Championship, and it seems like they always know where the other is on the ice. Like a lot of Russian forwards, he likes to challenge defensemen one-on-one and has a great variety of dekes that can make opposing defensemen look foolish. However, at times he can try too much and those end up in turnovers going the other way.

Although he's a smallish forward, Tkachev doesn't shy away from the tough areas of the ice, as he scored many goals this year from 5 feet from the net. Liked his compete level as well. He was probably following in Barbashev footsteps, but Tkachev can surprise the opposing team with some hits on the forecheck. Unlike Barbashev, though, his size gives him limitations of what he can do physically. As he got stronger, I expected his shot to get stronger as well, but as of now he needs to be close to the net to score. Adding a powerful shot to his repertoire would make him an even more dangerous threat going forward.

Quotable: "Had a great look at him in the first round of the playoffs against Blainville-Boisbriand and was very impressed by his skill level, but also his will. He battled hard all series long and scored some big goals for the Wildcats. Size is an issue, but you can't teach his vision and playmaking abilities." - HP Scout Jerome Berube

SEASON	LEAGUE	GAMES	GOALS	ASSISTS	PPG	PIM	HP RANKING
2012/13	MHL	47	13	22	0.74	20	72
2013/14	QMJHL	20	10	20	1.5	16	

Tornqvist, Henrik
RW – Linkoping (SWE) – 6'1" 165

Tornqvist is a big winger with decent feet who has a great shot. He's a good compliment to skilled linemates as he works hard and plays a good team game. Not without some skill as he shows the ability to get away good shots, including off the rush. He plays physical and wins puck battles. He jumps all over loose pucks wining races. He would be a later round pick if he is selected.

Quotable: "Scored a goal at the U18 after going wide with a backhand to the short side." - Mark Edwards

SEASON	LEAGUE	GAMES	GOALS	ASSISTS	PPG	PIM	HP RANKING
2012/13	U20 S.Elit	15	4	3	0.47	2	152
2013/14	U20 S.Elit	40	5	7	0.3	30	

Tryamkin, Nikita
LD - Avtomobilist (RUS) - 6'7" 229

Eligible for the third time, this year Tryamkin was able to showcase himself at the U20 WJC and at 6' 7" he probably didn't go unnoticed. A full time KHLer by now, what makes him an interesting prospect is the way he can move around the ice his 230 pounds. There is certainly room for improvement on his footwork and his skating looks awkward at times, but overall he is very mobile for a player of his size. Along with strength and great reach, he possesses a hard slapshot that he can get off pretty quickly.

SEASON	LEAGUE	GAMES	GOALS	ASSISTS	PPG	PIM	HP RANKING
2012/13	MHL	28	8	10	0.64	58	NR
2013/14	KHL	45	1	6	0.16	38	

Tuch, Alex
RW – USNTDP (USHL) – 6'03" 216

Tuch is a rare blend of sheer, hulking size, speed, and skill. While skilled in his own right, Alex does a lot of the dirty work. He battles hard in the corners and in board battles for the puck, plays really hard on the forecheck and always is aggressive. He uses his big body to protect the puck well and he creates a lot of offensive chances for that line at the ground level.

Aside from doing the dirty work, Tuch has some offensive flair of his own. He possesses excellent vision, and for a big body he has really good speed and agility. Combining his skating capability with his sheer size and strength, he can bull and power his way to the net for scoring chances. Tuch has a nose for the net and is no stranger to driving hard to it with or without the puck. Always a physical presence, he's extremely difficult to defend against. He has an excellent wrist shot with a great release.

Tuch plays a physical game and has some nastiness in him. It will be interesting to see how he adapts to playing against more players who are his size or close to it. Often, even in the USHL, he is a man amongst boys. He plays an emotional game, and sometimes that gets the best of him. He is prone to taking over-aggressive and retaliatory penalties. He will need to learn to keep his emotions in check and not take bad penalties.

Tuch has a chance to be the first USNTDP player taken in the 2014 NHL Entry Draft this summer. His attributes are a rare combination. Players in the skilled power forward mold who can skate like him don't come around very often.

Quotable: "I love his blend of size and skill. Some NHL scouts have told me they think he lacks skill but I disagree. He remind me a bit of Max Pacioretty" - Mark Edwards

SEASON	LEAGUE	GAMES	GOALS	ASSISTS	PPG	PIM	HP RANKING
2013/14	USHL	26	13	19	1.23	36	11
2013/14	(U18)USDP	61	29	35	1.05	70	

Turgeon, Dominic
LC – Portland Winterhawks (WHL) – 6'02" 196

Dominic is a strong two-way player who has shown a good understanding of both his offensive and defensive areas of responsibilities. He is a very fluid skater with good size and decent compete level. Dominic has excellent skills in the faceoff circle and has been counted on to win key face offs in all situations. He is not a very flashy player but seems to play a very consistent game in all three zones. Has shown to possess some offensive potential, his good size and skating allows him to gain space and set up scoring chances or battle for loose puck in the crease. Dominic has decent vision and hands. He protects the puck well. Dominic has shown a strong compete level and is calm when making plays under pressure. His strongest asset is his abilities to win face offs and use his size to create time and space for his line mates. Dominic plays a very sound defensive game, he has shown to possess a good understanding of his defensive areas of the ice. He is strong down low and uses his size to box out his opposition and force them to the outside, he uses his stick to take away the passing lane and his good defensive positioning and pressure on the puck carrier tends to lead to turnovers for his team to pounce on.

Quotable: "He's a riser for us." - NHL Scout

Quotable: "Among the numerous young Winterhawks, it was Turgeon that seemed to impress me most down the stretch. He has good size and reads the play well too.

He lacks the high-end offensive game, but there's no doubt that his skills translate to the next level and he still has good upside." - Scott McDougall

SEASON	LEAGUE	GAMES	GOALS	ASSISTS	PPG	PIM	HP RANKING
2012/13	WHL	54	3	5	0.15	2	113
2013/14	WHL	65	10	21	0.48	31	

Ustaski, Matt
LC – Langley (BCHL) – 6'05" 209

After a solid rookie season with the Langley Rivermen last season, Matt really elevated his game this season and showed the ability to contribute offensively on a regular basis. Matt has massive side at centre and is very effective in the slot battling for space and dominating defenders at this level. He is able to pick up several garbage goals due to his positioning and makes lives difficult for goaltenders trying to see the shot. In addition to this, Matt has good power in his shot and can beat goaltenders. Matt is physical but doesn't possess a huge mean streak and generally keeps it within the rules of the game. Ustaski will be joining the University of Wisconsin this September 2014.

SEASON	LEAGUE	GAMES	GOALS	ASSISTS	PPG	PIM	HP RANKING
2012/13	BCHL	55	11	16	0.49	38	173
2013/14	BCHL	54	29	20	0.91	30	

Valentine, Dallas
RD – Moose Jaw Warriors (WHL) – 6'03" 195

Dallas is a tall, slender defenseman. He has proven to be effective on the penalty kill and is willing to sacrifice his body when the situation calls for it. Valentine does well to clog up passing lanes. Defensively, he competes hard and often wins puck battles along the boards. He has good defensive positioning and as the season went along he appeared to get more ice in key defensive situations. The one area I would like to see Dallas improve is his gap control. He has the skating ability to give a little less space and step up with a good check or use his stick to cause a turnover. Dallas shows good mobility on the point and mixes that with good passing ability. He will rush the puck if the decision calls for its. He is an average skater who doesn't possess that explosive extra gear and could improve in this department. He moves the puck fairly well and has a decent point shot and is all around reliable in all situations, but doesn't really standout in the skills area.

SEASON	LEAGUE	GAMES	GOALS	ASSISTS	PPG	PIM	HP RANKING
2012/13	WHL	13	0	1	0.08	4	194
2013/14	WHL	69	3	11	0.2	44	

Vanier, Alexis
LD - Baie-Comeau Drakkar (QMJHL) - 6'05" 214

Selected 13th overall in the 2012 QMJHL Draft by the Baie-Comeau Drakkar, Vanier took great steps on his way on becoming a bona fide hockey player. Last year, his coach barely used him in the playoffs and he is now getting regular even-strength ice time, and PP time as well. He was the only QMJHL defenseman named at the BMO Top Prospects Game. He has a booming shot that hits the net often. Most of the time, his slapper is low and hard, which makes it tough to stop for goaltenders. That explains why his point totals went up drastically this season. He likes to play aggressively and to force plays. In his case, it can pay off sometimes.

When he tries to establish himself as a tough dude along the boards, he can get caught out of position when he is facing agile skaters. He needs to make better decisions in those situations, thus playing within his limits. In all of our viewings, he's been good playing one-on-one as he plays the man accordingly. That wasn't necessarily the case last season. His long reach is also helpful in his zone, as he covers plenty of space. It allows him to keep his opponents on the outside. Vanier also has a mean streak that is well-known among Q players. He's clearly not afraid to get in scrums after the whistle and we never saw him back down from anybody. He also likes to rush the puck and because of his large frame, he is successful. Vanier is a good straight-line skater for a big guy, but he does not have the required skating level to get back at times when he forces a rush or when he gets caught not moving his feet. Most of his breakouts come from using the windows, but we saw an improvement in his decision-making. The St-Constant native had a shoulder injury that kept him out of the QMJHL playoffs. He clearly won't get recognized as a quarterback, but Vanier has sure progressed enough to find his niche in the first three rounds of the 2014 NHL Draft.

SEASON	LEAGUE	GAMES	GOALS	ASSISTS	PPG	PIM	HP RANKING
2012/13	QMJHL	53	0	8	0.15	66	75
2013/14	QMJHL	61	15	21	0.59	52	

Vanko, Alec
LD – Chicago Steel (USHL) – 6'02" 185

2012 Draft Eligible, Vanko came on strong the second half of the season. Spending the previous season with the Janesville Jets of the North American Hockey League, this was Vanko's first season in the USHL. He is committed to Minnesota State University next year to begin his collegiate career.

Vanko is a rock solid defender with some offensive upside. He makes no mistakes in his own end, and while he fits more of the stay-at-home defenseman mold, his 29 points in 50 games points to more offensive potential down the line. He has good size and uses it. Always finishes his checks. He is an intelligent player, always make the good, safe first pass to get out of his own zone, but has the ability and vision to hit the home run stretch pass to spring forwards on a breakaway, which he did a number of times this season. Knows how to pick his spots for that and other offensive chances. He knows how to sneak in behind coverage in the offensive zone for backdoor-type plays. Good skater with a smooth stride and smooth feet, moves well laterally and in transition. Maintains good gaps, has a knack for anticipating passes and jumping the passing lanes in all zones. Just a rock-solid defenseman. Maybe a bit of a late-bloomer but worth a late-round pick or eventual free agent look out of college.

SEASON	LEAGUE	GAMES	GOALS	ASSISTS	PPG	PIM	HP RANKING
2012/13	NAHL	36	1	16	0.47	48	NR
2013/14	USHL	50	9	20	0.58	68	

Verbeek, Ryan
LW – Kingston Frontenacs (OHL) – 6'00" 188

Ryan was traded to the Frontenacs from the Windsor Spitfires early on this season. Verbeek's game is taylor made for a checking line role. He's not huge, but he is very strong, and finishes his checks with authority. He hits hard every opportunity he gets, and doesn't look off opportunities to take the body. He provides a good forecheck, and is a pretty good skater allowing him to pressure opponents on the forecheck that much better.

In addition to his checking abilities, he shows underrated offensive ability handling the puck well, challenging defenders in one-on-one situations, and has a very powerful shot. He likes to open himself up in the offensive zone, and make himself available for shots. Verbeek is a physical player who understands his role, and can chip in a little bit offensively. This should make him a valuable pick later on in the 2014 NHL Entry Draft.

"Ryan has a lot of value because he knows who he is and plays within that role. He's one of the most consistent checkers in the entire OHL and has a shot to go with it." - Ryan Yessie

SEASON	LEAGUE	GAMES	GOALS	ASSISTS	PPG	PIM	HP RANKING
2012/13	OHL	49	3	5	0.16	41	116
2013/14	OHL	43	12	12	0.56	29	

Virtanen, Jake
LW – Calgary Hitmen (WHL) – 6'01" 210

Jake is a right-shooting forward that has played all three forward positions this season. Virtanen predominantly played wing and does project best as a winger as he is able to get the most out of his tremendous speed there. Jake is a physically punishing forward with exceptional top-end speed and good footwork. He is one of the very elite prospects this year in terms of skating. He possesses a lightening quick first step which allows him to pull away from opponents very quickly. His agility and top speed often catch opponents flat-footed. When combined with his dogged determination of driving to the net and goal-scoring areas, it is easy to see why Jake was able to score over 40 goals this season. His speed and size is very effective in overpowering defenders which makes him almost impossible to contain in all three zones. He does not shy away from contact and actually often initiates it even if he's the puck carrier. He is quick to be involved in post-play scrums as it is usually his over-zealous play that drives opponents crazy. His soft hands and big frame has allowed him to score a lot of goals inside the circles this year. He has a very heavy wrist shot that he loves to use from anywhere in the offensive zone. He also has a big slapshot. His accuracy is generally okay, but can vary as he likes to take shots from impossible angles, off stride, etc…

He is an aggressive power forward who likes to make plays at top speed and always seems to be in overdrive. His strong stick-handling skills and speed allows him to control the puck though traffic and beat most defenders 1-on-1 on any given night. His high compete level and physical play has created havoc in the battle areas all year for defenders.

While Jake possesses almost everything you want from a prospect, he needs to improve on a few aspects. The first is that he is starting to learn that he needs to use his teammates better. Because he's always had success in creating offense by himself, he can be prone of trying to take on too many people at once. This can result in some turnovers that can be costly in transition. His inability to use his teammates may just be a learning thing, but looks to also be a result of some selfishness and tunnel vision. Jake had a spurt of a few weeks where he was using teammates consistently and he became extremely potent to defend against, however we'd like to see him to do that with more consistency. Finally, Jake needs to learn to think the game at as high of a level as he plays it. Very few people can skate the way he can and if he can learn to think it at that top speed, it'll be something to behold. Jake can be outright dominant at times offensively with his blend of size, skill and speed. He has the potential to be a dynamic power forward with an excellent scoring touch.

Quotable: "Jake is one of the most electrifying players you'll see in junior hockey. A tremendous skater that is able to accelerate away from opponents. He loves the physical play and has made numerous highlight reel checks. When he's on his game, there's a lot to like.

I do have some concerns as to how well he sees the ice and whether he'll ever be able to think the game as quick as he plays it. That being said, I've also seen him for stretches where you can't help but think that the sky is the limit for this kid."
- HP Scout Scott McDougall

Quotable: "First time I ever saw him, he was one of the worst players on the ice because of a lack of effort. The very next game he stepped it up and was the best player on the ice." - Mark Edwards

Quotable: "I thought he did some good things at the U18 in Finland. He made me feel more confident that he can succeed at the next level. - Mark Edwards

SEASON	LEAGUE	GAMES	GOALS	ASSISTS	PPG	PIM	HP RANKING
2012/13	WHL	62	16	18	0.55	67	18
2013/14	WHL	71	45	26	1	100	

Vrana, Jacub
LW/RW – Linkoping (SWE) – 5'11" 185

It seems like we have been watching Vrana for a very long time because he played on the Czech national team as a double under-ager. He is now just weeks away from his NHL Draft day and he finished on a high note after a strong performance at the World U18 in Finland back in April.

Vrana has fantastic speed that he uses effectively through the neutral zone and into the offensive zone. He has great hands and likes to show them off dangling around defenders. Much like Kevin Fiala (as an example) we like the way Vrana can make plays and think the game at high speed. He can dazzle with the puck to beat defenders but will also make the simple chip play to put the puck past defenders and then use his speed to gain possession. Vrana can score. He has a lethal shot that is accurate and he also includes a great one timer in his bag of tricks. He makes good choices on shot selection and anticipates the movement of both goalies and defenders well. He does a great job of not telegraphing his shots. His hand eye is very good, he uses great stickhandling skills along with quick feet to buy himself time to make plays. We have seen him complete some elite passing plays showing high-end vision and a great hockey IQ.

His play without the puck on his own side of the red line can leave you wanting more at times. While Vrana is effective pressuring the puck with his speed on the forecheck., he's not all that spectacular in his own zone. Most of his problems are due to mental breakdowns or a drop in his compete level. While his effort meter reads high on the offensive side of the game, he shows lapses in the defensive game.

Vrana is not afraid to win some pucks in one on one battles and he generally competes ok in this regard. It's obvious he understands the game and is not a dumb player. He will however try to do too much on his own at times when he has options to move the puck. Vrana is an offensive minded forward who will most likely need to crack the top six to stick in the NHL.

Quotable: "He is our top Euro." NHL Scout

Quotable: "He was awesome in our interview." - NHL Scout

Quotable: "Gave us agent prepared scripted answers to our questions." - NHL Scout

Quotable: "I expect him to go in the 20-25 range." NHL Scout

Quotable: "I wouldn't touch him until the 2nd round." NHL Scout

Quotable: "I think North American scouts like him more than most Euro based scouts do." - Euro NHL Scout

Quotable: "I loved him at the U18 in Brno, thought he was average at best in Sochi and then he played really well this year with the exception of one game where I thought he was just o.k." - Mark Edwards

SEASON	LEAGUE	GAMES	GOALS	ASSISTS	PPG	PIM	HP RANKING
2013/14	U20 S.Elit	24	14	11	1.04	26	30
2013/14	SHL	24	2	1	0.13	2	

Walcott, Daniel
LD – Blainville-Boisbriand Armada (QMJHL) – 5'11" 168

Walcott is a dynamic defenseman who came out of nowhere this season after playing last season with Lindenwood University in the ACHA before joining the Armada prior to this season. His best asset is his skating abilities, as he loves to rush the puck in the offensive zone and brought another dimension to the Armada's transition attack with his great speed. He makes good decisions with the puck and he logged a ton of ice time for the Armada. After only 15 games in his major junior career, he was chosen to represent the QMJHL at the Super Series vs Team Russia.

The 1994-born defenseman is not the biggest on the ice, but he's very strong on his skates and tough to knock off them. He protects the puck very well both in the defensive and offensive sides of the game. Can be a dangerous open-ice hitter thanks to his great skating abilities; he possesses great lateral agility that helps him be all over the ice. He's a great athlete but at times can get caught in the neutral zone trying to be too aggressive. He needs to pick his spots better physically. You can see Walcott make a good play deep in his own zone and will start an end-to-end rush all the way to the opposing net. He has a nice, smooth skating stride.

We loved his work on the PK where he showed tons of nice attributes; his anticipation is second to none. He reads the play very well and makes good work of his active stick, breaking plays and blocking passing lanes. Even on the PK, he won't hesitate to go towards the offense if he sees a good scoring opportunity. Can be overmatched down low in his zone versus bigger forwards but we love his compete level and he won't back down from a challenge. He thrives playing versus the opposing team's better forwards. A perfect example was a game against Halifax where he was matched up versus Drouin and Ehlers. He made sure to play physical on them every time they were on the ice. He's tough to beat one on one; he always keeps a good gap control and doesn't give much room to opposing forwards to make plays. He has great footwork, which allows him to adjust and change directions quickly.

His slight frame is a concern for us, how much bigger will he get is a big question mark. At the junior level he's fine, but once he turns pro that could hurt him. Quarterbacking the Armada power-play all year long, he sees the ice well and makes good decisions. He also has a good, accurate slapper from the point. We like his poise with the puck and his ability to remain very calm under pressure. Walcott usually played with Nikita Jevpalovs on the point, and those two really developed a nice chemistry on the powerplay, working on set plays where Walcott would set up Jevpalovs for one-timers.

Quotable: "Our Montreal based scout told me to pay attention to him on my first visit to Blainville this year, I was impressed. Walcott made smart decisions with the puck and he is a great skater. I liked that he didn't make any mental mistakes." - Mark Edwards

Quotable: "Our staff has mixed feelings on him, I really like him but not everyone thinks he is draft worthy." - NHL Scout

Quotable: "Saw this kid many times this season and very few times did I come away unimpressed. He can change the momentum of a game in various ways. He can provide offense, he can defend, and plays with an edge." - HP Scout Jerome Berube

SEASON	LEAGUE	GAMES	GOALS	ASSISTS	PPG	PIM	HP RANKING
2012/13	ACHA	33	4	9	0.39	30	91
2013/14	QMJHL	67	10	29	0.58	71	

Wallmark, Lucas
LC – Lulea (SWE) – 6'0" 176

We ranked him last year just outside the top 100, he slipped through the draft but excellent playing for Sweden at the World Jr Championship this past year. He is an excellent playmaker with fantastic hands, able to create time and space for his teammates with deft stick handling along the boards. He has a good shot but tends to look for a passing option first. He's a good back checker and has a good understanding of his defensive zone responsibility. Where he's limited is with his skating. He's agile in the offensive zone with good starts and stops, but in open ice he's slow-footed and awkward, limiting his ability to carry the puck up ice, forecheck, and back-check.

Quotable: "Had a great year but skating is still his issue." - Mark Edwards

SEASON	LEAGUE	GAMES	GOALS	ASSISTS	PPG	PIM	HP RANKING
2013/14	SHL 2	11	1	7	0.73	6	125
2013/14	SHL	41	3	7	0.24	2	

Walman, Jake
LD – Toronto Junior Canadiens (OJHL) – 6'1" 175

Walman is an elite skilled defender from the Toronto Junior Canadiens. Jake is currently committed to play NCAA hockey at Providence College. He shows poise with the puck in all areas of the ice especially when being pressured in the defensive zone. Jake has the skating ability to skate himself out of trouble while also leading the offensive rush whenever he gets the opportunity. He makes hard crisp passes and is constantly looking to jump into the rush as the high trailer. He has a very smooth skating stride and almost makes it look effortless at times to step around the opposition. Jake also displays a heavy shot from the blue line and is good at walking to the middle of the ice to open up shooting lanes and get shots through traffic. He is the powerplay quarterback and shows good vision and understanding of puck movement in the offensive zone. He can sometimes appear a little to nonchalant in the defensive zone which allows aggressive attackers to force him into bad reads. While his passes are hard he sometimes struggles with accuracy and needs to work at hitting his teammates in stride.

While very offensive, Walman is also not afraid to get dirty and does not back down from anyone in the defensive zone and in front of the net. He actively uses his stick to dish punishment to opponents that attempt to set up in front of him. Walman would benefit from adding some weight to his frame in order to help physically down low against bigger players at the next level. Walman had an extremely impressive season in the Ontario Junior Hockey League; he has all the tools to be successful at the next level whether it be the OHL or the NCAA. He should look to hear his name in the early-to-mid round at the upcoming draft.

Quotable: "We got good feedback from his interviews at the combine. Teams told me he was up front and very honest. He got better with every one of our viewings this season." - Mark Edwards

SEASON	LEAGUE	GAMES	GOALS	ASSISTS	PPG	PIM	HP RANKING
2012/13	GTHL	23	3	9	0.52	11	55
2013/14	OJHL	43	7	26	0.77	87	

Walsh, Jared
RD – Mississauga Steelheads (OHL) – 5'11" 172

Jared is slightly undersized for the defensive position and relies on his smooth skating ability to make an impact for his team. Jared is a solid puck rushing defenseman with a smooth stride and evades checkers in the neutral zone with the puck. He also displays good mobility. He has a laser release on his wrist shot from the point. He likes to pinch from the point quite often but can be a little dangerous with this at times. He moves the puck well and benefits in all three zones due to a good reaction time. Jared was very hit or miss in the defensive zone. In one on one match-up's he is very aggressive which has garnered mixed resulted. He is at his best when using his stick in these situations but despite his good skating ability, his timing on his pivots one on one needs to be refined. He struggled in 2 on 1's seemingly not knowing how exactly it should be played. This happened multiple times and did result in goals and scoring chances against. He played on the penalty kill and did an admirable job for an offensive defenseman. He blocks shots and gets on loose pucks clearing them down the ice very well.

One major concern for the slightly undersized Walsh, he can get outmuscled and get hit hard regularly. His lack of strength and his knack for exposing himself to big hits are a little concerning long term. Walsh has a moderately good chance of being selected and shows potential as a puck rushing defenseman.

SEASON	LEAGUE	GAMES	GOALS	ASSISTS	PPG	PIM	HP RANKING
2012/13	OJHL	49	4	17	0.43	24	NR
2013/14	OHL	66	5	16	0.32	14	

Watson, Matthew
RD – Kingston Frontenacs (OHL) – 5'09" 170

Matthew missed the majority of the season with a knee injury, but before this occurred he looked very good in limited action. He is a smooth skating defenseman capable of rushing the puck up ice, and does so intelligently. He is an offensive defenseman who has a powerful wrist shot, and slap shot from the point. He controls the puck well using his speed to buy time if an option doesn't present itself. Defensively, however, was a different story. Watson is adequate positionally but the concern is getting outmatched, and out muscled by much bigger opponents. He also struggled one-on-one on a regular basis despite his skating ability. Watson isn't expected to be selected at the 2014 NHL Entry Draft, as he really hasn't gained enough experience at the OHL draft nor does he have the size at the defensive position for the NHL. That is not to say he won't be able to one day reach that goal, but it will be an uphill battle, and he will need to continue to develop in the OHL before being considered for the NHL Draft.

SEASON	LEAGUE	GAMES	GOALS	ASSISTS	PPG	PIM	HP RANKING
2012/13	GOJHL	45	11	8	0.42	42	NR
2013/14	OHL	30	2	5	0.23	13	

Watson, Spencer –
RW – Kingston Frontenacs (OHL) – 5'09" 170

Spencer put together a very impressive rookie season in the OHL last year. We expected him to continue this trend entering his second season and playing a key role. He got off to a great start at the Ivan Hlinka camp in July, and had one of the most impressive performances in camp. Unfortunately he wasn't able to maintain this high level of performance on a game-by-game basis, and has had many highs, and lows in his game this season.

Spencer is an excellent skater with explosive acceleration and a great top speed. If he can beat the defender one-on-one he's very dangerous on the breakaway. When he's on his game he's also very good at handling the puck through traffic. He is capable of opening himself up for chances in the offensive zone, and can fly under the radar and get into good scoring position. He is fairly one-dimensional and for the most part is strictly a speedy skilled offensive forward. He has a shoot first mentality, and has a deceptive shot with good accuracy.

Watson may not go as high in the draft as his skillset suggests. If he makes the NHL it would have to be as a top-six forward because he doesn't possess the style, mindset or the size to play a bottom-six role. This brings a little risk to his selection, and labels him as a boom or bust prospect for the NHL. If this doesn't happen Spencer should still continue to be an outstanding junior player, and will get his chance if not in the NHL then elsewhere.

SEASON	LEAGUE	GAMES	GOALS	ASSISTS	PPG	PIM	HP RANKING
2012/13	OHL	63	23	20	0.68	18	131
2013/14	OHL	65	33	35	1.05	16	

Wegwerth, Joe
RW – USNTDP (USHL) – 6'03" 229

A big, physical presence and strong skater, Wegwerth is more of a defensive forward. He has decent puck handling skills and will occasionally have a good drive to the net and chip in some points here and there, but he is largely more suited to be in more of a defensive role.

Wegwerth finishes his checks, plays a really strong game along the boards and in the corners, gives a maximum effort level every shift and plays a sound defensive game all with some snarl and angst. As an NHL'er, he would probably be a good fit in the bottom six in a more shutdown, defensive role. He is committed to the University of Notre Dame.

SEASON	LEAGUE	GAMES	GOALS	ASSISTS	PPG	PIM	HP RANKING
2013/14	USHL	25	2	1	0.12	78	NR
2013/14	(U18)USDP	60	3	6	0.15	123	

Wesley, Josh
RD – Plymouth Whalers – 6'3" 195

Wesley is a big defensive defender from the Plymouth Whalers. He generally makes a simple first pass on breakout situations and excels when keeping things simple in the defensive zone. Josh has slow choppy feet and struggles when caught flat footed against a speedy offensive attack. He compensates for his lack of speed by understanding when to leave the offensive blue line and starting getting into a defensive mode. He has a good stick and a long reach which helps when facing on-coming attackers. Wesley shows good moments of physical play but needs to work on consistency issues in this area. He occasionally starts to run around in the defensive zone and thus sometimes ends up caught in traffic leaving open lanes and open opponents in key scoring positions.

Wesley would also benefit from improving his gap control which would cut down on opportunities for opponents to beat him wide with a quick burst. He has a big shot from the point but needs to work at getting into better shooting situations and understanding the offensive zone.

SEASON	LEAGUE	GAMES	GOALS	ASSISTS	PPG	PIM	HP RANKING
2012/13	USHL	38	0	1	0.03	14	170
2013/14	OHL	68	2	7	0.13	62	

Weyrick, Blake
G – USNTDP – 6' 3" 203

Weyrick is huge in net, and that's on account of not only his size, obviously, but his solid angles and aggressive nature in challenging shooters. He's a big body, but he's very athletic with quick legs and an exceptional glove hand. He holds his ground down low on the ice and is very strong, doesn't lose his net. Puck handling is not a strong suit of Weyrick's. He's not very good at it, and he makes bad decisions when doing it. That's really the only major strike on Weyrick. His size combined with athleticism will make him a desired target in June in Philadelphia.

SEASON	LEAGUE	GAMES	GAA	SV%	W	L	SO	HP RANKING
2013/14	USHL	11	3.04	0.884	NA	NA	NA	NR
2013/14	(U18)USDP	18	2.80	0.888	10	4	1	

White, Patrick
LC – Sarnia Sting (OHL) – 5'11" 163

Patrick is in his OHL rookie season after spending last year with the Gloucester Rangers of the CCHL. Patrick has filled into a bottom six role for the young Sarnia team. He provides a defensive first mentality and consistently hurries back to take care of his own end. Despite lacking experience at the OHL level the Sting made White a consistent presence on their penalty kill and he has not looked out of place. He is a shoot first player who showed flashes of offensive ability in Minor Midget but has yet to produce much in the way of offense thus far in his OHL career. While he is a player who understands his role and doesn't get caught trying to do too much, he currently lacks the ability of a player we expect to see selected at the 2014 NHL Entry Draft. Patrick missed the final two months of the season with a neck injury.

SEASON	LEAGUE	GAMES	GOALS	ASSISTS	PPG	PIM	HP RANKING
2012/13	CCHL	58	21	16	0.64	21	NR
2013/14	OHL	37	4	0	0.11	2	

Wilkie, Chris
RW – Tri-City Storm (USHL) – 5'11" 185

After a strong 2012-2013 campaign with the USNTDP U17 program and a great World U17 tournament in which he put up nine points in six games, Chris made his way to Tri-City this season and had yet another solid showing.

His stride can look a bit funky but Chris has good speed and gets to his top gear in a hurry. He's pretty fleet-footed and shifty and is able to weave in and out of traffic well with the puck. Really good hands a ton of creativity and confidence, Chris creates a lot of havoc in the offensive zone.

Excellent playmaking ability, can thread passes through tight areas and land right on the tape, puts a lot of zip on them. Dangerous player in close around the net. He can handle the puck in tight in traffic well, and has a quick burst first step that allows him to change his shooting angles and open things up. He probably attempts more wrap-arounds than any player viewed this season, but he pulls it off. Extremely quick in short bursts and his hands keep up with his feet. Great offensive instincts and one of the players where the puck just always seem to find them and be on their stick. Shoots the puck well, accurate. Always involved. Plays the point on the power play and is good at directing traffic and controlling the puck up high. Strong slap shot, has some zip.

Away from the puck, plays a fairly physical game and gets involved defensively. A bit turnover prone in the neutral zone. Decision making as to whether to carry the puck, head-man, chip, etc. can be cloudy. Tries to skate through people too often and causes rushes back the other way.

Early on in viewings there were times his foot speed and overall speed were in question, but over time it was realized that is was a matter of effort. Effort and compete level can be inconsistent, and when it's off it's noticeable. He looks slow and sluggish and it can be mistaken for that being his overall skill level if you didn't know any better. However, when he's on he's a difference maker, so hopefully he finds more consistency to that part of his game going forward. He will be joining teammate Austin Poganski at the University of North Dakota next season.

SEASON	LEAGUE	GAMES	GOALS	ASSISTS	PPG	PIM	HP RANKING
2012/13	USHL	38	7	7	0.37	38	NR
2013/14	USHL	57	17	19	0.63	39	

Williams, Devin
G – Erie Otters (OHL) – 6'00" 165

Devin split time in net with Columbus Blue Jackets prospect Oscar Dansk, however, he took over the starting role in the playoffs with an impressive performance in the first two rounds. Devin is slightly below average size for a goaltender. He does a great job centering to the shooter, and is consistently in position when a puck carrier comes into the offensive zone. He regularly stops the first shot. Williams has a strong glove hand, and directs rebounds away fairly well. He gets into trouble when players are able to get him moving side to side opening him up. He gets beat with quick cross-ice passes as his side-to-side movement struggles, and a lot of the goals he allows seems to go five-hole on him. He also drops to the butterfly far too early, which can expose the upper part of the net unnecessarily. He handles the puck very well, even under pressure making the smart play. With some very strong performances, we expect Devin to get drafted at some point, but will be a long-term project for whatever team selects him.

SEASON	LEAGUE	GAMES	GAA	SV%	W	L	SO	HP RANKING
2012/13	OHL	33	464	0.886	8	17	1	NR
2013/14	OHL	31	2.57	0.905	23	5	5	

Willman, Max
LW – Williston-Northampton (HS-MA) – 6'00" 181

Max is a re-entry player for the 2014 NHL Entry Draft. He is a very flashy skilled player. He has excellent speed and one on one moves. He can beat defenders and goaltenders at will. He handles the puck very well and is capable of creating plays for both his linemates and himself. He loves using his speed to push the pace of the game and make plays as many players at his level struggle to keep up with him. When he isn't distributing the puck among his linemates, he displays a hard accurate shot.

The biggest concern for him moving forward would be improvements to his defensive game. He doesn't really take care of his own end and will need to improve his two-way contributions. Max is slated to join Brown University in September 2014.

SEASON	LEAGUE	GAMES	GOALS	ASSISTS	PPG	PIM	HP RANKING
2013/14	USHS	25	21	23	1.76	NA	130
2013/14	Midget	11	5	13	1.64	6	

Wolanin, Christian
LD – Muskegon Lumberjacks (USHL) – 6'01" 174

Son of long-time NHL'er Craig Wolanin, Christian started the season in Green Bay before being traded to Muskegon in December. Christian's play has improved immensely as the season wore on this past year. I have liked him all season long, but his play took a noticeable upward climb upon arriving in Muskegon, where he put up 21 points in 32 games, compared to his five in 23 games with Green Bay prior to his trade.

Christian's defense is rock solid, but could still improve. Some of that may come from his mind being on offense so much, and he excels in that regard. With that said, again, his defense is solid, but I feel it could improve and that he has the hockey sense and ability to improve. He makes some really good plays on some really good players and is virtually impossible to beat one-on-one, but has the occasional lapse in judgment and will turn the puck over trying to skate it out himself. Very physical, loves to hit. Not afraid to mix it up and get in your face. Big, strong body.

His offensive ability is high end. He's a very fluid skater. He navigates the defensive and neutral zones extremely well and so smoothly. His hands are slick, as are his feet. Good length. Likes to rush the puck up ice and gains zone entry really well, has good hands in tight and is able to get past defenders at/inside the offensive blue line. At the same time, he's smart and sees the ice and will chip the puck in if he has no space to enter the zone or is outnumbered. He rarely ever gets caught up ice with the rush going back the other way.

Excellent power play weapon, is on the top unit typically. Christian has a heavy slap shot and is very accurate. With his hands and mobility he creates a lot of high quality open looks for himself. Moves the puck well and has good offensive zone instincts. Finds the open ice and likes to play give-and-go. Quick first step allows him to burst in those situations. Strong presence on the offensive blue line. Very confident with the puck there, creates a lot of offense. Has numerous great keep-ins on a nightly basis, very athletic and quick. Also an above average wrist shot and will use it when in need of just a quick puck on net.

I find Wolanin to be one of the more intriguing prospects going forward. He was passed up his first time around in the draft, but his game has grown immensely and with his combination of speed, size, skill, toughness, and instincts, his upside is good. As of this writing, he is uncommitted and his OHL rights are held by the Plymouth Whalers.

SEASON	LEAGUE	GAMES	GOALS	ASSISTS	PPG	PIM	HP RANKING
2012/13	USHL	54	0	8	0.15	70	204
2013/14	USHL	55	6	20	0.47	74	

Wolff, Nick
LD - Eagan High School (HS-MN) - 6'04" 200

Wolff is about as tough as they come when it comes to high school hockey. Nick is built like a tank and enjoys running over opponents whenever possible. He doesn't hesitate to deliver a check, even if it is a little bit questionable. He really plays with little mercy and is a nightmare to be matched up against physically.

Nick's strength also shows in his shot as he has a cannon from the point. He will need to improve his footwork moving forward as he can get beat by speedy forwards who are too quick for him to contain due to a lack of lateral mobility. He can also be forced into making unnecessary mistakes with the puck. Nick is slated to join the University of Minnesota-Duluth in September 2015.

SEASON	LEAGUE	GAMES	GOALS	ASSISTS	PPG	PIM	HP RANKING
2012/13	USHS	24	4	18	0.92	36	181
2013/14	USHS	41	11	16	0.66	86	

Wong, Tyler
RW – Lethbridge Hurricanes (WHL) – 5'09" 160

On a team that struggled to get much momentum going, Tyler provides an exception compete level and will battle hard for pucks. He combines this with excellent skating ability to make life difficult for opponents. He has been able to force a lot of turnovers and turn them into immediate scoring chances. He isn't very big or strong but he is willing to finish his checks regardless and try to disrupt puck possession. When he has the puck on his stick he is capable of both finishing and moving the puck with moderately good skill.

Along with his lack of strength, Tyler has trouble handling contact at times and his small size can cause him to get knocked off the puck a little too often for our comfort. Regardless, if Tyler is selected late in the 2014 NHL Entry Draft it would be as a project for a team who is looking long term at Wong's potential.

SEASON	LEAGUE	GAMES	GOALS	ASSISTS	PPG	PIM	HP RANKING
2012/13	WHL	54	5	8	0.24	37	NR
2013/14	WHL	52	17	14	0.6	56	

Wood, Kyle
D – North Bay Battalion (OHL) – 6'5" 229

Wood is a player who got better as the year went on, and stepped up even more in the postseason. He played regularly during 5-on-5, and took regular shifts on the powerplay and penalty kill. He's positionally sound in the defensive zone, and anticipates the play well. Wood uses his long reach to disrupt plays, and get in the passing or shooting lanes. He uses his big size to separate players from the puck, and is good defending in 1-on-1 situations.

Wood reads the play well and, though he doesn't do it often, knows when to jump into the play and help create offense. He's big, but skating would be our concern for the NHL level. While he looked fine in a straight line, his mobility slipped when he had to move laterally or make quick direction changes.

SEASON	LEAGUE	GAMES	GOALS	ASSISTS	PPG	PIM	HP RANKING
2012/13	OHL	16	1	1	0.13	8	209
2013/14	OHL	33	2	10	0.36	21	

Yakimowicz, Chandler
RC – London Knights (OHL) – 6'03" 195

Yakimowicz started the season with the Wilkes-Barre Scranton Knights U18 team with a short stint at the U.S. National Team Development Program.

Chandler joined the Knights after the Christmas break, and made an immediate impact on the fourth line for the Knights, showing a willingness to do anything for his team. He was quite raw coming into the OHL, and remains that way, but the Knights have done an excellent job shaping him into a legitimate NHL prospect.

He already possesses an excellent frame. His overall skating ability can be a little clumsy in regards to technique, but generates average speed. He finishes every check, and forechecks hard striking fear in smaller defenders when pursuing pucks in the corners. With limited ice he maximizes his potential by skating hard every second, and provides a tireless backcheck. He has blocked shots in the defensive zone, and sells out defensively to try and remove pressure in his own zone.

Chandler's toughness was also on display, as he dropped the gloves a handful of times in the final months of the season beating down some very tough opponents. His shot has improved immensely since coming to London, as he used to provide a weak shot that he put low to create rebounds. Chandler now has quite a bit of zip in his shot, and surprised goaltenders on a few occasions. Regardless, his offensive upside at the next level is very limited.

Ultimately Yakimowicz is a bit of a dark horse for this draft, but we really like what he shows in the mould of a hard working, bottom six player who knows who he is, and will consistently compete, block shots, win battles, drop the gloves and do what it takes to win. These players are very valuable at the next level, and when combined with a near 6'3" 200lb frame, Yakimowicz has a great edge as an excellent sleeper pick at the 2014 NHL Entry Draft.

"Chandler impressed me with the U.S. program earlier this year. The move to London really helped improved areas like his shooting ability but my favorite part about his game is he's so coachable. He uses his size extremely well and will go through a wall for his teammates." - Ryan Yessie

Quotable: "He has a good grasp of who he is as a player. I like when players give me a good self evaluation of their game." - Mark Edwards

Quotable: "Who is number 21? I like him." - NHL Scout (during Memorial Cup)

SEASON	LEAGUE	GAMES	GOALS	ASSISTS	PPG	PIM	HP RANKING
2012/13	MetJHL	37	11	13	0.65	26	118
2013/14	OHL	33	3	4	0.21	45	

Yazkov, Nikita
LW – Windsor Spitfires (OHL) – 6'01" 187

After a fairly successful World U17 Championship performance with Russia, the Windsor Spitfires selected Yazkov at the 2013 CHL Import Draft. Yazkov was given good ice off the bat, and combined decent size with strong skating ability. He has powerful acceleration, and a good top speed. He displays great hands, and is very elusive with the puck.

Yazkov is willing to challenge opponents one-on-one, which has seen mixed results. He has good offensive tools, but struggled to convert at times which saw his ice time drop as other players performances started passing his. Yazkov needs to get stronger, and become more of a consistent threat in the offensive zone to become a more legitimate NHL prospect.

SEASON	LEAGUE	GAMES	GOALS	ASSISTS	PPG	PIM	HP RANKING
2012/13	MHL	17	1	1	0.12	0	NR
2013/14	OHL	66	6	15	0.32	25	

Zwerger, Dominic
LW – Spokane Chiefs (WHL) – 6'00" 205

Dominic came over from Austria to join the Chiefs and had a moderately successful rookie season. Zwerger has a powerful shot which he can get off quickly. He likes to drive the net but will also pass the puck when he sees an available lane. He plays a power forward style and is built solid but doesn't possesses the height desired for this role. He is capable of doing a little bit of everything for his team whether it is producing scoring chances, using his size to protect the puck or playing a physical game finishing his checks. He kept it simple in his first season and showed some real signs of being an NHL prospect. He has a shot at being a late round sleeper who could really develop into a great player as more opportunities open up for him in his second season in North America.

SEASON	LEAGUE	GAMES	GOALS	ASSISTS	PPG	PIM	HP RANKING
2012/13	SWI Elite Jr.A	21	6	11	0.81	6	NR
2013/14	WHL	53	16	10	0.49	20	

NR = Not Ranked in our top 210 prospects for the 2014 NHL Draft

2015 NHL DRAFT TOP 30

2015 NHL DRAFT TOP 30

HP	PLAYER	POS	TEAM	LEAGUE	HEIGHT	WEIGHT
1	Connor McDavid	C	Erie	OHL	5' 11"	170
2	Jack Eichel	C	USNTDP U18	USHL	6' 1"	185
3	Noah Hanifin	D	USNTDP	USHL	6' 3"	195
4	Kyle Connor	C	Youngstown	USHL	6' 1"	170
5	Colin White	C	USNTDP	USHL	6' 0"	175
6	Travis Konecny	C	Ottawa	OHL	5' 10"	166
7	Mitchell Marner	C	London Knights	OHL	5' 10"	155
8	Oliver Kylington	D	Färjestad	SHL	6' 0"	181
9	Daniel Sprong	RW	Charlottetown	QMJHL	5'10	170
10	Jérémy Roy	D	Sherbrooke	QMJHL	6' 0"	186
11	Lawson Crouse	LW	Kingston	OHL	6' 3"	201
12	Zack Werenski	D	USNTDP	USHL	6' 2"	201
13	Mikko Rantanen	C/W	TPS Turku	SM-Liiga	6' 4"	195
14	Dylan Strome	C	Erie	OHL	6' 2"	170
15	Jeremy Bracco	RC	USNTDP	USHL	5'9"	154
16	Rasmus Andersson	D	Malmo	Allsvenskan	6' 0"	207
17	Matthew Barzal	C	Seattle	WHL	5' 11"	165
18	Nikita Korostelev	RW	Sarnia	OHL	6'2"	176
19	Pavel Zacha	LW	Bili Tygri Liberec	Czech	6' 2"	196
20	Nicholas Roy	RC	Chicoutimi	QMJHL	6' 4"	190
21	Yevgeni Svechnikov	LW	Bars Kazan	MHL	6' 1"	179
22	Paul Bittner	LW	Portland	WHL	6' 4"	195
23	Jordan Greenway	LW	USNTDP	USHL	6' 5"	205
24	Radovan Bondra	C	HC Kosice	SVK	6'4"	212
25	Ryan Gropp	LW	Seattle	WHL	6' 1"	163
26	Tommy Novak	C	St Thomas HS	MINN	5' 11"	178
27	Nick Merkley	RC	Kelowna	WHL	5' 10"	176
28	Julius Nattinen	LW	JYP U20	Jr. A SM-liiga	6' 2"	192
29	Erik Cernak	D	HC Slovak	Slovak	6' 2"	200
30	Kyle Capobianco	D	Sudbury	OHL	6'1	170

2015 NHL DRAFT PROSPECTS

Addison, Jeremiah
RW – Saginaw Spirit (OHL) – 6'00" 183

In his second season with the Spirit, Jeremiah provided a consistent hard working effort on a nightly basis. Commonly found in Saginaw's bottom-six, Jeremiah consistently finishes his checks on a regular basis. He keeps it simple, battles hard for pucks, gets in the face of opponents, and plays tough. He isn't a great skater, but gets around effectively. He provided a solid backcheck, and will work hard in all three zones. Due to his late birthdate, Jeremiah is ineligible until the 2015 NHL Entry Draft. We expect his role to increase with the Spirit with the graduation of a few forwards from the team. He has shown flashes of the ability to contribute offensively, but hasn't really had much opportunity to show it more consistently, which he may be able to do next season.

Ahl, Filip
LW – HV71 J20 (SuperElit) 6'3" 207

Ahl already has a pro frame to work with and plays a powerful game. He's powerful skater who has great puck protection along the wall, and he's tough to move from the front of the net. He's not a speedster but when he hits his top speed off the wing he's tough to handle for defensemen. He won't hesitate at taking the puck to the net; he's strong as a bull, and tough to knock off his skates. Ahl is a skill player with the puck, and capable of pulling some off some nice dekes around opposing defensemen. He plays a power forward game, and in 24 games against older competition in the SuperElit league he had 10 goals and 19 points. At the U17 hockey challenge he had 4 points in 5 games, and during the season also made his debut in the Swedish hockey league playing his first game in the top league in Sweden.

Aho, Sebastian
LW – Kärpät U20 (Jr. A SM-LIIGA)

Aho is a speedy, skilled forward from Finland who has really improved his game over the course of the last two seasons. He's a good skater with nice acceleration, and can fly off the wing. He has good hockey sense and makes smart play with or without the puck all over the ice. He had a lot of success offensively this year with his club team in Finland with 59 points in 44 games with Karpat U20 team. Aho played at the recent U-18 world championship as an underager and scored twice in 5 games there. Aho is also a good stickhandler, has a great shot, and quick hands.

Andersson, Rasmus
RD – Malmo (Allsvenskan) 6'0" 214

Andersson is solid two-way defensemen who played in the 2nd men's division in Sweden, and already has a nice frame to work with. He's not very tall, but is very strong on his skates, has good footwork, and is an above average skater. He's very active in the offensive zone, as he always tries to make something happen offensively, makes smart pinches, and he's very creative from the backend. His shot is solid and accurate from the point. Andersson makes good decisions with the puck, and doesn't get in trouble too often. Defensively he's solid in one-on-one coverage thanks to his good footwork and good active stick. He could be more physical along the boards and be more assertive. He's a good stickhandler, and can rush the puck from his zone to the offensive zone with ease. Andersson is cool under pressure, and doesn't panic when he feel pressure on the forecheck. This season with Malmo in the Allsvenskan had 13 points in 43 games.

Artemov, Artem
LW – Chicago Steel – 5' 11" 200 (2015)

The Moscow native had an excellent first season in the USHL, registering 33 points in 56 games. His play only continued to improve as the season went on, which could be said for most of his teammates as the Steel started the season 0-10, only to come within a couple of points of making the playoffs.

At 5'11, Artem's size doesn't blow you away but he plays a much bigger game than his height would suggest. At 200 pounds, he's solid as a rock. His wide base and low center of gravity make him a bear to defend, especially along the boards and in front of the net. He wins a lot more puck battles than he loses, and rarely does he get knocked off the puck, regardless of the defender's size. He is a right-handed shot but played his off-wing in every viewing. In addition to his physical strength, his quick feet and good puck handling skills are the ultimate compliment. He's very creative with the puck and has excellent playmaking ability on account of his vision and awareness combined with his physicality and skill. Puts passes through defenders' legs and sticks regularly. Rarely isn't tape-to-tape. Great saucer pass ability. Capable of beating defenders one on one. His stride is smooth and with his low center of gravity he's exceptionally shifty. Can turn on the jets and beat defenders wide and is not afraid to drive the net. Plays really well on the point on the power play. He handles the puck well along the blue line, and has the ability and creativity to beat defenders there one-on-one to create open shots and passing lanes for himself. Adept at making little passes to himself to evade defense and is very elusive. Exceptional patience with the puck, poise in spades.

His being on the point as a forward speaks to his defensive abilities and his coaching staff's trust in him to defend. Plays a strong defensive game in all three zones. He's strong and aggressive on the forecheck, backchecks hard, often catching opposing puck carriers, picking their pockets, and going in transition back the other way, and plays sound positionally in his defensive zone. Knows when to drop down and support his defensemen and line mates. He causes a lot of turnovers with his active stick and has a knack for clogging up passing lanes and intercepting or deflecting passes away. He always finishes his checks and can be trusted to play in any situation. Never takes a shift off. All in all, an excellent two-way player.

Askew, Cam
RW – Drummondville Voltigeurs (QMJHL) – 6'3" 202

Askew was the surprise of last year's QMJHL draft, as his selection (11th overall) was unexpected: he was originally committed to play college hockey at Northeastern and then at Boston University before making the choice to play major junior hockey in the CHL.

In his first year in the QMJHL, the Boston native was able to show off his skills even though he saw limited ice time on a veteran team. Played most of the year on the Voltigeurs 3rd or 4th line, and he was at his best when he played with skilled guys on his line, such as Georgs Golovkovs. Did get some power play time during the year, usually on the 2nd power play unit where he was used on the left side so he could be set up for one-timers. Askew already has a great frame and projects very well once he gets stronger, during the season it was clear that added strength would have been useful for the young American when he was battling for the puck or space in front of the net. Was drafted out of Cushing Academy as a centerman, but played the majority of the year on the right wing for the Voltigeurs. The best attributes to Askew's game are his hands. He's got soft hands and a quick release on his wrist shot. We saw him pick corners on goaltenders with his NHL-caliber wrist shot. He sees the ice well and has nice poise with the puck, in addition to being an underrated playmaker. Doesn't have the quickest of feet, an area he will need to make some improvements in as he continues to progress. The same goes for his top speed. Although he has a nice, power forward frame, he doesn't really play a physical game, and we would like to see him play with more jam. He will hit guys, but his lack of strength enables him to have less of a physical impact.

Bachman, Karch
F – Culver Military Academy (IN) – 5' 11" 165 (2015)

He plays with jump in his stride and makes some good offensive opportunities happen. He is a strong skater and stick handler and almost looks a bit European in his style.

He likes to make strong stop/start moves in offensive zone with speed. He will also drive puck to the net to make things happen and score. He played at Culver Military Academy and looks to be headed to the USHL in his draft year with the Tri-City Storm.

Baker, Tarek
F – Omaha Lancers U16 – 5' 11" 185 (2015)

Barker is a fairly decent skater in a wide stance with some nifty hands. He shows that he has some scoring promise as he can rip a good shot off or can score in tight and has solid offensive instincts. He can play physical style as well. He is committed to the Minnesota Golden Gophers (Big 10 Hockey).

Barwell, Jesse
LC – Mississauga Steelheads (OHL) – 5'10" 176

Barwell is a speedy skilled forward who had to take on a bit of a different at times, while playing on Mississauga's third line this season. Jesse is a smooth skater who can evade checkers and beat defenders one on one. He competes hard and has good vision and puck skills. He is more of a play maker and likes to create scoring chances for his linemates more than finishing scoring chances. It's expected Barwell will play a more offensive role for the Steelheads with a year in the OHL under his belt and atleast one departure on the Steelheads top six lines and is a player to watch for the 2015 NHL Entry Draft.

Barzal, Matthew
RC – Seattle Thunderbirds (WHL) - 5'11" 172

The 1st overall pick in the 2012 WHL Bantam Draft, Barzal is an offensively-gifted playmaker that possesses tremendous hands and elite vision. Barzal has excellent hockey IQ and is able to think the game at a much higher level than his peers. Barzal is very good on his edges and is able to create space for himself based on his exceptional ability to quickly turn or start and stop forcing defenders to match his footwork. While he has good acceleration and speed, that should further increase when he is able to add more strength and generate more power in his stride. Barzal attacks defences and tries to lure defenders to him before dishing a nice pass to an open teammate. He is able to thread accurate passes through traffic and is able to operate at high speed. He is a very good stickhandler and will take the puck to the net if the pass isn't available.

Barzal's shot is just okay. He has a pretty good release, but he isn't able to put a whole lot of velocity behind it. Much like his skating, Barzal could benefit in this regard by adding some bulk. Barzal is a threat both off the rush and within the offensive zone where he is able to identify gaps in coverage and exploit them. Defensively, Barzal is quite capable of defending and has a knack for stripping the puck from opponents. He can however be caught cheating up ice and will have to work on the consistency aspect of his defensive play.

Barzal is a special talent with similar attributes and skillsets of former 1st overall NHL draft pick Ryan Nugent Hopkins. This makes him among the best offensive prospects the WHL has produced in recent history and a strong candidate to be a high pick in the upcoming 2015 NHL Entry Draft.

Beauvillier, Anthony
LC – Shawinigan Cataractes (QMJHL) 5'09" 168

Drafted 2nd overall by the Shawinigan Cataractes, the younger brother of Rouyn-Noranda player Francis Beauvillier has been one of the only bright spots on his team this season. After the trade period, he got more responsibilities offensively, and he delivered in our opinion. Some may think the contrary, but unlike others in his draft class, we have to keep in mind that he was the main offensive weapon on his team.

He has the instincts of a natural goal scorer, always trying to get in the slot to take a shot. He is very agile on his skates, and creates a lot of space for himself with quick direction changes. His skating is fluid and precise with great acceleration. He buys time and space with elite stick handling in the neutral and offensive zones. These abilities, along with his creativity, make him a constant threat on the ice. He also showed good vision on the ice, and has superior hockey sense. He can execute high-level plays and spot teammates easily. He is also very shifty, and shows good awareness, keeping himself out trouble by keeping his head up and knowing who is around him on the ice. He can bring his intensity level up a notch, making him more aggressive and very hard to contain. He also creates more turnovers when he plays this way. Defensively, Beauvillier plays with his head on a swivel and is very aware of the situation out on the ice. He puts himself in a good position to take away plays from the point. An excellent skater with a knack for scoring goals, there is no doubt Beauvillier will be able to increase his offensive production in the QMJHL next season.

Bear, Ethan
RD – Seattle Thunderbirds (WHL) – 5'11" 188

Bear is a steady two-way defenseman that has already been entrusted to play key powerplay minutes for the Thunderbirds as a 16 year-old. He has a heavy slap shot that he's successfully able to get on net through traffic and above average vision. He prefers to keep things simple in his own end and doesn't often lead the rush as he prefers to use outlet passes. He won't really jump into the play unless a can't-miss opportunity presents itself or if his team really needs a goal. He's a stocky kid that effectively uses his size. He forces opponents outside and will press against guys in the corners to wear them out. His skating can be sluggish at times, but he can generate decent speed. As his skating improves, that will increase his ability to be a dynamic player from the point. Bear had a very respectable 19 point rookie season and is worth tracking for the 2015 NHL draft.

Bell, Jason
LD – Cape Breton Screaming Eagles (QMJHL) – 6'2" 190

The 12th overall pick in the 2013 QMJHL draft, Jason Bell is a gifted offensive defenceman with great skating abilities and a powerful shot from the point. In 2012-2013, Bell played for the Laval-Montreal Rousseau Royal and helped his team win the bronze medal at the Telus Cup.

Bell is a defenceman who thinks about offense all the time, and will lead or support the rush as much as possible. A good skater whose great top speed and good acceleration makes him dangerous in the offensive zone. He also likes to have puck on his stick and make plays. A big threat on the power play, as he can absolutely shoot the puck which is his number one weapon. His slapshot is very powerful, and it doesn't take much time to get the puck off his stick. He's very impressive with the puck, with quick and soft hands, which is a result of playing forward growing up, as he also did at this year's U-17 Hockey Challenge when he was used as a forward by the Team Quebec coaching staff. As a defenseman, Bell remains extremely raw with his defensive game, he likes to support the offense which can leave a big hole when there's a turnover. One thing we noticed in his first year in the QMJHL is he uses his stick well in his zone, is not known for his defensive prowess but breaks up plays with his active stick in front of his net. Battled some injuries this year and only played in 37 regular season games with the Screaming Eagles. More will be expected from him next year. His hockey sense and decision-making will need to improve as well, as he gets himself into trouble when pinching in the offensive zone; sometimes, he can try to do everything all by himself. We noticed this in Midget last season and he hasn't made the adjustment yet at the QMJHL level. Bell has a nice frame to him as well, but he's not a physical player at all in his own zone, another area that will need to be addressed.

Birdsall, Chris
G – Youngstown Phantoms – 5'11" 174 (2015)

He is average in size so some NHL teams might be hesitant as he is under the 6-foot mark but shows his strong techniques and athleticism. He seemed to always be tracking pucks, limiting his rebounds, and challenging the shooters. Now in recent seasons since playing in the USHL, his game is getting questions on his mental stability. It seems that when Birdsall is on, he is one of the best goalies at his age but when a goal or two is allowed the wheels fall off the wagon quickly. Birdsall is committed to Boston College (Hockey East).

Bittner, Paul
LW – Portland Winterhawks (WHL) - 6'4" 195

Bittner is a late-born '96 birth that really announced his presence to the hockey world with a break-out performance at the 2013 Memorial Cup. Bittner has tremendous size and is tough to contain. The left winger plays a physical game where he plays in the dirty areas of the ice and forces opponents to try to move him out of scoring position. He's good in the corners and likes to lean on guys. Bittner is not a fighter, but isn't afraid to mix it up with heavyweights when he feels as though they've taken a few too many liberties.

For a big guy, Bittner has a nice array of offensive tools. He has good awareness of the play, along with very good vision and passing skills. He has the strength to get to the tough areas and the soft hands required to finish. Bittner has shown that he can produce offense both off the cycle and off the rush with his long reach and good skating ability. Bittner is able to generate very good top-end speed and his acceleration is good for his size. While he is a particularly good skater for his size, it would be good to see some improvement in the agility department.

Bittner's tremendous upside and ability to produce in numerous situations make him a valuable contributor. Good chance you will hear Bittner's name called in the 1st round of the 2015 draft.

Blackwood, MacKenzie
G – Barrie Colts (OHL) – 6'4" 204

Blackwood's first full season in the OHL was a huge success, as he started 45 games for a playoff team in the Colts, was their playoff starter and named to the OHL's First All-Rookie Team. Blackwood is a very big goaltender with an ideal frame, and has the size to cut off angles and take away a lot of space in the net. Due to his size he can cover a good portion of the top of the net even when in the butterfly. He's pretty athletic, and while his rebound control isn't great at times, he always battles and is capable of making second and third saves. He's also a good puckhandler, and isn't afraid to leave his crease to play it. One knock on him is that he looks a little awkward in his net at times, and looks to be still growing into his body, and learning how to use it. At times he struggles with far-side shots taken at the opposite post when squaring up to a shooter coming down the wing. With more starts and experience he should get better with this. Overall going into the 2015 NHL Entry Draft Blackwood has a ton of potential as one of the top goaltenders out of the OHL.

Blaisdell, Doug
LD – Kitchener Rangers (OHL) – 6'02" 179

On a young Kitchener Rangers team Blaisdell showed good maturity for a 16-year-old when he made appearances during our Kitchener viewings. He has good size, and takes the body well against big forwards. He consistently plays a safe, smart defensive style of game using his size against opponents without playing an overly physical style. He is smart with the puck, and keeps it very simple, consistently making the smart play preventing turnovers, and advancing the puck. He should take on a bigger role for the Rangers next season, and is definitely a player to watch, as he is already mature beyond his years for a rookie defenseman playing in a limited role.

Boka, Nick
D – USNTDP-17 – 6' 1" 196 (2015)

A good-sized kid and has a lot of upside to his game. He is not a flashy offensive-defenseman although he moves the puck well and isn't afraid to skate it up either. He is quite mobile and plays aggressive. Boka shows physical play at the back-end and plays sound position as well as controlling gaps. He looks to have pretty heavy shot from the point too. Boka chipped in six goals and 13 assists in 52 games played this past season.

Bondra, Radonovan
RW – Team Slovakia U18 (Slovakia2) 6'4" 212

Bondra plays a power game but mixes in some skill. He's a big kid and sports some pretty quick feet for a kid his size. While we have somewhat limited viewings of him, he managed to impress us by taking the body all over the ice. Bondra is effective on the penalty kill and helps create some space that assists in creating some scoring chances. Bondra was one of the most consistent and effective forwards on his U18 team in Finland this past April. His first few steps could improve but overall he's a pretty good skater and showed himself to be a smart hockey player in our viewings. Bondra fshowed off some skill including several great passes. Bondra looks to have the tools to be a high pick In a strong class for the 2015 NHL Draft

Booth, Callum
G - Quebec Remparts (QMJHL) - 6'02" 196

Drafted by the Quebec Remparts in the third round out of Salisbury High School, Booth is a big and tall left-handed goalie that plays a fairly robotic standard butterfly style with tremendous attention to details and accurate positioning. He is calm in front of his net and compacted. The adjustment to the QMJHL has been a little tough for Booth, but he has done an admirable job adapting his game. He relied way too much on his sound positioning in order to makes saves and he had to work on his side-to-side movements as they were not quick enough. We've seen improvement in that regard thus his save percentage went up. Booth works hard to track pucks through traffic, spot pucks at his feet when he gives up rebounds and will rarely back down during a game whether it's a blowout or a tie game. He has also displayed good hands and the ability to catch any pucks and deflect away shot to the corner with his blocker. Another one of Booth's strengths is his ability to play his angles very well. He will rarely gets too deep in his net. He shows a calm coolness that is usually not seen as a rookie and that has an effect on his teammates' play around him. He has the ability to quick recover after giving up a rebound and making a huge save because of his quickness. He also has a wide butterfly, and takes up a lot of space when down on his knees. Booth will get the opportunity to shine next season as the Quebec Remparts will be hosting the Memorial Cup next year. We think we will get to see him more often between the pipes.

Bouchard, Jérémy
LW – Chicoutimi Saguenéens (QMJHL) 5'07" 170

After being the sixth overall pick of the 2013 QMJHL Draft by the Chicoutimi Saguenéens, Bouchard has done a good job adapting his game. In QMAAA, he was recognized as an offensive threat and it wasn't that easy for him to play on his team's third line. He has now become a two-way player who can be used in both offensive and defensive situations. There is no doubt in our mind that he possesses a high level of hockey sense. In his own end, he keeps placing his stick in a perfect position to create turnovers when he pressures opponents. He reads the play quickly and anticipates like few can..His wrist shot is good and very accurate, but he doesn't use it nearly enough. When used with good players that matched his offensive awareness. he has displayed good vision and playmaking abilities. He also doesn't hesitate to go around the net to knock in rebounds and is active in puck battles. He is very stable and agile on his skates and has shown the ability to make quick changes of direction although his straight-line speed can still be improved. Despite his small size, he is willing to battle on the boards to retrieve the puck and is not afraid of getting hit, using a low center of gravity to his advantage.

Bourque, Simon
LD - Rimouski Oceanic (QMJHL) - 5'11" 174

Bourque was one of Rimouski's 2nd round selections in the 2013 QMJHL draft. He played his midget hockey with Collège Charles-Lemoyne.

Started the year not getting a lot of ice time with the Oceanic, but the more the year progressed, the more he was getting ice time and winning the coaching staff's trust. At times with injuries and suspensions, Bourque ended up playing north of 25 minutes a game and did very well in those contests. He's a competitive defenseman who can play against the top lines of opposing teams and already did so on some occasions this season as a 16 year old. He's capable of playing big minutes at five-on-five and shorthanded, is tough to beat one-on-one as he uses his stick well to poke pucks away, and has above-average mobility to not get beaten wide. He has okay top speed and can rush the puck at times, but does it safely and gets caught rarely. He's a smart defender who uses his smarts to defend instead of playing a physical game where he could be overmatched due to his lack of strength. Bourque, who hails from Longueuil, played for Team Quebec at the recent U-17 Hockey Challenge in Cape Breton. He's a steady performer from game to game, and can stabilize a defense corps with his calm and poise on the blueline. Can play on the power play if needed, and moves the puck safely but his slapshot is just average, as it lacks velocity. But he does a good job of getting the puck on net.

Bracco, Jeremy
F– USNTDP-17 – 5'9" 155 (2015)

He led the USA NTDP-17 team in points as was a leader on the ice in setting teammates up or scoring a big goal. He is on the smaller side but skates well with some speedy wheels, good vision, and likes to have puck on his blade. He shows off his great edge work as he circles offensive zone simply handling biscuit making things happen. His skating ability is second to none. He has great offensive instincts, creativity, and above-average playmaking for sure. He produced 17 goals and 54 assists in 54 games. He can finish as he has a good shot, but he is unselfish and creates more opportunities for his teammates as he delivers crisp, tape-to-tape passes for goals. Bracco is a bit undersized but you cannot question his skill set and hockey IQ. He recently decided to commit to Boston College (Hockey East) after originally being recruited by Harvard. We expect him to be a player who continues to rise as next year unfolds.

Bricknell, Jake
RW – Belleville Bulls (OHL) – 5'11" 191

Jake joined the rebuilding Bulls as a 16 year old due in large part to his exceptional work ethic and consistency in this department. Jake is a strong skater and provides a relentless forecheck on a shift by shift basis and always found a way to be noticeable in our viewings of the Bulls this season. Jake hits hard and crushes opponents along the wall whenever he gets a chance. While he played a limited role primarily on the third and fourth lines for Belleville, he showed some intriguing offensive upside reading plays well and making intelligent passes. Jake already projects as a safe prospect for the 2015 NHL Entry Draft because he has the ideal mindset for a third line grinder at the pro level. He already has decent size, great strength, a strong powerful stride and the mentality to hit anything and everything that gets in his way. The big question at this point is whether or not Jake has the offensive upside to produce good numbers at both the junior and professional level. This should become more evident in Jake's draft year as his role with the Bulls should increase with the graduation of a few key players.

Brisebois, Guillaume
LD – Acadie-Bathurst Titans (QMJHL) – 6'1" 160

Brisebois was the 5th overall pick in last year's QMJHL draft by the Acadie-Bathurst Titan. The former Antoine-Girouard defenseman played a regular shift with the Titan this year and also represented his province at the recent U-17 Hockey Challenge in Cape-Breton.

Brisebois is an excellent two-way defenseman who has always played under the radar due to his style of play, and who is now playing in a small market team that doesn't get much exposure. In midget, he played with Jeremy Roy (Sherbrooke) and Anthony Beauvillier (Shawinigan) who were getting all the fanfare, but Brisebois has proved last year and this year that he is a very steady defenseman that doesn't get his team in trouble. He possesses great footwork and agility that make him tough to beat wide, he always has a great gap control and he is very smart, with a good active stick, defending in his zone. Brisebois has underrated offensive abilities; he's a good skater with good top speed, has a good first pass out of his zone and a low level of panic, even when pressured by the forecheck. Not a flashy player by definition, and on the transition he will take the smart option most of the time. The St-Hilaire native has grown quite a lot since the start of the 2012-2013 season and still needs to get stronger, as he can find it difficult facing stronger players in front of the net, or along the wall. By getting stronger, we expect his shot to gain more power, and we would like to see him get his shot on net quickly. Brisebois is still improving his physical game since last year, as he's getting stronger and more comfortable with his frame.

Burke, Cal
F – Nobles Prep (MA) – 5' 11" 175

He can fire the biscuit pretty well as that may be his best strength. Although skill sets overall are pretty good in skating, stick handling, and thought process. He has grown in recent years and has found success in the New England Prep School league at Nobles and will take his game in the upcoming season to the Cedar Rapids RoughRiders of the USHL.

Burns, Andrew
LD – Windsor Spitfires (OHL) – 5'11" 177

Andrew began the season with the LaSalle Jr. B Vipers, but also received time with Windsor including every playoff game for the Spitfires. Burns is a smooth skating defenseman who isn't extremely explosive or overly fast, but is very fluid in transition, and skating up the ice rushing the puck. He did well on the powerplay, making smart passes, and usually gets his shot from the point on net choosing the right times to shoot. Defensively he was fairly hit or miss. His positioning is moderately good, but he can chase the play at times, and get overwhelmed during heavy pressure. This could have been attributed to his lack of experience and youth, but will need to become more comfortable defending skilled offensive threats in his sophomore season.

Bushnell, Noah
RW – Sarnia Sting (OHL) – 6'02" 201

Bushnell had an excellent rookie season playing primarily on the third and fourth lines, with a little time on the second line when the Sting were consumed with injuries. Noah is a big physical winger who loves to finish his checks. He punishing opponents and really seems to enjoy playing this style of game. He wins more battles on the wall than almost any 16 year old this season. He's not shy about dropping the gloves and will do so without hesitation against much bigger and older opponents and generally will fair well in these fights. He also shows a scoring touch around the goal area. He has a powerful shot that has moderate accuracy and can sometimes catch goaltenders off guard. He has a very shoot first mentality and lacks offensive creativity, but is most effective with the puck in the slot or in a good shooting lane in the offensive zone. Noah just needs to get quicker as his mindset is great, he just needs to get to where he's going a lot quicker than he currently does.

Capobianco, Kyle
LD – Sudbury Wolves (OHL) – 6'01" 170
After being selected in the 1st round of the 2013 OHL Priority Selection Draft, Kyle was caught behind the veteran depth of the Wolves blueline, and had to remain patient, and take advantage of opportunities when they came. With a full line-up, Capobianco primarily played on the powerplay with a few five-on-five shifts here and there. However, when injuries arose, Kyle received ice in all game situations, and did his best with these opportunities. He displays intelligent puck moving ability in all three zones, and is particularly effective on the powerplay. He moves the puck intelligently, and has a good shot, but only utilizes it when he has a clear lane. Defensively he does a good job of competing along the wall, and getting his stick in lanes. He maintains positioning, and really doesn't try to do too much in his own zone. With the graduation of multiple defenders out of Sudbury, expect Kyle to play a much bigger role, and put his hockey sense, and two-way ability on display leading up to the 2015 NHL Entry Draft.

Carignan-Labbe, Julien
RD – Drummondville Voltigeurs (QMJHL) – 6'0" 185
Carignan-Labbé was selected in the 2nd round by the Voltigeurs in the 2013 QMJHL draft, and he brings lots of toughness to the table. He is a rugged defenseman who loves to hit and who is tough to play against. Even at 16, he didn't back down from anyone, and got into a couple of scraps. The former Seminaire St-Francois midget player was not intimated by making the jump to the major junior level at the beginning of the year, due to his strength and willingness to play a physical game. As a rookie defenseman, Carignan-Labbé didn't get a ton of ice time, but had enough to keep progressing and developing his game. When in the lineup, he played on Drummondville's 3rd pairing, and saw limited time on the penalty killing unit and no time on the man advantage. He does take care of things in own zone, is not afraid to block shots and pays attention to details. We would like to see him be more active with his stick in defensive situations, which would help his game. His puck skills are average, as he is not a natural puck mover from the back end. Can panic when pressured on the forecheck. He's an average skater, but needs to keep improving his footwork and quickness to keep up with quick forwards.

Carlo, Brandon
RD – Tri-City Americans (WHL) - 6'5" 185
A stay-at-home defender with tremendous size. Brandon is a late-born 1996 with a long reach and good defensive positioning. Not much in the way offense, but he makes up for it with his good defensive play and awareness. He has very good speed and decent mobility to a guy of his size. He is able to keep forwards to the outside and does a good job of finishing his checks. Can be prone to giving up too large of a gap off the rush, but has made progress in that area and has improved in his ability to take away space using his long reach. For such a tall player, Brandon is pretty thin. He will need to add weight and develop more strength in order to be a more intimidating presence going forwards.

Carlsson, Lucas
LD – Brynas J18 (Allsvenskan) 6'0" 182
Carlsson was quite effective at the 2014 world under-17 hockey challenge for team Sweden. He moved the puck very well to ease the transition game, and didn't hesitate starting or joining the rush. He's a smart defender, and rarely gets caught out of position. Even when he does, he has the skating ability to get back defensively. In the offensive zone he makes smart decisions with the puck, and showed good poise. On the transition if he doesn't see any open forwards he won't force a play. He'll either clear it up the boards or move it to his defense partner. In his zone and on the penalty kill he's capable of blocking shot in front of the net. He covers a lot of space on the ice, as he can cover for his defense partner if he gets caught pinching. There's a nice fluidity to his skating

stride. Carlsson doesn't have much of a physical game, and will need to get stronger. This season Carlsson split time between two teams in Brynas' system, and collected 32 points in 34 games at the under-18 level

Cascagnette, Jacob
LW – Kitchener Rangers (OHL) – 6'02" 179

Jacob split his season between the Kitchener Jr. B Dutchmen, and the OHL's Kitchener Rangers. Playing in a bottom-six role, Jacob did a great job providing a strong work ethic, and compete level for his team. He has good size, and skates moderately well for his size and age. He finishes his checks, and pressures hard on the forecheck. While we saw flashes of his offensive ability in Minor Midget last season, Jacob's strongest asset moving forward is his competitiveness. We expect Cascagnette to play a similar role on a much more consistent basis next season with the Rangers, and should be a legitimate prospect for the 2015 NHL Draft if he continues to develop, and improve at his current pace.

Joseph Cecconi
RD – Muskegon Lumberjacks – 6' 1" 198 (2015)

With his rights traded from Green Bay to Muskegon in December of this past season, Cecconi made his debut with the Lumberjacks not too long after, going on to play 28 games with the club. He is a product of the Buffalo Junior Sabres Midget program.

What impresses about Cecconi so much is his uncharacteristic cool and calm for a young player. Very poised, never seems nervous or rushed or unsure of himself; very confident young player.

Cecconi has excellent mobility. He gets up and down the ice with ease and makes everything seem easy. Solid decision-maker, always makes the good first-pass out of his own zone. He is not overly physical but he always takes the body and his angles are good. For a young player just coming up his adjustment period was remarkable small. Good shot blocker, and always willing to take a hit to make a play. Good size and uses his body well to protect the puck and win board battles. Really good compete level, battles hard.

His offensive upside is excellent. He managed six points in 28 games in his first stint of USHL play, and he is capable of more as his confidence grows and development continues. He makes good decisions at the offensive blue line, never forces anything, always makes the smart play. Doesn't take many chances yet but he will learn to as time goes along and will learn to pick his spots. The instincts are there. Again, remarkable poise.

I came away thoroughly impressed with Cecconi's season since being called up. He is slated to attend the University of Michigan starting in 2016, but his OHL rights are held by the Oshawa Generals. Wherever he plays going forward, it will intriguing to see his continued development. He has tremendous upside and as is stands today is a fine two-way defenseman.

Cernak, Erik
RD – HC Kosice (SVK) 6'3" 203

Cernak is a big boy who has been talked about as the next big prospect coming out of Slovakia for the last couple of years. Not only is Cernak huge, but he's also a fairly good straight-ahead skater for a player of his size. He moves the puck well with simple passes to his forwards, and on the power play can be useful thanks to his powerful slapshot. He played this year at the World Junior Hockey Championship, and at the recent U-18 world championship where he struggled when pressured in his own zone. His footwork is sluggish, as he was beat on the outside by quick players. His struggles at the under-18 made dropped him in our ranking, but the upside still remains high. This season Cernak split time between HC Kosice men's team, their U20 team, and the Slovak National U20 team. He had 7 points in 41 games playing against much older competition.

Ciccarelli, Matteo
LW – Sarnia Sting (OHL) – 5'09" 181

Matteo completed his first full season with the Sting and despite lacking in a few key areas of his game such as skating ability and high end puck skills, Matteo displayed a relentless and admirable work ethic game in and game out. He competes very hard for loose pucks and wins some battles against older and bigger players and has proven to be a very pesky player to play against. He also displays a willingness to play a complete 200ft. game. He is hit or miss when it comes to decision making with the puck and has served up numerous dangerous turnovers and has his most success making the basic, low risk, low reward type of plays. He lacks puck skills consistent of an offensive player at the OHL level but has shown a few flashes of puck handling ability and can jump on rebounds in the slot effectively. Matteo will need to get bigger and stronger and really needs to correct his skating stride before legitimately challenging as a prospect at next year's draft but to his benefit, he knows who he is; a hard working role player who is willing to sell out for the team by battling, making/taking hits and blocking shots.

Chabot, Thomas
LD - Saint John Sea Dogs (QMJHL) - 6'01" 177

Drafted in the second round by the Saint John Sea Dogs in the 2013 QMJHL Draft, Chabot had a good rookie year to say the least. Playing on a rebuilding team can also be beneficial and the Sainte-Marie native took it the right way. He mostly played with Olivier Leblanc and he even got some quality icetime on the powerplay. When he was playing Midget AAA, we have rarely seen him miss a pass. That's still the case in the QMJHL. His breakouts were on tape most of the time and he was able to rush the puck a bit effectively as well. His puck handling abilities are good, he can make his way around players easily with slick moves, displaying confidence when bringing the puck up. He is willing to jump down low into the slot in the offensive zone to provide scoring options off the rush and then can also get back to tie-up his man on the back-check to nullify the opposition's opportunity. He still needs to improve on his footing and his first few steps going backwards in order to react properly when facing opponents down the rush. Chabot does not possess a very good shot, and will certainly have to improve on it to be more of a threat from the blue line and not be one-dimensional. His positioning in his zone is solid, with an active stick and good reads. He makes few mistakes though he does get burned from time to time. He really needs to get stronger in order to be more effective down low in his zone, where he gets outmuscled thus losing battles he shouldn't lose.

Connor, Kyle
LC – Youngstown Phantoms – 6' 1" 170 (2015)

Even in a draft as strong as 2015's is expected to be, Connor will be a no-brainer in the 1st Round. A great USHL season followed by a dominant performance at the World U18's, Connor is an elite offensive talent with massive upside.

He plays with a lot of drive and creativity in his game. He consistently flashes his slick stickhandling skills and creativity with the puck. He is a good skater who can accelerate into another gear. He has great hockey sense and knows how to put himself in good scoring situations. Connor has been showing scoring since his Belle Tire days and also for the last two seasons in the USHL with the Youngstown Phantoms. So his strong performance at the U18 World Championships was not a surprise.

Along with his high-end offensive abilities, he plays a solid defensive game. He takes hits to make plays and despite his slight build, he still takes body positioning on opponents and takes hits well. Rarely is he flat out hit hard and knocked to the ice. He backchecks well and is a really good pickpocket in the neutral zone and quick in transition going back the other way.

He will need to fill out and get stronger, but that will come in time. He's expected to return to Youngstown next season and is committed to the University of Michigan in 2015.

Craievich, Adam
RW – Guelph Storm (OHL) – 6'0" 197

Craievich is a skilled offensive winger from the Guelph Storm. Adam was the third round pick of the Storm in the 2013 OHL Draft. He was in and out of the lineup this season due to the elite depth the Storm had up front. Craievich has a nose for the net and the puck seems to find him in the slot. He has a lethal wrist shot and a quick release that is able to fool goaltenders with its velocity and accuracy. Adam struggled with his skating at the minor midget level but really put in an effort in the offseason and showed considerate improvement. His stride is still choppy and it takes him some effort to work up speed however he uses his smarts to get to good areas in the offensive zone where he can utilize his finishing ability. He is good at driving to the net and getting his stick on point shots to create tip opportunities. With the graduation of a number of Storm forwards. Craievich should expect to play a much larger role next season. If his skating continues to improve as it did last season he will be an interesting prospect for the 2015 NHL Draft.

Crawley, Brandon
D – Selects Academy U18 (CT) – 6' 2" 201

He has good size already listed at 6'2" 201lbs. and brings a pretty solid all around game game. He will show some offensive flash as he will jump up into the rush. He has a great shot but needs to get it through more often. Impressed with his vision on the ice as he made some fantastic seam passes. He is not afraid the throw his body around, he wins battles along walls. Crawley is very raw and is clearly in need of some proper coaching, many of the flaws in his game are mostly a result of simply not being aware of defensive coverage etc. We see the potential for big upside. He recently signed to play with the London Knights (OHL) for next season and should get a good opportunity to earn icetime with a Knights team which will be retooling after hosting the Memorial Cup.

Crouse, Lawson
LW – Kingston Frontenacs (OHL) – 6'03" 200

Lawson went through a bit of an adjustment period early on for a young 16-year-old joining a skilled veteran OHL team in the Frontenacs. After getting his feet wet Lawson has continued to skyrocket in regards to his play and his stock for the 2015 NHL Entry Draft. Lawson really slimmed down in comparison to his Minor Midget physique, which has really helped his mobility. His skating was already pretty decent for a player his size, but it has noticeably improved over the last 12 months. Lawson plays a power forward style of game. He hits hard, and goes hard into the corner. He wins a lot of battles, and shows a good work ethic in the offensive zone. He protects the puck well in the offensive zone, and can buy time for himself to make a decision by cycling the offensive zone with the puck. Lawson has good offensive tools, which he was unable to show very much this season due to the depth in the Frontenacs lineup. He should get a better opportunity next season. Lawson has a hard shot, and will drive the net looking for rebounds. Crouse already played a key role in the penalty kill for Kingston willing to do whatever it takes to help his team out getting into passing lanes, blocking shots and getting the puck down the ice. Lawson has a ton of potential, and projects to be a top prospect out of the OHL for the 2015 NHL Entry Draft.

Dahlström, John
LW/C – Frolunda J18 (J18 Allsvenskan) 6'0" 183

Really enjoyed Dahlström's performance at the U17 in Cape-Breton. He used his size well to protect the puck, and took the puck to the net every time he had a chance. He was very good at creating scoring chances from cycling the puck, as his board play was excellent. Dahlström showed some nice finish in tight, and has underrated vision. He made some slick passes during the tournament to set up his linemates for goals. He supports his defensemen well coming back deep in his zone, and always made himself available to receive a quick pass from his defensemen to start the rush. Dahlström split his season between Frolunda's two J18 teams, and finished the year with 40 points in 39 games.

Davies, Jeremy
LD – Lac St-Louis Lions (LHMAAAQ) – 5'11 157

Davies was selected in the 6th round of the QMJHL draft in 2013 by Victoriaville. On talent alone, he should have been in the top two rounds, but the NCAA was and still is an option for the swift-skating defenseman. Davies was our 24th ranked prospect in our QMJHL draft guide last year and was recently drafted in the USHL in the 13th round by Waterloo.

The Montreal native went back for a second year of midget this season with the Lac St-Louis Lions and had an up-and-down year, like his team, but was great in the 2nd half of the season and in the playoffs (also like his team). The Lions qualified for the playoffs in the last game of the regular season, but caused two upsets in the first two rounds of the playoffs and eventually lost in the semifinals. Davies logs a lot of ice time, playing on the number 1 pair of defensemen and quarterbacking the power play. He possesses great feet, can really move smoothly around the ice, and loves to rush the puck out of his zone. A real key for his team's transition game with either his skating or passing plays, as he possesses great hands and he's a great puck handler who can make opposing defenders look foolish with his one-on-one moves. At times, he can be a little bit too fancy with the puck one-on-one, and that can lead to turnovers. However, his poise with the puck is above-average, as he never seems to be in trouble and never seems to panic with the puck, even under pressure. Often Davies will act as a 4th forward, as he often leads the rush in the offensive zone. Doesn't own a powerful shot from the point, but it's fairly accurate and will touch the net most of the time. Will need some work in his zone when he gets to a higher level than Quebec Midget AAA, and gets by with it now because he's as skilled as anyone and can outskate the majority of players in the league. Getting stronger will be a key as well for Davies, who will be in tough in higher levels versus bigger and stronger forwards in front of his net or along the wall, battling for position and the puck. It will be interesting which route Davies will take to continue his career.

Davidsson, Jonathan
LW – Djurgarden J20 (SuperElit) 5'11" 172

Davidsson caught our eyes with his intensity at the U-17 hockey challenge in Cape Breton. He has a non-stop motor; his feet are always moving, and he's tenacious on the forecheck. Davidsson brought a lot of energy to the Swedish team in every game we saw. He possesses good speed, and gets the puck to the net. He finishes every check he can on the forecheck, and can create turnovers with his hustle all over the ice. Davidsson has good hockey sense, and makes good reads while applying pressure on the forecheck. He also takes good angles in his puck pursuit. He's more an energy player than a skill player. This season back home he played at three different levels in the Djurgarden system amassing 62 points in 35 games at the U18 level, and one point in 11 games at the U20 level.

Davies, Mike
LW – Kitchener Rangers (OHL) – 6'02" 195

After being taken in the first round of the 2013 OHL Priority Selection Draft, Davies didn't quite live up to the billing of a first round pick. He has decent size, however, looks smaller than his 6'2" listing. Mike has a tremendous shot, and is extremely dangerous when in a good scoring area. This did not happen often, as his five goals this season suggest. In his defense, Mike didn't play many offensive situations, commonly receiving fourth line ice with no powerplay action, so his most effective area was physicality. Davies was consistently finishing his checks, and never let up on a chance to take the body. He provided a steady forecheck, backcheck, and was also willing to throw his body in front of shots in the defensive zone. However, he can be limited in his effectiveness when the pace of the game picked up, because his skating ability is a major concern at this point. He lacks any initial quickness, and takes several seconds before being able to reach his top speed, which isn't very good, either. When the pace of the game picks up Davies often gets left behind chasing the play.

Davis, Kevin
LD – Everett Silvertips (WHL) - 6'0" 180

Davis is smooth-skating defenseman with good size for his age. He has good skill, but is content to keep things simple and distribute the puck rather than try to do everything himself. He makes an accurate first pass and shows good awareness at both ends of the rink. Defensively, he combines using his good positioning and stick work with limiting his own mistakes in order to force opponents to earn scoring chances. A calm and poised defender, he can go unnoticed for large portions of games due to his high defensive awareness and simple play. If Kevin is going to be a puck-moving, stay-at-home style defenseman, it would be good to see some development in the physical aspect of his game.

De Farias, Joshua
RD – London Knights (OHL) – 5'11" 172

Joshua split his 16-year-old season between the Knights and the Waterloo Jr. B Siskins. In limited action De Farias was able to focus on a more steady defensive game in comparison to his puck rushing offensive game in Minor Midget the previous season. Joshua's skating is effortless, and became comfortable later on utilizing his skating to advance the puck up ice. He battled hard, and was able to keep up with the play for the most part at the OHL level, while in Jr. B he was capable of playing all game situations in a top-4 role receiving a fair amount of ice. He is smart, and creative on the powerplay, and is capable of distributing the puck among teammates rather quickly. De Farias will likely become a full time OHLer next season, and if he can get stronger, and continue to improve in his own zone while applying his offensive skills, he looks to be a legitimate prospect for the 2015 NHL Entry Draft.

Dergachyov, Alexander
C – SKA-1946 St. Petersburg (MHL) 6'4" 201

Dergachyov is a big center that came into his own this season in the MHL, and was a strong performer for Russia at the February five nation, and at the recent World Under-18 hockey championship. This season with his MHL team he recorded 21 points in 46 games, but Dergachyov's game is more than just points. He's an excellent player without the puck, and excels on the penalty-killing unit with great anticipation, and a good active stick. He's always the first forward on the backcheck, and supports his defensemen very well down low. He's a fine skater for someone his size, but could still work on his starts, and improve his top speed. He's not afraid to play a physical game. Dergachyov's a very strong kid who's willing to take a hit to make a play. He's willing to take punishment in front of the net if he has to; he's strong on his skates, and tough to move from there. He does some good work along the wall, protects the puck very well, and uses his size effectively. He's not afraid of taking the puck to the net, and can bulldoze himself there. On the powerplay he can either screen the goalie's view in front of the net, or play the playmaker role on the half wall. He showed nice poise with the puck, and an ability to find his teammates. He has a good shot with a great release on it, and is capable of putting the puck in the net. He's the guy that Russian coaches always used in key moment of the game, for an important faceoff or to kill a penalty.

Dermott, Travis
RD – Erie Otters (OHL) – 5'11" 195

Few get under the skin of the opposition better than Otters defenseman Dermott. His late birthdate has pushed him into the 2015 NHL Draft class, and while he does possess some skill, his strongest area is frustrating opposing forwards. He is slightly undersized for a defenseman but is built solid, and delivers both open ice hits, and hits along the wall with authority. Aside from his physical game, Travis is a smooth skating defenseman who handles the puck well, and can rush up ice with it. However we noticed he could get chased back by a forechecker far too easily for a good puck rushing defender. His puck play is consistently inconsistent, as he will make some excellent plays, and some questionable plays with the puck on a game-by-game basis. He has mishandled the puck in all three zones leading to chances against his team, and has also made great plays in all three zones leading to offensive chances. While he is strong, he can get outmuscled in the corners against older forwards with more size. Travis was able to put up great numbers as a rookie this season, and we look to see him improve more consistently with the puck, as his potential is high.

Deschênes, Luc
RD – Charlottetown Islanders (QMJHL) 5'11" 197

Drafted by the Victoriaville Tigres in the 2013 QMJHL Draft, he was traded by midseason to a rebuilding Charlottetown Islanders squad for Phoenix Coyotes prospect Yan-Pavel Laplante among other things.

Deschênes may not be the biggest player in the ice, but he's not afraid to play physical or go head first into puck battles. He stays aggressive between the blue lines with his gap control, and gives opponents very little room to try to go wide on him. He moves fluidly, helping him with timing his hits. He also gave up many odd-man rushes to the opposing team by pinching aggressively in the neutral zone, rather than smartly to hit the puck carrier. He is another player that likes to join the rush and he has very good abilities with the puck. His reads the play very well and finds teammates quickly with accurate passes. On the powerplay, his number one weapon is his slapshot from the point, it's lethal and already on a pro level. Although he did a good job on the transition, he needs to show more awareness and improve his decision making as he is prone to turnovers.

Dhooghe, Jason
F – Chicago Mission U18 – 5' 8" 150 (2015)

He shows good hockey instincts as must be in the family trait as his younger, Sean, is a top '99 who like his older brother is destined for Ohio State. He is not overly fast or gifted, but does the right things out there on the ice. The size might be a factor in the family genes as well, as neither Dhooghe are blessed at this point with height.

Dostie, Alex
LC – Gatineau Olympiques (QMJHL) 5'09" 159

Alex is an undersized yet tenacious talented forward who has developed up through the Magog Cantonniers' system before being drafted in the first round of the QMJHL Draft by Gatineau. He likes to keep his play simple in the offensive zone by executing efficient plays. He is a good two-way player who is good in the cycle game with agile stops and starts. In our viewings, he showed good puck distribution off the rush, and has some hands. He reads the play well and reacts quickly to make himself available and create passing options for teammates. He doesn't mind being physical, and doesn't pick his targets when it's time to hit. His hockey sense is also well displayed in the defensive zone, as he places his stick in the perfect position to create turnovers when he pressures opponents, reads the play quickly and anticipates like few can. He provides great support for his defensemen in his zone, allowing them to recuperate a good number of loose pucks after contact and to start the transition quickly. He always seems to be a step ahead of his opponents, even in the defensive zone. Dostie doesn't have astonishing top speed but it's fairly good for major junior, however, it will need to be better for pro hockey. Furthermore, his physical endurance doesn't seem very high and he wears down quickly as the game goes on when he plays this type of game. However, we believe he has what it takes to enjoy a successful second year under Benoit Groulx.

Dove-McFalls, Samuel
LW – Saint John Sea Dogs (QMJHL) 6'01" 193

Though still very raw, Dove-McFalls intrigues with good skating mechanics and skill to go along with a projectable frame. The Montreal native has played sparingly on his team's fourth line this season, but he was good enough to get his feet wet in the QMJHL at 16 yo straight from MESP. Dove-McFalls gets around fairly quickly for a big guy. He wins battles along the boards and works hard winning more than his share of battles. He is surprisingly creative and can beat defensemen one on one and possesses a strong wrist shot. He reads the ice well enough to effectively use his teammates. Samuel is good at using his size shielding opponents from the puck with his body before cutting to the net. He was a little inconsistent with his work ethic, but we've seen improvement over the past two years. He shows good backcheck and gets involved defensively. We look to see him continue to play a power game and increase his offensive input. His straight-line speed is average and we'd like to see him improve it a bit as well.

Dunda, Liam LW
Plymouth Whalers (OHL) – 6'4" 215

Dunda is a big rugged winger from the Plymouth Whalers. Liam was the sixth round pick of the Whalers in the 2013 OHL Draft. He is a big strong winger who looks to dish out physical punishment on the fore-check whenever he gets the opportunity. He was a longshot to make the team out of training camp but really worked his way into the lineup where he managed to play a large majority of the games this season. Dunda has a good skating stride for a big guy and shows the ability to get pucks deep into the offensive zone where he is able to use his size to win puck battles against older defenders. He excelled at the minor midget level opening up space for more skilled linemates and looks to be able to do the same at this level. Liam needs to work on his puck skills in the off-season in order to help him capitalize on the opportunities that his size allows for him. Dunda also showed a willingness to drop the gloves this season and is good at getting under the skin of his opponents. If he can work to add some offensive touch in the offseason he should certainly expect to see his name called in the 2015 NHL Draft.

Dunn, Vince
LD – Niagara Ice Dogs (OHL) – 6'00" 185

After being selected in the 6th round of the 2012 OHL Draft, Dunn really emerged this season after earning every inch of ice he received starting out with limited ice and eventually playing himself into key offensive situations. Vince is a smooth skating defenseman. He is extremely elusive with the puck and has a good top speed which he used to jump up in the rush without the puck. His skating ability is hands down his strongest area and he utilizes it extremely well. He makes smart passes up ice and could set up partial breaks and odd man rushes with quick accurate passes up ice. On the power play he was an impact making good decisions under pressure and has a strong shot. He is also willing to pinch at appropriate times which resulted in goals for his team. His hockey sense is high and was noticeable in all game situations. He is fairly strong and was willing to play the body and finish his checks despite not being the biggest defender on the ice. Defensively he was moderately good but without the puck he did have a few mental lapses and mistakes here and there which is understandable as a rookie and would usually recover. His one on one play needs to improve because he gives the forward too much space in these situations, resulting in him getting beat where his skating is strong enough to close the gap. Dunn is a very intriguing prospect for the 2015 NHL Entry Draft and could really boost his stock by taking his game to the next level.

Eichel, Jack
RC – USNTDP – 6' 1" 190 (2015)

An instant franchise-changer, Eichel will likely battle it out with Connor McDavid for the top pick in next year's draft. A dominating player in every facet, Eichel has a highly mature, polished game already at the age of 17.

He has great speed and quickness. Eichel moves around the ice with the greatest of ease. He is a very powerful skater as he has that extra gear to just blow by defensemen and drive the puck hard to the net Everything he does look completely effortless, but that should not be mistaken for actually having a lack of effort. Eichel plays hard, and for a player who gets so much attention and praise at such a young age, his attitude and work ethic on the ice are all the more impressive.

Magic hands, unmatched vision, and spades of hockey sense compliment the skating ability and make for as complete a player as you will see. He uses his teammates really well on the ice and is an excellent playmaker. He has good strength, solid frame, protects puck well, and can rip a hard, accurate shot quickly. He anticipates plays well and will beat goalies with those re-direct goals going hard to net or with a wicked wrister. He has all the tools from hockey IQ, shooting, skating, playmaking, physical play, with defensive know-how as well.

Eichel plays a professional game already, and it's unlikely he will be at Boston University for more than a season. He is a generational talent along with his CHL counterpart McDavid, and he will instantly change a lucky organization's fortunes the day his name is called at the podium.

Estephan, Giorgio
RC – Lethbridge Hurricanes (WHL) - 6'0" 184

Estephan has been one of a few bright spots in an otherwise dismal year for the Hurricanes. Giorgio has good talent and the former 4th overall WHL Bantam selection will be of interest to NHL teams next year. Giorgio looks poised to become a leading offensive threat for the team. He has good hands in tight and a knack for being able to finish his chances. Giorgio is smooth with the puck on his stick and is able to create his own shot. He shows good poise and awareness in the offensive zone. He generates good speed and is an overall good skater for his age. He is strong on his feet and can be tough to knock off the puck.

Giorgio is a competitor. He works hard, and at times, has overcome both physical pain and the mental anguish of lopsided scores to work through adversity and do whatever he can to help his team win. Defensively, Estephan has room for improvement. While he has shown that he is capable of backchecking, he has been known to float through the neutral zone. He also can be prone of leaving the defensive zone prematurely at times when he cheats up ice ahead of the play.

Evers, Christian
D – USNTDP-17 – 6' 2" 201

Evers is a nice size D-man with decent mobility, strong, and carries a big-time shot too. He also has exceptional vision as distributes the puck well can find the forwards with a few dandy stretch passes. He covers a lot of area in own zone too with long reach. He plays with a bit of a nasty streak too. He played with the NTDP-17 this past season and is set to step on the campus of North Dakota in the fall of 2015.

Fitzgerald, Casey
D – USNTDP-17 – 5' 10" 175

Another player with NHL bloodlines as father is Tom Fitzgerald who played 17 years in the big leagues. A very solid, and steady, two-way defenseman who loves to deliver laser beam passes to teammates' sticks. An active player who sees the ice well in making that stretch passes for the break-a-way or quarterbacking the power play, and possesses good shot. Fitzgerald is not an offensive powerhouse but will chip in with points and consistent on the back-end. Like his older brother at BC right now, he could aid his game with more strength and size. He should be a promising college player on the blue line in Chestnut Hill in the coming years at Boston College.

Fortin, Alexandre
LC – Collège Esther-Blondin (QMAAA) 5'11" 150

A second round pick by the Rouyn-Noranda Huskies, Fortin has a good mix between intensity, physical play and finesse play. Playing in the QMAAA again this season, he really had a great season with the Collège Esther-Blondin Phénix, where he registered 72 points in 47 games. He's a disturbing player to handle when he decides to give it his all, both offensively and defensively. His skating allows him to be very tenacious on the puck-holder and to be on time on the backcheck. Fortin is an agile skater, an asset he uses to carry the puck into the offensive zone whenever possible. He shows skill in bursts, with nifty dekes and a quick release on his wrist shot, but his puck-handling needs refining, as he's prone to giveaways. During the playoffs, he showed us that he does not belong with the QMAAA anymore, and that he's ready for major junior. We won't be surprised if he's a part of Rouyn-Noranda's second line next season.

Fournier, Jordan Ty
LW – Lac St-Louis Lions (LHMAAAQ) – 6'2" 186

Jordan is the younger brother of Stefan (Canadiens) and Dillon (Blackhawks) and was selected in the 2nd round by Victoriaville in last year's QMJHL draft. This season, he played his second season with the Lac St-Louis Lions, averaging over a point per game in the regular season and in the playoffs. He also had a five-goal game in the first round of the playoffs.

Very similar skillset to his older brother Stefan's; not the prettiest skater or flashiest player, but has a strong understanding of where he needs to go to score his goals. Never far from the opposing net, he will score most of his goals around the net. He was used on the power play in front of the net because he can create havoc there. He has good size and can be challenging for opposing defensemen to move in front of the net, as he is tenacious with the puck. He battles hard for pucks deep in the offensive zone, and protects them well, shielding away opponents with his frame. Fournier has decent hands and an underrated vision, and makes quick decisions with the puck. He's a hard worker at both ends of the ice, though his lack of speed hurts him in some defensive coverage situations. He will need to improve his quickness and his top speed as his skating is the biggest area that needs improvement at the moment. Plays a power forward game and goes up and down his wing. He should play full time next season with Victoriaville.

Franzen, Gustaf
C – HV71 J20 (SuperElit) 5'11" 165

We first saw Franzen last season during the 2013 World under-17 hockey challenge in Drummondville and Victoriaville, where he helped Sweden win the goal medal. In that tournament the young Swede had 10 points in 6 games. This season he was the captain of his club team, where he recorded 18 points in 36 games. He was also the captain of the national team at the World Under-18 hockey championship. He is a skilled forward that has a high hockey IQ, and understands the game well at both end of the ice. Franzen works hard in the defensive zone, and also makes good use of his active stick in the neutral or defensive zone to create turnovers or block passing and shooting lanes. He's an above average skater who can beat defensemen wide with a good burst of speed. He's as good of a shooter as he is a passer, possesses good hands, and a good release on his shot. He controls the puck well in tight, and has a strong work ethic. He could improve the velocity on his shot, but that could come once he gets stronger physically. He can struggle when playing against bigger players who can outmuscle him in front of the net or along the wall. Due to his lack of strength he plays more on the perimeter when trying to create offense.

Gabriel Gagné
RW - Victoriaville Tigres (QMJHL) - 6'04" 182

Picked in the second round by the Moncton Wildcats in 2012, he was involved in the Philippe Danault trade and was the key player in this transaction for the Tigres. In his first season with Victoriaville, Gagné had a pretty good season, starting the year on the bottom-six of the roster but finishing the year as one of the key Tigres players offensively.

He has a tall and lanky frame, and he's still filling into his 6'4", 182-pound frame. He has learned over the course of the season to use his size more in front of the net or to cycle the puck in the offensive zone. He is still not physical like you would expect a player with that big frame to be, but he has made progress in that area this year. He has a long reach which helps him keep defenders away. He won most of his one-on-one battles for the puck, as not many defensemen in the QMJHL can handle his size. His skating is average, but he has a long stride that makes him look faster. He just needs to get more power behind those pushes to improve his acceleration and agility. Gagné has a shoot-first mentality when he has the puck in the offensive zone, and has a good, accurate wrist shot. He also has a hard backhand in his shooting arsenal. He makes a lot of plays by rushing the puck or from the cycle. The St-Adele native, who played with St-Eustache of the Quebec Midget AAA in 2012-2013, has a bright future ahead of him if he keeps improving his quickness and physical game.

Gabrielle, Jesse
LW – Brandon Wheat Kings (WHL) – 5'11 201

The former 5th round bantam draft looks to be another homerun for the Wheat Kings as Jesse had a very successful rookie season where he was able to impact the game in a variety of ways for the Wheat Kings. Jesse has a high-energy motor and is not often out-worked. He's versatile and can play multiple forward positions. He isn't the tallest player, but he's thick. He is very strong for his age and is very efficient along the walls in puck battles. He readily throws the body. He is tough and more than capable of holding his own in a fight. He is also willing as witnessed by his 10 fights this season. Jesse is tenacious when chasing after pucks, has seen some success on the draw and has developed a good scoring touch when he has the puck.

While all of the above attributes scream gritty bottom 6 plug, Gabrielle is able to combine that intense compete level and toughness with very good skill making him an intriguing power forward option for teams drafting next year. He fights hard in front of the net and has seen some success in tight to the goalline as a result. With the puck, he is able to create space for himself and then to uses his good vision to identify whether to make a hard, accurate pass or use his heavy shot.

Jesse has a lot of tools at his disposal, but like all prospects, he has some items he needs to work on. He has seen some success with the aforementioned shot, but he will need to improve both the release and accuracy of it. Jesse isn't the most explosive skater, but gets where he needs to go around the ice. While he isn't a bad skater, he has some room to all-around improve in that aspect.

Jesse's strong play this season has started turning heads and he was even selected as part of this season's KHL draft. NHL teams are aware of what he can do and Gabrielle could position himself as a top pick if he is able to continue to show the type of improvements he's shown this past season.

Galipeau, Olivier
LD – Val-d'Or Foreurs (QMJHL) 6'01" 198

Drafted in the first round by the Val-d'Or Foreurs in the 2013 QMJHL Draft, Galipeau has been eased into the league playing third pairing on a contending team. He had a solid rookie season with the Foreurs moving up to the top four when injuries occurred. He plays a physical style of game. Despite this, he is fairly mobile for his age and size and handles one on one situations well. He wins most of his battles along the boards and makes the safe plays to get the puck out of his zone. His coverage is generally good, with particularly strong positioning against the rush where he angles off effectively and finishes his checks well. He is willing to sacrifice his body to block shots and he covers passing lanes fairly well. He tends to be overaggressive at times and that allows forwards to catch him off guard. He pinches aggressively to keep the puck in and get shots on net. He limits mistakes and is able to circle the puck effectively with quick and accurate passes in the offensive zone. Galipeau is also clearly one of the best open ice hitters we have seen in the Quebec area. He also played for Team Quebec during the WU17 and his physical game was a factor of his team's good showing at the tournament. He likes to get involved in scrums as well and he is clearly not getting intimidated. In fact, his overall game is always getting better when games gets tougher. His offensive game is somewhat limited, but he plays tough and we love his defensive acumen and his skating abilities.

Gawdin, Glenn
RW – Swift Current Broncos (WHL) - 6'1" 181

Gawdin is a talented forward with speed and skill. He can play both center and right wing, though he played as a winger this past season. He reads the play very well in the offensive zone and is able to get himself into scoring areas. Glenn has good stickhandling ability and is able to operate with the puck in traffic and at top speed. Glenn shows good promise in the offensive end, but can sometimes be too cute in making East-West plays.

Glenn still has work to do in his own end as he seems to have lost his confidence in his ability to use his body physically. He has good size, and at the midget level, Gawdin was really able to assert himself physically in order to create turnovers, but he seemed to shy away from contact at times this season.

Glenn has all the tools needed to become an elite player, but will need to put them all together on a consistent basis if he wants to be in the conversation as an early round pick next year.

Gicewicz, Carson
F – Nichols School – 6' 3" 210 (2015)

He is the younger brother of RJ Gicewicz and his older brother is a SLU recruit as well. Good sized kid with decent strength, good mobility, and all-around decent game. He shows good thoughts, makes the right passes, and can shot fairly well. He needs to gain a quicker step for the next levels and although has decent puck skills, they are not elite.

Gignac, Brandon
LW – Shawinigan Cataractes (QMJHL) 5'10" 159

A secound round pick by the Shawinigan Cataractes, Gignac had a good season with good chemistry alongside Anthony Beauvillier throughout the whole year. He showed top-end bursts of quickness and agility, and he reaches his top speed in no time. His speed is already comparable with other players at higher levels, which makes it easy for him to beat defenders outright. He has fairly quick hands and an effective shot that makes him a threat. He controls the puck well and can stickhandle around opponents. He shows good poise with the puck and shows good passing vision as well. When he's on his game, he engages well along the boards and wins more than his share of battles thanks to his shiftiness. However, he has shown us these strengths in brief flashes, generally over a few shifts, then will disappear for long extents. His physical strength is limited and puck protection situations are very tough for him. At the very least, he did still work hard, even during his team's meltdowns. However, he's a smart player who's conscious of his positioning defensively. Brandon's penalty killing ability has greatly improved throughout this season. He's intelligent position-wise and always gets his stick in the lanes. His quick reaction pays off here as well, allowing him to clear the zone when his team is under pressure.

Goberis, Zach
F – Colorado Thunderbirds U16 – 6' 0" 181 (2015)
He is a good sized kid and uses it to his advantage as well as he protects puck and likes to throw his weight around a bit. He played both ends of the rink showing strong two-way game. He will go into the dirty areas but will also show some nice stick skills. He is headed for the Lethbridge Hurricanes next season in the WHL.

Greenway, Jordan
F – USNTDP-17 – 6' 4" 215 (2015)
He is a good size player who skates well and knows how to protect the puck too. He displays some dominating performances on the ice as can show his keen vision in finding open teammate, uses his big frame to play with physical edge in corners or front of net, or by releasing a quick, accurate, hard shot. He can score on re-directs on the edge of the crease or dangle with his slick stick handling. He is a strong body with long reach and solid on his skates. Greenway brings those two elements of size and skill. He is part of the strong Boston University recruiting for incoming classes.

Greer, A.J
LW – Kimball Union Academy (USHS) 6'3" 198
A.J. made the jump from the QMAAA to New England Prep for the 2012-13 season, suiting up for powerhouse Kimball Union Academy. He brings an interesting skillset, with the tools to be a quality power forward, though he's very raw. He's strong on the puck, on his skates and possesses good protection skills. His hands and footwork in tight are quick and effective, allowing him to work well in a cycle. He goes hard to the net, and battles for loose pucks in the goalmouth. He has the size to dominate in the corners, but does not always put in the effort. He floats too often, and when he does move his feet his skating is awkward. He moves OK for his size, and shows good lateral agility, but he lacks straight-line speed and acceleration. He's a responsible penalty-killer, and shows good defensive awareness, but his lack of foot speed sometimes puts him a step behind where he should be. He plays the body, and shows an active stick on the forecheck, and in the neutral zone. He possesses an excellent wrist shot, good passing skills, and makes good decisions in outnumbered attack situations. He has the potential to be a top talent, especially if he improves his skating, and continues to get stronger. Greer, who is originally from Montreal, is committed to play college hockey at Boston University.

Guryanov, Denis
LW – Ladia Togliatti (MHL) 6'2" 183
Guryanov is another member of team Russia from the U-17 hockey challenge who had great reviews from our scouting staff. He's a big winger who uses his size well to protect the puck in the offensive zone, he's strong on his skates, and tough to knock down. He's a strong skater, can reach his top speed very quickly, and is also very agile. He can make quick sharp turns. With his speed, strength, and long reach he can be hard to contain when he takes the puck to the net. Guryanov also showed a strong commitment to the defensive game, and can be a threat to score shorthanded. This season he played in the MHL for Ladia Togliatti, and had 16 points in 37 games. He was also drafted 42th overall by Ladia Togliatti men's team in the KHL draft. He showed great playmaking skills at the U-17 playing on a line with Artur Tyanullin and Denis Alexeev, one of Russia's better lines at the tournament where Russia eventually won the bronze medal game vs team Quebec.

Gropp, Ryan
LW – Seattle Thunderbirds (WHL) - 6'3" 190
Gropp is a late 1996-birth year player that gave up his NCAA scholarship by jumping from the Pentiction Vees of the BCHL to the Thunderbirds in October. Gropp is a gritty power forward with

excellent size and offensive potential. He is willing to go to the tough areas and get involved in the physical play. He doesn't get too cute with the puck and prefers to play a North-South game. He is good at setting up in front of net and providing a screen while also able to slip away from coverage off the far side of the goal mouth in order to position himself for rebounds.

Ryan sees the ice well and does well to anticipate where to go. He does require some work on his skating so that he can get to those places a step quicker. Ryan had a bit of a slow start to the season, but was nearly a PPG player after Christmas before getting an invite to play for Canada at the U18 World Championships.

Guhle, Brendan
LD – Prince Albert Raiders (WHL) - 6'2" 178

The 3rd overall pick from the 2012 Bantam draft, Guhle has just barely scratched the surface of his potential. He had a pretty quiet season offensively for the Raiders, but has shown a strong ability to skate the puck out of trouble and lead the rush. For a big player, Guhle is a smooth skater that handles the puck very well. He is very mobile and is comfortable on his edges. He uses his skating and reach very well to force opponents to the outside where he is able to gain possession of the puck. He is not overly physical, but does not shy away from contact and is willing to hit (or be hit) to make a play. Guhle has an active stick and generally maintains good gap control. He can be sometimes caught flat-footed when he doesn't read the play about to transition, but he has looked quite comfortable defending at the WHL level.

Guhle has been a steadying presence in his own end and that combined with his skating, size and smarts will make him valued at the upcoming draft.

Hanifin, Noah
LD – USNTDP – 6' 2" 201 (2015)

Connor McDavid and Jack Eichel grab all of the headlines when it comes to the 2015 NHL Draft, but trailing right behind them is none other than Noah Hanifin.

Hanifin plays the most mature game for a defenseman of his age that I have ever seen. His game is so refined and so polished, you often have to remind yourself that you're watching a 17 year old. He plays with so much poise and control, never panics in any situation. Exceptional skater and puck handler, he can rush the puck from goal line to goal line at will. His size and speed combined with his hands and vision are just simply unfair. His slap shot is a rocket, and he has a great wrist shot to supplement his goal scoring arsenal. His hockey IQ is sky high, so he puts himself in position to fully utilize his entire skill set at all times.

Hanifin's defensive game is as polished as his offense is. His gaps and angles are perfect, and with his length and lateral agility he is nearly impossible to beat one-on-one. He often is able to poke the puck away before even having to body opposing players, but when he does body them they remember it. He is a boy in a man's body, and has delivered some of the biggest hits you will see all season. His positioning is flawless, and he always makes the good first pass to get out of the zone, though he knows when to pick his spots and take it up out of the zone himself.

He plays a pro caliber game already as a 17 year old, so the sky is the limit for him. One of the best prospects on the planet as it stands today.

Harkins, Jansen
LC – Prince George Cougars (WHL) - 6'1" 170

Harkins is a legitimate scoring threat playing for the Prince George Cougars. He started off the season very slow, but had an excellent 2nd half of the season where he wasn't too far off from scoring at a PPG pace. The young centerman is very talented and matches a high skill level with a nose for the net and a good compete level. Harkins is able to generate chances both off the rush and off the cycle. He is a threat to both pass and shoot the puck. He has good vision and distributes the puck very well, but also has a very good release on accurately-placed shots. He is able to stickhandle in traffic and uses his reach to protect the puck. He is a strong skater with good acceleration and top speed.

Jansen works hard at both ends of the rink and is a two-way player. He demonstrates good leadership abilities and is willing to go to the tough areas of the ice. Harkins needs to improve his strength and physicality as he can be overpowered by bigger, stronger players.

Harding, Sam
RC – Oshawa Generals (OHL) – 5'11" 170

Sam made the Generals as an undersized but skilled forward. He exceeded expectations this season despite playing in a somewhat limited role for the top seed in the OHL's Eastern Conference. Sam is a great skater who has an explosive first step and can beat defenders one on one using his speed. He is extremely elusive with the puck and becomes very difficult to contain once he gets going. He is creative in the offensive zone and can distribute the puck as well as shoot it with a lot of power. Sam showed all the signs of a player who could excel next season with increased ice and should only improve his stock going towards the 2015 NHL Entry Draft.

Heid, Nick
D – Omaha Lancers U16 – 6' 4" 194 (2015)

He is a good size D-man who skates well and can handle the puck. He will make good outlet passes and shut down the opposition with his strong physical presence. He can really fire the biscuit from the point.

Henley, David
LD – Charlottetown Islanders (QMJHL) 6'04" 181

After being drafted by his hometown team (Val-d'Or Foreurs) in the first round of the QMJHL Draft this past June, he asked for a trade by midseason and he found himself playing for the Charlottetown Islanders.

Henley has excellent size and is willing to play physical. Even though he plays with an edge, he does not constantly take undisciplined penalties, and will not lose his composure easily to go after an opponent and put his team on the PK. He uses his body effectively, and is hard to knock off the puck. Against the rush, he's hard to beat with good feet and long reach. He is good at poking pucks away with his good reach and does not give opponents much in the slot. Henley also shows a willingness to block shots and is good on the penalty kill utilizing an active stick to disrupt passing lanes. However, he still has a hard time dealing with explosive skaters when they come out wide on him because he lacks backward speed and lateral mobility. The Val-d'Or native is a decent skater and is good at transitioning from forward to backwards skating and vice versa. He shows adequate hockey sense and focuses on a defense first aspect when he is on the ice. He is also at his best when making the simple plays with the puck. He takes a lot of chances and the neutral zone and often tries to get the puck out of his zone in risky places.

Henderson, Jacob
F – Omaha Lancers – 6' 2" 190 (2015)

Definitely a power forward as he is a big body that plays like a tank. He is a decent skater, yet not overly fast, but will drive that puck hard to the net. He will grind it out in corners, down the wall, and out front using his solid mass to his advantage. Henderson is another '97 player out the St. Louis Jr. Blues organization who recently completed his rookie USHL season with the Omaha Lancers. He is headed off to Providence College in the fall of 2015.

Henley, Troy
RD – Ottawa 67's (OHL) – 5'11" 192

Troy was essentially a first rounder in the 2013 OHL Priority Selection Draft that fell to the Ottawa 67's as the first pick in the 2nd round. Henley got off to a bit of a slow start, a trial by fire in the OHL, but over the course of the season did an excellent job to adjust, adapt and learn from his mistakes. For a 16-year-old, he was one of the most reliable defenders on the 67's blue line. He skates well in all directions, and displays good mobility. Consistency was the key for Henley, and while he made the occasional mistake, he was for the most part very consistent, and reliable for his team. He is composed with the puck, and moves the puck hard, and accurately. Troy is pretty quick in one-on-one situations, and won the majority of these match-ups, but also got walked pretty bad in a few of our viewings. He was solid in his own zone, displaying good positioning, and did a good job down low battling, and competing with bigger, older forwards. He was also an effective shot blocker. Troy has shown all the development improvements we were hoping to see. Next season he should get an increase of ice time, because he already appears to be passing some of his teammates in terms of effectiveness, and reliability. We expect him to be a good prospect for the 2015 NHL Entry Draft if he is able to continue his improvement and development.

Holwell, Adam
LD – Moncton Wildcats (QMJHL) 5'11" 177

This QMJHL season has been one where many 97's made an impact on their respective team. Holwell has been a valuable top 4 defenseman with the Moncton Wildcats. He plays a refined two-way game, with deft stick handling and good puck decisions to go along with smart positional play in his zone. When pressured, he makes strong simple crisp breakout passes and moves the puck quickly. He rejoins the rush very wisely and when he doesn't have the puck on the breakout, will offer himself as a great passing option for his teammate without hesitating to jump in the play. He can play as a passer on the powerplay, but he doesn't have the shot required t be the shooter. He has average speed, and when he plays against opponents that are faster than him, he has a difficult time catching up to them, thus losing footraces he shouldn't. His high hockey IQ allows him to catch up sometimes, but he really needs to get his legs stronger in order to reach his top speed quickly. However, he is pretty well positioned in his own zone, getting his stick in passing lanes and following the play effectively. Holwell is more of a passive defender as he knows he doesn't have the body yet to continually engage himself physically. He will then rely on his anticipation to break plays.

Hughes, Cameron
LC – Spruce Grove (AJHL) - 5'11" 160

Cameron is a slick-skating center with great speed. He is able to handle the puck at top speed and has the vision and high IQ to both identify and assess his options. He plays at high pace and is able to catch defensemen by surprise with his speed. He is a very good puck distributor that creates space for himself using the aforementioned speed and passing abilities. Cameron shows a strong awareness of where to be in the offensive end. He isn't the biggest guy, but he's willing to finish his checks and is not afraid of going to the tough areas of the ice. He is still unrefined defensively as he needs to better recognize his check in his own zone, but has the speed and tenacity to create issues for opponents on the forecheck and through the neutral zone.

Jackson, Robby
LW – Chicago Steel – 5' 9" 165 (2015)

Drafted 153rd Overall by the Tri-City Americans in the 2012 WHL Bantam Draft, Robby opted for the USHL route and was subsequently drafted by the Steel 31st overall in the 2013 Futures Draft. As of this writing he remains uncommitted to an NCAA program.

Possessing a high, high hockey IQ, Robby is definitely one of the smartest and most cerebral players you will witness. He has exceptional anticipation of the play and puts that skill to use on both sides of the puck. Smallish in stature, he is a bull to play against and you will lose count seeing how many times players bounce off of him when attempting to check him. Conversely, he never passes up an opportunity to throw a check and isn't afraid to get in your face and under your skin. Plays with a definite edge but usually stays on the right side of the edge. He doesn't take dumb penalties and is adept at drawing them with both his antagonistic tactics and his physical abilities as a hockey player. Very elusive and slippery with the puck, Robby is a tough target to catch. He has high end speed and is extremely shifty. Great quick burst ability. He's especially effective in tight in the offensive zone. Has the ability to walk out of corners or off the boards around defenders and drive to the net. Extremely quick first step, beats defending players regularly in tight. Has a good shot and can pick corners, as evidenced by his 28 goals. He's not afraid to camp out in the slot or in front of the net, and isn't above putting away rebounds and "garbage" goals. He can score them in any way, shape or form. Uses his teammates well, has some playmaking ability. Finds the soft areas in coverage well and is very good at giving his line mates support t and an out option.

Robby's equally skilled on the defensive side of the puck. He is a tenacious forechecker and causes a lot of havoc in the offensive and neutral zones on that side of the puck. Picks pockets with the best of them. In the defensive zone he is always in position and always covering his responsibilities well. Effective penalty killer on account of his intelligence, speed, and aggressiveness. He knows when to pick his spots to take a chance and try and create an offensive opportunity while on the kill.

To call Robby a high-motor guy is a bit underscoring his abilities, but is true no less. His feet are constantly churning and he never stops moving, but it's always effective and isn't wasted energy. His size is a bit of a concern going forward, but being 16 still he has some time to potentially grow. He also needs to learn when and when not to do things all by himself. He is prone to turnovers at the blue lines, either trying to carry the puck out of his own zone past a defenseman or forechecking forward, or trying to take a defenseman on one-on-one and getting the puck chipped away and having the play go back towards his own zone. Taking size out of it, his speed, build, intelligence, and attitude could allow him to overcome the size obstacle at the next level. He is a great combination of speed, skill, hockey sense, tenacity, attitude and scrappiness . He is not against dropping the gloves and will stand up to anybody. This combination of traits are why he was named USHL Rookie of the Year. It was a well-deserved honor and something Robby surely will build upon.

Jones, Caleb
D – USNTDP-17 – 5' 11" 184 (2015)
He is a pretty good skater who makes good break-out and initial passes. He looks to be more defensive mined, and not overly dynamic especially when comparing to older brother, Seth Jones. He is following the same footsteps of his older brother as played this past season in Ann Arbor with NTDP-17.

Joseph, Mathieu
LW – Saint John Sea Dogs (QMJHL) 5'10" 143
Joseph began the season in MAAA, and early on, he was a key contributor to his team's offensive success. Even though he played in Minor Midget last year, Joseph was good enough to get himself drafted in the third round of the QMJHL Draft. A natural winger, his MAAA coach made him play center, and that has been a blessing for Joseph, as his defensive game was almost nonexistent last season. He became more aware of what he has to do without the puck and he now uses his assets (speed, above-average hockey sense) effectively in his own end. Recalled in the midseason, Joseph displayed a high skill level with the puck and explosiveness in major junior, finishing the season with a respectable 11 points in 30 games on a rebuilding team. He loves to rush the puck in the neutral zone, and he executes things well in the offensive zone.

We would love to see him more involved in the physical game, as he struggled when facing tougher defenders, losing many one-on-one battles. While he still needs to add a few pounds on his slight frame, Joseph might have what it takes to get under NHL scouts' radars next season if the numbers are there and he improves his puck protection.

Juulsen, Noah
RD – Everett Silvertips (WHL) - 6'1" 165
Noah is a hard hitting, physical defender who moves the puck well and likes to jump into the play.

Karrer, Roger
RD – GCK Lions U20 (Elite Jr.A) 5'11" 176
Karrer is not the biggest defenseman out there, but he showed at the U18 world championship that he could play a physical game, as he threw some good hits during the tournament. He's good in his one-on-one coverage, didn't back down from Alex Tuch in a situation where the American forward is much more bigger, and stronger than him. He was paired with Siegenthaler at the U18, and both did a fairly good job even as underagers. He made some good pinches on the powerplay, and moveed the puck pretty well. He's smart defender with great wheels, and he can move the puck out of his zone pretty efficiently. He's also a right-handed shot who can play on the powerplay, and those are always hot commodities by NHL teams at the draft. This season with his club team Karrer had 4 points in 32 games, and also played at the Calgary macs midget tournament over the holiday where he had 11 points in 7 games.

Kase, David
LW – KLH Chomutov U20 (Czech) 5'10" 150
Kase is the younger brother of Ondrej, who's eligible for the 2014 NHL draft. The younger Kase played this year internationally both at the U17 and U18 level for his country. He also played with his club team at the U18 & U20 level, where he collected a combined 61 points in 49 games. He was one of the better Czech players at the U17 hockey challenge, and finished the tournament with 6 points in 5 games for a Czech team that eventually finished 7th in the tournament. Kase also had success at the U18 level playing at the February five nations, and the U18 world hockey championship where he scored the overtime winner in the semi-final versus Canada. Kase is a very skill forward who skates well, and can make sharp turns on his skates. He's very agile going east west. He's also very creative with the puck, and makes his linemates better. Even undersized, he was able to protect the puck decently at the U17 level, but struggled more to make an impact when he made the jump at the U18 level, where his lack of strength was more evident. He has a good hockey sense, and knows where to be on the ice, and he makes smart plays in the offensive zone. Kase lacks velocity on his shot but we like his release, as it doesn't take much to get the puck off his stick. He'll need to work harder in the defensive zone, and become a better two-way forward. His puck skills are very easy to see on the ice, but at times he was a victim of trying to do much with it and turned the puck over.

Karlsson, Gabriel
LD – Linköping J18 (SuperElit) 6'3" 176
Karlsson is a defenseman with a lanky frame who played for team Sweden at the U17 hockey challenge in Cape-Breton, where Sweden finished 6th. He has nice confidence with the puck on his stick, but gets in trouble sometimes when he gets fancy while rushing it, as his decision-making can be poor at times. He can take too much time to make a decision with the puck on his stick, and this can lead to turnovers. In the offensive zone he has a good shot, and is quite effective at getting puck on net, but tends to always look for passes before shooting the puck. During the tournament he played on the 2nd powerplay unit. His passes are accurate, and helpful for the transition game.

In his zone he's not afraid to finish his hits. Though he has not filled his 6'3" frame yet, he's capable of pinning his man to the wall, and does a good job in front of the net. Poor decision-making can also affect him in the defensive zone, and that can lead to him chasing players in the defensive zone and being out of position.

Kashtanov, Ivan
C – Krasnaya Armiya Moskva (MHL) 5'10" 205

Kashtanov was the captain of team Russia at the U-17s, and was one of the most consistent forwards for Russia during the tournament, even though he didn't score as much as others during the event. He competes hard at both ends of the rink, and was an effective forechecker. He has a strong stick. In the bronze medal game he was one of the few Russians who showed up in the first two periods of the game, and gave an honest effort. He's strong on the puck, and protects the puck very well due to his good frame. He's a good stickhandler, likes to challenge defensemen one-on-one, and showed some impressive dekes during the tournament. Kashtanov showed good poise with the puck in the offensive zone, and can find his open teammates with ease. He sees the ice well, and is good on the powerplay. He's capable of playing a physical game, is strong on his skates, and tough to knock down. This season with his MHL team he collected 16 points in 35 games. He was recently drafted 5th overall in the KHL draft by CSKA Moskva.

Kolesar, Keegan
RW – Seattle Thunderbirds (WHL) - 6'1" 216

Keegan is a polarizing player to watch. With his size and skill, Keegan has the ability to be dominant, but the problem is that he is very inconsistent and is sometimes seemingly unengaged. Keegan is a proto-typical power forward that loves to throw his weight around. He is a punishing hitter and he is strong along the walls.

On top of his tremendous size, Keegan has a good skillset where he is able to generate offense with the puck on his stick. He has good top speed, but his agility and acceleration both need work despite noticeable improvements in those areas this season. When he has generated speed, he is able to drive to the net at will as there are very few players that can contain him.

Keegan's downsides include his limited vision as he tends to drive through people instead of even looking for options to distribute the puck and the effort/consistency issue. The latter issue is mostly apparent in his play away from the puck where he tends to float and limits the time spent in his own end. Keegan has all the skill and strength to succeed as a pro, but will need to improve his effort and consistency.

Kolias, Vasili
D – Chicago Mission U18 – 5' 10" 155 (2015)

He is a little undersized sized for a D-man but has decent hands and makes good initial breakout passes. He seems a bit odd in his skating but efficient enough. He shows some offensive notions as will get in on the score sheet although at times will play too loosey-goosey and passive on the 1-on-1 situations on the defensive side. He needs to play more aggressive as well as add strength and size. He is committed to BU (Hockey East).

Knott, Graham
LW – Niagara Ice Dogs (OHL) – 6'03" 180

Graham was a third round selection of the Ice Dogs and fought his way onto the team with a strong work ethic mixed in with some skill. Knott made an impression for himself finishing his checks hard and driving the net with the puck. He controls the puck well for a big forward and really improved his skating from the previous season, although there is still room for improvement in that area. He has a very powerful shot and good positioning in the offensive zone making him a threat when his line gains the offensive zone. Despite this he is very defensively reliable and will back-check and compete in his own zone. Combined with great size Graham just needs to add a little more muscle to his frame and he will be ready to continue to raise his stock for the 2015 NHL Draft.

Kodola, Vladislav
LC – Sarnia Sting (OHL) – 5'10" 155

Vladislav came over to Sarnia after being selected at the 2013 CHL Import Draft. He got off to a bit of a slow start displaying flashes of speed, elusiveness and puck skills but never put it all together on a consistent basis. As the season progressed these flashes became more evident and he began making more of an impact on the team. He is undersized but is generally capable of evading checkers in the neutral zone with the puck allowing him to take the puck up ice. He is willing to distribute the puck amongst his linemates and is a very pass first type of player. Moving towards the next draft he has a bit of an uphill battle because he looks very tiny on the ice and will drastically need to add muscle and preferably grow a little bit. He is pretty quiet on his side of the red line so if he is going to be an offensive first player he is going to need to play to his top potential on a much more regular basis in order to reach his potential and hear his name called at the 2015 NHL Entry Draft. Vladislav may also want to consider converting to the wing during the offseason as his faceoff percentage throughout this season in our viewings was around the 10-15% range.

Kohn, Mason
LC – Kitchener Rangers (OHL) – 5'10" 176

Mason was a very pleasant surprise for us, and surely the Rangers this season. After going in the 10th round of the 2013 OHL Priority Selection Draft, Mason made the team out of camp, and was for the most part their best, and most consistent 16-year-old this season. Mason isn't the biggest player, but he is a quick skater, and does a great job providing pressure on the forecheck. He forced several turnovers in our viewings, and showed a consistent, effective work ethic. Mason also showed us offensive upside possessing quick hands, good puck control, and a powerful shot. He showed signs of being able to take his offensive game to the next level. Mason is a very intriguing prospect for the 2015 NHL Entry Draft, and will have to battle some older players for ice, but has certainly shown the potential to be a key player for the young upstart Rangers.

Konecny, Travis
RC – Ottawa 67's (OHL) – 5'10" 166

Travis was the first overall selection at the 2013 OHL Priority Selection Draft out of the Elgin-Middlesex Chiefs program. Travis came into the 2013-2014 season with very high expectations, and he did not disappoint. He is a smooth explosive skater with very shifty moves, and can change direction on a dime. He changes gears very quickly; combined with his excellent puck handling ability he can be extremely hard to defend. Travis is very dangerous in the goal area with the puck. He has a quick accurate release on his shot, but is also capable of scoring highlight reel goals. Despite his goal scoring ability, Konecny is very unpredictable with the puck, and commonly chooses the smart option. He is a gifted playmaker, and can thread the needle on even the most difficult of passes. Generally if you play shot, he'll find a pass, and if you play the pass he can beat defenders one-on-one and gets power in his shot. Despite a lack of size, Konecny plays with an intriguing edge finishing his checks, playing with a little grit, and isn't afraid to take the hit for his team. Ultimately Konecny is a top prospect for the 2015 NHL Entry Draft, and gave NHL Scouts a preview of his talent at the U18 in Finland this past April. We will look for him to improve his strength over the summer.

Korostelev, Nikita
RW – Sarnia Sting (OHL) – 6'02" 176

Nikita was selected in the first round by the Sarnia Sting and due to joining a young team was able to exhibit his excellent offensive upside right from the start with his outstanding first career OHL goal. Nikita has an NHL level shot right now and is extremely dangerous when given any chance to shoot the puck from anywhere that could be considered a decent scoring area. He is also dangerous on breakaways and in shootouts because of his excellent hands combined with his powerful shot. What goes underrated about Korostelev is, much like Goldobin who also has strong finishing ability, Nikita is capable of making creative and intelligent passes and has created a wealth of scoring chances as well as goals for his linemates. Korostelev will challenge defenders one on one and is usually successful. His forecheck can be a little inconsistent but when he's on he shows great determination and is capable of forcing turnovers. His physical play is also inconsistent, but when he's in the mood for it, he can hit fairly hard. His skating is effective for someone his size and age but has room for improvement, particularly his first few steps. Nikita will need to improve on his consistency with his forechecking and physicality in addition to improving his first few steps. However with that said, he is among the most pure offensive talents expected to come out of the OHL at the 2015 NHL Entry Draft and possesses more size than those who are ahead of him at the moment.

Kotsovos, Anthony
RD – Windsor Spitfires (OHL) – 6'00" 180

Anthony split time this season with the OHL's Windsor Spitfires, and the London Jr. B Nationals. He played a limited role with Windsor when they were facing lots of injuries, and chipped in physically making basic puck plays. With the Nationals, Anthony was a big minute defenseman who played all game situations. While he is only average size on the blueline, he is extremely strong, and loves to punish opposing players. He is very aggressive, and battles hard along the wall. Kotsovos is generally very positionally sound in the defensive zone, but can chase the puck carrier at times. He is limited in the offensive department, but his shot is fairly good, and he generally makes the smart decision with the puck. His first pass is very good, and he consistently delivers hard, accurate passes. Kotsovos is expected to make the Spitfires full time next season, as he appears ready for the next step, and could become a player to watch for the 2015 NHL Entry Draft.

Kovacs, Robin
RW – AIK J20 (SuperElit) 6'0" 163

Kovacs is late-96 birthday that played in the SuperElit U20 league this season with AIK J20, and finished the year with 28 points in 40 games. He also played three games in the Swedish Hockey League without registering a single point. His number one attribute is his vision, as he's an excellent passer who can find his linemates with ease on the ice. We first saw Kovacs at the 2013 world under-17 hockey challenge where he helped Sweden win the gold. He has good hands, and is capable of manufacturing offense with his great speed. He still needs to add weight on his frame, as he can struggle against bigger players in puck battles in the corner and in front of the net. He has good anticipation, and a good active stick, which makes him a strong penalty killer. Kovacs plays a sound defensive game, and works hard in his own zone.

Kreis, Matthew
LW – Barrie Colts (OHL) – 5'11" 175

Kreis had a relatively good rookie campaign after being selected in the first round of the 2013 OHL Draft by the Colts. For the most part Kreis played in a bottom-6 role, but he was still able to produce some offense and contribute. Kreis is a good skater who's shifty with the puck, and hard to contain. He has very good hands, and can regularly stickhandle his way around opposing players. Kreis sees the ice well, and does a good job of passing to teammates as they hit open ice or before they reach a certain spot on the ice. He backchecked regularly for the most part, and tried to help the team in any way he could. One thing Matthew will need to work on is bulking up and adding strength, as against bigger, older opposing players he was pushed off the puck quite easily at times. With a regular shift in the top-6 of the Colts next year, Kreis will have more opportunity to produce and showcase his offensive skills to scouts.

Kylington, Oliver
LD – Färjestad (SHL) 6'0" 181

Kylington is a dynamic defensemen who brings a lot of offense from the blueline. The first thing you notice with Kylington is his speed and footwork. He can really fly on the ice, and loves to rush the puck into the offensive zone. He makes quick decision with the puck on the powerplay, and he's an excellent puck mover. At 16 years old, Kylington played in the Swedish Elite league this season becoming the youngest player in the league history to score a goal. He finished the season with two goals and six points in 32 games with Färjestad this season. He also played with his team in the exhibition tournament versus AHL teams. We saw him in Toronto against the Toronto Marlies, where he showed excellent poise and confidence with the puck. He was not afraid to carry the puck and did make some mistakes, but we really like the fact that he didn't play scared and played like he belongs there. In the AHL all-stars skill competition he showed off how quick his hands are scoring a very nice shootout goal. His puck skills are excellent, and as he showed there he's very dangerous one-on-one with a goaltender. At times he can be a victim of trying to do much with the puck, and can turn the puck over. This is due to being inexperienced, and playing against much older and more experienced competition. Due to having already a key role on his club team, Kylington didn't play in any of the major tournaments with his age group during this season. Adding strength would make him a more complete player, as he can be outmuscled for the puck in his zone, and in front of the net.

Laczynski, Tanner
F – Chicago Mission U18 – 5' 10" 161 (2015)

He shows some good offensive ideas and scoring senses. He possesses decent stick skills too and led the Chicago Mission U16 in scoring and also played some time as an under-ager with the U18 club. He will need to add size and strength but Ohio St. has recruited Laczynski's services in a couple of years.

Larsson, Jacob
LD – Frölunda J18 (J18 Allsvenskan) 6'2" 181

Larsson is a very mobile defenseman with good footwork who makes a lot of smart decisions on the ice. He's a strong passer, and is able to make some tough passes while under pressure. He's capable of starting the rush either by rushing the puck up ice, or making quick outlets to start the transition game. He's not afraid to jump into the play and join the rush. He showed great confidence with the puck. He's not an overly physical player, but he's capable of throwing a good hit here and there. He could add mass to his frame to win more puck battles. On the powerplay, he has shown a good, accurate, low, hard slap shots from the point. Larsson's also displayed good confidence playing the point on the powerplay. He has quick feet, and can use those quick feet to get out of trouble easily. Defensively he's solid, and always keeps an active stick to get in the passing lanes, and block shots. This season with his club team Frölunda, Larsson played with three different teams but mostly played at the U18 level where he had 25 points in 38 games.

Lazarev, Leo
G – Waterloo Siskins (GOJHL) – 5'10" 160

Lazarev was drafted 24th Overall by the Ottawa 67's at the 2014 OHL Priority Selection Draft. Leo is a 1997 born Russian goaltender who gained residency status in Canada, which allowed himself to be selected by the Ottawa 67's in the 2014 OHL Priority Selection Draft after spending this past season with Jr. B Waterloo Siskins. Leo is extremely meticulous of his routine, more than any OHL goaltending prospect of recent memory. He has a lengthy routine when going out to his net, which really sets the tone for the style in which he plays. Lazarev is lightning quick, and has exceptional reflexes. He does an excellent job on breakaways, and is nearly impossible to beat on the lower half of the net. He holds his glove very high, but is effective with the glove hand. He sets himself in position extremely early in comparison to most goaltenders, and centers himself very well towards shooters. His side-to-side movement is also excellent, and well above the average goaltender his age.

While Leo has a wealth of strengths, which make him very intriguing as a prospect for the OHL, he has his share of concerns. Almost every shot that hits him becomes a rebound. For a goaltender that is very aggressive towards the puck carrier when entering the zone, he will come well out of his crease to eliminate angles. Unfortunately this combined with his lack of rebound control can put him too far out of position at times, even for his outstanding recovery abilities on the second shot. He looks much smaller than his listing (closer to 5'8"- 5'9"), and can commit a little early dropping into the butterfly exposing the top of the net in a way that skilled OHL snipers will be able to exploit. He is also aggressive with the poke check, which has had its positives when he is successful, but when he misses it exposes a lot of net. Leo also loves to play the puck, however this is certainly not one of his strong areas, and fairly often resulted in a turnover. It should be an interesting year to see how Lazarev transitions to the OHL as a rookie because it will also be his NHL Draft Eligible season as well.

Lemcke, Justin
RD – Belleville Bulls (OHL) – 6'02" 198

Justin was the Bulls 1st round selection at the 2013 OHL Priority Selection Draft. He was almost immediately given key ice time for the young and rebuilding Bulls team playing on the team's power play and penalty kill in addition to his 5 on 5 ice. Justin is a big physical defenseman who likes to take the body whenever possible without going overboard. He is physically more mature than most players his age which helped him develop the ability to contain opponents along the wall despite being only 16 years old. He has a huge shot from the point which made him effective on the power play, however he needs to get more accurate with his shot. This year was a great development for Lemcke and will put him in a better situation for the 2015 NHL Entry Draft. His skating is still a main concern for us and while he has improved in his decision making he can still be pressured into making mistakes and will need to continue to reduce these occurrences if he would like to be among the top defenders taken out of the OHL next year.

Lalonde, Bradley
LD – Cape Breton Screaming Eagles (QMJHL) – 6'0" 194

Lalonde, who was selected in the 2nd round of the QMJHL draft by Cape-Breton, made a big jump playing full-time in the league after playing last year in Midget Espoir with the Lac St-Louis Royals. We have always been very impressed with Lalonde's smarts, as he is very steady from shift to shift but won't wow you with any of his skills. He has good hockey sense, and always makes quick decision with the puck. Not a flashy player, but will take the safe route in his puck movement. Lalonde is tough to beat one-on-one, thanks to a good footing, although he lacks top speed and need to work on his explosions to become an even better all-around skater. He's tough on his skates, and we like his competiveness but won't describe him as an aggressive defender. Not an offensive defensemen either, but makes good passes and is able to rush the puck on occasion. Lacks the hands and offensive instincts that his teammate Jason Bell has. Has a good slapshot from the point that can be useful on the powerplay. The Saint-Anne- de- Bellevue native represented his province at the U-17 Hockey Challenge in front of his home fans in Cape-Breton. Lalonde was playing a regular shift on defense for Team Quebec, and played mostly in defensive situations.

Lanoue, Vincent
LD – Quebec Remparts (QMJHL) 5'10" 178

He is an undersized defender who provides physical implication for his team. He's strong and keeps other teams honest with his ability to deliver some clean hits along the wall. He is always well positioned and executes details well in one-on-one situations. His awareness on the ice is good, always adjusting to his opponent's positioning in all 3 zones, staying on the defensive side of the puck. He offers good coverage in front of his net and is not intimidated there. He makes good first passes out of the zone, but lacks creativity and offensive skill to do much damage. He keeps it very simple with the puck, and does not try to take many chances from the blue line. He has below average hands, and his shooting ability is just average. He gets outmuscled by bigger forwards in puck battles, but his high tenacity gives him a chance to win some. He lacks dynamic skating, but he moves laterally well. He keeps his stick active and gets his body in front of shots and passes.

Lauzon, Jeremy
LD – Rouyn-Noranda Huskies (QMJHL) – 6'0" 179

The Huskies drafted Lauzon 20th overall in the 2013 QMJHL draft, after seeing him play a midget season with the Amos Forestiers in the Quebec Midget AAA league. Lauzon saw quite a bit of ice time in the 2nd half of the season with Rouyn-Noranda after the team's top defenseman, Dillon Fournier, had to have season-ending shoulder surgery.

Lauzon is a solid two-way defenseman with good attributes to contribute offensively. He's a strong skater with good top speed who likes to rush the puck from his zone. His footing is decent and he would need some upgrades with his quickness and fluidity, which would help him in his defensive zone coverage. Already at 16, he was used quite often on the power play, and even more in the 2nd half of the season after Fournier went down. He has nice qualities as a power play quarterback, as he has a good, accurate shot from the point and makes strong tape-to-tape passes. His decision-making has improved this season; he makes his decision quicker with the puck now. The Val-d'Or native is quite active on the power play, as he doesn't stand still and that makes him tough to defend. Made a quick adaptation to the major junior level, which helps in gaining his coaches' trust and getting more ice time. He's a strong player on his skates and can play a physical game when needed. It also looks like he has gotten a whole lot stronger since last year. In his zone he's effective in using his stick and blocking passing lanes, and he has become a good shot-blocker over the past two seasons. He's a player with no glaring weaknesses or strengths, but did progress a lot this season. Lauzon was not selected to play for Team Quebec at the U-17 Hockey Challenge in Cape Breton.

Léveillé, Loik
RD - Cape Breton Screaming Eagles (QMJHL) - 6'0" 218

Loik Léveillé has already been traded twice during his two year stint in the QMJHL. Originally drafted by the Baie-Comeau Drakkar in 2012, he was sent to Chicoutimi along with a couple of picks for Jérémy Grégoire. Chicoutimi traded him to Cape Breton during mid season to complete a deal made earlier for Nicolas Roy.

What we like about Léveillé's game is that he likes to join the rush and his offensive passing skills are also very good, creating plays with solid crisp cross-ice passes in the offensive zone. He is a smooth skater who's very strong on his feet with great footwork. He has a booming shot from the point and moves the puck well on the power play. He has very good hands that he is able to use to maneuver around opponents as he is skating at full speed while rushing the puck. Defensively, he has done a good job blocking shots in his own end and uses his stick to challenge the puck carrier and to knock the puck away from the opposition. He plays with some good physicality along the boards to separate his man from the puck and also makes some big hits at times to knock his man over. His biggest weakness is his consistency with his decision making. In some games we have seen he always made good decisions and on other nights, he panicked and made the life hard on himself and his team. That was the case especially in this year's playoffs against the Gatineau Olympiques where he really struggled. When he does so, he takes too much time to take his decisions and causes a lot of turnovers. He seems to think too much at times and he just needs to execute. He has the physical tools and the skillset to have an impact offensively next year in the QMJHL.

Lindberg, Brandon
LC – Sarnia Sting (OHL) – 6'00" 188

Brandon joined the Sting midway through the season from the Saginaw Spirit. Lindberg played very limited ice on the Spirit generally seeing ice time on the fourth line but graduated to the second and third lines on the rebuilding Sting and ultimately worked his way into top penalty killing minutes. Brandon is an outstanding penalty killer for his age and does an exemplary job shutting down opponents with great positioning, getting his stick in lanes and creates more scoring chances short handed most games than he does 5 on 5. He is an excellent skater who is capable of possessing the puck then separating from defenders on the penalty kill to get short handed opportunities, some of which resulted in goals. Five on five Brandon does a modest job creating offense usually moving the puck to his linemates in scoring areas. He can make some mental mistakes in the offensive zone from time to time but his outstanding backcheck combined with his speed allows him to recover from these mistakes. Going into the 2015 NHL Entry Draft Brandon doesn't show us anything that makes us believe he will be an offensive player at the NHL level but if he continues to get stronger and adds a bit of a physical element to his game, he's going to look like an excellent potential option as a two-way forward.

Lizotte, Cameron
LD – Peterborough Petes (OHL) – 6'02" 196

The 2013-2014 season was a good learning experience for the young defender in Peterborough. He has good size and is very strong but went through his share of growing pains. He battles hard and uses his strength along the walls but can lose proper positioning impeding his ability to win as many battles as he could. He can sometimes take undisciplined penalties as well. He had plenty of hit and miss situations in the defensive zone but seemed to improve in his consistency. Offensively he is very limited but is capable of making the simple pass and has a powerful shot from the point. He needs to pick his spots when utilizing this shot as he can put it into the opponents shinpads. Lizotte will see increased ice with the Petes next year. He already has the size and the physical mentality and if he can improve some of the concerns in his play he could turn into a very solid NHL prospect.

Malgin, Denis
C/RW – GC Küsnacht Lions (NLB) 5'9" 176

Malgin is an exciting young forward from Switzerland. He's a very good puckhandler, and likes to challenge opposing defensemen one-on-one as he has a great arsenal of dekes. Malgin is tiny and lacks strength, but he competes hard, and can create offense out of nothing. He's a decent skater but has a nice burst of speed down the wing, and can make him look opposing defensemen slow. The best quality of Malgin's game is his playmaking ability. He's very poised with the puck, and can control it very well on the powerplay. He can either play on the wing or at center, and he's willing to hold on the puck for an extra second to make a play. This season in the NLB, Malgin had 19 points in 38 games, and at the world under-18 championship had seven points in five games. He did very well with Kevin Fiala & Noah Rod at the tournament. Malgin dad's is originally from Russia and you can see in Denis game there's some Russian influence in the way he can stickhandle in a phone booth. Malgin struggles when the game gets physical, and he has to face tough physical matchups due to his lack of strength.

Marner, Mitchell
RC – London Knights (OHL) – 5'10" 164

Marner was the first round selection of the London Knights at the 2013 OHL Priority Selection Draft. He made an immediate impact, receiving ice on virtually every line on the Knights this season, earning some rare top-six ice as a 16-year-old on a stacked London team. Mitchell is a slightly undersized, but extremely skilled forward who possesses explosive speed, the ability to change directions on a dime, and elude checkers with ease. His most impressive skill is his vision. He reads plays at a rate quicker than most players in the OHL, and can create something out of nothing with the puck. He has the hockey sense to read when he can beat a defender, when the best option is to pass off, and while he appears to be a pass first player, he is capable of scoring some beautiful goals. Mitchell is one of the best players in the OHL eligible for the 2015 NHL Entry Draft. He should focus on getting stronger over the off-season, as there is really no glaring weakness to Marner that can't be resolved by strength or size, only one of which is in his control.

McAvoy, Charles
D – USNTDP-17 – 5'11" 189 (2015)

He is a smooth skater and covers ice fairly well for averaged sized D-man with adequate positioning and good use of body. He makes good initial passes and plays poised with puck. He needs to get stronger but shows a promising game. He plays with NTDP in Ann Arbor, MI and is headed to Boston University (Hockey East) is a couple of seasons.

McBride, Nick
G – Prince Albert Raiders (WHL) - 6'3" 176

Nick is a big goalie that uses his size well. He moves well and is able to quickly go post to post. McBride is a goalie that's found success everywhere he's gone and this past season, he learned the ropes this season as the backup to veteran Cole Cheveldave. Late in the season, McBride was outplaying the vet and earned numerous starts along the playoff stretch run including the playoff play-in game against Red Deer in which the Raiders won to earn the final playoff spot. He has a good compete level, makes himself big and battles for pucks. Nick is arguably the WHL's top goalie prospect for 2015.

McCool, Hayden
LW – Niagara Ice Dogs (OHL) – 6'03" 195

Hayden was selected in the first round of the 2013 OHL Priority Selection Draft but did not quite play up to his potential this year. Hayden has excellent size and is a very good puck protector but needs to add some more aggression and intensity into his game. He has the size of a power forward but aside from driving the net with power he plays a game suited for someone much smaller than he is. He showed puck skill but wasn't able to finish this season. He is a capable passes and can hold the puck for long periods of time due to his size and wait for the right opening. He will also compete defensively. In order to start reaching his potential Hayden will need to start thinking the game faster. This is easier said than done and was our major concern going into his rookie season. If he can either think the game faster or become a mean physical winger that opponents hate to play against then you should be able to see McCool's name rise up the 2015 NHL Draft list.

McDavid, Connor
LC – Erie Otters (OHL) – 6'00" 185

Connor is a top prospect for the 2015 NHL Entry Draft, and has done everything in his power to maintain his place among the best prospects over the past few years. He is a dynamic offensive talent who displays excellent skating ability. He has one-step explosiveness, and can catch defenders flat footed. He is extremely dangerous one-on-one for even the most experienced and effective defensive defenders at the OHL level. In addition to his speed he has outstanding creativity with the puck, and sees things that most players simply don't see. He can take a nothing play and turn it into a goal, and just when you think you have him beat, he will find a passing lane, and make it look easy. McDavid is much more of a playmaker than a scorer, but is capable of putting the puck in the net. He doesn't have an overly powerful shot, but has a quick release with excellent accuracy, finding the perfect spot. He is also an exceptional stick handler, and can make goaltenders look ridiculous with his puck handling ability. This is how he scores most of his goals. McDavid doesn't really have much in terms of glaring weaknesses. He isn't overly physical, but he isn't expected to provide that style of game. He does need to improve the consistency of his backcheck. He also had short stretches of the season where lacked some consistency. While it is difficult to play at that high level game in and game out, he will want to boost that consistency up a little going into what is very likely his final junior season.

McFadden, Garrett
RD – Guelph Storm (OHL) 5'10" 186

McFadden is a skilled offensive defender from the Guelph Storm. Garrett was the first round pick of the Storm in the 2013 OHL Draft. He saw limited time this season due to the elite depth on the blue line for the Storm. When he did see time he was very impressive. He is a strong skater with a fluid stride that makes rushing the puck look easy. McFadden showed a good understanding of defensive zone positioning and uses his smarts to break up plays and get his stick into passing lanes. He would benefit from adding some strength in the off season to help play a more physical role in the corners. He is an excellent passer and makes a strong crisp first pass to spark quick breakout opportunities. Garrett is extremely poised when controlling the puck and seemed to fit right into the lineup when given the opportunity. The Storm certainly has high expectations of McFadden for next season and he appears ready to step into the role.

McKenzie, Brett
C – North Bay Battalion (OHL) – 6'1" 192

After being selected in the first round by the North Bay Battalion, McKenzie jumped right into the line-up for the eventual 2014 Eastern Conference Champions. Brett has good size and uses it well to protect the puck and cycle down low. He finishes his checks effectively and plays with an edge but needs to continue to get stronger because despite size gets knocked around a little when opponents deliver checks to him. He has good power in his shot and has a bit of a shoot first mentality but is capable of creating rebounds with his shot. He has a good top speed but his first few steps could use some improvements. Brett primarily played a bottom six role for the Battalion this season and did moderately well statistically. With the graduation of a few key forwards, McKenzie should be able to push his way into atleast a partial top six role and show the offensive side of his game as well as the physical play leading into the 2015 NHL Entry Draft.

Miller, David
RC – SOO Greyhounds (OHL) – 5'09" 169

Miller has been on our radar for a long time after his outstanding performance for the Mississauga Rebels two seasons ago. Miller has continued to improve his game and despite being a little undersized he made a great impact for the Greyhounds regularly being relied upon for offensive contribution. He has excellent puck handling skills and is very dangerous in one on one situations. He has a quick release on his shot and gains deceptive power. He received plenty of power play ice and moved the puck extremely well in these situations making intelligent choices based on the situation. Miller shows great offensive intelligence and talent but can get knocked around a little due to his lack of size and strength. Miller should be a fun player to watch going into the 2015 NHL Entry Draft. He possesses a lot of skill and speed but lacks size and strength and should play a slightly increased role with the Greyhounds.

Meier, Timo
RW – Halifax Mooseheads (QMJHL) – 6'0" 200

Meier was the 12th overall selection in the 2013 CHL Import Draft by the Halifax Mooseheads, who also selected Nikolaj Ehlers with the 6th overall pick. Meier is a very different player in comparison to Ehlers, as he's not as flashy or speedy, but does a lot of dirty work along the wall and pays attention to small details. The Swiss forward plays a very North American game and likes to get involved physically in games; the more the year progressed, the more he was involved and comfortable with that style of play. For most of the year, Meier played on a 3rd line with the high-powered Mooseheads, and didn't get as many opportunities on the power play to show off his offensive skills as a guy like Ehlers did. Plays a powerful north and south game, and he's not very tall, but is sturdy on his skates and takes the puck to the net. The North American game suits him well, as he is not a great puckhandler and can lack confidence at times with the puck, but he does work in tougher areas of the ice. With a better supporting cast on his line, he could see his production improve next season. Seeing him earlier this season, his skating was worrisome as he didn't have great speed and his footing was average at best. He has since made some strides in this department, not that he's suddenly a great skater, but he made some nice progress and it will keep getting better as he keeps getting stronger. He has a good wrist shot as well, but we would like to see him make quicker decisions with the puck on his stick and improve his release as well.

Meloche, Nicolas
RD - Baie-Comeau Drakkar (QMJHL) - 6'02" 195

Meloche has been one of our favorites all season long. Drafted in the first round by the Baie-Comeau Drakkar in the QMJHL Draft, he logged a lot of minutes this year on a contending team. He was named to the QMJHL All-Rookie Team along Jérémy Roy.

For his size, he has fairly good skating abilities. He has very good speed and his footwork in tight areas is exceptional. Meloche can maintain a tight gap against opponents and gives them very little opportunity to score off the rush. He won a lot of battles along the wall and he's steady and relaxed on the penalty kill, maintaining a presence without chasing the play. He protects his goalie and teammates, coming to their aid after whistles. He will drop the mitts when necessary. He has a mean streak and it shows in his physical play. He is not afraid to deliver big hits and is clearly not intimidated to play against older players. Meloche pinches in from the point at the right time making him dangerous during sustained pressure. He makes very intelligent decisions with the puck, and very rarely ever misplays it. We really liked his poise. He's not especially dynamic but he's very effective at protecting the puck and reacting to pressure. When he doesn't have a lane to break the play out himself, his outlets and stretch passes are excellent. The Rosemère native moves the puck extremely well up ice and can be relied upon to make the smart decision on the point on the power play. He has a good shot from the blueline and uses it well on the powerplay. His hard slap shot is always low and often finds his way to the net. Consistency will be an important area for him to improve upon moving forward. He can be laid back sometimes and it can affect his game.

Merkley, Nick
RC – Kelowna Rockets (WHL) – 5'10" 176

Nick had a brilliant rookie season for the Rockets this year where he earned the WHL Rookie of the Year award over notable players such as Nikita Scherbak and Matt Barzal. Merkley thinks the game at a very high level and also has the matching skill to execute on that advantage. He isn't overly large big, but doesn't shy away from traffic. He can handle the puck at top speed and in traffic. He sees the ice well and is a very good puck distributor that's also not afraid to go to the net. Nick is a smooth skater with very good speed and agility. He's able to generate good lower body strength and is strong on his skates. Merkley never stops moving his feet.

Defensively, Nick hustles back and is a strong backchecker. He has excellent awareness both with and without the puck. He is particularly dangerous in transition as his ability to force turnovers and pick off errant passes gives him scoring chances when opponents are most vulnerable. He uses that good awareness to break up plays and quickly transition up ice.

He is the rare 16 year-old that is able to have offense run through him rather than to just contribute as a complimentary piece. Nick is a favorite to be a 1st round pick in the 2015 draft.

Samuel Montembeault
G - Blainville-Boisbriand Armada (QMJHL) - 6'02" 164

Montembeault is tall, lanky goaltender who was a favorite of ours in last year's QMJHL Draft, and backstopped his midget team to the Dodge Cup championship in 2013. He was selected in the 3rd round by the Blainville-Boisbriand Armada in last June's draft. This year, he was the backup to Étienne Marcoux with the Armada and didn't get a lot of playing time, playing in 14 regular season games and one playoff game. The Bécancour native is very solid down low, plays a butterfly style, has long legs and is very quick to cover the lower part of the net. Has a good, quick glove, but needs to do a better job tracking the puck with traffic in front of him, as he can get caught out of position and could do a better job anticipating the play. He has a nice projectable frame for a goaltender, as he was listed at 6'2", 164 pounds at the beginning of the year and still grew this season. He came in relieve to Marcoux in Game 7 in Rimouski in the second round, and we really loved how he reacted and was super confident in his crease. With Marcoux graduating next season, Montembeault should get plenty of playing time next year. If he keeps progressing, he could be one of the best QMJHL goaltenders available for next year's draft.

Moore, Ryan
LC – Windsor Spitfires (OHL) – 5'07" 155

Ryan is an undersized but skilled forward, who was the first player selected by the Windsor Spitfires at the 2013 OHL Priority Selection Draft. While caught behind older forwards on the Spitfires, Moore played a reduced bottom-six role for his team this season, playing primarily on the fourth line in our viewings. Moore is an excellent skater with explosive acceleration, and a good top speed. He is shifty, and controls the puck well in traffic. Ryan embraced the energy line role well for a small skilled forward, and was willing to physically compete with much bigger players, and finish his checks. Ryan will look to play a bigger role for the Spitfires next year, and use his speed, and puck skills to contribute more offensively. In regards to the 2015 NHL Entry Draft, Moore certainly has potential but drastically needs to grow to reach his true potential.

Morrison, Brad
LC – Prince George Cougars (WHL) - 5'11" 161

He has just average size, but Brad is a very slippery player that shows good offensive acumen. He thinks the game at a high level and finds seams in coverage. Morrison likes to keep his feet moving and has good speed and agility. Good bloodlines as his father played pro hockey.

When Brad's at his best, he can be a force. He scored nearly half of his points in just four multiple point games, despite dressing for 55 games total. Brad needs to find a way to succeed against bigger players as his lack of strength is an issue. He also needs to do a better job of being willing to pay the price to make a play. For him to garner interest as a top prospect, he'll also have to show better consistency and finds ways to contribute when he isn't scoring.

Morrison, Lochlan
RD – Calgary Hitmen (WHL) - 6'1" 212

Morrison played most of the season for the Telus Cup-winning Prince Albert Mintos of the SMAAAHL where he was captain. He was a key piece to the championship team as a nearly PPG defenseman that was used in all situations. Lochlan was able to get into a handful of games with the Hitmen where he showed that he belonged. A two-way defenseman with good upside, Loch showed a strong ability to make an accurate first-pass and was entrusted to even play some special team minutes as part of his call up. Morrison has a strong shot and he thinks the game at a higher than average level. As a result, he's been able to have some success as a trigger man on the power-play.

While Morrison has offensive upside, he also is strong defensively. Morrison has very good size and uses it well along the walls and when defending against large players. He plays a rough and tough game as defined by his 122 penalty minutes with the Mintos in just forty games. That being said, Morrison realized that players are bigger and stronger in the WHL and he will need to continue to get stronger. Morrison showed good positioning against the rush and he uses his strong awareness to locate and eliminate the potential for scoring chances. Morrison is an average skater and will need to work on all aspects of his skating from mobility/pivots, acceleration, and top speed.

Moynihan, Connor
LW – Halifax Mooseheads (QMJHL) – 6'3" 203

The younger of the Moynihans to join the Mooseheads this season, Connor is a big, strong forward who plays a real power forward game. The 92nd overall selection in the 2013 QMJHL draft showed very quickly that he wouldn't be intimated by finishing his checks, dropping the gloves at times and overall, bringing some good energy to his line this season. Played mostly on the Mooseheads' 4th line this season, but the young American was able to show strong puck protection when using his size to shield opponents away from the puck, and he's a good in the cycle. He's tough to handle down low, and will be even tougher once he gets stronger physically. The biggest weakness in his game right now is his skating. He needs to improve his quickness and footing, but that should come once he matures into his body and gets stronger. It also remains to be seen how much of a goal scorer he will become, as he goes in the right areas of the ice to score, but his hands remain average. Will score a lot of dirty goals in front of the net, where he will be tough to move from by the smaller defensemen across the league. Has a powerful shot, but needs to get it off quickly and make quicker decisions while in possession of the puck. We expect him to increase his production next season with an expanded role on the Mooseheads.

Murray, Troy
LD – Kootenay Ice (WHL) - 6'1" 175

With a mid-September birthday, Troy is one of the youngest players available in the 2015 draft. The younger brother of Ryan is a cerebral defenseman with poise and skill. He has decent size and good mobility. He plays a simple, steady game, but he is always learning and has become more and more dependable as the season has progressed. He shows good patience with the puck and he makes tape-to-tape passes. Troy focuses on his own zone first and foremost. He doesn't often jump into the play offensively, but as the season progressed, he showed a greater propensity to joining the play and aiding his forwards.

Troy has an active stick and does well to keep opponents to the outside against the rush. He is tough to beat off the rush and generally makes smart reads in his end. That being said, Troy can be affected by a strong forecheck – whether that means he forces an inaccurate pass or makes a bad decision. Especially early in the season, Troy was tentative at times. However, he has shown some improvements against the forecheck.

Troy also needs to add strength for when he's battling in the corner and he needs to improve his first few steps. He is a steady, reliable defender that will garner some interest next year.

Musil, Adam
RC – Red Deer Rebels (WHL) - 6'3" 193

Musil showed great progress throughout the course of the season. He had a slow start to the season where he was tentative and needed to adjust to the speed of the WHL pace of play. By the end of the season, he was one of Red Deer's more dangerous forwards. Adam is a very good skater for his age and he owns tremendous size and skill to go along with that.

The son of former NHLer Frank Musil uses his strength and reach to protect the puck. With the puck on his stick, Adam sees the ice well and is a good puck distributor. He has soft hands and is able to feather passes through traffic or stickhandle around opponents. He likes to shoot, although he owns just an average shot at this time. That being said, he flashes through the slot quickly enough that he gets opportunities to score before anyone covers him. He's very opportunistic and gets his share of garbage goals. Adam is able to cycle the puck well and he wins his share of puck battles. His top end speed and agility are good, but he could improve his acceleration.

Adam has high offensive upside, but he is still trying to work out the rest of his game. Like many young players, consistency is an issue with him. He can dominate for a shift and then be invisible for a period. He needs to show more from game to game and even shift to shift. His play away from the puck needs help. He works hard to backcheck, but doesn't seem to know where to be when defending in his own zone. His mental fortitude also needs to improve as we have seen players get under his skin through the course of the season – effectively rendering him useless as he seems more interested in retribution than playing his game.

Adam really has all the tools you could want in a young centre, he just needs to put them together on a regular basis. Right now, Adam is knocking on the door for being a 1st round pick.

Myers, Philippe
RD – Rouyn-Noranda Huskies (QMJHL) – 6'4" 186

Myers, who hails from Dieppe, New Brunswick, was drafted in the 4th round by Rouyn-Noranda in last year's QMJHL draft. He's a player who we had placed higher up in our rankings for our 2013 QMJHL draft guide who was very impressive at the 2013 Gatorade Challenge in Boisbriand, playing a very complete game for Team New Brunswick. Myers grew two inches this year and is a big-sized defenseman who likes to punish opposing forwards in the defensive zone. Look for him to continue to get bigger and stronger and become a more dominant, physical force on the Huskies' blueline. His footing will need some improvement; as of now it remains his biggest drawback. He can get caught flat-footed, getting beaten on the outside by speedy forwards. His puck skills are average. He won't wow anyone with his stickhandling, but makes good decisions with the puck and keeps his game simple. Defensively, he has a long reach that he uses well to block passing lanes and can block shots as well. We love his battle level along the wall in his zone and he's tough to play against. Myers played for Team Atlantic at the recent U-17 Hockey Challenge in Cape-Breton, where they finished 8th in the final standings.

Nättinen, Julius
C – JYP U20 (Jr.A SM-Liiga) 6'2" 187

Nattinen is big center who we first saw last year in the province of Quebec for the World Under-17 hockey challenge when he played as an underager. He showed flashes of a potential there with an already impressive frame for a 15-year-old. This year we got another look at him at the Macs midget tournament in Calgary. He's a hard working center who plays well at both ends of the rink, and can be used in all situations during a game. He's a good skater with a nice and heavy shot. He has good offensive instincts, strong playmaking skills, and a good vision. Nättinen is the younger brother of Canadiens prospect Joonas (Nättinen). He played for JYP U20 team, and had 27 points in 32 games this season.

Newhouse, Ben
D - Benilde-St. Margaret's School (MN) – 5' 8" 165
He is a player small in size but skates quite well and has elusive puck skills from a blue liner. He is quite poised with the puck and has sweet set of hands. He makes good decisions with puck and completing a break-out pass or knowing when to rush the puck. He will need to get stronger, but very shifty on his boots with excellent vision. NCAA Champion Union Dutchmen received his commitment for Fall 2016.

Noël, Nathan
RC - Saint John Sea Dogs (QMJHL) - 5'10" 174
Selected 3rd overall in the 2013 QMJHL draft, Nathan had an immediate impact for the Saint John Sea Dogs this year. The St-John's, Newfoundland native played for the famous prep school Shattuck St-Mary's for two years before joining the Sea Dogs this season. He played on the second line and on the second power play for the biggest part of the year. He has a pretty interesting mesh of jump and quick hands that helped him become really tough to play against in tight areas. He has good offensive instincts and sees open space quite easily. With his package of skills, he could be very dangerous in the offensive zone, and he's an unpredictable player because he can pass the puck or shoot just as well. At times he can have a tendency of holding onto the puck too long trying to create offense, and he likes to rush the puck. Even if he's recognized for his offensive tools, Nathan has worked hard from both ends of the ice. If he didn't have this high-end skill level, he could play a grinder role, because of his high compete level and his motor that never stops. He has a high hockey IQ, he's a good skater with great acceleration and above-average top speed. He can be intimidating for defensemen when he can gain his top speed in the neutral zone and challenge opposing defense in full strides. He has used his speed to come back quickly on the backcheck and support his defense well. He's a spectacular player who can bring fans out of their seats with some impressive rushes and great one-on-one dekes.

Niku, Sami
LD - JYP U20 (JR.A SM-LIIGA) - 6'0" 174
Niku is good puck moving defensemen from Finland who we first saw at the 2013 U17 hockey challenge in Drummondville and Victoriaville, where Finland finished in 7th place. This season he played for his country in various tournaments including the recent U18 world hockey championship, the February five nation tournament, and the Ivan Hlinka tournament in August. He also split time with his club between the 2nd highest men's league in Finland, and the junior club at JYP. Niku moves the puck well from his zone with some good accurate passes, and makes quick decision with the puck. He's a good asset on the powerplay for his team, has shown good poise with the puck, and a good ability of getting the puck on net with a simple wrist shot. Niku doesn't possess a great shot from the point, but always finds a way of getting the puck on net on a regular basis. He's not afraid of rushing the puck from his own end, but needs to be careful as sometime can turn the puck over mishandling it. In the offensive zone he can be victim at time of bad pinches, trying to force things, but has good enough speed to get back defensively after those mistakes. He lack strength due to his slight frame, and this hurts him in battles along the wall and in front of the net. He's also not a real physical guy in his zone.

Norman, Ryan
F – Shattuck St. Mary's Prep – 5' 10" 165

He is a good skater with average size but quite stable on skates with good gears and shows speed. He plays tough on the PK as uses his strong skating and stick to create havoc and break plays up. Norman has all the tools with good stick handling skills, skating, awareness at both ends of the rink, and playmaking ability. He is a late '96 so not draft eligible until 2015, but a player to keep your eye on for the future. He has produced well at Shattuck for two years at the prep level. He is set to step on the campus of Minnesota Golden Gophers in 2015.

Novak, Thomas
C– St. Thomas Academy (MN) – 5'11" 177 (2015)

Invited to the USNTDP ad will either be with hem or with Waterloo in the USHL. He shows what we would describe as high-end hockey sense and skills. He produced great numbers at Minnesota High School ranks at St. Thomas Academy thanks to great creativity and playmaking ability. He truly makes players around him better. He competes hard and makes things happen. He has good speed, and stick skills. He will skate the puck, showcase nifty moves, display his good shooting ability, and will also take the puck to the net. He is pretty decent sized player as well standing close to 6-feet and will need to continue to develop on the defensive side of the puck.

Osburn, Zach
D – Victory Honda U18 – 5' 11" 180 (2015)

He likes to show off his skating abilities and will skate the puck up and distribute nicely. He is a smooth skater and puck handler. He is a threat to score from the point with his shot and dangerous as well in finding the open teammates for the goal. He will drive the puck from the back-end to the net or exhibit his vision and creativity. He plays with good awareness and decision making. He is committed to Michigan State (Big 10).

Ott, Donovan
F – Select Academy U16 – 6' 1" 185

He plays physical, good size, and likes to shoot the puck. He has some nice hands, and creative thoughts, although really likes to snap the puck on net. Donovan has been recruited by Cornell Big Red (ECAC Hockey).

Pawlenchuk, Grayson
LW – Red Deer Rebels (WHL) - 6'0" 180

Pawlenchuk has become a bit of a favourite of ours this season. While he may not have the offensive upside of some of the other top prospects available for the 2015 draft, Pawlenchuk is a player that always gives a good effort and is versatile enough to contribute in a variety of ways. He started the season on fire before suffering an early season injury that caused him to miss a chunk of the season. Upon his return, Grayson picked back up where he left off and was entrusted to play tough minutes as a 16 year-old. Brent Sutter regularly went to him for defensive zone starts and as a first option on the penalty kill.

Grayson has great defensive zone awareness and he plays a very responsible game everywhere on the ice. He is able to thrive in a shutdown role where he shadows other teams' top scorers. He has decent size and is strong on his feet. He plays larger than his listed size and has good strength for his age. He hustles and often outworks bigger, stronger players.

Offensively, Grayson is good puck possession player. He is good along the walls and protects the puck well. He skates well and has pretty good pickup in his stride. He sees the ice well and makes a good pass. He goes to the tough areas of the ice and will pay the price to fish for rebounds.

Pernsteiner, Frank
D – Cleveland Barons U18 – 5' 10" 170

Pretty strong D-man as played good positioning, defends 1-on-1s well, and shows good use of stick in breaking up plays. Displays some offensive instincts from the back end as jumps up on the play occasionally but is not going to put up too many points. He possesses a decent shot from the blue line as well.

Pilipenko, Kirill
RW – HK MVD JR (MHL) 5'9" 168

This young Russian forward has played many times internationally for his country over the past two years, from the U17 hockey challenge in 2013 to last April's U18 world championship. Pilipenko is a player with a high-end skill level who has a quick wrist shot, and he's dangerous around the net. Alone with a goaltender he makes it look easy to beat them, shows great patience with the puck, and knows how to find holes placing the puck where he wants it. He also has a great release on his one-timers, is agile on his skates, and can dangle the puck with the best of them. He lacks a top gear to create more separation from opposing defenders. He see the ice well, is an accurate passer, and very creative with the puck. At his best you see him work hard on the forecheck using his speed to win races for the puck, and using an active stick to create havoc for opposing defensemen. Pilipenko's also very good at reading the play, and has the capability of being able to get behind defensemen for the stretch pass. He lacks consistency from game-to-game, as he can be invisible, and fail to create much offense. He'll need to work on improving his game without the puck as well. In his zone he can be lost at times, and needs to keep getting strongerm as he can get outmuscled for the puck along the wall at times. But having said that, Pilipenko doesn't need a lot of time or space to create offense, and that makes him a hot commodity.

Phelan, James
C – Shawinigan Cataractes (QMJHL) – 5'10" 171

Phelan, who played his midget hockey with the 2013 Telus Cup bronze medal-winning Laval-Montreal Rousseau Royal, is an energetic forward with great speed. The Laval native has great, active feet. Although he's not a big player, he plays much bigger than his size indicates. Phelan gets involved in traffic and brings a lot of energy to his team. He can play a bottom-six role within a team. Shawinigan drafted him in the 2nd round, 21st overall last year, and he played all of this year with the Cataractes. He only scored one goal this season, playing mostly on a 4th line and playing on the PK as well. Offense won't ever be Phelan's calling card, but we would like to see him improve his shot, which would help him score more goals. Improving his puck skills would also help; he's just average with the puck on his stick. We see him as an energy player with a lot of speed that can play a big role on the PK. He represented his province at the World U-17 Hockey Challenge playing that grinding and PK role for Team Quebec. Although he's not big or strong, Phelan protects the puck well using good technique, and he's good on the forecheck. He has terrific work ethic, and he's a smart player in all three zones. He's a natural center, but has the smarts and the speed to play on the wing. Will be interesting to see him progress next season and to see whether or not his role is expanded with the Cataractes.

Picco, Andrew
RD – Rimouski Oceanic (QMJHL) – 6'3" 224

Picco, who is originally from Newfoundland, was Rimouski's 5th round pick in last year's QMJHL Draft, but would have gone higher if not for his NCAA options. The Marystown native left his home at an early age to go play for the famous Shattuck St-Mary's program in Faribault, Minnesota. Picco played his last two seasons with the Prep School. With the Oceanic already having a lot of depth on defense, ice time was really hard to get for Picco, and mixed with an injury, he only saw action in 21 regular season games. Still trying to find his rhythm in the league, Picco has excellent size. Listed at 6'3" and around 220lbs, he is still growing into his body. His footwork and quickness are a big question mark, as he has a tough time keeping up with speedy forwards off the rush. Can play a rugged game in his own end, and has the size to be dominant in that area. Picco has some decent qualities as a puck-moving defenseman coming into the QMJHL, but didn't get much of a chance to show those qualities this year. He also owns a powerful slapshot from the point. To continue to develop, Picco will need to stay healthy, as he has battled concussions issues the last two years. Picco played for Team Atlantic at the recent U-17 Hockey Challenge in Cape-Breton.

Pilon, Ryan
LD – Brandon Wheat Kings (WHL) - 6'2" 212

Ryan is a big defender who plays a gritty defensive game while also having some puck-moving skills. He has a late 1996 birthday. He makes a good outlet pass and likes to join the rush. With the puck on his stick, he thinks the game at a high level. He makes safe, simple plays in his end and saves his creativity for the offensive zone. Ryan has seen found some success on the powerplay by both making smart decisions to either distribute the puck with an accurate pass or by using his cannon of a shot from the point. The shot is quite hard, but he'll have to improve his release as he has a big windup.

Ryan shows good defensive awareness and he plays a reliable enough defensive game that he truly is a two-way player that can play in all game situations. That isn't to say he is a perfect player. Ryan can be guilty of making bad pinches from time to time and his footwork is sloppy. His skating is below average and will need to improve in all aspects as he can be beaten wide and he sometimes struggles to maintain a tight gap with shiftier players.

He has shown that he can be a leader at a young age, although the reason he is currently in Brandon is that the former Hurricanes assistant captain went home after demanding a trade – effectively forcing Lethbridge's hand. Now he was just one of many people that asked out Lethbridge this past season and NHL teams will need to do their homework and decide whether this is a character issue or just an unfortunate circumstance. Either way, the move to Brandon has definitely rejuvenated Pilon and resulted in improved play as the season wore on.

Ryan is a talented two-way player that is really only limited by his skating. If he can improve that aspect, he will be highly sought-after next year.

Platonov, Alexei
LD – Atlanty Mytischi (MHL) 6'5" 203

Platonov is a huge kid standing already at 6'5", and could still be growing. We saw Platonov at the recent U-17 hockey challenge in Cape-Breton. This season with his MHL club he collected 16 points in 36 games, and with that he had 85 penalty minutes. With his size, Platonov is an intimidating presence on the blueline, and loves to hit opposing forwards while clearing the front of the net. He has decent mobility, and uses his long reach well to control his gaps. With the puck he moves it up ice fairly well, and has a big shot from the point. He's still very raw as a prospect with that size and puck moving ability, but the potential is there. He was one of the better Russians defensemen at the U-17 hockey challenge; he has the endurance to log a ton of ice time. He was drafted 73rd overall in this past year KHL draft by Atlanty Mytischi.

Price, Ethan
F – Portland Winterhawks – 5' 10" 183

He is a shooter for certain although he played a limited role in his rookie WHL season in Portland. He likes to get that puck on his stick and fire away a quick, snap shot. He handles the puck well and has some decent speed. Price will need to play more minutes and show more production during his draft year.

Provorov, Ivan
LD – Cedar Rapids Roughriders – 6' 0" 194

The highly skilled Russian defenseman had a solid USHL debut season, registering 19 points in 56 games with Cedar Rapids. High end offensive skill and equal skating ability, Ivan has enormous upside as an offensive blue liner. As with many offensive-minded defensemen at his age, his defensive responsibilities need improving. However, he has good awareness and at least at this level, his exceptional skating ability allows him to recover for mistakes he may make. His stride is text book; strong, wide base and very quick feet, low center of gravity. Very shifty and has excellent control of his body through his feet. Really good in transition. He loses no speed or mobility when handling the puck, as his hands match his feet as far as skill level and ability. Very smooth with the puck, has the ability to weave through traffic effortlessly and sees the ice very well. Often is the puck carrier to start power play rushes up the ice, gains zone entry with ease. Works the puck at the blue line with great poise, never any panic. Seems to slow the game down when he has the puck.

Unfortunately for Cedar Rapids, Ivan left the team in late March in order to try out and eventually make Russian U18 roster, and did so with very little notice. According to the staff at Cedar Rapids, this decision was made by his father. At the time of this writing, it was reported he would be returning to Cedar Rapids next season, but speculation is he may opt for the CHL. It's also worth noting he was drafted 120th overall by Lokomotiv Yaroslavl of the KHL, which also happens to be his hometown.

Rantanen, Mikko
RW – TPS (Liiga) 6'4" 196

We are big fans of Rantanen's game and we have him ranked highly in our early 2015 NHL Draft rankings. Mikko is a big kid, much like another Finnish star, Alex Barkov of the Florida Panthers. Mikko is relentless along the walls and has a great compete level overall. He's not without skill and his skating is solid for a big kid, it can take time for big kids to reach their skating potential after big growth spurts. He showed us to be a very smart player and can play in every situation. He plays smart hockey on the PP. He has good hands, flashed a good shot in our viewings and drives the net with authority.

Rantanen uses his size effectively, especially while winning battles and protecting the puck. He made a few bad reads on the defensive side of the puck but there was no lack of effort.

Reddekopp, Chaz
LD – Victoria Royals (WHL) - 6'3" 215

Reddekopp is a big defenseman that moves exceptionally well considering his age and size. He makes good decisions with the puck and has high upside at both ends of the rink. He makes a good first pass and has the ability to skate with the puck if required. He shows good poise with the puck and with further maturation, he'll become an all-around steady player. He's big and he uses his size well. He likes to finish his checks and he uses his strength to his advantage along the walls. He's not a big fighter, but he has shown some good toughness. He uses his long reach well in defending the rush. He anticipates his opponents' attacks and positions himself to break up neutral zone passes. He still requires time to consistently put his game together, but Reddekopp has the physical abilities that NHL teams are looking for at the draft.

Richard, Anthony
LC - Val d'Or Foreurs (QMJHL) - 5'08" 168

Richard, who centered the Foreurs' second line this season, had a good second season in the QMJHL. The "kid line" didn't get all the power play time they might have on another team, thanks to the Anthony Mantha line getting the majority of those minutes. Still, Richard and his linemates were able to produce enough to give the Foreurs some secondary scoring and a lot of energy. Richard, who is a late '96 birthday (making him eligible for the 2015 NHL Entry Draft) is a very speedy forward with quick feet who is always moving on the ice. He makes things happen with his speed, uses his speed well to forecheck and harass the puck-carrier, and makes defensemen back off with his speed. He's already one of the best skaters in the league, and will only get better as he gets stronger physically. The Trois-Rivières native has a high compete level and doesn't mind the physical game right now, but has trouble in one-on-one battles versus bigger players because of his lack of size and strength. He has developed a very nice chemistry with Nicolas Aubé-Kubel (2014) over the last two seasons, as both were drafted in the same draft, and worked their way up the Foreurs' depth chart. He does a good job on the penalty killing unit, using his speed and anticipation to steal pucks and even be dangerous in those situations.

He was chosen 16th overall by the Foreurs in the 2012 QMJHL Draft out of the Trois-Rivières Estacades' midget program. Richard loves to have ice time, though he had problems adjusting to the QMJHL in his first season while getting limited ice time on a 4th line and left the Foreurs to go back to midget for about a month only to return afterwards. He's a player who thrives on getting more responsibilities. He has a surprisingly good wrist shot and can surprise opposing goaltenders with his quick release. With the entire Val d'Or first line not expected to return next year, Richard's role and ice time should increase a lot next season as he should be the team's top center and will continue to be used in all situations.

Rook, Austin
D – Rivers School (MA) – 6' 3" 201

He stands big, skates fairly well for large body, and plays with physical edge. He shows good smarts in having stick in passing lanes and sound positioning in own zone. He also has some offensive talents as well on a play by jumping up on rush and firing his shot. He could improve upon his lateral mobility a bit.

Roslovic, Jack
F – USNTDP-17 – 6' 0" 173 (2015)

He shows a bit of jump in his game as he can skate well and has some decent puck skills as well to go along with that speed. He posted some decent numbers with NTDP-17 this past season with 15 goals and 16 assists in 54 games played.

Roy, Jeremy
RD – Sherbrooke Phoenix (QMJHL) – 6'0" 182

What a season it was for Jeremy Roy, who scored the most points by a 16 year old defenseman since the late 80s in the QMJHL. He didn't need a big adjustment period coming from Midget AAA; in September he was already used over 20 minutes per game and was Sherbrooke's number 1 defenseman. Another facet that was very impressive from Roy's season was that he was consistent from beginning to end. This is rare for true rookies in this league. Usually rookies have an up-and-down rollercoaster ride during their inaugural season, but this was not the case for Roy, who was solid throughout. Roy's potential is enormous, as he is an extremely mobile defenseman with strong and powerful skating abilities. He's tough to beat one-on-one because he's a very smart defender with great lateral mobility.

He is very aggressive in his coverage defensively. He likes to pressure the puck carrier immediately once they enter his zone with the puck. His best attribute is his offensive game. He acts as a 4th forward very often and is very active in the offensive zone. A threat on the power play, he possesses a powerful slapshot from the point and he's a gifted passer who will find his teammates with ease. His passing game is top-notch, and rarely will you see him miss an outlet pass to his teammates. It's usually tape-to-tape, and he helps the transition game so much for his team. Jeremy is not a giant, but he's extremely strong on his skates and will play a physical game along the boards.

He has a strong lower body that helps him in that facet of the game. Jeremy has great work ethic and doesn't take any shifts off. He's so much more advanced in his game than any other 97-born defenseman from the QMJHL; we feel he could have played in the league as a 15 year old and still outplay all 96-born defensemen this year in the league.

Jeremy was also a key member for Team Quebec at the 2014 U-17 Hockey Challenge in Cape-Breton. Quebec finished 4th in the tournament and as their captain, Roy was a big reason for that. He was also named to the tournament's All-Star team. In April, he also got named to the original roster for Team Canada for the World Under-18 Hockey Championships as an underager, but was hurt in the preliminary games before the tournament and was sent home.

Roy, Nicolas
RC - Chicoutimi Saguenéens (QMJHL) - 6'04" 190

Nicolas Roy was selected first overall at the 2013 QMJHL Draft by the Cape Breton Screaming Eagles, but he was traded before the beginning of the season to the Chicoutimi Saguenéens for three first round draft picks. He had a good season with this rebuilding team where he earned 41 points in 63 games.

There is no doubt in our mind that his biggest quality is his anticipation and his vision. He's always in the right place and he does many things that only well-rounded forwards can do. He blocks shots on a regular basis and he supports his defensemen well down in his zone. Most of the time, he will be the one able to get the puck out of his zone on his line. One of the things we likes about Roy is that he shows excellent offensive instincts and is adept at picking off passes through the neutral zone creating quick counter attacks and odd-man rushes. When he's entering in the offensive zone, he will often slow down right after the opposing blueline hoping to find open teammates, which he does successfully. If not, he will step in towards the middle off the rush to get shots from scoring position and drives hard to the net looking for his opportunities in tight. He also uses his body well deep in the zone to win puck battles and to create space for teammates. Roy has tremendous puck-handling skills and excels when he has time and space. He is fluid with the puck and will beat defenders 1-on-1 if they try to play the puck against him.

The Amos native has a strong wrist shot and gets into good scoring positions coming off the wall on the cycle. He is also a good playmaker and shows great awareness and vision finding teammates with a variety of creative passes. He handles contact well and looks to be fairly strong for such a young kid allowing him to control the puck with contact and keep going. He's a lanky skater that lacks jump right now. However, he moves fairly well and once he'll get stronger, his long strides will no doubt be more powerful and effective. Roy has for sure the smarts to progress and work ethic to progress well in the next seasons.

Ruggiero, Steve
RD – Youngstown Phantoms – 6' 3" 174

We came away most impressed by how mobile Ruggiero is at his size and age. He is very good skater, moves well in transition and laterally, and while his foot speed could be improved a bit it's still solid as is. Ruggiero moves the puck up ice really well and is very comfortable handling in all three zones. He has nice touch and a lot of poise as a young defenseman with the puck. He takes perfect angles on defenders and his gaps are always good, and he steps up on his man at the right time. Heavy hitter when he gets the chance. He always finishes his checks and has some mean in him. He possesses excellent vision and is an above average passer. He sprung forward on breakaways a handful of times this season with the stretch pass. He's strong on the offensive blue line and plays with a lot of confidence on the offensive side of the puck. He is committed to Penn State starting in 2015 and by all accounts is expected to return to Youngstown, but the Ottawa 67's own his OHL rights and I am sure they would be more than happy to have him.

Saarela, Aleksi
C – Lukko U20 (Jr.A SM-Liiga) 5'10" 194

Saarela is player who we first saw last year at the 2013 U-17 hockey challenge playing as an underager on Finland. This season he split time between Lukko's Under- 20 team, and the men's league. He missed time with injuries for a second straight year. He also played two games for Finland at the last World Under-18 hockey championship scoring one goal. During the season with Lukko U-20 team he amassed 22 points in 17 games. Saarela is an impressive skater and has quick feet with a great burst of speed. He likes to challenge opposing defensemen wide while using his speed. His hands are very quick, and he can put the puck in the net with the best of them, as his puck skills are high end. He has a really strong wrist shot, and a great release. He works hard all over the ice. We first saw him as a 15-year-old and were very impressed with his work ethic in his own zone, and solid play on the penalty kill. He can be a threat to score shorthanded with his great speed and anticipation. Saarela has solid playmaking skills, and sees the ice very well. We like his poise with the puck on the powerplay, and his ability to make players around him better. He won't back down from the physical game and competes hard, but at times in the offensive zone can be victim of playing on the perimeter.

Salituro, Dante
RC – Ottawa 67's (OHL) – 5'08" 185

Due to his late birthdate, Salituro is ineligible until the 2015 NHL Entry Draft. He already has two seasons under his belt with the Ottawa 67's, and has produced very good numbers for playing on a non-playoff team over the last two years. Dante is undersized but build very solid. He plays with an edge, and finishes his checks hard for a player his size. He will need to control himself, as he can take some undisciplined penalties at times. He is a powerful skater who is capable of protecting the puck extremely well for such a small player because of his solidly built frame. Dante has good puck skills, and can create scoring chances. Dante has a pretty balanced effort of passing, and shooting, and provides a deceptively quick shot. Salituro's upside is limited by his size, but he has proven to be a skilled player at the junior level. If he should grow over the next 12 months, it will certainly boost his projection for the NHL Draft. He will be one of the go to players for the Ottawa 67's, as they look to take the next step in the rebuild.

Sandström, Felix
G – Brynas J18 (J18 Allsvenskan) 6'2" 187

Sandström is a big goaltender who has represented Sweden internationally often already in his young career playing as a 15-year-old at the 2013 U-17 hockey challenge when we first saw him. He's a goalie with good size, and he uses it very well to cover his net. He doesn't stay too deep in his net, and likes to challenge shooters. He controls rebounds well, covers the lower part of the net very well, and is very calm in his crease. He was strong in shootout during this year U-17 vs Quebec, where he would never commit before the shooter showing great composure. He also has been impressive with his puckhandling ability, and was not afraid to make passes to his defensemen or forwards and help the transition game. Improving his glove side and concentration are two things he should work on leading to next year.

Seagraves, Bailey
G – Ohio Blue Jackets U18 – 5' 11" 175

He does not have the big, NHL goalie frame as just 5'11" although he positions himself well on shooters, athletic, and decent techniques. Seagraves played up this past season with the Ohio Blue Jackets U18 team.

Schemitsch, Thomas
RD – Owen Sound Attack (OHL) – 6'03" 201
Thomas is the bother of former Attack defenseman Geoffrey, who was selected fourth round by the Tampa Bay Lightning in 2010. Thomas is bigger than his brother, but has a long way to go before reaching his potential. On the positive, Thomas was effective in the offensive zone on the power-play pinching from the point at the right times, and was a dangerous option in the offensive zone that opponents needed to keep an eye on. Defensively it was a bit of a challenge. His skating is a bit of a struggle, particularly his first few steps. This affected him in one-on-one match-ups, and resulted in him getting walked. However, he pivots at the right time, and has a good stick, which has saved him on some occasions. He needs to handle the puck better when under pressure. This year was a good learning experience for Schemitsch, and with a late birthdate he isn't eligible until the 2015 NHL Entry Draft.

Schlichting, Connor
LD – Sarnia Sting (OHL) – 6'03" 205
Connor's rookie season in the OHL has been a bit of a learning process for the big 16 year old defenseman. He shows clear improvement throughout the season but also had to battle through injuries and played a lot more ice than most 16 year old defensemen due to suspensions, injuries and playing for a rebuilding team. He is effective on the wall battling for pucks despite not showing much of a mean streak to his game. He can contain and wins a fair share for someone his age. He has shown flashes of playing physical and certainly has the strength to deliver solid checks but he is highly inconsistent in this area and can look off checks at times. One on one play improved throughout this season maintaining a good stick, but generally gets beat when he tries to make the first move too early. He is at his best when keeping his puck decisions simple as he is not an offensive defenseman and is capable of completing simple high percentage plays. He has some mental lapses with the puck either throwing it up the middle or showing panic when pressured firing it off the wall towards opposing players resulting in turnovers. He has decent skating ability for his size and even showed interest in jumping up in the rush occasionally later on in the season. Connor shows a lot of promise due to his size and flashes of capabilities he's shown this year but has a lot of work ahead of him to reach his potential. 2014-2015 should be a very interesting season and an opportunity for him to show what he is capable of.

Siegenthaler, Jonas
LD – GC Küsnastch Lions (NLB) 6'2" 218
Siegenthaler is a huge kid already (6'2" 218) and just turned 17 at the beginning of May. Even as an underage player at the world under-18 hockey championship, he played top minutes on the backend with Roger Karrer. He's more of a shutdown type defenseman, as he's very strong physically and will clear the front of the net. With the puck his skills are average. He'll make simple accurate passes, but won't rush the puck or try anything overly fancy with it. He makes smart pinches to keep the puck in the offensive zone. Overall he makes good decisions with the puck, and can play on the powerplay, as he did for the Swiss at the Under-18. Siegenthaler is not a natural powerplay quarterback, but gets the job done with some simple quick puck movement. He doesn't possess the quickest of feet, and can get caught flat-footed in the neutral zone. Opposing forwards who have nice speed can take advantage of his lack of mobility by going wide on him. With his size he could be more physical in his own end than he already is which would help him make more of an impact. This season he played 40 games with his club in the NLB, where he had 8 points and also made his NLA debut with ZSC coached by former NHL coach Marc Crawford.

Spacek, Michael
RW – HC Pardubice U20 (Czech U20) 5'10" 181

Spacek, who has no relation to former NHL defenseman Jaroslav, is scoring winger from the Pardubice program. This season with the U20 team he had 28 points in 31 games. He was not at the U17 hockey challenge, but played with the U18 national team at the five nations in February, and at the U18 world championship in April where he had 7 points in 7 games as an underage player. His effort was missing at times during the tournament, where he would lose the puck too easily, and was not involved in the play enough. Other times you saw some good play from him, although he's not blessed with great size he went to the net hard, and pounced on a rebound to score a goal. He's a fine skater, and has a good top speed. Spacek reaches top speed quickly while rushing the puck, and loves to have the puck on his stick. Spacek 'sbest asset is his ability to find open spaces in the offensive zone, which lead to scoring chances. Defensively he has things to learn, and needs to take less risk with the puck and play a simple game.

Speers, Blake
RW – SOO Greyhounds (OHL) – 5'11" 162

Blake was selected in the first round of the 2013 OHL Priority Selection Draft by his hometown Greyhounds and didn't disappoint in his rookie season. Blake is a strong skater who has a great top speed and is very elusive beating opposing defenders as well as goaltenders. Blake is a flashy player who can pass as well as finish. He moved around all four lines for the Greyhounds this season seeing a little power play action here and there and was effective adding speed and jump to whichever line he was a part of. Blake has some intriguing offensive potential for the 2015 NHL Entry Draft and is definitely a player to watch next season.

Spencer, Matt
LD – Peterborough Petes (OHL) – 6'02" 196

After being selected third overall at the 2013 OHL Priority Selection Draft, Spencer had a decent first year in the league, but didn't quite live up to the hype and expectation. First and foremost, Spencer is a great skater for big defenseman. Few defenders have his combination of size and speed. He had more success in the offensive zone this year showing a knowledge of when to pinch and can make some solid passes in the offensive zone to create scoring chances. Defensively he struggled with the puck early in the season, making bad giveaways and serving up risky plays resulting in several scoring chances for the opposition. He was hit or miss in one on one situations showing the ability to skate with talented players but can try to be too aggressive making the first move resulting in him getting beat. On the positive side, Spencer showed good positional play and was willing to sacrifice his body for his team to block shots. Despite those concerns, Matt played much better in the last third of the season and if he can continue to trend upward, he could put himself in a position to be a 1st round selection.

Soy, Tyler
LC – Victoria Royals (WHL) - 5'11" 168

Tyler is a talented two-way center that is able to contribute all over the ice. He has good vision and thinks the game at a high level. He is a strong, speedy skater, and is able to finish scoring chances by utilizing a quick release on his shot. He is not overly big, but protects the puck well. While he has decent strength for his size, he will definitely need to get stronger in order to better compete for loose pucks and in front of the net. Tyler was mixed in with a largely veteran forward group in Victoria where he wasn't given top minutes, but produced very well (30 points) in a lesser role.

Sprong, Daniel
RW - Charlottetown Islanders (QMJHL) - 5'10" 177

Daniel Sprong was selected in the 1st Round of the 2013 QMJHL Draft by the Charlottetown Islanders out of the Lac-St-Louis Tigres MESP Program. In his rookie year, he scored 30 goals and earned 68 points in 67 games, thus he got named to the QMJHL All-Rookie Team.

Sprong is an elite puck handler with extremely quick hands. When he is in possession of the puck in the offensive zone, he has the ability to score goals all by himself and to set up spectacular plays. His superior speed makes him really dangerous. His first few strides are really what distinguishes him from other players, he can get to top speed with a few strides and get past a defenseman before he starts thinking about pivoting. An elusive player, he is also a very agile skater, twisting and turning to gain space while still keeping control of the puck. He is good in tight areas and has quick starts and stops. He navigates through traffic well and flashes a powerful wrist shot with a quick release. The Dutch native has also shown the ability to include his linemates very well especially on the rush making great passes and set up a few goals this season. With the speed and skills he possesses, he can play an East-West game in the QMJHL and can gain space and time easily for himself. He is relentless hounding pucks and doesn't get enough credit for how strong he is in puck protection and winning battles. He is nearly unstoppable on the powerplay when he has room to work with and shows off excellent passing, a great variety of hard, accurate shots, and fantastic poise.

Sprong also has improved his defensive game and his work ethic. Last year, it wasn't rare to see him float on the ice and suddenly, he would get that extra gear in no time flat when he had the puck. In our viewings, we saw him backcheck with intensity and he was sometimes willing to sacrifice his body to get the puck out of his zone. Sure, he's still cheating a bit leaving the defensive zone early and there's still room for improvement defensively, but Sprong is clearly a game changer at the QMJHL. There's a lot to like about him, but if there was anything we'd like to see him improve upon it's being more physical.

Stephens, Mitchell
RC – Saginaw Spirit (OHL) – 5'11" 182

As a former 1st round pick in the 2013 OHL Priority Selection Draft, Mitchell had a moderately successful rookie season. Generally playing on the third line for Saginaw, Stephens displays excellent skating ability. He is an explosive skater who reaches top speed quickly. He has a powerful wrist shot, and can hit his spot in the net effectively. His offensive tools especially his hands, and ability to evade checkers was impressive for a 16-year-old. Mitchell provides a lot of flash in his game but can run around a bit positionally. He can also panic under pressure, and doesn't always read situations well when he doesn't have the puck on his stick. Mitchell showed he can contribute offensively at this level, but his hockey sense will need to improve in order to really make an impact next season. Mitchell will be looked to, to provide more offense next season in his draft year, and early on looks to have the potential to be selected at the 2015 NHL Entry Draft.

Strome, Dylan
LC – Erie Otters (OHL) – 6'02" 178

Dylan, brother of New York Islanders forward Ryan Strome, went second overall in the 2013 OHL Priority Selection Draft. Dylan joined the Otters, and quickly was given the opportunity to produce. He moved around the Otters top-nine forwards showing his wide range of talents. Strome's skating has improved greatly over the passed 24 months, but still has a way to go before reaching his goal. His stride is smoother and he has a decent top speed, but more specifically his first few steps need the most work. He had good positioning in the offensive zone, and has a powerful shot. Despite being an offensive leader in Minor Midget, Dylan was relied upon to play a bit of a defensive role at times, which he did very well in. He competes hard for pucks, and uses his size to protect the puck, and get it out of his own zone. He makes life difficult for opposing forwards, and wins battles in his own zone. Offensively he has a good shot, and displays good creativity, and vision allowing him to work with his linemates in creating scoring chances. The ceiling is very high for Strome, but he has a lot of work ahead of him over the next year to reach his potential heading into the 2015 NHL Entry Draft.

Svechnikov, Yevgeni
LW – Bars Kazam (MHL) 6'2" 185

Svechnikov is big power forward who made a real first good impression in North America with a great performance at the 2013 U17 hockey challenge scoring 7 goals in 6 games. He has played for the past two seasons with the Bars Kazan MHL club in Russia, and also represented his country in various tournaments. He's very strong on the puck, and uses his size very well to protect the puck. He can be unstoppable at times when he's driving the net. He's a decent skater but he's not a speedster. Svechnikov could still work on improving his starts, but once he gains his speed he's tough to contain due to his strength, size and willingness to attack the net. He's very strong on his skates, showing good balance, and it's tough to take the puck away from him, as he excels in his puck protection down low. He's a shoot first type of player, likes to shoot from anywhere in the offensive zone, and his shot is deadly. Even as a shoot first type of player he's able to find his linemates on the ice as well. On the powerplay he can really make some nice passes to his teammates. Like many young Russian forwards, Svechnikov will need to play better without the puck, and become more responsible in his zone. He has battle inconsistency, as he can be downright dominant or totally invisible on the ice. He can be undisciplined in his physical game with some selfish penalties. He was very good at the recent U18 world championship, and showed signs of brilliance where he would dominate with the puck on his stick. He's expected to play for Cape-Breton in the QMJHL next season; the Screaming Eagles drafted him in last year's import draft 60th overall.

Svoboda, Martin
LW – HC Sparta Praha U18 (Czech U18) 5'6" 172

Svoboda is an undersized forward who has a good skill level and plays bigger than his size. He battles hard all over the ice. Even at his size he doesn't lose a lot of puck. He plays with a lot of heart, and can make things happen offensively with his energy on the forecheck and active stick. He sees the ice very well, and is an excellent passer. He's more of a passer than a scorer. Svoboda's very poised with the puck on his stick, and makes good decisions. In one game at the U17 he made a very nice stretch pass to David Kase for the game-winning goal in one of their games. Even if he's small, he doesn't mind the rough stuff, he's fearless and drives the net. This season with Sparta Praha U18 team he had 51 points in 40 games, and 110 penalty minutes.

Szypula, Ethan
RC – Owen Sound Attack (OHL) – 5'11" 163

Ethan was the first round selection of the Attack at the 2013 OHL Priority Selection Draft, and while he was a regular in the Attack line-up, he didn't receive a lot of time or offensive opportunities as a 16-year-old. Ethan is a smooth skater with good offensive skill. He has good hands, and can beat defenders one-on-one. He possesses good hands, and is dangerous with the puck in the offensive zone. In addition to his offensive ability, Ethan provides a hard forecheck, and is willing to go into the dirty areas to fight for pucks despite a lack of size and strength. He shows good heart, and is willing to play an energy role when asked. With the graduation of several players this year, Ethan should be able to check into an offensive role, and will hopefully show what he is capable of entering his draft year.

Texeira, Keoni
LD – Portland Winterhawks (WHL) - 6'0" 194

Keoni is a mobile, two-way defenseman with decent size. He has strong puck-moving skills and is very calm and poised with the puck on his stick. He is good on his edges and is able to use his skating to give himself time and options on the ice. He sees the ice well and makes good decisions. He owns a big shot from the point. Texeira is able to use his weight to his advantage. Keoni is a physical player that makes things difficult on opponents. He is pretty steady in his own end and does well to limit his mistakes.

Thompson, Will
RD – Saint John Sea Dogs (QMJHL) 6'00" 178

Thompson is a right-handed defenseman that took some time to adjust his game to major junior but has been better throughout the season. He is an above average skater and has the ability to skate himself out of trouble in the defensive zone. He has the speed it takes to follow the play effectively. He is not an explosive skater, but he has good footing that allows him to be anywhere on the ice in time. He shows good confidence carrying the puck, but needs to make quicker decisions on where to move it. He handles the puck well and is not a liability on the transition. Thompson stabilizes the play defensively when he's on the ice, as he reads the play well and shows good positioning. He has excellent reaction time when clearing out rebounds and is intelligent getting in passing lanes. His hockey sense and mobility allow him to be effective in one-on-one situations and he can also back up his teammates when they make mistakes. He got outmuscled a bit this season and that's the reason he lost some battles along the wall. He is also smart enough to support his forwards in the offensive zone and we would like him to do so more. He doesn't take many risks, playing a steady, simple and physical game. In summary, Thompson is a smart defenseman, playing the gap well, executing smart plays with the puck from his own zone when he is under pressure with poise in his game, which you rarely see from a 16 year old. He was mostly used on the third pairing this year and we believe and he will earn more ice time next season.

Tkachuk, Matthew
F – USNTDP-17 – 5' 11" 185 (2015)

He skates average at best as seems to be a step behind in his stride with no quickness. His stick skills are decent, plays a smart game in knowing where his teammates are and seeing the play develop. He has some good vision to his game. He is the son of former NHLer and BU star, Keith Tkachuk. He is committed to Notre Dame and finished up his NTDP-17 season potting 13 goals and adding 19 assists in 53 games played.

Tremblay, Olivier
G – Rimouski Océanic (QMJHL) 5'10" 179

After a stellar first half season with the Jonquière Élites in QMAAA, Tremblay got called up by the Rimouski Océanic that drafted him in the second round in the QMJHL Draft this past June.

The technical game of the Chicoutimi native is quite solid. He has good active arms to knock rebounds away to the corners, and is good at catching pucks coming to his glove hand. He cuts on his angles pretty well and he is aggressive in his crease. He is good at tracking pucks through traffic, but it is something that he will have to keep working on. A great athlete, Olivier is a very quick goalie. We have seen him make saves on superb post-to-post movements displaying his flexibility. His legs are strong and quick helping him in the rebound control area and in his lower- net coverage. He's very strong mentally and he's not affected when he lets a bad goal in. He keeps fighting to make saves and it is difficult to shake his confidence. Although he's still a small goalie, he was Team Quebec's starting goaltender during the WU17.

Tretiak, Maxim
G - Krasnaya Armiya Moskva (MHL) 6'2" 203

Maxim is the grandson of Russian legend Vladislav Tretiak. One thing playing in Maxim's favor is his size as he's already 6'2 and over 200 pounds. The young Tretiak use his size well in his crease, and covers his angles well. He doesn't give the shooter a lot to shoot at, as he looks big in his net. He gets in trouble when he has to move post-to-post. He lacks quickness in his lateral movement, and can be exposed there. As well we have seen him give real soft goals, which really hurt his team's momentum in a game. He lacks concentration on those soft goals he gives up, and his reaction time for those shot is not quick enough. Maxim is playing in the MHL with Krasnaya Armiya Moskva for a second straight year, and played for team Russia at various international tournaments. He has a lot of things to improve on with his techniques before next season, which will be his draft year. His play has been really inconsistent over our viewings the last two seasons.

Trottier, Brenden
RW – Sarnia Sting (OHL) – 5'11" 160

Trottier spent most of this season with the Lambton Shores Jr. B Predators but joined the Sting after his team was eliminated in the playoffs. He put up moderately good numbers at the Jr. B level and displays good two-way work ethic as a player who can make the smart play with the puck in the offensive zone, but will backcheck hard and pressure the puck carrier on the forecheck. Brenden will likely join the Sting full time next season in a bottom six role, which is the type of player he would project as if he were to make the NHL level. He has a lot of work ahead of him and will need to get bigger and stronger this off season, but he didn't look out of place in limited OHL action and should prove to be a tough player to play against next season.

Tweten, Tanner
F – East Grand Forks HS (MN) – 6' 2" 190 (2015)

He is a player that works extremely hard at both ends of the ice making for a nice two-way player. He possesses good size and plays the power forward style. He shows some decent skills around the net, makes good decisions with the puck, and is willing to play physical especially on the forecheck.

Tyanulin, Artur
RW – Irbis Kazan (MHL) 5'9" 165

Tyanullin is a small but very dynamic forward who was a star at the 2014 world Under-17 hockey challenge for Russia with 12 points in six games. He has great puck skills, and can dangle it with the best of them. He's solid skater with an extra gear, and he's also very shifty on his skates. He's purely an offensive player who loves to have the puck on his stick in the offensive zone, and he's a very creative player with the puck. He's deadly on the powerplay with more time and space to make plays. At even strength when he battles in the corners or in front of the net he's easy to push him off the puck, as he lacks strength. He's the type of player who only needs one scoring chance to score. He can be invisible in a game and on one shift he can make a great play for a goal. His effort level can be lacking at time, as he can go through stretch where is invisible on the ice. Tyanullin doesn't get involved in the physical part of the game very much as he's still physically immature. This season with his club team in the MHL he had 21 points in 23 games, and was also selected 131st overall in the KHL draft by AK Bars Kazan.

Vande Sompel, Mitchell
LD – Oshawa Generals (OHL) – 5'10" 180

Mitchell was noted in Minor Midget for his ability to play both defense and forward and while he is a defenseman the majority of the time, he did an admirable job filling in at forward when there was injuries or a suspension. Mitchell is a smooth skating defenseman who rushes the puck well and loves to jump up and get involved offensively. This is enhanced by his playmaking ability and intelligence with the puck. He creates plays in the offensive zone on a regular basis and has above average vision. He was a consistent presence on the power play and was effective under pressure. His defensive play was moderately effective but needs to get stronger and had trouble handling bigger forwards. While size is a bit of a concern going forward, Vande Sompel shows intriguing potential for the 2015 NHL Entry Draft.

Vladar, Daniel
G – HC Kladno U18 (Czech U18) 6'5" 185

Vladar is a huge goaltender with great athleticism that played very well for his national team at the U17 hockey Challenge. He was also named to the Under 18 world championship roster, but didn't get to play in the tournament. During the Under-17 he was a star in first game of the tournament against Sweden where he made 41 saves, but eventually loss 3-1. He has great size, covers his angles well, and doesn't play deep in his net resulting in not giving the shooters a lot to shoot at. He controls rebounds fairly well, and covers the lower part of the net with his long, quick legs. He's very athletic in his crease, and moves extremely well for a goaltender of his size. He was one of the most impressive goaltenders at the U-17, and with his size it screams potential. It should be interesting to see how he develops in next two or three years.

Wahlin, Jake
F – White Bear Lake HS (MN) – 5' 10" 170

He exhibits some nice offensive abilities and creates a lot of opportunity in knowing where to go with great anticipation. He scores in a variety of ways whether it's showing his strong shot, patience with the puck which makes the goalie commit early, or showing nifty hands on the breakaway. Wahlin is average in size but seems to be growing still and recently committed to St. Cloud State (NCHC).

Warren, Brendan
F – USNTDP-17 – 6' 0" 181

He is a player with some good upside in his game for the future. He plays a solid, all-around game with skill and strength. He shows sound offensive abilities this season again at NTDP-17 by producing 14 goals and 26 assists in 54 games. He possesses a solid shot that gives him the ability to wire shots in the net. He is scheduled to stay in Ann Arbor after his USA Hockey National Player Development Program stint as committed to Michigan.

Webb, Mitchell
LW – Peterborough Petes (OHL) – 6'02" 190

Mitchell played a very limited role with the Petes this season. When he was in the line-up he played 4th line and did very well in a limited checking role. He is a decent skater with good size who pressures the puck carrier hard. He finishes his checks and can hit fairly hard for a 16 year old. Webb has some offensive ability but it is only moderate and wasn't really on display this year. Mitchell should get an increased role with the Petes' next season and with some improvement he could be a potential NHL prospect as a bottom six checker/grinder.

Welsh, Nick
RD – Shawinigan Cataractes (QMJHL) – 5'9" 174

The Halifax native was drafted 33rd overall by the Shawinigan Cataractes in the 2013 QMJHL draft. Welsh is an undersized, offensive-minded defenseman. He's an excellent skater with good footing and with good fluidity in his movements. He's very active on the ice and likes to lead or support the rush, and if he gets caught he has enough speed to get back defensively. He has quick hands and get pucks on net very quickly, and although he's not very big, he has a great slapshot from the point. As previously mentioned, Welsh is not a big defenseman, but we like his compete level and how he battles hard along the wall and in front of the net; he plays much bigger than his size. He gets into trouble when he faces bigger players that can outmuscle him away from the puck and win positioning in front of the net. Defensively, he can have an aggressive coverage thanks to his strong skating abilities, and likes to challenge players in possession of the puck immediately and not give them much room to make plays. As he continues to develop, we feel Welsh will become an impact defenseman in the QMJHL and have a major influence on his team's power play. Also played for Team Atlantic at the recent World U-17 Hockey Challenge in his home province in Cape-Breton.

Werenski, Zach
D – USNTDP-17 – 6' 1" 205
He could build into a top prospect with his size and skills. He is mobile as moves well with and without the puck. He plays with confidence and makes a good physical presence out on the ice as tough to beat with his strength. Werenski is not afraid to handle the puck, makes good solid passes, and will try to get involved offensively. Many scouts and hockey personnel are sold on Hanifin as the best American prospect on the blue line, but others believe Werenski as just as good as a promising prospect for the NHL game. He is uncommitted at this point and it is said the London Knights (OHL) are aggressively pursuing now.

White, Colin
RW – USNTDP – 6' 0" 179
Part of the young crop of '97-born US players that had a phenomenal season as a group, White had an excellent first season with the USNTDP.

White plays a big, physical, tenacious game of hockey. He is an absolute bear to play against and defend. Any of the ice in the offensive zone from the net to the end boards belongs to him. He owns it. Few players viewed this season dominate battles and body positioning in that area of the ice better than White. He has good size but he plays even bigger than he actually is at this point in his career and development. He takes the occasional dumb penalty, being

White, Colton
LD – SOO Greyhounds (OHL) – 6'00" 181
Colton made the Hounds line-up despite several older defenders ahead of him and while he received limited ice this season he showed the potential we liked with the London Jr. Knights Minor Midget team. He is a smooth skating defender and plays somewhat similar to current Hounds defender Kyle Jenkins. Both have average size as young defenders and both are capable of skating the puck up ice and moving the puck intelligently in the offensive zone. Colton showed good positional awareness when he didn't have the puck on his stick and moved around well. With so many returning defenders for Sault Ste. Marie Colton will hopefully not get caught in the depth and receive the ice to show what he can do leading towards the 2015 NHL Entry Draft.

Wilkie, Zach
LD – Niagara Ice Dogs (OHL) – 6'00" 185
Wilkie was a favorite of ours in Minor Midget and made the transition effectively to the OHL. He is a powerful skater who showed excellent puck rushing ability. He has quick hands and is capable of creating offense for his team. He sets up will in the offensive zone but will get a little risky with his pinches from time to time. While he doesn't have ideal size and strength just yet, Zach does a great job of battling along the wall and playing a physical style of game. He was effective but not

Wotherspoon, Parker
LD – Tri-City Americans (WHL) - 6'0" 170

With a late August 1997 birthday, Parker is one of the youngest players available for the 2015 draft. The brother of Flames prospect Ty Wotherspoon, Parker is a smooth-skating defender who seems to adapt to the style of game being played. Parker is poised with the puck and has shown good maturity in his game. While he focuses on defense first and foremost, Parker has decent offensive potential and has shown the ability to skate the puck out of trouble and lead the rush. He makes a good first pass.

He has good size, but needs to add strength as he can be knocked off the puck at times. He is a mobile skater that is able to use his edges well. He maintains good gap control and keeps his opponent to the outside. He can use some more experience in his defensive zone coverage as he can have lapses not understanding who to check. He shows a strong compete level.

Yan, Dennis
F – USNTDP-17 – 6' 0" 185

Yan possesses some gifted hands, powerful skating, and pure sniping abilities. He has very good hockey awareness and creativity. He played with the NTDP-17 team this past season and not sure his production of 12 goals and 14 assists in 48 games is indicative of his game. He has grown over the last couple of years but still stands to add strength to his game, a bit more sandpaper, and more sound defensive awareness. He was recently drafted in the KHL to in the 2nd round to Lokomotiv Yaroslavl.

Young, Spencer
D – Philps Exter Academy (MA) – 5' 10" 168

He is not overly big or strong, though he shows good patience with the puck with decent stick skills and vision from the blue line. He shows his offensive side by joining the rush on occasion, but will not being establishing big numbers on the score sheet. He has been honing his game in the NE Prep circuit at Philips Exter the last two seasons and will joining Hockey East's Providence College in a couple of seasons.

overly aggressive or acting out of frustration. Exceptionally strong and solid on his feet, he is an immovable object. The exception is when he chooses to move, and in that case he has great wheels and a high motor. His feet are always moving and he's very shifty for a big body. He plays a real intense game and his effort level is never in question. Add a good pair of hands and a scoring touch and White is the total package. You need no more evidence than his 18 points in six games at the World U17's. Slated to enter Boston College in 2016, White will be a fun player to watch develop the next few years.

Zacha, Pavel
C/LW – Bili Tygri Liberec (CZE) 6'3" 201

We first saw Zacha at the 2013 World Under-18 hockey Championship where he played as a double underage player for the Czech team. This season the big forward played in the men's league with Liberec, and in 38 games he scored four goals and added four assists. He also played at the world junior hockey championship, Ivan Hlinka, five nations & world under-18 hockey championship last April. At the U18 in our viewings we felt that Zacha was average, as he mishandled the puck at times, and played too passive. He was also not very good at the WJC, but being one of the youngest players there we gave him a pass. He's a natural center, but we saw him play LW this year mostly. Zacha is a big body that possesses a powerful stride, and an extra gear that helps create separation between him and the opposing team's defenders. He sees the ice well, and can move the puck quickly in the offensive zone. He is quite creative in offensive situations, and on the power-play. Zacha can be dangerous in the offensive zone thanks to his good shot, and has great velocity on his one-timers. He already he has nice size, and is quite strong while protecting the puck very well along the wall by using his size to shield opponents away. He's strong on his skates, and can be physical if needed. Zacha is a smart player in his zone, and has the ability of playing on the penalty kill thanks to his hockey sense. Consistency remains Zacha's biggest issue, as he can play some great games, and in other games he can be invisible.

Zeppieri, David
LC – Sudbury Wolves (OHL) – 6'02" 190

David played a bottom-six role for the Wolves in his first season in the OHL, which was a good situation for him because of his effective two-way style of play dating back to Minor Midget. Zeppieri provides a strong forecheck, and plays with a ton of energy. He forces his opponents to make mistake possessing an intimidating frame when barreling down on the puck carrier. He doesn't hesitate to finish his checks whenever possible. David also goes hard into corners, and wins battles. He plays a 200-foot game, and works hard defensively helping out in his own zone. While he didn't play a very offensive role for his team, he showed flashes of puck skills, and puck handling ability. David will look to take the next step in his career next season with an increase of ice time, and more opportunities to chip in offensively.

Zhukenov, Dmitri
C – Avangard-97 (Youth-Ural) 5'11" 159

Zhukenov was very impressive at the U-17 hockey challenge in Cape-Breton, posting 10 points in 6 games. He impressed our scouting staff with his willingness to compete at both end of the rink, showing strong effort on the backcheck. He's a good skater with a great burst of speed, and loves to rush the puck. He's very creative with the puck in the offensive zone, and has great playmaking abilities. He makes good decisions with the puck, and he's pretty quick at analysing the options he has in front of him. Zhukenov is more of a passer than a shooter, and was successful playing on Russia top powerplay unit at the U17 tournament. He's a dangerous player one-on-one, and can dangle pretty well with his great arsenal of dekes. He was drafted 15th overall by Avangard Omsk in the KHL draft this year.

2016 NHL DRAFT PROSPECTS

Allard, Frédéric
D – Chicoutimi Saguenéens (QMJHL) 6'00" 150

After being selected in the first round by the Chicoutimi Saguenéens, Frédéric Allard has been a pleasant surprise for this squad. He was labelled by some Sags fans as the best defender of their squad and we clearly do not disagree. He's not flashy by any means, rather he is very effective and steady on defense in our viewings of Chicoutimi. He has a highly developed hockey sense and displays it well when paired with his solid positional game and quick decisions while under pressure. His great footing provide him great one-on-one coverage giving opponents very little room to work with. He has a good stick to knock away passes and to take away passing lanes. He's more of a passive defender that relies on sound positioning and vision to be effective down low. He will rarely get caught turning the puck over, demonstrating his composure. Surprisingly at first sight, he regularly played on the first powerplay unit. He founds his teammates and most of the shots he takes get to the net. We would like to see him use his slapshot a bit more, but he has a hard, accurate wrist shot and he likes to use it. A fairly good puckhandler, Allard also isn't afraid to get deep in the offensive zone in keep the puck there. The one area of improvement for him would be his strength. He has a hard time maintaining body position against bigger opponents in the slot, and may have a hard time tying up bigger and physically mature players at the pro level.

Allen, Sean
LD – Guelph Jr. Gryphons (OMHA) – 6'01.75" 182

Sean was selected 41st Overall by the Kitchener Rangers at the 2014 OHL Priority Selection Draft. Allen is a big defenseman who played a ton of minutes for the Guelph Jr. Gryphons, and was their most relied upon defenseman in all-game situations. Sean has excellent size, and is capable of playing physical; we liked the fact that he played with a nasty streak on occasion. He generally uses his size, most effectively below the goal line in corners on the boards. He displays moderately effective defensive zone positioning, and will stick to his area, and won't chase hits. He is a good skater for his size. Allen is willing to rush the puck, and will even drive wide like a winger at times protecting the puck, and taking it to the net. While he can be effective at this, he can sometimes try to do too much with the puck, resulting in turnovers. He has a good wrist shot, and a powerful slap shot, which has helped him contribute offensively. He likes to shoot the puck whenever possible.

Anderson, Joey
F – Hill-Murray HS (MN) – 5' 11" 174

Anderson has good speed and utilizes his strong shot well along with some nice vision and stickhandling ability. A top '98 recruit out of the State of Hockey that seems to be a step above his competition.

Ang, Jonathan
RC – Markham Waxers (OMHA) – 5'10.25" 148

Jonathan was the offensive leader for the Markham Waxers this season. He did an excellent job keeping his team competitive in some tough match-ups with his combination of speed and skill. Ang is a very strong skater with excellent speed driving the outside, and can catch defenders flat footed at times. He has scored a few goals by driving the net, and creating a chance for himself with good hands, and strong puck skills. One of his greatest assets is his ability to control the puck under pressure using his small frame to the most of its ability to fend off checkers. He controls the puck for long stretches of time, and is capable of opening things up for his teammates by drawing in opposing players. He is smart positionally in the offensive zone, and is capable of creating chances for both himself and others. One concern for Ang moving forward is his lack of interest to go into the dirty areas, and battle for the puck. While he is comfortable competing with the puck, we'd like to see him get a little more tenacious without it. Jonathan will need to add muscle, as he should be able to make the jump to the OHL level next year. For him to do that he'll need to deal with bigger, stronger and older defenders, and must get his strength up to continue to have the type of success he's had in Minor Midget. We would also like to see him improve his consistency on the backcheck. He projects to be a talented offensive minded forward who utilizes his speed and puck control ability to contribute at the next level.

Balmas, Mitchell
LC - Cape Breton Tradesmen (NSMMHL) - 5'11" 168

Mitchell Balmas has come off an extremely successful set of Bantam seasons where afterwards he was invited to the All-State All Canadians camp. His Midget team this year, the Tradesmen, was one of the weaker teams in his league and there was instant pressure on the rookie to perform. Balmas was moved to the wing for most of the season and given top minutes, both even-strength and special teams (including powerplay and penalty kill time) although he seems equally comfortable as a pivot. It is likely that he played upwards of 20-25 minutes in every game, a tall order for any player. Balmas has a mature frame with good size and athleticism. On his skates, he shows as a strong, power-forward type player with a long stride that can burst into acceleration while in motion. He is a very good puckhandler and can create time and space anywhere on the ice to make a play to a teammate. He has a very good release, one of the quickest in the league, and can catch goalies sleeping with it. Balmas is a powerplay specialist and can captain any man-advantage situation with ease until the pieces are in place to convert. Defensively, Balmas can be positionally sound once on the right side of the puck, but shows a lack of commitment at times, even though he possesses the tools to chase down almost any player in the league. He will need to renew his commitment to the whole ice in order to impress upon scouts his desire. He has all the tools to jump into a lineup and contribute. On a very positive note, Balmas was invited to the World U-17 Team Atlantic selection camp and was named to the final roster. He competed in five games and registered two assists as the only underage player on the final roster.

Bastian, Nathan
RC – Mississauga Steelheads (OHL) – 6'02" 185

Nathan is a late 1997 birthdate, which means he should be able to rack up three seasons of OHL experience before being eligible for the 2016 NHL Entry Draft. Nathan split this past season with the OHL's Mississauga Steelheads and Brantford Jr. B 99ers. Bastian has great size and combines this with excellent work ethic. He provides a tenacious effort on the forecheck and battles hard for loose pucks. His work ethic should be a determining factor in his ice time with the Steelheads as he's expected to play full time next year and would provide a solid two-way presence for the Steelheads.

Barron, Travis
LW – Toronto Jr. Canadiens (GTHL) – 6'01" 175

Barron was drafted 3rd Overall by the Ottawa 67's at the 2014 OHL Priority Selection Draft. Travis is a strong, physical winger who plays a north-south game. He is not going to dazzle you with his skating or his puck handling, but he gets around the ice efficiently, and wreaks havoc on the forecheck. He has a good motor, and plays with a fearless tenacity. He finishes his checks and is willing to sacrifice his body, whether it is to chip a puck out of the zone, or to block a shot. Uses his size, and strength to maintain puck possession along the wall. Travis drives the net hard with or without the puck. He goes to the dirty areas on the ice, and will likely have to rely on scoring his goals at the next level from the area around the net. Barron is not the most creative player, but he is a smart hockey player. He finishes well around the net, and shows many intangibles in his game that coaches will love. Travis would benefit by continuing to work on his offensive skills to maximize his value to both his OHL team and for himself, as he begins the next stage of his development leading up to his NHL Draft eligible season.

Belisle, Brad
LC – Thunder Bay Kings (HNO) – 6'02" 195

Brad provided a good two-way presence for the Thunder Bay Kings in our viewings. He likes to finish his checks hard and has good size to work with. He battles very hard down low in the offensive zone and is capable of cycling the puck. He is smart positionally and finds the right areas to go for high percentage scoring opportunities. He was excellent in the face-off circle in our viewings and won more than his share of draws. He also is effective getting his stick into passing lanes in the defensive zone to break up chances. Brad was selected 53rd Overall by the Sarnia Sting at the 2014 OHL Priority Selection Draft.

Bellows, Kieffer
F – Edina HS (MN) – 6' 0" 190

He plays like his father as kind of a bull on skates but does possess skills as well. He has the pro-build formulating along with scoring ability. He will play the aggressive, physical game but at times steps over the line. He recently helped Edina Hornets win the Minnesota HS Class 2A State Championship.

Bitten, William
RC - Ottawa Jr. 67s – 5'09" 151

Bitten was drafted by the Plymouth Whalers and was a favorite of all our scouts going into the 2014 OHL Draft. His compete level is fantastic in all three zones and is refreshing to watch. Bitten is a smart hockey player with an exceptional skill-set. He is a great skater with great short area quickness.

He is agile and showed off an ability to be very elusive with an without the puck. He worked hard both offensively and defensively and flashed his skating ability a few times catching opponents from behind while applying back pressure. Bitten has parts of his game which reminded us of two players selected in last years OHL Draft, Travis Konecny of the Ottawa 67's and Mitch Marner of the London Knights. He has both scoring and playmaking skills, displaying good on ice vi- sion. On the character front, he is of the charts in a positive manor. If Bitten slides past the 10th pick in the draft we think he starts to become a possible steal in this draft in our opinion.

Bourque, Trent
LD – Hamilton Jr. Bulldogs (OMHA) – 6'01" 176

Trent was selected 51st Overall by the Sudbury Wolves at the 2014 OHL Priority Selection Draft. Bourque was one of our biggest risers as the season progressed. He made strides in many different facets of his game. Trent is a smart player who understands the position, and more often than not makes smart plays with the puck. He showed us an ability to keep a good gap, and showed confidence in his skating ability to do so. Speaking of his skating, it's very good, and will allow him to transition to the OHL more easily than many of his peers. His lateral movement is good, and he showed us good short area quickness. Although Trent might not be quite elite in any one specific area of his game at this point of his development, he is also with any major areas of weakness in his game. We liked the confidence, and poise he shows in all three zones. He made especially good decisions in the offensive zone in our viewings. Trent showed us to be a worthy defender with good OHL offensive puck moving ability, and he also showed off some very good offensive upside. Outside of the odd high-risk play, he picked his spots pretty well both joining rushes, and pinching in the offensive zone. He supported his partner well, making it easier on them to have a solid outlet while under pressure. We project Bourque as a solid two-way defender in the OHL with big upside in many areas of his game, especially offensively.

Brown, Logan
LC – Indiana Jr. Ice U16 (USA) – 6'04.5" 210

Logan was selected 6th Overall by the Niagara Ice Dogs at the 2014 OHL Priority Selection Draft. Brown's 2013-14 campaign was an injury-plagued one at the start, but that didn't stop the 6'4" forward from putting together a good season. Brown is gifted with great size, skill, and NHL genes from his father, Jeff, the long time NHL'er and current coach of the Indiana Ice of the USHL. There are times he relies a bit toomuch on those things alone, however. Brown can have shifts where he floats and goes through the motions and relies solely on his skill to get things accomplished. That can work at times at the AAA level, but it won't at the next level. With that said, those shifts are usually in the minority and when Brown does up his compete level he is simply on a completely other level from most of the rest of his competition.Between his size, his hands, and his skating ability, he has all the tools. He sees the ice really well and is an excellent passer, and he has the hands to beat players one on one to create scoring chances for himself. He has shifty feet and moves well for a kid with his size, and because of his long stride he has deceptively decent speed. Defensively, he also plays a solid game. He backchecks hard and between his skating ability and his reach, many times he breaks up rushes through the neutral zone, often on the backcheck by pick-pocketing the puck carrier and taking it back the other for an offensive zone possession. At the end ofthe day, Brown has the potential to be a great player at the next level, whether that is in the OHL or with the USNTDP, it's just a matter of "want to". If the effort and compete level are there, he has a chance to be a dominant player. The motor needs to be turned on more often.

Brown, William
RD – Ottawa Jr. Senators (ODHA) – 6'01" 158

Brown was drafted 43rd Overall by the Ottawa 67's at the 2014 OHL Priority Selection Draft. Willam was, in our opinion, the best player on the Ottawa Jr. Senators this season. He has good size and good feet. We liked the progression he made in the physical part of his game. He pretty much threw a "no hitter" in the first half of his season, but he started to make strides in that department in the second half of the season understanding that he needed to develop that part of his game. It's still largely a work in progress but at least he became aware of the weakness in his game. He's a big strong kid with some offensive abilities that need more "push back" in his game. Tools and potential are there.

Brushett, Ryan
RW - Lac St-Louis (LHMAAAQ) 5'11" 168

Brushett is an offensive player who can play both on the wing and at center. He had a good season with the Lions in 2013-2014. Originally from Verdun, Brushett can be a very effective player offensively, due to his high skill level and great wrist shot. He can pick corners with great accuracy already and has a good release on his wrist shot; he's dangerous when he gets the puck in the slot. He sees the ice well and he's among the best in the province of Quebec at manufacturing offense, but consistency is a big issue with his game. One game he can look like a potential top-10 pick in this draft, and the next game you barely notices him. Finding a consistency in his game will be key for Brushett at the next level, and he might need extra time at the Midget AAA level. He's a decent skater with good feet, but will need to work on improving his top speed which would allow him to create more space for himself and create more separation between him and his defenders. Ryan does a good job on the forecheck, he's a smart player who uses his stick well and can steal pucks from opposing players on the forecheck or in his puck pursuit. He's not overly physical at the moment; he lacks strength and prefers to play a finesse game. We still feel Brushett would benefit from playing less of a perimeter game in the offensive zone and get more involved in the tough areas of the ice instead of waiting to get the puck back. Without the puck, he can be lazy with his defensive-zone coverage at times and tends to focus on the puck and lose track of his assignments. It still unknown what Brushett's plans are for next season: he could play major junior, might lean toward playing another year in Midget AAA or go the prep route like many other Lac St-Louis kids have done in the past.

Bunnaman, Connor
LC – Guelph Jr. Gryphons (OMHA) – 6'00.5" 196
Connor was selected 31st Overall by the Kitchener Rangers at the 2014 OHL Priority Selection Draft. Connor showed the best OHL Draft upside as far as forwards go on his team every time we saw Guelph play. Although his skating would probably grade out as average, he has pretty good skills, and he competes hard. Connor did have times through games where he left us wanting more as far as consistency goes, but for the most part we liked what we saw. We would like to see him develop a 2nd gear as far as his skating goes; Bunnaman lacked any sort of explosiveness. Overall, there was a lot to like, and he made a positive impression on our scouts.

Campoli, Michael
LD - Lac St-Louis Lions (LHMAAAQ) 6'02.5" 189
Campoli came with much hype from the bantam level and didn't have the year a lot of folks expected, due to injuries and inconsistent play. He did, however, have a strong postseason with the surprising Lac St-Louis Lions, who went all the way to the Quebec Midget AAA semi-final when they finally got healthy as a team. The Pointe Claire native is a big blueliner with above-average mobility; he has quick feet that help him keep up with speedy forwards coming off the rush, and has good lateral agility to cover a lot of space defensively. Not many players in Quebec have this combination of size and skating abilities on the back end. Campoli can dish out big hits in open ice and has a good sense of when to step up in the neutral zone without getting caught being too aggressive. In his zone, he could be more of a physical player down low, as he has the strength but needs to play a more consistent, mean game. It remains to be seen how much his shoulder separation injury at the beginning of the season affected his play during the rest of the year, mostly at a physical level. One of the best aspects in his play in his zone is his active stick, with which he breaks up a lot of plays or passes. Campoli is more of a stay at home defenseman who does possess a big slapper from the point, but he needs to use it more frequently. On his team, he didn't get the chance to play on the powerplay often or at all, so his offensive game still remains raw at this point. His play was on and off with the puck this season, as he could make some good decisions with it (quick, simple, short, tape-to-tape passes) but when pressured in his zone you could see him panic a bit and throw it away. As a dual citizen, Campoli elected to take part in USA's Hockey U-17 camp in Ann Arbor, Michigan this March and was eventually selected as part of the 2014-2015 NTDP team, which will surely affect his draft stock on draft day.

Candella, Cole
LD – Vaughan Kings (GTHL) – 6'01" 180
Cole is a very offensive minded defender. He is a great skater and shows high confidence when skating with the puck through traffic. He has strong acceleration and can skate himself out of trouble with ease. Candella shows good poise with the puck and is able to elude fore-checking defenders with quick feet. He is constantly looking to push the play and generates numerous offensive chances from his rushes. Cole shows good puck skills and is creative in 1-on-1 situations. He excels at driving to the net with the puck and is able to add an extra burst of speed to beat many unsuspecting defenders wide or up the middle. He has a big slap shot and is able to get it on target through traffic seemingly with ease. Candella is also a physical player and is constantly looking to initiate contact and is a player that other teams know is on the ice. He does need to improve his defensive zone awareness as he sometimes gets caught standing around or over pursuing the puck carrier. Our biggest issue with Cole is that he seems to lack hockey sense. He needs to improve his decision making in many situations. Too often he forces passes into tight areas or skates himself right into trouble when better options are available. These decisions often result in turnovers and

quick counter attacks. He also needs to work at reading the play better when he's attempting to hold the offensive zone. Cole played up with the Junior "A" Milton Icehawks and kept his game simpler. He picked his offensive rush spots much better than with the Kings. Cole was selected 23rd Overall by the Belleville Bulls at the 2014 OHL Priority Selection Draft.

Chychrun, Jakob
LD – Toronto Jr. Canadiens (GTHL) – 6'02" 195

Jakob played a step above his competition this season. He uses his size, skating ability, and puck handling skills to control the flow of the game. He is a strong skater who uses his powerful stride to jump into the offensive rush, often leading the rush himself. Jakob shows tremendous poise with the puck and makes an excellent, crisp outlet pass. He passes the puck like someone well advanced of his age. He also shows good touch when making a saucer pass. He plays with his head up and has very good vision and instincts. Jakob's hockey sense is very apparent, as he is usually a step ahead of the competition. He can quarterback a powerplay and be equally effective on the penalty kill. He has a very hard, heavy shot and a keen ability to get his shot through from the point and he keeps it low for tips and rebounds. He shows very good balance on his skates and was difficult to knock off the puck. Jakob also shows that he can be a physical force when he needs to use his size and play a physical game. He shows good gap control and does not give up his lines as easily as most players his age. He has a good active stick in his own end and finishes his checks well. Towards the end of the season he began to play a little too casual at times and sometimes overhandled the puck. Like many kids his age, Jakob still has room for improvement on his defensive zone coverage; he lost his man at times and didn't read plays quickly enough. Overall, he shows maturity and ability beyond his years. We have been very impressed with Jakob was selected 1st Overall by the Sarnia Sting at the 2014 OHL Draft.

Crossley, Brett
LC - Shattuck St-Mary's (Prep) - 6'0" 160

A product of the Cole Harbour minor hockey program, Brett has spent the last two years at Shattuck St Mary's in Minnesota. He comes from a hockey family; his sister plays at University of New Hampshire, while his father has been with the Dartmouth Subways (Newbridge Gladiators) as head coach for many years.

Brett has blossomed into a high-end prospect. He is an excellent skater and demonstrates speed down the wing. While he is not a punishing forward, he is not afraid of traffic and will take a hit to make a play. He possesses a high hockey IQ and plays a cerebral game. Skilled with the puck, Brett is more of a playmaker than shooter. He reads the ice well and does a great job of jumping into open ice and reading seams to get himself into good support positions. Would like to see him take more risks offensively and improve his one-on-one play when he attacks the opponent's defense. Brett played an important role with Hockey Nova Scotia while playing on its top line with Mitchell Balmas and Michael O'Leary at the Gatorade Challenge. It should also be noted that he was selected as team captain. Brett projects as a second-line center who can earn an opportunity as a special-teams player. His only deficiency is that he appears to have a slight frame. If he adds the necessary strength and weight required, he will be a good major junior player. It is unknown at this moment if Crossley will leave his prep school to play major junior.

Day, Sean
LD – Mississauga Steelheads (OHL) – 6'02" 216

After receiving exceptional player status and being selected 4th Overall at the 2013 OHL Priority Selection Draft, Sean played his first season in the OHL as a 15 in the league. He didn't look out of place at all generally playing second pairing minutes and seeing action in all game situations to give him a very good amount of ice without overwhelming him. Day showed us many consistencies in his game during our viewings both good and bad. First and foremost, Sean is an excellent skater who does an excellent job on the rush. He evades checkers and possesses an effortless stride. He also has a good frame which he utilizes to protect the puck very well on the rush. In the offensive zone he generally makes good decisions with the puck. Considering his puck rushing ability, he can sometimes be forced to retreat all the way back to his own net if he's being forechecked by a strong skating forward. While he makes accurate tape to tape passes regularly without pressure, he was fairly consistently pressured into rushing his decisions and turning the puck over when a hard forecheck pressure is put on Sean. Moving forward this season with a success for the young 15 year old. Moving forward we will look to see him improve his decision making under pressure. His physical game was virtually non existent this season which is understandable for an underager in the OHL but is something we hope to see develop now that he has a year of experience in the league.

Dineen, Cam
D – NJ Rockets U19 – 5'10" 160
He plays a steady game on the back-end as he is committed defensively and will also find players in transition and through the seams to start the offense. A Yale recruit out of the NJ Rockets program.

Dubois, Pierre-Luc
LW - Albatros du Collège Notre-Dame (LHMAAAQ) 6'00" 161
Son of Eric Dubois, coach of the Rimouski Oceanic, Pierre-Luc is a forward who was able to contribute very well on the scoresheet this season. His excellent puck control at high speed is one of the main reasons for his success. During each of our viewings, he was able to beat defenders in the offensive zone to create room, then driving the net. Also, he possesses very good vision. He's able to make low percentage passes with ease. He has no hesitation with slowing down the pace and trying to find better options. His wrist shot is deadly and can be fired very quickly. He amasses a lot points on the man-advantage where he has more room to maneuver. This Rimouski native is a natural scorer and has one of the most dangerous shots in the Quebec Midget AAA league. Dubois is also able to rush the puck with ease in the offensive zone. He keeps in head up and he's an explosive, fluid and powerful skater. He never shies away from going in the tougher areas of the ice and loves to compete in one-on-one battles. However, as he plays aggressive, at times he can lose control of his emotions and be undisciplined. This leads him to be in the penalty box at the wrong time. His play in his zone is fine, but he still needs to be more involved, as he showed at the end of the season. Dubois is a player whose talent is without question and who will bring his scoring abilities with him to the next level.

Dhillon, Stephen
G – Buffalo Regals (OMHA) – 6'02.75" 163
Stephen was selected 52nd Overall by the Niagara Ice Dogs at the 2014 OHL Priority Selection Draft. Stephen has good size and is technically sound. He looks good in the butterfly position and shows himself to very strong covering the bottom of the net. His rebound control is fine for a goaltender this age but is an area he has room for growth. We like the way he doesn't overplay the shooter and is balanced and controls his movements in the crease, pucks just seem to hit him due to good positioning. Dhillon always seemed to keep his team in games and showed good consistency during the season. He was also solid at the NTDP camp.

Dorval, Zack
LC – SOO Thunder (NOHA) – 5'11.25" 167
Zack was selected 35th Overall by the Kingston Frontenacs at the 2014 OHL Priority Selection Draft. Zack is slightly undersized, and displays strong skating ability, but plays bigger than his size with

good physicality against bigger opponents. He is willing to go to the dirty areas, and has delivered some solid checks. He has good hands, and is able to beat defenders one-on-one, and has the patience to buy time. He has a good shot, and has a bit of a shoot first mentality. He is willing to put in effort in the defensive zone, but needs to be more aggressive on the high point in the defensive zone.

Felhaber, Tye
LC – Ottawa Valley Titans (ODHA) – 5'10.25" 174

Tye was selected 10th Overall by the Saginaw Spirit at the 2014 OHL Priority Selection Draft. Tye was one of the most exciting, and purely talented players available for the 2014 OHL Priority Selection Draft. He has explosive skating, and exceptional quickness, which allows him to reach top speed almost instantaneously. He doesn't even seem to break stride when evading checkers faking one way, and going the other in the neutral zone. He is capable of driving the puck end-to-end almost at will, and does so on a regular basis when he picks up the puck from his own end. He has excellent puck skills, and is extremely dangerous on the breakaway. Tye has been able to score some absolute highlight reel goals bringing a "wow" factor on some individual plays, and can finish in so many different ways. However, despite his excellent skill level, hockey is still a team sport, and Felhaber has had great difficulty throughout our viewings distributing the puck and including his linemates in the play. He very rarely passes, and assuming he doesn't take the puck end-to-end, once he acquires the puck, the play usually ends good or bad, based on what he does with it himself. Unfortunately we've seen many highly talented players struggle as they move up a level when they play this individual style, and this is our only real concern with Felhaber. His compete level drops off a bit the further he gets from the opposing net. He can also make risky plays in his own zone with the puck attempting to do it all himself. Tye's skill level alone puts him among the best players in his age group, however, his seemingly unwillingness to pass the puck could affect him at the OHL level, and eventually for the NHL draft. He needs to take the next step in his development by learning to trust his teammates, and begin to pass the puck. He will obviously have better talent around him in the OHL, and he will quickly find out that good things can happen when you pass.

Fitzpatrick, Evan
G – Newbridge (NSMMHL) 6'2" 194

After moving from Newfoundland to Nova Scotia a couple of years ago to attend Newbridge Academy in Sackville, Fitzpatrick put together two excellent Major Bantam AAA seasons and was invited to the All-State All Canadians camp. Fitzpatrick split time in between the pipes with second-year goalie Aaron Mantle, and in the end registered three shutouts with a 2.31 GAA and 0.920 SV% in 17 games. You are immediately struck by his size and athleticism, as he is a tall and strong goalie with fast reflexes and good symmetry in his movements. He is a pure butterfly and relies heavily on positioning and speed to cut pucks off. He is the strongest-skating goalie in the Atlantic region by a margin for his age. If his glove hand is tested, you will notice that he displays good reflexes and can make guaranteed goals disappear with a flash of his glove. In scrambles, he can display extreme flexibility and agility and make impossible saves. Likewise, his deflection control is excellent, easily the best in the Atlantic area, with purpose to control the play at every instance. Compared to all of the goalies in the league, he is of average ability when handling the puck outside of his crease and this would be a definite area for improvement, as witnessed on several occasions. There are two sides to Fitzpatricks' mental game, as he almost always appears calm and steady no matter how big the stakes, however, at times you will get a sense of distraction and in those games he becomes vulnerable to attack and perhaps loses focus on the task at hand. This can be more evident with higher-stress situations. Fitzpatrick is the top-rated goalie going into the draft and it is our feeling that whichever team drafts him will have a solid piece to build around for the next few years. Fitzpatrick was named a league First Team All-Star in the NSMMHL and also named to Team NS for the Under-16 Gatorade Challenge

Fortier, Maxime
RW – Lac St-Louis Lions (LHMAAAQ) – 5'10" 168

Fortier was a Halifax 2nd round pick in the 2013 QMJHL draft, and played another year of midget this season with the Lac St-Louis Lions this season. The Lachine native did play three regular season games with the Mooseheads, and was called up to stay with the team in the playoffs after his midget team was eliminated from their own playoffs. Fortier was arguably the best skater in his league this season, an excellent skater who can reach his top speed in two or three steps. He can be very dangerous if he goes untouched in the neutral zone when rushing the puck, as his speed is very tough to contain at this level. He's a shoot-first type of player, has a quick release on his shot and won't hesitate to let it go from anywhere in the offensive zone. Scored 40 goals in 40 games this season with his midget team and scored once in 6 games with Team Quebec at the World Under-17 Hockey Championships. At this tournament, Fortier was playing on the first line with last year's top overall pick, Nicolas Roy, and was part of Quebec's best line during the tournament.

One strong attribute of Fortier's game is that he's very good at getting open to receive a pass, either in the offensive or neutral zone. He was used on the penalty killing unit this season as well, and he was a constant threat to score there with that great speed and anticipation. Fortier's hockey sense is just average, as he can create a lot of offense with his speed and shot, but he's not a natural playmaker and tends to keep the puck. Fortier has yet to mature physically, and that's one of the reasons he went back to midget for an extra year. Can get outmuscled by stronger players in corners or in front of the net and will lose those one-on-one battles at the junior level if he doesn't get stronger. Although Fortier is not afraid, he will even initiate contact at times in midget, it remains to be seen what type of physical game he will have at the junior level. Without the puck, he tends to stop moving his feet and gets a little bit lazy in his own zone at even strength.

Fox, Adam
D – LI Gulls U16 – 5'9" 155

He is not a big blue liner physically but handles the puck and skates well. He quarterbacks the power-play and distributes the puck up ice using good decision making skills and vision. He can wheel around the offensive zone to be the playmaker and likes to join the rush as the 4thforward frequently. He looks to be in good position to make the team. Fox could strength up of the defensive side.

Garin, Will
F – Holy Family Catholic HS (MN) – 5'9" 171

He is a bit on the smaller side, yet he competes hard and gives an honest effort. He has some nice wheels and handles the biscuit pretty well too. He shows good hockey sense, protects the puck well, and has good offensive thoughts. He could play a bit more physical. Garin is committed to UConn in a couple of years.

Gauthier, Julien
RW – Val d'Or Foreurs (QMJHL) – 6'3" 220

Gauthier was the 6th overall selection in last year's QMJHL draft by the Val-d'Or Foreurs and is also the nephew of former NHLer Denis Gauthier. Like his uncle, Julien has great size and won't turn 17 before October 2014. Played majority of the year on the Foreurs' 3rd line, and got some power play time as well. He was physically ready to start his junior career, unlike many of his draft class. Already possessing a NHL frame, Gauthier has all the tools to become a solid power forward in the next couple of years. He's an excellent skater for his size, has great top speed and has quick light feet as well. He excels in puck protection and on the cycle, and it is really tough to get the puck away from him. He's at his best when he plays an aggressive type of game, as not a lot of people can match him with that size and speed.

His consistency is an issue, as we would like to see him more involved in the play on a regular basis. He could be a dominant force with that combination of speed and size. He played for team Quebec at the World Under-17 Hockey Championships, and was not very noticeable during the tournament. He was one player Team Quebec was counting on.

His hockey sense is average at best; he doesn't seem to know where to go in the offensive zone to get open. He has a great wrist shot with a quick release, but he's often not in the right position to take a shot. He's an underrated passer, but there again, he takes too much time to make a decision with the puck and that is costly at this level. Without the puck, he made some progress this year, but he does have some lazy shifts in his zone where he stops working and moving his feet. Nevertheless, Gauthier is an intriguing prospect to keep an eye on, due to his combination of size and speed which is rarely seen in Quebec.

Getson, Keith
LC South Shore Mustangs (NSMMHL) 5'11" 178

Getson is coming off a Midget season where all eyes were on him to see if he could repeat a performance like last years' Bantam performance, where he shattered the league record and recorded 50 goals. His Midget year would prove to be more difficult, but in some ways perhaps made him a more complete player. On paper, his offensive punch seemed to drop, as he managed 18 goals this season. However, this places him second amongst rookies by only one goal. Getson continues to use and develop a powerful skating stride, built on a foundation of great strength. He can explode forward, with or without the puck and he can frequently catch defenders flat. His puck control is confident and with great timing, he can shift pucks through defenders while powering past. Getson possesses a very developed shot. It is hard and accurate with a great release. This season, he has a renewed passion for realizing his role and place on the ice and was committed to developing his defensive game. He was much more engaged in the defensive end towards the middle and end of the season, and he benefited on the scoresheet. There were some tremendous displays of strength this season, times when he could not be knocked off the puck during board play. The upside for Getson is big and he would project immediately into any teams' lineup. Getson was placed on Team NS U16 Quebec Challenge Cup Roster.

Girard, Samuel
LD - Élites de Jonquière (LHMAAAQ) 5'9" 156

Girard was able to have a great impact this season in the Quebec Midget AAA league. We think he has enormous potential. This Élites de Jonquière product is an offensive defenseman with phenomenal skating abilities. He's a fluid skater that always keeps his feet moving, which allows him to be at the right place to retrieve pucks. He anticipates the play like few players can, and it explains in some way his success on the ice. He likes to rush the puck end-to-end and he's really exciting when he does it, showing high end puck skills, a good burst and a great hockey sense. He easily finds openings when he rushes the puck because he keeps his head up all the time. Also, rarely does he get caught off-guard when in possession of the puck. It does happen that you will see him turn back and go on his strong side to escape the forecheck while still being conscious of his surroundings. If not, he will take a quick and efficient decision and just pass the puck to an open teammate in a similar situation.

When he's used on the power play, Girard acts as a quarterback. He's the one controlling the puck and because of his excellent footwork and out of this world vision, he's capable of finding his open teammates with ease, proving that he can make passing lanes by himself. It's not a secret for anyone that the power play success of the Élites de Jonquière rest on the shoulders of this Roberval native. His slapshot, although accurate, could be more powerful to be more of a threat with goalies at a higher level. He often finds a way to be efficient along the boards, in the middle of the ice or in tight spaces. He plays one-on-one confrontation very smartly and with patience. He doesn't get caught often and his good mobility helps him to not get beaten wide and to always be in position between his goal and the opposing forwards. Even if he's not the biggest, Girard is stable and is able to use his body to separate opposing players from the puck. He barely gives big bodychecks, but they are well synchronized and efficient. He also likes to be aggressive in his coverage and put pressure on the puck carrier in the defensive zone. In one-on-one situations deep in his zone, he does fine at the moment, but we are well-aware that his size could give him trouble at the major junior level. Finally, Samuel is a player that has a strong work ethic and plays better the bigger the moment is.

Gleason, Ben
LD – Detroit Honeybaked U18 (HPHL) – 5'11.25" 157

Ben was selected 36th Overall by the London Knights at the 2014 OHL Priority Selection Draft. Ben is a smooth skating two-way defenseman who, despite making the jump from Bantam to playing up with the U18 program this year was a defenseman who could do it all from the back end. Ben has quick feet, and is extremely mobile. He was very effective rushing the puck up ice, showing elusiveness, and intelligence on the rush. He has a great point shot, which is low and deflectable, and gets through to the net on a regular basis. He moves the puck well, and is very smart, and precise with his passes. He also has good patience with the puck, and doesn't force plays.

Ben was very reliable defensively, and will retreat early if it's clear the play will end up going up ice. He has excellent positional awareness in the defensive, and neutral zones, and is consistently where he should be. He lacks strength, which effects him in battles against bigger, and older players but he utilizes his stick well to offset this disadvantage. Ben looks like an excellent option for a smooth skating two-way defenseman who simply needs to get stronger.

Green, Luke
LD – Newbridge (NSMMHL) 5'11" 168

Luke Green has been in the eyes of scouts for years as he continued to improve through Bantam and into Midget. He was invited to the All-State All-Canadians camp after his senior Bantam season. Green is perhaps the best skater in the '98-born group from Nova Scotia and arguably the rest of the Atlantic region. There is not a lot of fault to be found with his technique and his speed and agility is elite. When watching him play, you are instantly drawn in and as you continue to watch, you become aware that his skating provides the foundation for solid puck handling skill that at times can leave you breathless. Every shift he is on the ice is a potential to make an amazing play with the puck. His offensive hockey IQ is perhaps the most developed out of this draft class, as he anticipates and reads the game at an elite level, creating opportunities where others do not see them. He can pass with pinpoint accuracy in a variety of ways, and he also can finish things with a fast release wrist or even a snapshot. His synergy and coordination level is very high, and he can shoot at full speed and while in motion, including a slapshot. In his own zone, Green can run into real difficulty.

Luke is most definitely an offensive defenseman and is frequently a fourth forward on the ice. This can lead to odd-man rushes for the other team and places a lot of defensive responsibility back on his other linemates. He seems to have some issues with cutting off the ice from attackers, and he won't use many sweeps and stick checks to try and separate players from the puck due to his weaker gap control or him being on the wrong side of the puck. He is much more effective a defender when simply having the puck on his stick, and defending with possession rather than aggression. Watching him protect the puck, you get a sense that he is stronger that stature would lead you to believe. With 17 goals and 20 assists in 24 games and being named the NSMMHL Top Rookie Defenseman, it's easy to see that people agree he is a desirable asset for any team.

Greenway, JD
D – Shattuck St. Mary's U16 (MN) – 6'4" 194

He surely brings an intimidating physical presence as he is a very solid body at 6'4" and 200lbs. who likes to punish opponents. The potential is untapped here.

Hellickson, Mat
D – Rogers HS (MN) – 5'10" 155

He is a solid all-around defender that does not have the flash, but a composed game at both ends of the rink.

Jones, Max
LW – HoneyBaked U18 – 6'2" 190

Max was selected 18th Overall by the London Knights at the 2014 OHL Priority Selection Draft. Jones possesses a relentless compete level, and works hard shift after shift. He uses the grit he brings to his full advantage; he has a bit of a nasty streak, which makes him difficult to play against. He forces turnovers because he takes away opponents ice so quickly. He skates well with a nice stride, and shoots the puck like a pro. He has good size, and will drive to the net with or without the puck. He constantly wants the puck, and shows the drive to do whatever it takes to get it. He finished the bulk of his checks in our viewings, although there were a few times near the end of shifts where he chose to wave his stick at opponents. The thing that jumps out at you with Jones is his high energy all over the ice combined with great skill. He forces turnovers because he takes away opponents ice so quickly. He protects puck very well with his body, and showed some poise buying time to make a play. As mentioned, Max has excellent power in his shot, and he can score, but he also showed us that he could distribute the puck as well. We like that Jones isn't a one-dimensional player. Jones played well with other great players at the NTDP, and showed he doesn't lag behind other top players in the hockey sense department. Jones was a bit hit or miss in positionally; sometimes smart others times he ran around. He also rushed moving some pucks in his own zone when he had more time. Jones is in the process of deciding whether to play for the OHL's London Knights or the United States National Team Development Program for the 2014-2015 season. In either situation he will likely get a lot of ice right away.

Hanley, Jack
LD – Whitby Wildcats (OMHA) – 5'10.5" 180

Jack is an offensive defenseman for the Whitby Wildcats. He has shown us a varying degree in work ethic, but when he's on his game he's an excellent puck rushing defenseman who acquires the offensive zone on a regular basis. He displays good lateral movement, and walks the line effectively. He also has great power in his wrist shot, and his slap shot, which he gets off from the point efficiently. Defensively he displays good positioning, and plays in all game situations. He reads plays effectively getting into passing lanes, and negating offensive chances against. Jack will need to become more consistent on a game-by-game basis, because he is an impactful player at this level when he plays to his potential. He will also need to get stronger. Jack was selected 64th Overall by the Belleville Bulls at the 2014 OHL Priority Selection Draft.

Henderson, Eric
LW – Sun County Panthers (MHAO) – 5'11.5" 167

Eric was selected 54th Overall by the London Knights at the 2014 OHL Priority Selection Draft. Eric looks like a pro with the way he drives the net. He displays patience, and slick hands along with cerebral finishing abilities, which make him a huge threat to score. While you don't see a great backhand shot in Minor Midget often, Henderson has a great move, and quick release on the backhand. Henderson's backhand shot has caught goaltenders off guard, and has resulted in some nice goals for him. He has slick hands, which allow him to create chances for himself, and others. He possesses the hockey intelligence to read plays, and always seems to quickly make the right decision with the puck. On the powerplay, he moves the puck very well, finding great positioning, and making effective decisions with the puck. He is effective along the wall using his size, and strength to come away with the puck more often than not. He is a reliable backchecker who will compete in his own end, and is very positionally sound. Henderson is one of the most exciting players in Alliance when it comes to NHL Draft potential, and is a player we feel could surprise at his team's camp this fall. While we would like to see him gain a little more explosiveness in his skating ability, gain a little more strength, and add in a little more of a mean streak in his game, there is very little that concerns us with Henderson at the OHL level. He is poised, mature beyond his years, and contains the hockey sense that gives him a great opportunity to succeed.

Katchouk, Boris
LW – Waterloo Wolves (MHAO) – 6'00" 169

Boris was selected 33rd Overall by the Sault Ste. Marie Greyhounds at the 2014 OHL Priority Selection Draft. Boris played a big part of the Waterloo Wolves top line that finished 1-2-3 in Alliance league scoring. Katchouk provided a little bit of everything for his team this season. He is a strong skater who is very elusive, and extremely difficult to contain. He excels at bringing the puck through the neutral zone, and reading the play deciding whether to pass or shoot. He does lean a little bit towards his shot, which is powerful, accurate and he shows the hockey sense to find good scoring areas without the puck, opening himself up for a pass. With that said, he is more than willing to pass, and will usually make the right play in relevance to the play in terms of passing or shooting. When he is moving the puck he shows excellent creativity, and has made some highlight reel passes that lead to goals. He isn't afraid to go into the corners, as he provides a hard forecheck, and wins a fair amount of battles for a skilled player. The only weakness with his skill is he can try to do a little too much at times. His work ethic had it's lapses, but overall he played most of his games with a high compete level, rarely taking shifts off. He provides a solid forecheck using his speed and tenacity to force turnovers. Defensively he has shown willingness on a few occasions to block shots, and will work in the defensive zone. Boris has the size and skill to make the jump to the OHL next year, and simply just needs to get stronger at this point. He needs to maintain consistency with his work ethic, and continue to keep the balance between utilizing his powerful shot and slick passing ability.

Keller, Clayton
C – Shattuck St. Mary's (HS-MN) – 5'08" 149

Clayton was selected 40th Overall by the Windsor Spitfires at the 2014 OHL Priority Selection Draft. Keller was one of the best in the players in the 2014 OHL Priority Selection Draft class. He sees the ice very well, not only in setting up scoring chances with quality passing, but also his ability to read plays. He anticipates the play very skillfully before it happens, therefore displaying his high hockey IQ. He is not really big in size, though it does not hamper his game at all due to his smarts on the ice. He plays all situations from the powerplay to the penalty kill, and is always dangerous on the ice. Keller is a skilled player that can score in a variety of ways. He can showcase his nice hands, dekes, and moves, and he can also fire it home with a quick wrist shot or powerful slap shot. He skates well, and is not afraid to get the puck in the corners or along the wall. He plays every shift with energy to track down the puck, or in an attempt to posses the puck, which leads to scoring chances. Keller shows great offensive instincts, and determination. He skates very well, he's agile, and has all-around good skill sets. He is always moving to get the puck, protect it, or get open for opportunity. He handles the puck quite well, knows how to protect it, will find the open man, and can release a nice hard shot too. Overall, he shows a great competitive nature out on the ice. He is one of two under aged players at Shattuck St. Mary's playing up on the Prep team rather than age appropriate U16 club. Clayton has committed to Boston University in the NCAA.

Khodorenko, Patrick
F – HoneyBaked U16 – 5'11" 185
He is one of the top forwards to play out of the HoneyBaked '98-born team for last few seasons. He is another smart, solid hockey player with a great future. He shows great patience, creates opportunity offensively, protects puck well, and has above-average vision for sure. He always looks dangerous with the puck.

Kirwan, Luke
F – USNTDP-17 – 6'1" 225
A very powerful skater and solid player with great stick skills and deadly shot. He plays an explosive up & down game utilizing his body well. He can score coming down off-wing using the defenseman as screen to just release an absolute laser beam or drive the puck hard to the net. Kirwan competes hard as well as built and plays ready for the next level. He has been described as "man-child" out on the ice with he makings for the pro game. He's uncommitted & drafted to the OHL.

Knierim, William
RW – Chicago Mission U16 (HPHL) – 6'03" 208
William was selected 32nd Overall by the Owen Sound Attack at the 2014 OHL Priority Selection Draft. Seemingly a man amongst boys at the U16 level, William is a tough player to miss on the ice. His size is among his top attributes, and he likes to use it to his advantage in all facets available. In addition to playing a physical style, and always finishing checks, he's equally adept at using his reach, and strength to protect the puck. He proves to be very difficult to defend against. His footwork, while it could be improved, is still solid for a bigger body at his age, and does nothing to hinder him outworking, and out-skating the competition. He has good speed in open ice, and combining that with his size, and compete level makes him nothing short of a headache to play against. He likes to agitate, and physically intimidate to boot, but is intelligent, and picks his spots. He always skates hard, always competes hard, and loves being in the tough areas of the ice. He handles the puck really well in tight around the net, and has excellent overall vision of the ice. Very intelligent, and despite being a big body, manages to find open areas of the ice offensively for open shots often, and is always in proper position defensively. His playmaking abilities are equally impressive, as there were numerous occasions he made passes few of his peers are capable of at all areas of the ice, but especially in the offensive zone. Greater still are his abilities to put the puck in the net. William has one of the best, and quickest releases we saw all season, and his shots come with a lot of zip and accuracy. He can flat out rip it.

Kutkevicius, Luke
LC – North York Rangers (GTHL) – 6'00" 148
Luke was selected 25th Overall by the Mississauga Steelheads at the 2014 OHL Priority Selection Draft. Kutkevicius is a big Center for the North York Rangers with plenty of skill. Luke flew under the radar for a large part of the season due to injuries. A strong performance at the OHL Cup really showcased a number of good qualities in his game. He is good at shielding opponents from the puck and working along the boards deep in the offensive zone. Luke showed a strong skating ability with a good level of speed beating a number of defenders wide off the rush. He is relentless in puck pursuit and is always looking to jump start quick counter attacks by back checking hard and creating turnovers. Kutkevicius has a heavy shot and a quick release allowing him to score a number of exceptional goals. He does not always venture into the dirty areas of the ice and would benefit from adding some muscle to his frame and improving his strength. Luke can occasionally be knocked off the puck fairly easily. He showcased his good smarts and vision on the power play quarterbacking it from the defense position. He makes his linemates better and was a key part of a surprising run by the Rangers at the OHL Cup.

Kyrou, Jordan
RC – Mississauga Senators (GTHL) – 5'11" 158

Jordan is a highly skilled center for the Mississauga Senators. He is exceptionally elusive with the puck and is very shifty once entering the offensive zone. Kyrou is able to slip checks with ease while showcase a variety of creative offensive skills. He is good in 1-on-1 situations and is a big task to handle for most defenders at this level. Jordan has a strong shot and a quick release that is able to catch many goaltenders off guard from the high slot. While highly skilled with the puck, Kyrou is also not afraid to get his nose dirty and can be found looking for scoring opportunities in front of the net and battling for loose pucks along the boards. He is a good skater but could benefit from working on his foot speed and edge work to really compliment his puck skills with speed. He is good at playing bigger than his size indicates which unfortunately led to a season ending injury early in the playoffs. He uses his size well to shield the puck but rarely looks to initiate any contact with opponents. Kyrou also has a good net presence and looks for tips and jam chances in tight. Jordan was selected 38th Overall by the Sarnia Sting at the 2014 OHL Priority Selection Draft.

Krys, Chad
LD - NJ Rockets U19 - 5'11" 165.

Krys is definitely a high-end talent at the '98 birth year in the USA. He actually has been turning heads for several years now. As a Pee Wee Major U12 playing for the Westchester Express, he singlehandedly won the New York State Championship with his elite skills and hockey sense. In fact, one top coach who is an ex-NHLer himself now coaching at a well-known program in the US, said Krys was the only kid he ever made a game plan around because he is head & shoulders above.

Krys is a talent that you recognize right away. He plays very poised with the puck on his stick and has a smooth skating stride as well. He is not overly big but average size and growing. He often looks effortless out there with his skating and dangerous from the back-end with his nifty stickhandling and above-average vision. He is a player that wants to have the puck on his blade and always looks to make a play. He has the ability to wheel the puck up ice himself or find the open-man for the scoring opportunity.

He has great offensive thoughts to his game as he can take the puck end-to-end using stride to blow around defenders allowing him to be the playmaker or finish the play himself. He does not have a booming slap shot, but utilizes his quick and accurate wrist shot to score goals. He does not play overly physical yet will play the body and uses an active stick and high-end hockey IQ to read plays along with quick foot work to close gaps quickly leading to turnovers in which he effectively transitions puck up ice.

He thinks the game a step ahead and is a "can't miss" prospect for sure. A few adjectives to describe his game are: dynamic, advanced for age, strong, student of the game, and relentless passion for the game. Right now he is deciding upon committing to the NCAA route to either Boston College or Boston University. Keep in mind his father played at BU, yet the 'Q' might be in his future as well. Next season he is headed to USA Hockey's NTDP-17 in Ann Arbor, MI.

Kunin, Luke
F – USNTDP-17 – 5'10" 183

He does possess some offensive skills although needs to be more consistent in his play each game and even each shift. The Wisconsin recruit improved his dependability this season as posted a very respectable 20 goals and 18 assists in 52 games played for NTDP-17. Kunin is average size at 5'10" but still only 16-years old at this point. He is a late 1997 birthdate in December so he is not even NHL draft eligible until 2016. He developed his game playing with the St. Louis Jr. Blues organization along teammate, Matthew Tkachuk, whose father former NHLer Keith Tkachuk coached the young '97s growing up.

Laberge, Pascal
RC - Grenadiers de Châteauguay (LHMAAAQ) 6'00 ½" 158

Laberge is without a doubt the most promising forward in this year's draft class from the province of Quebec. He was a standout performer in the regular season with the Châteauguay Grenadiers and helped them win the playoff championship, eventually losing to Prince Albert in the Telus Cup final in the third overtime period. The St-Martine native is an offensive forward who oozes with potential, with his great skating abilities and lethal shot that he can release extremely quickly. His quick hands make him a threat to score every time he's on the ice. He can score in many different ways; he can win positioning in front of the net, use his speed off the rush, or just use his big shot from anywhere in the offensive zone. When he can get free lanes to skate into the neutral zone, he can gain his top speed quickly and he's extremely tough to contain off the rush for any defenseman at this level. He can expose them by going wide on them. Coming in with that speed, he can be downright intimating for defensemen and makes them back off, which gives him more room with which to manoeuvre in the offensive zone. Laberge already has good puck-protection skills, using his size and long reach to shield opponents away from the puck. Those skills will only improve once he gets physically stronger, as versus bigger players he can lose puck battles along the boards due to lack of strength. Laberge has a great, projectable frame going forward, but he's still physically immature at the moment. Laberge is at his best on the power play, where he can show his poise with the puck and control it from the half-wall on the left side of the ice, and he can hurt you with his shot or playmaking abilities. Laberge is more of a finesse type of player, we would like to see him get more involved in the play and go in the tougher areas of the ice. Inconsistency is another area of his game that will need some improvement at the next level, as he can go hot and cold in his performance from game to game

Lawr, Jake
G – Halton Hurricanes (OMHA) – 6'02" 150

Jake established himself early on as one of the better goaltenders available in the 2014 OHL Priority Selection Draft. He has excellent size, and seems to always put himself in ideal positioning. He isn't very quick, but is very technically sound in his positioning. He is particularly difficult to beat on the lower half of the net, yet covers a lot of the top with his size. He needs to improve his rebound control, and his recovery ability because both are below average. The combination of the two can get him into trouble some games. He is very good at handling the puck, and makes smart, quick decisions when playing the puck. He will need some time at the lower junior levels before making the jump to the OHL. When one of either his rebound control or his recovery improves, Jake will be able to make the jump. In the meantime he'll need at least one of those two areas to improve to begin realizing his potential.

Lauzon, Félix
LC – Cantonniers de Magog (LHMAAAQ) 5'8" 170

Félix had a real good end of the season, and a great postseason as well. He was Magog's leading scorer in the regular season. It is worth noting that he was given an exemption to play his last bantam year in Midget AAA last season. He possesses good hockey sense that makes him efficient in all three zones. He can play on the first powerplay unit as well as the first penalty killing unit without any problems. Many times, Félix was used on the point on the powerplay. Defensively, Félix is excellent at retrieving pucks, supporting his defensemen well and is also good in terms of puck protection. In a game situation where's there a big faceoff, he was the player called upon to win that important draw. He possesses great anticipation and excellent vision; he showed during the season that he was ready for the next level. Félix has a wrist shot that opposing goaltenders don't like because he's capable of placing the puck in tight spaces wherever he wants to and it leaves his stick very quickly. However, he's not the quickest skater or explosive on the ice, but with his anticipation and reads place him at the right position at the right moment, and he's also the first forward on the backcheck. Félix played at the beginning of the year with an injury which slowed him down, but once past it, he was back to his top form. One of the most complete players in the draft without any doubts. He's the kind of player that we can see more in a 3-2 win in overtime than in a 7-2 win. He's a clutch player, a player that raises his play for big games.

Lindgren, Ryan
D – Shattuck St. Mary's Prep (MN) – 5'11" 190

He is the stockier, solid side frame that moves well, defends his own end hard, and also has a great booming shot from the point. He uses his stick well to break plays up and shows aggressive, sandpaper nature to make life difficult on opponents. A Minnesota Golden Gopher commit.

Luce, Griffin
D – Salisbury Prep (CT) – 6' 2" 201

Many scouts and coaches are sky high on the young Luce. No question he brings a strong physical presence on the ice with his large frame. At this age he surely is an intimidating player but will need to keep improving his feet to help his overall game. He will punish players and can fire the biscuit. Michigan has already offered him a verbal scholarship.

Maher, Jordan
LC - Central Ice Pak (NLMMHL) 5'11" 164

This was Maher's second year in Major Midget despite being a '98-born, as he played with the Ice Pak last year as an underage player. He was nearly a point-a-game player as an underager, and this season he put out an impressive 1.95 points per game including 23 goals and 24 assists over the 24 game schedule. Numbers don't do justice to what Maher brings on the ice almost every shift. He is an explosive and fast skater, able to instantly accelerate, and he can perform this with the puck as well, seemingly not able to slow down. He exhibits good edge control, but like almost all skaters his age, with more size and strength he will gain even more improvements in this area. In stride he can pinpoint passes and improve his position, always looking to be in a first-class scoring lane. His shot is extremely accurate and on net. He is one of the few players his age comfortable with all types of shots while in motion. He is comfortable in the periphery or at the net and will take abuse to get there. Defensively, he doesn't drop off, much as I was able to witness his willingness to backcheck and the result of his efforts. He frequently would chase down puck-carriers as they tried to enter his zone and strip them of the puck, or separate them from it so a teammate could recover it. He was an Alternate Captain on his team and it's clear by the maturity of his play and vocalization that he is a natural leader on the ice, whose understanding of the game is very high. Over the season, he has improved his game, getting better in every aspect. Maher is a playoff performer as well, as he has led his team to both a provincial title and a berth in the Atlantic Championship. Maher was an invite to the World U-17 Team Atlantic selection camp as an underage player but was not named to the final roster.

Mascherin, Adam
LC – Vaughan Kings (GTHL) – 5'09" 197

Adam was selected 2nd Overall by the Kitchener Rangers at the 2014 OHL Priority Selection Draft. Adam is a highly skilled center. He possesses the hardest shot in the age group, and combined with a lightning quick release, was able to produce a large number of true highlight reel goals. While not the tallest player, Mascherin is certainly built very thick, thus making it hard for opposing defenders trying to knock him off the puck. He is very strong on his skates, and rarely ever falls down. Adam is a strong skater, and uses quick powerful strides to get himself into open areas of the ice. He is a big time shooter, and is the triggerman on the powerplay in all situations. His wrist shot is very deceptive, and has been able to beat goaltenders from literally all areas of the offensive zone. He is absolutely lethal from the middle of the circle, and can launch a puck upstairs in a hurry. Mascherin does not shy away from physical contact, and initiates contact of his own if presented with the right opportunity. He is strong in the faceoff circle, and seems to have a good understanding of positioning in all three zones of the ice. He was also able to dominate with the Georgetown Raiders of the OJHL scoring a number of points in a playoff run, and essentially stepping right into the focal point of the first powerplay. He would benefit from adding some offensive creativity to his game, as sometimes he relies on his shot too much, taking some very low percentage outside shots. Mascherin posted big numbers this season without the benefit of having other high-end offensive stars surrounding him on the Kings roster.

Matthews, Auston
F – USNTDP-18 – 6'0" 200

A very skilled offensive player that scores in a variety of ways. He is a good skater and decent sized at 6-foot. He shows great hockey sense and is reliable in his own zone as well. He was called up to the NTDP-18 team mid-season and certainly did not disappoint as he scored 12 goals and 21 assists in just 24 games played. He also started to raise more eyebrows on the international scene at the U17 World Challenge and U18 World Championships as displayed his offensive talents and slick scoring abilities. There is no question he will go high in the 2016 NHL Entry Draft. He is uncommitted to any NCAA school and well sought after by many top D1s but some have the feeling he might end up WHL bound.

McAvoy, Charles
D – USNTDP-17 – 5'11" 190

He is a smooth skater and covers ice fairly well for averaged sized D-man with adequate positioning and good use of body. He makes good initial passes and plays poised with puck. He needs to get stronger although late '97 birthdate so probably still growing. The former NJ Rocket product has been recruited by Boston University (Hockey East).

McInnis, Luke
D – Hingham HS (MA) – 5'10" 165

He shows good skill sets and skating ability like his father. The young McInnis has a good head for the game as he sees the ice well and plays that playmaking style.

McPhee, Graham
F – Shattuck St. Mary's U16 (MN) – 5'11" 165

The skilled scoring forward with gifted hands and strength that can set plays up or put on the finishing touch himself. He is a Boston College commit.

McLeod, Michael
RC – Toronto Marlboros (GTHL) – 6'01.25" 175

Michael was selected 5th Overall by the Mississauga Steelheads at the 2014 OHL Priority Selection Draft. Michael is a high end offensive talent for the Toronto Marlboros. He is an exceptional skater and uses long powerful strides to beat almost any defender to the outside or up the middle when he is on his game. He flies around the offensive zone with ease and is very shifty and slippery in tight. McLeod uses his size to shield opponents from the puck before utilizing a quick acceleration to beat them wide before cutting to the net. He has elite puck skills and excels at winning 1-on-1 situations before dazzling opposing goaltenders with a variety of dekes. Michael also has a big shot and is able to get it on target from all areas of the offensive zone. He does not shy away from physical contact and is relentless in the corners after loose pucks. McLeod combines size and elite puck skills to consistently be one of the best players on the ice. He does sometimes struggle with consistency over the course of a full game, but can be a game changer at any moment. He would benefit from cutting inside with more regularity because he sometimes ends up deep in the corner after the start of the rush seemed promising. McLeod is excellent on the power play and is a great playmaker setting up his teammates all over the ice. He had a consistent season and excelled in the playoffs. He finished the season on a high note winning the OHL Cup MVP award. Michael has all the tools to be highly successful at the next level and with a relentless commitment to the game he should continue to just get better.

Mete, Victor
LD – Owen Sound Attack (OHL) – 5'08.75" 157

Victor was selected 8th Overall by the Owen Sound Attack at the 2014 OHL Priority Selection Draft. Victor has elite level, effortless skating, and is a slick puck moving defenseman. He uses his excellent skating to create time and space for himself, and he can skate himself out of trouble in the defensive zone when necessary. At times he is a one-man breakout. He makes a good outlet pass, and also moves the puck well to his defense partner. Victor has a high hockey IQ, and shows good on ice vision, and awareness. Mete has a knack for knowing when to jump into the offensive rush, and sometimes leads the rush when given space in the neutral zone. Victor has excellent recovery speed, and works hard to get back into position after joining the offensive rush. He shows poise, and confidence when handling the puck. Victor walks the blue line well in the offensive zone, and shows an ability to get his shots through to the net. However, he does not possess a booming shot. Mete exhibits good balance on his skates for a smaller defender. As an undersized defenseman he can struggle in puck battles with bigger forwards along the boards, and in front of his own net. This will be his biggest challenge as a rookie at the next level.

Middleton, Keaton
LD – Huron-Perth Lakers (MHAO) – 6'05" 207

Keaton was selected 50th Overall by the Saginaw Spirit at the 2014 OHL Priority Selection Draft. Keaton is an absolute giant on the blueline, and was easily one of the biggest players eligible for the 2014 OHL Priority Selection Draft. Scouting Keaton was one of the bigger challenges because he has so many intriguing raw tools, but there is a lot of room for improvement as well. Keaton is most effective on the wall. He is dominant in puck battles, and very difficult for opposing players to handle in the corners and along the boards. He also does a good job of boxing out opposing players with his size. He isn't always an overly physical defenseman, but he has shown signs of having a real mean streak. He can really punish players at this level, and will be able to be an imposing defenseman at the OHL level as well. His footwork needs improvement, as he can get up, and down the ice, but his feet are very heavy, and it takes him some time to get moving. Pivoting can be a bit of a challenge sometimes, which results in him being beat one-on-one. Puck play is an adventure at times Middleton. He has streaks where he makes solid, accurate first passes. However, he can also be rushed into puck playing mistakes or try to force passes that simply are not there. Keaton has an absolute cannon of a shot from the point and utilizes it liberally. It is easily one of the hardest shots in the draft. This has developed mixed results over the course of the season, as he can score or create a rebound with it. He doesn't pick his spots very well and a lot of times, if a player was brave enough to get in front of his shot, they were able to block it. His shot was inaccurate on occasion. He does a great job holding the line utilizing his size, and his long reach to keep the play going in the offensive zone. Because he has so much to work on, he will take a while before he can make a positive impact on a team. That patience should pay off as Keaton could develop into an excellent defenseman if he is able to refine his required areas of improvement.

Neveu, Jacob
RD - Forestiers d'Amos (LHMAAAQ) 6'1 ½" 194

Jacob Neveu played last season in the Midget Espoir league with Abitibi-Temiscamingue at the age of 14 and we noticed him right away. This season, he improved during the season to become a premium defensive defenseman. This Rouyn-Noranda native is a physical player that doesn't give any room to opposing forwards. This defenseman with an imposing frame loves to play physical along the boards and in front of his net. He makes opposing forwards pay the price and becomes an imposing player on the ice. Also, he's often involved in scrums that happen after whistles. Defensively, he's very solid one-on-one, as he doesn't let opposing forwards go around him without making a strong effort of using his stick and his size at the right moment. Very good on the penalty killing unit, Neveu covers a lot of space and showed a great understanding of the game, blocking shots and passing lanes. When he's in possession of the puck in the defensive zone, he uses often the boards to get the puck out. His transition game is simple; he makes short passes and doesn't take risks. We have seen him play on the power play and at his best when he can unleash his powerful one-timer slapshot. He's a powerful skater that is strong on his skates, but needs to work on his pivots. Neveu can play a lot of big minutes and can be efficient late in games. We believe that he's ready to play in the QMJHL next season in a defensive role and could be used on the penalty killing unit.

O'Leary, Michael
LW/C - Salisbury Prep School (CT) - 6'1" 175

Scouts often use the expression "some players just look like they were built to play hockey." This expression applies to Michael. He is a player who has been off the QMJHL radar for most of this season because he played for the Salisbury Prep team. His recent showing at the QMJHL Gatorade challenge showcase was no surprise to those who have watched Michael develop as a player in the Halifax Minor Hockey system. O'Leary was also selected to play in the NHLPA sponsored All State Program last summer, where he showed well. If we were to choose one word for O'Leary it would be "winner." He has been part of a dominant group of '97-'98 born players in Halifax, and has won countless championships. His winning tradition continued this year in Salisbury with his team winning the Tier 1 New England Prep School championship.

As a player, he is a prototypical power-forward who has a knack for scoring big goals. He projects as a top-six forward but is also proficient in his own end. He is an athletic player who excels at many sports, but we are thankful that he has chosen hockey as his passion. O'Leary is a centre but can also play the wing. O'Leary is a player who competes hard and has the will to win. His greatest strengths lie in the offensive zone, where he thrives in the corners and loves to go to the blue paint. We have witnessed an improvement in his skating but this is the one area that needs to get better. His straight-away speed is ample but his first few steps and lateral agility may prevent him from being a top line centre at the next level. It still unknown if O'Leary will stay in school or join the QMJHL. If he does report to his QMJHL team, this team will get a player who thrives in critical situations and brings an element of grit and determination that is prized in an otherwise east west style league.

Paquette, Christopher
RC – Kingston Jr. Frontenacs (OMHA) – 6'00.75" 174

Christopher has a great combination of size and skill, which makes him a very intriguing prospect for the 2014 OHL Priority Selection Draft. Paquette is a strong puck handler who can evade checkers in the neutral zonem and beat defenders in one-on-one situations. He prefers shooting to passing, but when he does pass he shows creativity and accuracy, making a few excellent passes to develop scoring chances for his team. His shot is intriguing. It has good power on it but it can be inaccurate at times. It's streaky. We've seen him both pick the smallest area top shelf and score, but also continuously shoot into the goaltenders logo. This will likely see him be a bit of a streaky goal scorer at the next level if he can't increase the consistency in his accuracy. He generates decent speed, and can really drive the net well with his skating, but lacks explosiveness. He finishes his checks, but doesn't really possess a mean streak. Paquette looks to be a pretty safe prospect advancing to the next level. We would like to see him improve his backcheck, and get a little stronger, as he is a bit lanky and has a lot of room to add muscle. But he brings a lot of different abilities to the table, and even if he stopped growing, his height is solid for both the OHL level and potentially one day to the professional game.

Pastujov, Nick
LW – Detroit Honeybaked U16 (HPHL) – 5'11.5" 186

Nick was selected 68th Overall by the Saginaw Spirit at the 2014 OHL Priority Selection Draft. One of the things that come across most impressive about Nick is his compete level, and passion. Even in games where his team was dominating. and the game well decided, Nick rarely took a shift off, and played hard passionate shift after shift. He is player that just flat out looks like he is having the time of his life playing hockey, and when someone that skilled carries all of those attributes it makes them all the more impressive as a hockey player, and as a young man. Possessing an excellent two-way game, Nick battles as hard defensively as he does flashing his offensive prowess. Exceptional speed, athleticism, and phenomenal hands all make him a treat to watch in every viewing. He creates so much space offensively, and makes would-be defenders miss regularly. Quick hands, and shifty feet, along with a solid frame make him beyond a handful to defend against. Pastujov is an excellent passer, even better shooter, he has a nose for the net, and is one of those players the puck just seems to "find" a lot. Equally good defensively, Nick uses that speed to backcheck hard, and regularly causes turnovers in doing so, often resulting in him taking the puck back the other in transition for odd-man breaks, and quality scoring chances. He makes great decisions, but is especially responsible defensively. Great player for the penalty kill, as he is defensively sound but has the quickness, and smarts to be able to create offensive opportunities on the kill. There is no situation he cannot handle, and is without a doubt one of the best players in his age group.

Pezzetta, Michael
LC – Mississauga Senators (GTHL) – 6'00.75" 201

Michael was selected 11th Overall by the Sudbury Wolves at the 2014 OHL Priority Selection Draft. Michael is a strong power forward for the Mississauga Senators. Pezzetta excels at pushing the pace of the play. He can really fly down the wing, and uses this speed to blow past many flat-footed opponents around the league. He also has shown a knack for finishing scoring opportunities with a heavy wrist shot, and quick release in tight. He is a very smooth skater, and shows good agility, and acceleration from a stand still. He is good at supporting his teammates on pinch opportunities as well as in scrums after the whistle. Pezzetta is also a dominant physical force, and finishes checks with speed, and authority. He is the type of player other teams are very aware of when he is on the ice. He excels at picking up a puck in the neutral zone, and driving to the net for a crash, and bang plays with authority. His offensive skills with the puck are underrated, and he works hard to get into scoring positions in the offensive zone. Michael is good at getting low in the defensive zone, and is able to support or carry pucks out of the zone with confidence. He does sometimes need to be careful about crossing the line, and taking penalties. Pezzetta has taken a few nights off over the course of the season, and needs to work at ensuring consistency, and compete level as he continues to move forward into his OHL career.

Picard, Miguel
LC - Albatros du Collège Notre-Dame (LHMAAAQ) 6'00" 167

Miguel Picard is a forward with a great hockey sense. He's always well-positioned on the ice in all three zones. When he plays centre, he's very helpful for his defensemen, as he supports them well and knows how to use his size to retrieve pucks. His offensive hockey sense is well-developed and he has an above-average vision. He finds his teammates in no time and possesses the ability to make plays look easy. He also doesn't shy away from the net to jump on rebounds and the physical game doesn't bother him, as he is rarely intimidated by the opposing team's pressure in his play-selection. Picard has quick hands in tight spaces and has good puck-protection techniques that help him increase the time of possession in the offensive zone. He excels along the wall and knows how to protect the puck, using his size well. Also, Picard gives an honest effort every time he's one the ice. However, his skating stride is not fluid, lacks explosion and will need some adjustments for him to play at the major junior level. But a player like him will get picked high in the draft regardless. If he improves his skating ability, he has the potential to become a very good two-way player in the QMJHL.

Pu, Cliff
C – Toronto Marlboros (GTHL) – 5'11.75" 168

Clifford is an elite offensive forward for the Toronto Marlboros. He is an exceptionally smooth skater and has one of the best accelerations in the entire draft. Pu moves fluidly all over the ice and has the quick burst ability to break away from defenders. He is very skilled with the puck and shows all types of creativity in the offensive zone. He has scored a number of highlight reel goals from in tight and has excellent hands in goal scoring areas. Cliff reads the ice exceptionally well, and is a great puck mover, making his linemates look better every shift. He is very elusive in the offensive zone and is a great finisher when the puck finds his stick in the slot. Pu is reliable in the defensive zone and helps out down low in all situations, picking the puck up and skating it out of trouble himself on some occasions. The biggest knock on his game is that Pu plays at the end of his stick and does fly by's too often rather than get involved in the physical element of the game. He needs to work at finishing checks and showing an overall higher compete level for loose pucks. Offensive consistency is also something that Cliff should look to improve on at the next level, as too often he became a perimeter player, which hurt his production as a consistent offensive performer.

Raaymakers, Joseph
G – Chatham-Kent Cyclones (MHAO) – 6'00.5" 169

Joseph was selected 37th Overall by the Sault Ste. Marie Greyhounds at the 2014 OHL Priority Selection Draft. Joseph is one of our top ranked goaltenders for the 2014 OHL Priority Selection Draft and is the top goaltender out of the Alliance area this season. He played a key role in the Cyclones making the semi-finals of the OHL Cup. Raaymakers displays good reaction time and challenges shooters very effectively. He has moderately good size, and has good vision through traffic. He also handles traffic very effectively, as teams try to crash the crease he's able to maintain focus and remain composed. We have seen him handle the pressure of a big game situation well and make key saves at important times in the game. For his size he's fairly quick, and rebounds have hurt him at times, but hasn't been a major concern for us looking at the big picture. His glove hand is a little inconsistent, as we've seen him get beat there frequently in comparison to other areas. At times he'll commit to the shooter too early. Joseph is a goaltender who is very well rounded for his age, and while we don't expect him to make the jump right away, he will just need some minor refinements at the junior level before being ready to make the jump to the OHL.

Raddysh, Taylor
RW – Toronto Marlboros (GTHL) – 6'00.25" 190

Raddysh is a powerful winger for the Toronto Marlboros. He uses his size exceptionally well, and shields opponents from the puck with ease. Taylor is much better player with the puck on his stick than without it. He shows great vision, and reads the offensive zone well, setting up teammates in highlight reel scoring situations. He makes strong crisp passes, and generally makes the smart pass rather than force something that is high risk. Raddysh has a good shot, and scores a large chunk of his goals from in tight. Taylor is a decent skater, and gets up and down the ice well. He might not be the fastest skater in the draft, but he is able to get going after the first few starting strides. He is lanky, and has a long reach which allows him to get his stick into passing lanes in the neutral zone, and create quick counter attacks. The biggest thing that Raddysh needs to improve is consistency in both effort level, and offensive production. He had an excellent start to the season before floundering at the midway point, but picked it up again with high-level playmaking abilities at the OHL Cup. He makes things look simple for his linemates, and produced large offensive numbers this season. There is also room for Taylor to grow into his body, and with a relentless commitment level he will be a very strong force at the next level.

Reynolds, Keenan
LC – Ottawa Jr. 67's (ODHA) – 6'01.25" 193

Keenan is a huge forward who has been ably to fly a little bit under the radar for the Jr. 67's with the great play of his teammate Will Bitten. He has good puck possession skills utilizing his huge frame to protect the puck, and can control it for long periods of time. He displays excellent hockey sense, and reads plays well. He has good speed for a player his size, and has deceptive moves, capable of beating defenders and goaltenders in one-on-one match-ups on a fairly regular basis. Reynolds also has an absolute laser of a shot. Despite his excellent release on his shot, Keenan can be unselfish to a fault, and always seems to be looking to make the pass. He has made some excellent passes, and created scoring chances with his vision, but will sometimes overlook an ideal shooting lane to force a lower percentage pass. He does a good job of taking up space, and creating a disruption in the slot with the reaction time to bang home rebounds. He has a good work ethic, and competes in all three zones taking away time and space. He finishes his checks, but doesn't possess much of a mean streak. Keenan has the size you love to see in a prospect. He is poised with the puck, displays good hockey sense, and projects very well to the OHL level, and beyond. If we could adjust anything in his game, we would like to see him shoot the puck more often, and play with a little more of an aggressive mean streak.

Rossini, Sam
D – Burnsville HS (MN) – 6' 1" 170 (2016)

He is talented with his fluid skating ability and capability of moving the puck in transition quickly while taking care of his own end too with tough defensive play. He is decent size and still growing as is his offensive potential. He is a Minnesota native staying in-state for his NCAA career with the Golden Gophers.

Saigeon, Brandon
LC – Hamilton Jr. Bulldogs (OMHA) – 6'00.75" 184

Brandon had a good but a little inconsistent start to the season, and didn't really play to his potential early on. As the season progressed he simply got better and better. He finished the year off with an outstanding performance at the OHL Cup, and solidified himself as one of the most talented players available for the 2014 OHL Priority Selection Draft. Brandon is effective in all areas of the game, but was at his best when shooting the puck. He has one of the best shots in the draft with a quick release, and an absolute rocket off his stick. His finishing ability in the goal area is among the best in his age group. He displays excellent vision, and while he is a shoot first style of player, he has shown the ability on many occasions to create something out of nothing for his teammates. He is extremely dangerous on the powerplay when given time with the puck, because he can move the puck so well. He can also exploit shooting lanes for goals. He isn't a player who tries to force plays very often and will cycle the puck or buy time with his puck control if the option isn't there. Despite all of his offensive attributes, he has done a great job on the penalty kill, skating with the puck, and buying a lot of time. He showed a willingness to play physical, but isn't an overly aggressive checker. We would like to see him play with the level of consistency in which he played late in the season. While he is suitable for the centre position, he has struggled in the faceoff circle in our viewings, and will need to improve in this area. Brandon was selected 4th Overall by the Belleville Bulls at the 2014 OHL Priority Selection Draft.

Salinitri, Anthony
C – Windsor Jr. Spitfires (MHAO) – 5'09.5" 153

Anthony was selected 17th Overall by the Sault Ste. Marie Greyhounds at the 2014 OHL Priority Selection Draft. Anthony was one of the most skilled and creative players available in the OHL draft. He displays great speed and elusiveness and is very difficult to contain. His puck skills are at a high level, and he is very creative. Many times when it appears the play may be done, he finds a way to elude the defender and make something happen out of nothing. He has great hands in traffic and remains calm under pressure, which allows him to beat defenders and finish in high percentage areas. In addition to his scoring ability, he has shown the ability to complete high difficulty passes.

What really stands out for Anthony is, along with his offensive ability, he has shown defensive responsibility using his speed on the backcheck. He does to be more consistent with this. Salintiri lacks size and needs to get stronger, but with his wealth of skills, and his ability to play with a fearless edge in physical match-ups, Anthony should debut in the OHL as a 16-year-old.

Sanchez, James
F – Chicago Young Americans U16 – 6' 2" 185 (2016)

Sanchez is a good sized player at 6'2" who shows nice hands, the set-up style, plus a solid two-way game. He is bound for Michigan University (Big 10).

Stanley, Logan
LD – Waterloo Wolves (MHAO) – 6'06.25" 209

Logan was selected 12th Overall by the Windsor Spitfires at the 2014 OHL Priority Selection Draft. Stanley is a massive defenseman for the Waterloo Wolves. He played a big role both offensively, and defensively for his team this season. Logan possesses outstanding size, and can finish his checks devastatingly hard. He has the size to protect the puck for a long period of time, allowing him all the time needed to make a decision. Offensively he likes to rush the puck. He is a little heavy on his feet, and not a great accelerator, but he generates good speed, especially for a defenseman of his size. He is usually at his best on the rush making a move, then getting the puck deep or passing it off. Too often he got in trouble trying to do too much with the puck, resulting in the puck being sent the other way. He moves the puck effectively on the powerplay, but very much prefers to shoot. He has a huge blast from the point, which was effective when it got through. Stanley's shot selection resulted in several shots being blocked.

In the defensive zone, Logan is extremely difficult to play against. He is big, strong and has a bit of a mean streak to him where he enjoys punishing opponents. He is tough in battles, and works fairly hard to win the majority them. He usually makes the safe smart first pass up the ice, but had a tendency to serve up dangerous passes, right up the middle on more than a few occasions.

Logan is at his best with the puck when he keeps it smart, and simple. Stanley's play has been widely inconsistent in our viewings. He shows flashes of being a star in the junior leagues, and beyond, but also shows signs of complacency, and can make some questionable decisions. He will also try to do too much after making a great play, ultimately negating his initial success.

With the Spitfires, he has the potential to thrive, and could easily become one of the best defensemen in the entire 2014 OHL Priority Selection Draft class. However, he will need to be reeled in a little, and required to focus on a defensive first game, which is where his long-term strengths are. He should eventually become a defender who can chip in offensively as well.

We love the potential Logan shows, but he will need to go through some growing pains before reaching that high level of potential.

Stillman, Riley
LD – Peterborough Jr. Petes (OMHA) – 5'10.5" 180
Here is a kid who is pure offense. We actually project him more as a forward in the OHL. Riley is a great skater who can really handle the puck. In general, he has great offensive instincts and loves to jump up into the play from the back-end but needs to do a better job of picking his spots. He cheats too often and gets caught more often than not. He's not great defensively, not an effective player in his own end, just too easy to beat in our viewings. While it sounds like we are pointing out a lot of deficiencies in his game, this is a player who can really skate and has great puck skills, including a great shot. As we said, we project him to be a better prospect as a forward. Has NHL Boodlines as his father is Cory Stillman.

Sylvestre, Gabriel
RD - Phénix du Collège Esther-Blondin (LHMAAAQ) 6'02½" 169
Sylvestre, who played on the talented Phénix squad who lost in the league finals is a very interesting prospect who doesn't have a lot of flaws in his game. Like his teammate Guillaume Beck, Sylvestre already has a nice frame and should only get bigger and stronger as he continues to progress. He's a player who earned his coaches' trust and was used all year in important parts of the game, playing big minutes all year long. Sylvestre is not a flashy player like his teammate Beck, but he's extremely smart and effective in a defensive role. He's strong on his skates and has a good physical game in his zone. He battles hard in the defensive zone and is not afraid about clearing the front of the net. For a player his size, he has an above-average mobility and footing, though he can get caught flat-footed in the neutral zone at times but this was more the case in the first half of the season. He has made some adjustments in this area in the 2nd half of the year, and in the playoffs. With the puck, we like his decision-making; he doesn't try any fancy plays and always chooses the easy outlet, or will just chip the puck by the boards if there's no open teammate. He has some ability to play on the powerplay and has a good shot from the point, but couldn't really show them this year with the Phénix as Beck was getting all the top powerplay minutes. Played for Team Quebec at the Quebec Cup AAA International in late December in Châteauguay, and eventually lost to team Finland in the final.

Thom, Matthew
RD – Mississauga Senators (GTHL) – 6'01" 191
Matthew was selected 71st Overall by the Kingston Frontenacs at the 2014 OHL Priority Selection Draft. Matthew is a solid two-way defender for the Mississauga Senators. He has good size, and is able to use a long stick to knock pucks free from opponent's sticks or ride them into the boards coming off the rush. Thom brings a nice level of physicality to his game, and can be counted on to finish checks in both open ice and along the boards. He works hard to clear the front of the net, and does not shy away from blocking shots. Matthew makes a solid first pass, and primarily keeps breakout passing options simple. He skates with big long strides, and is able to jump into the rush with ease but chooses to pick his spots better than other defenders. His footwork and transition speed are sufficient enough to compete at the AAA level, but he may want to quicken things up a little bit to compensate for more elite opposition. He has a booming shot from the point, but lacks a quick release, and requires time for a large wind up. Although he is a physical player, it sometimes seems forced, and he should look to ensure that his compete level is constantly high.

Timms, Matthew
LD – Hamilton Jr. Bulldogs (OMHA) – 5'08.75" 172
Timms has been an impact player from the blue line for the Hamilton Jr. Bulldogs this season, and improved throughout the year. Matthew is a smooth skating defenseman who is capable of rushing the puck end-to-end with a good top speed, and evasiveness in open ice. Once in the offensive zone Matthew is a dangerous player due to his ability to read plays, and make the right pass. He also has

one of the hardest shots of any defenseman available in this draft, and uses it whenever possible. Defensively he is usually strong in one-on-one situations, however, he can from time to time be a little passive with his gap resulting in a scoring chance. He may not have a lot of height, but he is one of the most punishing checkers in this draft. He will regularly find any reason to crush the opposing team's top players when possessing the puck along the boards. He is tough along the wall, and wins a ton of battles with his surprising strength. He is willing to block shots, and generally does whatever it takes to win with a high competitive nature. Our only concern at this point is his lack of size. If he were a few inches taller he would arguably be one of the best defensemen in his age group. If he can grow, then his potential is endless. We have also had some concerns with his decision making with and without the puck, which on occasion resulted in turnovers being served up to opponents.

Wells, Dylan
G – Niagara North Stars (OMHA) – 6'01" 172

Dylan put together a great string of performances this season, and has been one of the most impressive OHL Draft eligible goaltenders we've seen in a while. Dylan's has good size, which is a little deceptive considering the way he stands with a very crouched down stance. He is lightning quick, and has excellent reflexes. He moves side-to-side very well, and handles direction chances quite well. He has exceptional level of recovery, which helps him make the second save when rebounds get out front. He has a quick glove hand, and can read shooters well. Wells wasn't a goaltender who got into bad habits, and seemed to learn from his mistakes both in game, and throughout the season. While rebound control isn't great, it isn't horrible either, and may be his most important area of improvement. Dylan shows a complete game that is as ready for the next level as much as any other goaltender selected early over the last few years. In our opinion he's was the top goaltender for the 2014 OHL Priority Selection Draft.

Zimmer, Max
F – Wayzata HS (MN) – 5'10" 165 (2016)

He is average in size although plays with a jump in his game. He displays good speed down the wing and possesses a good shot as well that allows him to pick his spots for goals. He is a scrawny kid that will need to get stronger but shows good offensive abilities.

SCOUTS GAME REPORTS

Aug 6, 2013. Canada vs. Sweden (Ivan Hlinka U-18)

Can #11 Sam Bennett: Bennett played a good game, scored a nice goal coming out of the corner with the puck, driving it to the net, and beating the goalie with a nice move. Not afraid of mucking it up in the corners and started the game with a big hit to set the tone. Will need to get stronger because he can get outmuscled by bigger opponents in one-on-one battles along the wall, but I like his determination. Can get away from defenders thanks to his skating ability and a variety of quick moves that create separation.

Can #5 Aaron Ekblad: Aaron had a load of ice time in this game, even though he struggled most of the time. Inconsistent would be a key word to describe this game, made some good plays and some other bad ones. He didn't miss too many power play shifts either, even though his play was sub-par. Not shy when it comes to rushing the puck in the offensive zone (mostly seen in the first half of the game), got caught with a bad pinch that led to scoring chance for the Swedes, and was more cautious after that turnover. In the defensive zone I would have liked to see him assert himself more in physical battles. He could be dominant in those areas if he used his size more. Can also get hypnotized by the puck and lose track of his man. Puck decisions, like the rest of his game, were inconsistent. He doesn't seem to get affected by a bad shift, however, as he bounce right back after a bad shift to make some good plays.

Can #12 Jared McCann : I thought McCann had a quiet game after scoring the opening goal. Got a pass from Lemieux, was all alone in the slot with the Swedish goaltender, and made a nice move on his backhand to put Canada up in this game. After that, I didn't notice much out of him other than one sequence on a two-on-one when he took too much time to take a decision and the Swedish defender was able to poke-check the puck away from him.

Can #21 Brendan Lemieux: Started the game with a great pass to McCann, who was all alone in the slot and put Canada up 1-0. Even though he's not the biggest guy, Brendan is willing to play a physical game and did so in this game. Skating looks fine compared to past viewings of last year.

Can #23 Daniel Audette: Daniel showed some good things with the puck in this game: he is a lot more dangerous when he has space and time to make plays, which makes him a threat on the power play. Has some good, quick feet, and can generate some good speed through the neutral zone, but needs work in his defensive game and can get outmuscled easily by bigger players in board battles.

Can #9 Robby Fabbri : Fabbri was solid and made things happen when he had the chance. A good skater with at least 3 good rushes in the 2nd period when he was successful deking opposing defensemen. Made Swedish defenseman #3 Laggesson look silly in one of them. Didn't get a goal but made things happen. Similar to Audette as he can be overmatched physically along the wall.

Can #4 Haydn Fleury: Like Edblad, Fleury was on & off in this game. At times, he was making some good smart plays and in others, was making weird ones. Fleury showed a good skating ability, rushing the puck on occasion in this game and a good physical game as well, throwing some good hits. Also made some weird passes that put his d-partner in trouble, including a risky one on the blueline on the power play.

Can #25 Roland McKeown: Was a steady presence on Canada blueline today, didn't stand out offensively except late in the game with Canada down a goal or two and was playing like a 4th forward on the ice and forcing plays. Has a real good first pass out of his zone, and it helped Canada's transition game when he was on the ice.

Can #1 Julio Billia: Billia was just okay. He kept Canada in most of this game but surely would like to have the Nylander goal back after Canada had gained momentum in the 3rd period. Can't blame him for the loss, but he's capable of better performances.

Can #19 Jake Virtanen: Virtanen was solid in this game. He has a powerful stride that can be used to beat defenders wide, like he did in the 3rd period when he beat one and crashed into the Swedish goaltender. On the power play, we saw him play the point on occasion. I like his patience with the puck and he has a strong release. Not shy to muck it up in the corners, or in front of the net. Virtanen's biggest problem is his consistency, very different play from shift to shift.

Swe #20 William Nylander: Nylander played well in this game but could have been much better; love to have the puck on his stick. Likes to go back deep in his own zone, stickhandle through the neutral zone, and beat forecheckers with his strong puck skills. Tries to do too much at times with the puck, look like the perfect pond hockey player at times. Would like to see him use his teammates more, as he can make some amazing passes. Scored a killer goal while Canada had great momentum in this game; took a pass in the neutral zone and fired a quick shot after entering the Canadian zone that beat Billia blocker side. Nylander was smart, using one of the Canadian defenders as a screen on that shot, still a shot I'm sure the Canadian goalie would like to have back.

Swe #17 Adrian Kempe: Kempe was very strong in this game. He plays a like power forward using his size and speed well. Showed real nice puck protection in this game using his big frame. He has some work to do with his hands' agility when receiving a pass that is not directly on his stick, and has problems adjusting to a bad pass. I like his skating stride. He is a very powerful skater and is very strong on the puck. I like when he gains top speed and uses his size and reach to beat defensemen wide.

Swe #23 Oscar Lindbolm: A quiet game for Lindbolm today, didn't notice him much other the time he tried to throw a hit on Ekblad but took the worst of the collision.

Swe #3 William Lagesson: A solid two-way game overall for Lagesson, who is not the most agile defender but is smart and knows his limitations. Got deked pretty good by Canadian forward Fabbri in the 2nd period, but overall, his defensive game was solid. Saw him use his size well and had a couple of nice blocked shots to help his goaltender out.

Swe #28 Anton Karlsson: Like Lindbolm, he was quiet today and one had to look hard to find him on the ice. Karlsson was a star at the U17 last year, but not so much in this game. Had a good shift in the 2nd period while on the forecheck: threw a big hit to create a scoring chance for his team.

August 9th 2013: Canada vs Russia (Ivan Hlinka semi-final)

#18 Brayden Point: Brought some nice energy to his line with his speed and hustle. Saw him get involved physically earlier in the game, but his play dropped off after the first period. Started the game on a line with Daniel Audette and Spencer Watson.

#19 Jake Virtanen : One of best Canadian forwards in this game, made good use of his outside speed many times, beating defensemen wide and charging the net. Rotated positions regularly on the power play; started on the point but ended up screening the goalie in front of the net. Saw him doing different things offensively either as a setup man or also challenging defensemen one on one.

#15 Spencer Watson: Watson played a good game, was very tenacious on the puck and a constant threat around the net. Scored the opening goal of the game on a rather weak shot that beat the Russian goaltender, and showed some good stickhandling work on that play. Likes to shoot the puck and did a good job of getting open in the offensive zone. Watson showed some good hustle away from the puck, not letting his man get away after a bad pinch from a Canadian defenseman.

#11 Sam Bennett: Bennett had an okay game, but did show how quick his hands are, deking one Russian defenseman, which made said defensemen fall on the ice. Scored Canada's 2nd goal, jumping on a rebound after a series of shots from the Canadian powerplay.

#22 Clark Bishop: Bishop did all the little things you want from a grinder: got into the shooting lane, showed good stick work in the neutral zone, poking the puck away from Russian players. He had a strong forecheck presence, as he did a nice job of running the clock holding onto the puck deep in the offensive zone late in the 3rd period. Scored the empty net goal that put Canada up 3-1.

#23 Daniel Audette: Again, Audette's best shifts came on the powerplay, was rather inexistent at even strength. Good puckhandler, but stayed too much on the outside and didn't develop any real good scoring chances.

#18 Eduard Nasybulin: The smallish d-man got a ton of ice time in this game and played in every situation. Can be a risk-taker at times with the puck. A willing physical player who is not always successful when stepping up trying to hit a player open-ice. Can be overmatched versus bigger players in physical battles along the wall or in front of the net. Played mostly on the left side on the powerplay but didn't show a great shot from the point in this game.

#11 Ivan Nikolishin: Nikolishin was okay in this game. He showed some nice flashes, but overall his play was not strong enough. A good skater with nice agility who loved to have the puck on his stick. Became vulnerable when trying to do too much with the puck and caused turnovers while rushing the puck. On some occasions he should just trust his teammates more and not try everything on his own. The most dangerous I saw him was when he was playing on the PP, as he looked to have more trust in his teammates in those situations and could really find his open teammates. Even at his best during this game, he still was a perimeter player.

#13 Kiril Pilipenko : Was quiet in the first half of the game but came on strong in the 2nd half with some real good rushes attacking the Canadian defense. Strong skater who likes to challenge opposing defensemen and has a nice arsenal of dekes. Made Canadian captain Aaron Ekblad look bad in one of them.

#28 Jevgeni Nazarkin : Had a real nice open ice hit on Canadian Robby Fabbri early in the first period. Big-sized defenseman with okay mobility. Didn't do much in the offensive zone or with the puck, but was a solid presence in his own end and played a physical game.

August 10th 2013 Canada-USA (Ivan Hlinka tournament final)

#17 Michael Dal Colle: Started the game with a strong forecheck that led to a turnover. Scored the game's opening goal after taking a feed from Spencer Watson and beating the USA goaltender with a good wrister from the faceoff circle. Did some good work along the wall, strong on the puck. Needs some work on his skating stride and does lack explosion in his first couple of steps. Best I've seen from Dal Colle in this tournament.

#15 Spencer Watson: Watson played a good game. He was always around the net and knew how to get open for scoring chances. Can get his shot away in no time and in different ways. Made a nice play on Canada's opening goal with a nice drop pass to Dal Colle while taking a big hit. Not afraid of going in the tough areas, even at his smallish size, and will battle in front of the net for those rebounds.

#19 Jake Virtanen: Virtanen was strong again for Canada, used his speed very well again. One of the best skaters on this year's Canadian team. Used his size well to protect the puck and cycle it. An underrated playmaker, as he can find open teammates with ease. With his size and speed I would have liked to have seen him step up his physical play, as USA was the more physical team and he could have been Canada's answer.

#11 Sam Bennett: Bennett was solid, showing interesting flashes offensively. Early in the 2nd period, he had a great rush, first by deking a USA player with a nice shoulder deke then taking the puck wide, beating the defensemen with his great speed and then centering the puck in front of the net for a quality scoring chance. Later, while on the power play, he made a nice cross-ice pass to Aaron Ekblad, who was hiding behind the USA defense.

#5 Aaron Ekblad The most safe game I saw Ekblad play all tournament long, as he didn't take risks with the puck or pinching like he did earlier in the tournament. Was solid overall in his own zone and moved the puck safely with short passes. Made a good read on the powerplay in the 2nd period, hiding behind the USA defensemen and getting open for a Sam Bennett cross-ice pass.

#18 Brayden Point: Played with his typical hustle and energy that we saw all tournament long. Point was good again at getting out of corners with the puck and taking it to the net, as he did so twice in today's game.

#9 Paul Bittner: Big-sized American forward out of the WHL who was good in this game, using his size well to win space battles in the Canadian zone. Tough to move in front of the net, will battle hard for those rebounds in front of the net. Will crash and bang. Skating stride needs some work and doesn't generate a lot of speed while skating with the puck.

#21 Ryan Wagner: Liked his energy and hustle. Threw some good hits, including one on Jayce Hawryluk at the Canadian blueline that left the Canadian player on the ice for an instant.

#18 Nick Schmaltz: Average game for Schmaltz as he was not noticeable much during this game, save one good shift on the powerplay where he showed his strong playmaking skills and vision. Other than that, he didn't show much compared to previous viewings earlier in the tournament.

#10 Kyle Connor: Connor was one of the best American forwards in this game. He is a very good stickhandler and an above average skater. Very smart with the puck, played the point on the powerplay for team USA. Very quick on his skates and can beat defensemen wide with that speed.

#2 Brandon Carlo: A willing physical player, Carlo is the youngest defensemen on the American team and brought a sound physical game. He is very strong, and showed it in those one on one battles versus smaller Canadian forwards. Threw some good open ice hits as well, like most of this American defense who was very active in the neutral zone. Didn't do a whole lot with the puck.

Sep. 8, 2013 – Green Bay vs. Dubuque Fighting Saints (USHL-Exhibition)

DBQ #9 Seamus Malone C (2014) – Picking up where he left off last season, Malone is having a solid preseason thus far. Plays in all situations. Phenomenal hands, does nothing but create plays. Not a lot of size but he plays big, doesn't back down and finishes checks. He's strong on his feet and isn't afraid to be in the tough areas. Aggressive and plays with a good edge. Feet are always moving. Probably the kind of guy you could put on a line with anyone and he'd make things happen, but being up on a top line with top line talent is all the more dangerous. Probably the best player on the ice despite only getting on the score sheet with one assist.

DBQ #28 Shane Eiserman LW (2014) – Physical, in your face game. Had a couple of big hits. Good game defensively, good effort. Always in position. Had two assists, created a lot of offensive opportunities. Excellent passing, saw the ice well. Good two-way game.

GB #20 Christian Wolanin L (2013) - Really strong game. Good size, plays tough. Finished his hits and isn't afraid to mix it up. Got into a fight in this game and was on the losing end of it, but still willing to go. He's a good skater, good feet. Intelligent player, always in good position and has good anticipation of the play. Jumped into passing lanes in the neutral zone a couple of times breaking up would-be breaks and leading the charge the other way. Maintains good gaps and is tough to get around entering his own zone. Likes to jump into the play offensively. Slick passer, sees the ice well. He has good hands, makes good little moves to make for better passing lanes and evading defenders. Good guy for the PP but defensively responsible all the same. Good two-way game.

FINAL SCORE: 5-1 Dubuque

SCOUTS NOTES:

Pretty good pace for an exhibition game. Dubuque's got a few games under its belt after playing over in Russia. They had a bit of a slow start with Green Bay having the better of the chances but remained scoreless after one period. From the second period on Dubuque carried more of the play and had the better of the chances, eventually exploding for five goals and after a softie first goal on a neutral zone dump-in. Green Bay eventually netted one late in the third after being down 5-0 but it was pretty much all Dubuque after the first period. Hayden Steward did make a few key *stops for Dubuque but all in all they carried the play as a whole. They appear to be a strong club again this season after winning the Clark Cup last season.*

September 13th 2013, Rouyn-Noranda Huskies vs Drummondville Voltigeurs.

Rouyn

#5 Jeremy Lauzon Def (2015): The 16 year old D-man didn't get a ton of ice time in this game but was noticeable. Made a good play breaking up a 2-on-1 by sliding and blocking a pass. Also had a good hit behind his net on a opposing forward that he was able to contain on the outside in an offensive rush.

#6 Philippe Myers Def (2015): The other 16 year old defenseman on the Huskies' blueline got less ice time than Lauzon in this game. We liked him last year for our QMJHL draft guide, but I couldn't get a good enough read on him tonight due to limited ice time.

#12 Gabriel Slight Rw (2014) Slight played a very physical game and was involved in lot of scrums. Useful on the powerplay when he parks himself in front of the net and can disturb the opposing defensemen and goalie. Didn't do as much in today's game, as he was used as a shooter and was hanging out in the slot. Had a glorious scoring chance but missed the net with a clear shooting lane. He needs to work on his accuracy and keep working on his hands to become a more a valuable player for the Huskies.

#18 Jason Fuchs Lw (2014): The Swiss rookie forward played a good 1st career QMJHL game. Fuchs loves to rush the puck in the offensive zone. Has the speed to beat defenders easily, in addition to a nice pair of hands and can stickhandle in a phone booth. Not overly big, got his bell rung a couple of times in the first period. Got hurt and stayed down for a couple of minutes on the 2nd big hit. Saw him play on the point on the powerplay on occasion, as the Huskies don't have a true puck-moving defenseman with Dillon Fournier at his NHL camp.

#20 Julien Nantel C/W (2014): Nantel played an okay game like the majority of his teammates. He didn't get a ton of ice time in the first period but played a regular shift the rest of the way. Played the half wall (right side) position on the powerplay, also saw him at center at even strength shifts. Nantel used his speed well on the forecheck and on the backcheck, showing his two-way game. Didn't get a ton of scoring chances tonight, but he did get a couple of chances in close to the net on the powerplay. Other than that, he was quiet.

#21 Alan Caron Def (2014) Caron played a regular shift on the Huskies' blueline but he's not the most flashy defenseman. His foot speed can get him in trouble, as well as his decision-making. Loves to use his body, as he showed on one particular sequence, stepping at his blueline and throwing possibly the hit of the game. Not very noticeable otherwise.

#24 Victor Baldayev Def (2014) My first viewing of the big Russian defenseman. I liked what I saw, as he's very active in the physical side of the game. Very active in his own zone and likes to finish his checks. Got involved in a good fight versus Jerome Verrier. did well, and didn't back down after being challenged. Had some iffy decisions with the puck and in other instances, he showed nice potential as a puck rusher. Undrafted in last year's NHL draft, but has some raw potential.

#27 Francis Perron Lw (2014): Perron was one of the best forwards for the Huskies in this game, as he used his speed and quickness to create things in the offensive zone. His slight frame hurt him in one-on-one confrontations against bigger and stronger players. Has real quick hands in close and can dangle the puck pretty well. He has nice vision on the ice and can find his teammates with ease, a good reason why he was used on the point on the powerplay.

Drummondville

#11 Joey Ratelle W : Scored the 2nd goal of the game after taking the puck out of the corner and driving it to the net, beating the Huskies' goalie. Played a fairly solid game afterwards, mucking it up in the corners and doing the little things to make his line successful.

#19 Cam Askew C: The young American had a decent first game in the league, Askew was good at getting open in the offensive zone, had a couple of good scoring chances in the game. Played the role of playmaker, played mostly on the 3rd line and also got some powerplay shifts. His skating will need some work, as he will need more explosion in his steps. Also stayed on the outside mostly in this game, will benefit using his size and go to the net more often.

#95 Georgs Golovkovs Lw: The young Latvian forward made a good impression tonight, doesn't have the quickest of feet but showed nice hand skills. Had a couple of real nice dekes. Looks bigger that what he's been listed and he's not afraid to go in the corner and win his puck battles. Also made some good plays in his own zone and looks to be a responsible two-way player.

#55 Sergei Boikov Def : The other Voltigeurs' import player also playing his first QMJHL game, Boikov showed some nice puck movement tonight. He started the game with a slick pass to send one of his teammates on a breakaway, which led to Drummondville's 2nd goal of the game. He's somewhat of an adventurer in his own end, lots of work to be done there. Needs to get stronger and play a more physical game, as he got outmuscled on multiple occasions in this game.

Sept 13, 2013. Québec Remparts vs Chicoutimi Saguenéens (QMJHL)

QUE #31 G, Booth, Callum (2015) Booth is being recognized by many as the best 16-year-old goaltender coming out of Quebec. In his first regular season game, Booth was not outstanding, but he was solid. He allowed four goals on 34 shots. He seemed laid back in his movements. He allowed a bad powerplay goal off a slap shot, as he didn't cover his net well, leaving a small hole between his right pad and the post. Booth's movements proved he's clearly a butterfly goaltender. He was able to track the puck well even though there were often Sags' players in front of him. Booth also showed great athleticism. At times he struggled to control rebounds, especially on point shots without a lot of velocity.

QUE #13 LD, Lanoue, Vincent (2015) He's a young defenseman that I really liked last season with Collège Esther-Blondin in MAAA. His makes a good first pass, and he didn't shy away from physical play. He landed a hard open ice hit early on in the first period. He closed his gap pretty well in one-on-one situations, and he showed good hockey sense in the defensive zone. However, he struggled down low against bigger forwards as he was often outmuscled. He was clearly the defenseman with the highest compete level on the team.

QUE #5 LD, Maheux, Raphaël (2014) Acquired from Shawinigan, Maheux was quite surprising. He still has the big frame that characterized him last year, but he's slimmer. He executed smart plays with the puck in transition. He looks quicker than he did last season, but I can't say that he was physical. He used an active stick to make some good defensive plays and he contained most of the opponents coming his way. His hockey sense was good, but not great. He scored on a wrist shot from the point that was deflected by Sags' defenseman Loik Léveillé. I considered him as Quebec's fourth best defenseman.

QUE #20 LD, MacIntyre, Duncan (2014) He played a typical Duncan MacIntyre-type game. He made some great passes on the breakout and he rushed the puck quite well at times. He was always positionally sound and his skating was very fluid. He showed ability to deliver some good checks along the boards when he wanted to be physical, due to his hockey sense. However, he relied on his hockey sense to stop any attack that came in. His strong footwork was displayed as it allowed him to fluently move around the ice. He was reliable and his play was steady all game long.

QUE #18 RD, Donaghey, Cody (2014) Quite frankly, his game was similar to the one played by Duncan MacIntyre, except that Donaghey's hockey sense was not as good. He was always used on the top powerplay unit as the only defenseman. He moved the puck efficiently throughout the game. He lost some one-on-one battles because of a lack of determination along the boards. That's something he must work on.

QUE #27 C, Shea, Brandon (2014) Shea played the best game I've seen from him in three years. The fact that he's now mentally healthy certainly helps his game. He skated pretty well in straight lines. He displayed a good power forward game. He was tenacious along the boards, and made some great passes from behind the opposing net. He finished the game with two assists on the night. His puck protection was quite good, and he was fairly good defensively, supporting his defenseman most of the time. He showed a desire to compete and had good chemistry with Fabrice Herzog (TOR). Shea was also solid at the faceoff circle as we won 18-of-32 faceoffs.

QUE #61 RW, Herzog, Fabrice (TOR 2013 draft pick) Herzog arrived about 30 minutes before the game and it certainly didn't show. He's a big guy, who's not an explosive skater, but his strides are powerful. He was strong on the puck and he wasn't afraid to get his nose dirty. He circled the puck well on multiple occasions on the powerplay while displaying slightly above average hockey sense. He scored a goal due to Billia's mistake behind his net.

CHI #26 C, Bouchard, Jérémy (2015) He was the Sags' most consistent forward and was buzzing around the net in the offensive zone. He showed great chemistry with Sylvestre. Bouchard always made the right decisions with the puck and his defensive play was quite good. He played like a veteran in the neutral zone by never giving the puck away as he dumped the puck in or dished it off to a teammate when he had to. He also created multiple scoring chances with his vision. He also showed a nice release when using his wrist shot.

CHI #55 C, Roy, Nicolas (2015) His biggest quality is his vision and anticipation. Even though he still has to adjust his game to the Q level (he didn't train with the team in the preseason, nor with the Screaming Eagles), he showed that he was a good puck handler. Roy almost scored a beautiful goal in the second period with a nice backhand shot that hit the post. He moves well for a big man, especially in an Olympic sized rink like the CGV. He was minus-2, but that is deceiving as he played well defensively. Roy took on his defensive responsibilities, and allowed his hockey sense and reach to do the work for him.

CHI #9 D, Allard, Frédéric (2016) He looked extremely nervous and was frequently exposed early on. He made some poor decisions with the puck, and seemingly gave the puck away more than all of his preseason games combined. He looked lost to start the game, but in the second period he was a little better, especially in the defensive zone. It was a bad game for Allard as on top of his poor decisions with the puck, he wasn't involved physically.

CHI #64 D, Liamkin, Nikita (2014) Liamkin played a fairly solid and simple game. He took the puck out of his zone quickly, was involved physically and he cut his turnover numbers down to zero. He did rush the puck up, but only when he was on the powerplay. His skating is still effortless and extremely fluid, allowing him to escape opponents and get out of pressure when he has the puck. His defensive zone coverage was quite good as well, as he was not caught out of position once. He was not used on the penalty kill, which is something that I don't really understand, especially because of how he played defensively.

CHI #24 C, Gignac, William (2015) A smallish forward, Gignac showed a good pair of hands. He made David Hunter looked like a fool in the third period with a spoon. Despite his size he was able to win most of his one-on-one battles using his smarts and his tenacity. However, he got pushed off the puck way too often. He showed good vision, but must improve his breakouts. I don't see him as a viable NHL prospect because he's barely 5'6" and not an elite skater, but he showed some flashes and he's eligible next year. He scored the winning goal and he was good at the faceoff circle.

CHI #12 LW, Sylvestre, Sébastien (2014) As a 20-year-old player, Sylvestre displayed a great pair of hands in traffic. He is very good when it comes to stickhandling. He was elusive along the boards, and he set up some nice plays for his teammates as well. He's an above average skater for his size (6'1") and showed a good burst in his stride. His defensive play was OK for a winger. I'm sure he'll earn a pro contract (AHL) somewhere down the road at the very least. He probably has the highest potential out of all 20-year-old players in the QMJHL.

Sept 15, 2013. Shawinigan Cataractes vs Chicoutimi Sagueneéns (QMJHL)

CHI #7 RD, Léveillé, Loik (2015) Léveillé had a bad game. His decision making with the puck was average at best. Something that showed me that he does not have the best hockey sense in the world is that he always forgot the man coming out of the penalty box. That problem led to two breakaways against. Overall, he seemed lost in the defensive zone. He was still physical and his hard slap shot from the point reached the net on some occasions.

CHI #19 LD, Roussy, Samuel (2014) A 19-year-old defenseman, Roussy is a big guy weighing 235 pounds. He was somewhat surprising in that he was able to cover Léveillé's mistakes in the defensive zone. His play with the puck was good, and he was able to start good breakouts. He was used on the powerplay, standing in front of the opposing goaltender. While doing that, he scored on a deflection in front. His skating ability isn't very impressive and his willingness to hit is questionable.

CHI #27 C, Dauphin, Laurent (PHO 2013 draft pick) He held on the puck way too much in the offensive zone. He didn't use his teammates, even when they were better options to make a play. He clearly saw them, as he was only making those passes when he felt he was surrounded. He wanted to do it all by myself. Dauphin had nice speed on the rush and was able to get the puck up out of his zone to start the breakout. He made the play of the night, getting past Cataractes' defenseman Nick Welsh with a beautiful deke and he then scoring on the backhand.

CHI #28 D, Lyamkin, Nikita (2014) Lyamkin showed improvement in his defensive play. He was not caught trying to be fancy and his defensive zone coverage was better. He showed that ability to rush the puck and he was good playing the point on the Sags' second powerplay unit. He registered two assists in the contest. He showed a good ability to find shooting lanes thanks to his exceptional footwork on the blueline. That was the case on Roussy's goal. He was willing to throw his body around, as well, and he was good on the breakout.

CHI #55, C, Roy, Nicolas (2015) Roy had a good game overall. He broke up multiple plays in the neutral zone thanks to his exceptional hockey sense and his long range. He was used on the powerplay and he showed some good vision. Defensively, he was quite good, helping his defensemen down low. He covered the third man quite well and he was always a good option for them to start the breakout. I'm eager to see him when he'll be in game shape.

CHI #17, LW, Tremblay, Simon (2014) Tremblay went hard to the net and battled really well for territory and loose pucks in front. He played well on the penalty kill, consistently willing to block shots. Tremblay also scored a nice goal with a quick wrist shot after winning his battle in the corner. On that play he made a pass to Jasmin Boutet, who instantly gave him the puck in front of the net.

SHA #37 RW, D'Aoust, Alexis (2014) D'Aoust was good again. He battled hard for the puck and he was always in good position to receive the puck. He has a good net presence and he made the simple plays quite well while cycling or screening the goaltender. There was a shift where he protected the puck quite well for 30 seconds, and he made a nice shot on Domenic Graham's right pad (D'Aoust was on the left side) that led to a scoring chance. His skating is average.

SHA #63 LW, Pawelczyk, Alex (2013) Pawelczyk really improved his skating ability. The game I saw in La Tuque was not an anomaly. He was really effective down low using his body to protect the puck and the decisions he made with it were somewhat surprising. Due to the bigger ice in Chicoutimi, he wasn't as good on the forecheck.

SHA #11 C, Gaudreau, Frédérick (2013) As a 20-year-old player, Gaudreau provided intensity and an effective two-way game tonight. He was once again the best player for Shawinigan. He's smart and speedy. He showed me that he was able to use his solid decision making on numerous occasions in the offensive zone, showing some vision. He's far from being a Mike Ribeiro in that regard, but he surprised me with his good decision making with the puck.

SHA #91 C, Beauvillier, Anthony (2015) Beauvillier showed tremendous hockey sense. He's always in good position on the ice and he was noticeable because of that. His skating was good for a 16-year-old kid, as he created a lot of space for himself with quick direction changes. He controlled the puck well even at top speed. Although he's willing to go in the corners, he was better when he worked on the perimeter.

September 20, 2013 – Plymouth Whalers at London Knights (OHL)

PLY #13 LW Dunda, Liam (2015) - In his OHL debut, Liam showed he wasn't the least bit intimidated provided good strong physical play early in this game. While he was consistently physical he can get a little too high with his hits putting him at risk for unnecessary penalties. He was very good at frustrating opposing players.

PLY #20 RD Wesley, Josh (2014) - Josh's play was very mixed tonight. He did a good job to force turnovers on several occasions in this game. However he also lost control of the puck a few times as well. He was initially not playing very tough in the slot allowing opposing players to screen the goaltender, but he played much more aggressive in this third period.

PLY #22 LW Mistele, Matt (2014) - Matt possesses a very hard shot but stuck mostly to the perimeter in tonight's game. He also made a great pass to set up a chance but outside of a few moments he was fairly quiet tonight.

PLY #27 RD Rathgeb, Yannick (2014) - Puck play was a bit mixed tonight, he made a mistake on the power play resulting in the play going the other way. Later on in the game he made a few great plays at the offensive line ot keep the play going. He is willing to play physical and delivered a solid open ice hit. He got beat too easily a few times one on one and prefers to take the body in one on one situations whenever he can. He likes to jump up in the rush and tried to get involved offensively when the opportunities were there.

LON #7 RD Stewart, Owen (2014) - Owen had a difficult game. While he possesses good size he pulled up going into the corner. He was willing to hit after the fact, but needs to be willing to take the hit to make the play. He lost his positioning multiple times in the defensive zone. He also struggled with the puck in all three zones and in general with the pace of the game.

LON #88 RD Centorame, Santino (2014) - Santino opened the game playing very well but was called upon to play a ton of ice and his play declined throughout the game. He won a battle early drawing a penalty. He then went out and showed a quick and smart puck play on the power play. He struggled a little defensively giving too much space one on one and got beat by skilled players. He pulled up in a puck race to the corner avoiding contact.

LON #91 C Platzer, Kyle (Edmonton) - Kyle scored the opening/game winning goal with a hard shot top shelf. He also scored the second goal shooting from the left circle making it 2-0.

LON #93 RC Marner, Mitchell (2015) - Mitchell made a beautiful pass to set up London's opening and game wining goal on the power play. He possesses great speed to lead the rush and continued to set up a few chances. All in all a solid OHL debut for Marner.

Scouts Notes: London did a very good job playing a solid 60-minute game slowly taking control of this game. Anthony Stolarz (Philadelphia) was solid when called upon and opened the season with a 3-0 shutout. In addition to the reports above, for Plymouth Francisco Vilardi (2014) displayed good speed and showed good puck possession skills. Alex Peters (2014) delivered a big hit late and had a very quiet game. For London Christian Dvorak (2014) showed a few flashes of his elusiveness with the puck. Aiden Jamieson (2014) possesses very good skating ability but got beat in one on one situations.

September 21, 2013, Kootenay Ice vs Red Deer Rebels (WHL Regular Season)

RD #4, Fleury, Haydn (2014) - Fleury has very good acceleration and top speed. Pivoting and edges need some work, but an overall plus skater. Good vision and first pass. Too large of a gap resulted in his man scoring the 2nd Koo goal. Passes were pretty accurate and easy to receive, but they could be dealt with more velocity. Fleury joined the rush at the right time and really used his body well to shield the puck. Showed good mobility walking the blue line on the point and creating traffic before getting belt high wrist shots on net. Good offensive instinct. Showed a bit of chippiness in some after whistle activities.

RD #9, Bleackley, Conner (2014) - Smart player. Strong on the puck and could generate offense with it off the half wall and on the rush. Needs to improve positioning on the offensive cycle. Showed good patience with the puck and while he preferred to shoot, he made several good passes while driving with the puck. Showed better strength along boards. Own zone reads were good. Generally good in his end although was caught behind his man once.

RD #16, Pawlenchuk, Grayson (2015) - Responsible in his own end. Good along the walls. Played key penalty killing minutes as a rookie. Has shown some offense early on this season to go with his defensive play.

RD #17, Mpofu, Vukie (2014) - Under-sized player with dynamic skating abilities.

RD #25, Musil, Adam (2015) - Opportunistic scorer with good size. Skating looks to have improved since last season. Very soft hands. Looks to be comfortable in offensive zone, but still needs work on his own zone play.

RD #30, Burman, Taz (2015) - Backup goalie. DNP.

Koo #10, Shirley, Collin (2014) - Good hustle and vision along sidewall to put the puck on teammates stick while Doetzel guarded him for Kootenay's 2nd goal. Has good size. Plays a well-rounded game with some offensive spark.

Koo #23, Reinhart, Sam (2014) - Very cerebral. Doesn't waste energy - every move has purpose. High puck IQ - the puck seemed to just follow him everywhere. Reinhart was the first player to every loose puck in front of own net and every puck battle on the walls. Showed very good touch on passes and used great vision to find openings. Consistently in scoring areas. Quick release allowed him to get shots off through heavy traffic while guarded in the high slot. Red Deer attempted to shut him down by using Winnipeg Jets 2nd round pick Lukas Sutter to shadow him. Dynamic on the powerplay, but only had limited penalty-killing minutes. Defensive play good, but could improve in that regard. Game's 2nd star.

Game Notes: Some poor goaltending combined with some tough luck for defenders made for a high scoring affair in Red Deer's home opener. Red Deer skated away with a 6-3 win although the game was closer than the score indicated. These same two teams played each other last night in Cranbrook with Red Deer winning 4-2 in the season opener for both teams.

September 22nd 2013, Drummondville Voltigeurs vs Sherbrooke Phoenix

Drummondville

#6 Julien Carignan Def (2015) Didn't get a ton of ice time but showed his willingness to play a physical game even though he was on the losing end of those contacts. Moves the puck fairly smartly, didn't get into too much trouble. Kept his game simple and didn't have any glaring mistakes.

#11 Joey Ratelle Rw (2014) Ratelle played mostly on the 3rd or 4th line. He is at his best when he's physical and plays a strong north-south game. Skating needs some work; he needs better acceleration to create more explosion in his stride. Finished most of his checks and got his nose dirty in front of the net.

#19 Cam Askew C (2015) The young American center centered Drummondville 3rd line and also saw shifts on the powerplay tonight. Didn't do a whole lot offensively, would have liked to see him use his size more to create more room for himself and do a better job a protecting the puck. Here again, his skating stride needs some work; he lacks an extra gear which would help him create more offense. On the powerplay you can see him positioning himself not far from the slot, looking for loose pucks or for passes. Doesn't look lost in the defensive end, he is not a liability there.

#55 Sergei Boikov Def (2014)

Boikov again played on the right side with the team's top defensemen on the power play and showed some good puck movement. Has a good shot from the point, where they like to set him up for his one timer, but the young Russian defenseman will need to work on his accuracy. Not an overly strong player, Boikov played the body more today than my previous viewing. Has a good pass out of his zone and can help the Voltigeurs with their transition game. Some work needs to be done with his defensive play and how he reads certain plays.

#95 Georgs Golovkovs C/LW (2014)

The Latvian forward was not as impressive as my first viewing of him last week, even though he scored a goal early in the 3rd period. Does a good job of using his size well to create room for himself and protect the puck. Skating is average at best, and he needs to work on improving his foot speed. Has a great wrist shot, but needs to use it more often, as he has potential to be a dangerous weapon. Played both at center and the wing tonight.

Sherbrooke

#7 Vladislav Lysenko Def (2014)

Lysenko played his usual physical game. He can really step up on guys at his blueline as he did in the first period, twice on the same shift. Was not as physical the rest of the game but he's a constant threat for an opposing forward coming down the wing in the Sherbrooke zone. Did a good job in the defensive zone and used his strength well to keep his man to the outside. With the puck, he kept his game simple, and didn't do anything significant with the puck or in the offensive zone. Lysenko went undrafted last year at the NHL draft, and with a strong 2nd year with the Phoenix, he could hear his name called this next June.

#15 Jonathan Deschamps Def (2014)

Deschamps played his typical defensive sound game with no real flashy moment. You have to look really hard to notice him as he get lost in the shuffle with the offensive Roy and Neil, and the ultra-physical Lysenko on this Sherbrooke defensive squad. Made some good decisions by pinching to keep the puck in the offensive zone Thought his skating and mobility was okay today but an upgrade could help him cover more space in his own zone. Would have liked to see him play the body more and be more intimidating. He was named captain of the team during Sherbrooke's training camp.

#28 Daniel Audette C (2014)

The younger Audette played a good game for the Phoenix tonight, and used his speed very well. Likes to rush the puck though the neutral zone and use his good wheels to get away from defenders. On some occasions he can hold onto the puck for too long but overall, tonight he did a good job of distributing it to his linemates. Played on a small line with Deslauriers and Wieser, and that line was very dangerous in the offensive zone near the net, created a lot of energy and buzz in the rink. Audette is at his best on the powerplay when he can control the puck with ease, has more time and space to manoever in the offensive zone and make plays. Audette took 3 minor penalties and all of them could be called bad ones, so it's a good thing to not back down from anyone, but you have to be smart about it.

#32 Carl Neil Def (2014)

Neil played a solid game tonight. He is really confident with the puck. Reads the plays well and makes smart decisions with the puck. Didn't do much offensively, as it was the Jeremy Roy show, but made some good passes on the powerplay and in the transition game. Not afraid to rush the puck deep in the offensive zone trying to make things happen. Played on the 2nd powerplay unit today, and similar to my viewings of last season, I saw that he can get into trouble when he stops moving his feet at the blueline while his team doesn't have the puck, and gets caught with opposing forwards behind him which can lead to a scoring chance on the PK.

#53 Tim Wieser Lw (2014)

The small Swiss winger had a good game, scoring his first QMJHL goal tonight (GWG). He took the puck in the neutral zone and, once in the offensive zone, cut to the middle and snapped a shot high-glove to beat the Drummondville goaltender. Wieser was manhandled along the wall on a couple of occasions. Showed a nice pair of hands with some slick moves with the puck, including one trying a deke between his skates. Wieser can get around the ice pretty easily, as he's a swift skater.

#71 Vincent Deslauriers Rw (2014):

The 3rd member of the Audette-Wieser line was also very good tonight, he doesn't have elite skills but was solid in all areas of the ice. Excellent on the backcheck, and always took his man out, which led to the Wieser goal in the 3rd period. Always finishes his checks and doesn't back down from anyone. Liked his speed, he made good use of his wheels on a play where he split through two defensemen to get in all alone with Drummondville's goalie. Showed a solid two-way game overall today, used his stick well to pokecheck away from opponents. Good team player, too, as he came to defend his teammates on a couple o occasions.

#73 Chase Harwell C/W (2015)

Harwell started the game on the 4th line, but as the game progressed, he got more ice time and some powerplay shifts here and there. I like the energy he brings to the table, can really skate and can beat defensemen wide as he did in the 2nd period, almost scoring on the backhand after beating one of Drummondville defensemen easily. Came really close to notching his first QMJHL goal, touching the post after a juicy rebound in front of the net.

#88 Trevor Stacey Lw (2016)

Stacey is a big rookie forward who loves to play the enforcer role, even though he just turned 16 last week. Always looking to initiate contact on the forecheck, but some work needs to be done to upgrade his skating, as he can get late or just miss guys with his hits due to this. He does have some skills, as I think there's more to him than just a tough guy. Was looking to fight all game long but couldn't find a partner, didn't get much ice time all game and barely any in the 3rd period.

#97 Jeremy Roy Def (2015)

Roy was outstanding tonight, played easily over 25 minutes and played in all situations of the game. He has so much confidence with the puck and didn't make many mistakes tonight. Calm and poised, he is such a lethal weapon on the transition game for a hockey team, whether he makes a crisp pass or skates with it end to end. Not shy to act as the 4th forward on the ice; there has been next to no adjustment coming from Midget AAA to the QMJHL for Roy. Got the first point in his career from a point shot on the powerplay that was tipped in front of the net. Later in the 3rd period, he added his first career goal after taking a wrist shot high blocker from the faceoff circle. Defensively, Roy covers a lot of ice thanks to his mobility and skating ability. Also very strong for a 16 year old and doesn't get overpowered by older players in the league.

Sept 27, 2013. Lethbridge Hurricanes vs Kootenay Ice (WHL)

KTY #23 C, Reinhart, Sam (2014) Reinhart had a pretty good game. When he stepped on the ice, he had an impact. He is a natural playmaker that uses the point quite well. He is strong on the puck and he gets open so easily it's frightening. He controls the puck with ease thanks to sound body positing and good lower body strength. He's good on the cycle and he wins most of his 1-on-1 battles. He can play at even strength, on the powerplay and even on the penalty kill. He has the desire and the versatility required to play any kind of role.

KTY #10 LW, Shirley, Colin (2014) Shirley is a big body that likes to dump the puck in the offensive zone and to chase it like crazy. He brings a physical presence when he wants to. He has surprising puck handling skills, as he deked a guy in front of the opposing net before shooting the puck wide on a powerplay. He is rarely the first forward back in the defensive zone.

LET #4 LD, Pilon, Ryan (2015) Clearly Lethbridge's best defenseman, Pilon is an excellent skater for a guy with his size. He possesses quick feet that allow him to go anywhere he wants to on the ice in time. He makes quick decisions with the puck and his hockey sense is pretty good. He knows where he needs to be and he can break plays in his zone with his long reach. He's a force along the walls and he's defensively sound. Pilon can play on powerplay without looking lost. He dishes the puck well and he has the ability to find the net with his point shot regularly.

FINAL SCORE: 4-3 KOOTENAY

September 27, 2013 – Peterborough Petes at Kitchener Rangers (OHL)

PET #10 RC Cornel, Eric (2014) - Cornel possesses good positioning in the offensive zone and a very quick release on his shot to wire the puck top shelf for Peterborough's second goal of the game. He is a smooth quick skater and uses it to hurry back defensively. He provided great pressure on the penalty kill. He created a few good plays on the rush utilizing his speed and skill.

PET #16 LW Lorentz, Steve (2014) - Steve worked hard and created a couple scoring chances including one where he beat the defenseman from the corner moving towards the front of the net.

PET #20 LW Ritchie, Nick (2014) - Nick had an excellent game tonight consistently creating scoring chances every single shift. He made an excellent play right on the first shift of the game forcing a turnover and turning it into a scoring chance for his team. He has very intelligent positioning in the offensive zone opening himself up for passes and skating to where the puck is going instead of chasing the puck and the play. He displayed a cannon of a one-timer to score Peterborough's first goal of the game. Nick then threw the puck out front to set up Peterborough's second goal. He also created Peterbrough's third goal making a great move one on one then fired a laser blocker side to score Peterborough's third goal of the game. He also delivered a few solid hits in this game. All in all Nick was a decisive factor in Peterborough's win and the best player on either side of the ice tonight.

PET #27 RD Spencer, Matthew (2015) - Matthew had a very up and down game tonight. He mishandled the puck a few times in the first period and generally looked very nervous. He made a great play on a two on one to break up a scoring chance after his defensive partner went way out of position. However he got walked pretty bad on a two on two turning it into a two on one in the slot. He struggled in battles despite his size. He also had a few issues with his positioning. He ended up being the hero with less than 10 minutes left in a tie game pinching off the point and banging home a rebound for the game-winning goal helping his team complete the comeback.

KIT #20 RW Magyar, Nick (2014) - Nick showed good puck protection and cycled the puck well to help set up Kitchener's second goal of the game. Although his skating really needs improvement he was able to elude a few players on the rush and carry the puck into the offensive zone making good decisions.

KIT #81 LD Sergeev, Dmitri (2014) - Dmitri showed a willingness to play physical against some of Peterborough's bigger forwards tonight.

Scouts Notes: Kitchener opened up with a great start to this game. Brent Pedersen (Carolina) utilized excellent position in the slot to bang home the opening goal of the game. Matia Marcantuoni (Pittsburgh) then scored on a good one-timer to give Kitchener a 2-0 lead. Despite Kitchener then taking a 3-1 and 4-2 lead, Peterborough scored three goals afterwards to steal a 5-4 win from the Rangers. Ryan MacInnis (2014) wasn't all that noticeable tonight, however he did use his size effectively to protect the puck. Darby Llewellyn (2014) was effective creating a few turnovers and utilizing his excellent hands to create a few chances.

Rouyn-Noranda Huskies vs Victoriaville Tigres, September 28th 2013

#5 Jeremy Lauzon Def (2015) : The 16 years old defenseman played mostly on the 3rd pairing today with some power play time. Saw him being paired with the team's top defenseman Dillon Fournier on occasion but mostly was paired with Allan Caron. Had a couple of offensive rushes that didn't result in anything but it was nice to see him trying to make plays with the puck. What I liked about his game today was that he didn't back down from a big physical team like Victoriaville and still got his nose dirty.

#18 Jason Fuchs Lw (2014): Fuchs again showed how good of a skater he is. You see it more with more room on the ice, like on a powerplay, rushing the puck deep in the offensive zone. Did struggle in this game versus a big team like Victoriaville and was unable to create much offense due to his lack of strength. Made a nice play in the 3rd period, stealing the puck at the Victoriaville blueline and giving it to his teammate Mathieu Lemay, who scored the 3rd Rouyn-Noranda goal (the eventual game winner).

#20 Julien Nantel C/Lw (2014) : Nantel played a good game overall, not a real threat offensively but played a strong game on both sides of the ice. A very smart player without the puck and is always the first forward to get back and help his defensemen out. I like how he used his speed on the forecheck. On one occasion, the Victoriaville goaltender got out to play the puck and Nantel caught up to him and stole it, which nearly resulted in a goal for the Huskies. Other good scoring chances for Nantel came when he touched the post after taking a shot from just inside the blueline with traffic in front of the net. Also liked how in the neutral zone, he makes quick, short passes to his linemates, which helps the transition game of his team.

#27 Francis Perron Lw (2014): Perron was okay today, made some real nice plays with the puck but was weak without it. An imaginative player with the puck, as he likes to set up his teammates and play on the point on the powerplay. Showed nice patience with the puck in the offensive zone, not a very fast skater but can make sharp turns on his skate to escape opponents and create space for himself. Due to his lack of size, he can get outmuscled along the boards and it showed today versus a much bigger Victoriaville team. Has a tendency of trying to do too much with the puck and that can lead to turnovers; he needs to be smarter and play the clock better as he was a victim of a bad turnover inside his zone with less than 4 minutes to go while his team was up by two goals.

#4 Petr Sidlik Def (2014): Sidlik has been passed over in the last two NHL Drafts, but with a strong final junior year, he could hear his name called next June. Sidlik played a strong game logging tons of ice time today, and played in all situations. Played a simple game, as he didn't get into trouble and made smart decisions with the puck. Moved the puck efficiently on the powerplay but doesn't own a big shot which can make him predicable. Sidlik was named captain of the Tigres this year, one of the rare European captains in the CHL.

#8 Tristan Pomerleau Def (2014) : The small rearguard was solid today for the Tigres, didn't do a lot of flashy things offensively but was rock-solid in his own end. Played on Victoriaville's 2nd powerplay unit, where he moved the puck smartly and kept his game simple. Undersized, but he's a battler in the corner, still in tough versus bigger forwards which was not really the case today versus a rather small Rouyn-Noranda team up front. Mobile on his skates and can get away from forecheckers with ease, such as when he used a spinorama move in his own end.

#15 Mathieu Ayotte Rw (2014) : Didn't show much at even strength for the Tigres today, was used also on the point on the powerplay and didn't wow me there either. I thought his decision-making was lacking and he doesn't own a big shot from the point. The only highlight from him in this game was a scoring chance early in the 3rd period when he had the puck all alone in the slot but couldn't beat Alexandre Belanger.

#27 Gabriel Gagne Rw (2015): Gagne is a tall lanky forward playing in his rookie year in the QMJHL, started the game on the Tigres bottom 6 but finished the game as a top 6 forward. Has an awkward skating stride and doesn't generate a lot of speed. Has a great reach; he's still growing into his body, but does a good job protecting and cycling the puck. Had an impressive shift in the 3rd period with his line cycling the puck and using their size to win puck battles for a strong 90 seconds. Came close to scoring a goal in the 3rd period after taking a pass in the slot and showing nice patience with the puck, waiting and waiting to make the goalie move but couldn't beat him in the end.

#45 Julien Proulx Rw (2014): Proulx is a huge forward standing at 6'5", 215lbs, playing the role of enforcer for the Tigres. Obviously a very willing physical player but his sub-par skating hurt him as he missed most of his hits, though he did get all of Alexandre Leclerc in a big open-ice hit in the first period. Made a real nice backcheck, stealing the puck away from Dillon Fournier, who was all alone in the slot. Didn't do much with the puck in the offensive zone.

#95 Jan Mandat C/W (2014): The rookie Czech forward played a sound defensive game today. He made a real nice defensive play coming back in front of the net, stealing the puck from a Huskies player who had an open net to shoot at. Offensively, he didn't do a lot to stand out, and on the powerplay the Tigres used him on the half-wall. Does a good job on the forecheck to harass defensemen, uses his size well to protect the puck and is not shy when the game starts to get more physical. He has a sluggish skating stride that will need work this season.

Sept 28, 2013. Val-d'Or Foreurs vs Québec Remparts

VDO #5 LD, Gélinas, Guillaume (2014) Gélinas, 20, was the best defenseman on his team. He got the puck out of his zone with ease, using the boards well when he was pressured. His puck skills were above average and he showed that he could control the puck on the powerplay. He wasn't afraid to join the rush and jump into the play, either. He was solid in his own zone as well, using his smarts to strip the puck away from opponents. However, bigger players often outmuscled him because of his lack of size.

VDO #20 LD, Henley, David (2015) Henley really needs to work on his pivots. He must be quicker. That was the thing that was most noticeable about him. However, he was able to close his gap effectively and his sound positioning showed that his defensive hockey sense is good. For a 6'4" defenseman, he can hold his own pretty well in most battles in the corners. He was able to make some simple breakouts, but it was harder when they became complex.

VDO #27 C, Sille, Timotej (2014) An average skater at best, Sille was able to protect his puck quite well thanks to his size. He lacks explosiveness, but he was effective down low, able to put on adequate pressure.

VDO #8, RW, Mantha, Anthony (2013 Detroit Red Wings draft pick) Mantha was very dominant. On the powerplay he made complex passes look so easy, it was dazzling. He showed off his quick release and his shot was powerful and accurate at the same time. He scored on a one-timer from up high and François Brassard didn't even finish his movement towards him before the puck went in high on the glove side. Mantha also looked good while killing penalties. He was effective in stealing the puck and clearing the zone. He scored four goals and had one assist. He still played on the perimeter, but he's well above everyone in the QMJHL in terms of skill. Thanks to his skating ability and size, he was able to get past Quebec's defenders with ease and had no problem getting to the inside. He drove the net pretty well when he had the occasion, almost three times per period. In a lopsided game like this, he sure looked like an NHL player, even though he wasn't involved in the corners. Though, he didn't really need to be.

VDO #9, C, Richard, Anthony (2015) Richard is shifty skater that likes to create things offensively thanks to his speed and his agility. He was tenacious and showed some good vision. Richard was pretty reliable in his own zone as well. He's a small, gritty forward.

VDO #16, RW Aubé-Kubel, Nikolas (2014) Aubé-Kubel was pretty good in this game. He was the one doing the right things offensively on his line. He controlled the puck in the neutral zone and in the offensive zone, finding open ice easily. He showed good puck handling skills in tight space, which helped him install the play. Most of the time, he was the first man back on his zone. Formed a nice duo with Richard.

VDO #12, RW, Gauthier, Julien (2016) Gauthier won most of his battles because of his explosive and powerful skating abilities. He showed tremendous puck handling skills in tight areas. He protected the puck quite well and he was able to drive the net effectively, even though he's pretty young. He's the kind of guy that lacks desire at times, but that wasn't the case in this game. He was motivated and he even played good defensively, stealing the puck on multiple occasions. He scored two goals and had an assist.

Overall Quebec looked pretty bad. Their forwards were atrocious, undisciplined and they lacked desire. Anthony Duclair kept turning the puck over in his own zone. All their defensemen looked lost in the defensive zone, except Vincent Lanoue who was the only one keeping it simple, even though he struggled a bit as well. Cody Donaghey was beat twice on the outside because of bad reads, Raphaël Maheux wasn't able to get the puck out his zone and you could compare Dillon Donnelly to an orange cone. Even Ryan Culkin, their best defenseman normally, was beat constantly by Anthony Mantha.

FINAL SCORE: 11-2 VDO

Sept 29, 2013. Drummondville Voltigeurs vs Chicoutimi Saguenéens

DRU #24 RD, Aubé, Frédéric (2014) Aubé was beat on the outside several times. I saw some potential in that kid. His first pass was effective and his puck skills were OK for that level, as he was able to control the puck well while under pressure. He needs to work on his footwork a bit.

DRU #55 LD, Boikov, Sergei (2014) An offensive minded defenseman, Boikov has good puck skills. His first pass was adequate and he circled the puck well on the powerplay. Defensively, he stopped moving his feet in one-on-one situations once again. I saw him get attracted to the puck way too much. He was often caught out of position and Drummondville gave up a number of scoring chances as a result. His slap shot from the point is powerful, but not accurate enough.

DRU #95 C, Golovkovs, Georgs (2014) Golovkovs was outstanding. He was good in the corners and he played with an edge. He cycled the puck with ease. He showed that he has a good hockey sense. It was very difficult to steal the puck away from him as he used his ability and his hockey IQ. He's not an explosive skater, but I was surprised by the fact that he won most of his races for loose pucks. He scored two goals with his wrist shot on very similar plays on the powerplay, receiving the puck on the right side of the net and then shooting high on the glove side.

DRU #10 C, Lalancette, Christophe (2012 San Jose Sharks draft pick) Lalancette was the best player on Drummondville's side in all three zones. He was always at the right place at the right time. Offensively, he used his fluid stride to get past defenders on a regular basis. He showed nice vision and he was willing to pay the price. He also showed good puck handling skills down low, but if he were more of a scorer, he would have scored at least two goals. He was effective defensively and was able to put some nice pressure in the neutral zone. He was also the first one back in his zone.

DRU #11 LW, Ratelle, Joey (2014) Ratelle carried the puck once in a while in this game. He was feisty and willing to pay the price in dirty areas. His puck skills are adequate and he can create things offensively on his own. He positioned himself well in the offensive zone, but he still has to improve on his work defensively. You can see that he gets his points by driving the net hard in spite of his small frame.

DRU #13, LW, Gauthier, Guillaume (2014) Gauthier had a good game. He displayed his great vision in the offensive zone and good hockey sense. He's clearly not the kind of guy that will be involved physically, but he can manage to register points by using his vision. He made a beautiful saucer pass to Golovkovs on his first goal. He was also the quarterback on the powerplay. He played on a line with Golovkovs and Ratelle and they did the dirty work for him. His puck skills are good, as he can slip away from opponents with the puck, and he showed a high level of creativity.

DRU #19 RW, Askew, Cameron (2015) Askew wasn't that noticeable. He is strong on his feet, but he lacked agility and desire. You see that he had a good hockey sense, but he's not quick enough to really play his game. Though, he can make some nice passes in the neutral zone.

CHI #9 D, Allard, Frédéric (2016) Allard had a good showing. His footing allowed him to provide great one-on-one coverage and to leave very little space to opponents. He was difficult to beat on one-on-one's and his first pass was accurate. He circled the puck well on the powerplay and he was used on numerous occasions at even strength, which is kind of unique for such a young defenseman in the Q. Actually, Allard offers steady play and I can say that he's the defenseman with the better defensive hockey sense on his team. He never gets caught out of position and he's able to steal the puck away thanks to his hockey IQ. He likes to use his wrist shot when he's on the point, but it lacks power.

CHI #64 D, Lyamkin, Nikita (2014) Lyamkin had a good game overall. He was good on the powerplay as he circled the puck well and was effective on the point. He found shooting and passing lanes easily thanks to his fluid footwork. He moved incredibly well on the blueline. I noticed that he was caught out of position on two occasions. While he was under pressure, he made some good decisions by keeping things simple, which was something I liked. He limited the number of turnovers in doing so. Previously, he would have tried to rush the puck up and ultimately lost it. He still gets outmuscled at times, but I was surprised by the way he stood up when opponents were too close to his goalie.

CHI #7 D, Léveillé, Loik (2015) Léveillé limited his defensive mistakes. He was tough to beat one-on-one and closed his gaps well. He was a force along the boards down low and he made some solid crisp passes to get the puck out of his zone. However, when he doesn't see anyone available, he tends to panic and he constantly gives the puck away. He displayed solid puck handling skills on the blueline. That's one of his main assets. He played a ton and he delivered. He was consistently good with his defensive zone coverage.

CHI #55 C, Roy, Nicolas (2015) He's clearly getting better with time. He was doing the simple things quite well. He had a good net presence and drove the net hard. Roy deflected a shot on a powerplay to score his first QMJHL goal. He also displayed some good puck handling skills. On one occasion, he beat two opponents while driving the net, which was nice to see. His play in the defensive zone was good. When his defenseman were in trouble, he was able to steal the puck away from an opponent and start the breakout right away.

CHI #10 RW, Hudon, Charles (2012 Montreal Canadiens draft pick) I really liked his play in the neutral zone. The passes he made and his positioning were a big part of his game. He broke up plenty of plays and he was great on the powerplay. He liked to get under Jerome Verrier's skin, as he always had something to say to him after the whistle. His slap shot from the point isn't overly heavy, but it's accurate. He made some nice changes of direction, as well, in order to create passing lanes. It was a typical game coming out of him.

FINAL SCORE: 4-2 CHICOUTIMI

September 28, 2013, Red Deer Rebels vs Calgary Hitmen (WHL)

Cal #2, Thrower, Josh (2014) - Tracked bodies well and made several solid open ice hits. Hard to play against. Comfortable with the puck on his stick. Made a bad pinch in the 2nd and didn't recover well for the rest of the shift. For a guy that plays a physical game, he needs to get stronger as he was knocked off the puck a couple times while skating back to retrieve it against the end boards.

Cal #18, Virtanen, Jake (2014) - An excellent skater with great explosion in his stride. Had his head down and skated himself into a corner on more than one occasion. Was still able to drive wide off rush and get get good chances on solo rushes. Needs to use his teammates better. High quality shot, but didn't choose his spots wisely. Too often shot into traffic with no hope of puck getting near net. Finished his checks. Looks much heavier this year. Went hard to net for rebounds and his chippy play often led to him being in the middle of scrums after the play was over.

Cal #29, Fazleev, Radel (2014) - Showed good character in standing up to Kayle Doetzel after the big Red Deer denfenseman high-sticked Virtanen. Was able to handle a few hot passes, but his hands just looked average on the night. Good passing ability and had his head up looking for options in offensive zone. Had good puck possession skills and was able to gain the offensive zone on the powerplay.

RD #4, Fleury, Haydn (2014) - showed good offensive awareness and ability in the offensive zone. Defensively, he looked better than his partner (and defensive specialist) Doetzel. Showed a little grittiness in front of own net.

RD #9, Bleackley, Conner (2014) - A well-rounded player that was used by Brent Sutter in all situations on the night. Smart and unselfish with puck. Made good touches and showed good vision with the puck. Not the most skilled guy, he works hard. Hands improving. Positioned himself well away from puck. Needs to improve how quickly he releases his shot.

RD #16, Pawlenchuk, Grayson (2015) - Continues to string together good performances to start the season. Has on the receiving end of an easy goal after a nice passing play. Outworked the much larger Hitmen captain Jaynen Rissling along the walls. Regularly out on penalty killing assignments and thrived against older players on 4 on 4 situations. Protected the puck well along wall. Good skater.

RD #25, Musil, Adam (2015) - After putting up four points in his first three games of the year, Musil was held in check tonight and was practically invisible through two periods. He was far more noticeable in the third period where he put together a couple nice shifts. Virtanen seemed to have gotten under his skin and Musil seemed more interested in getting back at him than anything else. Good size and nice hands. Very nice skater for his age. Backchecked well and did well to breakup an odd man rush, but his own zone play generally needs improving.

RD #30, Burman, Taz (2015) - Backup goalie - DNP

Game Notes: Tonight's game was the Hitmen home opener. Calgary completely controlled the play and the result was never in doubt. Shots on net: 14-3 after 1, 21-7 after 2, 35-13 after 3.

Oct 1st, 2013. Victoriaville Tigres vs Chicoutimi Saguenéens (QMJHL)

VIC #4 LD, Sidlik, Petr (2014) Sidlik was pretty good. He's their best defenseman at the moment, without a doubt. He played a ton and he delivered. He's really tough to beat one-on-one and isn't afraid to engage physically. Sidlik always has good gap control. He knows what to do with the puck, almost always choosing the safest option. His breakout passes are on tape most of the time and he's well positioned in his own zone. He broke up numerous plays down low thanks to his hockey sense. He's also good on the powerplay, as he offers good support. He's the Tigres' captain and he acted like one. He gave it his all the entire game and he was a steady presence on Victoriaville's blueline.

VIC #8 LD, Pomerleau, Tristan (2014) Pomerleau displayed good puck handling skills on a blueline. You can clearly see that he's at ease when used on the powerplay. He's a small, but stocky defenseman. His breakout passes were good and I really like the way he uses his body to fool opponents when he has the puck. He never gets beat out wide and is not afraid to jump into the rush when he has the opportunity. He improved on his decision-making based on what I saw last year. He uses his body positioning and an active stick to break plays in his zone.

VIC #23, LD, Boucher, Félix (2014) Boucher had a surprisingly good night. He moves well for a big defenseman, has good footing and his first pass is not bad. At times he struggled with the puck, but I like the way he played one-on-one. Boucher has good gap control as well.

VIC #95, C, Mandat, Jan (2014) Mandat possesses good hand-eye coordination. Even when the puck isn't on the ice, he's able to control it in tight areas. He's an average skater, but he understands the game pretty well. Mandat's always in good position to receive a puck and he finds open ice quite easily. Mandat is a threat on the powerplay, as he can easily control the puck. He still needs to work on his defensive positioning when he's playing center, though.

VIC #15, RW, Ayotte, Mathieu (2014) Ayotte is still small and skinny, but he showed a pretty nice combination of puck handling skills and vision. He played the point on the powerplay. He's good when he slows down the play. When he does that, he holds on the puck a bit and he's able to find an open man quite easily. Ayotte lost plenty of battles because of his small frame.

VIC #27, LW, Gagné, Gabriel (2014) Gagné is a 6'4" left wing that will only get bigger. It would not hurt him at all. I saw him last year and he had a three-goal night in MAAA. He still has that shoot first mentality and that's not a bad thing. He protects the puck well and he's able to get in position to shoot with good body positioning. He wins most of his battles for loose pucks in the corners. However, he's clearly not the kind of guy that will be involved physically.

VIC #31, G, Whitney, Brandon (Chicago Blackhawks 2012 draft pick) Whitney was simply outstanding. His lateral movements were fast and well done. You clearly see that he's in full control of his body now, which was not the case four years ago. He kept his focus all game long and he made some astonishing saves in the second period when his team was trailing. A goalie with that size combined with great athleticism will always be sought-after.

CHI #9 D, Allard, Frédéric (2016) Allard was the best defenseman for the Sags once again. He understands the game quite well, he never gets beat on the outside and he is well positioned in his own zone thanks to his great defensive hockey sense. He broke up numerous plays in the corners even though he doesn't want to get involved physically. His first pass was good and when he was in danger, he always found a way to get the puck out of his zone.

CHI #64 D, Lyamkin, Nikita (2014) Lyamkin had a good game overall. On one occasion, he controlled the puck about 10 seconds in the neutral zone, beating four defenders in that occasion. He then put the puck down in the offensive zone. He's a fluid skater and it helps him a lot in his defensive coverage. When the game gets physical, you see that he doesn't shy away from it, but he tends to get knocked off the puck at times. When you see him in these situations, you understand that he still has to fill out. His breakout passes were good as usual.

CHI #7 D, Léveillé, Loik (2015) Léveillé is at his best defensively when he can hit the puck holder. When he doesn't, things can get out of control sometimes. He made some solid crisp passes to get the puck out of his zone. He made a mistake on a powerplay when he allowed Carl-Antoine Delisle to go in alone as he was trying to keep the puck in the offensive zone. Delisle scored on a breakaway and it was the game-winning goal.

CHI #60 G, Graham, Domenic (2014) Graham had a pretty good game. I like the way he battles in his crease even when things are out of control. He fights hard and he displays good athleticism and quickness. He did a good job covering his angles. Graham is a good puck handler and I like the way he plays out of his net.

FINAL SCORE: 2-1 VICTORIAVILLE

Rimouski Oceanic vs Drummondville Voltigeurs, October 5th 2013. (QMJHL)

#6 Beau Rusk Def (2014): A big physical presence in front of his net that uses his size and strength well to clear forwards in front of his goalie. Not a natural with the puck, as he was victim to turnovers and put himself and his D-partner in trouble. Not very mobile on his skates, was part of the Oceanic's 3rd pair of defensemen.

#15 Anthony DeLuca Rw (2014): DeLuca was quiet in the first two periods, as Rimouski was outplayed by Drummondville, but came alive in the 3rd with 2 quick goals. The first goal came when he tipped in a shot from the point, and the 2nd came after finishing a pretty passing play at the side of the net. When things don't go well for DeLuca, he can be a frustrating player, as he's a shoot-first mentality player and his shots tend to always get blocked when he rushes things with the puck, as he did in the first two periods. A lot more effective when he shares the puck and gets his linemates involved like in the 3rd period. His skating has improved vastly compared to last year and his overall game is still progressing since last year, where at the start of the year he was a liability without the puck.

#21 Nicolas Hebert C/W (2014): Hebert played on the Océanic's 3rd line, where he had a quiet game with Michael Joly and Samuel Courtemanche. Hebert worked hard in all three zones in today's game. He doesn't do a lot in the offensive zone or with the puck. A very responsible player without it, as he is always the first forward to get back on the backcheck to help his defensemen out. Skating looks like Hebert's biggest weakness, and I do not see a lot of improvement from last year. However, he looks much stronger than last year, and it showed in his puck battles along the wall, where he doesn't get outmuscled as much as last year.

#24 Simon Bourque Def (2015): Bourque was excellent for the Océanic tonight, where he played a ton with Samuel Morin injured and Jimmy Oligny getting kicked out of this game. Paired with team captain Ryan MacKinnon, the young 16 year old defensemen showed tremendous poise with the puck. Obviously Bourque lacks strength at this stage of his career but showed great competiveness and courage in this game as he played with a target on his back when a veteran Drummondville forward tried to get him to drop the gloves in the 2nd period. I like how he plays in 2 on 1s, letting the shooter cut to the goalie while taking care of the 2nd forward. I also like how he always skates with his head up, and is very mobile as well.

#42 Andrew Picco Def (2015): Picco was used on the 3rd pairing with Beau Rusk today. His mobility is just okay, as he needs to get stronger on his skates. Does keep his play simple with the puck and didn't have it easy today, being paired with Rusk who had a tough outing. Strong in his physical battles and won most of them, and he will become even better when he matures physically and gets even stronger. Made a real simple play on the Océanic's 2nd goal, taking a simple shot from the point which was tipped by DeLuca, who started the Océanic comeback in the 3rd period.

#11 Joey Ratelle Rw (2014): Ratelle scored the game opening goal today, a rather flukey one that somehow got behind the Rimouski goaltender. Ratelle was aggressive on the forecheck for the first 2 periods but then, like the rest of his teammates, just sat back and watched Rimouski make their comeback. I liked the level of grit he showed during this game, where he was involved in the physical play in the corners and always involved in scrums after the whistle. Showed some nice patience with the puck in the offensive zone on one particular play, as he outwaited a Rimouski defender which led to a scoring chance. Skating is still an area where Ratelle needs to upgrade, as he doesn't generate a lot of speed and his first three steps are average at best.

#19 Cameron Askew C/Rw (2015): This was Askew's best game of the three I saw so far this season: he was a lot more aware of his surroundings and better in his own zone. Still didn't get a lot of ice time, playing on the team's 3rd or 4th line with some power play time. but he made most of it by scoring a goal in the first period with a excellent quick wrist shot, high glove. Came very close in the 2nd period while on the powerplay to scoring his 2nd goal, but was robbed by a sliding Peter Trainor who saved a goal for a quick instant. However, Drummondville ended up scoring anyway, just seconds later.

#55 Sergei Boikov Def (2014) : Boikov was paired at even strength with 16 year old rookie Julien Carignan-Labbé today. I liked his work ethic even though he didn't win all his puck battles; he hung in there and competed. But that remains Boikov's biggest issue: his lack of strength hurt in his physical confrontations. Moved the puck well, but didn't see him as much on the powerplay today as previous viewings.

#95 Georgs Golovkovs C (2014): This was the worst I have seen the Latvian forward so far this season in three live viewings (not that he was not involved, but he just didn't seem focused). Got run over in the neutral zone by Jan Kostalek and didn't look interested after that hit. I was surprised he stayed in the game after that. You can see he has great hands as he likes to try to deke defensemen while entering in the offensive zone but it just didn't work out for him today for some reason as he lost the puck. Drummondville used him on the power play on the half wall position, he has a nice shot and vision and can be a double threat from that position.

Oct 5, 2013. Baie-Comeau Drakkar vs Chicoutimi Saguenéens (QMJHL)

BAC #3 LD, Vanier, Alexis (2014) Vanier has improved on his puck handling skills. He looked confident with the puck and he was not afraid to try things offensively. His slapper was quite effective (low and heavy), hitting the net on multiple occasions. He played on the first powerplay unit along with Dominic Poulin. Vanier's pretty big and is also tough to beat when the play is along the boards. His footwork and his backward skating still need improvement. He was past on the outside several times, as he was not able to get a proper reach on some of Chicoutimi's speedsters. I consider him as a viable prospect for the upcoming NHL draft.

BAC #21 RD, Meloche, Nicolas (2015) Meloche is a tough customer. As a defenseman, he doesn't shy away from physical play and he's already nasty as a 16-year-old. He can control the puck quite well on the point, as he was used sporadically on the second powerplay unit. His passes are always hard and accurate. When there was someone in front of his goaltender, he pushed him right away. In the third period, he showed that he's willing to drop the gloves, which is something worth mentioning. He needs to contain his nastiness, as it resulted in some bad penalties. I haven't seen him get caught in the defensive zone.

BAC #15 RW, Imama, Bokondji (2014) Imama is what I consider a pure athlete. He has a really thick frame. He was able to rush the puck in the offensive zone with his strength. He protects the puck well using sound body positioning and surprising speed on the outside. He beat Loik Léveillé that way once. He does not possess elite vision or sublime puck handling skills, but he is an effective power forward in the Q.

BAC #61 LW, Gorbunov, Denis (2014) Gorbunov is in his first year in the Q. He has good hands and he finds teammates easily when he posts himself near the hash marks. He is an above average skater and he's not afraid to work in the corners. His defensive play is good and he is still a good option for his defensemen to start the breakout.

CHI #9 D, Allard, Frédéric (2016) Allard is a steady defenseman. You know what you can get out of him. He makes a good first pass and is pretty tough to beat on one-on-one. He never gets beat on the outside and he is able to break up a lot of plays down low. He is used on the first powerplay unit, which says a lot about his offensive abilities and his decision-making.

CHI #64 D, Lyamkin, Nikita (2014) Lyamkin continues to get better. His hockey sense in general is good for that level. His skating ability really helps him, as he made some great rushes up in the offensive zone. His play along the boards is better as well, as he used his body to separate the puck from his opponent on a regular basis. He was good on one-on-one situations in the open ice as he used his stick well. Lyamkin made quick decisions with the puck, which is something I liked about him in this game.

CHI #7 D, Léveillé, Loik (2015) Léveillé played with an edge in this game. He hit Félix Girard pretty hard in the third period behind his net and his passes were, as always, hard and accurate. His play in his own zone was good overall. He almost always played the body and his defensive coverage was adequate. He tried complex plays when pressured in an effort to make breakout passes rather than keeping it simple. He's a good puck mover, but he needs some polishing.

CHI #55 C, Roy, Nicolas (2015) Roy scored a rebound goal on a powerplay in the first period, but his skating (his strides are not that powerful, his legs needs to get stronger) limited him against the Drakkar. He showed some good patience with the puck in the offensive zone and was not a liability in the defensive zone. His hockey sense really helped him in that regard. He blocks passing lanes, offers good support down low and he always kept an eye on the third man.

FINAL SCORE: 4-2 BAIE-COMEAU

October 5, 2013, Seattle Thunderbirds vs Lethbridge Hurricanes (WHL)

Sea #4, Foulk, Griffin (2014) - Good game from Foulk who was passed over last year. Played top four minutes on the night. Showed good all-around abilities on the night but lacked any dominating traits for a pro game.

Sea #11, Troock, Branden (Dallas 2012) - Had a strong first period showing good hands and skating to go along with his power forward game. Was injured at some point and left the game on a stretcher during the 1st period intermission despite not obviously being hurt during any play.

Sea #13, Barzal, Matthew (2014) - The former 1st overall WHL Bantam draft pick showed nice vision and patience in finding the trailing forward on an odd man rush in the first. Continued that type of play throughout the 1st and was almost too selfless as he passed out of a partial breakaway - although a fortuitous break resulted in a goal on the play anyways. While his defensive game is good for his age, he did make a couple of noticeable mistakes in his own end. Has very quick hands and is able to feather passes through traffic. Showed a quick release and could have easily scored a couple goals if not foiled on good chances. Extremely mature game from the 16 year-old. At even his young age, he was able to control the pace of the play on numerous occasions. Played heavy minutes on Seattle's top line and 1st PP unit. His excellent skating, high IQ, vision, and hands make him reminiscent of Nugent-Hopkins. Finished as the game's 2nd star after a 4 assist night.

Sea #17, Theodore, Shea (Anaheim 2013) - Seemed to rarely come off the ice. Often double-shifted with a load of PP time. A very good skater that was able to control the play in the offensive zone as he was always a threat with the puck and walked the blue line with ease. His passes were delivered with precision and perfect timing. His aggressive play in joining the rush did put him out of position in transition several times. Showed good composure in own end but needs to work on positioning and board play.

Sea #25, Bear, Ethan (2015) - The right-handed defenseman is one of two 16 year-olds on Seattle's 1st PP unit (the other is Barzal). Really didn't show a lot on the night. First step needs to improve. Seemed very average on the night.

Sea #28, Kolesar, Keegan (2015) - A very large player for his age. Showed improved agility from last season playing midget hockey. Explosiveness has improved too. Once at top speed, he's a handful to deal with as he's strong and drives hard to the net. Typical power forward. Threw a massive hit in the second as a result of his speed and strength to drive his opponent into the boards with force. Willing to go to the tough areas and did well in puck battles. Limited vision with the puck as he constantly skated with his head down.

Sea #33, Hauf, Jared (Philadelphia 2013) - A poor game from the hulking defender. Poor body positioning and body control allowed much smaller players to strip him of the puck. Played a little better late in the game and was part of Seattle's goon lineup that was employed late in the game along that included two other 6'6 skaters.

Leth #4, Pilon, Ryan (2015) - Not draft eligible until 2015, Pilon is already an anchor on the Lethbridge blue line and wears an 'A' for the Canes. Has a heavy point shot and nearly scored a couple times from the point after ringing a shot off the post and narrowly missing on a couple other shots. Used his forwards well from point. Thinks the game well with the puck on his stick but his footwork was pretty sloppy. Made a couple bad pinches that resulted in quality chances for the T-Birds.

Leth #29, Estephan, Giorgio (2015) -Showed some resolve early after he took a puck in the mouth early but came back right away. Good hands and skill shown on the night. Creative offensively and seemed to work hard.

Leth - Duke - DNP - injured

Game notes: Lethbridge started well before a bad break resulting in a goal resulted in a first period implosion and eventual 4-0 hole at the end of the 1st period. Shots were close in number but Seattle had much better chances and skated away with a 5-2 win. Seattle's defence pairing of Hauf and Douglas may be the largest in junior hockey as both are listed at 6'6.

Oct 5, 2013. Prince George Cougars vs Kamloops Blazers (WHL)

PG #29 LD, Grewal, Raymond (2014) Grewal is a dime of a dozen stay-at-home defenseman. A late birthday, he showed some good coverage along the boards and he was willing to play the body down low. He made simple decisions with the puck in order to put it out of his zone. Most of the time, he was behind for loose pucks. His footwork needs work, most notably his pivots, because he lost many races for loose pucks as a result. His positioning was fine.

PG #27 LD, Carvalho, Joseph (2014) Carvalho is an offensive defenseman who makes a good first pass. He is able to drive a powerplay and he has the necessary hockey sense to pinch at the right time in order to keep the play alive. He lost too many battles along the boards and it's very easy to get rid of him, as he was outmuscled more than once. He also forgot a man coming out of the box in the second period. His slapper on the powerplay lacks velocity and power, but it hits the net. Carvalho is a fluid skater, but he's not explosive.

PG #35 G, Edmonds Ty (2014) I admire Edmonds' athleticism and flexibility. I came away impressed by his performance. He covered the lower part of the net effectively and he was not afraid to defy shots. A butterfly goalie, he possesses good mental strength. His lateral movements must be quicker for the next level.

PG #13 RW, Pochiro, Zach (St. Louis Blues 2013 draft pick) Pochiro was the shining man in that game for me. He protected the puck well and he kept making good decisions with the puck on his stick. He played the point on the powerplay and he was the designated shooter. He's a good man to have in the corners and he displayed some nice power moves one-on-one. His strides are powerful. I wouldn't call him a speedster, but he can make defensemen look like fools when he gets going on the outside.

KAM #9 LW, Shynkaruk, Jesse (2014) Shynkaruk caught my attention on his first shift. I noticed his high compete level and his willingness to drive the net. He played with Bozon and he was able to create things offensively with him thanks to his speed. Even though he's small, his strides are good and he can add that extra gear in order to be the first in his races for loose pucks.

KAM #29 LD, Harlacher, Edson (2014) Harlacher is a big defenseman. When he was pressured, he was able to regularly able to safely get the puck out of his zone. He's a lanky guy who at times gets too focused on the puck, instead of covering his man in his zone. He can get the puck out of his zone.

KAM #5 RD, Thomson, Jordan (2014) Thomson possesses a good first pass. Used in most situations (powerplay, penalty kill, 5-on-5), he does not excel in anything, but I'd say he was reliable tonight. He closed his gap well on one-on-ones and he was able to rush the puck up in order to dump it in. He can get beat by quicker guys on the outside, but he has the hockey IQ to not let them on the inside. I noticed that he raises his stick a bit too high before a slap shot. He was stripped of the puck twice because of that. Otherwise, I'd say Thomson is a good puck mover that we have to keep an eye on.

FINAL SCORE: PRINCE GEORGE 3-0

October 5, 2013 – Niagara Ice Dogs at Sarnia Sting (OHL)

NIA #2 RD Graham, Jesse (NY Islanders) - Jesse made a bad giveaway early on which lead to Sarnia's first goal of the game. He recovered with a good wrist shot from the point to score Niagara's second goal of the game and utilized his excellent speed.

NIA #4 LD Dunn, Vince (2015) - Vince showed good speed and used it to jump up in he rush. He made an excellent pass to set up a partial break and was generally good offensively. He gave too much space in one on one match-ups allowing him to get beat wide from time to time.

NIA #5 RD Siebenaler, Blake (2014) - Blake possesses great speed and jumped up in the play regularly. He showed good offensive instincts and a big slap shot from the point.

NIA #11 LW Perlini, Brendan (2014) - Brendan looked great early and often creating scoring chances all game long. He shows excellent skating ability and has great size. He evades checkers confidently. Brendan nearly went end to end with the puck while shorthanded and does a great job of getting his stick in lanes while shorthanded. He does however need to attack the puck carrier quicker in these situations to take away time and space. He likes to cut across the middle entering the offensive zone using his size and speed to open things up. He controlled the puck fairly well but his hands look like they need to catch up to his feet at times. Perlini was possibly the best player on either side of the ice tonight.

NIA #17 RC Protapovich, Alexander (2014) - Alex was strong on the forecheck and uses his stick very well to disrupt passes and skating paths and did a good job forcing turnovers. He blasted a one-timer to score the game tying goal with 36.4 seconds left.

NIA #29 LD Mikulovich, Aleksandar (2014) - Alex was hit or miss in one on one situations. While he used his size and played a tough game at times, he also did a little embellishing trying to sell penalties.

SAR #7 RD DeAngelo, Anthony (2014) - Anthony had a very up and down game. He threw the puck away early resulting in a chance for Niagara. He was also handling the puck a lot but remaining on the perimeter. Despite this he made some good passes to set up chances, particularly on Sarnia's second goal of the game. He went end-to-end late in the game with the puck then made a good pass to set up a big scoring chance. He even made a few good plays in the slot to clear the front of the net.

SAR #11 RW Hargrave, Brett (2014) - Brett showed a few flashes of his skill level but didn't really accomplish anything with it. He made a few great passes in this game, but showed very little urgency getting back defensively when the play went the other way.

SAR #22 RD King, Jeff (2014) - Jeff made the smart first pass out of the zone for his team and was willing to block shots.

SAR #27 RW Goldobin, Nikolay (2014) - Nikolay didn't make as huge of an impact as he normally does, but he was using his great speed and hands to create scoring chances for his linemates.

Scouts Notes: In a battle between two teams at the bottom of the standings this was actually a very exciting game. The lead changed hands four times back and forth between the two teams. After taking a 1-0 lead into the second, the Sting found themselves trailing 2-1. However, after two goals from Nickolas Latta (Free Agent) in 1:53 midway through the third period it looked like Sarnia would take the victory. A last minute goal followed by the only goal in the shootout would give Niagara the 4-3 win.

Oct 8, 2013. Vancouver Giants vs Prince Albert Raiders (WHL)

PA #29 C, Draisaitl, Leon (2014) Draisatl was clearly the best player in this game, there was no doubt in my mind. He really had an effect on the game. At even strength, he was able to slow down the pace of the game to install plays offensively. I'm truly amazed by his playmaking abilities. He made some outstanding passes. He made a fabulous cross ice pass on a 3-on-1 and on a powerplay in the second period, he made a backhand pass, without even looking, directly to Josh Morrissey who was in the high slot. He protected his puck well along the boards using sound body positioning. He handled the puck like an NHL player, and in his zone he helped his defensemen immensely. He didn't give the puck away and he used his reach to cover large spaces near his net. He scored on a beautiful one-timer that went just under the crossbar on a powerplay in the middle of the second period. He scored a beauty goal in the shootout, too, where he displayed the Benoit Pouliot move.

PA #19 RW, Gardiner, Reid (2014) Gardiner had a good game overall. He's a gritty two-way player that has underrated offensive abilities. He can circle the puck well on the powerplay and he's a good puck protector. When he's on the rush, he likes to chip the puck in. He was also tenacious in the corners. Gardiner scored while his team was short handed and he also had the game-winning goal. Strong on his skates, he makes simple decisions with the puck. Most of the time, he's the first forward back in his zone. I like his work ethic. He used his speed well on the outside. Defensively, he cut numerous passing lanes due to his active stick and he covered his point well.

PA #17 RW, Yaremchuck, Lance (2014) A small forward who can surprise opponents with short bursts, Yaremchuck didn't look out of place as Leon Draisaitl's linemate. He displayed good offensive hockey sense as he was at the right place at the right time. He scored a goal thanks to Dalton Thrower's soft play in front of his net. On the other hand, it was tough for him to get the puck out of his zone due to his lack of size. He needs to make quicker reads when he's not moving on the ice.

VAN #16 LW, Foster, Thomas (2014) Good defensively, Foster interfered with passes on a regular basis due to sound positioning. He started some simple breakouts and he was able to get the puck out of his zone on a regular basis. Don Hay used him a lot on the penalty kill. He had a nice shift near the end of the game in overtime where he drove the net using his quickness and speed that he gained in his two first steps.

VAN #6 RW, Atwal, Arvin (2014) Normally a defenseman, he played right wing early in the game. He had an assist in the first period as he instantaneously shot on a bad give away from Cheveldave. He made a good pass on a 3-on-1. Atwal played with intensity and was willing to throw his body around. He didn't look out of place as a forward. Atwal took some shifts as a defenseman in the third period. When used on the powerplay, he displayed good pick skills and a good footwork for a big man.

FINAL SCORE: PRINCE ALBERT 4-3 SO

Oct 9, 2013. Calgary Hitmen vs Swift Current Broncos (WHL)

SWF #6 RD, Honka, Julius (2014) Honka's a smooth skater who gains his top speed in his first two steps. His footwork is excellent as his skates are always moving. His defensive coverage is quite good, as he was always on his man. Honka made some fantastic rushes from his end displaying his quickness, ability to avoid pressure and his great vision on the ice. I like the way he handled the puck even in tight areas. As an example, he spooned Jesse Zgraggen down low and he then made a nice pass to one of his teammates at the opposite side. He's not afraid to pinch in order to keep the puck in the offensive zone. He played a lot with Dillon Heatherington and there is no doubt in my mind that he was the most effective defenseman for his team.

SWF #5, LD, Martin, Brycen (2014) Martin had a really rough night. It was tough for him to get the puck out of his zone. He fumbled the puck when pressured. Defensively, he had trouble containing forwards that were quicker and more agile than him. He was beat way too many times on the outside one-on-one. He was attracted to the puck even when his team was shorthanded, consequently leaving opponents open in front of his net.

CGY #29 LW, Fazleev, Radel (2014) Fazleev drives the net on a regular basis and scored two goals that way. He is a big body who struggles when moving laterally. Fazleev always finished his checks. He protected the puck well using his size, but he must make better decisions with the puck down low. The puck found him on a regular basis.

CGY #18 RW, Virtanen, Jake (2014) Virtanen is a big winger with good puck protection skills. He put his great skating ability on display as he had some nice rushes on the outside. He can get that extra gear when he needs it and that's what I like about him. Virtanen's play was inconsistent shift-to-shift. Sometimes, he was just wandering around the ice, floating back to his zone. On the other hand, I saw him dish out some good checks and put pressure on Swift Current's defensemen. When he did, it led to turnovers. He also had a nice back check where he broke up a 2-on-1.

FINAL SCORE: CALGARY 5-4

October 10, 2013 – London Knights at Sarnia Sting (OHL)

LON #10 LC Dvorak, Christian (2014) - Christian possesses good speed and is a strong skater. He also has a good wrist shot. He was able to use it to create a rebound for London's first goal. He scored a great goal later on using his speed to open things up, waited for the goaltender to make the first move then used his quick wrist shot to score top shelf.

LON #74 LD Jamieson, Aiden (2014) - Aiden showed very good skating ability but lost too many battles, particularly in the defensive zone.

LON #93 RC Marner, Mitchell (2015) - Mitchell showed his elusiveness down low in the offensive zone and used it to create scoring chances for his team. He was also very tough to contain defensively in one on one situations. He controls the puck consistently with confidence and quickness. At one point he got hit in the head after falling. He was willing to get back into the play which resulted in his team scoring.

SAR #5 RD Hore, Tyler (2014) - Tyler was most noticeable in battles along the wall. He uses his strength along the wall to win battles and uses his size to box out opponents well. He finishes his hti along the wall and made the simple play at the line.

SAR #7 RD DeAngelo, Anthony (2014) -Anthony played a fairly solid overall game. He was getting his stick in lanes and was defensively a lot better than usual. He was even willing to block a couple shots. He showed good creativity on a few occasions with the puck making the smart play and didn't try to do too much. Late in the game he intelligently jumped up in the play for scoring chances.

SAR #10 LC Kodola, Vladislav (2015) - Vladislav was elusive in the neutral zone and good some good quick smart plays with the puck to set up a few scoring chances. He also stepped in and out of traffic well on the power play to set up his powerful shot. Despite the shot that he has he will look off good shooting options to try and force the pass. On one of these occasions the bad pass ultimately lead to a goal against his team. Kodola won't use his body in any battles but will engage with his stick.

SAR #11 RW Hargrave, Brett (2014) - Brett made a good play taking a hooking penalty to save a goal for Sarnia. He lacked determination on the forecheck and lacked confidence with and without the puck resulting in him playing a little more on the perimeter. He looked frustrated with himself and didn't play the game that made him successful in pre-season.

SAR #27 RW Goldobin, Nikolay (2014) - Nikolay showed he can evade checkers even while standing still utilizing his hands. In the 3rd period on the rush during a power play he made a great play evade two checkers but was cross checked from behind to end the play. While he created a few great chances he made a few mental mistakes throwing the puck away in the offensive zone.

SAR #35 RW Korostelev, Nikita (2015) - Nikita showed good evasiveness despite his size beating defenders and getting off his exceptional shot. He beat Stolarz twice but just missed hitting both the post and the crossbar in separate situations. He also had a great scoring chance but forced the goaltender to make an excellent save. He needs to be more aggressive on the puck carrier in the defensive zone.

Scouts Notes: Sarnia opened up a 1-0 lead in the first and took it into the second half of the game. However London was able to capitalize on a few chances and walked away with a 4-1 win after scoring a late empty net goal. Noah Bushnell (2015) was effective in finishing his checks hard. As the game went on some opponents actually avoided him in battle. Craig Duininck (Free Agent) was particularly impressive blocking at least a half dozen shots in the first period alone and continued this throughout the game. He also handled some of London's top players very well one on one.

October 11, 2013 – Belleville Bulls at London Knights (OHL)

BEL #5 D Lemcke, Justin (2015) - Justin likes to use his body whenever possible but his skating is a struggle. He possesses a big point shot.

BEL #11 LW Cramarossa, Michael (2014) - Michael showed good work ethic especially along the boards. He provided a strong forecheck with good speed.

BEL #23 C Petti, Niki (2014) - Niki displays excellent skating and he's explosive after one step. He also possesses good power in his shot. He was always the first to jump up in the offense but the last forward to get back defensively all game long.

BEL #26 RW Bricknell, Jake (2015) - Jake plays with an exceptional about of energy and work ethic. He's a strong skater and puts relentless pressure on the forecheck. He also showed some intriguing offensive tools. He made a few excellent passes to set up some scoring chances. He also was willing to drive the net without the puck.

BEL #31 G Graham, Charlie (2014*) - Charlie showed an excellent glove hand and made a few highlight reel saves to keep his team in the game as long as he could. He has great reflexes and exceptional quickness. He gets to the top of the crease to compensate for his size.

LON #10 LC Dvorak, Christian (2014) - Christian was willing to take the hit to make the play for his team. He was skating very well in and out of traffic both with and without the puck.

LON #16 LW Domi, Max (Phoenix) - Max showed on multiple occasions flashes of his dominant puck skills. However he got caught trying to do too much on his own.

LON #24 RW McCarron, Michael (Montreal) - Michael struggled with the puck today getting knocked around by much smaller players and lacks the speed or puck protection to maintain puck control for long periods of time.

Scouts Notes: Remi Elie (Dallas) scored early to give Belleville a 1-0 lead after the first period and played an excellent game against his former team. However a five goal second period by the London Knights launched them to a big 6-1 victory over the

Bulls. Despite the score Charlie Graham (2014*) played outstanding in this game making several great saves.

Oct 11, 2013. Acadie-Bathurst Titan vs Québec Remparts (QMJHL)

BAT #11 RW, Boivin, Christophe (2014) Boivin is a really small forward who was well positioned most of the time. Despite of his size, he was able to get the puck out of his zone even when pressured. He is faster in straight lines now. He likes to create plays from the half wall. However, he is not strong enough to be a viable NHL prospect right now.

BAT #27, LD, Gingras, Anthony (2014) Gingras was playing on Acadie-Bathurs's first pairing. He needs to improve his footwork, as he can get beat by guys with quick changes of direction when he is directly facing them. Overall, he has good hockey IQ. He is able to keep his man on the outside most of the time. He rarely panics when he has the puck and I like the fact that he was willing to block shots. He's not the kind of guy that likes to play physical. He instead relies on his positioning to break up plays.

BAT #55, LD, Brisebois, Guillaume (2015) The first pick of his team in the last QMJHL draft, Brisebois is a smooth skater. He covers his man well and his stick is always active. I noticed that he was keeping things simple and making safe decisions with the puck. He's not strong enough to maintain his man along the boards, but he's aware of the zones he needs to cover. He impressed me when he forced an explosive Anthony Duclair to stay on the outside after the New York Rangers prospect intercepted a pass from Brisebois' partner.

QUE #5, LD, Maheux, Raphaël (2014) Physical along the boards, he rarely loses confrontations when he gets near his man. When opponents have space to get around him, it's more difficult for him to contain them. He's not speedy enough. A big man weighing 214 pounds, you understand why he struggles in that area. His skating needs work, both backwards and forwards. The thing that makes him a good prospect is his booming and heavy shot from the point on the powerplay. He found good shooting lanes and he made smart decisions with the puck on a regular basis. When he plays like this, he's a valuable prospect to keep an eye on.

QUE #18, RD, Donaghey, Cody (2014) Donaghey makes a good first pass and displayed it on several occasions. He also joined the rush several times. His shot from the point was easy to block, though. He had a terrible shift near the end of the first period where he fumbled the puck once and where his breakout passes were intercepted twice. However, he bounced back pretty well, showing good mental strength. I really like his backward skating. He's a tough guy to play against because of the way he moves on the ice (his agility, mostly) and he understands the game.

QUE #32, LD, Chevalier, Maxime (2014) Made an intelligent pass, perfect for a deflection, from the point in the first period. Chevalier lost battles with his man along the boards often, meaning that he needs to get stronger. He also had some problems to get the puck out of his zone while pressured.

QUE #96, RW, Moody, Zachery (2014) An average straight-line skater, Moody is a hard working guy with an average skillset. He is willing to compete for the puck in the corners. He understands his role and his skating is adequate at this level. He is often at the right place at the right time down low.

Scouts notes: Anthony Duclair (New York Rangers draft pick) scored a heck of a goal. Showed his extra gear on the penalty kill, beating the defender on the outside. He then cut towards Bathurst's net and beat Jacob Brennan with a nice move that concluded with a wrist shot. Talking about him, Jacob Brennan had a solid game. He made several quality stops, saving his defensemen's mistakes. Had to face a few breakaways and situations where his team was outmatched. He fought all night in his crease. Adam Erne (Tampa Bay Lightning prospect) made a great rush where he *out-skated a Titan's defenseman and he put the puck in the back of the net with an astonishing reverse shot.*

October 11, 2013 - Moose Jaw Warriors vs Brandon Wheat Kings (WHL)

Bdn #2, Pulock, Ryan (NYI 2013) - An anchor on the Wheat Kings' blue line. Steady in his own end and a key part of the power play. Big shot from the point.

Bdn #8, Hawryluk, Jayce (2014) - Great energy early on. Not the biggest player, but is tenacious on the puck and skilled enough to capitalize on the turnovers he creates. Scored on a 2-on-1 in which he kept the puck and scored. Keeps his feet moving all the time. Not afraid to go into the corners and he won numerous puck battles. Good speed. Some Brendan Gallagher is his game. Used his body well to protect the puck. Used his stick very well to impede passing lanes. When matched up against Point, Hawryluk looked noticeably larger. Displayed great hand-eye coordination after reacting to a puck sailing waist high through the goal crease and quickly connecting on a shot on net through traffic. Strong game - finished with two points and a shoot out goal.

Bdn #13, Bukarts, Rihards (2014) - Had a few shifts where his speed and puck-handling skills were evident, but overall had a fairly quiet game. Fought through a few checks, but strength needs work.

Bdn #22, Shmyr, Braylon (2015) - DNP.

Bdn #33, Papirny, Jordan (2014) - DNP - back up goalie.

MJ #1, Paulic, Justin (2014) - Was up to the test as he faced shots early and often. Used his size well at times, but was overly deep in his crease at times. Protected the top of the net well. A battler. Made over forty saves on the night in a 3-2 shoot out loss. Kept himself square to the shooter. Footwork could use help as he was vulnerable down low. Slow to recover after making an initial save.

MJ #2, Sleptsov, Alexey (2014) - Gave up a little too much space to Hawryluk on a 2-on-1 in which a goal was scored. Skated pretty well. Thinks the game pretty well and has a little skill too. Made a lot of simple plays and didn't showcase his talents as much as he could've. Was beaten a couple times on stretch passes but recovered well and obstructed scoring chances with an active stick.

MJ #19, Point, Brayden (2014) - Was buzzing the net early on. Highly-skilled and able to make plays with the puck in traffic. Very small, but his smarts and speed allowed him to anticipate the play and win some loose puck battles that he would likely have lost otherwise due to his small stature. One of the more dangerous offensive players in the game despite the lack of points.

MJ #31, Sawchenko, Zachary (2016) - DNP - back up goalie.

Game Notes: An entertaining game in Brandon in which the home side carried a lot of the play but needed the help of a suspect penalty late to score the tying goal before winning 3-2 in the shoot out. Hawryluk and Point both shone in a match up of early round prospects for the 2014 draft.

Oct 12, 2013. Acadie-Bathurst Titan vs Chicoutimi Saguenéens (QMJHL)

BAT #11 RW, Boivin, Christophe (2014) Had a rough night. In one occasion, he showcased good patience with the puck. However, he lost the majority of his battles due to his lack of size, not for a look of effort.

BAT #27, LD, Gingras, Anthony (2014) Almost everything went bad for him today. He had trouble getting the puck out of his zone while his team was shorthanded. He was manhandled along the boards and, like I noticed in my previous viewing, he was beat by quicker guys with effective bursts. When Gingras had time he made good breakout passes.

BAT #55, LD, Brisebois, Guillaume (2015) Brisebois was one of the few Titan's defensemen that was able to play well on Chicoutimi's rink due to his good agility. At the beginning, he had trouble with defensive zone coverage but was better later on. He showed good offensive instincts. On his team's first goal, he intercepted a pass in the offensive zone, held onto the puck long enough to let a Sags' defenseman compromise himself. He then made a pass to Dominic Beauchemin that left him all alone. He was outmuscled on some occasions, but he was able to redeem himself with good positioning. His breakouts were not as effective compared to my last viewing, though.

CHI #7, RD, Léveillé, Loik (2015) Léveillé had a good showing. He scored the game-tying goal when he took a chance as he went deep in the offensive zone. He showed his good offensive instincts in that sequence. His shot from the point was heavy, but he rarely hit the net. When he saw his options, the passes he made were fast and on the tape. At times he tries to complicate breakouts when feeling confident. He had good positioning in his own zone and played with an edge along the boards.

CHI #28, LD, Lyamkin, Nikita (2014) Lyamkin played with an edge in this game. He was involved in some scrums after the whistle, and he was very physical when clearing the front of his net. Lyamkin made some defensive mistakes when he had the puck, mainly by giving the puck away on the boards on bad rims. One-on-one, he was fairly solid. He displayed his excellent mobility and footing in these occasions.

CHI #58, RD, Allard, Frédéric (2016) Allard constantly made intelligent plays with or without the puck. He's clearly not a risk taker. He kept his stick active and he was way more physical than usual in this game, which was surprising. He was able to take the puck away from the opposition rather easily. His breakouts were effective and he showed good puck control. He needs to improve his wrist shot power.

CHI #55, C, Roy, Nicolas (2015) I really liked his defensive zone play. He covered his defenseman pretty well, was always in a good position to block passes and in the shooting lanes. Roy was good at the faceoff dot in the first two periods. He had a tendency to try some fancy breakouts; making some iffy passes to his closest winger even he is covered. He needs to keep it simple in order to get the puck out of his zone, even if it means to use the boards. In the offensive zone, he made some good plays without the puck. He had some of the best scoring chances in this game and he had a great net front presence.

CHI #26, RW, Bouchard, Jérémy (2015) Bouchard made some good plays with the puck in the offensive zone. Displayed solid offensive hockey sense and he was a tireless worker.

Scouts notes: Janne Puhakka (2014) scored two goals in this game. He made a beautiful play on his first goal where he dazzled. He took control of the puck behind Jacob Brennan's net and he was able to sneak in the high slot. He then scored on a low wrist shot on the stick side. Like in his last game, Brennan was outstanding, even though he was pretty bad on Puhakka's second goal.

Oct 16, 2013. Moncton Wildcats vs Saint John Sea Dogs (QMJHL)

MON #2 LD, Holwell, Adam (2015) Holwell made simple breakouts all game. He covered his zone quite well. He was used against Sea Dogs' first line and he was able to knock them off the puck regularly. He didn't turn the puck over, and his footwork was adequate because he was facing slower skaters tonight. When he gets stronger, he'll be a good defenseman in the Q.

MON #5 LD, White, Tucker (2015) He is way too slow. White needs to improve both his forward and his backward skating. He played on the third pairing. His poor skating does not help him at all in any aspects of his game. He can't cover his guys properly and I noticed that his breakouts were not that good, as well.

MON #8 LW, Garland, Conor (2014) Garland had difficulty getting the puck out of his zone. This smallish forward was good once again along the boards. He drew a call on him for cross-checking halfway through the first period, as he controlled the puck using while displaying great agility. Garland played as a defenseman on Moncton's first powerplay unit. It was clearly not his place. He was not at ease. Most of the shots he took from the blueline were blocked. He was pushed off the puck way too often. In the second period, he made a nice pass on Mark Simpson's goal. He waited for his teammates on a counterattack and he found Simpson alone in front of Auger's net.

MON #22 C, Barbashev, Ivan (2014) I loved his work ethic once again. He finished his checks just as he did the game I saw against the Remparts. He was able to control the puck easily in the offensive zone. I didn't see him on the ice after the first half of the first period, though.

SNB #3 LD, Leblanc, Olivier (2014) Leblanc was able to keep players along the boards even though he is undersized. He played a smart but aggressive game. While shorthanded, he was able to reach teammates twice for breakaways, showing his good vision. He was the most reliable defenseman on Sea Dogs' squad. He made a nice toe drag to create a good passing lane on the last Sea Dogs' powerplay, showing good puck skills. He broke up a lot of plays in the neutral zone and he gave his all the entire game.

SNB #5 LD, Chabot, Thomas (2015) Chabot showed good offensive instincts, as he liked to join the rush early in the first period. That was also the case in the third period. He seldom missed a pass. They were always on tape. He had some defensive lapses in his coverage and one-on-one but he was good overall.

SNB #7 RD, McQuaid, Alexander (2014) McQuaid had a bad game. He constantly made bad breakouts. Even when his team was shorthanded; he showed his incapacity to clear the puck out of his zone. He made a bad pinch that resulted in Moncton's third goal. He was not able to catch up. On the other hand, he played with an edge.

SNB #12 LW, Richard, Joey (2014) Richard is big winger who is a below average skater. His puck skills are average, but he can protect his puck well down low in the offensive zone. His passes were mostly out of reach.

SNB #15 C, Highmore, Matthew (2014) I really liked his hockey sense. Always well positioned, he also anticipated offensive plays on a regular basis. He crashed the net when needed. His defensive play was good. Highmore worked well along the boards and he was able to help his defensemen in any way he could. He took many dangerous shots in this game and they were pretty accurate. He scored a beautiful goal switching from the backhand to the forehand and then shooting top shelf.

SNB #16 LW, Dove-McFalls, Samuel (2015) He won a battle along the boards. Dove-McFalls finished his checks early in the first period. After that, I barely noticed him.

SNB #18 C, Smallman, Spencer (2014) Smallman displayed some nice moves on the rush. He played on a line alongside Nathan Noel.

SNB #25 C, Noel, Nathan (2015) Noel made a nice rush in the first period. A pretty dynamic skater, he showed his great vision when he made a nice pass to Connor Donaghey on Alex Dubeau's right side of the net from behind. He liked to cut towards the front of the net when he was in possession of the puck. Noel made a nifty move at full speed in the third period. He got rid of Jacob Sweeney easily and then cut towards the net before getting off a good shot. Five minutes later, he then beat another defender with his blazing speed before making a center pass. He had his coach's trust as he was on the ice in the last minute of the game.

Gatineau Olympiques vs Drummondville October 18th 2013 (QMJHL)

#3 Marc-Olivier Crevier-Morin Def/F (2014) : Crevier-Morin played a sound 1st period in his own zone, made some smart plays and moved the puck smartly. I liked his physicality in the game that he used either with his size or his stick. Had 2 or 3 shifts at forward in the 2nd period as well but went back to defense and stayed there for the rest of the game. Not a flashy performer but did what he was asked to do.

#8 Alexandre Carrier Def (2015) Carrier is already wearing an A on his jersey which proves how important he is to this squad. Was paired with the big Mikael Beauregard at even-strength and played on the first power play unit for the Olympiques. I like how he battles, even if he can get outmuscled at times, he never quits on a play. I also like his decision making, as he moves the puck smartly up front with quick, short passes. I also like how he joins the rush, and never got into trouble when he did so. On one occasion, he rushed the puck all the way to the side of the net from his own blueline and made a nice feed to a teammate in the slot, who couldn't finish the play. On the PK, he showed some nice stuff getting in the shooting lane all the time and not being afraid of blocking shots.

#13 Alex Dostie C (2015); Speed is the number 1 asset that Dostie brings to the table. Can get to top speed in no time. His acceleration in the neutral zone got the attention of the Drummondville defense very quickly. Still very young and very light on his skates, but things get rough for him versus bigger, older players. Doesn't have the strength or experience to compete right now versus those bigger players. Scored the Olympiques' 3rd goal after jumping on a loose puck in the slot and firing a quick shot from the top of the faceoff circle.

#18 Vaclav Karacabek Rw (2014) Karacabek was good tonight, showed some nice flashes of skills. I like his puck protection and how he can get the puck in the corner while also being able to get out with it and take it to the net. Not a strong skater, needs some work on his acceleration to bring more overall speed to his skill set. A good passer, his passes were tape to tape most of the night. Didn't see a whole lot of physicality from his game. Scored the game-winning goal by coming out of the corner with the puck and firing a great wrister from the top of the faceoff circle past by the Drummondville goaltender with 7 minutes left to play in the 3rd period.

#40 Tommy Lapierre Lw (2015): Lapierre played on Gatineau's 4th line and had a good scoring chance in the 1st period when he got the puck in the slot but took too much time to get his shot though and it was eventually blocked by a Drummondville defenseman. That's one adjustment that young players coming from midget AAA have to make: to get their shot though quicker. I liked his physical game but he will need to work on his skating to become a more effective player on the forecheck. Can play a pest role, as he can lead the other team to take penalties on him like I saw late in this game.

#6 Julien Carignan-Labbé Def (2015) Had some iffy moments with the puck in the offensive zone, where he had a good chance to take a shot but started fumbling the puck when he felt the pressure of a Gatineau player getting close to him. Again, I really liked his physical game in tonight's performance. Doesn't back down from anyone, and almost got into a fight with Tommy Lapierre after a whistle.

#11 Joey Ratelle Rw (2014) : Ratelle was solid tonight, and played in all situations of the game. Made a great play on the PK stealing the puck at his own blueline and attempted to beat the other defenseman wide, but couldn't, due to his sub-par skating ability. Finishes his checks and works hard all over the ice. One negative from his game tonight was that he took too much time to make a decision with the puck. His skating issues can cause him problem on the forecheck, and he can't time all of his hits properly.

#19 Cam Askew C/RW (2015) Askew didn't get much ice time in today's game. Played on the 3rd or 4th line for the Voltigeurs. Had chance to get involved physically with a big hit in the offensive zone but put the brakes on before hitting the player. He was a little bit too soft along the wall for my liking, and had one good scoring chance in this game but took too much time to get his shot though and was eventually blocked in front of the net.

#55 Sergei Boikov Def (2014) A quiet game from the Russian rearguard, who was paired with Frederic Aubé and both had a very quiet first period. Used on the 2nd power play unit with Dexter Weber. Got run over by Mikaël Beauregard in the 2nd period while entering the offensive zone with his head down. Started the 3rd period with a big hit of his own, which I wish I could see more of out of him on a regular basis. Can get caught playing the puck in one on one confrontations, as he was on occasions in today's game.

#95 Georgs Golovkovs C (2014) It was not a good showing for the Latvian forward, who did show some good moves in a sequence in the first period which led to a Gatineau penalty, but that was honestly the only good thing Golovkovs did in this game. His play has cooled off since a big hit he received 2 weeks ago from Rimouski's Jan Kostalek. He was used on Drummondville 2nd PP unit this time.

Oct 19, 2013 Kamloops Blazers vs Everett Silvertips (WHL)

EVT #89 C Nikolishin Ivan (2014) Started out the 1st period a little sluggish, but his game improved over the next two periods. Played well defensively along the boards but could have been more physical. Was very effective on the Powerplay creating time and space with puck patients and vision. Had a couple good scoring chances but was looking to dish the puck before shooting.

EVT #10 RW Sandhu Tyler (2014) His defensive play was solid, was feisty and aggressive along the boards and on the forecheck was a hand full for Kamloops defense. His speed to the outside created a scoring chances off the rush. Needs to finish his scoring chances.

EVT #12 LW Leedahl Dawson (2014) Was physical both ends of the ice tonight. Punished the Kamloops defense on the forecheck winning the one on one puck battles. Had a nice feed to Kohl for Everett's loan goal of the game. Would like to see him use his size and speed to create more scoring chances off the rush.

KAM #29 D Harlacher Edson (2014) Looked slow and out of place most of the game. Was caught flat footed on a few occasions and beat wide. Under pressure on Everett's forecheck he tend to panic turning the puck over. Looked timid holding the offensive blue line. Had opportunities to make a play or put the puck on net but would dump the puck back into the corners.

Kam #24 D Rehill Ryan (2014) Tough kid, can throw the mitts. Played a good hard physical defensive game until ejected in the 2nd for an open ice hit on Everett player. Was very affective along the wall with his size and positioning. Will join the play off the rush or skate the puck out of zone to create offensive chances.

Kam #25 D Clouston Conner (2014) Good size player, Moved the puck well for most of the game. Played physical at times but could have been more aggressive on the puck and play in the corners. Decent skater for the most part, had ok defensive angles. Not much offensive upside to his game. Played a safe defensive game tonight.

Oct 19, 2013 Kamloops Blazers vs Everett Silvertips (WHL)

EVT #89 C Nikolishin Ivan (2014) Started out the 1st period a little sluggish, but his game improved over the next two periods. Played well defensively along the boards but could have been more physical. Was very effective on the Powerplay creating time and space with puck patients and vision. Had a couple good scoring chances but was looking to dish the puck before shooting.

EVT #10 RW Sandhu Tyler (2014) His defensive play was solid, was feisty and aggressive along the boards and on the forecheck was a hand full for Kamloops defense. His speed to the outside created a scoring chances off the rush. Needs to finish his scoring chances.

EVT #12 LW Leedahl Dawson (2014) Was physical both ends of the ice tonight. Punished the Kamloops defense on the forecheck winning the one on one puck battles. Had a nice feed to Kohl for Everett's loan goal of the game. Would like to see him use his size and speed to create more scoring chances off the rush.

KAM #29 D Harlacher Edson (2014) Looked slow and out of place most of the game. Was caught flat footed on a few occasions and beat wide. Under pressure on Everett's forecheck he tend to panic turning the puck over. Looked timid holding the offensive blue line. Had opportunities to make a play or put the puck on net but would dump the puck back into the corners.

Kam #24 D Rehill Ryan (2014) Tough kid, can throw the mitts. Played a good hard physical defensive game until ejected in the 2nd for an open ice hit on Everett player. Was very affective along the wall with his size and positioning. Will join the play off the rush or skate the puck out of zone to create offensive chances.

Kam #25 D Clouston Conner (2014) Good size player, Moved the puck well for most of the game. Played physical at times but could have been more aggressive on the puck and play in the corners. Decent skater for the most part, had ok defensive angles. Not much offensive upside to his game. Played a safe defensive game tonight.

Oct 20, 2013   Swift Current vs Everett Silvertips (WHL)

EVT #89 C Nikolishin Ivan (2014) Played a good two way game. Battled hard is his defensive zone supporting his defense throughout the game. Showed physical defensive coverage keeping the play along the boards, used aggressive stick positioning to shut down the scoring areas. His offensive vision and crisp passing generated good scoring chances off the rush. Could have played more aggressive on the forecheck. Added a PP goal with a quick release off a cross ice feed. Ivan played an overall decent game with limited mistakes needs to add a little speed/quickness to his game.

EVT #10 RW Sandhu Tyler (2014) Played a quiet game adding a goal and assist. Used his speed to sneak into the scoring areas with a couple good scoring chances but needs to finish. Played hard along the boards and was aggressive on the forecheck winning a few battles for loose pucks. Was pushed around a bit due to his lack of size.

EVT #12 LW Leedahl Dawson (2014) Energy forward, physical on the forecheck. Did the little things well tonight (chip pucks, block shots). Would like to see him get more creative offensively. Good size with decent hands has potential to be decent power forward. May be a surprise player later in the season.

SC #6 D Honka Julius (2014) Offensive minded swift skating defenseman who showed poise and patients with the puck in all 3 zones. Not overly physical tonight but reads the play well and kept the play to the outside with good defensive positioning/angles. Good first out pass and didn't panic under pressure. Likes to jump into the rush and is an offensive threat. Can play in all situations. Had a PP goal.

SC #5 D Martin Brycen (2014) Played a stay home style defensive game jumping into the rush on occasion. His play along the boards was decent using his size and reach to gain puck possession. Tough in front of the net always aware with head on a swivel most of the game. Good first out pass and seemed calm with the puck. Has offensive upside to his game. Could of played more physical in the defensive zone.

SC #3 Harris Jordan (2014) Played an overall decent game. Physical player who needs to work on his defensive positioning. His play along the wall was good, and moved the puck out of the zone well with a few good head man passes. Got caught a few times watching the play but recovered well. Player to watch throughout the season.

October 20, 2013 – Ottawa 67's at Guelph Storm (OHL)

OTT #3 RD Henley, Troy (2015) - Troy was very reliable for a 16 year old defenseman. He skates well in all directions and moved the puck hard and accurately up ice. He displayed good positioning in the defensive zone. While he reacts quickly one on one and won some of these battles he got walked pretty bad for Guelph's second goal of this game. He did a good job down low and out front containing bigger forwards.

OTT #6 LD Duchesne, Jonathan (2014) - Jonathan likes to play physical and is at his best when he's finishing his checks along the wall. He showed effective aggression on the penalty kill especially in the slot and battles hard. He also wins his share of the battles along the wall. He lacks vision with the puck and needs to improve quite a bit in this area, but will go glass and out when pressured. His skating is also a clear area of improvement for Duchesne and doesn't seem to get enough power in his strides.

OTT #10 LC Dulong, Trevor (2014) - Trevor kept it simple and battled physically in the defensive zone delivering several good hits and playing a very responsible two way game. Skating is decent.

OTT #17 RC Konecny, Travis (2015) - Travis displayed good skating ability and intelligent positioning in the offensive zone. While he wasn't a big impact in this game, he made some excellent passes; especially on the power play.

OTT #21 LD Middleton, Jacob (2014) - Jacob had a pretty slow start to the game and didn't make much of an impact positively or negatively early on. He made some smart passes and moved the puck well without forcing plays as the game went on. He made some good one on one plays against some speedy opponents. He also shows a good shot from the point. With that said it seemed on numerous occasions that Jacob struggled a little with the pace of this game.

OTT #40 LD Lintuniemi, Alex (2014) - Alex received a ton of ice for Ottawa today and played a big role in all game situations. He moved the puck well on the powerplay making good hard passes. He showed the ability to skate with forwards in one on one situations but doesn't always activate his stick resulting in easy cross ice passes and gets burned by skilled forwards and resulted in multiple scoring chances. He panics with the puck under pressure and made a very bad giveaway behind his own net throwing the puck out front which immediately resulted in Guelph's first goal of the game.

GUE #6 LD Baltisberger, Phil (2014) - Phil took the body effectively in the corners. He displayed a hard low slap shot and a quick, powerful wrist shot and he gets these shots off quickly. He made a great defensive play on a puck race to negate a potential scoring chance. Overall he played a very smart game.

GUE #9 LC Fabbri, Robby (2014) - Robby moved the puck very well on the power play. Without the puck he did a great job opening himself up on the power play for chances. He showed flashes of his speed and skill and made some god passes but struggled handling the puck in prime scoring areas. He did eventually score for Guelph giving them a 5-3 lead and putting this game away.

GUE #15 RW Stevens, Marc (2014) - Marc received good time on the penalty kill and he pressures the point very well. He was willing to block shots and when he got ice 5 on 5 he provided a solid forecheck and finished on a few checks.

GUE #22 LC Suter, Pius (2014) - Suter was noticeable for his quick skating ability. He also helped set up Guelph's first goal of the game. While he didn't see much ice, he was fairly impressive when he was on the ice.

Scouts Notes: Goaltending was a little rough in this Sunday afternoon match-up. Teams exchanged goals for the first forty minutes. However in the third the Guelph Storm proved to be too much scoring three goals and escaping with a 7-3 victory. In addition to the reports above, for Ottawa Dante Salituro (2015) showed good protection in this game, especially for his size. Joseph Blandisi (Colorado) scored the opening goal while short handed driving the net then beating the goaltender top shelf.

October 20, 2013 – S.S. Marie Greyhounds at Oshawa Generals (OHL)

SOO #6 LD White, Colton (2015) - Colton displayed good skating ability and had very smart positioning without the puck. He competed hard along the wall winning battles against bigger forwards. He did make a puck mistake which directly turned into a scoring chance against.

SOO #14 RW Pastorious, Nick (2014) - Excellent backcheck to break up a two on one chance for Oshawa. After helping out defensively Nick provided a little offense for his team as he banged in a bit of a soft goal in the slot to score the Greyhounds' third goal.

SOO #18 RC Speers, Blake (2015) - Blake utilized his skating at multiple points in this game but was for the most part neutralized by Oshawa defenders. He struggled in the face-off circle losing most of his draws.

SOO #19 LC McCann, Jared (2014) - Jared made quick decisions early on the power play point making good passes and showing a good shot. He also played forward on the power play and battled hard down low. As the game progressed he started to make a few bad decisions in the offensive zone. Jared possesses a hard accurate shot. He provided a hard forecheck but always leads with his stick and wouldn't finish his check. He made a good shootout move but was stopped when he ran out of room. The only word to describe Jared's work in the face-off circle is exceptional. In regards to face-offs won by the centreman, Jared won 12 out of 13 and was absolutely dominant whenever he took the draw.

SOO #22 LD Spinozzi, Kevin (2014) - Kevin provided a smooth first pass up ice. He was poised with the puck and played extremely physical in this match-up.

SOO #26 LW Hughes, Brandon (2014) - Brandon put together a strong forecheck for his team and moved the puck intelligently on the rush.

SOO #51 LD Jenkins, Kyle (2014) - Kyle moved the puck accurately on the power play. He put together a few decent puck rushes, but needs to make harder and more precise passes on the rush. He possesses above average skating and a decent shot.

OSH #14 LW Latour, Bradley (2014*) - Bradley made a positive impact early in this game making a great pass after stealing the puck on the penalty kill to set up a breakaway and Oshawa's first goal of the game. He provided great physical play and received ice in all game situations. Despite his excellent work ethic he made a few questionable decisions with the puck.

OSH #15 RW Hore, Matt (2014) - Matt showed great work ethic when he got on the ice by finishing his checks and providing an excellent forecheck.

OSH #19 RW Cassels, Cole (Vancouver) - Cole showed great work ethic on Oshawa's second goal showing a willingness to battle then made a nice move out front to score. He threw the puck away a little bit in the offensive zone and while he work's hard in all three zones, he also turned the puck over in all three zones.

OSH #21 C Laughton, Scott (Philadelphia) - Scott played an outstanding game tonight for the Generals and were a huge reason they won tonight. His speed is much improved. He played top minutes in all game situations. He received several scoring chances short handed finally scoring on his third short handed chance. He showed his outstanding shot later on wiring an absolutely picture perfect shot after beating the defenseman one on one to score Oshawa's fourth goal of the game.

OSH #58 D Vande Sompel, Mitchell (2015) - Mitchell made some very intelligent passes in this game. He liked to jump up in the rush and get involved offensively.

OSH #71 LW Dal Colle, Michael (2014) - Early on Michael did a great job jumping up on the rush turning it into a two on one but couldn't finish his chance after skating off the defenseman Nurse. He controlled the puck very well in traffic. This was most evident when he made an outstanding play to evade multiple defenders, cut across the crease to score a great goal. In the shootout he did a good job outwaiting the goaltender, however he missed the net afterwards.

OSH #89 C Harding, Sam (2015) - Sam is a great skater but really wasn't using his speed to his advantage in this game. He has a powerful release in his shot and did great in the face-off circle winning the majority of his draws despite being one of the youngest players on the ice tonight.

Scouts Notes: This was an excellent game tonight. Both the Greyhounds and the Generals went back and forth all game long. Just as Oshawa appeared to have this game locked down, the Hounds came back late in the third to force a shootout. After both Matt Murray (Pittsburgh) and Daniel Altshuller (Carolina) made saves in the first three rounds, Cole Cassels (Vancouver) scored the game winning goal in the shootout. Sergey Tolchinsky (Carolina) scored two goals for the Greyhounds. On *the first goal he quickly picked up a rebound and scored. On the second he made a nice backhand move to beat the goaltender.*

October 20, 2013 - Lethbridge Hurricanes vs Calgary Hitmen (WHL)

Cal #2, Thrower, Josh (2014) - Skated well. Good physicality along the boards. Made good first passes. Entrusted to play key minutes late in the game. Scored an empty net goal to close out the game.

Cal #18, Virtanen, Jake (2014) - Very strong first period - he had a hat-trick less than nine minutes into the game. Good speed and puck protection to get in alone for his 2nd of the game. Pro-level release on his wrist shot. Just threw the puck on net for a soft 3rd goal. On shifts he where he was constantly moving his feet, he was very dangerous. Had a few shifts where he was essentially stationary in the neutral zone and turned over the puck as a result. Had a shoot-first mentality. Is much harder to knock off the puck this year. Opponents have difficulty preventing him from going where he wants.

Leth #4, Pilon, Ryan (2015) - Pilon played a pretty steady game. Made simple, smart plays with the puck. Understands the game and positioned himself well for the most part. Foot speed is a concern as he was beaten wide on a couple occasions. Pivots weren't strong. Has a good shot but takes too long to unload it. Scored on a weak wrist shot that was deflected by two Hitmen sticks. Passing skills good, but weren't as sharp today as usual.

Leth # 5, Wong, Tyler (2014) - Extremely hard-working player that constantly created chances off the forecheck. Skates well, but is very under-sized for the pro game at this time. Constantly a thorn in the side for all opponents. Outworked a much bigger and stronger Jaynen Rissling along the boards and often came out of scrums along the walls with the puck. A coaches player who will do whatever is needed to win. Currently leading Lethbridge in scoring and a lot of that is out-hustling opponents, forcing turnovers and going hard to the goal.

Leth #16, Duke, Reid (2014) - Soft hands and showed an ability to handle the puck in traffic. Played the point with the man advantage where he was able to make use of his good passing abilities. Positioning was awful both while playing the point and forward today. Far too aggressive on defense and did not stop the puck carrier from driving to the net on at least two occasions. Had troubles with positioning in his own end. Average size. Got better as the game progressed and was starting to create offence in the third period.

Leth #29, Estephan, Giorgio (2015) - Very good skater for his age. Has good hands. Is poised with the puck and was able to create several good chances. Has good size for his age and is strong on his stick. Has good offensive instincts and a knack for scoring.

Game Notes: This game was never in doubt as Calgary controlled the play for the vast majority of the game. Lethbridge didn't ever quit, but were clearly out-matched. A late empty-netter made it a 6-3 final.

Oct 20, 2013   Swift Current vs Everett Silvertips (WHL Regular Season)

EVT #89 C Nikolishin Ivan (2014) Played a good two way game. Battled hard is his defensive zone supporting his defense throughout the game. Showed physical defensive coverage keeping the play along the boards, used aggressive stick positioning to shut down the scoring areas. His offensive vision and crisp passing generated good scoring chances off the rush. Could have played more aggressive on the forecheck. Added a PP goal with a quick release off a cross ice feed. Ivan played an overall decent game with limited mistakes needs to add a little speed/quickness to his game.

EVT #10 RW Sandhu Tyler (2014) Played a quiet game adding a goal and assist. Used his speed to sneak into the scoring areas with a couple good scoring chances but needs to finish. Played hard along the boards and was aggressive on the forecheck winning a few battles for loose pucks. Was pushed around a bit due to his lack of size.

EVT #12 LW Leedahl Dawson (2014) Energy forward, physical on the forecheck. Did the little things well tonight (chip pucks, block shots). Would like to see him get more creative offensively. Good size with decent hands has potential to be decent power forward. May be a surprise player later in the season.

SC #6 D Honka Julius (2014) Offensive minded swift skating defenseman who showed poise and patients with the puck in all 3 zones. Not overly physical tonight but reads the play well and kept the play to the outside with good defensive positioning/angles. Good first out pass and didn't panic under pressure. Likes to jump into the rush and is an offensive threat. Can play in all situations. Had a PP goal.

SC #5 D Martin Brycen (2014) Played a stay home style defensive game jumping into the rush on occasion. His play along the boards was decent using his size and reach to gain puck possession. Tough in front of the net always aware with head on a swivel most of the game. Good first out pass and seemed calm with the puck. Has offensive upside to his game. Could of played more physical in the defensive zone.

SC #3 Harris Jordan (2014) Played an overall decent game. Physical player who needs to work on his defensive positioning. His play along the wall was good, and moved the puck out of the zone well with a few good head man passes. Got caught a few times watching the play but recovered well. Player to watch throughout the season.

Oct 24, 2013. Shawinigan Cataractes vs Rouyn-Noranda Huskies (QMJHL)

SHA #26 LW, Gignac, Brandon (2016) Gignac is a beautiful skater. He's really explosive, but he did not played often. He made a beautiful pass in a three-on-two to Francis Beauvillier. He used his speed on the rush and he beat Alexandre Leclerc on the outside before making his pass a cross-ice pass to the older Beauvillier. He needs to be more consistent on a shift-to-shift basis. He can have a few good shifts and some awful ones in a short period of time.

SHA #37 RW, D'Aoust, Alexis (2014) D'Aoust displayed good puck protection skills along the boards all game long. He played on Shawinigan's first powerplay unit and he was used in front to bring a net presence. He did fairly well in that department. He was good on the penalty kill as well. He has a good hockey sense overall, as he was in good position most of the time. He's pretty average with the puck, as he won't "wow" you with his stickhandling abilities.

SHA #61 LW, Hodge, Kris (2014) Hodge was good on the forecheck and I liked the compete level in this game. He crashed the net in the first period and created a good scoring chance thanks to his hard work in the second. Otherwise, he's not the kind of guy that will initiate offensive plays down low on a regular basis. He's more of a third liner.

SHA #63 LW, Pawelczyk, Alex (2014) Not as noticeable compared to my latest viewings. He seemed to be always a step behind.

SHA #77 RD, Welsh, Nicholas (2015) Welsh likes to get involved in the offensive zone and acted as the fourth forward on some occasions. He made some nice rushes and he was able to circle the puck well in the offensive zone. Defensively, it was tough for him on some occasions because on he's pretty small and skinny, but his skating abilities helped him in his coverage. I really liked his footwork.

SHA #91 C, Beauvillier, Anthony (2015) Beauvillier needs to work on his defensive play. He was able to create some things on the rush with good puck handling moves, but he was clearly not willing to go in the dirty areas to retrieve loose pucks.

SHA #96 RW, Zinoviev, Ilya (2014) Zinoviev made good decisions with the puck while on the rush. He scored Shawinigan's only goal right after Frédérick Gaudreau won his faceoff late in the first period. He was not noticeable after that, though.

SHA #52 G, Phaneuf, Storm (2014) Good athleticism. He does not follow the puck well and he seemed lost positionally sometimes. Phaneuf was fairly good in the first half of the game. He choked once again in the third period, showing his poor mental strength. He went down on the butterfly way too early on Dea's goal.

ROU #5 LD, Lauzon, Jérémy (2015) Lauzon intercepted passes in the first period. He rushed the puck up about twice per period. He made a good end-to-end rush in the middle of the second period, displaying his good puck control. I was impressed when I saw him being able to maintain Pawelczyk, a six foot six winger, along the wall. Lauzon scored in the third period on a turnover made by Lukas Pozgay. He used his slapper to beat Phaneuf top shelf. Defensively, he covered his zone properly.

ROU #6 RD, Myers, Philippe (2015) He must get quicker with his pivots. Myers used his body properly along the boards and he controlled his gap well one-on-one. He made simple decisions with the puck on the breakouts. He had an assist tonight on Jason Fuchs' goal when he intercepted a breakout pass just before sending Fuchs all alone near Storm Phaneuf. When he had the puck on the opposing blueline, he was able to find good shooting and passing lanes on a regular basis.

ROU #18 LW, Fuchs, Jason (2014) He's a quick skater that plays an East-West style. Fuchs finds open ice well. He scored a pretty goal when he was left alone in front of the net. The goal came after a turnover created deep in the defensive zone by Julien Avon. He went on his forehand and then quickly on his backhand to completely undress Phaneuf.

ROU #20 RW, Nantel, Julien (2014) He played on a line with Mathieu Lemay and Maxime St-Cyr. Nantel was good in the corners, along the boards and was strong on the puck. He possesses a great stride with good balance. He can reach his top speed in his first few steps, which helped him a lot to rush the puck in the offensive zone, something he did on numerous occasions in this game. He constantly made good decisions with the puck and showed good puck protection, especially in his last shift in the first period. He was efficient in his own zone as well. He's not one who will initiate plays. He's more at ease when he is in support.

ROU #27 RW, Perron, Francis (2014) This former first round draft pick in 2012 is a pretty good playmaker at this level. He has a good knack to find his teammates with good outlet passes. He fought well in the corner to regain control of the puck and he then made a nice pass to Jean-Sébastien Dea in the first period. Perron is also a good stickhandler through traffic. I really like his hockey sense as well. He was always aware when the defenseman on his side wanted to pinch, therefore being at the right place. He was outmuscled at times. He also played on the point on the powerplay.

FINAL SCORE: 4-1 ROU

Oct 25, 2013. Cape Breton Screaming Eagles vs Chicoutimi (QMJHL)

CAP #4 LD, Bell, Jason (2015) Bell is a smooth skater who likes to rush the puck. He can close his gap pretty well and his breakouts were good. He was able to find good shooting lanes on a regular basis. There are only a few defensemen that can dangle the puck like him at his age. On the other hand, he is way too attracted by the puck, leaving players alone in his coverage on the way to it. At the end of the second period, he made a risky pinch that paid off big time. He poke-checked the puck near his blueline and then he crashed the net. With a second left in the period, he scored a goal on a pass received from Charles-Éric Légaré. Defensively, he was beat by a normal spoon on numerous occasions. He's a risky playe, but he possesses some untapped potential. He just needs to simplify his game a bit. He played on the second powerplay unit with Bradley Lalonde.

CAP #12 RD, Lalonde, Bradley (2015) Lalonde is a solid puck mover that doesn't possess a major weakness in his game, but doesn't excel in anything. He made simple and quick decisions with the puck all game long. Defensively, I really like how he handled himself against bigger guys than him. He never gave them an inch. He rarely found himself in trouble in the defensive zone in terms of positioning.

CAP #18 LD, Haché, Justin (Phoenix Coyotes 2012 draft pick) Haché was the steadiest defenseman for his team tonight. His skating abilities helped him big time in his defensive coverage. Paired up against Laurent Dauphin and Sébastien Sylvestre, he didn't look silly at all against them. He was quick and smart enough to follow and to maintain them on the perimeter. On the powerplay, he displayed his good puck handling skills. The breakout passes he made were quick and effective as well all game long. He made a few mistakes with the puck when he was exhausted and under pressure, but that was only a small sample of his game.

CAP #2 RD, Leduc, Loic (New York Islanders 2012 draft pick) Leduc is a beast physically. When he wants to crush someone, he simply does it. He broke up numerous plays thanks to his long reach. For a guy that tall, he sure needs to work on his footwork, but I wouldn't say it's a liability in a big rink like in Chicoutimi. On the other hand, the breakouts he initiated were bad to say the least.

CAP #27 LW, Pelletier, Julien (2014) I barely noticed him. He played on the first powerplay unit and was a fixture on the penalty-killing unit as well. Pelletier possesses average puck skills. He can control the puck along the boards effectively, but nothing more than that. He's not that involved in the game. He's good at getting open in the offensive zone, though.

CAP #10 C, Simard, Timothé (2015) I liked his game. Simard is very intense and he's the kind of guy that completes his checks whenever he has the opportunity. He did that four or five times. His defensive play was good, as he supports his defensemen and he covered his man well down low in the defensive zone. He crashed the net on several occasions, but you see that he's limited offensively.

CAP #19 C, Darcy, Cameron (2014) Darcy had a good showing. The guy constantly works hard and he was solid in all areas. He protected the puck quite well and I noticed that he liked to slow down the play in order to reach a teammate left alone in the offensive zone. He scored the last CAP's goal of the game with a good low wrist shot on the glove side.

CHI #28 LD, Lyamkin, Nikita (2014) Lyamkin had a pretty bad game. He made some stupid decisions with the puck, including one that resulted in Cape Breton's second goal. It seemed like he wasn't aware of what happened in front of him in his breakouts. In his zone, he followed his man well, but he was not aggressive enough in order to strip the puck away from the puck carrier. I'll put that in a part of his growing process.

CHI #7 RD, Léveillé, Loik (2015) Léveillé was dominant in the first period. He made great decisions with the puck, he was physical and he acted like a number one defenseman in his zone. He had a nice setup on Gobeil's goal and he showed his great offensive instincts on Dauphin's goal. Otherwise, his start faded as the game went on. His pinches were not calculated; he made dumb plays with the puck on the breakouts and so on. He lost control of the puck at his blueline on a powerplay in the third period when the pressure was not even there.

CHI #58 RD, Allard, Frédéric (2016) Allard had an OK showing. He made the simple plays, but his breakouts passes were not accurate early in the game. One of his shifts on the PK when he blocked about three passes in a row in a moment where the Sags were in big trouble.

CHI #55 C, Roy, Nicolas (2015) Roy had a good game. I liked his compete level and he was always in a good position to be an option for Sébastien Sylvestre in the offensive zone. Defensively, he was pretty good as well. He's smart with the puck and he knows what to do in order to help his team in both zones. Once he gains more speed, he'll be able to be more dominant in the offensive zone, as he sometimes lost his races for loose pucks. He's doing the right thing, but he's just not fast enough.

Scouts notes:

William Carrier competed for the first time ever in front of me. He was involved physically and after the whistle as well. He was able to get under the skin of multiple players. He displayed his great vision on the powerplay and his really good puck *handling skills at even strength. Alex Bureau (2014) was awful tonight. He allowed four goals in the first period only. Three of them were gifts given to the Sags. A showing like that in front of 30+ scouts won't help him for sure.*

FINAL SCORE: 5-4 CHI

Oct 25, 2013. Halifax Mooseheads vs Acadie-Bathurst Titan (QMJHL)

HAL #6 LD, Jacques, Jacob (2014) Jacques made good decisions with and without the puck. He pinched at the right time and the breakouts he made were good. His poor footing put him in a position where he was sometimes not able to catch up against faster forwards.

HAL #12 C, Moynihan, Danny (2014) The older Moynihan is sound defensively. He was not afraid to use his body to knock the puck off of puck carriers in his zone. He used his speed and he protected the puck using his strong lower body effectively. He has done a good job centering Mooseheads' third line. He only lost two faceoffs in the entire game.

HAL #24 LW, Ehlers, Nikolaj (2014) He had a few nice backchecks in the first period. Somebody told me his defensive play was almost inexistent, but in this game, it wasn't the case based on what I saw. He was a fixture on the Mooseheads' penalty kill because he anticipated well. He's an above average skater at this level. He displayed his agility and he made some finesse plays in the offensive zone. Early in the second period, he had a beautiful rush on the powerplay where he went behind the opposing net. He then passed to Brent Andrews, who was left alone by Anthony Gingras. Ehlers was accurate with his one-timers on the powerplay. He formed a nice duo with Jonathan Drouin. At times he does shy away from tough areas. He was the game's third star.

HAL #32 LW, Shewfelt, Andrew (2014) Shewfelt is good on the forecheck. Had a nice chance early in the second period when used his speed well to lose a defender. He accepted a pass from Andrew Ryan and he got a nice shot off that was stopped by Jacob Brennan's right pad. He didn't create a lot of things offensively, but he was an effective grinder.

HAL #71 LW, Moynihan, Connor (2015) The younger Moynihan is a big winger that likes to complete his checks. He turned it over in the defensive zone by giving the puck away on some occasions. Moynihan understands the game quite well, but he had trouble dribbling with the puck. If he works on that, he can be an effective power forward in the Q.

HAL #96 RW, Meier, Timo (2015) Scored a first period goal on a beautiful play made by Jonathan Drouin. He just had to tap the puck in. I liked the way he was always in good position offensively. He made simple plays with the puck and was effective when cycling the puck or crashing the net. Drouin also initiated on Meier's second goal. On that play, Meier pressured the puck carrier effectively. Drouin took the puck then lost the two defenders with astonishing dekes. Ultimately, Meier scored with a nice wrist shot that went high on the glove side.

FINAL SCORE: 5-2 HAL

October 25, 2013 – Barrie Colts at Sarnia Sting (OHL)

BAR #4 RD Dotchin, Jake (Tampa Bay) - Dotchin played an excellent game for Barrie, Dotchin directly impacted all three of Barrie's first goals to open up a 3-0 lead on Sarnia, making strong passes to help create the first two goals, then unloaded a cannon of a slap shot from the point to score Barrie's third goal. Dotchin made solid plays in one on one situations. He prefers to assert himself physically in these situations but was effective in utilizing his stick. He was outstanding along the wall in battle and finished his checks hard at every opportunity.

BAR #5 RD Ekblad, Aaron (2014) - Ekblad didn't have his best performance tonight. He did show flashes particularly with his puck rushing ability and the ability to evade checkers at his size was very impressive. He has an excellent point shot utilizing both wrist shots and slap shots. He chooses which shot to use intelligently and generates an exceptional amount of power out of them. He used his shot to score the eventual game winning goal on a 5 on 3 power play. Aside from these, Aaron really struggled. He turned the puck over a lot in his own zone and lost battles to both Bryan Moore and Nick Latta on a regular basis. Both are much smaller than Ekblad but both simply outworked Aaron and it resulted in scoring chances for Sarnia. At one point in the second period during a battle with Goldobin, Ekblad got frustrated and threw a punch. A penalty was promptly called by the official but Ekblad was not taken to the box. Directly on the ensuing face off to open the power play he two handed Bryan Moore to give Sarnia a 5 on 3 power play with the Colts leading 5-4. Aaron was frustrating in scrums after the whistle. He consistently initiated and threw the first few shots, but when opposing players responded Ekblad quickly backed off, resulting in one of his smaller teammates stepping in for him. Overall while Aaron showed some reasons why we consider him one of the top prospects for the 2014 NHL Entry Draft, his play tonight was largely frustrating.

BAR #12 LW Labanc, Kevin (2014) - Kevin was very good with the puck for the most part tonight. He consistently made great passes and processed the play very quickly. He set up a few scoring chances, one of which resulted in Barrie's fifth goal of the game. LaBanc showed good elusiveness along the boards evading checkers while maintaining puck control. He got a little too over confident with the puck which did result in him throwing the puck away on a behind the back play in his own zone directly resulting in a scoring chance against his team.

BAR #21 LW Lemieux, Brendan (2014) - Lemieux scored going hard to the net and launching a powerful one-timer for Barrie's fifth goal of the game. Earlier in this match-up he dropped the gloves with Josh Chapman and got worked over pretty bad. Although Brendan took a ton of damage in this fight, he hung in there for the whole fight and landed a couple good shots of his own. Skating needs improvement but he's very willing to finish on his checks every chance he got.

BAR #26 LW Mangiapane, Andrew (2014) - Andrew put together a very solid performance on the fourth line and saw his ice time increase as the game went on. He was very slippery and would win battles against bigger players and became very difficult to contain, even along the wall. He showed flashes of very good offensive ability. At one point he beat a defender then made an outstanding pass to set up his linemate who missed on the scoring chance.

SAR #7 RD DeAngelo, Anthony (2014) - DeAngelo ran into one of his teammates left shoulder early on and left the game in pain. When he returned he seemed frustrated. He was seen slamming his stick on the ice in frustration on multiple occasions as he seemed to be getting upset and Barrie fed off this and continued to push him off his game. He was generally reliable on the point on the power play showing excellent evasiveness and helped set up Sarnia's fourth goal, despite not receiving an assist. However a bad turnover on the point on Sarnia's power play also resulted in rush that ended with Barrie scoring their third goal. He showed a good stick in one on one situations vs. speed. He was very good working on a 5 on 3 penalty kill but after Barrie scored at no fault of his own he started slamming his stick again.

SAR #10 LC Kodola, Vladislav (2015) - Vladislav displayed good skating and vision passing the puck, but he missed on a few trying to get a little too fancy. Overall he showed some god flashes and some bad giveaways in this game. Kodola did very well in the face-off circle today.

SAR #15 LC White, Patrick (2014) - Patrick was noticeable on the penalty kill getting in passing lanes and getting the puck down the ice. He played a very defensive responsible game when he was on the ice regardless of the situation. He struggled in the face-off circle for the most part in this game.

SAR #17 LW Renaud, Alex (2014) - Alex struggled handling the puck and looked out of his element trying to produce offense for the sting. He was at his most effective when finishing his hits and keeping his game simple.

SAR #19 LC Ciccarelli, Matteo (2015) - Matteo took the hit to make the play on multiple occasions in tonights game. He was also effective creating a few turnovers. He won a couple draws in this game and got a little more ice than usual as Sarnia was playing with 10 forwards.

SAR #20 LD Schlichting, Connor (2015) - Connor struggled with the puck tonight throwing it up the middle at one point immediately resulting in a scoring chance against. He turned the puck over either throwing it away or losing control when he was pressured by opposing players. Connor was noticeable making a huge defensive play saving a partial break and ending a potential big scoring chance for the opposition.

SAR #22 RD King, Jeff (2014) - Jeff showed excellent speed and elusiveness on the rush on multiple occasions handling the puck well regularly. He made a deflection in his own slot putting his goaltender out of position directly resulting in Barrie's second goal of the game.

SAR #23 LD Core, Zachary (2014) - Tonight's game starting out well for Zachary but his play dropped off as it went on. He did a great job battling out front of his own net keeping the crease clear and staying aggressive on opposing forwards. He made an excellent pass to set up Sarnia's second goal of the game. He showed good moves on the rush, but he got caught too deep in the offensive zone for odd man rushes. He started to misplay the puck later on in the game and gave up several bad turnovers late with his team down a goal, all of which were in his own zone.

SAR #27 RW Goldobin, Nikolay (2014) - Nikolay played a huge part in keeping the team in this game and looked like the player he has the potential of being. He was in on four of Sarnia's five goals tonight. He was creating offense all night with his puck possession and passing ability. He did a great job driving the net with a Barrie defenseman all over him but maintained puck control for a great scoring chance. He made several outstanding passes in this game. He sent the puck up ice with a perfect pass to set up a chance. He made an absolutely outstanding play to set up Sarnia's third goal. Nikolay scored Sarnia's fifth goal of the game. He can get caught at times standing around on the ice.

Scouts Notes: This was a very interesting and exciting game that start out looking like a blowout. Barrie jumped out to an early 3-0 lead but the Sting did a great job fighting back as the Colts' seemed to fall asleep tying the game at 3's. Barrie would score the next two goals, and while Sarnia responded, the Colts would go on to win this game 7-5. Both starting goaltenders Brodie Barrick (2014*) for Sarnia and Daniel Gibl (2014*) struggled in this game giving up a few soft goals.

October 25, 2013 – Kitchener Rangers at London Knights (OHL)

KIT #17 RW Kohn, Mason (2015) - Mason put together a good hard working effort. He got the puck deep and forechecked hard. He put forward some hard hits despite his size. He showed some good moves one on one and reads plays effectively.

KIT #20 RW Magyar, Nick (2014) - Nick showed good hockey sense in this game and was very smart positionally. He hurries back defensively, however he is slow. He made good passes in the neutral zone and showed quick puck decisions in the offensive zone on limited power play time.

KIT #27 LW Llewellyn, Darby (2014) - Darby showed good skating, speed and awareness in all three zones. He read the play well getting the jump on the play for a breakaway opportunity which he didn't score on. He showed a strong forecheck using his speed to take away time and space. He was excellent in the defensive zone 5 on 5 which earned him some time on the penalty kill. He has smart defensive positioning and consistently takes care of his own zone.

KIT #44 RD Hora, Frank (2014) - Frank skates well and showed good speed with the puck. He has a good wrister from the point, not a ton of power but deflectable. He made some dangerous passes in his own zone, one through the slot nearly got picked off. He used his size well enough in battles but at one point he couldn't contain a London forward and held him for a penalty. He went back to the box after throwing the puck over the glass when under pressure.

KIT #72 LC MacInnis, Ryan (2014) - Ryan tends to chase the play a little bit. He protected the puck well but rushed his decisions. He got power play ice time and made the smart simple play. He has great size but doesn't use it nearly enough especially when it comes to opportunities to finish his check. He made a bad no look pass in his own zone setting up a scoring chance for the opposition. Ryan was very effective in the face-off circle winning a lot of draws.

KIT #81 LD Sergeev, Dmitri (2014) - Dmitri shwoed good speed to jump up in the rush. He made strong passes up ice to set up offensive chances. He was positioned safely at the line and would get back defensively but also jumped up at the right times. He forced his shot from the point into shin pads of the defending forward in front of him. He didn't play much of an impact in this game and just gave up on the play late in the third down 3-0 giving London an unchallenged breakaway.

KIT #93 LW Davies, Michael (2015) - Michael struggled with the pace of the game when the puck was moved quickly. He was willing to finish his checks along the wall whenever possible. He also backechecks hard but was constantly chasing the game.

LON #10 LC Dvorak, Christian (2014) - Christian provided a great forecheck and cycled the puck very well. He forced turnovers in the neutral zone on multiple occasions. He also showed good moves to give himself a partial break which he didn't score on.

LON #16 LW Domi, Max (Phoenix) - Max banged home the puck in the slot for London's second goal of the game beating Iafrate in a battle in the slot. Max really turned it on in the third period with his creativity and helped keep the momentum in his team's favour.

LON #53 LC Horvat, Bo (Vancouver) - Bo picked up a rebound created by Kitchener defenseman to score the game winning goal. He forced turnovers in the neutral zone and showed great hockey sense in all zones and all game situations.

LON #88 RD Centorame, Santino (2014) - Santino did a good job showing speed to get to the red line and effectively got the puck deep. He tried to force his point shot and shot into the shinpads of the forward in front of him. Defensively he got beat one on one, particularly bad on one play.

LON #93 RC Marner, Mitchell (2015) - Excellent on the cycle for his team. He provided a fast pace to this game and made quick decisions with the puck. He showed a willingness to go into the corners without hesitation despite his size. He displayed outstanding puck control to create plays for his team and was constantly a positive impact in this game for his team.

Cape-Breton vs Baie-Comeau Drakkar, October 26th 2013. (QMJHL)

#4 Jason Bell Def (2015): Bell played a regular shift at even strength and received power play time as well. Showed some impressive speed rushing the puck on a couple of occasions and can gain top speed very quickly. Had some trouble in own zone covering his man down low. Made a nice play in his own zone after a bad turnover by his goaltender, making a nice dive in front of his net to block a pass in a 2-on-1. Decision-making on the power play was lacking a bit, as he made some bad passes in his power play stints with the other 16 year old, Bradley Lalonde.

#10 Timothé Simard C (2015): Simard played a decent game tonight, where he was active in all three zones. Got a pass in the slot from Justin Haché and his backhand shot was tipped in front of the net by Charles-Eric Légaré to put Cape-Breton up 2-0 in the game. I liked his positioning in the defensive zone and he was quite successful in the faceoff circle. Also liked his cycling game with his line today, on one sequence they did a great job of cycling and later on, Simard came out of the corner with the puck and got into the slot untouched, but missed his shot. Nice work on the PK, as he was not afraid to block shots.

#12 Bradley Lalonde Def (2015): Lalonde played his typical steady game, and it seems he made the big jump from Midget Espoir to major junior this year with ease. Playing on the 3rd pairing, he got power play time with the other 16 year old, Jason Bell. Played a smart game tonight, always keeping it simple with his outlet. Had a great scoring chance in the 3rd period with an open lane to shoot on net on the power play, but missed his shot.

#27 Julien Pelletier Lw (2014): Pelletier, a natural center, is playing left wing this season with the

Eagles. Has a short stride with average speed, and didn't generate much offense tonight. Did throw a big hit in the 2nd period, stepping up in the neutral zone on a player who had his head down. Was involved in the play in all three zones, but couldn't get anything going offensively.

#3 Alexis Vanier Def (2014): Vanier was quiet in the first period, didn't touch the puck a lot and was not involved in the play. Started getting into the game in the 2nd period, with a big hit in the neutral zone that created a 2-on-1 rush for Cape-Breton. Later got a boarding call on William Carrier for a big hit in the corner, a type of penalty that coaches will call a good one for targeting the opposing team's top player. With the score tied at 4 with less than 10 seconds in the game, Vanier made a great read, hiding at the left side of the net, and got a perfect pass from Frédéric Gamelin to score the game-winning goal with 5 seconds left in the game. Played on the team's 1st PP unit with 16 year old rookie Nicolas Meloche.

#15 Bonkondji Imama Lw (2014): Did a good job with his line of keeping the puck deep in the offensive zone and tiring the Cape-Breton defense. Imama still needs to get quicker on his skates which would help him in his forecheck pursuit. A powerful player who is tough to knock down or get the puck away from. Played a strong physical game that night.

#21 Nicolas Meloche Def (2015): Played a regular shift with 19 year old veteran Dominic Poulin and played on the 1st power play unit with Alexis Vanier. Very poised and calm with the puck in his own zone; there was no sign of panic which is rare for a 16 year old defenseman in the QMJHL. Meloche finished the game with 2 assists, his first one came after he took a shot from the point that was blocked but got onto Valentin Zykov's stick at the side of the net which made it 2-1 for Cape-Breton. His 2nd assist came by following the puck carrier all the way to the Cape-Breton net and took a weak shot on net that eventually got back to Zykov, who got his 2nd goal of the game at the side of the net which put Baie-Comeau up 4-3. Didn't see much physicality out of him tonight but he showed some real strong passing in his game, and doesn't play like a rookie.

#61 Denis Gorbunov C (2014) Gorbunov was undrafted last year and decided to join his countryman Zykov in Baie-Comeau. Gorbunov is centering Baie-Comeau's first line with Boudreau and Zykov. Had a tough game in the faceoff circle, but the Russian center is very quick and can change directions very quickly. Dangerous in the offensive zone, very quick to get to loose pucks and benefit from Boudreau's speed and Zykov's power game. Although he is undersized I still like his compete level in regards to battling in the corners. Late in the 2nd period he took advantage of a bad line change for Cape-Breton, hiding at the blueline and getting a long pass from the goalie Cadorette before making a great pass to Frédéric Gamelin on a 2-on-1 opportunity to put the Drakkar up 3-2. Overall, a strong game from Gorbunov.

Oct 26, 2013. Saint John Sea Dogs vs Chicoutimi Saguenéens (QMJHL)

SNB #3 LD, Leblanc, Olivier (2014) Leblanc is an aggressive defender that likes to throw his body around. He was by far the best defenseman for the Sea Dogs in this game. Defensively, his great footwork allowed him to follow the puck carrier, and he was smart enough to cover anyone coming his way. I really liked his ability to create passing lanes from the point on the powerplay. He scored a goal using his slapper on the powerplay. He can control the puck quite well; however he did give the puck away on some occasions while under pressured. His breakouts were fast and accurate.

SNB #5 LD, Chabot, Thomas (2015) Offensively, there is not much to dislike about his game. His passes were almost always on tape and he created offensively on a regular basis, even when pressured. He was always aware of what the Sags forwards were giving to him. Defensively, he made good use of his stick, but he was outmuscled occasionally. He was beaten by Janne Puhakka in a one-on-one because he stopped moving his feet for a second, letting him go with a wrist shot good for a goal. Other than that, he had a good showing for such a young kid.

SNB #7 RD, McQuaid, Alexander (2014) McQuaid is a tough player that is able to contain almost anyone along the boards. He displayed the willingness to clear the front of the net and he was effective doing so. However, his skating abilities aren't good enough for this level. While going backward, he was always getting beat by almost anyone. His passes were barely on the tape as well.

SNB #12 LW, Richard, Joey (2014) I barely noticed him in this contest. He clearly lacks explosiveness, but he was able to create some plays near the half-wall. Defensively, he was a bit of a liability as most of the plays were going on his lane because he wasn't fast enough to get in the defensive zone.

SNB #15 C, Highmore, Matthew (2014) I really liked his game, notably his work ethic. Highmore played with an edge in the corners, as he was not afraid to use his body to regain control of the puck. He displayed his good vision by making some quick passes to his wingers on the rush. When he was down low, he cycled the puck quite well and he was the one controlling the play on his line. He was at the right place at the right time on most occasions offensively and defensively. He was a constant pain in the ass in the neutral zone. He can control the puck effectively, but that's not a big part of his game. He's a slightly above average skater in the Q. His starts are good and that makes him a threat on the rush. He was in the middle of a lot of scrums, which was a part of his game that I discovered. He's on the rise, in my opinion.

SNB #18 RW, Smallman, Spencer (2014) You may not like my pun, but he was a small man last year. He grew up a lot in the off-season, being now near 6'. He possesses good hockey sense that allows him to be a good complement on an offensive line. His vision is adequate. He displayed good speed on the rush.

SNB #16 C, Dove-McFalls, Samuel (2015) Dove-McFalls is a guy that is a good when cycling the puck. He would be more at ease on the wing, as it seems natural for him to play within his lane. Not loaded with a lot of talent, but he's a responsible two-way player.

SNB #25 C, Noel, Nathan (2015) Noel is clearly the best forward on his team. He played a ton and he delivered big time. He's a dynamic skater who oozes potential. He understands the game like nobody else. He was always in a good position to help his defensemen down low and he was able to make quick transitions for them. I really liked the release on his wrist shot that he used a lot when rushing the puck. His shots were accurate, hitting Billia's pads or body in order to create a fortunate rebound. He can control the puck really well and he showed his elusiveness on multiple occasions. I saw him break up approximately 10 plays in the neutral zone just by keeping his stick active. He made a great pass to Smallman on a two-on-one, but he was unable to score. He's pretty vocal on the ice and on the bench as well. His work ethic is really good.

CHI #7 RD, Léveillé, Loik (2015) Léveillé did a good job limiting his turnovers in this game. Most of the time the breakout passes he made were fast and accurate. He delivered some good checks along the boards. He attempted a cross-ice pass in the offensive zone with twenty seconds remaining in the third that almost cost the game for his team.

CHI #28 LD, Lyamkin, Nikita (2014) He had a halftone showing. On some shifts, he played his man pretty well, was tough to beat in his one-on-one, avoiding pressure with his tremendous skating abilities once he regained the puck's control. Otherwise, he seemed indolent, letting his man go without reason. He played on the first powerplay unit late in the game and he seemed comfortable.

CHI #55 C, Roy, Nicolas (2015) He had his best game in the season. Roy covered passing lanes in the neutral zone well. He was able to create opportunities for himself in the high slot with his good stick handling abilities and his reach. He protected the puck quite well almost everywhere on the ice. He's more of a pass-first guy as he was always looking for his teammate to set up a perfect play.

CHI #30 G, Billia, Julio (2014) He displayed his great quickness in this game as he made some key saves throughout the game. The shots that went high were easily blocked or picked up and he followed the play very well, even when there was traffic in front of him. He absorbed most of the shots that came his way without a rebound. Even after he gave up the tying goal late in the third, he was able to regain his focus and he was solid in overtime and during the shootouts, showing his good mental strength.

Oct 27, 2013. Gatineau Olympiques vs Quebec Remparts (QMJHL)

GAT #3 LD, Crevier-Morin, Marc-Olivier (2014) The first time I noticed him in this game was when he closed his gap well on a Nick Sorensen with full speed in the middle of the first period. I was sure he would get beat, but that wasn't the case. His defensive zone coverage was good overall. His footing is average at best, but he compensates with his willingness to play the man. Opponents had to fight for every inch in his battles. When he gives too much space on the ice for the puck carrier, his backward skating's lack of speed is exposed. Offensively, I saw him gave the puck away on a regular basis and every time he had the puck in the neutral zone, he just dumped it without looking for any options.

GAT #8 RD, Carrier, Alexandre (2015) Carrier circled the puck well in the offensive zone. He was able to cover his defensive partners' mistakes on many occasions. Carrier was the smartest defenseman on his team. His stick is always in a good position to break up a play, whether it's in a one-on-one or to cover passing lanes. Also, he was often well positioned in his zone, as he never left his man alone. Most of his breakouts were fast and accurate. When he was pressured with the puck, I'd say about 90% of the decisions he made were good. On the other hand, I noticed that it was tough for him to contain Fabrice Herzog, who's way bigger than him. Clearly the best defenseman on his team once again.

GAT #14 LD, Henry, Jared (2014) He played on the second powerplay unit. Didn't hesitate to try the backdoor play in the offensive zone. He was able to circle the puck as well. Defensively though, he was too aggressive, leading to some two-on-one situations for his defensive partner.

GAT #13 LW, Dostie, Alex (2015) Dostie was good on the rush. He made accurate outlet passes in the offensive zone that displayed his good vision. He is also an explosive skater that needs to get bigger. He was outmuscled way too often along the boards. He worked hard and his defensive play was good for a 16-year-old.

GAT #18 RW, Karabacek, Vaclav (2014) Karabacek possess good hands in tight areas. He had a nice rush where he took control of the puck in the neutral zone, protected it and then cut towards the net. He attempted a pass to Alex Dostie, who followed him well on a two-on-one. He doesn't lose his speed when he has the puck, which is something rare at this level. When he has the chance to fire the puck, he does not hesitate. He clearly has a shooter mentality. In the second period, he had five or six shots. Early in the third, he scored on a one-timer from the high slot. Karabacek was the most dangerous player in the offensive zone in the entire game. He tends to shy away from physical play, though.

QUE #13 LD, Lanoue, Vincent (2015) Lanoue was not that noticeable, but that's a good sign for him. He limited his turnovers and he was good in his one-on-one battles. Played on the first pairing with Ryan Culkin.

QUE #18 RD, Donaghey, Cody (2014) Donaghey looked like a fool early when Martin Reway surprised him with his blazing speed in the neutral zone. As the game progressed, his breakouts were good and his defensive zone coverage was more than adequate.

QUE #20 LD, MacIntyre, Duncan (2014) It was his first game in over a month and it looked like he didn't miss any time. He was pretty good defensively. His pinches were good and he was solid in his one-on-one. MacIntyre played with an edge and I liked that, especially when you know he's coming off a wrist injury. The decisions he made in the offensive zone were good. I liked his ability to join the rush when necessary.

QUE #32 LD, Chevalier, Maxime (2014) Showed some good offensive instincts pinching at the right time. He scored his first QMJHL goal on a weak wrist shot from the point.

QUE #96 LW, Moody, Zachery (2014) Moody showed good anticipation on the forecheck. He was a pain in the ass for Gatineau's defensemen. His hard work paid off in the first, where on the same shift he had a breakaway and he deflected a shot for his goal. He displayed good puck protection skills all game long.

QUE #30 G, Booth, Callum (2015) Booth was always in the right place at the right time in his crease. He faced opposing shots properly, covering all the spaces he could. He didn't move excessively and he controlled his rebounds like a pro. He made some key saves on M-O Broullard and on Émile Poirier displaying his athleticism and his quick lateral movements. He allowed two quick goals early in the third period, but he kept his focus for the remaining of the game.

FINAL SCORE: 4-2 QUE

October 29, 2013, World Jr 'A' Challenge Canada West Selection Camp Black vs Red

Black #4, Stoykewych, Paul (2014) – Passed over in last year's draft. Good-sized defenseman that played a solid all-around game. Was very calm under pressure. Made good first passes. Very steady in his own end. Was given some power play time, but projects as more of a defense-first guy.

Black #6, Hickey, Brandon (2014) – Arguably the top draft-eligible player in the entire group based on his play today. Very good mobility combined with great size. Walked the blueline expertly and had a heavy, accurate shot from the point. Can quarterback the powerplay. As a '96-born player, Hickey was one of the youngest players in camp.

Black #11, Gardner, Rhett (2014) – One of the higher profile draft-eligible players at camp, but was largely invisible on the night. Made a few nice plays, but didn't do much to separate himself from the pack.

Black #14 Hannoun, Demico (2014) - Small, but highly skilled forward was able to dangle against slower opponents. Scored a pair of nice goals. One was on a nice 1-on-1 rush, while the other was a perfect shot from the slot in traffic. Had very good hands and an overall high skill level.

Black #15, Rockwood, Adam (2014) – Rockwood was very creative and elusive. Had a great first step, quick feet, and good vision. Processes the game at a high level and is not afraid to make simple safe plays rather than force something and cause a turnover. Has a slight build, but looked to be taller than expected (around 5'10). Extremely skilled, but can sometimes shy away from contact. Could be in the mix as a late-round draft pick.

Black #31, Dillon, Alex (2014) – Goalie with great size. Looked composed in the net and used his size well to take away space from shooters. Tended to drop to his knees a bit early and was saved by a couple pucks going over his shoulder but hitting the post.

Red #4 Ripley, Luke (2014) – Twice passed over at the draft, Ripley's game was much more refined than many other defensemen at camp. A rangy defenseman that was able to outmuscle opponents and take away space defensively, but was also able to pick his spots well offensively. Above average skater for his size.

Red #12, MacMaster, Tanner (2014) – Small, but very shifty. Excellent speed. Can turn on a dime and larger players can't skate with him. However, he was often kept to the outside and was pushed off the puck frequently. Expected him to be the top small, skilled player, but he didn't have a memorable game.

Game notes: Much faster pace of play than the White vs Gold game played earlier in the night. Entertaining game as both teams attempted to push the play up ice quickly in transition. Black won 4-2.

October 29, 2013, World Jr 'A' Challenge Canada West Selection Camp White vs Gold

Gold #5, Birks, Dane (Pit 2013) – A big defenseman that skated well. Controlled the pace of play at times and had several dominant shifts. One of the best players in today's game. Could skate with the puck, made a reasonable first pass and used his size well to defend. Finished his checks.

Good pivots.

Gold #8, Wight, Jeff (2014) – Large forward with a heavy shot. Has good speed, but acceleration needs to improve. Willing to step up for a teammate when things got a little chippy. Pretty raw, but has some long-term potential.

Gold #12, Hughes, Cameron (2015) – A good puck distributor. Part of the top line for Team Gold along with Jones and Bowles that did most of the damage for Team Gold. Good speed and was able to stick handle in traffic.

Gold #14, Jones, Nicolas (2014) – Was able to control the puck and showed some good smarts by getting to open areas to continue the cycle. Great vision to find Bowles at the far side of the net for a tap-in goal through traffic. Had great chemistry with Bowles and had four assists on the night.

Gold #15, Bowles, Shawn (2014) – Third member of the top line for Team Gold. Good-sized winger that has good vision. Had excellent chemistry with his linemates and had numerous chances. Potted a couple goals and was heavily involved in a pair of other goals but didn't get on the score sheet for them. Played a pretty simple North-South game, but the skill is there. Not afraid to chip and chase and worked hard in the corners. Anticipated the play well and found holes in the defensive coverage. Worked hard in his own end, but was running around too much. Bowles often looped around the ice instead of executing quick starts and stops. Hands are above average, but he's not a puck dangler by any means. Complimented his smaller, skilled linemates well by maintaining puck possession off the cycle, drawing opponents to him, and then setting up near the goal mouth. Was passed over in last year's draft, but may draw some late round interest if he continues to play like he did today.

White #6, James, Connor (2015) – Good skating defenseman. Was able to skate the puck out of trouble and gain the offensive zone. Not overly big and wasn't strong enough to push opponents off the puck along the boards. Not ready for this team at this point, but there is definite offensive upside and should have a good chance to crack this team a year from now.

Game notes: Slow, hesitant pace to the opening game of the night between Team White and Team Gold. The Gold Line of Bowles, Jones, and Hughes were able to create chances at will, although chances were otherwise limited on both sides. Scoring was aided by poor goaltending. Team Gold ended up winning 5-3.

Kootenay Ice vs Red Deer Rebels WHL Regular Season, October 30, 2013

Koo #2, Murray, Troy (2015) – Tentative at times and lost a couple puck battles deep in his end. Murray has decent size, but needs to gain strength as he can be knocked off the puck without much effort. Did well to force opponents wide while defending the rush. Showed good composure with the puck later in the game.

Koo #9, O'Connor, Kyle – Kootenay's 4th line center did well along the boards and was involved in a goal mouth scramble to tie the game late in the 3rd period. Has good size and seemed to get around the ice alright in limited viewing.

Koo # 11, Martin, Jon (2014) – Passed over in the 2013 draft. Winger with very good size and decent speed. Looks to really filled out and is tough to move off the puck. Has good speed, but his agility is limited and he isn't able to quickly shift directions. Tough and always finishes his checks. Had a decisive win in a fight with Kolton Dixon.

Koo #12, Philp, Luke (2014) – Late 1995-birth year. Small, quick, and skilled player. Kootenay's 2nd line center, plays powerplay minutes on the point. Puck jumped his stick while on the point, leading to a Brooks Maxwell short-handed breakaway goal. Seemed to work a lot harder than he needed to as he wasted energy with some questionable positioning away from the puck at times.

Koo #14, Descheneau, Jaedon (2014) – Small, but was willing to drive to the net and was rewarded with a couple goals for his efforts. Needs to get stronger as he can be knocked down rather easily. Has good skill.

Koo #16, Elyniuk, Hudson (2015) – Plays with some truculence. Choppy skater, but has some good size and is willing to throw it around.

Koo #23, Reinhart, Sam (2014) – Kootenay's captain. Tremendous vision. Very quick hands and has the intelligence to match. Able to make smart plays under pressure with limited time and space. Supported the puck well in the defensive zone. Made safe plays in his own end. He won a majority of the draws that he took on the night. Exceptional at both ends of the ice tonight. Scored in the shootout off a slapshot.

RD #4, Fleury, Haydn (2014) – Excellent mobility for a large defenseman. Very calm on the ice. Jumped into the play at opportune times. Shot seemed to be just okay tonight. Wasn't able to create as much offensively as he is capable of, but he did create a couple chances. Defensively he kept opponents to the outside and was steady defending the rush. Would like to see a bit more grit in his game.

RD #9, Bleackley, Conner (2014) – A heart and soul player. Gave complete effort at both ends of the rink. Heavy wrist shot that he tries to use as often as he can. Good instincts away from the pucks. Great first few strides to accelerate into scoring areas ahead of his opponent. Bleakley has shown much better vision than he did last season. Used his teammates well. A leader for the Rebels. Failed to score in the shootout when he attempted a wrist shot.

Game Notes: Red Deer controlled the game early, before Kootenay pushed back in the 2nd period. Red Deer went ahead 3-1 in the 3rd period before eventually blowing the lead and succumbing 4-3 to the Ice in a shootout. 1993-born Rhyse Dieno had a good game. He has looked good in recent viewings and may garner some attention as a free agent if he can continue to make plays at high speeds. Dieno earned an invite with the Minnesota Wild earlier this summer.

Kootenay Ice vs Red Deer Rebels WHL Regular Season, October 30, 2013

Koo #2, Murray, Troy (2015) – Tentative at times and lost a couple puck battles deep in his end. Murray has decent size, but needs to gain strength as he can be knocked off the puck without much effort. Did well to force opponents wide while defending the rush. Showed good composure with the puck later in the game.

Koo #9, O'Connor, Kyle – Kootenay's 4th line center did well along the boards and was involved in a goal mouth scramble to tie the game late in the 3rd period. Has good size and seemed to get around the ice alright in limited viewing.

Koo # 11, Martin, Jon (2014) – Passed over in the 2013 draft. Winger with very good size and decent speed. Looks to really filled out and is tough to move off the puck. Has good speed, but his agility is limited and he isn't able to quickly shift directions. Tough and always finishes his checks. Had a decisive win in a fight with Kolton Dixon.

Koo #12, Philp, Luke (2014) – Late 1995-birth year. Small, quick, and skilled player. Kootenay's 2nd line center, plays powerplay minutes on the point. Puck jumped his stick while on the point, leading to a Brooks Maxwell short-handed breakaway goal. Seemed to work a lot harder than he needed to as he wasted energy with some questionable positioning away from the puck at times.

Koo #14, Descheneau, Jaedon (2014) – Small, but was willing to drive to the net and was rewarded with a couple goals for his efforts. Needs to get stronger as he can be knocked down rather easily. Has good skill.

Koo #16, Elyniuk, Hudson (2015) – Plays with some truculence. Choppy skater, but has some good size and is willing to throw it around.

Koo #23, Reinhart, Sam (2014) – Kootenay's captain. Tremendous vision. Very quick hands and has the intelligence to match. Able to make smart plays under pressure with limited time and space. Supported the puck well in the defensive zone. Made safe plays in his own end. He won a majority of the draws that he took on the night. Exceptional at both ends of the ice tonight. Scored in the shootout off a slapshot.

RD #4, Fleury, Haydn (2014) – Excellent mobility for a large defenseman. Very calm on the ice. Jumped into the play at opportune times. Shot seemed to be just okay tonight. Wasn't able to create as much offensively as he is capable of, but he did create a couple chances. Defensively he kept opponents to the outside and was steady defending the rush. Would like to see a bit more grit in his game.

RD #9, Bleackley, Conner (2014) – A heart and soul player. Gave complete effort at both ends of the rink. Heavy wrist shot that he tries to use as often as he can. Good instincts away from the pucks. Great first few strides to accelerate into scoring areas ahead of his opponent. Bleakley has shown much better vision than he did last season. Used his teammates well. A leader for the Rebels. Failed to score in the shootout when he attempted a wrist shot.

Game Notes: Red Deer controlled the game early, before Kootenay pushed back in the 2nd period. Red Deer went ahead 3-1 in the 3rd period before eventually blowing the lead and succumbing 4-3 to the Ice in a shootout. 1993-born Rhyse Dieno had a good game. He has looked good in recent viewings and may garner some attention as a free agent if he can continue to make plays at high speeds. Dieno earned an invite with the Minnesota Wild earlier this summer.

Oct 31, 2013. Rimouski Océanic vs Chicoutimi Saguenéens (QMJHL)

RIM #24 LD, Bourque, Simon (2015) Bourque had a fairly good game. He applied good pressure on the puck carrier while on the rush near his blueline. He anticipated plays quite well. He played within his abilities with the puck. He made short breakouts passes and when he was under pressure, he simply used the boards to get out of trouble. Bourque sometimes got beat by explosive skaters on the outside. His coverage was sound for 16-year-old. He lost some one-on-one's along the wall, but he was always aware of what surrounded him.

RIM #15 RW, DeLuca, Anthony (2014) DeLuca clearly has that shoot-first mentality. Every time he has the occasion to take a shot, he won't miss it. He's more at ease playing on the perimeter and most of his scoring chances came on a rush. He won't go in the dirty areas to retrieve loose pucks. He finds open ice easily and teammates on a regular basis. His defensive play is a bit above what I expected, but it still not good enough. He floats way too much. He had a breakaway along with Scott Oke coming out of the penalty box in the second period. When he was near Domenic Graham's crease, he went on the backhand before passing the puck to Oke between his legs for a goal.

RIM #22 C, Boland, Tyler (2015) Boland displayed his speed on numerous occasions on the rush. He's an above average skater in a straight line. A dedicated player, his defensive play was efficient. Not a good puck handler, he did beat Lyamkin with a spoon before shooting on Graham's left pad. Played on the penalty kill and centered the Rimouski's third line.

CHI #64 D, Lyamkin, Nikita (2014) Lyamkin had a rough night. He barely played being the Sags' defenseman who logged the fewest minutes. He made terrible decisions with the puck. He did give the puck away three times per period. It was difficult to control his gap on one-on-one's. He kept playing the puck and it put him out of position constantly. He seemed lost on the ice.

CHI #7 D, Léveillé, Loik (2015) He played a typical Léveillé game. He made quick and effective breakouts. He played physical along the wall and he was able to circle the puck on the powerplay. At times he lost his man in his zone and coming out of the penalty box, showing poor defensive hockey sense along the way.

CHI #55 C, Roy, Nicolas (2015) Roy was the best forward on the ice in all three zones. He was always supporting his defensemen when necessary and he was able to get the puck out of his zone regularly. He displayed good puck control early in the first when he came off of the wall deking two players back-to-back before taking a shot on the right post. He also made a great pass to the far side for Victor Provencher on the powerplay earning an assist. Roy completed his checks and he intercepted plenty of passes in the neutral zone. He played a well-rounded game.

CHI #26 C, Bouchard, Jérémy (2015) A fixture on the Sags' penalty killing, he displayed his anticipation breaking up passes. Bouchard was able to get some good scoring chances out of it. He was feisty and he was a threat on the forecheck. The pressure he applied was intelligent, as he never gave the easy option for the puck carrier. He scored the winning goal when he pounced on Jérémy Carignan's rebound before shooting the puck top shelf on the stick side.

FINAL SCORE: 3-2 Chicoutimi

Nov 1, 2013 Brandon Wheat Kings vs Everett Silvertips (WHL)

EVT #89 C Nikolishin Ivan (2014) didn't look like he was firing on all cylinders until the third. Played a decent game defensively taking away the middle and playing physical along the boards. His puck patients and vision lead to a couple scouring chances. But was unnoticed most of the game.

EVT #10 RW Sandhu Tyler (2014) His defensive play was rocky tonight, but was feisty and aggressive on the forecheck winning battles along the boards. Used his speed to create scoring chances off the rush. Had a nice tip goal in the third. Needs better hands around the net.

EVT #12 LW Leedahl Dawson (2014) Played a hard first shit until getting ejected for a hit from behind penalty.

EVT #26 D MacDonald Cole (2014) Was move up to wing and played there the whole game. He brought a physical presence and energy every shift for Everett. Was aggressive in all 3 zones using his size, not much offensive upside to his game. He is versatile, but lacks a few tools.

BRN #8 LW Hawryluk Jayce (2014) Offensive threat every shift. Used his speed to create scoring chances, Showed tremendous offensive upside. Was aggressive and physical at both ends of the ice. Good hands and puck protection around the net. Finished with 3 goals and 1 assist. Best player on the ice. Is underrated in my opinion.

BRN #13 LW Bukarts Rihards (2014) Showed good speed on the rush and 1 on 1, had 1 goal and 1 assists. Decent offensive skills set, could have been more physical this game but showed good aggression on the puck. Was reading the play well and intercepted and few passes.

BRN #17 C Quenneville John (2014) Looks sluggish/lazy most of the game. Was coasting back into his own zone, or just floating around his offensive zone most of the game. Showed some spark on a few shifts, battles hard when trying to gain puck possession. Has offensive upside to his game. Very good on the draw winning all key faceoffs. Just an off night for John.

Nov 1st, 2013. Blainville-Boisbriand vs Chicoutimi Sagueneéns (QMJHL)

BLB #77 LD, Beaudoin, Guillaume (2014) Beaudoin was good on the powerplay. His breakout was effective as well. Defensively, he had a bit of trouble trying to maintain bigger opponents along the wall. His footwork was adequate and he was aware of what was around him. Had two assists and played with Daniel Walcott on BLB's first pairing.

BLB #5 LD, Halbert, Nathanael (2014) A Stouffville Spirit's product, Halbert is a defensive minded defenseman. His footwork is OK and I really liked how he closed his gap. I was surprised to see him join the rush on some occasions. While on the point on the powerplay, he was able to create good passing lanes.

BLB #85 LD, Walcott, Daniel (2014) In his first year in the QMJHL, Walcott oozes potential. He's a fluid skater and he played like a number one defenseman all game long. He was quick on the transition and he played with some edge. His shot from the point is hard and fairly accurate. Defensively, his quick feet helped him a lot in his coverage. He still needs to get quicker to put his stick on the puck on one-on-one's. He's definitely a riser as I could see him being drafted.

BLB #9 LD, Schingh-Gomez, Olivier (2016) Schingh-Gomez was playing his first game in the QMJHL. He looked fairly good. Like most BLB defensemen, his first pass was effective and he controlled the puck quite well. A good-looking backward skater, he tried to keep it simple. He was caught at times in his zone because he was too attracted by the puck.

BLB #8 C, Aronsson, Emil (2014) Centered BLB's first line between Clapperton and Roy. He was willing to crash the net and he was responsible defensively. He finished his checks and he was able to protect the puck quite well along the boards. Not an impressive stick handler…He's always in the right place at the right time though.

CHI #28 LD, Lyamkin, Nikita (2014) His first two periods were awful. He was bad on one-on-one's and he turned the puck over way too much. In the third, he played more due to the overwhelming score and he was more confident. He rushed the puck twice and was effective doing so.

CHI #30 G, Billia, Julio (2014) He was exposed in this game. Most of BLB's shots were high. Had trouble with his glove. His lateral movements were quick and in control. He fought in his crease in order to make saves. Despite the fact he allowed seven goals, I wouldn't say he was bad. He was beaten by quality shots that he couldn't stop due to his small size or because perfect plays were executed on the powerplay.

FINAL SCORE: 7-2 Blainville-Boisbriand

November 1, 2013 – Sudbury Wolves at London Knights (OHL)

SBY #23 LD Capobianco, Kyle (2015) - Kyle received limited ice in tonight's game, playing primarily on the power play. Capobianco controlled and moved the puck effectively on the power play for the Wolves tonight.

SBY #27 RC Schmalz, Matt (2014) - Matt possesses tremendous size and showed occasional willingness to finish checks showing decent strength on the wall. He is capable of generating speed but his footwork is a consistent struggle and affects him in battles and when trying to handle the puck in his skates. His reflexes were also slow as there were a few situations where he could have had a positive impact on the play, but simply couldn't react as quickly as opposing players. Matt was effective playing limited second unit power play when he took up space out front. While he wasn't overly aggressive he was very difficult to move and created a screen that the 6'6" goaltender Anthony Stolarz wasn't used to having to compete with.

SBY #36 LD Cummins, Conor (2014) - Conor was noticeable for his skating ability and moves well in all directions. He was hit or miss with the puck today turning it over a few times in his own zone. He also showed varying results in one on one situations as he handled bigger forwards with his reach but got beat wide by speed and skill.

SBY #52 LD LaBlanc, Stefan (2014) - LaBlanc showed strong puck rushing ability on a few occasions and moves well backwards and side to side as well. He showed good compete out front despite not having great size or strength and was able to tie up opponents sticks well. He was penalized in the third flipping the puck over the glass.

LON #10 LC Dvorak, Christian (2014) - Christian showed flashes of his skill and was able to get involved in a couple chances, but he was most impressive competing hard low in his own zone battling and breaking up chances acting almost as a third defenseman under sustained pressure.

LON #55 LD Bender, Tim (2014*) - This was Bender's OHL debut and he put on a very solid performance for someone playing their first game in the league. Right off the bat he showed good puck handling ability. He was confident rushing the puck and passing it up ice and showed accurate puck moving ability. He skates very well and shows good awareness opening himself up and making himself available for passes. He generally was safe on the rush not jumping up ahead of the play. He competes hard defensively and was willing to finish his checks, although he needs to add muscle. He takes away time from opposing forwards and will attack the puck and the body.

LON #88 RD Centorame, Santino (2014) - This was not one of Santino's best games as he mishandled the puck under pressure on a few occasions, lost his positioning and lost battles. He did have a few flashes of strong play and separated the puck using his stick in one on one situations, but needs to put together stronger performances if he is to continue to receive regular ice on the Knights blueline.

LON #93 RC Marner, Mitchell (2015) - Marner looked excellent tonight as he has in most viewings of the Knights this season. He impresses with his puck skills and the quickness in which he reads the play and makes his decisions. One of these quick puck decisions sent Max Domi in on a breakway to open the third period as Marner recorded an assist on the game winning goal due to his quick pass. He has explosive quickness and is very slippery and tough to contain.

Scouts Notes: Both teams struggled to finish on their scoring chances and puck playing mistakes killed momentum on both sides as Franky Palazzese (Free Agent) and Anthony Stolarz (Philadelphia) put on outstanding performances for their respective teams. Max Domi (Phoenix) scored the game winning goal just 9 seconds into the third period showing his lethal finishing ability and outstanding hands and skating to walk in and score. Ryan Rupert (Toronto) also got on the scoresheet making an excellent defelection off a shot coming from the point.

Nov 1, 2013 Brandon Wheat Kings vs Everett Silvertips (WHL Regular Season)

EVT #89 C Nikolishin Ivan (2014) didn't look like he was firing on all cylinders until the third. Played a decent game defensively taking away the middle and playing physical along the boards. His puck patients and vision lead to a couple scouring chances. But was unnoticed most of the game.

EVT #10 RW Sandhu Tyler (2014) His defensive play was rocky tonight, but was feisty and aggressive on the forecheck winning battles along the boards. Used his speed to create scoring chances off the rush. Had a nice tip goal in the third. Needs better hands around the net.

EVT #12 LW Leedahl Dawson (2014) Played a hard first shit until getting ejected for a hit from behind penalty.

EVT #26 D MacDonald Cole (2014) Was move up to wing and played there the whole game. He brought a physical presence and energy every shift for Everett. Was aggressive in all 3 zones using his size, not much offensive upside to his game. He is versatile, but lacks a few tools.

BRN #8 LW Hawryluk Jayce (2014) Offensive threat every shift. Used his speed to create scoring chances, Showed tremendous offensive upside. Was aggressive and physical at both ends of the ice. Good hands and puck protection around the net. Finished with 3 goals and 1 assist. Best player on the ice. Is underrated in my opinion.

BRN #13 LW Bukarts Rihards (2014) Showed good speed on the rush and 1 on 1, had 1 goal and 1 assists. Decent offensive skills set, could have been more physical this game but showed good aggression on the puck. Was reading the play well and intercepted and few passes.

BRN #17 C Quenneville John (2014) Looks sluggish/lazy most of the game. Was coasting back into his own zone, or just floating around his offensive zone most of the game. Showed some spark on a few shifts, battles hard when trying to gain puck possession. Has offensive upside to his game. Very good on the draw winning all key faceoffs. Just an off night for john.

November 2, 2013 – Sudbury Wolves at Sarnia Sting (OHL)

SBY #19 LW Burgess, Connor (2014) - Burgess got a chance early positioned at the side of the net but couldn't finish. He generates acceptable speed for the OHL level but his skating is very awkward and he uses way too much energy on his first few steps to get moving. He showed an effective forecheck in the limited ice he saw, even forcing a turnover or two against bigger opponents. Was able to be effective by keeping it simple and providing a forecheck for his team. Lacked puck skills to handle the puck effectively when pressured, but was able to get a few scoring chances when going to the slot, but couldn't finish.

SBY #23 LD Capobianco, Kyle (2015) - Kyle kept it pretty simple tonight receiving a fair amount of ice 5 on 5 after the injury to de Haan. He won races to the puck and competed hard along the wall. He made the smart simple play with the puck and didn't try to do too much. He was also utilized on the Wolves power play.

SBY #27 RC Schmalz, Matt (2014) - Matt was noticeable out front battling creating a disruption out front. However he didn't do this enough. Matt's footwork is not very good at all and struggles with his steps and with his balance. He can however generate good speed when given enough ice and was able to drive the wing, beat the defender wide. On another situation he was able to get in on a breakaway and made a good move but was stopped. He was hit or miss along the wall which isn't good enough for a 6'6" forward. His balance affected him as he was effectively knocked off the puck by smaller opponents. Matt did a good job in the face off circle tonight winning the majority of his draws.

SBY #36 LD Cummins, Conor (2014) - Conor delivered a few solid hits in one on one match-up's and was moderately effective defensively. However he really struggled with the puck making risky passes in his own zone and at times firing the puck down the ice when there were passing options available to him.

SBY #44 LC Zeppieri, David (2015) - David received limited ice playing on the fourth line, but he was very effective on the forecheck playing with a ton of energy and taking away time and space effectively. He was also going hard into the corners and battling very hard against older and stronger players. David handled the puck on very rare occasions in this game, but during these moments he showed effective puck handling skills and generally good hands.

SBY #52 LD LaBlanc, Stefan (2014) - LaBlanc played a very strong game tonight. He was very consistent with his play. He shows very good intelligence with the puck choosing the right times to rush and the right times to pass the puck. He is smart without the puck generally maintaining ideal positioning and while he's not an overly physical player he is willing to finish his check and willing to compete in battles. He rarely makes a mistake and was very solid for Sudbury in tonight's game. He possesses good vision and intelligence on the ice and while he is slightly undersized for the defensive position he was consistently solid and reliable.

SBY #61 LW Pancel, Nathan (2014*) - Nathan is a re-entry player, however he was a game changer for the Wolves' tonight getting in on 5 of the 6 goals, 4 of which came directly because of him. He scored early with a big wrist shot giving the Wolves' a 1-0 lead. He then was able to bury in the slot area to give Sudbury a 2-1 lead in the second period. He followed this up with an outstanding pass from the corner to set up Mathew Campagna and create Sudbury's third goal. Finally he wrapped up the hat trick on a bit of a deceptive wrist shot that gave Sudbury a 6-3 lead. In addition to his offensive input he worked hard along the walls. He was also very good defensively willing to get into passing and shooting lanes both on the penalty kill and 5 on 5 breaking up a number of chances for the Sting. He is listed at 6'0" 190 at the moment. His size prevented him from being selected initially, but if he has in fact grown and continues to play such an effective two-way game, he could hear his name called in 2014.

SBY #77 Crisp, Connor (Montreal) - Connor came to the defense of his teammate Evan de Haan after he got absolutely leveled with a clean hit by Alex Renaud. Crisp picked a fight with the smaller, younger Renaud and destroyed him pretty bad landing several huge punches. In addition to the fight, Crisp was effective throughout the game showing very well in battles along the wall and finishes his checks hard. Crisp is built huge and makes his presence known physically at every opportunity, but also showed a pretty good shot as well.

SAR #5 RD Hore, Tyler (2014) - Tyler struggled tonight with the puck throwing it away on multiple occasions. He also shot it down the ice on more than one occasion despite passing options available to him. At one point he threw the puck up the middle from deep in his own zone which directly resulted in a scoring chance. Overall his puck moving ability is a work in progress. He is effective in one on one situations particularly when his opponent lacks speed and will drive them into the boards. He was however beat wide in a one on one match-up as well. Tyler was most effective tonight when the battle came to the wall. He showed a good comfort level with the level of physicality and likes to finish his checks. He was able to win a fair number of battles due to his tenacity and size along the wall.

SAR #6 RW Bushnell, Noah (2015) - Bushnell was noticeable showing a tenacious forecheck forcing turnovers. He also finished his check and took the body whenever it was remotely possible and was a strong physical presence.

SAR #7 RD DeAngelo, Anthony (2014) - Anthony put together a solid performance tonight. He kept it simple early making the smart pass and maintaining good defensive positioning. He was strong in a few one on one match-ups at one point driving a Sudbury forward hard into the boards after forcing him outside. He was consistently effective on the power play showing good calm and composure when pressured high on the point. He also scored firing a wrister top shelf with a heavy screen in front of the Sudbury net.

SAR #10 LC Kodola, Vladislav (2015) - Kodola was noticeable showing flashes of his elusive skating ability and puck handling skills. He will get the puck deep if he doesn't trust his path instead of trying to force a low percentage rush skating into opponents. He made some solid passes, but was able to get on the scoreboard with his first OHL goal following up on a rebound scoring Sarnia's second goal of the night.

SAR #17 LW Renaud, Alex (2014) - Renaud landed one of the biggest hits of the year absolutely destroying Evan de Haan with a beautiful and massive clean hit deep in the offensive zone. Renaud accepted a fight with the much bigger and stronger Connor Crisp on his very next shift and took a beating. He hung in there taking a lot of big punches but was able to land a few of his own. Renaud was effective when playing a physical style, but struggled on the cycle and when entering the offensive zone because he lacks vision and made some blind passes and drop passes that went right onto Wolves' sticks with no teammates even close to the puck on some occasions.

SAR #19 LC Ciccarelli, Matteo (2015) - Ciccarelli played one of his best games tonight for the Sting providing a strong forecheck and forcing turnovers. He contributed on Sarnia's second goal of the night after taking a bad tripping penalty he left the box and joined the rush. He opened himself up for passes then went hard to the net causing a disruption allowing Kodola to sneak in and score practically into an empty net undefended as the focus was on Matteo. While his footwork drastically needs work, he showed speed in enough open ice and nearly got a breakaway chance. He was ultimately penalized because he lost the race by a few feet and had to slam on the breaks to avoid running Palazzese, spraying him with snow.

SAR #20 LD Schlichting, Connor (2015) - Connor continues to struggle adjusting at the OHL level. Too often he's taking a light swing at a puck or chasing the play trying to catch up to the play. This is most destructive when his man is left open in the slot which resulted in a few huge scoring chances. At one point he jumped right infront of his own goaltender as Sudbury was preparing to shoot completely screening his own goaltender resulting in a goal. His physicality is inconsistent, but when he does go into the corners he shows good strength and utilizes his size intelligently. Connor shows some panic with the puck and will throw it away far too quickly when he's unpressured. Some of these things should come with experience and a comfort level with the league, but at the moment he's struggling with the pace of the league.

SAR #23 LD Core, Zachary (2014) - Core struggled with the puck tonight turning it over several times, particularly putting the puck on the tape of Wolves' forwards on two occasions directly resulting in scoring chances. He tends to only be effective when going boards or glass and out and can rush the puck a little bit as he uses his body very well to protect it. While his puck play was overall a huge struggle tonight, the one area he is certainly not lacking in is work ethic. He makes up for some of his mistakes by purely putting in a ton of effort competing extremely hard and went to war against any Sudbury player in his area and competing for the puck and for ice.

SAR #27 RW Goldobin, Nikolay (2014) - After an outstanding performance last weekend, Goldobin really struggled in tonights game. While he made his usual excellent passes and showed flashes of brilliance his work ethic was below the level it needs to be at. Whether it was lacking hustle getting out of the zone on a delayed offside or not competing for a puck, he just wasn't working hard for the majority of this game. He also turned the puck over a lot more than usual making a lazy casual pass resulting in a few turnovers.

SAR #35 RW Korostelev, Nikita (2015) - Nikita was noticeable in flashes. He skates very well for such a big 16 year old and shows shiftyness that is rare in such a big forward. He rushed the puck up ice and did a good job getting open. He tied the game 3-3 on the powerplay accepting a pass and quickly releasing his exceptional shot top shelf for the goal. He nearly caught Sudbury off guard seconds later again with his shot but just missed.

Scouts Notes: While Sarnia hung around for most of this game, the Wolves just seemed to be a step ahead all night. Sudbury benefited from turnovers and a consistent work ethic from all four lines. Sarnia was able to create offense but once Sudbury made it 5-3 in the third period, their persistence dropped off.

November 3, 2013 – Erie Otters at London Knights (OHL)

ERI #5 LD Felker, Justin (2014) - Felker noticeable a limited amount of times today but he was effective along the boards winning battles working tenaciously to take the puck away a few times. He also wasn't shy about utilizing his size to finish a few very solid hits.

ERI #15 LC Pettit, Kyle (2014) - Kyle played on the fourth line tonight, but as the Knights pulled away, he received more ice time. Kyle was excellent on the forecheck pressuring opposing forwards and went into the corners hard. He showed good hands on the cycle down low and used his body to protect the puck very well deep in the zone. He was effective every time he came on the ice due to a very strong work ethic in all three zones. He was also very effective in the faceoff circle tonight.

ERI #19 RC Strome, Dylan (2015) - Dylan was moderately effective playing on the second line. He was effective keeping up with the pace of the play, finished his checks a few times, but generally didn't get many opportunities with the puck. His skating with smooth and he has an OK top speed but lacked explosiveness.

ERI #37 LW Wood, Travis (2014) - Travis received limited ice but when he was out there he showed god speed and provided a hard forecheck and finished his checks along the boards. He showed an absolute cannon of a slap shot, but missed the net.

ERI #44 RD Dermott, Travis (2015) - Travis struggled in one on one situations and down low today getting outmuscled in both areas. He shows smooth skating ability and handled the puck well when carrying it up ice, but was chased back far too easily. He was hit or miss with the puck making a few solid passes but he also threw the puck away on a couple occasions as well. Dermott got into it with Marner today a few times tonight. At one point he gave him a nudge after the whistle and Domi threw his gloves off and punched Dermott several times. Travis declined to drop the gloves and his team scored on the ensuing power play.

ERI #97 LC McDavid, Connor (2015) - Connor was far from his dynamic self tonight. He possessed the puck very rarely and chose to make the simple pass instead of challenging defenders on the rush or in one on one situations. He battled down low early on in the game but his compete level dropped off dramatically throughout this game, particularly when London scored their fourth goal. By the time his team was down 5-2 he showed absolutely no compete or interest in the play, even when it was happening in front of him. For a player with the talent of McDavid this game can't be considered as anything but a write off for him, as we know exactly what he is capable of and this was either an off game, or the result of a player who is playing injured.

LON #10 LC Dvorak, Christian (2014) - Dvorak worked hard defensively in this game. He showed good strength on the puck protecting it under pressure. He made a great hit along the wall then made a pass to set up a sure goal that was negated by a penalty by Erie.

LON #16 LW Domi, Max (Phoenix) - Domi made an outstanding behind the back pass to give his linemate Tierney a perfect shot in the slot. Later on he made another outstanding cross ice pass to set up Welychka on the power play. Both assists were very high level and very few players at this level could have the vision and awareness to make one of those plays let alone two. Domi removed himself from the game for a little bit defending Marner by throwing his gloves off and fed an initially unsuspecting Dermott with several punches to the face who didn't drop his gloves or his stick in the altercation. This gave Erie a power play and the Otters were able to tie the game in the second period during the power play that came from this decision.

LON #55 LD Bender, Tim (2014*) - Tim was consistently smart with the puck making very solid passes up ice and moving it well in the offensive zone. He was capable of flipping the puck out of the zone while under heavy pressure He possesses good power in his shot. Bender weaved into the corner in puck races instead of taking the direct route.

Scouts Notes: This game got off to quite the slow start. Neither team was capable of creating much of a scoring chance in the first period. Connor Brown (Toronto) was able to score the opening goal by going to the net after making a pass and battled in the crease eventually beating the goaltender. In the second however, the Otters and Knights got off to a very physical start which included Michael Curtis (Free Agent) dropping the gloves and beating Alex Basso (Free Agent) who doesn't fight very often. Later on Dane Fox (Free Agent) and Josh Anderson (Columbus) dropped the gloves. Despite Anderson's size advantage Fox won this fight rather easily. However this would be the only thing the Otters would win in the final 40 minutes as the Knights went on to score four unanswered goals en route to a 6-2 victory today. Hayden Hodgson (2014) didn't have much of an impact today as he was noted for mishandling the puck on the rush a few times

Nov 6th, 2013 Kamloops Blazers vs Everett Silvertips (WHL Regular Season)

EVT #89 C Nikolishin Ivan (2014) Played a responsible defensive game, using his angles and checks to keep the play along the boards. Was tough on the draw winning key faceoffs. Looked like he was on cruise control through the offensive zone not playing to aggressive on the puck. Had a nice PP goal in the 1st period.

EVT #10 RW Sandhu Tyler (2014) Played very aggressive along the boards tonight winning 1 on 1 puck battles. His speed was creating a scoring chances and hard for the younger d-man to control most of the game. Had two assists.

KAM #29 D Harlacher Edson (2014) Looked slow and out of place most of the game. Didn't show any spark to his game. Tends to throw the puck away when under pressure on the forecheck. Had a couple physical shift throughout the game but was not much of a impact.

Kam #24 D Rehill Ryan (2014) Was very aggressive in the defensive zone. Made a couple good first passes out of the zone. Shows some offensive flare with a couple good rushes. One of Kamloops better players tonight.

Kam #25 D Clouston Conner (2014) Good size player, Moved the puck well for most of the game. Played physical at times but could have been more aggressive on the puck and play in the corners. Decent skater for the most part, had ok defensive angles. Not much offensive upside to his game. Played a safe defensive game tonight.

November 7, 2013 – Guelph Storm at London Knights (OHL)

GUE #6 LD Baltisberger, Phil (2014) - Phil competes hard along the wall but was hit or miss in terms of winning those battles. He finishes his hits regularly. His skating is manageable but he lacks explosiveness and overall his skating is slightly below average.

GUE #11 LC Dickinson, Jason (Dallas) - Jason was fairly reliable in this game at both ends of the ice. He also did a great job following up on a rebound to score Guelph's third goal of the game. However he mishandled the puck which directly resulted in London scoring their fifth goal and sending this game to overtime.

GUE #15 RW Stevens, Marc (2014) - Marc received very limited ice but when he was on the ice he showed an excellent forecheck, strong skating and great pressure on the puck carrier. He is reliable defensively and makes smart decisions around his positioning when his team is pinned.

GUE #22 LC Suter, Pius (2014) - Suter started out on the fourth line but as the game progressed and he put together a strong consistent effort his ice time drastically increased in the second half. Pius skates well and provides strong forecheck pressure but consistently pulls up when he gets too close and needs to make contact to complete his forecheck. Regardless he was able to force some turnovers and created some offensive chances both with his shot and with his passing ability tonight. Suter struggled in the face-off circle, but overall he became a strong presense for the Storm tonight.

GUE #31 G Mancina, Matt (2014) - Matt made some good saves due to following the play well. He also displays good vision. His reflexes seem a little behind the play when facing some of London's top shooters.

LON #10 LC Dvorak, Christian (2014) - Christian doesn't need much space to create offense and was able to create some chances with his puck handling skills. He battles deep in the offensive zone and while he's usually reliable in the defensive zone he was stripped of the puck which Guelph turned into a scoring opportunity. He was able to force turnovers but mishandled the puck in this game a few times as well.

LON #55 LD Bender, Tim (2014*) - Tim pulls up while going into the corner. He's willing to make contact and get involved in battles but refuses to be the first one in. He will however skate in the way of an opponent trying to get into the corner and delay their involvement. He made some very smart passes both in the neutral zone and offensive zone. He was hit or miss in one on one situations making some solid plays with his stick. But there was also occasions where he got beat pretty bad.

LON #88 RD Centorame, Santino (2014) - Santino made the smart simple play with the puck tonight. He was hit hard and couldn't recover in time partially resulting in Guelph's second goal of the game.

LON #93 RC Marner, Mitchell (2015) - Mitchell handles the puck in his feet very well showing good coordination, quickness and calm under pressure. He made a good pass in the slot then showed good reaction time to score London's third goal on the rebound.

Scouts Notes: London put forward a dominant performance in the first period and appeared as they were going to coast through this game. However they sat back in the second and Guelph really turned it on showing great resiliency and tied the game up. After exchanging goals in the third period both teams earned a point. After struggling for most of the game, Dakota Mermis (2014*) took the puck end to end making a great move and burning Matt Finn (Toronto) to the outside to score the game-winning goal in overtime on an impressive rush.

Nov 7, 2013. Czech Republic vs Russia (WJA Challenge)

CZE #7 LD, Rasner, Alex (2014) One of the things that I liked about Rasner's game is that he always kept his head up. He is always well positioned and executes details well in one-on-one situations. He has to move his feet faster though as he can get beat by faster opponents on open ice.

CZE #19 F, Vesely, Radek (2014) Vesely showed some good passing ability, drawing coverage and then finding seams. Nice wrist shot. Set up at the low circle on the powerplay and acted as a triggerman. Guilty of being too stationary, waiting for the puck to come to him rather than rotating around to attract defensive attention and give his teammates an option. Still liked his game though.

CZE #22 F, Zohorna, Radim (2014) Tall lanky kid. Kid has potential that's for sure but he needs to move the puck rather than taking long outside shots. Zohorna protected the puck really well on the wide drive and put good pressure on the forecheck. He was clearly effective playing that kind of hockey.

CZE #24 LD, Pyrochta, Filip (2014) He made a lot of difficult plays look easy throughout the game, he has long strides when he's trying to reach his top speed, got open easily in the neutral zone with that speed. Pyrochta moved the puck well on the powerplay. He needs to have a better puck management when under pressure though.

RUS #20 G, Tretiak, Maxim (2015) Tretiak allowed a bad goal from center ice looking really out of place, but he had a really solid game. He never gave shooters much to look at and gets around the crease well for a big man. He kept his focus after his bad goal. Tretiak has a good glove and he relies on it a lot.

RUS #12 F, Kraskovski, Pavel (2014) Good puck protection, goes in front of the net. Likes to give hits as well. He was able to get the breakout started with some good passes out of the zone and put great pressure and physicality on the forecheck to force turnovers then move the puck out front to a man in the slot.

RUS #13 F, Pilipenko, Kirill (2015) Really elusive with the puck. He scored on a one-timer on a powerplay. He has a superb hockey mind and gets open easily in the offensive zone, offensive execution is off the charts, will rarely miss the net when he shoots towards it whether those are backhands, wrist shots or one-timers.

RUS #16 F, Kamenev, Vladislav (2014) Kamenev had a pretty good game tonight, showing some nice skills with the puck down low and protecting the puck well to come around the net out front to put a good shot on net, then jump on rebounds in a hurry. He uses his body and strength nicely to win battles along the boards and create space for himself. He has some pretty nice agility and above average top speed, which makes it easier for him to get around opponents with the puck. Could use more burst in his step to make him more dangerous in the offensive zone. Kamenev displayed some excellent passing and vision to find an open man in the slot to create some good chances. He was able to hold up off the rush after gaining the offensive zone to move the puck to a trailing player, and was distributing the puck well on the power play.

RUS #18 RD, Nasybullin, Eduard (2014) Gave a good hip check at the beginning of the game. Played well in his zone, clearing the front of his net and winning most of his one-on-one battles. He was making the first pass out of the zone most of the time. He does like to cheat some time and got beat by speed. Needs to watch his pinching and seal off the boards better. He was one of the better players for the Russian team tonight.

FINAL SCORE: 3-1 RUS

Nov 9, 2013. Rouyn-Noranda Huskies vs Quebec Remparts (QMJHL)

ROU #6 RD, Myers, Philippe (2015) Myers really needs to improve his footwork. It's not really adequate for the Q level. I was surprised by his poise and his decision making with the puck. He executed the simple plays well. He was also good along the board.

ROU #17 RW, Lemay, Mathieu (2014) Lemay was the best player on his team without a doubt. He was intense, played well along the wall and he was creative around the net. He was the one initiating offensive opportunities. He shot a lot and had several quality scoring chances.

ROU #20 C, Nantel, Julien (2014) I was not impressed by his showing. He looked disinterested and he didn't really know what to do in the neutral zone. He was playing with Jason Fuchs and Steve Mercier, and it was very visible that was not a perfect match. Nantel needs teammates that can follow him on the rush and be at the right position when necessary. I like his skating stride. His defensive play was honest. When he was F3, he did a fairly good job.

QUE #13 LD, Lanoue, Vincent (2015) Lanoue was bad on one-on-one's. He was outmuscled along the wall by mostly all Huskies' forwards. He played a ton alongside Ryan Culkin.

QUE #18 RD, Donaghey, Cody (2014) Donaghey had a very bad first period. Most of his breakouts were out of reach and his coverage was awful. In the second period, his game was better and he made a great cross-ice pass to Anthony Duclair that led to Alexandre Boivin's goal.

Scouts notes: Anthony Duclair (New York Rangers 2013 draft pick) had a great game. He earned two goals and an assist. He used his speed efficiently especially on the rush. Yanick Turcotte (2014) scored his first QMJHL goal and engaged a hell of a fight against Quinn O'Brien. François Brassard (Ottawa Senators 2012 draft pick) had a good performance overall.

FINAL SCORE: 5-2 QUE

Baie-Comeau Drakkar vs Drummondville, November 10th 2013, QMJHL

Baie-Comeau

#3 Alexis Vanier Def (2014): The big defenseman played a decent game this afternoon, scoring the game's opening goal from an heavy shot from the point that went through the Drummondville goaltender. Vanier was also very involved in the physical game in this contest, not shy to use his size and strength in the corners and showing he was more than happy to clear the front of his net. In his zone, he tends to focus on the puck too much and can forget to cover his man in front of the net. Played in all situations of the game, got a lot of ice time on the power play and also a regular shift on the penalty kill unit. Would like to see him more involved in the play, as he didn't touch the puck often at even strength.

#15 Bokondji Imama Rw (2014): Imama played a typical Imama game, as he was intense and finished every check he could. Tried to set the tempo of the game with some good hits on the forecheck early in the game. Skating is still rough for him as he needs to get quicker to become more effective on the forecheck. Not a lot of offensive chances for him today, and being a better skater would also help him in that department. Was involved in a lot of scrums and took 2 roughing penalties after whistles.

#21 Nicolas Meloche Def (2015): Was paired with Vanier at even strength and on the power play. Liked his poise and calm with the puck. He doesn't look like a 16 year old rookie out there. He was the most active puck-rushing defenseman on the Drakkar this afternoon, his first pass out of his zone was hard and precise. Can find himself in tough along the wall as he still lacks some strength and needs to fill his 6'2" frame. Scored a nice goal on the power play after blocking a clear attempt by Drummondville, where he let go of a solid wrist shot from just inside the blueline with heavy traffic in front of the net to put his team up 3-0.

#61 Denis Gorbunov C (2014) Gorbunov came to North America this season after being passed over in last year's NHL draft. A late '94 birthday, Gorbunov has taken no time adjusting to the

QMJHL. Centered the team's first line and also played the point on the first unit of the power play paired with veteran D-man Dominic Poulin. Showed good creativity with the puck on the point and has a nice vision, finding his teammates with ease. At even strength play too much a perimeter game from what I saw today, did showed nice patience with the puck and was willing to wait an extra second to make a play.

Drummondville

#6 Julien Carignan-Labbé Def (2015): Played a decent game with the limited ice time he received. Showed he is very strong on his skates and doesn't get overpowered in the defensive zone and along the wall versus the bigger and older forwards. Doesn't mind mixing it up in front of the net with opposing forwards, and even got into a fight with Sharks' draft pick Gabriel Paquin-Boudreau.

#11 Joey Ratelle Rw (2014): Worked hard in all three zones, finished his checks as much as possible on the forecheck. An honest effort out of him tonight with not much flash in his game, however, he did play in all situations. Skating still an issue with his game.

#15 Nikolas Brouillard Def (2014): Brouillard didn't bring his "A" game today, as he made some errors with the puck, tried to do much with it on one sequence which led to a turnover, although he had enough speed to get back and take the puck away from a Drakkar player who had a breakaway. Was in tough in his own zone versus a big, physical team like the Drakkar who doesn't give you much time to make a decision with the puck with their hard forecheck. One of the few Voltigeurs' players who was able to get his shot through the net, as Baie-Comeau had a great job blocking shots all night long. Took a shot from the point that was tipped by Christophe Lalancette in front of the net to put the score at 3-2 Baie-Comeau in the 3rd period.

#19 Cam Askew C/Rw (2015): Didn't get a ton of ice time in the first 2 periods. The 3rd period saw him starting getting shifts with players from the top 2 lines, as Drummondville was looking for some goals and played their most skilled forwards together. Didn't generate much in terms of offensive chances for Askew though, but he made a nice play in his zone, covering his man and taking the puck away from him.

#55 Dimitri Boikov Def (2014): Boikov delivered a big hit just inside his blueline that led to a scrum, after it he looked like he got hurt, but stayed in the game. Played on the Voltigeurs' 2nd power play unit, where he made a real nice play with his stick after his team was pinned down in their zone for a good minute, and he was able to get the puck away from a Drakkar player with a nice stick check. Late in the game, he was hurt again after taking a hit in his zone, and didn't see a lot of ice time in the 3rd period.

#95 Georgs Golovkovs C (2014): Liked his compete level in this game, had some impressive shifts while holding onto the puck for a long time in the Baie-Comeau zone. Has great puck protection skills. Without the puck, he can be a troublemaker as he gave the puck away on more than one occasion in his own zone when he was pressured. Golovkovs is great in open spaces when he has time and space to skate with the puck, but I didn't see much of it today. Got hit really hard by Charles Poulin of Baie-Comeau, who caught the Latvian with his head down entering the Drakkar zone.

#96 Dexter Weber Def (2014): Played on the first power play unit with Nikolas Brouillard for the majority of the game until the 3rd period when he was replaced with a forward on the point. Like his decision making and level of calm in this game, didn't try any flashy plays with the puck. Didn't get into trouble and was also smart in his own zone, and didn't lose too many battles. Had trouble today getting his shot through the net as Baie-Comeau did a real nice job of getting in their way.

November 11, 2013 – Kootenay Ice vs Calgary Hitmen (WHL)

Koo #2, Murray, Troy (2015) – Good read to jump a passing route and break up a 3-on-2. Had trouble maintaining his balance today and lost an edge a couple times. Maintained composure under pressure, but made a few soft plays in his own end. First pass and skating still need work.

Koo #12, Philp, Luke (2014) – Played centre at even strength. Good speed from the outside. Played the point on the 1st power play unit and was able to thread a few passes through traffic to teammates in scoring positions. Not overly big, but he showed some skill, defensive awareness and a good amount of hustle.

Koo #14, Descheneau, Jaedon (2014) – The diminutive winger passed over at last year's draft continued his strong offensive play. Parked himself beside the net and was rewarded with a pair of goal mouth tap-ins on the night. Exceptional passing skills – showed he was able to connect on some long passes to hit teammates in stride, as well as make precise passes through traffic. Good vision.

Koo #16, Elyniuk, Hudson (2015) – Had limited ice-time on the day. Was on the receiving end of a couple big hits. Has a good-sized frame, but needs to get stronger. Skating needs to improve – particularly his first few steps.

Koo #23, Reinhart, Sam (2014) – Good awareness away from the puck. Strong position play at all ends of the rink. Excellent awareness and touch to spring Deschenau for a partial breakaway after Reinhart drew a defender to himself. Used often on the penalty kill today. Reinhart was heavily involved in creating a couple good scoring chances that eventually resulted in goals despite him not being credited for assists. Showed good patience with the puck.

Cal #2, Thrower, Josh (2014) – DNP

Cal #16, Babych, Cal (2015) – Showed flashes of skill and good hands, but still doesn't look comfortable playing at this level yet. Had a couple turnovers on bad passes.

Cal #18, Virtanen, Jake (2014) – Used at center today. Didn't outright win draws, but was often successful at tying up his opponent until his wingers recovered the puck for him. Was around the puck a lot on the night, but wasn't able to do much with his passes. He was very casual with the puck, but kept things pretty simple and made sure he was able to clear his own zone. He was more successful when he carried the puck up ice. Is able to handle the puck at high speed and drives hard to the net (perhaps too hard on the night as he was assessed a couple goalie interference penalties). One of the few Hitmen able to create scoring chances on the night.

Cal #29, Fazleev, Radel (2014) – Kept the puck moving in the right direction, but is still adjusting the WHL style of play.

Game Notes: Despite a roughly even shot count, Calgary was sluggish and drastically out-played on the night in a 5-1 Kootenay win. Kootenay's top line controlled the play for the most part. That line was able to score some key goals at both even strength and on the power play that effectively took Calgary right out of the game.

Vancouver Giants vs Everett Silvertips November 11, 2013 (WHL Regular Season)

Evt #10 C Sandhu Tyler (2014). Not much to his game tonight, Looked like he showed up and was just another body on the bench in my opinion. Had a few strong shifts, using his speed to create a couple good scoring chances off the rush. Played a pretty consistent game on the defensive side.

Evt #89 C Nikolishin Ivan (2014). Unleashed that quick cannon and was rewarded with a nice goal. Kids has decent hockey IQ. Set up a couple golden scoring chances with crisp passing. Was decent on the draw tonight winning 50% of his face offs. His defensive play was strong supporting the D down low. Showed good compete level battling in the corners.

EVT #12 W Leedahl Dawson (2014). Brings energy to his team, played his typical crash and bang style. Couple decent scoring chances but couldn't pull the trigger tonight. Kid works hard and plays with an edge, needs to open up more offensively.

VAN #6 D Atwal Arvin (2014.) Good size defender with decent skating. Played an aggressive game, did not shy away from the physical play. Showed a good active stick shutting down the scoring lanes. Got burned a couple times tonight and needs to have head on a swivel more often. Nothing to special about Atwal tonight.

Van #5 D Morrison Tyler (2014). Had a couple good shifts battling in the corners. Made a few good outlet passes out of the zone. Nothing stood out about his game that say WOW look at me. Stay home defenseman who played a quite but productive game.

Regina pats vs Everett Silvertips November 13, 2013 (WHL Regular Season)

EVT #10 Sandhu Tyler (2014). Played with passion tonight, looked the energizer bunny in all three zone banging anything that touch the puck. Reginas defense struggle to keep up with sandhu quickness most of the game. He snipe 3 goals tonight and his offensive touch is starting to show. His defensive game struggled at times tonight.

EVT #89 C Nikolishin Ivan (2014). He brought strong presence to his defensive game tonight, shutting down the passing lanes with an active stick and throwing his weight around along the wall. He played like that fly on wall you just can't get to go away. Nice crisp passing in all 3 zones. Strong on the face off. Very patient with the puck always looking to make a play. In my opinion he needs to pull the trigger a little more and unleash the booming shot.

EVT #12 W Leedahl Dawson (2014). Not his best game, looked tired tonight. Couple good shifts with energy but just not much there tonight.

REG #29 C Hunt Dryden (2014). 2 goals and 1 assist. This kid is a very shifty player, he seems to slide into the scoring areas untouched. Had a couple golden chances to finish off the hat trick but just could not finish. Is not afraid to be physical and battles hard in the corners. Has some offensive talents that have yet to blossom full scope. Has lots of offensive tools to play with. I do question his defensive responsibilities, needs to focus on both side of the puck at times.

November 15, 2013, Kootenay Ice vs Prince Albert Raiders (WHL Regular Season)

Koo #2, Murray, Troy (2015) – Steady young defenseman. As the season has progressed, Murray has looked more comfortable at the offensive end. Nothing spectacular about his game, but the tenth overall pick in the 2012 WHL Bantam Draft has shown that he can contribute at the WHL level. Another steady game for the youngster tonight.

Koo #16, Elyniuk, Hudson (2016) – A good energy player that likes to crash and bang when he can. Elyniuk needs to improve his first couple steps. Once he gets going, he can pick up good speed, but he struggles on his edges too. Skating as a whole could improve. Was pretty quiet on the night.

Koo #23, Reinhart, Sam (2014) – Kootenay's captain. Reinhart was able to release a hard shot while at top speed. Continues to see the ice extremely well. Was able to support own zone breakouts on a couple occasions by finding empty space to dump the puck where only his teammates would be able to get it. Had a couple decent chances in the first period, but was held in check with just a single second assist on the night.

PA #4, Guhle, Brendan (2015) – The #3 overall pick in the 2012 WHL Bantam draft has looked at home in his first WHL season. A very smooth skater in all aspects. Has excellent size and he uses it well to force forwards to the outside, while defending. Is not overly physical, but uses his stick very effectively. Defended very well. His offense hasn't yet translated at this level. Despite the lack of offense at this time, Guhle will still be valued by NHL teams in 2015 for his combination of steady defensive play combined with good smarts, size and skating abilities.

PA #5, Andrlik, Tomas (2014) – A late '95-born Czech defender. Andrlik was hesitant with the puck and didn't really show any defining qualities on the night. Average size, made a decent first pass, average skater.

PA #19, Gardiner, Reid (2014) – Good size. Was able to create turnovers on the forecheck. While he gets around the ice alright, Gardiner's skating could use some improvement. Worked hard and read the play well off the rush. Had a few good chances in the slot due to his ability to understand where the puck would be. Could use some work on his shot regarding both his strength and release.

PA #21, Gennaro, Matteo (2015) – Big winger had a couple good chances on the night. Has a heavy shot and does well to put himself in scoring position. Has a long stride and is able to generate speed pretty quickly for his size. Worth watching for 2015.

PA #29, Draisaitl, Leon (2014) – Wears an 'A'. Raiders' #1 center since arriving in Prince Albert last season. Great size and he sees the ice well. A solid all-around center with good passing abilities. His main weakness is his skating ability as he lacks an explosive first step. Draisaitl looked passive at times as he doesn't needlessly use energy. That being said, a little more urgency when engaged in puck battles would be welcomed. Had a pair of assists on the night – one was a simple 2nd assist while the other was a nice saucer pass through penalty killers to Morrissey for a PP goal.

PA #33, McBride, Nick (2015) – Backup goalie. DNP.

Game notes: This key game showcased a pair of potential lottery picks in the upcoming draft competing head to head in the Reinhart vs Draisaitl matchup. Reinhart had the early advantage with superior skating and willingness to work in the corners. By the end of the game, both players played good games, but it was Draisaitl helping his team walk away with a 3-2 win over the visiting Ice with a pair of assists.

Portland WinterHawks vs Everett Silvertips November 15 2013 (WHL)

EVT #10 C Sandhu Tyler (2014). Had a nice gino tonight. Looked like a spark plug tonight firing on all cylinders, had a couple good scoring chances in close but couldn't pull the trigger. His quickness just creates offense chances. Was strong in the defensive zone, blocked a couple shots and made good first passes out of the zone was patient with the puck and not forcing the play.

EVT #89 C Nikolishin Ivan (2014). Was waiting 3 periods for him to get fired up. Not his best game so far but did the little things tonight for the win. Was strong on the draws again tonight and is always an offensive threat when he has possession of the puck, showed his vision with pin point passing.

EVT #12 W Leedahl Dawson (2014). Brings energy to his team, played his typical crash and bang style. Waiting for his offensive talents to blossom this year.

PORT #9 C De Leo Chase (2014) Mighty mouse was left off the score sheet but played a very consistent game. He moved the puck well through all 3 zones, very dangerous off the rush with his speed and offensive creativity. Would like to see him get more physical in the defensive zone/corners. All-around player with lots of tools to use in his tool box.

PORT # 22 W Schoenborn Alex (2014). Big power forward with some offensive upside to his game. Likes to battle and compete. Crash and bang style player around the corners and boards. A little more polished then Iverson in my opinion.

PORT #13 W Iverson Keegan (2014). Big strong power forward type. Protects the puck well and can be very tenacious around the corners and along the boards. I would have like to see him drive the net more often and fight for space in the scoring areas.

PORT #23 C Turgeon Dominic (2014). Decent two way type center. Looked somewhat timid to physical play in the corners. Was ok at best in the faceoff circle tonight. Nothing really stood out from this game.

Prince George Cougars vs Everett Silvertips November 16, 2013 (WHL Regular Season)

EVT #10 C Sandhu Tyler (2014.) Used his speed to slide into the scoring areas but could not finish tonight. Good puck protection and was showing patients trying to set up rather than force the play. Average game on the both side of the puck for Sandhu tonight.

EVT #89 C Nikolishin Ivan (2014). Played an average game nothing stood out and said look at me tonight. Was consistent in all 3 zones, played the body and used good angles. Was strong on the draw winning a good percentage.

EVT #12 W Leedahl Dawson (2014). Nothing special tonight, played a consistent game on both side of the puck. Had a couple shifts with good offensive chances but couldn't finish. Played solid in the corners winning the battles.

PG #29 D Grewal Raymond (2014). Strong D-man who plays with an edge. Overall had a decent game, played the body well and used decent angles. Needs to shut down the passing lanes more often with an active stick and keep his head on a swivel. Has some tools in the shed but they need some polishing.

Nov 16, 2013. Charlottetown Islanders vs Moncton Wildcats (QMJHL)

CHA #4 LD, Laliberté, Kevin (2014) Laliberté is a fine young defenseman used mostly at even strength. On some occasions, he was caught out of position in his zone as he was trying to retrieve possession of the puck. I liked his backward skating, as he never lost his balance. His skating was fast enough that no Moncton Wildcats' player not named Barbashev was able to beat him on the outside. He grew and that helps him in his battles deep in his zone. HIs footwork is efficient at this level and his breakouts passes are fairly good.

CHA #10 C, Kielly, Kameron (2015) Kielly played a well-rounded two-way game. He was the best Islanders center in this game. He worked tirelessly all game long taking away the puck from opponents. He was strong on his skates protecting the puck pretty well along his way to the net. Showed great chemistry with Daniel Sprong displaying his passing skills. He made some great decisions with the puck in the offensive zone.

CHA #11 RW, Sprong, Daniel (2015) This guy is really a threat offensively. He was always around the puck, controlling it like a seasoned veteran. He is already the best puck handler in the Q next to Jonathan Drouin. He set up some great plays on the powerplay where he was really dangerous. He's a dynamic skater who gains his top speed quickly. With his quick changes of direction, he can get free spaces in a second, which allowed him to create good shooting lanes. Compared to last year, he really improved on his defensive game. He knows where to go to help the transition game, although he does cheat a bit. He scored a heck of goal in the shootouts and he made a great cross-ice pass on Anthony Cortese's goal.

CHA #19 C, Goulet, Alexandre (2014) Goulet is almost the same player I saw last year in Midget AAA. His speed allows him to beat defenders on the rush on the outside. After he beat them, he often takes a shot good for a rebound. When the play is set up in the offensive zone, he is an adequate passer. He was responsible in his zone and was successful in the faceoff circle.

CHA #26 LW, Pépin, Alexis (2014) He's really taken a step back since last season. He is nowhere near as fast than he was and that affects his game overall. He's always late on the play and he became somewhat of a liability in his zone. He's still making quick decisions with the puck and he's great protecting the puck. When he has the time to take a shot, his wrist shot is hard and accurate.

MON #2 LD, Holwell, Adam (2015) Holwell is pretty calm with the puck, gets his shot through to the net and doesn't rush or panic to make a play. He's also very well positioned on the ice relative to the situation. Played on the first powerplay unit with Ivan Barbashev and Conor Garland.

MON #8 LW, Garland, Conor (2014) Garland showed his quick feet more than once when he is around the wall. When a defenseman is fast and quick enough to get close to him, he's easy to push around. He is extremely creative and has pretty good hands. He was also smart enough to offer teammates options in the offensive zone and he plays in the traffic.

MON #22 C, Barbashev, Ivan (2014) I have rarely seen a guy that committed both ways. His strides are powerful and he's a great skater when going a long distance. He created great offensive opportunities for his teammates with vision and made some beautiful one-touch and drop passes. He used his body well to create spaces for him in the offensive zone.

FINAL SCORE: 3-2 CHA SO

November 17, 2013 – S.S. Marie Greyhounds at Kitchener Rangers (OHL)

SOO #14 RW Pastorious, Nick (2014) - Nick received limited action in this game but provided a good physical presence. He dropped the gloves and threw several good shots. He took a few as well but the shots he took didn't really seem to affect him.

SOO #17 RC Miller, David (2014) - Miller has great hands and controlled the puck well in small spaces. He did a great job using his puck control ability to score the Greyhounds' third goal of the game. He took a checking from behind penalty in this game, but did so to save a goal. His lack of size hurt him a little as he got knocked around a bit in this game.

SOO #19 LC McCann, Jared (2014) - Jared made a few creative passes to set up scoring chances for his team. He mishandled the puck on several occasions. He reads the play extremely well and gets himself into great positions to do some damage but isn't finishing when he's getting these chances. Regardless of this he was extremely impactful in the face-off circle and won a ton of draws for his team.

SOO #20 RW Mallette, Trent (2014) - Trent showed very good skating ability and pressure on the forecheck. He was strong on the Greyhounds' penalty kill applying pressure on the point very well.

SOO #22 LD Spinozzi, Kevin (2014) - Spinozzi provided great physicality in this game. He was physical down low and finished his checks every chance he got. He was also very tough battling in the slot. He did go out of position to finish one of his hits which directly resulted in a two on one chance for Kitchener. He protects the puck well using his size to fend off checkers. His skating is decent but he could benefit from getting quicker.

SOO #27 LW Bunting, Michael (2014*) - Michael did a little bit of everything in this game. He showed good moves with the puck driving the wing. The end of the play resulted in the Greyhounds' second goal of the game. He was willing to finish his checks, hustles back defensively and puts pressure on the puck carrier.

SOO #51 LD Jenkins, Kyle (2014) - Kyle displayed good skating and mobility in all directions. He made great simple decisions with the puck making short passes and getting the puck deep. But he also made a perfect two line pass to set up a partial break. He isn't the biggest defenseman but he got surprising power in his hits.

KIT #10 RD Schmidt, Logan (2014) - Logan has progressed well for the Rangers this year. He possesses a hard shot from the point and keeps it low and deflectable. He skates effectively well and rushes the puck well. He generally makes the smart safe play with the puck consistently, however he seems to get a little rattled under pressure and can mishandle the puck when pressured.

KIT #17 LW Kohn, Mason (2015) - Mason was pretty good tonight using his quickness to pressure opponents. He also showed quick hands and a hard shot.

KIT #20 RW Magyar, Nick (2014) - Nick was impactful in this game scoring two goals for Kitchener, one of which was the winning goal. He holds down smart positioning in the slot and created disruption in this area. On his first goal he initially got robbed, but stuck with the play and scored the rebound. He scored the second goal from almost the exact same spot. He reads the play well and seems to be one step ahead all the time. He also showed some passing ability moving the puck up ice from his own zone. Nick also helped set up the game winning goal for his team.

KIT #27 LW Llewellyn, Darby (2014) - Darby made a few great passes in this game, some of which his linemates couldn't finish on. However he did play a big part in setting up Kitchener's game winning goal. He was fairly reliable defensively for his team and skates well. He needs to look before passing at times because he turned the puck over multiple times due to not taking a look before making the play.

KIT #44 RD Hora, Frank (2014) - Frank was able to make a few solid simple plays with the puck under pressure. He was pretty reliable defensively tying up opponents in the slot area and good stick in a one on one rush. He received good power play ice but was a little hit or miss with the puck. He has a good powerful shot that hits the net about half the time. His shot created a rebound that resulted in Kitchener's second goal of the game. He did however made a few bad decisions resulting in the puck heading down the ice.

KIT #72 LC MacInnis, Ryan (2014) - Ryan got a several good scoring chances due to strong positioning but couldn't finish a lot of those chances. He did however use a powerful wrist shot with good accuracy to score mid blocker side for the eventual game winning goal in the third period. His skating needs improvement.

KIT #93 RW Davies, Mike (2015) - Mike provided good work on the forecheck and finished his checks. He was also willing to throw himself in front of a few shots in the defensive zone. He did struggle with the puck in all zones and showed limited puck handling ability. He got into position for a few offensive chances but missed on them.

Scouts Notes: Kitchener came to play today and were the better team in the first period. However, after Sault Ste. Marie scored two goals on Jordan DeKort (2014*) that were a little soft, they would take a 2-0 lead into the second period. Kitchener continued to apply pressure but Matt Murray (Pittsburgh) did an outstanding job robbing Kitchener over and over again. Eventually in the third the Rangers' attack got to the Hounds. When it was all over Kitchener overcame 2-0 and 3-1 deficits and scored 5 unanswered goals to take a 6-3 win over Sault Ste. Marie.

November 22, 2013 Youngstown Phantoms vs Lincoln Stars (USHL)

YNG #7 Letunov, Maxim C (2014) – Great work on power play. Had two points, PP goal and assist on the night. Scored with a rocket top-shelf from the circles off a feed from Kyle Connor in the closing stages of the second period to bring the Phantoms back within one. Worked relentlessly on the backcheck causing multiple turnovers in the defensive zone. Caused a turnover in the neutral zone which led to Connor's goal. Showed great vision on the ice and incredibly smart with the puck. A truly top-notch performance from Letunov on the night.

YNG #12 Piccinich, JJ (2014) RW – Showed flashes of great potential mixed in with some questionable decisions. Gave the puck away more than once and took some ill-advised shots from low percentage areas. Not afraid to shoot from anywhere on the ice, sometimes to the point of bad decisions leading to turnovers in the offensive zone. Solid skater. Needs some polish before jumping to the next level. Worked well with Letunov and Connor on the Phantoms first PP unit.

YNG #18 Connor, Kyle (2015) C – Was probably the best player on the ice as a '97. Great skater, could beat anyone on Lincoln one on one. Had two points on the evening, scoring a goal and adding an assist to go with it. Assist on Letunov's second period goal displayed his skating ability and vision to see Letunov streaking in the middle of the ice and find his stick for the goal. Connor's goal came off a Lincoln turnover in the neutral zone on a 2-on-1 with Letunov who passed it Connor for the finish. Very impressive performance from Connor.

LIN #4 Daniel Willett (2014) LD – Willett didn't get much playing time on the night. He's on Lincoln's third pairing. His size is definitely what's holding him back. He's got a good head on his shoulders and his hockey sense is there, he just can't be a physical force on the back end and he just can't take long enough strides to keep up once he gets beat. He had a secondary assist on Lincoln's second goal and won the game on a nice shootout goal.

Scout's notes: This was a very exciting game to be at. To see Youngstown's NHL prospects (Connor and Letunov) step up and play well was a treat. Lincoln jumped out to a 2-0 lead in the first but Youngstown just kept with them eventually tying the game at 3-3 with five minutes left in the third. After a scoreless overtime, Lincoln's Daniel Willett (2014) scored on a great shootout goal to win the game.

November 22, 2013 – Erie Otters at London Knights (OHL)

ERI #11 RW Hodgson, Hayden (2014) - Hayden didn't play a huge factor in this game one way or the other. He delivered some solid hits along the wall and finished his check effectively. He skates moderately well and showed decent puck handling skills. There really doesn't seem to be any glaring weakness in his game. However he doesn't seem to possess any standout skills either.

ERI #15 LC Pettit, Kyle (2014) - Kyle was effective for his team tonight playing limited ice. He delivered a number of punishing hits in this game in all three zones. He has outstanding defensive positioning and was extremely reliable in his own zone. He was rewarded with a little short handed action and faired well.

ERI #19 RC Strome, Dylan (2015) - Dylan was noticeable on a few occasions working hard and battling. He didn't create much offensively and was out of position in the defensive zone. He also struggled at times to keep up with the play. He showed flashes of his skill level in this game but will need to continue to work at keeping pace with the action on a regular basis.

ERI #24 D Raddysh, Darren (2014) - Darren skates well in all directions. He keeps up with quick skaters while maintaining his defensive positioning. He is also capable of skating the puck out of trouble. While he received a lot of ice and played an important role for Erie he didn't make a big impact on the play positively or negatively.

ERI #44 RD Dermott, Travis (2015) - Travis played a gritty and agitating role for Erie getting under the skin of the opposition. He struggled with the puck on a few occasions at the offensive line which resulted in his team losing their presence in the offensive zone. He also mishandled the puck a few times in his own zone which got his team into trouble.

ERI #97 LC McDavid, Connor (2015) - In the first period Connor picked up a lose puck in the neutral zone and exploded for a breakaway chance but got robbed going five hole. He showed great hands in the slot making a quick and precise pass to create a great scoring opportunity. He started out a little slow in this game but started creating more offense as it went along despite not touching the puck quite as often as he usually does.

LON #11 RW MacDonald, Owen (2014) - Owen is an undersized forward but he put together an excellent performance with limited ice time tonight. He forechecks hard and works intensely along the wall winning battles against much bigger players. He is a strong skater and used this ability on the forecheck and on the backcheck competing in all three zones. Despite his size he delivered a couple of solid hits.

LON #14 LW Elie, Tristan (2014) - This was Tristan's OHL debut and he played a pretty solid game with limited ice. He skates well and battled hard on the wall beating veteran opponents along the wall. He also plays physical despite not having the size his brother Remi possesses.

LON #93 RC Marner, Mitchell (2015) - Marner utilized his speed and skills on a few occasions in this game to open up a few scoring chances. He made an excellent pass through a defenseman to set up London's third goal.

Scouts Notes: London showed their new look defense in this game and received a great effort from Zach Bell (Free Agent) and Nikita Zadorov (London) making their regular season debut for the Knights. Oscar Dansk (Columbus) looked very shaky to open the game which eventually lead to London putting two goals on the board in the first twenty minutes. He played better after settling in for the last 40 minutes. Santino Centorame (2014) lost a battle directly resulting in the Erie Otters cutting the Knights lead to 2-1. However goals from Bo Horvat (Vancouver) and Chris Tierney (San Jose) along with an outstanding goaltending performance from Anthony Stolarz (Philadelphia) the Knights were able to lock down the 4-1 win.

November 23, 2013 – Windsor Spitfires at London Knights (OHL)

WSR #11 LW Yazkov, Nikita (2014) - Nikita was noticeable tonight for his quick hands and his good first step. He has great quickness and is very elusive, he does however get ahead of himself from time to time and loses the puck.

WSR #19 LC Foss, Ryan (2014) - Ryan provided good pressure and uses his stick well on the forecheck. He played the puck off the wall instead of looking for options when initiating the rush. He panicked with the puck in his own zone under pressure in the first period putting it over the glass. London scored their second goal on the ensuing power play.

WSR #40 LC Moore, Ryan (2015) - Ryan is an excellent skater and possesses explosive speed. He's a little undersized but is willing to hit much bigger opponents.

WSR #66 RW Ho-Sang, Josh (2014) - Josh made some slick passes early on and at several different points in this game. He is very good at leading the puck to where his intended target will be making him very dangerous in all zones with the puck. He also gets the puck deep effectively instead of trying to take on the whole team. He was frustrating when it came to battles as he wouldn't engage along the wall. He occasionally forced a turnover with his stick but evne on the power play where he used his great speed on the rush, but lost the puck he showed no compete to try and get it back. He also would just stand around when his team didn't have the puck a few times. He was way too easily knocked around by opposing defenders on the power play in the slot and behind the net. He left on the power play after taking a big hit behind the net. However he returned a few shifts later. He did cover for his defensman well showing a very good stick when momentarily playing the defensive position. While there is no questioning Josh's skill level, he does a lot of things that are extremely frustrating and will need to be worked out of his game before he has a chance of being successful at the next level. He also took several face-off's despite opening the game at right wing, but lost most of those draws.

WSR #81 LW Verbeek, Ryan (2014) - Ryan showed good positioning in the offensive zone and kept his feet moving opening himself up. He also showed decent skills and a good move one on one for a scoring chance. While he flashed a little skill he still seems to be at his best when playing a hard checking game.

WSR #96 LW DiGiacinto, Cristiano (2014) - Christiano's skating is very uncomfortable as he looks like he's running on ice. He showed a good two-way game tonight hurrying on the backcheck to break up a few plays, however his reaction time needs to improve as he was caught observing on one scoring chance he likely could have prevented. He was also willing to block shots for his team. He got involved a few times offensively, most notably a two on one break but tried to force the pass back to his teammate instead of taking the shot which was the much clearer option.

LON #10 LC Dvorak, Christian (2014) - Christian provided another strong two-way presence tonight hurrying on the backcheck and always seemed to be the first forward back defensively every time. He showed good moves one on one and added in some excellent passes to create chances. He did however try to force a few plays throwing the puck away in the offensive zone a few times.

LON #11 RW MacDonald, Owen (2014) - Owen skates well and isn't intimidated by bigger players delivering some solid hits down low. Despite playing in limited action he was involved in a few scoring chances making a great pass early in the game to create a chance. He was also set up for a great opportunity but couldn't finish on it. Owen proved he would easily be a top 9 player on most OHL teams, but is caught by the great forward depth of the Knights. However he is taking advantage of the playing time he is being given.

LON #16 LW Domi, Max (Phoenix) - After playing maybe his worst game of the season last night, Max responded with possible his greatest effort of the season. Max directly set up three of London's four goals in this game. The first he mishandled the puck but recovered and quickly made a strong centering pass out front. The second was an excellent cross ice pass on the power play to set up Bo Horvat. He also factored into the fourth goal making a great pass to set up Chris Tierney. Every single shift he was flying using his elusiveness and excellent vision to create plays for his teammates. After a few performances this year that were a little unbecoming of his talents, Max showed tonight why he can be a game breaker for his team this year, and why he deserved to be a high selection in last year's draft.

LON #53 LC Horvat, Bo (Vancouver) - Bo had a great game tonight and played a factor in his team's victory. He forced several turnovers, was strong in the face-off circle and unloaded a massive one-timer for London's second goal. He then followed that up with a great pass to set up London's third goal. While Bo is most recognized for his strong two-way play he showed tonight exactly how underrated his shot is.

LON #93 RC Marner, Mitchell (2015) - Mitchell played outstanding all game long and was a huge impact on the Knights and easily one of the best players in this game. He went hard to the net on the rush and finished on a pass to score London's first goal. Right after the centre ice face-off following his goal he took the puck in and made a great pass to set up a big scoring chance. Throughout this game it seemed every time he was on the ice he was creating offense and easily could have factored into a few more goals with the chances he created. He can make great passes from his own zone up the ice as well and set up partial breakaways. In the third he made yet another outstanding pass to create the play that directly resulted in the Knights' fourth goal.

Scouts Notes: The London Knights played an extremely impressive 60 minutes of hockey tonight. While the Windsor Spitfires came into Budweiser Gardens and put forward a strong effort the Knights just suffocated the life out of the Spits and never gave them an inch all game long. Anthony Stolarz (Philadelphia) recorded his third shutout of the season. While he played strong when needed, he was rarely challenged due to a tight defensive effort by the Knights'. Alex Fotinos (2014) was chased after the fourth goal of the game but deserves a ton of credit as he made some excellent saves in this game and really didn't have much of a chance on any of London's four goals. While the final score was 4-0 for London, the Spitfires didn't play a bad game at all. London was simply able to capitalize on some picture perfect plays.

Nov 23, 2013. Moncton Wildcats vs Chicoutimi Sagueneéns (QMJHL)

MON #2 LD, Holwell, Adam (2015) Holwell was his usual self in Chicoutimi. He has a high hockey IQ and was a fixture on the first powerplay unit of his team once again. His coverage overall was pretty effective. He still needs to improve his footwork a bit.

MON #4 LD, Sweeney, Jacob (2014) Sweeney is logging a lot of minutes. He didn't look bad in close range battles and his breakout passes were surprisingly good. His vision is somewhat limited, but he can reach his closest teammate with an accurate pass. With his large frame, I was amazed by how he was able to maintain his gap properly on a bigger ice surface like in Chicoutimi.

MON #8 LW, Garland, Conor (2014) Garland had a quiet game. Was still creating some good opportunities from the boards thanks to his shiftiness. Otherwise, even if he had plenty of space, he played more on the perimeter.

MON #11 C, Olivier, Mathieu (2015) Olivier is more suited on the wing as he has tunnel vision. His work ethic is great and his two-way game is well above average for a 16-year-old forward. He can follow the pace of a QMJHL game and is great on the forecheck.

MON #22 C, Barbashev, Ivan (2014) Barbashev played a strong two-way game once again. He finished his checks every time he had the opportunity. He displayed his great offensive hockey sense all game long, but you see that he lacked that extra gear in order to create spaces faster.

MON #26 C, Simpson, Mark (2014) He is a lanky kid that played in the MHL last year. He's six-foot-five and his skating stride is a bit awkward. He proved to me that he could use his long reach effectively on the forecheck. His straight-line speed is OK and I liked his intensity. His hockey sense in general is quite good and he played a ton of minutes.

CHI #44 RD, Carrier, Scott (2014) Carrier had a good game for a guy that was undressed most of the time this year. He played the body often in his battles along the wall and he used the boards effectively in order to get the puck out of his zone. He played a steady, simple and physical game.

CHI #28 LD, Lyamkin, Nikita (2014) The more I see him, the more I'm disappointed. On some occasions, it seems like he does not know how to play defensively. He can't control his gap and he is all over the place in his zone. In order to be effective, he needs to rush the puck but his coach doesn't allow him to do so. When he started rushing in the third, his confidence level went up and his defensive game was better.

CHI #24 C, Gignac, William (2015) Gignac created some great chances on the rush playing with Charles Hudon and Simon Tremblay and he really gave his best in this game. He has high hockey IQ, but he's way too small at the moment in order to be considered as a viable NHL prospect.

FINAL SCORE: 2-0 MON

Blainville-Boisbriand vs Drummondville Voltigeurs (QMJHL) November 29th 2013

Blainville-Boisbriand

#5 Nathanael Halbert Def (2014): Used in a shutdown role tonight, paired with Daniel Walcott who is the more offensive of the two. Halbert was strong in his zone, liked his gap control and he understands how to play in a shutdown role with strong positioning plays. Doesn't have the quickest feet, which can get him into trouble when he's immobile on the ice. Needs to keep his game simple with the puck as he got into trouble trying to do too much with it tonight on a couple of occasions. Also saw ice time on the power play.

#18 Julien Bahl Def (2014): Not the best game out of Bahl tonight, as his passing game was off, and I saw him miss easy passes. On one shift, he tried to do too much with the puck, which resulted in a neutral zone turnover. However, defensively he was good and never panicked when he was pressured deep in his zone. Used in a shutdown / PK role, where he's at his best.

#85 Daniel Walcott Def (2014): Saw a lot of ice time again tonight, as he played in every situation of the game. Walcott covers a lot of space on the ice thanks to his great skating ability; I saw him join and lead the rush many times tonight. Although he is not a huge player, he can still throw some good hits, and his powerful lower body helps with that. On his team's first goal he made the whole play happen by taking a loose puck in front of his net and making a quick pass to Philippe Sanche, who chipped the puck into the boards back to Walcott, who went end to end to create a 2 on 1. He missed his original shot, but was able to get a 2nd crack at it by sending the puck right to Frederic Bergeron's stick in front of the net to tie the game at 1. Liked how he used his stick in the defensive zone, he is very active and has a good gap control versus opposing forwards on the rush. Made a great defensive play on the PK late in the game with the scored tied at 2, by blocking a shot, finishing his hit, and then blocking a pass right in the slot where he was able to clear the puck out of his zone. Loved the anticipation he showed on that play.

#8 Emile Aronsson C (2014): From his first shift, you could see the Swede has a strong hockey IQ, coming back deep in his zone to help his defensemen often during the course of this game. Aronsson was strong in the faceoff circle as well tonight and was used in every situation of the game by his coach, Jean-Francois Houle. Didn't create a lot of offense but I did appreciate how he protected the puck in the offensive zone and kept it in the Voltigeurs' zone.

#71 Nikita Jevpalovs C (2014): The Latvian forward was good for the Armada tonight; made a real nice little pass to Philippe Sanche by attracting one defenseman to him which led Sanche to a 2 on 1 for the second Armada goal. Showed throughout the game that he has quick hands and a fast release on his shot.

#92 Marcus Hinds Rw (2014) Hinds has a defensive role on the Armada squad and was very effective in this game. He was tremendous on the PK, blocking shots and breaking up plays with an active stick. Up and down winger with nice size, he's tough to contain along the wall and did a great job on the forecheck. Uses his size well to protect the puck in the offensive end.

Drummondville Voltigeurs

#4 Frederic Aubé Def (2014): Played on the Voltigeurs' 3rd pair of defensemen, Aubé's first pass was decent tonight and he kept his game simple. Got caught on one occasion with his feet not moving, which led to an odd man rush for the Armada. A non-flashy player that does his work without much fanfare. As a rookie, he doesn't see a lot of ice time on the special teams' units, but I could see his PK minutes increase as he gains experience.

#6 Julien Carignan-Labbé Def (2015): Was paired with Aubé on the Voltigeurs 3rd pair. One thing is clear with Carignan-Labbé: he likes to play a physical game and will clear the front of the net. On the flipside, he got caught trying to be too aggressive at his blueline going for a big hit. Saved an Armada goal when the puck went through his goaltender and he took it just before it could cross the red line.

#96 Dexter Weber Def (2014): Used in all facets of the game, used on the 2nd pp unit for the Voltigeurs and I like how he didn't hesitate at putting pucks on net. Moved the puck well to his forwards, and is very helpful to his team's transition game. Liked his footwork; when he rushed into his own zone, he was able to get enough separation between him and a forechecker and made a quick pass to get out of danger. He had a good, active stick on the PK as well tonight.

#11 Joey Ratelle Rw (2014): Didn't notice him in the first 2 periods, but he came alive in the 3rd with some real good shifts from his line. Not known for his skating abilities, but showed some nice speed going wide on an Armada defenseman, and seconds later came close to scoring by crashing the net and failing to materialize on a juicy rebound in front of the Armada goal. On another sequence, I liked how he cut into the middle of the ice after passing the blueline to give himself a better shooting angle, unfortunately, he was robbed by the glove of Etienne Marcoux of the Armada.

#19 Cam Askew C/RW (2015): Like Ratelle, I didn't see a lot of him in the first 2 periods, but he started being more active in the 3rd . His line did a terrific job putting pressure on the Armada defense and keeping the puck deep in their zone. Not much in terms of scoring chances came from Askew but he did stuff a coach will appreciate in this period. Made a real nice steal in the period as well, anticipated a pass from an Armada defenseman in their zone, but couldn't convert this into a scoring chance.

#95 Georgs Golovkovs C (2015): Quiet game from the Latvian forward, didn't notice him much at all during the game. He is at his best when he has the puck, but he barely touched it all night. Saw some good puck protection from him but it resulted in no offensive chances.

#55 Sergei Boikov Def (2014): Compete level was higher tonight from previous viewings, he worked harder along the wall to win more one on one battles. He needs to keep his play simple with the puck as he got into trouble trying to do too much when rushing it.

#15 Nikolas Brouillard Def (2014): Brouillard got tons of ice time, was featured on every power play and is very good at moving the puck on the man advantage. I thought that tonight his pass accuracy was lacking a little bit, as I have seen him do much better in this area. Not shy to join the rush, as he did in the 3rd period when he followed the rush to the net and had a grade-A scoring chance, but couldn't get enough wood on the puck after a weak rebound. Defensively, though, he struggled with opposing forwards challenging him wide and taking the puck to the net, and his lack of size showed in those sequences.

Saskatoon Blades vs Everett Silvertips November 30 2013 (WHL Regular Season)

EVT #10 C Sandhu Tyler (2014). Played an overall decent game, was very affective on both sides of the puck tonight. Used his speed to create offensive and get into scoring position. Was physical all the boards and played a solid defensive game.

EVT #89 C Nikolishin Ivan (2014). Ivan showed up tonight 1 goal and 2 assists. Was nothing but an offensive threat tonight, the puck seem to find his tape. He was threading the needle, nice puck protection to defend off and delivered a couple beauty sauce passes but Everett couldn't bang it home. Best player on the ice tonight in my opinion.

EVT #12 W Leedhal Dawson (2014) Played a solid physical game, made some good hits in the zone to force odd man rushes. Good compete level tonight and was tenacious around the corners winning the battles. Always brings energy to every shift.

SASK #27 W Scherbak Nikita (2014). Very underrated player in my opinion. Lots of offensive tools and plays a very defensively sound game. He can dangle and dazzle in tight, or bang along the boards. Likes to have the puck on his stick. High Hockey IQ and decent skater. Might have to make a trip up North to see him play again.

SASK #2 D Coghlan Ryan (2014). Good size d-man, played a physical game, likes to bang and punish. Has some offensive talents. Ryan is a player to watch throughout the year.

SASK #16 C Revel Matt (2014). Ryan was kept off the score sheet tonight, which was a surprise. He was all over the ice, he reminded me of a little pest that won't go away. Showed a tremendous offensive upside to his game and knows the key task to playing a defensive game. Another player in my mind to watch this season.

Sask #55 D Nogier Nelson (2014). Big shut down defender who likes to use active stick to shut down the lanes. Has some decent hockey IQ and was reading the play off the rush forcing everett players to the outside with good 1 on 1 coverage. Played his angles well and does not mind getting physical. Looks to be some offensive upside but looks for like a stay home dman. Player to watch develop throughout the year.

November 30, 2013 – Prince Albert Raiders at Brandon Wheat Kings (WHL)

PA #16 RC Vanstone, Tim (2014) - Vanstone was noticeable on a few occasions in this game for the Raiders by providing a strong forecheck and finishing a few checks deep in the offensive zone.

PA #29 Draisaitl, Leon (2014) - Leon was credited with the opening goal of the game after crashing the net, the puck just happened to hit his skate and went in giving him the goal. Leon showed a strong two way game tonight forcing turnovers in the defensive zone and continuously willing to get deep in the defensive zone to compete for pucks. He was able to create a few chances throughout this game using his passing ability and positional knowledge for scoring chances. Despite his offensive hockey sense he isn't physical, doesn't hit and very rarely uses his size. He was a little streaky in this game in terms of his performance, but certainly saved his best work for the final minutes of the game. He was able to protect the puck in the offensive zone with less than a minute down a goal near the blueline keeping the puck in the offensive zone. He then took the puck out of the corner and made a great pass out front to create the tying goal with only 12 seconds left in the game. Then only 18 seconds into overtime he created the winning goal rushing end to end then making a great pass to set up the overtime winning goal. He showed very good speed on the rush despite his footwork and quickness needing work as he takes quite a bit of time to get going.

BDN #6 LD Pilon, Ryan (2015) - Pilon was pretty quiet early playing it safe but as the game went on he started playing more aggressively with the puck and jumping up in the rush. He showed good elusiveness carrying the puck up ice and his skating has showed clear improvements. His skating also allowed him to get involved in the offensive zone without being a defensive liability. He also showed a good first pass under pressure.

BDN #7 LD Roy, Eric (Calgary) - Eric made an outstanding pass from his goal line to the offensive blue line creating a breakaway chance. He moved the puck well on the power play, but was very risky on multiple occasions in regards to his positioning and at one point completely lacked hustle on what turned into a good scoring chance against his team.

BDN #8 RC Hawryluk, Jayce (2014) - Jayce did a great job on draws when on the wing helping centre get the win. He was extremely elusive along the wall all game long evading contact and slipping away from opponents. He was able to use this ability to help set up Brandon's third goal. He can also cycle the puck intelligently. He made an outstanding move in the first period to beat two defenders and nearly score on the backhand. He is smart and creative with the puck, calm under pressure and possesses quick hands that forces opponents to back off a little. He showed some grit on a few occasions putting a lot of force in his checks and was willing to engage with bigger opponents without hesitation.

BDN #13 LW Bukarts, Rihards (2013) - Bukarts showed skill with the puck and smarts without the puck. He has quick hands and used them to create a few scoring chances. He was hit or miss on the fore check, but was at his best when using his speed. He was a little apprehensive around contact. He possesses excellent positional play in the offensive zone. He was constantly finding ideal positioning in the offensive zone. He practically had an open net on one chance but fanned on the shot. On a few other occasions his teammates didn't realize he was open. He scored later in the game winding up and blasting a slap shot from the top of the circle.

BDN #17 LC Quenneville, John (2014) - Quenneville fired a wrister from the top of the circle to give Brandon their girls goal of the game. He shows decent skating ability and prefers to shoot over pass whenever the opportunity arises. He had a few flashes in this game but was pretty quiet for the most part.

BDN #22 LW Shmyr, Braylon (2015) - Braylon had a few flashes of brilliance in this game showing good speed and hands, particularly in the neutral zone on the rush.

BDN #33 G Papirny, Jordan (2014) - Jordan had a decent game despite allowing five goals. Every goal was either one he had little chance on or was a point blank shot. He does a good job getting to the top of his crease and playing his angles well. He showed good recovery on rebounds he should have had and was fortunate his lack of rebound control didn't affect him more. He made a few very solid good glove saves but was beat primarily glove side point blank when he was scored on.

Scouts Notes: A very back and forth match-up in Brandon as the Raiders jumped out to a 2-0 lead early on. However the Wheat Kings responded with four consecutive goals giving Brandon a 4-2 lead late in the game. It appeared they would hold down the victory but three unanswered goals including one with just 12 seconds left in regulation and another 18 seconds into overtime to give Prince Albert a 5-4 overtime victory. In addition to the reports above, for Prince Albert Josh Morrissey (Winnipeg) scored the second goal of the game after a great rush as he utilized his speed and puck skills to beat the defender then the goaltender.

Portland WinterHawks vs Everett Silvertips December 3 2013 (WHL Regular Season)

EVT #10 C Sandhu Tyler (2014). 1 assist for the speedy winger. Was average tonight and played an excellent two way game. It was good seeing Tyler doing the little things tonight (Blocking shots, Chipping Pucks and Winning battles).

EVT #89 C Nikolishin Ivan (2014). 1 goal and 1 assist tonight. Seen some PP time and was very effective. Probably the best player on the ice for Everett. Ivan played with a little edge tonight was more physical than normal and this type of play created some excellent scoring chances tonight.

EVT #12 W Leedahl Dawson (2014). Nothing more than crash and bang, hitting everything that moves. His game never really changes, his play is mostly consistent every night. You get what you see, a hard working player who brings energy. Still waiting for his offensive upside to blossom.

PORT #9 C De Leo Chase (2014) finished the night with 1 goal and 1 assist, played a very consistent game in all 3 zones. Always very dangerous with his speed and offensive creativity. Played with a little edge tonight throwing around his small frame. Lots of talent, just needs a little size to his small frame.

PORT # 22 W Schoenborn Alex (2014). Had a nice goal tonight, was all over the ice creating some decent offensive chances. Good offensive upside to him game and its starting to show. His defensive game was decent, was aggressive on the 1 on 1 battles winning the puck more often than not. Lots of potential to his game

PORT #13 W Iverson Keegan (2014). Had a nice assist and finished +2. Played physical in the corners and was showing a good compete level tonight. Strong kid who needs to use his size more and battle in front of the net and bang home some garbage.

PORT #23 C Turgeon Dominic (2014). Decent two way type center. Played a sound defensive game, worked hard on both sides of the puck tonight. Could be more physical.

December 4, 2013 – S.S. Marie Greyhounds at London Knights (OHL)

SSM #13 RW Goetz, Keigan (2014) - Keigan played great tonight for the Hounds displaying great energy. He finishes his checks hard and delivered about a handful of massive hits deep in the offensive zone. He provides an excellent forecheck, but also backchecks hard and forces turnovers. He didn't show anything offensively but in terms of a physicality and work ethic he was excellent.

SSM #17 RC Miller, David (2014) - David was strong for Sault Ste. Marie tonight moving the puck extremely well on the power play. He made quick decisions and was at his best when leading the rush making smart passes and quick decisions. He scored the Greyhounds first goal of the game by blocking a horrible puck play by Brady Austin in the slot as the puck went off his shin pad and into the net.

SSM #18 RC Speers, Blake (2015) - Blake received a lot more ice time than in previous viewings this year and made the most of it. He showed flashes of his talent on a few occasions making a great pass to set up a scoring chance and showing good power in his shot. He also provided strong pressure on the backcheck.

SSM #19 LC McCann, Jared (2014) - We certainly saw two sides of Jared McCann tonight. He struggled early and often in the first forty minutes. He turned the puck over in his own zone. He made a good play on the wall to force a turnover but then threw the puck away and down the ice ending the pressure in the zone. He showed his vision creating a few good plays. He was also effective in his own zone competing hard down low, maintaining good positioning and was able to force multiple turnovers. Overall the first two periods were a struggle. McCann really picked it up in the third period especially with about five minutes left he made an outstanding move to split the defensemen then another great move to beat the goaltender to score the Greyhounds second goal and bring them within one goal with 5 minutes to play. He played the majority of the final five minutes of the third and had some great shifts making some excellent passes, getting in great positioning and even made a great deflection that got robbed to give his team a chance. He also has decent skating ability. In addition to this he was outstanding in the face-off circle winning 75% of draws in terms of face-offs won by the centreman. Despite this he was utilized as a winger in the final minute of the game where the Greyhounds lost 3 out of the 4 key draws against the Knights.

SSM #22 LD Spinozzi, Kevin (2014) - Kevin was pretty quiet for the first two periods of this game keeping it simple but he was a lot bigger impact in the third for Sault Ste. Marie. He made a good pinch off the line to get a good scoring chance. He also made some smart passes and held the line very well to keep the play going in the offensive zone. Skating is average at best and while he has good strength he wasn't overly physical today.

SSM #51 LD Jenkins, Kyle (2014) - Kyle is a smooth skating defenseman and showed good patience on the puck rush on multiple occasions. He wasn't a big impact in this game but after taking a penalty in the neutral zone, he got out of the box and received a partial breakaway where he opted to pass to the trailing man and set up a scoring chance.

Scouts Notes: In what will end up being one of the most exciting games of the OHL Season, the Knights were able to hold on to the 3-2 victory in a rare midweek match-up. The action went back and forth but it was Anthony Stolarz (Philadelphia) who made some huge saves early to allow the Knights to take a 1-0 and 3-1 lead. Jared McCann (2014) scored a highlight reel goal to bring it to a 3-2 score but the Greyhounds were unable to score in the final few minutes despite maintaining consistent offensive zone pressure late in the game.

Dec 5, 2013. Baie-Comeau Drakkar vs Chicoutimi Saguenéens (QMJHL)

BAC #3 LD, Vanier, Alexis (2014) Vanier likes to get involved physically along the wall. Whenever he sees the opportunity, he will try to crush the puck carrier at the cost of being out of position. His slapper from the point is really heavy, but it wasn't accurate. His long reach gives him room to adjust himself in open ice confrontation. He played within his limits and that helped him a lot on a bigger ice surface. His size and his point shot are the reasons why we can consider him as a viable NHL prospect.

BAC #21 RD, Meloche, Nicolas (2015) He played with Alexis Vanier. His breakouts are quick and effective. He played the man well on one-on-one's, especially against faster forwards. He's strong enough to not get pushed around during battles for loose pucks. I really like his balance and his footwork allows him to get rid of the pressure. It's also easy for him to take good low hard shots through traffic. He earns big minutes and he delivers. He was their best defenseman in this game.

BAC #15 RW, Imama, Bokondji (2014) When he gets control of the puck, Imama will usually dump it in the offensive zone and he will chase it. He's not overly fast, but he's strong on his skates and he's intimidating the opposition. He made a nice saucer pass on a two-on-one to Félix Girard. Otherwise, you don't notice him that often.

CHI #28 D, Lyamkin, Nikita (2014) He played on the powerplay early in the game. He was able to take effective shots good enough for scoring chances. His lack of strength hinders him in his one-on-one battles and he's not playing that often. He recorded his first assist in about 28 games or so.

CHI #26 LW, Bouchard, Jérémy (2015) He scored a beautiful goal near the end of the first period when he took possession of a loose puck in the offensive zone and he fired it top shelf. He was also a fixture of the first penalty kill unit. He covered passing lanes effectively in those situations.

CHI #55 C, Roy, Nicolas (2015) He displayed his stick handling abilities when he deked two men before using his backhand to put the puck to the net on the second powerplay given to his team. He's sound defensively as he constantly helps his defensemen to ease the transition. I was quite impressed when I saw him reach Victor Provencher quickly with a long pass good for a breakaway out of his zone.

CHI #24 C, Gignac, William (2015) A small sized forward, Gignac used his explosiveness and his high hockey IQ to create scoring chances. He went in the traffic and he was always around the puck. He earned two assists in the game.

CHI #30 G, Billia, Julio (2014) He wasn't tested a lot early in the game. Things started to get tough for him in the middle of the second period. He allowed three back-to-back goals. All those shots taken went above his shoulders. Zykov's two goals were clear shots from the high slot that nobody could have stopped in the Q. He was well positioned but his size hindered him to make those tough saves. He wasn't bad. He displayed quick reflexes at times and I liked his reaction after the second period. He was solid afterwards.

FINAL SCORE: 4-3 BAIE-COMEAU

December 6, 2013 – Saginaw Spirit at Kitchener Rangers (OHL)

SAG #3 LD Prophet, Brandon (2014) - Brandon displays good toughness in the slot and along the boards punishing opponents who enter his space. He helped set up Saginaw's second goal pinching in and putting a shot on net creating the rebound for the goal. He does a good job of keeping his feel moving on the offensive line to open himself up as a passing option.

SAG #10 LC Sadowy, Dylan (2014) - Dylan showed a good combination of size and skating. He was effective getting the puck deep in the offensive zone. Defensively he was willing to throw his body in front of shots from the point and shows a good compete level.

SAG #31 G Serebyrakov, Nikita (2014) - Nikita does a very godo job of cutting down angles well and challenging shooters. He didn't have much of a chance on a few goals scored by Kitchener but on one occasion he allowed it to snowball into a second goal which he shouldn't have allowed. A lack of rebound control resulted in one of the goals allowed tonight.

KIT #8 RD DiPerna, Dylan (2014) - This was a bit of a rough game for DiPerna. He generally sticks to using his stick and wouldn't take the body in several situations that called for it. He chased the play a little on the penalty kill and struggled a little positionally. While he has an effective shot from the point he tried to force it putting it into the opposing players shinpads and out of the zone.

KIT #10 RD Schmidt, Logan (2014) - Logan has shown great improvements since the start of the season. He continues to be a great skater and is capable of skating the puck out of trouble. He was also effective on the power play rushing the puck into the offensive zone from his own end. He makes quick passes in all three zones and made good decisions while under pressure.

KIT #20 RW Magyar, Nick (2014) - Nick scored on his first shift of the second period with hard work going after a rebound then eventually banging the puck home. He was physical at moments in this game but was penalized for a great hit down low. Magyar's skating is improving but still needs work.

KIT #27 RW Llewellyn, Darby (2014) - Darby continues to show a strong two-way game and it was strongly accentuated in tonight's game. He was willing to block shots and put good pressure on the point during the penalty kill. He did take himself off the ice on one of the penalty kills taking a bad hooking penalty. He checks opposing players' sticks effectively but isn't tough along the wall and in battles. Darby scored twice in this game. His first surprised the goaltender when he quickly shot off the draw. He scored what would be the eventual game winning goal going to the net and banging home the rebound.

KIT #72 LC MacInnis, Ryan (2014) - Ryan showed good positioning in this game but in reference to his skating, his first step is still a struggle. He also gets knocked off the puck by smaller opposing players.

Scouts Notes: Kitchener seemed to catch the Spirit on an off night as they dominated the majority of this game and took home a 5-3 victory. The physical play *dropped off later on as clean textbook hits were being called for penalties. In addition to the reports above, for Saginaw, both Brandon Lindberg (2015) and Jeremiah Addison (2015) were noticeable delivering some solid hits along the wall and provided good energy for the Spirit. For Kitchener Brandon Robinson (2014) threw a bit of a questionable hit resulting in Sean Callaghan (2014*) initiating a fight with Robinson which Brandon didn't fair well in.*

December 8, 2013, Portland Winterhawks vs Calgary Hitmen (WHL)

Port #7, Bittner, Paul (2015) – Showed a good first couple steps for a big guy. Fast and very strong on his skates. Great size. Played on the top line and 1st powerplay unit. Heavy shot, but not overly accurate. Would like to see him drive to the net a little harder. Used his body well to screen netminders and protect the puck, but for a big guy he's wasn't all that physical.

Port #9, De Leo, Chase (2014) – Big hit early on against the much bigger Alex Roach. Good acceleration and puck handling abilities. Centered Portland's 2nd line. Generated a couple good chances on the night. Defensive effort was generally there, but on one shift he was beaten back into his own zone by Greg Chase, who ended up driving to the net for a goal.

Port #13, Iverson, Keegan (2014) – As a big guy with a power forward mentality, he wasn't able to win nearly as many puck battles as would be expected. Effort level wasn't consistent. Projects to be a grinder with reasonable defensive abilities. Skating and hands were slightly above average.

Port #19, Petan, Nic (Winnipeg 2013) – Outside of Bjorkstrand, Petan was Portland's next best forward. Showed good anticipation on the penalty kill where he was able to break up a Hitmen pass for a breakaway opportunity. Was very good at finding the trailer on the rush. Created numerous chances on the night.

Port #22, Schoenborn, Alex (2014) – Started the game with very limited ice time. Made the most of his opportunities and was eventually entrusted to kill a 4-on-3 penalty as the lone forward late in the game. Had a good inside-outside move to drive around a Calgary defenseman and get a good shot on net. Good size and skated well.

Port #23, Turgeon, Dominic (2014) – A good skater who centered Portland's third line. As Portland struggled to catch up late in the game, Turgeon's line saw their ice time cut. Looked to play a strong 200 foot game but had limited offensive success.

Port #27, Bjorkstrand, Oliver (Columbus 2013) – Scored early with a wrist shot through traffic. Distributed the puck particularly well. Had numerous one-touch passes to open teammates for one-timers. Portland's most dangerous player on the night.

Port #44, Texeira, Keoni (2015) – DNP.

Cal #2, Thrower, Josh (2014) – Did not play a lot, but looked fairly steady on the night. Moved the puck well.

Cal #18, Virtanen, Jake (2014) – Good skater. Strong on his feet. Defensive play was good on the night. On multiple occasions Virtanen was able knock pucks out of the air and turn them into good scoring chances. Consistently went hard to the net.

Cal #29, Fazleev, Radel (2014) – Fazleev is starting to look more comfortable on the NHL-sized rink than he has earlier in the year. With some additional confidence, Fazleev is now handling the puck cleaner and showing better vision. Lacks a top skating gear and while his puck handling has improved, he is not able to dangle through opponents though he often tries. Limited upside.

Game notes: This game was the third in three days for the Winterhawks. While Portland started off strong, they seemed to run out of energy after the first period. Captain Taylor Leier missed the game with the flu. Several others looked to be bat-

tling fatigue or illness. After being a pretty even game for the first 30 minutes, Calgary eventually started to control the play and pulled away for a 4-1 win.

December 13, 2013 – Guelph Storm at London Knights (OHL)

GUE #9 LC Fabbri, Robby (2014) - Robby has excellent speed and he uses it on the rush to create scoring chances. He weaves through traffic very well with the puck, controlling it effectively. He scored Guelph's second goal making a great play controlling the puck through his legs in the slot then making a quick release on his shot to score.

GUE #13 RW Craievich, Adam (2015) - Adam's skating has improved, primarily in his top speed but he still struggles quite a bit with his first few steps. He played a good role for the Storm finishing his checks whenever possible and possesses good size.

GUE #15 RW Stevens, Marc (2014) - Marc finishes his checks hard and provided a good forecheck on the Storm fourth line tonight. He showed decent skating ability and even a few moves with the puck.

GUE #27 D McFadden, Garrett (2015) - Garrett played very well tonight. He handles speed very well in one on one situations. He always keeps his feet moving and has great awareness of his surroundings. He was also very god in the slot utilizing both his stick and his body to defend. He skates very well for a defenseman built as strong as he is and despite his good offensive qualities he was very consistent and strong with his defensive zone coverage. Garrett also finishes his checks whenever possible.

LON #10 LC Dvorak, Christian (2014) - Christian shows good speed and makes smart decisions on the rush. On one rush he went hard to the net without the puck and quickly banged in the rebound showing good hands on London's second goal. In the offensive zone he uses his hands and his puck skills to buy himself extra time in the offensive zone. He also showed a willingness to stand up for his teammates in the post whistle scrums. Christian received an increase in playing time and was very effective with the ice he was given.

LON #11 RW MacDonald, Owen (2014) - Owen displayed excellent work ethic every shift. He possesses good speed and challenged defensemen one on one with the puck on the rush but was unsuccessful.

LON #93 RC Marner, Mitchell (2015) - Marner showed good positioning in the slot early on to earn a scoring chance. He then carried the puck into the slot late in the first to score the opening goal of the game with 5.9 seconds left in the first period utilizing his patience and made a nice move to beat the goaltender. He has decent power in his shot and needs to use it a little more frequently. He made a good pass on the rush which lead to London's second goal of the game.

Scouts Notes: Guelph Storm visit London Knights in a battle of two of the top four teams in the Western Conference. The first was exactly as expected with a lot of back and forth action with both teams playing fairly evenly. However, in the second period the London Knights exploited a few weaknesses in Justin Nichols (2014*) game allowing them to take a 3-0 lead. The Storm would battle back but the Knights would take this game 5-2. In addition to the reports above, Pius Suter (2014) wasn't very noticeable tonight but showed good work ethic and good speed. Josh DeFarias (2015) showed good skating to consistently stick with the play but got pushed around a little physically. Max Domi (Phoenix) made a very heads up play while being taken down to set up London's third goal which was the eventual winning goal. He scored London's fifth goal late in the game.

Vancouver Giants vs Everett Silvertips December 14 2013 (WHL)

Evt #10 C Sandhu Tyler (2014). 1 assist tonight. His speed every game creates good scoring chances, he should have pulled the trigger on a few chances tonight but decided to look for a pass option first. Was smart on the defensive side of the puck tonight.

Evt #89 C Nikolishin Ivan (2014). 1 assist tonight. Was strong on the draw tonight, some dirty sauce passes through traffic off the rush but everett couldn't burry the biscuit. Was very shifty in the corners showing a few dangles that left the dman flat footed.

EVT #12 W Leedahl Dawson (2014). 1 assist tonight. Good hard physical game for Dawson. Always doing the little things each shift.

VAN #6 D Atwal Arvin (2014.) Played an aggressive game, did not shy away from the physical play. Showed a good active stick shutting down the scoring lanes. Was the best dman on the ice for Vancouver.

Van #5 D Morrison Tyler (2014. Had a couple good shifts, was physical at times. Played an overall decent game, would like to see him get more physical and compete in the corners.

Rouyn-Noranda Huskies vs Blainville-Boisbriand Armada, December 14th 2013 (QMJHL regular season)

Rouyn-Noranda

#5 Jeremy Lauzon Def (2015): Lauzon played a regular shift today for the Huskies, and even saw time on the 2nd power play unit. Uses his size well, had some good hits in the game, and was able to pin down opposing forwards on the wall. Looks to have grown quite a bit since the beginning of the season, and looked much stronger. Had some issues with his footwork and agility in this game, and was beat on the outside on a couple of occasions.

#6 Philippe Myers Def (2015): Myers saw limited ice time today, as he was used as the team's 7th defenseman, although he did see some ice time on the power play. When on the ice, he kept his game simple and didn't get into trouble. Made some good pinches as well to keep the puck in the offensive zone.

#7 Justin Guenette Def (2014): Undrafted last year, Guenette played a good game today. Used his speed well to rush the puck and forced the Armada to take a penalty on him in one of his rushes. Made a real good long stretch pass to send Marcus Power on a breakaway. This was a solid game overall from Guenette.

#12 Gabriel Slight Rw (2014): Slight, who was undrafted last year as well, is a huge kid that used his size well today, winning puck battles and space in the offensive zone. Used on the first power play unit and his role was pretty simple, as he was told to stand in front of the net and make life tougher for the opposing goaltender and defensemen. On the Huskies' 1st goal, he didn't get any points on the scoresheet, but played a big role battling in front of the net with Daniel Walcott, pushing him out of the way. When Walcott got hit by a slapshot from the point, the puck found Marcus Power's stick and he put the Huskies up 1-0. Puck skill and skating ability are still two areas of concern in Slight's game, and I have not seen a lot of progress since last year.

#20 Julien Nantel Lw (2014): Nantel was okay today, played a sound two-way game and worked hard. Had his best chance on a 2-on-1 where he received a perfect pass from Marcus Power, but missed the net with his shot. Liked his speed; he's first on the puck often on the forecheck, a strong player that is tough to handle along the wall.

#27 Francis Perron Lw (2014): Perron is likely the most creative player on this Huskies' team and is being used on the point on the powerplay, as the Huskies don't have much in term of puck-moving defensemen other than Dillon Fournier. Perron was dangerous on the powerplay, using his good vision to find teammates, and also did a good job getting pucks on net with a simple wrist shot from the point. His lack of strength hurt him at 5-on-5 as he was not very noticeable there. Also did some good work on the PK as he has good speed and anticipated the play well.

Blainville-Boisbriand

#5 Nathanael Halbert Def (2014): Halbert was good this afternoon, he's a smart player who won't get his team in trouble and move the puck well to his forwards. Was tough to beat in one on one situation and was matchup versus one of the top player in the league Marcus Power and did very well. Played on the Armada 2nd power play unit and was good at putting puck on net.

#8 Emile Aronsson C (2014): Aronsson played a decent two-way game, a smart player who is very responsible in his own end and understands the game well. Had a below-average game in the faceoff circle though, and this is where he is usually strong. Not a flashy player offensively but liked his puck protection and how he uses his size well to protect it.

#18 Julien Bahl Def (2014): Played a decent game, saw some good puck movement from Bahl today. Nothing flashy about his game today, would have liked to see more power on his shot from what I have seen today. Defensively he was sound, good gap control and not afraid to block shots.

#85 Daniel Walcott (2014): Walcott sees a lot of ice time, as he's used on the 1st powerplay and penalty kill units. A superb skater with quick feet that allow him to cover a lot of space on the ice. Saw him go end-to-end on the powerplay. Although he's not the biggest, he can deliver some good hits, and has good timing with his open-ice hits, as he showed today. Tough break on the first goal by Rouyn-Noranda, as he was pushed from behind by Gabriel Slight and then got hit in the visor by a slapshot from the point, only to see the puck end up on Marcus Power's stick which put the Huskies up 1-0. Showed nice patience with the puck on the powerplay late in the game, which led to a goal to tie the game at 1.

USA NTDP-18 vs Utica College – 12/14/2013 7pm (Utica Memorial Aud)

USA NTDP-18:

#1 Blake Weyrick (G) – He is the only player on the NTDP without a college commitment and there might be a reason why after watching the game. Weyrick made 27 saves on 31 shots for a decent outing, though I question two goals given up because of poor rebound control on the 2nd and 4th goals. The 1st goal against was off a bad clearing attempt/turnover by defenseman #6 Collins on the penalty kill that landed puck right on Utica player's stick at top of circle in which he fired quickly on net to beat Weyrick high glove side. The 2nd goal was even strength goal which Weyrick failed to control a point shot. He kicked it right out to a player standing left-front side of the net. The left-handed Utica player quickly fired far side, under Weyrick's blocker for the easy tally. The 3rd goal against cannot be blamed on the tender. After a costly turnover at the blue line on the breakout, the Utica defenseman quickly fired a shot towards the net, which was tipped by a teammate coming back into the play out of the corner. Weyrick received little help on this one. All three of these goals came in the 2nd period. The final and 4th goal in the 3rd period again was on the penalty-kill. A low point shot made its way on net through some net traffic, but again Weyrick was unable to cover the puck. The Utica player corralled the puck and potted in the open net as Weyrick was down and unable to recover. Although he made some difficult saves in tight, his mechanics looked average on the night. He got beat glove side, blocker side, and the tracking and control of pucks was a bit of a struggle. As mentioned his rebound control for low shots, working through screens was in question (2nd & 4th goals), recovery (4th goal), and reaction time (1st goal). He is a good sized goalie with decent net coverage, but you wanted him to make the saves to keep team in it especially versus an NCAA D3 team that did not have any real guns.

#2 Jack Dougherty (D) – This D-man has been gaining a lot of attention in the early part of the season after a solid USA Hockey Select 16s in 2012 outing and All-American Prospects Game this past September. He pairs up with the undersized #5 Fortunato on defense and also plays PP on the 1st unit. He was average at best this night and actually took two bad penalties that led to Utica power-play tallies. In the 1st period he took a tripping call on player going to the net looking for the pass and then in the 3rd period, a sort of a back-breaker penalty that led to Utica's 4th goal. While playing the forward 1-on-1 down the wall he looked to be in good position and closed the gap, but then unwisely got a bit too aggressive and kind of kicked the feet out of the forward when he no longer was a scoring threat. He is willing to play the body and defensive positioning was OK. Honestly, he did not really show much and looked mediocre.

#4 Ryan Bliss (D) – Bliss isn't anything special but he made some good hits on the night showing his physicality. He popped a couple of players with some nice 1-on-1 hits. He is not much for offensive production yet he can distribute puck up ice and will get shots to the net. He plays a steady game without the flash at both ends of the ice.

#5 Brandon Fortunato (D) – He is the smallest of the bunch on the blue line for NTDP, yet he might be the smoothest and smartest. He makes good decisions with the puck in distributing up ice on the break-out or when he is quarterbacking the PP at the point. I have seen him play in various settings since age 16. He is a good skater and he handles the puck with good poise. Where he does get lost sometimes is being able to keep up with the physical play needed in the defensive zone. He really needs to gain strength not only in playing the body, but also in his shot. He is definitely a pass first player because he has the vision but also his shot is weak. On the PP in the 1st period he shot one from the point that fluttered in on the goalie. As mentioned, that's not the first time I have seen this happen while watching Fortunato. If he was a few inches taller, 50 lbs. heavier then scouts would be having a field day for his services. He is that specialty PP guy that will not blast goals in but can set the table well. Comparisons are always tough and not always justified, though Fortunato could be that next Torey Krug going undrafted, attending college, and maturing at a later date.

#6 Ryan Collins (D) – He is a big body and that is really all. He is a step behind and questionable mobility. His lateral mobility and pivoting could use some work especially when playing faster competition. He just seemed a step behind in the thought process department in distributing puck. He made a costly turnover in the 2nd period on the PK as he rounded the net his clearing attempt went to Utica player parked on the top of the circle who fired it quickly by the handcuffed USA goalie #1 Weyrick. He has to be one of the weaker D-men in the program.

#7 Andres Bjork (F) – He showed some good offensive thoughts on the night playing on wing alongside #19 Larkin and #21 Hitchcock. Yet he kind of stayed on the outside of really creating any scoring chances and making an impact.

#8 Jack Glover (D) – He had been getting a good deal of 1st round draft pick talk as the season began, but I am beginning to wonder if he is really that caliber. He took bad roughing penalty after the play late in 1st period that led to Utica PPG early in 2nd period. He also received a 10-minute slashing misconduct penalty in 3rd period. Some of his decision making is questionable and that was evident to in 2nd period. He forced a breakout pass up the middle as he tried the saucer in which centerman couldn't handle and that led to turnover to D-man at blue line and Utica's 3rd goal. Also with his size you would like to see more punishing plays in defensive zone. He also had a shot blocked on the PP from the point in which he gave up break-a-way chances and his slashing penalty negating the man advantage. One play on the PK he did read the play well and had stick in passing lane to break-up and send biscuit length of the ice. He will play the physical style with awareness in his own end. Honestly overall, did not walk away impressed.

#9 Shane Gersich (F) – He is the one forward like #21 Hitchcock that is flying well below the radar. North Dakota has a nice commit in Gersich as he will continue to grow and add strength which is his downfall right now. It's not that he gets outmuscled but he's on the smaller to average size. He was clearly the best player two summers ago in 2012 at USA Hockey's Select 16s. Gersich was one of the best forwards this past fall at the All-American Prospects Game too. He has all the tools from high hockey IQ, skating, stick handling, passing, and shooting. From my viewpoint he had some limited ice time and he as well as his team would benefit more if he played center because of his advanced skill sets. In the 2nd period he anticipated a puck going to the point and smartly tipped it out into the neutral zone. With his speed he easily out raced the D-man to create a 2-on-1 situation in which he played well by faking pass but fired it high missing the net. He also took a late hit in the corner in 2nd period by big D-man but he battled through it finished his shift and continued to play in the game. In the 3rd period he wisely had good stick position away from the puck to block/intercept pass at point too again create a scoring chance the other way using his skating ability and stick skills. He then nicely laid a drop pass for the D-man joining rush in the high slot, but teammate over skated killing the opportunity. There are a few others getting most of the attention though Gersich should be watched closely too.

#10 Joe Wegwerth (F) – He is a gritty, physical player with a limited role. He did not create any real scoring threats as offensive capabilities seem restricted at this level now. He along with line mates #13 Wagner and #22 Fiegl play that hold, sandpaper style game. He is a blue-collar player for sure.

#11 Jack Eichel (F) – Right off the bat you notice his game and it brings back good memories of his game at USA Hockey's Select 16s Camp in the Summer of 2012. I actually was kind of amazed he was in the line-up on a very, very snowy night in central New York because he had to be in Minneapolis, MN for the USA WJC Camp in less than 24 hours. On the first power-play opportunity he was handling and distributing the puck with ease and authority. He seemed to play a rover position between the defensemen #2 Dougherty and #5 Fortunato at the top and in between in order to get open. He shows good vision and quick decisions in moving the puck on the PP. He was always making crisp, tape-to-tape passes and then realized his chance to fire away. On the second PP opportunity in the 1st period he got himself open at the top of the circle and received pass down low from the goal line by #27 Milano. He immediately one-timed the shot that rang hard off the post/cross bar then bouncing off goalie in the crease allowing #17 Tuch to tap in for the rebound goal. On the blast, it actually sounded like the puck spilt in two because Eichel has such torque on his shot. He ripped a shot high from the same area in the 3rd period that again sounded like it cracked the glass, so you know he can shoot the biscuit hard. His stride is strong, powerful and he has the explosive gear that allows him to wheel past defenders. Each time I watch him skate, I think he must have had power skating lessons at a young age the way he extends legs and motions arms. His entire skating is very solid form in acceleration, speed, balance, and mobility. He showed this in the 2nd period as he easily stickhandled through the neutral zone avoiding players and then took to the outside around the D-man creating a good scoring chance and then almost scoring on his own rebound. Eichel has very good hockey sense as he is aware of players and defenders around him and always is dangerous on the ice. He is good size, can play a physical game, and also not be affected by hits. His hands actually seem to have gotten even softer over last few years as he is craftier than when he was 15 years-old. In the PP in 3rd period, he was at the top of point. A pass intended across ice went in front of Eichel about 1-foot off ice and he easily tapped it down out of mid-air on his stick with ease to again set-up a play. Overall, Eichel displays high level of offensive awareness that reads plays well and will get himself into a variety of scoring situations. He possesses a laser, quick release, good playmaking abilities, willingness to play defense, and go to the dirty area too. He holds strong puck skills, competitive nature, hockey IQ, physical play, efficient defensive play, and displays leadership and confidence. Even though NTDP lost 4-1 on the night, Eichel is a difference maker. He is a gifted player that no question will be highly sought after in the 2015 NHL Draft and BU definitely hit the jackpot on this recruit.

#13 Ryan Wagner (F) – He is a smaller sized forward that is willing to play all areas of the ice. I saw at USA Hockey's Select 17s this past summer and his game of energy and relentlessness is still the same. He plays a solid two-way game and for NTDP definitely plays a more 4th line, grinding role. He made good play in 1st period by stealing puck off D-man at defensive blue line to create a 2-on-1 opportunity, although the finish on the play did not amount. He may be one of the NTDPers that is bypassed in the draft.

#14 Dylan Pavelek (F) – He kind of buzzed around the ice but it didn't amount to much of anything. When it was too late and NTDP realized that they were about to lose to a NCAA D3 team, Pavelek started to throw the body around in the 3rd period. He looked average on this night just as he was at USA Hockey's Select 17s in the summertime.

#16 Jonathan MacLeod (D) – MacLeod is just coming off injury and seemed to have some limited ice time on the night. He played steady and simple game. He made a big open ice hit in the 2nd period and doesn't shy away from the physical play.

#17 Alex Tuch (F) – He is a good sized forward playing on the wing with #11 Eichel and #27 Milano as NTDP's top line. He also plays in front of the net as a screen on the first unit power-play and scored USA's only goal on the night in the 1st period doing a great job in his role with the man advantage. After #11 Eichel ripped a shot off the post/crossbar Tuch quickly reacted and banged home the rebound lying in the crease after bouncing off the back of the Utica goalie. He utilizes his big frame well as will work the puck low, get into the greasy areas, and he also isn't afraid to lay the body on his opponents as he caught a few players with some solid hits on the night. He possesses a good, powerful shot. His skating is decent and stick skills are average too as he isn't one to wheel the puck up ice and showcase high-end moves, but will show a toe-drag every now and then. He plays that north-south game, keeping things simple, and capitalizing on his opportunities. Scouts love because the tools and mind are there along with big frame to make the pro level.

#18 Nolan Stevens (F) – He was just average at best. I actually would like to have seen #9 Gersich at center rather than Stevens as he did not display the skill and leadership at center to make a difference out on the ice. There isn't anything special here and he might be another that is bypassed at the draft.

#19 Dylan Larkin (F) – I have certainly seen Larkin play better than he did on this night, but that's not to say he isn't talented and one of the better players on NTDP-18 team. He is certainly a good skater and handles the puck well. He was pretty good at the face-off circle on this night and also was playing tough defensively. He smartly and efficiently played the body in 2nd period on a back-check as he angled player out on boards just inside the blue line to break up any scoring chance. On the offensive side he also displayed his wheels as he flew down the wing then stopping on a dime then quickly firing a shot that the goalie struggled to handle but the official quickly blew the whistle, it could have led to USA's second goal. In the 3rd period, on the cycle he received a pass at the top of circle and quickly released a shot on net, yet took a solid hit to the shoulder that left him stung. He is a shoot first player and I have seen plenty of finish in the past which should excite NHL teams.

#21 Ryan Hitchcock (F) – He is overall a very good player as he possesses a fine skating stride, good hands, a high hockey sense with worthy offensive instincts and solid defensive knowledge. He is of average size yet will play the body, can use his shot to create scoring opportunities, and also has the ability to distribute the puck. He made a good play in 1st period coming down 2-on-2 as he held puck long enough to draw D over then quickly dished to a teammate joining rush, then went to the net for the rebound but unfortunately failed to convert. He has good vision, quick thoughts as he thinks ahead, and will control puck on stick to make things happen. I thought #11 Eichel and Hitchcock were the best players on the ice for NTDP. He has also played solid in my previous viewings. You just wish he had some more size and sky could be the limit. Hitchcock is one of the more underrated players like #9 Gersich on NTDP-18.

#22 Jared Fiegl (F) – I have yet to ever really see any offensive upside and why naming to NTDP in Fiegl. He is a defensive style player with limited offensive thoughts. When down a couple of goals already in the 3rd period on the penalty-kill, he had opportunity to spring #9 Gersich on a break-a-way by banking pass off boards but failed to either recognize the situation and/or lacked the touch to make indirect pass to teammate. Nothing of real pro potential here.

#24 Louie Belpedio (D) – He is sort of like #28 Billitier whereby he can skate well with good mobility and poise with puck by handling it or breaking up ice yet never does anything beyond. He will make the hits when necessary and pretty solid on the defensive side. He uses stick well and did so in 2nd period in negating scoring chance on a rush, but then failed to continue with play, as his man stepped out of corner and re-directed a shot from the point for Utica's 3rd goal. Again, you think perhaps Belpedio could bring his game to the next level but rather settles in each shift rather than taking game beyond.

#27 Sonny Milano (F) – Milano has been one of the better '96-born USA players for some time though he does not always showcase his skills consistently. Against a NCAA D3 team he was average. Of course you see that he can handle the biscuit quite well and skates fluidly too. But here on this night, I thought Milano played to perimeter and did not engage well enough for a potential 1st rounder. Like #11 Eichel and others they can really move the puck well on the power-play. Milano picked up a PPA on #17 Tuch's goal as he feed the puck up high to #11 Eichel from down low on the goal line perfectly for the one-timer. So the hands, vision, and offensive thoughts are definitely apparent, yet he needs to be more physical and finish his checks. Added strength and grit to his game would do wonders. A few times he was lazy on the back check and lost some battles along the wall. He was finding open teammates in the offensive off the cycle while protecting puck down low, but sometimes failed to move his feet to breakaway and give that extra effort. Overall, you would like to see a more two-way game with added consistency.

#28 Nathan Billitier (D) – He is a good skating, undersized defenseman. He plays a simplified game with good outlet passes and handles puck fairly well. He doesn't do anything more than that. He sometimes is slow in getting to the loose pucks and definitely could become stronger along the boards in battling for the puck. Sometimes he overcommitted on PK to open up opportunity, but otherwise makes decent decisions with and without the puck. He did not show any real offensive thoughts or advances. On one play he joined the rush on a 2-on-2 situation and was left a drop pass by #9 Gersich to walk into but he was not ready with stick on ice and thus chance was lost and puck was quickly turned up the other way. He isn't that nasty, shut-down D-man nor is he that highly skilled offensive blue liner. You walk away thinking he is holding back and has more to offer, but each time doesn't show the next-level material.

December 15, 2013 – Kingston Frontenacs at London Knights (OHL)

KGN #2 LD McEneny, Evan (Vancouver) - Evan really struggled today despite making some really good plays one on one. McEneny made a very bad play with the puck at the offensive line which required him to hurry back to have a chance but stopped skating which resulted in London's second goal. Even if the goal wasn't scored on the breakaway, his lack of backcheck would have allowed for a second chance opportunity. He also took two careless penalties in the third period of a tie game.

KGN #9 LW Verbeek, Ryan (2014) - Ryan gets good power in his shot and utilized this to score Kingston's fourth goal of the game. He is primarily a checker but has shown pretty good hands when controlling the puck. He did however have a little trouble with hard passes on the rush. He finished a few hits and was generally effective for the Frontenacs today.

KGN #20 RD McKeown, Roland (2014) - Roland displays excellent skating for his size. He did a good job in the slot on the penalty kill playing his man well but also making sure the goaltender was able to follow the play. He struggled with the puck tonight on several occasions. Primarily trying to force passes on the rush and struggled with his first pass.

KGN #55 RD Watson, Matthew (2014) - Matthew unleashed a quick wrister from the point which found it's way through for Kingston's second goal. He then made a great play to step up and intercept a pass in the neutral zone. He then rushed the puck into the offensive zone and unloaded a hard slap shot. The rebound created from the shot directly resulted in Kingston's third goal. While Matthew is a good skater he got beat consistently in one on one situations, including against unskilled forwards.

KGN #67 LW Crouse, Lawson (2015) - Lawson is a decent skater for his size but needs to continue to work on getting quicker on his first few steps, but it is decent for his size and age. He received plenty of ice on the penalty kill and was much more assertive along the wall than previous viewings at this level. He seems more comfortable playing his physical game and it helped him make a more positive impact for his team.

KGN #93 LW Bennett, Sam (2014) - Sam struggled early on with distributing the puck trying to force shots from bad angles looking off multiple clear passing options to force a shot that didn't get on the net. He did however show the ability to make some excellent passes and move the puck much better when choosing to utilize his line mates. With the power Bennett gets in his shot he becomes a much more dangerous player when he utilizes his passing skills. Sam initiated Kingston's run of four straight goals making an outstanding move to beat two defenders then score while off balanced in the slot.

KGN #96 RW Watson, Spencer (2014) - Spencer utilized his speed and smarts to open himself up a few times in the offensive zone and made a few good plays but was for the most part unnoticeable in this game.

LON #11 RW MacDonald, Owen (2014) - Owen was very effective on the cycle and competes hard to win battles and overcome his size. He skates very well. He made a very bad play with the puck in his own zone resulting in a scoring chance against his team. At this point Owen does not appear to be a legitimate prospect for the 2014 NHL Entry Draft due to a lack of size and the lack of offensive ability to overcome that size. He is a very good player at the OHL level.

LON #12 RD DeFarias, Josh (2015) - Josh played very well defensively on the rush using his speed and stick to negate potential chances. He battled hard in the defensive zone and kept it simple all game long.

LON #14 LW Elie, Tristan (2014) - Tristan was noticeable in this game delivering a few very solid hits along the boards and provides speed to his forecheck. He appears to have grown since training camp.

LON #1 G Herbst, Liam (2014) - Liam made his OHL debut midway through the second period after Kingston's third goal. Liam went about 18 months without playing up until this October. Liam did a good job getting in front of shots and following the play. However he struggled controlling shots and looked nervous in the net. He got caught going the other way and couldn't recover quickly enough resulting in a late second period goal. He did not return for the third period.

Scouts Notes: This was a Sunday afternoon match-up between two good teams that had an exciting finish after a wild start. The London Knights jumped out to a 4-0 lead and looked poised to cruise to victory. However the skilled Frontenacs team kept coming at the Knights and were able to score a few beautiful goals and a few soft goals to tie the game up. The game contained atrocious officiating which really played a factor as the game entered the third period. London would score the game winner with less than four minutes left on the clock. An empty net goal would make this game end with a 6-4 result. Max Domi (Phoenix) scored twice for London tonight scoring the first with a great move on the breakaway. He then showed great puck control and patience on his second goal.

December 20, 2013 – Niagara Ice Dogs at London Knights (OHL)

NIA #4 LD Dunn, Vince (2015) - Vince showed great elusiveness with the puck due to his great skating ability. He was very good under pressure and was able to make the intelligent play despite the situation. He was also willing to play the body when the situation arose despite a lack of size. Aside from a few mistakes here and there, Vince played a strong game tonight. He pinched in from the point and quickly scored to give Niagara the lead with less than three minutes left in the game.

NIA #5 RD Siebenaler, Blake (2014) - Blake showed good skating ability in all directions and uses this to his advantage in the netural zone. He made a few mistakes rushing the puck in the defensive zone but at times showed the knowledge to skate backwards and create time and space when there were no options. He showed some good offensive skills but wasn't very aggressive in one on one situations.

NIA #11 LW Perlini, Brendan (2014) - Brendan has an excellent combination of size and speed. He showed a willingness to provide a two-way presense as he showed a solid back check on multiple occasions. He has very good power in his shot and made a great move to score Niagara's third goal of the game. He then showed his excellent shot with just one minute left in a tie game as he shot a laser top shelf to score the game winning goal. While there were features in Perlini's game that was very impressive this game, he was not engaging at all on the fore check. He constantly took the route that would result in the least contact possible even if it meant not getting the puck. For a player his size it was constantly surprising watching him avoid initiating or being involved in any contact and is a major concern for him as an NHL prospect.

NIA #20 LD Wilkie, Zach (2015) - Zach showed strong skating ability and a great puck rush. He utilized his rushing ability and quick hands to help create Niagara's first goal early on in this game. He battles effectively along the wall despite not having great size. He was also willing to sacrifice his body to block shots. Overall this was a very good game for Wilkie as a 16 year old against one of the top teams in the league.

NIA #28 RD Haydon, Aaron (2014) - Aaron showed good physicality in this game finishing his checks hard and playing very aggressive on the wall. His skating has shown clear improvements over last season and is not a real concern for us at this point. He moved the puck quickly when given ice on the power play. He played a strong defensive game tonight for the most part but made one glaring mistake on London's first goal where he didn't play the man or the pass and could have easily prevented the goal by doing one of these things.

NIA #29 LD Mikulovich, Aleksandar (2014) - Aleksandar showed improved skating and skated well backwards in transition. His skating still looks uncomfortable but it is effective. He handled size very well in one on one match-up's and was consistently strong defensively. He maintained good positioning for the most part of this game. Although he is a defensive first defenseman, he showed the ability and intelligence to jump up in the rush at the right times. In the second period he clearly dove in his own end to try and draw a penalty, instead it directly lead to a scoring chance for London.

NIA #31 G Moran, Brent (2014) - Brent had one of his strongest performances of the season stopping well over 50 shots in this game. He did a great job of getting into position to make the initial save. While he was doing a very good job getting in front of the inntial shot regularly he was sloppy at times making some of these saves. He was also fighting the puck a little at times as well. This resulted in a few rebounds that he probably should have had. He did a good job tracking the play but after making the initial save, he did a times lose track of the rebound putting him out of position. He seemed to have trouble with balance at times and has a very odd tendency to lay down on his back when he should be getting to his knees or even back on his feet.

Scouts Notes: Niagara jumped out to a nice 2-0 lead, but Matt Rupert's (2014) two second period goals along with a few atrocious calls to give London two questionable 5 on 3 power plays lead to the Knights trimming the lead to 3-2. Both teams alternated goals twice giving Niagara a 5-4 lead going into the final two minutes. It was with two minutes remaining that Zach Bell (Free Agent) jumped up in the rush and launched a quick, hard wrist shot top shelf to tie the game at 5-5. London then went short handed quickly thereafter as Matt Rupert (2014*) took a selfish penalty delivering multiple cross checks to the face of a Niagara player. This was followed by an atrocious phantom call resulting in Niagara gaining their own questionable 5 on 3 power play. The Ice Dogs wasted little time as Brendan Perlini (2014) fired a laser past the Knights goaltender for the eventual game winning goal as the Ice Dogs beat the Knights 6-5. Also of note in this game, Cody Caron (2014) scored Niagara's second goal in this game. It was a wrist shot off the wall and was a bit of a soft goal.

Dec 20, 2013. Charlottetown Islanders vs Blainville-Boisbriand Armada (QMJHL)

CHA #4 LD, Laliberté, Kevin (2014) He had trouble containing Samuel Hodhod on one of his multiple rushes in the middle of the first period. His breakouts were not that good early on, but they were better as time passed. When paired against third liners, he proved that he could be effective at the QMJHL level.

CHA #10 C, Kielly, Kameron (2015) Lost the puck early in the first period in his zone. A PK specialist, he was good at covering shooting lanes with his active stick and his feistiness. He was good along the wall and was able to retrieve puck possession when he was engaged in a battle for a loose puck. He showed a good level of creativity on a two-on-one late in the second period when he dished a perfect backhand pass to Bursey who missed the open net.

CHA #11 RW, Sprong, Daniel (2015) Tended to cheat defensively in the first period. He tried to jump too early offensively. When the play was set up down low thanks to Goulet's speed, he was able to reach teammates quickly around the opposing net. He had a quiet game.

CHA #19 C, Goulet, Alexandre (2014) His speed allowed him to be good on the forecheck. He's at his best as a centerman. That way, he doesn't have to compete along the wall on a regular basis. Goulet had a breakaway that resulted in an unsuccessful penalty shot in the first period. I liked his quick feet and his strides were powerful. In my mind, he is a pure rusher. His decisions with the puck are quick and effective and I liked his compete level in this game, which is something he has improved over time. He scored in the second period on a powerplay with a low shot.

CHA #26 LW, Pépin, Alexis (2014) Displayed his good ability to control the puck early on. He's thinner compared to the last time I saw him back in Moncton. He improved his speed and that helps him overall. He's still making quick decisions with the puck, which allows him to create good scoring chances. He had a tendency to stop moving his feet in the offensive zone near the high slot. It didn't allow him to get in good position to receive pucks good enough for scoring chances. His passes were always on the tape.

BLB #5 LD, Halbert, Nathanael (2014) He was good on one-on-one's in the first. Used his quick feet in order to rush the puck twice in the first period. Besides that he wasn't noticeable.

BLB #8 C, Aronsson, Emil (2014) A big body, Aronsson isn't the kind of guy that will amaze you with his skills. He protects the puck effectively and he likes to crash the net. I liked the way he paid attention to details without the puck. He never seemed lost on the ice and he knows what to do to be effective. He was pretty good on the forecheck thanks to his sound body positioning in those situations.

BLB #19 RD, Bahl, Julien (2014) A fairly good passer, I didn't notice him turn it over early in the game. He plays a simple game and I liked his poise with the puck. He rarely panicked and he was effective in the defensive zone. He's not explosive by any means, but his smarts are really intriguing.

BLB #25 RW, Strong, Joseph (2014) Had a good opening fight against Mike DiPaolo with five minutes played in the first period. He's your typical tough guy who needs to improve his speed to play at the next level.

BLB #85 LD, Walcott, Daniel (2014) Really liked the guy once again. He's a superb skater that likes to get involved physically. He never hesitates to pinch and he uses that to his advantage on most occasions. He is strong on his skates and that helps him to protect the puck along the wall in his zone. Acted like a number one defenseman all game long. His mobility helped him big time in his coverage

FINAL SCORE: 6-2 BLB

Dec 21, 2013. Chicoutimi Saguenéens vs Québec Remparts (QMJHL)

CHI #28 LD, Lyamkin, Nikita (2014) He's getting better in his zone. When he was in control of the puck, he chose to skate with it through the neutral zone and that allowed him to gain confidence. He cut down on the turnovers and he communicates better with his teammates on the ice. He was used on the third pairing along Scott Carrier and he saw limited action on the powerplay.

CHI #55 C, Roy, Nicolas (2015) Roy won important faceoffs in his zone and he was excellent covering the high slot and his man when necessary. He used his long reach at his advantage covering the neutral zone thus creating multiple scoring chances. I remember a particular shift in the second period where he anticipated the play so well that he blocked a pass from Olivier Archambault that resulted in a two-on-one. He was the most consistent forward for the Sags.

CHI #58 RD, Allard, Frédéric (2016) Allard was his usual self. He was pretty good on one-on-one's controlling the distance between him and the puck carrier. He played a simple game and he was able to make quick and wise decisions with the puck. He kept his blueline effectively as well. He was used on the first powerplay unit and he scored his first QMJHL goal thanks to a beautiful cross-ice pass from Laurent Dauphin.

CHI #30 G, Billia, Julio (2014) Early in the first period, he was surprised by a weak shot from the blueline taken by Kurt Etchegary. Late in that period though, he made a key glove save getting away from his crease defying Maxime Chevalier who joined the rush on a three-on-two. He made another big glove save on Anthony Latina early in the second period on a breakaway. He didn't commit and he followed Latina really well. He gave his team a chance to stay in the game in that period. He was not afraid to leave his net to stop the puck and to start breakouts on his own.

QUE #18 RD, Donaghey, Cody (2014) Most of his passes were accurate and I liked the way he handled himself well on the powerplay. He was going back and forth in the offensive zone thus getting in good position. Defensively, he was fine.

QUE #20 LD, MacIntyre, Duncan (2014) MacIntyre anticipated the play well. He broke some plays in the neutral zone and he was tough to beat on one-on-one's. He was not flashy by any means, but he was following his man pretty well and he kept him on the outside most of the time. I would like him to be more aggressive to regain puck possession, though.

Scouts notes: Anthony Duclair (NYR 2013 draft pick) used his speed efficiently creating multiple scoring chances for himself. He gets that extra gear so fast, it's astonishing. Olivier Archambault was his usual self. He's a great rusher, but most of his rushes ended up in the corner and he kept the puck way too long although he looked like a wizard with the puck in that game.

FINAL SCORE : QUE 4-2

Finland U17 vs Lloydminster Bobcats, December 28, 2013

LMB #1, McGrath, Austin (2015) – The Medicine Hat 4th round Bantam pick in 2013 made some good saves and stayed square to the puck as much as he could as he faced a barrage of cross-ice one timers amidst a Finnish shooting gallery. The biggest issue with his game today wasn't his inability to stop the puck (even after letting in nine goals), it was the extra heartache he created for himself whenever he tried to play the puck as he constantly turned the puck over to opponents and had his defensemen confused by what he was trying to do with it.

LMB #10, Clague, Kale (2016) – As a 15 year-old playing against the Finnish U17 team, Clague looked very calm and composed. The 6th overall pick in the 2013 WHL Bantam draft is a very smooth skater with excellent vision and poise with the puck. He always kept his head up looking for passing and skating lanes as showcased by a great stretch pass that led to a breakaway on the Bobcats' first goal. While skating the puck out of his end, Clague saw a small gap open up and right away fired a perfect pass up the middle to set up the scoring chance. Clague has a good jump in his step and moves the puck as well as any 15 year-old defenseman. His outlet passes were very accurate and firm. Early on, he had a couple wobbles early on in his own end, but Clague was arguably the game's best defenseman by the end of the game. Clague thinks the game at a high level and boasts good size to go along with his strong skating and passing abilities. Defensively, he kept the Finns to the outside, wouldn't give anyone a chance to drive to the net and always kept to the strong side of the puck. Offensively, Clague led the rush on a few occasions and showed the ability to handle the puck at top speed as well as to stickhandle through traffic. He showed excellent awareness by twice finding open teammates after utilizing a slap pass. Excellent vision and hockey smarts.

LMB #3, Koep, Andrew (2015) – Oil Kings 2nd round bantam draft constantly kept his feet moving. Doesn't have great size, but has some skill and worked hard. Not afraid of contact. Good shot, but wildly off target.

LMB #18, Braid, Chasetan (2015) – One of the few bright spots for the Bobcats was the play of Braid. He played hard and physical against the Finns. Braid drove to the net and wasn't afraid to go to the tough areas. Was rewarded with a hat-trick for his efforts.

FIN #3, Jarvinen, Ville. A big defenseman that did well to use his size to separate opponents from the puck. Liked to play the body, but didn't always pick his spots wisely. Fist pass wasn't always on target. Liked to jump into the play offensively and had a pretty heavy shot. Shot accuracy wasn't a strong point as most attempts went right towards the netminders. Skating was choppy. Was arguably the Finns grittiest player on the day and possesses a bit of mean streak.

FIN #7, Juolevi, Olli (2016) – As a '98-born playing on the Finnish U17 team, Juolevi showed that he more than capable of playing with the older guys. He already is quite tall and has some room to fill out. Juolevi played a pretty simple game where he was able to use his strong skating skills to retrieve the puck and good, accurate passing skills to push the puck up ice. He wasn't overly physical, but his puck skills were high end and he kept the play moving in the right direction. There's still some rawness to his game, but with his size, combined with his strong passing and skating skills make him worth tracking as a potential puck-moving defenseman for the 2016 NHL draft.

FIN #8, Ruuskanen, Walterri (2015) – DNP

FIN #9, Saarijarvi, Vili (2015) – A good skating defenseman with puck handling abilities. Saarijarvi would spin off opposing forwards while working the point on the PP. An excellent skater and a constant threat with the puck. Saarijarvi loved to one-time the puck from the top of the point as he had numerous chances during Finnish powerplays. While Saarijarvi has some good skills, he must get stronger as he is quite small and was easily knocked off the puck.

FIN #24, Vainio, Veeti (2015) – Vainio is a good skating defenseman with a solid all-around skill set. Probably Finland's best defenseman on the day, Vainio was able to control the play from the backend. He was very patient with the puck to the point that he seemed to be toying with the Bobcats. Puck skills were good, but its unclear of how high-end they are. Defensively, he was overly confident in his own end a couple times and incoming players' speed caused him to have to turn his hips early and caused a bit of trouble for him. Vainio understood when to jump into the play and he effectively read the play and timed it well whenever he decided to be the trailer on the rush. Good offensive instincts, but a little raw in his own end.

Fin #25, Nattinen, Julius (2015) – Big center that uses his size well. Skating was good and he was able to weave through opponents with ease. Nice hands, heavy shot and good offensive instincts. Nattinen put up 4 points and was the best player on the ice today along with Laine. Worked well at both ends of the rink, although his defensive play got a little sloppy once the game was well out of reach and he was trying to pad his stats. Used in all situations for the Finns. Voted the game star for the Finns.

Fin #27, Laine, Patrik (2016) – 1998-born forward. A very big player that was constantly pushing the play up ice. Laine always seemed to be in good position. He showed an ability to stickhandle through traffic. Played the body nicely and consistently finished his checks. Skating was okay, but first step could improve. Right-handed shot playing on the left side. Big shot although he had a couple misfires. Laine was easily one of the best players on the ice along with linemate Nattinen. Finished the game with three points.

Game Notes: The Finnish team was clearly the dominant team in this game (and the entire tournament thus far), but Lloydminster has some success early by keeping the Finns to the outside with physical play and team defense. Once the Finns got going, the play became a bit of game of keep away in which the Finns moved the puck effectively looking for a one-timer chance. They were able to do this not only with the man-advantage, but also at even strength and occasionally short-handed. Finland was content to roll four lines once they got a couple goal cushion and let many of their better players get a break as this was each team's 3rd game in three days. The play got chippier as the game tilted more and more in Finland's favour. Finland ultimately won 9-3. Finland has won all three of their games, outscoring their opponents by a combined score on 31-4.

Switzerland U17 vs Vancouver NW Giants, December 28, 2013

VNW #8, Schultz, Ty (2015) – Willing to block shots while on the penalty kill. Puck moving defenseman with good (not great) skating skills. Was a little too soft to play against today.

VNW #9, Szeto, Justin (2015) – Wears an 'A' for the Giants. Played forward on the night. Has offensive skill, but is still quite small and thin. Went to the net and did well along the boards, but there is a lack of push back whenever any rough stuff occurs. For his size, he doesn't play mean enough which just allows opponents to get in extra shots against him. Skated well, but top end speed could improve.

VNW #20, Benjafield, Quinn (2016?) – A nice power move to take the puck around the net and slide it through the crease. Attempted a slap pass that would've worked had he put more on it. Showed flashes of a power forward-type game. Would like to see him improve his first few steps.

VNW #22, Fabbro, Dante (2016?) – Right-shooting LD. Nice skater with great agility and ability to quickly turn the play up ice. Plays a mature game and was entrusted to play key minutes for Vancouver. As a 15 year-old, Fabbro was the best defenseman on his team (on a solid veteran team boasting an older 1st round WHL bantam pick in Schultz among others). Fabbro was exceptionally good 1-on-1 and showed great poise with the puck once he collected possession of the puck. Had a nice rush where he dangled a Swiss player before wrapping around the net and feeding a teammate with a pass in the slot. Had a pair of well-earned assists in the game. Was very effective at either end of the rink and was one of the best players on the ice despite being the youngest. Made a pair of picture perfect stretch passes where only his teammates could reach the puck.

SWI #2, Karrer, Roger (2015) – Right-shooting defenseman. Above average size and has good mobility. Kept square to his opponent and showed good pivoting. Jumped into a lane late as a trailer and scored on a nice shot over Tavin Grant, the Giants netminder's glove hand. Blasted a slapshot from the point past Grant for his 2nd goal of the game. Finished the game with three points. His own zone play needs a little work, but there were some similarities between his game and that of Swedish 2nd round NHL pick Robert Hagg at this point in his development.

SWI #11, Haberstich, Fabian (2015) – Captain of the Swiss team. A big player for his age, Haberstich used his size well and finished his checks. Created numerous chances early on. Moved pretty well, but his stride was a little choppy. Seemed to be a stride behind Impose all the time.

SWI #15, Diem, Dominik (2015) – Average size. Good speed. Had a few good chances off the rush. Supported the puck well for the most part, but made a couple glaring mistakes in his own end.

SWI #25, Heughebaert, Stephane (2016) – A late '97 born forward who is an excellent skater and able to handle the puck at top speed. Created several opportunities early on using his speed and body to shield the puck. Showed good vision with the puck and was able to keep his head up to look for openings even under pressure.

SWI #28, Impose, Auguste (2015) – A dynamic-skating player that loved to drive the play. Played both forward and defense early on as he was particularly good at retrieving the puck and skating end to end. Often played the point on the powerplay for his ability to skate the puck into the offensive zone. Showed good mobility and he was able to maintain the puck while moving all directions. While he is a good skater, he lost an edge a couple times early on while trying to shift directions. Impose has good hands and is creative with the puck. A ball of energy, Impose finished his checks and created a lot of chances with his strong skating skills. Strong shot. He often looked for teammates that can read the play as quickly as he can as he tries to keep the puck moving at high speed in order to create space, but found limited help at times.

Game Notes: In an exciting game, the Swiss held on for a 4-3 win versus last year's finalists. Vancouver actually controlled the play for most the game and outshot the Swiss 36-20, but were stymied by the Swiss defense. Switzerland had the lead for most of the game. Due to the tournament format, Vancouver now needs help to qualify for the knockout round as these two tournament heavyweights were both placed in the same pool and only the pool winner is guaranteed through to the knockout round. Only three of the five 2nd place finishers move on to the next round.

Dec 28, 2013. Slovakia vs United States (WJC game)

USA #3 LD, McCoshen, Ian (2013 Florida Panthers draft pick)

I didn't like McCoshen's game that much. He was undisciplined (kneeing an opponent in the second period) and his defensive zone play was average.

USA #4 LD, Butcher, Will (2013 Colorado Avalanche draft pick)

Butcher had an active stick in his zone. Made a nice tee-in pass on Hartman's goal. I liked the decisions he made with and without the puck.

USA #7 RD, Grzelcyk, Matt (2012 Boston Bruins draft pick)

He isn't afraid to take chances in order to produce offense. He moves the puck fast and his breakouts were almost always on tape. His play in his own zone was effective. He won't be the one using his body to regain puck possession, but he uses his smarts and his stick to retrieve it.

USA #9 RW, Copp, Andrew (2013 Winnipeg Jets draft pick)

A big body who showcased his passing skills in the third period. He had two assists on two goals he initiated: one on a three-on-one and another from the corner.

USA #10 RW, O'Reagan, Daniel (2012 San Jose Sharks draft pick)

Scored a goal on the powerplay with one second left in the first period. Didn't notice him much afterwards.

USA #11 C Barber, Riley (2012 Washington Capitals draft pick)

Barber made a great move on the rush while he outskated a Slovak defenseman in the first period. He was on his backhand and he went on his forehand and he then quickly took a low shot. He has a low center of gravity, which explains why he is so great protecting the puck in the offensive zone. He played on the penalty kill as well and he was covering shooting and passing lanes effectively.

USA #13 RW, Hinostroza, Vince (2012 Chicago Blackhawks draft pick)

A shifty skater and good dangler, Hinostroza was effective when his team was shorthanded. He used his speed effectively and he hustled hard to get first on loose pucks. He was good on the forecheck as well.

USA #15 C, Eichel, Jack (2015)

He scored on a powerplay with a low shot underneath Sabol's right pad. He has a great vision that few players possess, even NHLers. The pass he made to Will Butcher on USA's third goal truly showcased it and he made some others that were similar later in the game. He controls the puck at high speed and his strides, although they seem awkward at first glance, are really powerful. He is really a true offensive dynamo with awesome hockey sense.

USA #17 LW, Kerdiles, Nicolas (2012 Anaheim Ducks draft pick)

Kerdiles broke a play in the neutral zone on a penalty kill in the middle of the first period. Showed good wheels and he created scoring chances off the rush on multiple occasions.

USA #21 C, Hartman, Ryan (2013 Chicago Blackhawks draft pick)

He earned a pass on Eichel's goal off the rush. Scored on a one-timer from the high slot that went above Sabol's shoulders.

USA #22 RW, Fasching, Hudson (2013 Los Angeles Kings draft pick)

He is a direct straight-line forward that likes to crash and bang. He protected the puck really effectively due to his large frame. Not overly creative, he only made the simple plays in order to cycle the puck properly.

USA #23 LW, Matteau, Stefan (2012 New Jersey Devils draft pick)

He is still the same player as last year during his one-year stint in the Q. Matteau likes to trash-talk after the whistle. He finishes every check whenever he has the opportunity and he really plays with an edge.

USA #32 G, Gillies, Jonathan (2012 Calgary Flames draft pick)

I really like his athleticism. He made some key saves all game long. He's tall, he moves fast in his crease and he has a good ability to track pucks through traffic. Still had to control his rebounds a tad better though. He heavily relies on his frame and his athleticism in order to make saves.

SLO #7 RD, Predajniansky, Jakub (2014)

This 19-year-old defenseman played a lot on the powerplay, but he was prone to turnovers all game long in his zone. He was effective moving the puck in the offensive zone. Was not bad on one-on-one's.

SLO #14 RD Cernak, Erik (2015)

A big body, Cernak played a ton. Used his long reach effectively on one-on-one's. He was quite good along the wall for a young kid at this stage

SLO #9 C, Kolena, Milan (2014)

Played on the powerplay alongside Martin Reway. Scored on a tap-in. He had a decent showing. He was good in his zone when he was F1.

SLO #10 RW, Reway, Martin (2013 Montreal Canadiens draft pick)

Reway is an east-west forward that can turn on a dime. I really like his shiftiness and his puck control in the offensive zone. He looked like a wizard, especially in the first period. He showcased a good sense of anticipation early on. He was quite noticeable in the first period as he was the most dangerous offensive threat for his team. Had a goal on a powerplay and another late in the third when he took a shot on his backhand after he received a pass from David Griger. He still shies away from physical play.

SLO #20 C, Dano, Marko (2013 Columbus Blue Jackets draft pick)

Dano knows how to get open in the offensive zone. I liked the way he played on a two-on-one in the second period where he took a shot on Gillies' left pad that led to a good scoring chance missed by Lunter. He had two great scoring opportunities in the third, including a breakaway, thanks to his smarts.

SLO #22 LW, Cehlarik, Peter (2013 Boston Bruins draft pick)

Cehlarik made good decisions with the puck down low. He was good on the cycle and used good body positioning in order to protect his puck. Had a great shift on his team's first goal where he made a great rush that led him to the high slot. He fired a wrist shot that Gillies couldn't control.

SLO #28 RW, Skalicky, Pavol (2014)

He had a nice check on Brady Skjei in the first period. Didn't really notice him afterwards.

Czech Republic vs Sweden U-17 Hockey Challenge December 29th 2013

Sweden

#7 Jacob Larsson Def (2014): Larsson showed some good footwork in this game, and I liked his lateral mobility on the back end. Has good speed, which I saw him use when he rushed the puck during the game. I liked his decision-making and his strong passing game as well. Good poise with the puck on the powerplay; he has a good, low, hard shot from the point.

#19 Linus Ölund F (2014): Scored the game's opening goal early in the first after going to the net to jump on his own rebound. Was arguably Sweden's best forward in the first period, as he showed a lot of energy and made some nice plays in the offensive zone. Good on-ice vision with some solid passes, and I liked his two way game. A hard worker who has good feet. Great blocked shot late in the 3rd while Sweden was down a man.

#11 Filip Ahl F (2014): Loved the way Ahl played today, He may not be the quickest skater, but every time he had a chance to take the puck to the net, he did. Strong as a bull; didn't mind making contact with the Czech goaltender. Showed off some interesting moves with the puck in the offensive zone; in the first period he pulled a toe drag in one of his rushes.

#10 Johan Dahlström F (2014): Showed some very interesting flashes in this game. His goal came from a beauty rush, where he showed quick hands and a willingness to go hard to the net. Almost scored another goal the exact same way by cutting to the net after beating a defenseman wide. Was not really noticeable the rest of the game, other than a dumb penalty late in the first period.

#14 Jonathan Davidsson F (2014): Liked his energy and the fact that his feet are always moving. Davidsson has good speed, and is willing to take pucks to the net. Good forechecker, will finish his hits and create turnovers with his hustle. An energy role player on this team.

#8 Jonathan Leman Def (2014): Decent poise with the puck on the power play, good mobility. Made a great saucer pass to send #13 on a breakaway, and that really caught my eye as a standout pass.

#5 Lucas Carlsson Def (2014): Liked his smarts in the offensive zone. He is a good skater that covers a lot of ice.

#1 Felix Sandström G (2014): Sandström played well today. His rebound control was good and he made look himself look big in net. Challenged shooters aggressively and didn't give them much to shoot at. Was beaten by a one-timer from the slot, can't blame him on that goal.

Czech Republic

#9 Filip Chlapik F (2014): Played a decent two-way game. He was good on the forecheck, creating some problems for the Swedish defense. Showed his passing abilities on one sequence where he made a nice saucer pass on a two-on-one, but was rather quiet outside of that offensively. Did most of his good work along the boards, without the puck. Smart player.

#22 David Kase F (2014): Thought Kase was the better Czech player today, as he showed a very impressive skill set with the puck. Liked his creativity with the puck; he made his linemates better and was able to find them with ease. An above-average skater who can make sharp turns on his skates. Protected the puck well even if he's undersized, and saw some time on the point on the power play. His goal came from a quick one-timer from the slot, where he showed a quick release and good positioning in the offensive zone. Was a victim of trying to do too much with the puck late in the 3rd when his team was desperate for a goal.

#23 Simon Stransky F (2014): Was paired with Kase most of the game, and it showed, as both of them were the Czech best players offensively. An average skater who is not as agile as Kase, but who is still a smart player. He showed some good patience with the puck in the offensive zone. Made good plays without the puck in the neutral zone, showing good commitment to the defensive game.

#18 Filip Suchy F (2015): Made a great backhand pass from behind the net to #22 Kase for the only Czech goal. Outside of that, he was not very noticeable offensively today. Showed some good speed and agility on his skates in some rushes.

#13 Martin Svoboda F (2014): A smallish player, outside of one real good scoring chance in the first period, Svoboda was not a big factor for the Czech team today. I thought he lacked energy late in the game after he was caught from behind in a two-on-one rush.

#30 Daniel Vladar G (2014): Tremendous game from Vladar, who was tested a lot in this game by the Swedes. Has great size, and doesn't give a lot to shoot at for a shooter. He doesn't stay too deep in his crease and will challenge shooters at times. Was very tough to beat down low thanks to his quick legs.

FINAL SCORE: 6-3 USA

December 29, 2013 Team Ontario vs. Germany (U-17)

Score: 8-1 Ontario

ON # 16, C, Stome, Dylan (2015) – Strome did a nice job holding the puck down low, and buying himself time before passing it to teammates, and creating chances around the net. He also made a nice feed to Blake Spears on the powerplay, which led directly to Ontario's 2nd goal. He was hitting open teammates on the tape all game, and was one of the best players on the ice. Strome also showed off his excellent release when going top shelf on an odd man rush in the 3rd period.

ON # 17, C, Konecny, Travis (2015) – Konecny had some flashes of brilliance in this game. He displayed his excellent release on numerous occasions, and showed some good speed beating defenders to loose pucks. He also made an excellent play knocking a German player off the puck, which led directly to Marner's goal in the 2nd. He also had a strong backcheck after an Ontario turnover, and carried it up the other way before dishing it to Marner for his 2nd goal of the night. Konecny was excellent in this game, though he did take two penalties within three minutes in the 2nd period.

ON # 9, C, Marner, Mitch (2015) - Marner displayed good speed throughout the game. He has a quick few first steps, and used that to blow by German defenders. He showed good vision and patience, waiting for lanes to open up before hitting teammates with good passes in scoring position. His game plan was more or less feed Konecny whenever he could, which seemed to work pretty well. Marner is known for his offense, but he also made a couple nice plays in the defensive zone breaking up plays before Germany could get a scoring chance. Marner showed nice finishing ability scoring a hat trick in this game. He was involved in some beautiful passing plays as well.

ON # 12, C, Mckenzie, Brett (2015) – McKenzie played real well on the penalty kill, and was able to establish a consistent forecheck throughout the night. McKenzie was in perfect position in the offensive zone while shorthanded, and was able to finish a play in front, taking advantage of a turnover from Germany.

ON # 21, LW, Crouse, Lawson (2015) – Crouse was able to get in on the forecheck, and finish his checks all game long. He used his size to create space for himself in front, and he had quite a few quality chances in front of the net. Crouse also had a nice assist to Marner in the 2nd period.

ON # 15, LW, Matthew Kreis (2015) – Kreis found twine early on as he went to the net, and showed nice hands in front finishing a play started by Sean Day.

ON # 7, D Chychrun, Jakob (2016) – At times his outlet passes weren't great, and he elected to skate the puck out of his zone several times instead. He was physical early, and engaged in body contact whenever he could. Chychrun made some smart pinches in the offensive zone, and scored his goal that way. He displayed his powerful shot on a few occasions, as well.

ON # 8, D, Vande Sompel, Mitchell (2015) – He was calm with the puck throughout the game, and consistently made good outlet passes to his forwards. He read the play well, and didn't try to force anything. Vande Sompel also did a nice job of safely carrying the puck into the offensive zone, and allowing his team to set up shop before making a play with the puck.

ON # 4, D, Day, Sean (2016) – Day's skating was brilliant once again. He was very calm under pressure, never panicked with a forechecker coming at him, and used his skating ability to avoid any kind of trouble. He blew by a few German defenders before getting it to Kreis in front, who scored the first goal for Team Ontario. Day was good on the powerplay, and very calm while walking the line, opening up lanes. Day also consistently made good outlet passes, and had a few beautiful end-to-end rushes.

ON # 6, D, Spencer, Matt (2015) – Spencer wasn't flashy, but I thought he played a real solid game. He was able to break up plays and get pucks out on the penalty kill, and always seemed to get the puck out of trouble. He made some nice outlets, skated well and overall played a good two-way game.

ON # 1, G, Timpano, Troy (2016) – Timpano wasn't tested regularly, but he was very good when called upon. He made some nice saves, and showed good athleticism getting pieces of his body on the puck, even when it looked like he was down and out. He stopped 15-of-16 (.938 save percentage) in the first 40 minutes before being replaced by Ben Blacker for the 3rd.

GER # 9, D, Glaessl, MAx – Glaessl wasn't afraid to throw pucks on net, and for the most part was able to get them through. He had a bad pinch in the neutral zone where he tried to hit Travis Konecny, completely missed, and Konecny jump-started an odd man rush during 4 vs 4 play. He missed some open players with bad cross-ice passes and overall his decision-making wasn't great with the puck on his stick. He played on the top powerplay unit for Germany, and did have a few nice holds in that situation.

GER # 6, D, Halbauer, Philipp – Halbauer was pretty quiet for the most part, but he had an excellent shift on a powerplay in the 1st that led to Germany's only goal. He had a nice hold at the line, and danced around a couple Canadian defenders before dishing the puck and eventually recording an assist on the play.

December 29, 2013, Sweden vs. Czech Republic (U17)

Score: 3-1 Sweden

SWE # 17, F, Grundstrom, Carl (2016) – Grundstrom is a good skater who can efficiently get around the ice. He's confident with the puck in the offensive zone, and plays the game quick. He reads and reacts well, knows where to go on the ice, and is strong on the backcheck as well. He made a couple nice plays pickpocketing the puck from Czech players.

SWE # 19, F, Olund, Linus (2015) – Ohlund isn't a big player, but he's not afraid of going into traffic, and has a nose for the net. He went to the net, and stayed with his initial shot before banging in the rebound for the 1st goal of the game. Ohlund also showed nice vision, and playmaking ability, hitting a streaking player towards the net with a tape-to-tape pass, which led directly to a Grade A scoring chance in front of the net. On another occasion Ohlund faked a shot that the defender bit on, then hit an open man in front to create a scoring chance. He easily could have had two or three assists. He also took a regular shift on the penalty kill, and had a nice block late in the game defending the lead.

SWE # 10, F, Dahlstrom, John (2015) – Dahlstrom used his size very well when protecting the puck. He had a nice rush where he took a pass, skated with it down the wing, and stepped around a defender before using his big frame to cut to the net, and finish in tight. Dahlstrom also made a nice feed to Ohlund on his goal.

SWE # 11, F, Ahl, Filip (2015) – Ahl is a good skater for his size (6'2"), and showed nice hands for a big man, dancing around a couple Czech defenders, and getting a backhand shot off in the slot after gaining the line. Ahl also made a nice power move where he skated down the wing protecting the puck before cutting and driving to the net.

SWE # 7, D, Larsson, Jacob (2015) – Has a hard, accurate shot. Larsson is a good skater who can skate the puck out of trouble whenever necessary. He's a good passer, and is capable of making long, cross-ice feeds to stationary or moving targets. He made an excellent play slipping by a Czech forward in his own zone before carrying the puck up ice, and sending a nice cross-ice feed to help his team enter the zone. Sweden scored just moments after. Larsson did a good job holding the line in the offensive zone on several occasions, and his backwards skating was fluid whenever he had to defend on the rush. He was also good while quarterbacking the powerplay. He's a good passer, and sees the ice well so he was able to hit open teammates and consistently set up scoring chances. One shift Larsson skated the puck out of his own then made a beautiful saucer pass through two defenders that led to a mini-breakaway for a teammate. Larsson also kept an active stick in the defensive zone and used it to break up or intercept passes from Czech plays on several occasions.

SWE #6, D, Carlsson, Gabriel (2015) – Carlsson is very confident with the puck. He's capable of making the outlet pass, but if it isn't there he has no problems carrying the puck up ice. When it gets to the offensive zone he likes to give it to a teammate as soon as he can, and he almost forced passes trying to do that. A couple times he tried to pass it to a teammate a few feet away while entering the zone, and it almost led to turnovers.

SWE # 5, D, Carlsson, Lucas (2015) – He made a good first pass, and was able to effectively start the rush on a regular basis. He showed good vision, and always put the puck in the right place. Carlsson was good skating with the puck, and wasn't afraid to jump into the rush and join the play, either. Carlsson is always able to get back whenever he pinches because of his skating ability. Carlsson has a calm demeanor, and never forced a play even when pressured by the forechecker. He was also able to use his skating ability to catch a Czech forward on an odd-man rush, lift his stick and steal the puck away.

SWE # 1, G, Sandstrom, Felix (2015) – He didn't have much work for the first 15 minutes or so, but Czech Republic really came on after that. His rebound control was good, and he was almost always in perfect position. Sandstrom made the saves he had to, and always seemed calm between the pipes. Sandstrom was also pretty good handling the puck, and making outlets when he had to.

CZE # 15, F, Wagner, Frantisek (2015) – Wagner took a regular shift on the penalty kill, and was good in that role. He blocked some shots, broke up a couple players, and made a nice stretch pass to give a teammate a chance shorthanded.

CZE # 13, F, Svoboda, Martin (2015) – Svoboda was one of the best Czech players in this game. He was pretty quiet for most of the 1st period, but as the game went on he continued to get better. He made a couple nice plays on the PP early in the 2nd hitting open teammates with passes in the scoring area as well as getting a couple scoring chances himself. He beat Felix Sandstrom five-hole but it somehow changed direction and ended up missing the net. Svoboda also backchecked regularly and was usually in position to break up a play in the defensive zone.

CZE # 18, F, Suchy, Filip (2016) – He was pretty quiet throughout the game, though he did make a beautiful feed to David Kase for Czech Republic's only goal. Suchy was standing in front of the net facing the blue line, and rather than trying a spinning shot, he made a perfect backhand feed to Kase who essentially had an empty net to shoot at.

CZE # 17, F, Dymacek, Roman (2015) – Dymacek played a solid game. He was good on the penalty kill, and showed solid speed when blowing by a Swedish defenseman to get himself a breakaway down a man. He also was able to deke around opposing players regularly, and was able to create space for himself to get shots off and create scoring chances.

CZE # 22, F, Kase, David (2015) – Kase was one all over the ice, and generated scoring chances consistently for the final 40 minutes. He had a couple great chances to tie the game up, and also scored Czech Republic's lone goal in this game. He's a smart player, was always in the right place at the right time and could skate pretty well, too.

CZE # 6, D, Krenzelok, Daniel (2015) – Krenzelok was the designated shooter on the Czech powerplay. On the 5-on-3 in the 1st period in particular, his teammates were really trying to set him up. He scored on a beautiful, hard, accurate wrist shot but the goal was waved off because the net was slightly dislodged.

CZE # 30, G, Vladar, Daniel (2015) – Vladar was the only reason his team was in this game. It took Czech Republic almost the entire 1st period to get a shot on goal, but because of his strong play the Czechs were within one goal after 20 minutes. His rebound control was good, and he made some athletic saves in front stretching and sprawling out to get a piece of the puck. Vladar also did a good job holding the post when Sweden players attempted wraparounds or jam plans in front.

Scout notes: Czech Republic was much better in the final 40 after a very slow start...Czech defensemen seemed to miss a lot of breakout passes.

Sherbrooke Phoenix vs Drummondville Voltigeurs, QMJHL, December 29th 2013

Sherbrooke

#53 Tim Wieser Lw (2014): Played with Audette today, has good speed at this level and can win races for the puck. Undersized and was put in check most of the afternoon when he doesn't have space to manoeuver. Had a great scoring chance late in the first period when Audette was able to create a turnover from a Drummondville defensemen just inside their defensive zone to send him all alone but couldn't beat the Voltigeurs netminder. Although not big, Weiser is not afraid of contact and will initiate some and will even jump to hit his opponents but doesn't have much impact into his hits. Saw him block at least 2 shots in the defensive zone with one leading to a breakaway where he was hooked which lead to penalty shot late in the 3rd period. Couldn't beat the Drummondville netminder after a nice deke on the backhand.

#15 Jonathan Deschamps Def (2014): Deschamps does a nice job in his zone as a defensive defenseman, strong on his skate and he's strong enough to pin his man down the wall. Had some struggles with the puck today and slow decision making with the puck. Know his limits and kept his game simple today, already captain of his team at 17 years old. Hard worker.

#19 Mitchell Lundbolm C (2015): The young American forward didn't got a ton of ice time 5 on 5 but saw him him get pp time and was use in front of the net due to his size. Skating stride need work and still need to get stronger. Good defensive awareness as a center he gets back deep in his zone to help his defensemen's out.

#28 Daniel Audette C (2014): Not Audette best effort today, his line had a hard time generating any offense and were off on many rushes. Even on the power play couldn't generate much, where he usually is at his best. Made a nice stickcheck at the end of the first period to strip of the puck one of the Drummondville defensemen which lead to his Tim Wieser being all alone in front of the net with the puck but couldn't finish it. You could see Audette was getting frustrated with the lack of success his line had in the game and saw him play a chippy game, on one occasion made sure referee was not looking and crosscheck a Drummondville defensemen in the ribs and late in the 2nd period gave a bad hit from behind in which he got lucky just getting a 2minutes. Barely played in the 3rd period.

#32 Carl Neil Def (2014): Showed nice patience with the puck at the blueline and made a nice fake shot and then throw puck behind the net which result in the first goal of the game earlier in the first period. Neil was used on the first power play unit in this game, would have like to see him make quicker decisions with the puck in his own zone. He's got good gap control ,used his stick to keep distance with opposing forwards. Made a good job of cleaning the front of the net on the PK and was strong in his battle along the wall. In the 3rd period, loss his man for a fraction of seconds in the slot wich gave him time to score the game winning goal.

#73 Chase Harwell C/Lw (2015): Inconsistent effort from the rookie American today, like the speed he showed on some rushes and he's a good stickhandler. Also showed with his linemates that he can play a gritty game with some strong forecheck presence late in the 2nd period after Drummondville tied the game at 3. But overall it was a rather quiet performance from Harwell.

#81 Gabriel Fontaine C (2015): Fontaine was call up from his midget team in Magog for this game with players missing with injuries and different international tournaments. Didn't get a ton of ice time in this one but made the most of it, made a nice pass to Jason Houde to send him to the net for Sherbrooke 3rd goal, that was Fontaine first career qmjhl points. Also like his forecheck presence later in the period, has good speed and used it well to make life hard for the Drummondville defense on that shift. After that didn't noticed him on the ice.

#88 Trevor Stacey Lw (2015): Didn't see much from Stacey in this game, don't think he got a lot of ice time. Saw him throw a weak hit in the 2nd period is where I first noticed him during the game. Other than that I didn't noticed him .

Drummondville

#4 Frederic Aube Def (2014): With some defensemen's out of the lineup Aube saw his ice time increase on the power play today, showed a nice low shot that he's tough for a goalie to see if he's screen and can be easily tip in front of the net. Kept his game simple even with the add responsibility, not a typical offensive defensemen but did fine today. Had some nerve earlier in the game with the puck and was taken off from the power play for a brief time but was back on it in the 3rd period and had an assist on the 5th Drummondville goal. His play in his zone was solid again; nothing flashy but does his job without any fanfare.

#11 Joey Ratelle Rw (2014): A good game for the 2nd year forward, nothing flashy about his game but played a sound two-way game. A hard worker who play hard and goes to the net to jump on any rebounds. Scored the game winning goal in the 3rd period after hiding away from Neil for a shot moment and getting a pass in the slot and beating the Sherbrooke goaltender. Was Drummondville 2nd best forward in this game in my opinion, even with the score 3-0 Sherbrooke he was working hard and trying to make things happen for his line.

#15 Nikolas Brouillard Def (2014): Brouillard was usual self today, made some real nice play with the puck and quarterback the voltigeurs powerplay. Try to force the play too much at time in the offensive zone and got caught but has the speed to get back defensively at this level. Used the spinorama often in the offensive zone to protect the puck and get away from defenders. Showed tremendous patience with the puck on one particular shift where he outwaited Audette at the blueline which made the Sherbrooke player fall on the ice trying to cover Brouillard. Great series of plays by him lead to Drummondville first goal of the game after a great breakout pass to Matthew Boudens he continued to skate and got the puck back just outside the Sherbrooke zone and then found a streaking Frederic Gaudreault between the two Sherbrooke defensemen who end up beating their goaltender.

#19 Cam Askew Rw (2014): Started the game on the 4th line and didn't see much out of him in the first period. Started to play better in the 2nd period with a nice give & go on a rush where he showed some decent speed. Was used in front of the net on the power play and almost got a goal but couldn't get enough power on his shot. Came close of scoring once again in the 3rd period after he receive a perfect pass at the side of the net form Georgs Golovkovs but was robbed by the Sherbrooke goaltender. Much better effort from him in 2nd & 3rd period after he moved into the 3rd line and was paired with Golovkovs.

#55 Sergei Boikov Def (2014): In the offensive zone, thought his decision making was lacking in the first half of the game. Taking too much time to make a decision with the puck and got into trouble at times because of this. Defensively he was sound, played a safe game in his own zone and threw 1 or 2 good hits. In the 3rd period his decision making were better and showed a nice slap shot from the blueline and even saw him take the puck deep in the Sherbrook end to apply pressure.

#95 Georgs Golovkovs Lw/C (2014): Was rather invisible in the first 2 period of this game but came alive in the 3rd period once paired with Askew. Made a sweet pass to Askew at the side of the net which would had been a goal if not from the great pad save from Desrosiers the Sherbrooke goaltender. Great play where he took puck of the corner and then deke a Drummondville forward around the faceoff circle and got away a great wrist shot. Good release on his shot, showed some nice stickhandling skill in the 3rd period as at time look like he stickhandle the puck in a phone booth.

Dec 29, 2013. Baie-Comeau Drakkar vs Chicoutimi Sagueneéns (QMJHL)

BAC #3 LD, Vanier, Alexis (2014) He had a bad night. He lost his man, Simon Tremblay, early in the first that resulted in Sags's first goal. He was soft all night long. In order to be effective, he needs to be involved physically. His lack of footwork is being exposed on a bigger ice surface like in Chicoutimi. He was used on the powerplay due to his heavy slapper. He lacked vision, which was showcased by the wrong decisions he made when he tried to take his time.

CHI #58 D, Allard, Frédéric (2014) Allard was the best defenseman on the ice. He was bright out there. Still needs to add weight to his slight frame, but he is being used in key situations. He's reliable in his zone, his stick is active and he was able to get the puck out of his zone quite easily despite the pressure applied by energetic and bigger Baie-Comeau forwards. He earned an assist on a powerplay.

FINAL SCORE: 3-0 CHI

Czech Republic vs Quebec U-17 Hockey Challenge December 30th 2013

Czech Republic

#13 Martin Svoboda LW (2015): Thought Svoboda was tremendous for the Czechs today, did a lot of nice things offensively for his squad. Even though he is listed only at 5'6", he was very strong on the puck against Quebec, and won most of his puck battles. Finished the game with a goal and an assist (although the scoresheet didn't give him the 5th goal for the Czechs, it was clearly scored by him). Love his passing game. He made a nice stretch pass to #22 David Kaze to send him on a breakaway for the game-winning goal at the beginning of the 3rd period. Scored his goal with less than 30 seconds left in the game; he took a pass at the blueline, beat Quebec defensemen on the outside and cut to the net to beat the Quebec goalie with a low glove shot. Love his game, tough to knock down as well and he battled hard all game long.

#17 Roman Dymacek Lw (2015): Has some flashes in the game offensively, scored a nice goal with a quick shot from the slot in the 3rd period. Made some nice passes during the game showing some nice creativity, but his play was inconsistent.

#18 Filip Suchy F (2016): Suchy had quite a start to this game, with two good scoring chances near the net, but was also hit very hard by Quebec's Olivier Galipeau with a huge open-ice hit. His play tailed off after the hit, but he still showed some nice speed on the rush and I liked his puck protection while battling in the corners.

#23 Simon Stansky RW (2015): Was the best Czech forward in the first period in my opinion, not a great skater, but always around the puck and makes things happen offensively. Scored a great goal at the beginning of the 2nd period, showing some serious puck skills and quick hands. Doesn't need a lot of space to make something happen offensively. Smart positionally in the offensive zone, as he showed some nice dekes in one-on-one confrontations.

#22 David Kase C (2015): Thought Kase was pretty quiet in the first two periods. He got good ice time during the game, but couldn't generate much offense until the 3rd period. Scored the game-winning goal early in the 3rd period where he hid behind the Quebec defense and received a superb pass from #13 Martin Svoboda that sent him all alone against Callum Booth. He beat Booth going roof on the backhand.

#1 Alex Stezka G (2015): Good game from Stezka today, who has nice size and covers the net well. Only goal he gave up was a five-hole goal from the side of the net on a Quebec powerplay, and for the rest of the game, he gave nothing to Quebec forwards. A calm goaltender with good reflexes and who generally control his rebounds well enough. For a big goaltender, he has quick legs and he's quick. Liked his battle level in the crease when Quebec was putting pressure on net, crashing his crease.

#12 Vojtech Budik Def (2016): One of the few '98-born defensemen in this tournament, Budik got some good ice time from his coaches today. Had some problems in the first period with his passing game, where he got caught being too aggressive in the neutral zone as well. Had quality ice time in this game playing on the first Czech powerplay unit. His game improved after the first period and he made better decisions with and without the puck. Liked his feet, he has good agility and good lateral mobility.

#9 Filip Chalpik C (2015): Played a good two-way game today, nothing flashy offensively but plays the right way. Gets pucks deep and gets the cycling game going. He has good reach and surprised the Quebec defense with some good stickhandling work. Hard worker that uses his size well to protect the puck well. As a center, I noticed he goes back deep in his zone to help out his defense. Came close to scoring after tipping a shot from the point in front of the net, but that was a real good reflex save by Callum Booth of Quebec.

#5 Jozef Zajic Def (2015): Noticed Zajic when he was going deep in the offensive zone with the puck trying to make thing happen offensively for the Czechs. Not a big defenseman, but has nice feet and good mobility. Made a great stickcheck at the side of the net on Quebec's #19 Brandon Gignac to prevent him for scoring in the 2nd period. Scored into an open net to put the Czechs up 4-1 in the last minute of the game.

#7 Martin Weinhold Def (2015): Liked his defensive qualities in this game; he had a good gap control and kept Quebec forwards close to him. Made an excellent play in a one-on-one confrontation versus Quebec's best forward Nicolas Roy. The Quebec forward tried to go around him and Weinhold finished the play with a good hip check.

Quebec

#12 Anthony Beauvillier C (2015): Scored Quebec's only goal early in the first period on the powerplay from his usual spot: in the faceoff circle at the left side of the goaltender. His puck management was lacking in the first two periods. He tried to do too much with the puck and caused turnovers in his zone. On the penalty kill, he had a tough time getting the puck out of his zone multiple times and his passing game was off as well. I either saw some selfish plays with the puck (with open teammates ready to receive a pass) or he simply just didn't see them out there, which showed a lack of vision.

#10 Nicolas Roy C (2015): Started the game well with a nice pass to #12 Anthony Beauvillier for the game's opening goal on the power play, showing good patience with the puck on that play. Roy's skating is rough and he doesn't have great top speed to create separation from defenders. Goes to the net with the puck when he has a chance. Showed his smarts in the defensive zone with good positioning in his zone. Used his reach well in one-on-one confrontations, and with his dekes, he can be a dangerous player to defend one-on-one.

#17 Maxime Fortier Rw (2016): Fortier had a good start of the game, using his speed well and giving the Czech defense some issues with his outside speed . Made a good stickcheck in his zone, stealing the puck away and keeping his feet moving for a loose puck, which caused a penalty to the Czechs. After this, he was pretty quiet until the 3rd period, where he had a great shift holding onto the puck behind the Czech net before making a sweet backhand pass to #10 Nicolas Roy, who was all alone in the slot for a good scoring chance.

#5 Guillaume Brisebois Def (2015): Played a simple game, making simple outlet passes to his forwards, nothing fancy. He played in all situations of the game. Good poise with the puck and a very consistent performer from shift to shift. Tough to beat one-on-one, as he keeps a good gap between himself and opposing forwards.

#7 Jeremy Roy Def (2015): Had some good moments in the first two periods, where he moved the puck well and was not shy to rush it in the Czech zone. Played in all situations and started forcing plays in the 3rd period, with Quebec down in the game, and found himself in trouble. Tried a cross-ice pass in his zone more than once and was cut down by a Czech winger playing the left wing lock to perfection.

#6 Nicolas Meloche Def (2015): Not a good game out of Meloche, thought he struggled with his decision-making. His passing game, which is a strong facet of his game, was off all game long. Was soft in his zone with his coverage. Made a good play in the 3rd period, where he followed Nicolas Roy in an offensive rush, got the puck and fired a quick shot on net from the top of the faceoff circle. Love Meloche's quick release on his shot.

#30 Callum Booth G (2015): Made a lot of saves in the first two periods, where Quebec was outplayed by the Czech squad, and kept his team in the game. His rebound control, which is usually excellent, was off in this game, but he still found a way to make most saves in the first two periods. In the first, I noticed high shots were the shots that gave him the most issues. In the 3rd, the Czechs found a way to put three behind him and I can't say he was to blame for any of them, as Quebec's defensive zone play was bad. Liked his calm demeanor in his crease; he moves well for a big goaltender as he showed on one sequence in the 2nd period where he moved post-to-post to steal a sure Czech goal.

Dec 30. 2013. Pacific vs West (World Under 17 Hockey Challenge)

PAC #31 G, Sawchenko, Zach

One thing that caught my attention at the beginning of the game was the fact that he freezes the puck a lot. He stays a bit deep in his crease and he looked smaller than he really is in his net. Sawchenko had trouble dealing with shots coming from the point early on. He was really weak on Hobbs' goal as he wasn't positionally and mentally ready. He controlled his rebounds better as the game progressed.

PAC #3 RD, Davis, Kevin

Played great on a 3-on-1 in the first period. He also displayed sound body positioning and good hockey IQ. He's willing to battle for puck possession in the corners. He's pretty quick on the transition as well. He had a great second period showing. His slapper is hard and accurate and I really like his footwork that allows him to slide well on the blueline and to cover a lot of spaces in his zone.

PAC #6 LD, Reddekopp, Chaz

He is a big defenseman with a lack of footing. He was caught on first Colton Conrad's goal being too aggressive on Matthew Campese instead of playing patiently. His lack of footing affected his game but used in a certain role, he's effective clearing his net.

PAC #8 LD, Wotherspoon, Parker

I liked the way he's always in good position on his one-on-one's. His breakouts are simple, but effective. His defensive coverage overall was excellent as he was a pain in the ass for the puck carrier. He was squaring up well to oncoming forwards all game long. He blocked multiple shots in this game. He moved the puck surprisingly well early in the third, even earning an assist on Matteo Gennaro's second goal.

PAC #9 F, Musil, Adam

Musil was great in terms of protecting the puck. He has the tools (speed, size, smarts) to become an effective power forward. I liked his smooth skating stride and his quickness for a big guy like him. He used his body effectively in order to create spaces for himself. He did score the fourth goal of his team burying a rebound.

PAC #10 F, Gennaro, Matteo

He made quick decisions with the puck. He is not overly fast, but he executes well in the offensive zone. He can create spaces for himself and the opposition tended to forget him in the slot. He deflected a nice shot coming from Noah Juulsen for his second goal.

PAC #11 F, Ronning, Ty

He gets in good position to receive pucks on the transition. I really liked his willingness to battle even though he's on the small side. He did try a toe-drag in the second period in a one-on-one that didn't work. He is weak physically and he gets pushed around way too easily.

PAC #16 F, Comrie, Ty

He applied good pressure on the forecheck. I liked the fact that his wheels were always in movement. He did not create a lot of things offensively, though. He was efficient in his zone covering his man effectively.

PAC #17 F, Merkley, Nick

He constantly creates scoring opportunities using his edges well. Merkley displayed a high level of creativity distributing the puck rather easily. He's a finesse player.

PAC #18 F, Estephan, Giorgio

Scored on a good forehand-backhand move on a powerplay. He won most of his faceoffs as well.

PAC #21 F, Soy, Tyler

He has shown good anticipation and utilizes this to create turnovers. That was the case on Pacific's first goal when he intercepted a pass attempted by Ethan Bear. He then took a shot and Matteo Gennaro took the rebound. He also prepared Estephan's goal by using his speed on the rush. He went behind Flodell's net and he made a nice backhand pass in front he didn't get credit for. Was good on the penalty kill as well thanks to his anticipation. I liked his two-way game as he back-checked hard. He scored a heck of a goal late in the game using his quickness to cut toward the net before shooting in the five-hole. Soy really had a strong showing in this game.

PAC #22 F, Harkins, Jansen

Harkins was the captain of his team. He took a bad slashing penalty early on, but he did compensate later on with his great hockey sense and his hard work. He was able to break up plays effectively in the neutral zone and he was the one who did all the work on his team's second goal. He always gets his nose dirty and he's willing to sacrifice his body to get things turned in his favor.

WES #2 RD, Bear, Ethan

Bear is a good-sized defenseman that finds opening when rushing the puck. He looked good carrying the puck, handling it with smooth and displaying nice hands. He's good enough to create shooting lanes from the point. He was used a lot by his coaches and he delivered. He's really tough to beat one-on-one.

WES #4 RD, Hobbs, Connor

He controls the puck quite well on the opposing blueline. On his goal though, he fumbled the puck twice before shooting on his backhand. He had a nice hip check on Ty Comrie.

WES #6 LD, Murray, Troy

Murray controlled his gaps effectively and his footwork helps him a lot with his coverage. He has good hockey IQ and he efficiently gets the puck out of his zone. He also made a lot of smart simple plays with his stick to break up plays in his own zone.

WES #9 F, Draude, Terrell

Draude is a big body with smooth hands. He can drive the net effectively.

WES #11 F, Halbgewachs, Jayden

He's a skilled player. He controls the puck well in tight and he sees the ice pretty well when used on the powerplay. Overall he was pretty much invisible.

WES #12 F, Campese, Matthew

I liked the agility he showcased when he got rid of Reddekopp early in the first period. He has good hands in tight and he uses his teammates well in order to create offensive opportunities. Campese was really at his ease near the half wall.

WES #14 F, Kolesar, Keegan

Kolesar is a big body that lacks explosiveness. He's bright and he plays within his limits. He was good along the wall and he protected the puck effectively.

WES #15 F, Conrad, Colton

Small forward who moves the puck well and who takes great shots on net. He did score a goal on a 5-on-3 powerplay.

WES #21 F, Keane, Jackson

He was good on the forecheck. He is a great passer and he has good vision. He's especially deadly on the powerplay when playing the point. He's been the best offensive weapon on his team.

FINAL SCORE: 6-3 Pacific

Dec 31, 2013. Canada vs United States (WJC game)

USA #15 C, Eichel, Jack (2015)

That kid has a natural scoring touch. He knows where to shoot the puck and he is particularly deadly on the powerplay. He finds passing lanes so easily it's frightening. He's really quick as he can get to loose pucks in a heartbeat. He owned Griffin Reinhart in one-on-one situation using him as a screen before taking a great wrist shot on Zach Fucale in the second period. Most of his shots were dangerous even though they came from the perimeter. His wrist shots are accurate and he fires them quickly.

CAN #5 RD, Ekblad, Aaron (2014)

He was a fixture on Canada's penalty killing team. He seemed to be in the right position to make a defensive play. Ekblad shows quick footwork but doesn't move anywhere particularly fast. He joined the rush once early in the second period where he took a shot that went directly into Gillies' chest protector. He could have been better on Barber's goal, but he used his stick effectively to break a three-on-one a bit later in the game. He showed man strength winning battles in his own zone.

CAN #23 RW, Reinhart, Sam (2014)

Reinhart had a bad first period, much like the rest of his team. He panicked with the puck giving the puck away twice when he was in the defensive zone zone. He used the width of the ice effectively to move the puck in the second period. Had a great chance early in the third period where he cut towards the net shooting wide. He played with more confidence with the puck and he was good in his own zone covering the high slot and his man.

CAN #17 C, McDavid, Connor (2015)

He played well as he created scoring opportunities off the rush finding his teammates and putting the puck to the net. McDavid scored on his rebound to make it 2-1. He was able to reach top gear in almost no time and he was elusive in the corners. He was defensively responsible.

FINAL SCORE: 3-2 CAN

Dec 31. 2013. Quebec vs Sweden (World Under 17 Hockey Challenge)

SWE #1 G, Sandström, Felix (2015)

He was always squared to the puck and he made 49 saves in this game, which is astonishing even though most of the shots taken were not overly dangerous. He wasn't caught too deep in his crease and I liked his recovery.

SWE #2 D, Anderberg, Alexander (2015)

Anderberg is a physical defenseman with great footwork. His breakouts were effective and he was good getting away from pressure. Had a great shift in the third period where he went on an end-to-end rush that led to a great scoring chance where he took a shot on Tremblay's right shoulder.

SWE #3 D, Alftberg, Philip (2015)

He was good on his one-on-one's and he moves well on the ice. He contained Nicolas Roy well in the third period.

SWE #4 D, Bouramman, Gustav (2015)

His breakouts were good and he was used in key situations for Team Sweden. Nothing extraordinary in his game but he is pretty effective. He plays the body accordingly and his coverage in his zone was consistent.

SWE #5 D, Carlsson, Lucas (2015)

He controls his gaps pretty well and he kept his stick active in his zone. He generally made quick and effective decisions in transition and he used his body properly when battling for puck possession in the corners. He was a fixture on Sweden's penalty killing team.

SWE #6 D, Karlsson, Gabriel (2015)

He's big and he's not afraid to play physical to retrieve possession of the puck. His hockey IQ is pretty good. Karlsoon was good clearing the front of his net.

SWE #8 D, Léman, Jonathan (2015)

He was used on the first powerplay unit. He can move the puck well but his coverage needs some work.

SWE #10 F, Dahlström, John (2015)

He made a nice one-touch pass on Eriksson El's goal. He was pretty effective along the wall protecting the puck.

SWE #11 F, Ahl, Filip (2015)

Ahl's long reach allows him to get on loose pucks. His strides were powerful and you could see that he was strong on his skates. He lacks explosiveness but it does not affect his game much right now. He protects the puck effectively down low and he showed good vision.

SWE #12 F, Asplund, Rasmus (2016)

Asplund is a big centerman who's pretty good at the faceoff dot. Like many Swedish forwards in this contest, his game is all about puck protection down low. Liked his two-way game as well.

SWE #14 F, Davidsson, Jonathan (2015)

He read the play really well and he created a scoring opportunity pressuring Jason Bell on a penalty kill at the beginning of the second period. He did the same thing to Jérémy Roy and was credited with an assist on Sweden's second goal.

SWE #15 F, Emanuelsson, Einar (2015)

I liked his speed. He was effective on the forecheck, but he kind of disappeared as the game went on.

SWE #16 F, Erixon, Oliver (2015)

Scored on an empty net after receiving Ölund's pass on his tape.

SWE #19 F, Ölund, Linus (2015)

A lanky skater, Ölund used his frame effectively along the wall and on the rush. Ölund made a great pass in front of Tremblay's net good for Sweden's second goal. A great net presence, he knows how to get open. His play improved as the game went on. From late in the second period, he was constantly dangerous, rushing the puck, cutting towards the net and being a cycling monster. He was Sweden's best offensive weapon.

SWE #20 F, Eriksson Elk, Joel (2015)

Scored Sweden's first goal on a quick wrist shot from the high slot. Was an effective cycler and he protected the puck well enough to create space and shooting lanes for himself.

SWE #22 F, Kalte, Anton (2016)

He was always the first forward on the ice during a penalty kill for his team. He won key faceoffs and he was covering the point effectively. He hustled hard all game long.

QUE #31 G, Tremblay, Olivier (2015)

He was scored on early in the first minute of the game, but he was better as the game went on. He cuts on his angles pretty well and he was aggressive in his crease. I saw regularly back in Jonquière in MAAA and he was his regular self. He challenged shooters and his lateral movements were really quick and in control. He was not quite as good in the shootouts, but overall his showing was impressive.

QUE #3 D, Galipeau, Olivier (2015)

Galipeau dished out some great bodychecks all game long. He had five or six game changing hits. He's tough as nails and his coverage in his zone was good. He's not overly fast, but his footwork allows him to get proper body positioning and to play aggressively on the puck carrier. He was involved in several small scrums after the whistle as well.

QUE #6 D, Meloche, Nicolas (2015)

Meloche displayed his strong puck control abilities all game long. He made some nice rushes and the passes he made were almost always on the tape. He makes the game look easy. He positions himself properly on one-on-one's, he plays physical when he needs to and he's good at keeping his blueline.

QUE #7 D, Roy, Jérémy (2015)

Roy is a natural talent. He easily played more than 30 minutes in this game. He's reliable in his own end and moves the puck very fast. He can do a bit of everything and he's been successful while doing it, whether being used on the penalty kill, power play, even strength, etc. His hockey sense is truly amazing and the decisions he made were constantly the right ones. I loved his footwork.

QUE #10 F, Roy, Nicolas (2015)

Pretty much the best forward for Team Quebec again. In that competition, his straight-line speed is above average opposed to what he's been facing in the Q, which allows him to create his magic. He cut towards the net regularly and his hockey sense was displayed on a particular play where he blocked a shot near the middle of the second period during a penalty kill. He then went on a breakaway scoring a beauty. He also earned an assist on Beauvillier's goal. Roy was as always pretty effective in his zone.

QUE #12 F, Beauvillier, Anthony (2015)

He scored on a one-timer going 5-hole in the first period. Played a bit on the perimeter.

QUE #14 F, Gauthier, Julien (2016)

He has all the physical tools to be dominant. He is a big body with great speed and great puck protection skills. He doesn't have much hockey sense, so most of his rushes or his plays ended up in the corners without being dangerous for Sandström at all.

QUE #15 F, Dostie, Alex (2015)

I liked his feistiness and he has good hands in tight. Played on the penalty kill a lot and he was able to break up some plays thanks to his high hockey IQ.

QUE #22 F, Blier, Samuel (2015)

He worked his ass off being the key element of his line. He was great putting pressure on Swedish defensemen keeping his stick active and being relentless.

FINAL SCORE: 3-2 SWE SO

December 31, 2013, Quebec vs. Sweden

Score: 3-2 (SO) Sweden

SWE # 10, F, Dahlstrom, John (2015) – Dahlstrom showed good vision on his assist in the 1st period, taking the puck, and quickly hitting Ek Eriksson, who was heading towards the net, before Ek Eriksson finished in front. He was good on the cycle, and protecting the puck along the wall. Dahlstrom used his size and strength along the wall to help win battles, and he wasn't afraid to crash the net. Dahlstrom was usually quick to get back to the defensive zone and more often than not was there as an outlet to help his defensemen exit the zone.

SWE # 20, F, Ek Eriksson, Joel (2015) – Ek Eriksson showed good awareness on the 1st goal, realizing his team intercepted a clear in the offensive zone before heading towards the net. He took a quick feed from Dahlstrom, then showed off a nice release beating Tremblay high glove and giving the Swedes a 1-0 lead.

SWE # 19, F, Olund, Linus (2015) – Olund was good on the forecheck in this game. He retrieved several dump-ins from his teammates, and was able to win quite a few puck battles along the wall. Olund pickpocketed Jeremy Roy on the backcheck on what probably could have been a penalty, which allowed Sweden to regain possession and score just seconds later. Olund did good work along the wall, and was good passing the puck from behind the net. On several occasions he hit teammates streaking towards the net with good passes in the scoring area.

SWE # 7, D, Larsson, Jacob (2015) – Larsson's fluent skating ability was on display once again. He showed good speed skating both forwards, and backwards. One rush Larsson was ahead of the play skating sideways along the wall before retrieving the puck at the blue line, and dumping it to an area Sweden could pressure on the forecheck. Larsson was able to jump-start the rush regularly, either via outlet pass or skating it out. Larsson jumped into the play a couple times to help create offense, and never hesitated to take an open shot, and put the puck on goal. At one point Larsson was caught pinching, but he used his great skating ability to get back defensively before Quebec could take advantage.

SWE # 5, D, Carlsson, Lucas (2015) – Carlsson did play as much as he did against Czech Republic, but he was effective when he did. He was good starting the breakout, and made some nice D-to-D passes to his partner to escape trouble in the defensive zone. Carlsson also blocked a few shots on shift when Sweden was hemmed in their own zone.

SWE #6, D, Carlsson, Gabriel (2015) – Carlsson moved the puck well, and took a regular shift on the powerplay, quarterbacking the 2nd unit. He wasn't afraid to shoot, but he was more of a passer. He made a good outlet pass, and was confident skating the puck through the neutral zone. Nicolas Roy blocked his shot in the offensive zone, and Roy was able to get a step on Carlsson going the other way before scoring to tie the game.

SWE # 1, G, Sandstrom, Felix (2015) – Sandstrom was really good in this game. He took away a lot of the net, was good down low and didn't allow many rebounds. At the start of the game he was making stops, though he looked a little shaky. Sandstrom seemed to calm down as the game went on and made big stop after big stop.

QUE # 10, F, Roy, Nicolas (2015) – Roy's skating was quite good, as he was able to generate good speed after just a few strides. He showed high hockey IQ, and good vision, as he always seemed to hit an open teammate with a pass on the tape. Roy made a nice pass to Beauvillier in front to assist on Quebec's 1st goal. Roy also showed good hands, as several times he was able to deke around Swedish defenders before taking a shot or dishing it off to an open man. Roy showed good speed breaking away from Gabriel Carlsson, and nice hands finishing in tight by sliding the puck through Sandstrom. Roy started the play by blocking a Carlsson shot.

QUE # 12, F, Beauvillier, Anthony (2015) – He doesn't have much size, but he's certainly not afraid of contact. He hit bigger opponents, and was consistently causing havoc on the forecheck. Beauvillier worked hard around the net as well as along the boards, and was able to create some scoring chances from winning battles. He always finished his checks, and was effective on the powerplay as he took a pass around the net and wired one through Sandstrom's 5-hole to tie the game. Beauvillier shot the puck whenever he had the opportunity.

QUE # 7, D, Roy, Jeremy (2015) – Roy failed to get the puck out along the boards, and it led directly to a Sweden goal. Roy showed good skating ability when jumping into the play, and was smart with his pinches, making a play with the puck and getting back before he could get caught. He showed good vision on the powerplay, and was almost always able to get the puck to the open man. He was hauled down in the 2nd period when he was exiting the zone with the puck, there was no penalty and Sweden scored shortly there after. Roy was excellent in overtime, particularly on the penalty kill when he blocked consecutive shots, and was able to get up hurting and still get the puck out.

QUE # 31, G, Tremblay, Olivier (2015) – Rather than covering the puck and getting his team a whistle, he played it to Jeremy Roy, who failed to get it out, and it resulted in the 1st goal. Tremblay looked a little slow and almost surprised by Ek Eriksson's shot on that goal. He was a little shaky early on, especially when handling the puck, but he really settled down during the rest of the game. Tremblay is a pretty small goaltender, but his positioning coupled with his speed and agility allowed him to make several great saves he probably shouldn't have made.

Victoria Royals vs Everett Silvertips December 31 2013 (WHL Regular Season)

Evt #10 C Sandhu Tyler (2014). Good puck movement tonight. Played with good intensity for most of the game. Needs to start playing more consistent every night. Showed flashes of offensive. Had the puck on the doors step a few times but just couldn't put the biscuit home.

Evt #89 C Nikolishin Ivan (2014). His lack of speed does not stop the strengths this kid bring every game. Showed good awareness and vision when under pressure. Can thread a needle through a maze and always seems to find the tape. Played a good two way game. Still needs to shoot more.

EVT #12 W Leedahl Dawson (2014). 1 assist tonight. Dawson played a physical game, the kids does the little things that go unnoticed. Needs to get more confidence in the offensive zone.

Vic #2 D Hicketts Joe (2014). Stocky defender who played a decent game. Is a workhorse in all game situations. Need to add some strength to compete with the bigger forwards. Overall decent game for the kids. Needs to work on the some basics.

Vic #25 RW Fushimi Brandon (2014). Had a strong game, Played physical at times. Needs to play more consistent with some tenacity. Has some good tools in the shed but does not utilize is game situations.

Final Victoria 3-2

December 31, 2013 Macs Midget Semi-Final #2 Finland U17 vs Okanagan Rockets

FIN #7, Juolevi, Olli (2016) - Lanky defenseman is smooth on his skates. Top end speed wasn't as apparent today although this was the 2nd game of the day for both teams.

FIN #8, Ruuskanen, Walterri (2015) - Good size, pivots were okay. Moved the puck reasonably well. Defended well. Constantly used his body to take away space from opponents. His feet were a bit heavy. He was caught with his head down for a big hit in which he was down on the ice for a while with an apparent head injury before needing help off the ice. He did return to the game.

FIN #9, Saarijarvi, Vili (2015) - Little defenseman is able to really step into his shots. Scored again tonight on shot from the top of the circle. Good offensive instincts, but size may limit his effectiveness at higher levels.

FIN #15, Palmu, Petrus (2015) - Pint-sized forward with exceptionally gifted hands. For his size, an improved first few steps would be helpful. Can be contained to the outside against bigger players. Scored a couple key goals late to seal the win. Had a quick shot released that seemed to surprise Okanagan's goalie. Finished the game with three points. Wore an 'A'. Was involved in some late game antics showing poor sportsmanship as he was involved in some verbal sparring and a feigned injury (now seen a couple times this tournament).

FIN #16, Ruotelainen, Artu (2015) - A little bigger than Palmu, but didn't look quite as skilled. Has been pretty quiet in this tournam. He did have some moderate success off the rush using well-placed wrist shots. Could be kept outside at times. He will need to make a habit of coming in closer to the net as his scoring chances are coming from too far away for continued success at higher levels of play.

FIN #24, Vainio, Veeti (2015) - Good size combined with strong skating skills. One of the more mobile players in the tournament. Strong two-way play. Had a couple good shots on net from the point on the powerplay in the 1st period. Does exceptionally well in transition. Won several puck battles in his end before being able to carry the puck up ice.

FIN #25, Nattinen, Julius (2015) - Big center wasn't given as much room to operate today and was kept to the outside in the 1st. Worked hard at both ends of the rink. Had a real nice touch pass assist on the power play that led to Finland's first goal. Struggled a bit in the faceoff dot tonight.

FIN #27, Laine, Patrik, (2016) - High skill level was evident today. Excellent toe drag in 1st period. A big winger that can play a strong north-south game, but also has the skating, smarts, vision and hands required to play a more skilled game. Used an inside-outside move to break in on a partial breakaway before firing a puck high and wide of the net. Highly skilled player in a good frame. For a big guy, he's still growing into his body and he lost a few puck battles to smaller players, but the compete level was there. Laine was Finland's best player on the night.

OKA #9, Jost, Tyson (2016) - Very impressive early on. As a 15 year-old Jost already wears an 'A' for the BCMML-leading Rockets. Gifted hands allowed him to navigate through traffic and strong vision helped him create chances out of nothing. A strong skater that is elusive. He doesn't need space to operate with the puck. Was used on the point on the powerplay. Had a unbelievable shift in the 2nd period, twice stripping Finnish players of the puck to set up chances. The second steal resulted in him scoring a breakaway goal that was called off due to the net coming off its mooring before the puck crossed the line. Jost had a supurb game until taking a bad checking from behind penalty that led to Finland's game winning goal and effectively ending a dream game by his Rockets team.

OKA #20, Browne, Tanner (2015) - Great stickwork on the penalty kill to impede pinching Finnish defensemen sneaking in from the point. Tried to finish his checks against the bigger Finns with limited success. Strong defensive awareness skills shown early on. Average size and above skating ability. Could have shown a better touch on a couple failed clearing attempts in his own end. Late in the game when his team was down a goal, Browne took a questionable interference penalty and a subsequent argument with the ref led to an additional unsportsmanlike penalty. Finland scored on the 4 minute man-advantage to ice the game.

OKA #12 Kryski, Jake (2016) - Generated good speed with his upright skating style. Played a pretty simple game, dumping and chasing the puck. Came back to his own end hard, but was curling too often when he should have been starting/stopping instead. Had a few chances off the rush.

Game Notes: In a high intensity game between Okanagan and Finland U17, the tournament favorite Finns were tested by a Rockets team that never quit and prevented Finland's vaunted offense from scoring for over 43 minutes. A 1-1 game until halfway into the 3rd period, Okanagan eventually self-destructed late in the 3rd with some poor penalties allowing Finland to break the game open with a pair of poweplay goals that turned the 1-1 game into a 3-1 lead. An empty netter and another late game goal closed out the scoring for Finland's 5-1 win that was far closer than the score indicated. Had Okanagan done a better job staying out of the box throughout the game, they legitimately could have taken this game. Coming into the game Finland had scored an amazing 50 goals in their five previous games. A common theme over the past few days has been some ugly finishes at the end of the Europeans' games as lots of words have been exchanged during the game and tempers flaring once the game had been decided and this game was no different.

Jan 2nd, 2014. Atlantic vs Russia (WU17 Hockey Challenge)

ATL #1 G, Mann-Dixon, Blade (2015) He is small but his lateral movements are extremely fast in his crease. Not drafted by a QMJHL team yet, he truly made some noise. He was aggressive and he looked confident. High shots will be a trouble for him at the next level. He had some trouble controlling his rebounds. Most of his saves were because of his reflexes.

ATL #3 D, Deschênes, Luc (2015) He was caught being too aggressive leading a 2-on-1 twice on the same shift. His slapshot was hard and accurate hitting the net on multiple occasions. He dished out an astonishing hit on Andrei Bannikov and he did it with his knee. He was thrown out of the game.

ATL #4 D, Lee, Cameron (2015) He is clearly an offensive defenseman. He rushed the puck behind Kolesnikovs' net more than twice. He has great wheels, but his defensive game is truly awful at this point. He can't be relied upon in his zone. He scored on a hard shot from the high slot on a powerplay early in the third period.

ATL #5 D, Myers, Phillipe (2015) He kept his stick active all game long. His long reach helps him a lot in his coverage. Looked good on the penalty kill. He had some nice rushes, which is something forbidden at the Q level for him.

ATL #6 D, Picco, Andrew (2015) Russian forwards were too fast for him obviously.

ATL #7 D, Thompson, Will (2015) Thompson was one of the few Team Atlantic defensemen that looked good in his zone. His breakouts were on tape more often than not.

ATL #8 D, Welsh, Nicholas (2015) Defensively, he looked lost early in the first period.

ATL #9 F, Balmas, Mitchell (2016) Played along Nathan Noel and Alexandre Jacob. Balmas has hockey sense that few possess. You don't see him that much, but you realize he's always around the puck. His compete level was higher than when I saw him back in the Monctonian. He has quick release on his wrist shot.

ATL #11 F, Bower, William (2016) He scored the first goal of the game and I didn't notice him much after.

ATL #15 F, Jacob, Alexandre (2015) A little speedster, Jacob used his quickness effectively to create scoring opportunities.

ATL #16 F, Noel, Nathan (2015) He protected the puck quite well along the wall and he can find openings while controlling the puck rather easily. He found teammates easily in the offensive zone on the delay. He was the one controlling the play in the neutral zone for his team and he won important faceoffs in his zone.

ATL #18 F, Pickard, Campbell (2015) I saw him protecting the puck properly along the wall.

ATL #21 F, Tower, Colby (2015) He worked very hard down low and had a shot go off the post in the first period. Deflected a Deschênes shot early in the second period.

RUS #1 G, Kolesnikovs, Nikita (2015) He controlled his rebounds effectively and he was tough to beat on low shots. He was not tested much as most shots were coming from the perimeter.

RUS #2 D, Platonov, Alexei (2015) Platonov is a big defenseman that likes to play the body. He is good clearing the front of his net. He took good shots from the point. He creates good passing and shooting lanes while patrolling the blueline. His long reach really helps him controlling his gaps and his breakouts were effective most of the time. He played a ton and he delivered. He was the best Russian defenseman in that game.

RUS #3 D, Sidorov, Mikhail (2015) He read the play well. I saw a particular shift where he played the body well on a 3-on-2. He was able to contain Nathan Noel at his full speed on a one-on-one thanks to his footwork, which was impressive considering who he was facing. He lost a battle in front of the net with Alexandre Jacob late in the third.

RUS #7 D, Rykov, Yegor (2015) He played the body effectively on one-on-one's. He was good on the transition as well. It was really tough to beat him on the outside. He did nothing exceptional.

RUS #8 D, Kozyrev, Alexander (2015) He was good patrolling the opposing blueline. He set up Zhebelev fnicely or his second goal, where he looked towards Mann-Dixon's net before passing the puck perfectly for a one-timer. His footwork is good.

RUS #11 F, Kvartalnov, Danila (2015) Showed he was strong on his skates on a shift where he outmuscled Will Thompson beating him on the outside. He then joined Kashtanov who was left alone in the slot.

RUS #13 F, Tyanullin, Artur (2015) Coupled with his natural offensive instincts, Tyanullin is a heck of a dangler, too. He's shifty and he is a clear offensive talent. Even though he's small, he was spectacular in the offensive zone. He caught my attention at first sight. He's easy to push around, though. He had two breakaways on the same shift while killing a penalty. If you give him open ice, he'll be deadly.

RUS #14 F, Byakin, Mikhail (2015) Another quick skater, I saw him cut towards the net on some occasions even though he's on the small side. He was good putting his stick on the puck.

RUS #18 F, Alexeyev, Denis (2016) Loved his two-way game as he complimented Tyanullin and Guryanov effectively.

RUS #19 F, Kashtanov, Ivan (2015) He has good speed on the rush and he's bright enough to know when to control the puck or when to shoot. He is really an East-West type of player.

RUS #23 D, Tsukanov, Denis (2015) His vision is not that good but he can get the puck out of his zone and he battles hard along the wall.

RUS #24 F, Yemets, Ivan (2015) He has good hockey sense. He knows how to get open and he used the ice effectively making nice cross-ice passes all game long. He's on the small side. Yemets had good puck control as well.

RUS #25 F, Guryanov, Denis (2015) A great playmaker with his big size, Guryanov displayed great chemistry with Artur Tyanullin and Denis Alexeev. He was posted in front of Mann-Dixon's net and he received a sublime backhand pass from Tyanullin that he buried on a wrist shot. His long reach and his two-way game are excellent for a winger. He knows where the defensive zone is and he creates great scoring opportunities while his team is shorthanded. I love the way he skates. He can get to full speed in his first few steps and he is by no means a knock-knee skater. He extends his legs properly while skating and he can turn on a dime easily. It was also easy for him to get the inside on the rush using his shoulder effectively against those Maritimers defensemen. He looked like the real deal in the first period.

RUS #27 F, Zhukenov, Dmitri (2015) High level of creativity displayed on several occasions. Earned an assist on Zhebelev's first goal where he made a backhand pass between his legs taking after gaining possession of a loose puck.

RUS #28 F, Rozhkovsky, Artyom (2016) He scored his team's first goal on a rebound.

FINAL SCORE: 5-3 RUS

Quebec Remparts vs Drummondville Voltigeurs QMJHL January 3rd 2014

Quebec

#13 Vincent Lanoue Def (2015): The rookie defenseman played at even strength with team captain Ryan Culkin, but didn't get much ice time on special teams. Kept his play with the puck pretty simple, he would either dump it in or make quick short passes to not get into trouble. Played fairly well in his zone by playing his man well. Got hurt at the beginning of the 3rd period after taking a hit behind his net, but didn't miss any shifts.

#18 Cody Donaghey Def (2014): Donaghey was inconsistent in his passing game tonight, as he missed some easy outlet passes in the neutral zone. Played on the Quebec 1st power play unit with Culkin, made some nice pinches to keep the puck inside the offensive zone. Good active stick in his zone to break up plays near his net. However, his footwork needs work, as he does not have the quickest feet.

#20 Duncan MacIntyre Def (2014): Started the game with a brutal giveaway in his zone where he should just have gotten rid of the puck earlier. Later on in the sequence, now in the offensive zone, he made a nice shot/pass to Duclair in front of the net for Quebec's 1st goal of the game. Good overall skater, if he gets caught out of position he has enough speed to get back defensively. Played on the PK with Culkin but didn't see any power play time.

#49 Lucas Batt Lw (2014): Played on an energy line with Trent Turnbull and Zachery Moody, but I didn't think he brought much energy to his team. Did a fine job at keeping puck deep in the offensive zone but didn't see much other than that. Not see much physical play out of him, either.

#96 Zachery Moody C (2014): Played an energy role but saw ice time on the power play and penalty killing units. Good forecheck presence from his line late in the 2nd period where they pinned Drummondville in their own zone. Not much to talk about on the offensive side of his game. Good job coming back as the centerman down low to help out his defensemen.

Drummondville

#4 Frederic Aube Def (2014): Increased ice time for him from previous viewings; saw him having a regular shift on the 2nd power play unit. Showed decent mobility and good straight ahead speed rushing the puck. Played at even strength with another 96' born defenseman in Sergei Boikov, made some good pinches to keep puck inside the offensive zone.

#11 Joey Ratelle Lw (2014): Played an agitating role in this game, had a big hit on Olivier Archambault and then tripped the Quebec goaltender in his crease. Played a physical game all night long, finished his hits on the forecheck and seeming to target key players with his hits. Screened the goaltender's view by positioning himself in front of the net.

#15 Nikolas Brouillard Def (2014): Brouillard was terrific in this game. He rushed the puck numerous times in the offensive zone from his zone with ease. Made smart plays in the offensive zone; rather to force the play, he just put pucks on net, looking for a rebound or tip like on the first Drummondville goal. Skated well today and made quick decisions with the puck which resulted in a quick transition game for the Voltigeurs.

#19 Cam Askew Rw (2015): Had some limited ice time on the power play in this game, played a regular shift with Golovkovs and Gauthier. Didn't show a whole lot in this game other than a real nice deke he put on Kurt Etchegary of the Remparts in the 2nd period in the offensive zone, and used his long reach to pull that move off. His skating is still rough and he is still playing a perimeter game.

#55 Sergei Boikov Def (2014): Played with Frederic Aube at even-strength and received limited power play time. Had some turnovers in the first half of the game, turning the puck over. Lots of times he gets hit and he's not in good position to take said hit. Not strong on his skates either, though he threw a good hit in the 3rd period but didn't look overly confident giving that hit.

#95 Georgs Golovkovs C (2014): Showed good puck patience in the offensive zone, and a good wrister with a quick release. Protected the puck well in the corners, but his lack of strength makes him lose puck battles versus bigger, stronger defenders. He has soft hands and good puck skills. Doesn't do enough when he doesn't have the puck to be a factor in a game. Dangerous when he has open space to make his plays, but can be invisible when he doesn't.

#96 Dexter Weber Def (2014): Didn't do a whole lot today; he got his power play time cut down in favor of Aube on the 2nd unit. At even–strength, he played with Brouillard and had to stay back often as his partner was rushing the puck often tonight. Didn't get a ton of chances to touch the puck. Didn't see anything wrong with his defensive plays, but it was not much of a physical game from him, either.

January 3, 2014, Pacific vs. Russia (U17)

Score: 7-3 Pacific

PAC # 9, F, Musil, Adam (2015) – Musil tried to get himself going, and provide Pacific energy on the first shift. He was able to get in on the forecheck, finish checks on a couple Russian defenders, and his pressure led to a turnover that turned into a scoring chance. Musil was knocked off the puck, and lost a puck battle in the offensive zone, which Russia grabbed and got quickly up ice where they were able to get a couple scoring chances.

PAC # 10, F, Gennaro, Matteo (2015) – Gennaro worked hard all game long, and was rewarded for his efforts 10-fold. He was good down low, and on the forecheck, and was sort of Johnny-on-the-spot when it came to Pacific's 4th goal, which turned out to be the game winner. Gennaro had a good net front presence, and was able to bang in a rebound in tight. His 2nd goal was scored on a beautiful backhander over Samsonov's shoulder, as Gennaro calmly walked out in front given the amount of space Russia left for him.

PAC # 11, F, Ronning, Ty (2016) – Ronning always knew where to be on the ice. He wasn't afraid to battle bigger players in the corners, nor was he afraid of going to the dirty areas of the ice or in front. He made a nice read off what his defenseman would do when he went to the slot, and stood in front of Samsonov while waiting to deflect a point shot. Ronning did a good job getting back defensively to help out the defensemen whenever he could. Ronning gained good speed in his first few steps, and combined with his shiftiness he was tough to defend. He put pucks on net whenever he could, and scored Pacific's 3rd goal on a perfect shot from the slot. Ronning was able to get into the shooting lanes regularly, and blocked a couple shots that way. He was also pretty relentless on the forecheck, and knocked bigger players off the puck in the corners several times.

PAC # 17, F, Merkley, Nick (2015) – Merkley was good on the forecheck, and wasn't afraid to go to the dirty areas to create offense. He had a nice deflection in front to score Pacific's 1st goal, as he tipped in Reddekopp's initial point shot. Merkley had a nice play in the 1st where he carried the puck in on what was an odd-man rush, and hit a streaking teammate in front of the net.

PAC # 19, F, Benson, Tyler (2016) – Benson kept his game simple, but it was very effective. He was able to get in on the forecheck consistently, and forced several turnovers by finishing checks, and winning battles down low. Benson was good controlling the puck on his stick, and hitting teammates with passes on the tape whenever open. Benson also showed nice hands, as a couple times he was able to deke himself out of sticky situations to help create space for himself.

PAC # 20, F, Morrison, Brad (2015) – Morrison got off to a good start in this game. He displayed excellent stickhandling ability when he danced around a couple Russian players coming from the half-wall, which led to a good scoring chance in front. Morrison displayed good speed when he got going through the neutral zone, and was able to generate scoring chances with his line almost every shift. Morrison kept his game simple, and never tried to do anything too fancy. He passed it to the open teammate whenever he could, and a simple pass to Juulsen at the point led to a goal.

PAC # 6, D, Reddekopp, Chaz (2015) – Reddekopp didn't have his best game in this one. He seemed to panic under pressure with the puck on his stick, and turned it over a couple times early by just throwing the puck at a teammate when he had time to make a better play. After Reddekopp's 2nd early turnover, he committed to one Russian forward on a 3-on-1 and left two players wide open in front of the net. Not only did Russia get an excellent scoring chance on the play, but also Ronning was forced to take a penalty on the backcheck trying to prevent a goal. He also turned it over near the blue line in his own zone, and Russia was able to get a great scoring chance from near the slot after it. Reddekopp made a nice play clearing the puck out of the net front area when there was a loose puck up for grabs. He did a good job getting pucks through from the blueline, and the first goal was scored as a direct result of that as Nick Merkley deflected it in front to tie the game. As the game went on, Reddekopp continued to get better. He made better reads with the puck, threw several shots on net, and seemed more calm with the puck in the defensive zone.

PAC # 8, D, Wotherspoon, Parker (2015) – Wotherspoon played a steady two-way game. He was positionally sound in the defensive zone, and made smart, simple reads with the puck to get it up ice, and out of the zone. He showed good vision, and passing ability, as he was able to hit streaking forwards with cross-ice passes regularly. He also did a nice job of holding the line in the offensive zone. Wotherspoon made a beautiful pass up the boards to Estephan, who fed Ronning in front for Pacific's 3rd goal.

PAC # 7, D, Juulsen, Noah (2015) – Juulsen had a very loud first 20 minutes. He scored Pacific's 2nd goal on a shot from the point, was physical whenever he could be, and laid a huge hit on Artem Vladimirov in the neutral zone after a couple turnovers by his team. Juulsen was a good side-to-side passer, and made good reads with the puck consistently. Juulsen was smart with the puck in the offensive zone, as whenever there was any traffic in front, he'd simply put the puck on net.

PAC # 31, G, Sawchenko, Zach (2016) – He wasn't peppered with shots, especially in the 2nd, but he was good when called upon. At times he allowed some juicy rebounds, but for the most part his control was OK, and he did a good job recovering with second and third saves.

RUS #19, F, Kashtanov, Alexei (2015) – Kashtanov showed good puck handling ability, and used his body well to protect the puck from Pacific players. He was good carrying it along the wall. He did a good job of using his deking ability to create space for himself.

RUS # 13, F, Tyanulin, Artur (2015) – Tyanulin made some very smart decisions with the puck on his stick. He showed good speed, vision and the ability to create. Tyanulin had an opportunity in front of the net, but didn't have the angle to take a shot so he made a nice pass to another Russian player in front, which gave the team an excellent scoring chance. He also had a nice burst of speed splitting through Pacific's defense, and scoring top shelf.

RUS # 27, F, Zhukenov, Dmitry (2015) – Zhukenov was an absolute force on Russia's top power-play unit. On the first PP of the game, Zhukenov picked up the puck behind his own net, and showed a good burst of speed flying down the wing, before deking his way towards the middle of the ice, and getting a shot off. After Pacific was able to get the puck out, Russia reset with the same play where Zhukenov picked it up from behind his net, and skated it. After realizing the side of the ice was sealed off, Zhukenov made a nice pass to an open player in the middle of the ice, and continued to skate up ice. There eventually was a nice rebound in front of Sawchenko, and Zhukenov showed good awareness, and compete level finding the puck, and battling his way to the front of the net where he banged it home on the door step. Zhukenov made a nice play carrying the puck up ice, keeping his head up the entire time, and hitting Zhebelev with a beautiful cross-ice feed on Russia's 2nd goal. One thing I liked about Zhukenov's game is that he backchecked, was willing to engage in battles along the wall and tried to play a 200-foot game. He made a perfect pass to a teammate wide open in front, who ensued to miss an empty net.

RUS # 24, F, Emets, Ivan (2015) – I like Emets' game in this one. He made some real heady plays with the puck, and did a nice job making a pass, reading the play, and reacting. He did a nice job finding open space in the scoring area, and showed a quick release getting some good shots off in front.

RUS # 16, F, Zhebelev, Aleksandr (2015) – Zhebelev is a good skater, who often found himself in the right place at the right time. After a Pacific turnover at the Russian blue line, Zhebelev quickly skated up ice and buried a Zhukenov pass in front for a nice goal off a 2-on-1.

RUS # 7, D, Rykov, Egor (2015) – For the most part, Rykov made good outlet passes to jump-start the rush. He was also willing to skate the puck out of trouble when necessary, and didn't force plays. Rykov was confident with the puck, and wasn't afraid to throw pucks on net whenever he was given the opportunity.

RUS # 30, G, Samsonov, Ilya (2015) – Samsonov showed great athleticism in this game, making several highlight reel saves when it looked like Pacific had a sure-fire goal. Russia was absolutely dominated in the 2nd period, and Samsonov made big save after big save to keep them in the game entering the 3rd period. The wheels sort of fell off then, but Samsonov was the only reason this game was even remotely close. He displayed a nice glove, making several excellent glove saves throughout the game. Samsonov also did a nice job of using his size to the advantage, as he took up a lot of the net. At times his rebound control wasn't great, and he struggled to see through screens at times, but overall he was very good in this game. It's hard to win when your team allows over 50 shots.

January 3, 2014, Sweden vs. Ontario (U17)

Score: 6-3 Ontario

ON # 16, C, Stome, Dylan (2015) – Strome did a good job of protecting the puck in this game. He used his size to create space for himself, and was able to make good decisions with the puck quickly. Strome displayed great vision sending passes to teammates as they found open ice, and put pucks where only his team could get them. He didn't record a point on Ontario's 1st goal, but he made a great play coming off the half-wall, and taking ice before feeding it to Knott, which led to the goal. Strome made a nice play in the 3rd period, as he intercepted a pass, skated in and roofed one over Sandstrom to give Ontario a 6-3 lead, and ice the game.

ON # 17, C, Konecny, Travis (2015) – Konecny did a good job creating offense, and showed off his impressive release on several occasions. He also backchecked hard all night, and was regularly the 1st forward back in the defensive zone. He also showed good vision, and passing ability with the puck, as he was able to regularly hit open targets. One play he made in particular that impressed me was when he outskated an oncoming Swede before sliding across a perfect cross-ice pass to Stephens, who drove the net, and drew a penalty. Konecny had a few nice plays where he sidestepped checks or opposing defenders, and safely carried the puck into the offensive zone. He had several excellent chances, and I think had three or four quality shots in the 1st period alone. Konecny made a beautiful backhand pass to Crouse in front on Ontario's 3rd goal. He wasn't afraid to be physical, either, as he had a couple nice hits, including a big one on Grundstrom.

ON # 9, C, Marner, Mitch (2015) - Marner may be small, but he's not afraid of contact or going to the dirty areas of the ice. Marner went to the net on the PP, and helped slide the puck to Vande Sompel on the 1st goal. He showed good speed, and was able to win races for loose pucks regularly. He's a pass-first player, and at times he tried to force a pass to a teammate who wasn't entirely open, but the creativity was there. Marner really showed his elite skating ability, and elusiveness on the powerplay in the 2nd period, as he was able to drift around several defenders before making a beautiful feed to Strome for a tap-in goal.

ON # 12, C, Mckenzie, Brett (2015) – McKenzie had a glorious chance shortly after the start of the game, as he was able to find open ice in front, and was given the puck all alone. McKenzie made a nice move, and had Sandstrom beat but slid the puck off the post, the net came off, and a golden opportunity was wasted. McKenzie made most of his noise around the net, as he had most of his chances there including his lone goal.

ON # 14, F, Knott, Graham (2015) – Knott doesn't look overly fast, but he gets around the ice well. He's a good passer, and was very unselfish, hitting an open teammate rather than shooting whenever he could. Knott had a nice give-and-go with Strome on their first shift of the game. Knott made a nice read from behind/beside the net on the PP, getting the puck into the scoring area on Ontario's 1st goal.

ON # 21, LW, Crouse, Lawson (2015) – As usual, Crouse used his size to his advantage. He was good protecting the puck on his stick, along the boards, and in the cycle game. Crouse got in on the forecheck, finished his checks, and wasn't afraid to crash the net. Crouse scored both of his goals within 6-feet of the net.

ON # 22, F, Stephens, Mitch (2015) – Stephens did a good job of creating offense on a pretty consistent basis. He only had one assist in the blowout win, but he had or setup chances almost every shift, and that total could have easily been higher. He distributed the puck well, and always seemed to make smart decisions with the puck. Stephens also read the play well, as he was able to intercept outlets or cross-ice passes from the Swedes on several different occasions. He was good creating offense on the rush, and wasn't afraid to put pucks on net if he had a lane. Another thing I liked about Stephens' game was when nobody was open in the offensive zone, he would simply put the puck in an area where there was open ice if his teammate was close enough to get to it and make a play. Stephens made a nice play driving the net after receiving a pass, fighting off a check, and drawing a penalty.

ON # 7, D Chychrun, Jakob (2016) – He was physical when he could be in the defensive zone, and wasn't afraid to engage in battles in the corners. On the power play he was effective, making smart plays with the puck, and passing to open players rather than forcing shots. He had a couple nice plays off the rush, and tried to put pucks on net when he could. One rush he through a puck on net, followed up grabbing the rebound, and hit McKenzie in front for a goal.

ON # 8, D, Vande Sompel, Mitchell (2015) – Vande Sompel was able to move the puck up efficiently throughout the game. For the most part his outlets were on the tape, and he'd hold the puck for an extra second or two if necessary to allow his teammates more time to get open. He also showed good skating ability, and didn't panic under pressure when the puck was on his stick. He made an excellent read without the puck on the PP, seeing his teammates had the puck down low on the opposite side of the ice. He pinched into the play, found open ice around the net, and made no mistake with the puck ripping it past Sandstrom for a goal. He was confident skating with the puck, and was to skate the puck out of trouble on a regular basis. I liked his decision making the puck; as if something wasn't there he'd wait until something opened up, or simply get the puck in deep. One play he made that was real impressive was when he grabbed the puck at the point, attacked the Sweden forward, did a fake shot, stepped around the defender and got a solid shot off. He did a good job of holding the line in the offensive zone, as well.

ON # 4, D, Day, Sean (2016) – A couple times things looked shaky in the defensive zone, but he always seemed to find a way to hang onto the puck, and skate it out of trouble. His passes were on target for the most part, and looked pretty good on the power play opposite side of Chychrun. As usual, his effortless skating stride, and good top speed were regularly on display. He was caught pinching in the offensive zone, but due to his exceptional skating ability Day got back in the play, and broke up an odd-man rush going the other way. He was also willing to throw his weight around, as he laid the body whenever he could, and had a huge open ice hit on Grundstrom.

ON # 6, D, Spencer, Matt (2015) – Early in the 1st period Ontario was pressing, and Spencer made a bad read in the offensive zone, forcing a pass that wasn't there. It led to a turnover, and too away some momentum that was building from a good Ontario shift. Spencer made some nice defensive plays using his stick to knock the puck off of Sweden forwards, before retrieving the puck, and starting the breakout.

SWE # 22, F, Kalte, Anton (2016) – Kalte had a pretty quiet game, though he did have a goal in the 1st period. He went to the net, and sort of planted himself in front. Carlsson pinched into the play, hit him with a good pass, and Kalte was able to finish the play.

SWE # 11, F, Ahl, Filip (2015) – Ahl played a real solid game. He was good on the forecheck, and won several battles along the boards for loose pucks. At times he was able to skate through checks from defenders, and made a nice play getting the puck in front of the net on Carlsson's goal. Ahl was confident skating with the puck, and was able to safely skate it into the offensive zone while maintaining possession on numerous occasions. At one point Jesse Barwell took a pretty healthy run at Ahl, and he was able to hold his ground, brace himself, and send Barwell flying the other way.

SWE # 12, F, Asplund, Rasmus (2016) – Asplund made a couple nice plays in the defensive zone, as he had an active stick, and wasn't afraid to get into the shooting lanes to block a shot. Asplund did a nice job crashing the net, and pouncing on a juicy rebound in front to get Sweden within two goals late in the 2nd period.

SWE # 19, F, Olund, Linus (2015) – Olund had chances offensively, but what I liked about his game was his commitment to defense, and work ethic on the wall. He wasn't able to get on the scoresheet, but he had a couple nice plays in the defensive zone, and battled for pucks along the wall.

SWE # 17, F, Grundstrom, Carl (2016) – Grundstrom was confident with the puck on his stick, and made some nice plays with it coming from behind the net or out of the corners. He showed good speed getting to loose pucks, and he always seemed to be in the right place at the right time. Grundstrom was good carrying the puck into the zone, as well, as due to his speed Ontario defensemen backed off, and he took what he could get, gaining the offensive zone with control of the puck.

SWE # 7, D, Larsson, Jacob (2015) - Larsson made good reads with the puck, and always had his head up, looking up ice to make a play. He hit most of his outlets, and made some tough cross-ice passes to teammates in stride. Larsson wasn't afraid to jump into the play, and was rarely caught pinching. He's not an overly physical player, but he knocked Ontario forwards off the puck on a couple different occasions before retrieving it, and starting the play up ice. He also showed shiftiness with the puck, and the ability to elude attempted hits from oncoming forecheckers. Larsson made a beautiful play on Sweden's 1st goal, stickhandling around a forward in his own zone before making a play up ice that started the breakout on what turned into a goal.

SWE # 5, D, Carlsson, Lucas (2015) – Carlsson complimented Larsson well on their defense pairing. Like Larsson, he can skate pretty fluently, and can move the puck well. Carlsson also likes to pinch into the play at times, but did a nice job covering for Larsson when he jumped into the play, as well. Carlsson made a nice read jumping into the play, and when he saw a man covered him at the point, he circled around the net, and was able to bang in a rebound to tie the game. Carlsson made another excellent play in the 1st when he carried the puck into the offensive zone, and hit Kalte on the tape in front before he scored Sweden's 2nd goal of the game.

SWE #6, D, Carlsson, Gabriel (2015) – Carlsson missed a few outlets in this game. They were close for the most part, but some could have been better. He wasn't afraid to use his big frame (6'3") to try and push opponents off the puck, and for the most part he did a good job in that regard. Carlsson had a bit of a tough go in the defensive zone at times, as a few shifts he was caught in his own zone, and spent most of it chasing players around the ice. He also fanned on a pass that was intercepted by Ontario, which led to a couple scoring chances.

January 5, 2014 Seattle Thunderbirds vs Calgary Hitmen (WHL)

CAL #32, Sanheim, Travis (2014) - Big, fluid-skating defenseman is really starting to heat up. Had been very solid over the past few weeks. Above average speed and acceleration. Good mobility, but balance needs to improve. Has shown better poise and made better decisions with the puck over the last several weeks. Raw, but has good potential. Own zone play has been good, but he is subject to occasional turnoves under light pressure. Is able to skate the puck out of his zone. Doesn't have a hard shot, but he is able to regularly get wrist shots on through traffic. He scored on a wrist shot from the point today and added an assist. With his recent strong play and huge improvements over the season, Sanheim has put himself on the radar for the NHL draft.

CAL #2, Thrower, Josh (2014) - Scratched. Is having a disastrous season as a prospect as he has been surpassed on the depth chart by fellow 2014 prospects Ben Thomas and Travis Sanheim.

CAL #11, Malenstyn, Beck (2016) - Above average size, but needs to add strength. While he was pushed down and knocked off the puck on a few occasions, Malenstyn never gave up on a play and kept plays alive by making plays from on his knees. Played for Okanagan Hockey Academy at the recent World School Hockey Challenge in Calgary where he was one of the tournament's best players. Good hustle and has the skill and vision to be dangerous with the puck once he gets it. Good leadership qualities.

CAL #5, Morrison, Lochlan (2015) - Good positioning against the rush. Good awareness. Strong defensive play from a 15 year-old. Identifies and eliminates his check quickly and efficiently. Has good size, but strength is a big issue as he can get pushed around by bigger, stronger players. Recorded his first career WHL point today.

CAL #23, Hyman, Aaron (2016) - Former 3rd round Bantam pick's first WHL game and the Hitmen didn't even have a name bar ready for him. Excellent size for his age as he's already one of the bigger players on the ice. Strength hasn't caught up with the frame yet as he spent most of the first period on his backside. Made a good defensive play in taking away a scoring chance after his teammate Sanheim tripped while trying to defend his man. Skating is pretty choppy and mobility is a bit of a concern.

CALL #18, Virtanen, Jake (2014) - The best player for either team on the night, Virtanen was constantly controlling the play. Seems to be turning a corner as he is finding a good balance on when he can drive with the puck up ice and when he's better off distributing it. Is showing some better patience with the puck and using this extra time to look for teammates to pass to. Had a drive where he skated wide around a defender and instead of taking a bad angle shot as he typically would do, he wrapped around the net and was able to find Helgeson open at the top of the slot for a goal. Able to skate around opponents at will. Is a much more valuable player when he's creating chances with speed and then looking to distribute the puck. Showed very soft hands while he scored on a very nice wraparound. He seemed to always have the puck on his stick and he was extremely dangerous with it. Showed that he can still be a bit of a pest as he drew a penalty behind the play.

CAL #27, Thomas, Ben (2014) - Has shown great improvements as the season has progressed. Is much more confident in his abilities. Has been good in his end for a while now, but his offensive game is really starting to develop. Not to overly downplay his passing ability, but even if he never becomes much of a big point producer, he'll still have value as a good puck moving defenseman that rarely makes mistakes in his own end and is able to make good decisions with the puck to keep the play alive. Good size, skates pretty well, makes a good first pass, but could be a bit more physical. Steady game from him today.

CAL #16, Babych, Cal (2015) - Didn't see a lot of ice time until the game was well out of reach. A bit of a sneaky player, Babych has been taking care of his end and not doing much of note until a couple odd man rushes late.

SEA #12, Gropp, Ryan (2015) - LW. Very good size and willing to go to the tough areas. Plays a strong North-South game. Set up in the low slot for Thunderbird powerplays and was rewarded with a rebound goal. Very upright skater. Lost an edge a couple times and balance looks to be a bit of an issue. Would like to see better explosiveness in his skating as both his top end speed and acceleration need work. Anticipated the play well through the neutral zone earning himself a breakaway in which he failed to convert on.

SEA #24, Delnov, Alex (FLA 2012) - Big, strong centerman for the Thunderbirds. Tough to move off the puck, was good on faceoffs and owns a good amount of skill. The Russian played a strong North American-styled game. Very strong down-low and had good hands when he didn't have much room to operate with. Had a pair of assists on the night.

SEA #27, Volcan, Nolan (2016) - Average size, but has good strength relative to the other 15 year-olds in today's game. Able to create pressure on the forecheck. A step slow in finding his check in his own end.

SEA #17, Theodore, Shea (ANA 2013) - It was quickly apparent how effortlessly he can move the puck. Is able to move the puck up ice with ease either with crisp passes or with his strong skating ability. While he oozes offensive potential, Theodore's game is still very raw. He let Calgary enforcer Joe Mahon drive wide against him. Once the puck is in the corner, Theodore does well to control his opponent and gain control of the puck. His game down low was much better than his defending off the rush. For a such a good puck mover, Theodore has brain farts handling the puck and coughed up the puck for a pair of high quality scoring chances in the 1st period alone (one of which resulted in a goale). Cleaned up his own zone play later in the game, but he still has much work to do on gap control and defensive zone play in general.

SEA #34, Elder, Kaden (2016) - The 15 year-old natural center did not look comfortable playing defense in his 3rd ever WHL game and was very tentative on the ice. Average size and skating abilities.

SEA #1, Mumaugh, Danny (2014) - Got the start today after being shelled for 7 goals against Edmonton last night. Wasn't square to shooters or aggressive enough in challenging Pavel Padakin on his breakaway goal. Not overly big and often went down too early leaving the whole top of the net wide open. Was pulled in the 2nd period.

SEA #35, Myles, Justin (2014) - Played in relief for Mumaugh. Didn't fare much better as he was also cheating to cover the low part of the net and Calgary shooters were scoring at will above his shoulders.

Game Notes: Seattle was playing in Calgary for the first time in a couple seasons. They were playing their 3rd game in three days and short numerous key players due to the U17 Challenge and injuries. After a great 10-1 run leading up to the Alberta roadtrip, the Thunderbirds have been dropped five straight and have been out-scored outscored 29-4 over the last four alone after dropping this contest 10-2. Calgary is really coming together as a team as of the last month or so and are starting to take a stranglehold on the Eastern Conference standings. They are now rated the #7 team in the country with a record of 27-8-2-3.

Portland WinterHawks vs Everett Silvertips January 8 2014 (WHL)

EVT #89 C Nikolishin Ivan (2014). His game was off tonight, seems to struggle offensively with the physical play of Portland defenders. His lack of speed showed tonight through the neutral zone with the speed of Portland shutting him down along the boards. Couple bad turnovers leading to good scoring chances.

EVT #12 W Leedahl Dawson (2014). Crash and bang was Dawson game, hitting everything that moves. Had 1 assist and was +1 tonight. Didn't see much ice time but utilized his time well. Dawson will chip in offense every few games but will show up every night and play with tenacity.

PORT #9 C De Leo Chase (2014). Kept of the score sheet, but that does not stop Chase from creating offensive with his speed. He is hard to hit down low because he is so shifty. Good offensive anticipation. Worked hard on the back check and was solid in the defensive zone. The kid has no quite in him.

PORT # 22 W Schoenborn Alex (2014). Starting to like this kid more every game. Has really blossomed throughout the year. Very underrated winger with lots of tools. Used his speed and was strong along the boards, hard to knock off the puck. I like his aggression and physical natures on the forecheck.

PORT #13 W Iverson Keegan (2014). 1 goal and finished +2. Played physical in the corners and was showing a good compete level tonight. Strong kid who needs to use his size more. Would like to see him drive the net and battle for garbage goals more often.

PORT #23 C Turgeon Dominic (2014). 1 assist and +1. Was strong the on draw winning some key face offs. His offensive game is starting to mature as he gains more confidence. Probably the best two way player on the ice tonight.

Final Portland 4-1

Tri City Americans vs Everett Silvertips January 10 2014 (WHL)

EVT #10 C Sandhu Tyler (2014). 1 assist for the speedy winger. Was average tonight and played an excellent two way game. It was good seeing Tyler doing the little things tonight (Blocking shots, Chipping Pucks and Winning battles).

EVT #89 C Nikolishin Ivan (2014).. Seen some PP time and was very effective. Probably the best player on the ice for Everett. Ivan played with a little edge tonight was more physical than normal and this type of play created some excellent scoring chances tonight.

EVT #12 W Leedahl Dawson (2014). Nothing more than crash and bang, hitting everything that moves. His game never really changes, his play is mostly consistent every night. You get what you see, a hard working player who brings energy. Still waiting for his offensive upside to blossom.

Tri #22 W Vickerman Taylor (2014.) Power forward who needs to drive the net and battle. Has decent speed and seems strong on the puck. Showed flashes of offensive but seem flat most of the game.

TRI #2 D Thrower Josh (2014). Physical defenders who loves to hit and punish. I like his tenacity and aggression in the corners. Plays a good 1 on 1 defensive game. Has some good tools in the box

Cape-Breton vs Blainville-Boisbriand Armada, QMJHL January 10th 2014

Cape-Breton

#4 Jason Bell Def (2015): Bell played on the 3rd defensive pairing tonight, with limited ice time on the power play. Made some good plays in his own zone using an active stick to break plays out near his net. Didn't do a whole lot offensively, though, and didn't have the puck on his stick very often.

#26 Loik Leveille Def (2015): Got much stronger on his skates since last year. In the first period, he was hit a couple of times and the opposing player took the worst of the hit. Played a regular shift at even-strength, and saw some time on the first power play unit. His puck movement was hit or miss tonight; he made some good, quick passes to help the transition game but other times he made some soft passes that ended up as turnovers. Played the puck instead of playing the man on Blainville-Boisbriand's first goal of the game…and also had some trouble in his zone in the 2nd period.

#10 Timothé Simard C (2015): Showed some nice bursts of speed during the game, including on one PK shift where he went wide on a defenseman and cut to the net, almost scoring a goal. Did a good job on the penalty killing unit, good positioning and good stick work.

#11 Clark Bishop C (2014): It was a good game from Bishop tonight, who used his speed very well to be a threat on the forecheck. Played a physical game all night long, including a highlight-reel hit in the neutral zone where he stepped up on his man just outside the offensive zone. Showed good puck protection, using his size well and taking the puck back to the net or the slot. A good neutral zone player with a good active stick, though he lacked some creativity with the puck offensively at times.

#17 Maxim Lazarev Lw (2014): Lazarev was quiet most of the night, but came through at the right time, scoring the game-winning goal with less than 3 minutes left with a great wrist shot from just inside the blueline. Got good ice time from the Screaming Eagles' coaching staff, played on the top two line, and got his share of power play time. However, he showed a little bit too much of a perimeter game on the power play, was not involved in the play as much as I would like and I saw nothing as far as physical play.

#19 Cam Darcy C (2014): Darcy is a '94-born rookie in the QMJHL coming from Boston who played a solid game and had tons of ice time. Strong player who protects the puck well using his size; scored a goal from a great slap shot from the blueline on the power play. A good two-way effort tonight from him as he stole puck away from an Armada defenseman and after skating behind the net, found Justin Hache coming down from the blueline in the slot for the 3-2 goal. He does have heavy feet and is not the quickest skater, but he is a strong player physically.

#27 Julien Pelletier Lw (2014): Pelletier showed some good feet and nice bursts of speed going wide on a couple of occasions against Armada defensemen. Did a nice job on the penalty killing unit, having been paired with Timothé Simard tonight. Capable of playing a physical game, as he did throw one of the game's biggest hit as F1 on the forecheck. Good work from him without the puck, smart game.

#31 Alex Bureau G (2014): Bureau was the #1 star of the game in my opinion, as he made many great saves to keep the Screaming Eagles in this game and eventually coming out on top. Very athletic in his crease, and never quits on a puck. Showed a quick glove taking a goal away from an Armada forward at the side of the net in the 2nd period.

Blainville-Boisbriand

#71 Nikita Jevpalovs C (2014): Played a solid two way game tonight, good effort in his zone to backcheck and help out his defenseman deep. Liked his chemistry with #85 Daniel Walcott on the power play; they could find each other very well on the ice. Possesses a great shot and was using it at will on the power play as he was set up often. Good wrist shot as well, with a quick release.

#92 Marcus Hinds Rw (2014): Hinds had a great first period as a threat on the forecheck and strong on the puck. Good bursts of speed in tight spaces, and he protected the puck well in the offensive zone. Good effort without the puck as well, strong commitment to come back into his zone. However, he was quiet after a great first period.

#5 Nathanael Halbert Def (2014): Was caught watching the puck on the first Cape Breton goal, leaving his man open at the left side of the net. Outside of that, Halbert was solid for the Armada tonight, and made some nice plays blocking shots in front of his net. He did a good job keeping the puck alive in the offensive zone with some nice pinches, nothing flashy but very effective.

#85 Daniel Walcott Def (2014): Good game from Walcott, who used his good skating abilities in different ways tonight. Didn't hesitate to join the rush when he could, was tough to beat one-on-one due to his great lateral mobility. Played a physical game, throwing some good hits in the neutral zone along the boards. Controlled the puck well on the power play and made smart decisions with it. Anticipation in the defensive zone was excellent to break plays out.

#77 Guillaume Beaudoin Def (2014) Played with Walcott at even-strength, has decent mobility and speed. Had a nice rush in the first period in the offensive zone before being stripped away from the puck near the net by Jason Bell of Cape Breton. Not a whole lot to see out of him tonight, as for being paired with Walcott, he let him do most of the work as far as moving the puck out of his zone.

Jan 10, 2013. Sherbrooke Phoenix vs Chicoutimi Saguenéens (QMJHL)

SHE #15 D, Deschamps, Jonathan (2013) A big defenseman, Deschamps is the captain. He always played the body on one-on-one's and he was not afraid to shake things up a bit in his goalie's crease. I really liked last year, but his offensive game hasn't stepped up since last year. He was missing easy controlled breakouts. He was willing to sacrifice himself, blocking shots all game long and his footwork clearly needs refining. It was evident especially when he was chasing forwards along the wall.

SHE #32 D, Neill, Carl (2013) His main asset is his ability to create offensive opportunities from the backend. He's able to reach teammates on a long distance with hard and accurate passes. He has low center of gravity and that helps him maintain his strength in his battles. He's a powerful skater, but he needs to improve his backward skating as he has trouble gaining speed in his first steps. He looked confused with speedy players coming at him and had trouble catching up to them. That was the case against Dominic Beauchemin in the second period. He played on the first powerplay and displayed his heavy shot several times.

SHE #18 D, Bahl, Julien (2013) Playing with Jérémy Roy helps a lot. He played within his limits and his first pass was quick and effective. His defensive zone coverage was good. I really liked his defensive IQ as he rarely turned the puck over under pressure. He was able to maintain players along the boards and he kept his stick active when he had to defend himself on two-on-one. He does not create openings thanks to his skating though as he's not a rusher unlike Roy.

SHE #97 D, Roy, Jérémy (2014) This young kid is truly amazing. He played key minutes and he looked like a number one defenseman. His mobility truly makes him attractive. He can rush the puck effectively and he is great quarterbacking the powerplay. His aggressive coverage helped him a lot regaining puck control. His breakouts were always on the tape and he was able to neutralize pressure with sound body positioning along the wall in his zone. He was strong on his skates and he was able to play physically. He's good maintaining proper gap as well.

SHE #28 C, Audette, Daniel (2013) On a bigger ice surface like in Chicoutimi, Audette really looks like a big fish in a small bowl. His speed and his agility are well above average. He is a pure rusher that likes to create scoring chances off the wing. He distributes the puck better than most players in the league. He won't slow the play down, but will create openings for his teammates off the rush. Compared to last year, he is clearly improving the way he plays in his zone as well as he was mostly the first man back and he was a great help for his defenseman. He gained his coach's trust as he was being used in all key situations (powerplay, 3-on-5, etc.) On the downside, he held onto the puck too long at times. When he doesn't see anyone available, instead of securing the play down low or waiting for his teammates, he'll use his speed skating around everybody in the offensive zone. When he did it, he often lost possession of the puck leading to a turnover most of the time.

SHE #73 RW, Harwell, Chase (2014)

This young American played with drive. Even though he's on the small side, he constantly crashed the net and it didn't hamper his ability of working the puck into the corners or down low in the offensive zone. He scored a goal late in the third period on a two-on-one.

CHI #58 D, Lyamkin, Nikita (2013)

Lyamkin scored on a powerplay with his wrist shot. Finally, I saw him moving the puck on some rushes and even though he gave too much room on one-on-one's, he's improving without the puck. He needs to be more aggressive, though. He saw some good quality ice time.

CHI #30 G, Billia, Julio (2013)

Billia was great. His lateral movements were fast and in control. Even though he boxed the puck early on, he did control his rebounds nicely on high shots. He showed lightning quick recovery and he never lost eye contact with the puck. He looked composed as well and he seemed mentally strong. Was superb on the three shots he faced during the shootouts, as he never overreacted.

SCORE: CHI 4-3 SO

Jan. 11, 2014 - Sioux City Musketeers vs. Chicago Steel (USHL)

SC #43 Waltteri Hopponen LW (2014) - One of the more noticeable players on the ice in this game. Always makes the smart play, heads-up passer. Linemates always have to be ready for a pass when on the ice with him, very creative. Adept at creating space for himself when in possession of the puck. Great weapon on the PP, had a PP goal in this game. Isn't afraid to be in front of the net, always crashes the net hard. Skilled player who isn't afraid to get physical and go to the dirty areas of the ice.

SC #5 Neal Pionk D (2013) - Very good all-around defenseman. Physical, always finishes his checks, likes to play chippy and with an edge. Very aggressive to the puck, eliminates opponents' space with the puck well. Moves very well, has quick feet, nice stride. Has some offensive upside, confident with the puck and makes good decisions. Good first pass out of the zone. Can play in all situations, with any D partner. Very versatile. High compete level, wins a lot of battles. Had a very strong game.

SC #10 F Jared Thomas F (2012) - Skilled player, very good hands, uses body well to protect the puck and create space for himself. Excellent playmaker. Defensively responsible, backchecks hard, supports defensemen down low in defensive zone. Has moments of floating a bit at times and his compete level can come into question but he had a good effort level in this game. Above average shot. University of Minnesota-Duluth commit.

SC #4 Ryan Mantha D (2014) - Big-bodied defenseman with good hockey sense. OK skater for his size, but his footwork needs improving. He doesn't get beat often but did get caught flat-footed to the outside by a forward for a good scoring chance against in this game. That will need to improve. Anticipates the play exceptionally well. Jumps into passing lanes and causes a lot of turnovers on account of his anticipation and his long reach. Good stick, smart and well-positioned in the defensive zone. Good puck-mover, very patient, makes good decisions with the puck. Got involved offensively a few times in this game. He likes to jump into the rush and find openings in the offensive zone, knows how to pick his moments without getting caught. Doesn't play soft but was not overly physical in this game.

SC #7 Bobby Nardella D (2014) - Pint-sized defenseman but exceptional skating ability and intelligence make up for a lack of size. Quick feet, good speed, moves very well in tight space with the puck. Can get overmatched physically but has a good stick and defends very well, uses his skating ability to his advantage. Looks very smooth and comfortable with the puck, has good patience. Makes a lot of subtle moves with puck to keep possession, keep plays moving, make defenders miss on the offensive blue line. University of Notre Dame commit.

CHI #20 Artem Artemov LW (2015) - Highly-skilled Russian forward, 2015 Draft Eligible. Was all over the ice for Chicago, had two assists. Easily could have had more points in this one. Great hands, very creative with the puck. Smooth stride and quick, shifty feet. Capable of beating defenders one-on-one. Tough to defend down low in offensive zone. Very strong on his feet, solid base. Very difficult to knock him off the puck. Has a very quick release. High-end offensive skill. Was Chicago's best player in this game.

CHI #31 Chris Nell G (2012) - His goaltending was a big reason for Chicago's win. Stellar effort. Moves very well laterally. Made a number of stops on high quality chances. He was very strong down low, excellent rebound control. Has decent size, maintains his angles and doesn't lose his net. Had an excellent game, 35 saves on 37 shots.

FINAL SCORE: 3-2 Chicago (OT)

SCOUTS NOTES:

This was one of the better games Chicago has played all season. Sioux City is the better team but Chicago had the better effort and got big saves when they needed them. Neal Pionk was probably the most noticeable player in this game despite not making the scoresheet. He was very involved any time he was on the ice. Plays in all situations so he's on the ice a lot, had a great game. Offensively, Hopponen and Artemov were treats to watch out there. High-end skill with intelligence to match. Great skaters, and the game in general had a very high pace. Sioux City has a lot of talent with a number of players worth watching, Chicago just got the better of them on this particular night.

Saint-John Sea Dogs vs Blainville-Boisbriand Armada, QMJHL January 12th 2014

Saint-John

#3 Olivier Leblanc Def (2014): Loved the way Leblanc played this afternoon, brought an in-your-face, physical game to the table. Threw a huge open-ice hit in the first period where he had to fight right after, even though the hit was legal, with no head contact on it. Was physical in his own zone as well, as he likes to hit and plays an agitating role for his team. Played in all situations of the game and is trusted by his coaches. Moves the puck fairly well to his forwards today, nothing flashy about his offensive game tonight though. On the Armada's overtime goal, he got outmuscled to the net by Jevpalovs, which is too bad because he didn't give much in his coverage on that play.

#5 Thomas Chabot Def (2015): Showed some nice things with the puck and has a great shot from the point. Had a tough time containing speedy forwards off the rush; he got beaten several time on the outside. Footwork needs work and he also needs to get stronger to win more battles.

#15 Matthew Highmore C (2014): Showed his strength in this game, as well as his quick feet. He didn't stop moving his feet in the offensive zone. Strong play without the puck, came back to help his defense out deep in his zone. On the first goal, he made a great play, knocking down a puck in the air (showing some great eye and hand coordination) in the neutral zone, which provoked a turnover. Then he got the puck back in the slot and let go of a backhand shot that was stopped, but Oliver Cooper was able to put the puck in the net on the rebound. Had a lucky assist for the 2nd Sea Dogs' goal after coming out from the corner with the puck, making a cross-ice pass that hit Cooper's skate to end up on Zilbert's stick, which tied the game at 2 midway the 3rd period. Good game overall from Highmore, who did have some struggles in the faceoff circle however.

#16 Samuel Dove-McFalls C/LW (2015): The big-sized forward from Montreal had limited ice time in this game, playing on a 3rd or 4th line role for the Sea Dogs with not much special team play. Good work along the boards using his size well to bang bodies and protect pucks. Goes to the net in search of rebounds. His skating needs some work, as he looked like he had heavy boots on. Showed his inexperience with a bad penalty late in the 3rd after crosschecking an Armada player after a legal hit.

#42 Mathieu Joseph W (2015): Started the game slowly, getting limited ice time but got better as the game went on. Showed his great hands, deking a veteran defenseman on the Armada with a great in-and-out move in the slot. Also had a great rush in overtime, using his speed and his will to take the puck to the net even if he got hooked and tripped on the play. Joseph played the first half of the season in Midget, but will play the rest of the season in the QMJHL.

Blainville-Boisbriand

#5 Nathanael Halbert Def (2014): Played a sound game defensively, with smart positioning in his own zone and blocked shots when needed. There was nothing flashy about his game with the puck, though. He showed good gap control, as he kept a good distance between him and opposing forwards. Good stickwork as well.

#71 Nikita Jevpalovs C (2014): He was one of the better players for the Armada tonight, as he scored the opening goal with a quick one-timer from the faceoff circle on the power play. Protected the puck very well tonight, used his back to shield away opposing defensemen from it. Can hold onto the puck for a long time, and he showed nice patience with it in this game. An agile skater, I saw him make some quick turns on his skates to get away from defenders deep in the offensive zone. Great play on the overtime goal where he made a spinorama move in a one-on-one confrontation to create separation from the defender, then drove to the net with the puck which ended up on Walcott's stick for the winning goal.

#77 Guillaume Beaudoin Def (2014): Was paired with Walcott again tonight. He showed some good gap control against opposing forwards on the rush. He has nice mobility, too, as he moved fairly well on the ice. Made some good pinches to keep puck in the offensive zone. Showed nice things in overtime on the power play, such as good poise with the puck and attempts to make offensive plays, which I didn't see during the first three periods.

#85 Daniel Walcott Def (2014): Played a strong physical game, had numerous big hits and was also hit hard in the 2nd period which resulted in him dropping the gloves. Elite skating ability makes him a threat to step up for a big open-ice hit. Love his anticipation in the defensive zone; very quick to cut spaces and gives no time to forwards with the puck. Good active stick to cut passing lane or strip pucks away. If he sees an opportunity to rush the puck in the offensive zone, he will take it, as he is such a fluid skater. Good read on the overtime goal where he followed through on the Jevpalovs rush to the net and had a free puck in front to score the overtime goal.

#92 Marcus Hinds Rw (2014): Terrific shift on a 5-on-3 penalty kill, won a puck race in the corner and was able to kill time deep in the Saint-John zone. Did great work all game long, deep in the Saint-John zone with his puck protection and pinning down the Sea Dogs deep in their own end.

Moose Jaw Warriors vs Everett Silvertips January 18 2014 (WHL Regular Season)

EVT #10 C Sandhu Tyler (2014). Used his speed to create chances and played a responsible defensive game. Didn't play with much aggression on the forecheck.

EVT #89 C Nikolishin Ivan (2014). Was good in the face circle tonight. Was calm with the puck, threading the needle. Needs to shoot the puck when given the chance.

EVT #12 W Leedahl Dawson (2014). I liked his poise tonight, was aggressive and taking chances offensively. Was strong on the forecheck and winning the little battles along the boards.

MJ #19 C Point Brayden (2014). 3 assists. He got some dirty dangles in his tool box, undressed a couple EVT defenders tonight. Keen offensive instincts and elusive dangles that with dazzle. Great foot speed and never stops moving. Not overly big but works hard. He seems to show up out of nowhere to receive passes and used his speed and touch to create scoring chances. Played a responsible defensive game.

MJ #2 D Sleptsov Alexey (2014). Composed defender who was calm and showed good poise with the puck. Always seem to make the right play coming out of his defensive zone. Decent transition passer and his skating ability allows him to rush the puck when there is no outlet. Could be more physical in the corners and along the boards.

Final Everett 4-3

Jan. 18, 2014 – Waterloo Black Hawks vs. USNTDP U18's (USHL)

US #17 Alex Tuch RW (2014) – Brought edge and physicality as is usually the case. Always finished his checks and had a couple really hard hits. High compete and effort level at all times, both ends of the ice. What I like about Alex is willingness to drive to the net with the puck, which he did a few times in this game. His size combined with his speed and strength allows him to drive to the outside on defensemen and edge them out to create a lane to the net. Only downside was a poor penalty taken far behind the play that lead to a power play goal against about five seconds into the power play. I like his edge but he has to be smart about it and not take it too far. He did that time and it cost his team a crucial goal against.

US #27 Sonny Milano LW (2014) – Milano was up to his usual tricks in this matchup. He is so creative and fluid with the puck, and his elusiveness is matched by few of his peers. One play in particular was a snapshot to what he is capable of. He picked up the puck in between the red line and his offensive blue line, circled almost completely around the entire neutral zone toward his defensive zone and back to the offensive zone and then turned on the jets to enter the offensive zone and blow past the defenseman wide for a great scoring chance. He drew a penalty on the play, as he often does with speed in beating defenders. He was physically engaged in this one, as well, getting in opponent's faces a couple of times and never shying away from anything physical.

US #11 Jack Eichel C (2015) – A bit of an off-night for the usually stellar centerman. Displayed some of his usual skill set but all in all had a rather average game. Seemed a bit "off" all game and didn't have his usual jump in his feet and hands. With that said, even an "off" night for Eichel equates to a pretty average game overall.

US #19 Dylan Larkin C (2014) – Larking scored the lone goal for the US late in the game while 4-on-4. He was camped out in front of the net and tucked home a rebound from a point shot. Larkin backchecked hard and was defensively responsible as always, and had a solid game offensively, as well. He's simply tenacious on the puck and refuses to lose battles. I love his compete level and will to win. High motor and effort level in this game which is always the case and his two-way game is fantastic. Played in all situations and is as versatile as they come.

US #2 Jack Dougherty D (2014) – Dougherty assisted on Larkin's goal. He placed a hard, low wrist shot on net and Larkin put in the rebound. It was a smart play instead of trying to wind up for a big slapshot like defensemen at all levels tend to want to do so often. The play illustrated Dougherty's intelligence and awareness. Had a strong game defensively. Rock solid in his own zone, particularly stingy in front of his own net. Had one nice check in particular, stepping up at a good time at his offensive blue line, knocking the puck carrier to the ice and allowing his team to regain possession of the puck and transition right back into the offensive zone. Was a beautiful play.

US #8 Jack Glover D (2014) – Glover had a so-so game. Was mostly average and struggled on a few occasions. On one shift in particular, he made a bad decision to pinch at the offensive blue line and missed both the puck and the puck carrier, leading to a rush the other way. On the same shift he got caught playing the puck instead of the body and got walked near the faceoff dot, giving up a quality scoring chance against that Weyrich bailed him out on. That was the worst of it, but overall fairly average and not very noticeable in this one.

US #22 Jared Fiegl C (2014) – Fiegl is a very skilled and speedy player and showed it in this game. Strong puck handler who likes to drive the puck to the net. He shields the puck particular well with his body and is tough to remove from the puck. Had a physical game, as well, with a few nice hits and is not shy about mixing it up and getting involved with the opposition. One of the better forwards in the game today on either side.

US #1 Blake Weyrich G (2014) – Weyrick was at the top of his game today. Waterloo had a number of high quality chances and Weyrick came up strong. Turned away a breakaway and made a highlight reel save post-to-post on a great chance while Waterloo was on a power play. Also made a phenomenal glove save late in the game on a laser beam from the point that got redirected. Big body and very good athleticism. Strong effort.

WAT #22 Tyler Sheehy C (2013) – Scored a beauty of a goal on the power play. He fired a high, hard snap shot from around the faceoff dot right past Weyrick. Did a great job finding soft spots on the ice in coverage, creating high quality chances for himself. Intelligent player, good hockey sense. Does a really good job at creating space for himself to operate, creative offensively. Very good speed, and used that speed for both sides of the puck. Made a couple of nice plays on the backcheck and had a strong game in his own zone.

WAT #51 Mark Friedman D (2013) – Strong, low, compact skater with a nice stride. Anticipates the play extremely well, evidenced by his breaking up passes on a few occasions in the neutral zone by jumping the passing lanes. Tough player; got hit extremely hard by Tuch in the 3rd period that shook him up but bounced back and didn't miss a shift. High hockey IQ and sees the ice well. Very noticeable.

WAT #33 Cameron Johnson G (2012) – Maybe the star of the game, Johnson was absolutely phenomenal, and the main reason for his team's victory. The US outshot Waterloo 47-32, and a high percentage of those were high quality chances. Excellent rebound control and very good laterally. Decent size and makes himself big in the net. Weyrich was excellent, but Johnson topped him.

FINAL SCORE: 2-1 Waterloo

SCOUTS NOTES:

I felt the US carried the play in this one for the most part but Waterloo certainly had no shortage of quality scoring chances themselves and made the most of them. A couple others players of note were Ryan Hitchcock (LW 2014) and Jonathan MacLeod (D 2014) for the US and Liam Pecoraro (F 2014) for Waterloo. Stellar goaltending on both sides and an all around entertaining game.

Everett Silvertips vs Kelowna Rockets January 22 2014 (WHL)

EVT #10 C Sandhu Tyler (2014). 1 assist. Was calm with the puck tonight with limited mistakes. Was strong on the forecheck but needs to be more consistent offensively.

EVT #89 C Nikolishin Ivan (2014). Needs to produce more offense consistently. Set up a couple decent scoring chances with some laser like passes. Great ability to find the player under pressure or through a maze of sticks. Played a sound defensive game.

EVT #12 W Leedahl Dawson (2014). Had good compete level tonight. Strong on the boards and physical in the corners.

KEL #14 C Chartier Rourke (2014). 1 assist. Rourke showed good speed and poise. Was relentless on the forecheck winning the small battles. Shifty player who can sneak into the scoring areas untouched. Played a solid game in all 3 zones.

KEL #23 W Kirkland Justin (2014). Didn't play.

KEL #24 C Baillie Tyson (2014). 1 goal. Aggressive player despite his size. Very shifty and agile which makes him hard to hit. Anticipates the play well and uses his quickness to attack. Does not seems to be consistent shift to shift but plays competitive.

KEL #3 D Stadel Riley (2014) Not very big but is calm and poise under pressure. Moves the puck well and does not seem to make many mistakes coming out of his defensive zone. Showed good compete level and aggression. I like his quickness to shut down 1 on 1 situations.

Final Kelowna 6-3

Jan. 25, 2014 – USNTDP U18 vs. Muskegon Lumberjacks (USHL)

US #17 Alex Tuch RW (2014) – Physical presence, created his usual havoc in the offensive zone. Created a lot of plays doing the dirty work in the corners and along the boards. That line has so much synergy, they dominate possession in the offensive zone. Potted US' third goal with assists from both his line mates.

US #27 Sonny Milano LW (2014) – Assisted on Tuch's goal. Line could've had more goals if not for some great saves by Schierhorn. So much playmaking ability and elusiveness. Had a good defensive effort, was backchecking hard. Line as a whole created a lot of chances.

US #19 Larkin LC (2014) – Strong, physical game. Drove the puck to the net a lot. Plays fearless. Tireless worker, never quits. Caused numerous turnovers and just simply overpowered opposing players in all three zones. His motor never shuts off.

US #2 Jack Dougherty RD (2014) – Smart decisions, safe with the puck and protected it well. Made really smart, good pinches to keep plays alive in the offensive zone. Had a few good shots on net; heavy slap shot. Couple solid, quick wrist shots. Got a power tally from the point. Really effective on the power play, moves the puck well and while his mobility is average-slightly above average, moves the puck laterally along the blue line well to open up lanes.

US #8 Jack Glover RD (2014) – Had a good offensive game but struggled elsewhere. Threaded a beautiful pass to Bjork on the second goal. Seems to have better awareness and instincts in the offensive zone. Had a rough game defensively. Was completely walked a couple of times by opposing puck carriers. Too often tries to poke check and play the puck as opposed to taking the body. His stick is slow, forwards exploit it and get in behind him. Happened to him twice on one shift about 20 seconds apart. Happened again the 3rd Period to the same player he turned the puck over to. Questionable decision making in the defensive and neutral zones.

US #9 Shane Gersich LW/C (2014) – Notched a power play tally in the 3rd Period. Strong offensive game, created a lot of quality chances, especially on the power play. Does everything at top speed, I like his quickness. Quick first step, gets to top speed in a hurry.

US #21 Ryan Hitchcock LW (2014) – Had a few shots on goal and created some chances but somewhat of a quiet game offensively. I really like his speed and how much space he creates for himself with the puck. His foot and hand speed combined are a handful to defend. Really shifty and creative.

US #22 Jared Fiegl LW/C (2014) – Played a real physical game, which is the norm for Jared. Chippy and aggressive but smart about it. Big body with the puck, protects it well. Solid game defensively, no mistakes.

US #10 Joe Wegwerth RW (2014) – Had a physical, bruising game as usual. Had a real good game in the offensive zone, strong puck control and protected it well, especially along the boards and down low around the goal line. Had a couple really nice drives to the net with the puck. He is able to just bull his way around with his size, skating, and decent hands. Got more engaged physically in the 3rd Period and was tangled up with Wolanin in an altercation. Strong physical presence.

US #7 Anders Bjork LW/C (2014) – Had a beautiful top-shelf goal on a nice pass from Glover on a turnover. Great play all around. Tied for a team-high five shots on goal. Great game with the puck, quality chances. Solid in all three zones.

US #11 Jack Eichel RC (2015) – Up to his usual tricks, playmaking and skating circles around everyone. Made a really nice play to set up the Dougherty power play goal. Smooth zone entries, dominating puck possession in offensive zone. As a line, him, Milano, and Tuch are so in tune with one another and so dominant. Almost scored one of his own on a laser of a slap shot. Makes the game look so easy, slows everything down.

US #2 Edwin Minney G (2014) – What more is there to say than the stat line: 38 shots, 38 saves. Many were high quality chances, stopped a couple of breakaways. Big body in net, was really aggressive, challenged shooters. Excellent rebound control. Fair share of shots were from the perimeter but was still tested plenty. Strong game.

MUS #6 Christian Wolanin LD (2013) – Smooth skater, quick feet, excellent hands. Had the puck on his stick a lot. Carried the play up the ice numerous times. Great poise with the puck, weaves through neutral zone traffic smoothly, never looks panicked. Always made good decisions on breakouts and is a strong passer. Finds the open man and it's always tape to tape. Really mobile and a lot of offensive confidence. Played the body well and had a couple of nice hits. Never got beat one on one.

MUS #29 Eric Schierhorn G (2014) – Score is deceiving, could've been much worse if not for him. Was hung out to dry a lot of the night. Gave up few rebounds but when he did, there were often second and third chances thereafter. Made a lot of saves on high quality chances in tight. Bad game for his team and on the score sheet but showed a lot of skill and athleticism.

MUS #11 Matt Iacopelli RW (2012) – Iacopelli had a game-high nine shots on goal. Minney shut him down. He has one of the best shots I have seen league-wide. World class. Snappy release, tons of zip, accurate. Minney just got the best of him. He uses his size really well to protect the puck and he's got wheels. Size-speed combo is difficult to defend. He tended to have more compete and a higher level of effort in the offensive zone than the others, and even there there were times he wouldn't engage as much in puck battles but clearly he has a nose for the net and the puck tends to find his stick. Simply snake-bitten tonight.

FINAL SCORE: 7-0 USNTDP

SCOUTS NOTES:

While the US did carry more of the play, the score is deceiving. Muskegon had no shortage of chances, but the US power play was too much for Muskegon tonight. Schierhorn was left out to dry a bit but still came up big for the Lumberjacks numerous times, just got torched on the power play. Game took a bit of a nasty turn in the 3rd Period. A lot of action after the whistle and play got chippy. I like the continued progress of Christian Wolanin. His game has really come along and he's become one of the more noticeable players in every game he suits up for.

Jan. 25, 2014 - Youngstown Phantoms vs. Chicago Steel (USHL)

YO #7 Maxin Letunov C (2014) - Skilled forward may have been the ice-time leader for either team. Played in all situations; huge power play threat but defensively responsible and gets penalty kill time. Had shifts at both center and left wing. I feel he's better suited and better utilized at center. His defensive play was as impressive as his offensive play. Creates offensive opportunities with his defensive play. Pick-pocketed opposition a couple of times in the offensive zone to create quality scoring chances. Broke up a pass in the offensive zone in the slot, toe-dragged a defender and fired a rocket snapshot on a quality scoring chance, quality stop by Steel goaltender Morris. Has a quick release. Great offensive zone entry both five-on-five and on the power play. He isn't the prettiest skater but he has very good speed, very deceptive. Lulls defenders into thinking they have him lined up and then instantly turns up the foot speed and makes moves to elude them and/or outskate them. Works hard, never takes a shift off. Really liked his play away from the puck, showed good hockey sense, always in the right position. Great all-around game.

YO #10 Trey Bradley LW (2014) - His smallish size is the second thing you notice about Bradley after the first thing that gets your attention in the first place; his speed and skating ability. He does everything at the top gear. Shifty feet, quick hands, very speedy. Won two or three one-on-one battles with his stickhandling in the offensive zone. He creates space well for himself and given his shiftiness is very hard to defend. "Slippery" comes to mind. He did get roughed up on a couple of occasions but generally he's very good at avoiding contact and putting himself in the best position to make a play before getting removed from the puck. Showed no hesitation to handle the puck or put himself in the tough areas of the ice. Has great chemistry with his linemates, assisted on the first goal on the power play.

YO #12 JJ Piccinich RW (2014) - Strong-skating forward had an excellent game. One of the more noticeable players on the ice. Always skated hard, high compete level, very aggressive at both ends of the ice. Saved a goal on one play on account of his hard backchecking and breaking up a would-be goal on what was a 2-on-1 until he was able to catch up to the play just in time. He's an excellent skater, has real good speed, quick feet. Low center of gravity, gets a lot of power out of his stride. Good offensive skill set. Scored on the power play in the second period, was camped out in the front of the net. Likes to be physical and isn't afraid to hang out in those areas. Played in all situations.

YO #18 Kyle Connor C (2015) - High end offensive skill. Potential first-rounder. Has excellent speed. Beat defensemen wide for quality scoring chances twice. The first time was a beautiful play, made a chip pass to himself and blew around the defenseman without even being touched. Has a thin frame and needs to fill out but as is he still looks strong. Won a lot of board battles, didn't get knocked around, doesn't shy away from the physical stuff. Was very good defensively. Always backchecked hard and thwarted what would have been a couple of odd-man breaks had he not skated hard to get back. Very intelligent player, sees the ice well. Was very patient with puck, never seemed rushed, doesn't force anything that's not there. Game is very mature, overall.

YO #57 Steven Ruggiero D (2015) - Really liked his game a lot. Big body, but moves very well. Long body, long reach, but very smooth. Good footwork and moves well in transition. Smooth constantly comes to mind. Was very patient with the puck, makes good decisions, always look cool and doesn't get rattled. Maintained good gaps and closes on the puck carrier very well. Difficult to get around. Has some offensive upside, nice hands, picks his spots well to jump into the play offensively. Never passed up a chance to throw his body on someone. Likes to be physical. A lot to like about his game.

YO #27 Luke Stork C (2013) - Strong, steady, smart player. Doesn't have blinding speed but moves well, physical, always involved in this game. Puck found him a lot. Works as hard as anybody on the ice. High, high compete level, played in all situations. Lot of ice time. Has good leadership qualities. Seems like a calming influence on the ice, always talking to teammates and communicating. Intelligent, great hockey sense. Heads up passer, set up a couple of breakaways. Solid game, does everything well.

CHI #20 Artem Artemov LW (2015) - Solid all-around game, which is often the case with him. His hard work down low creating his scoring opportunity which he cashed in on. Took a couple of hits and bounced off another. Always patient with the puck, just never gets rattled. Had a great wrist shot from the dot in the third period that hit the post. Has a great release. Always makes good decisions, very smart player. Took hits a couple of times in order to make a play. Not afraid to sacrifice himself. Very unselfish player.

CHI #23 Robby Jackson LW (2015) - Had a nice game for Chicago. High-motor player, always moving at high speed. Made a couple really nice cross-ice passes, one for a breakaway from his own zone and another in the neutral zone to help a teammate gain zone entry in behind the defenseman. Sometimes tries to be too cute, cost him a couple of turnovers. Tried to make too many moves on his own and another time tried to make a fancy pass, giving up a quality shooting opportunity. Responsible otherwise. Always supports defensemen down low. High energy guy linemates seem to feed off of.

CHI #17 Fredrik Olofsson RW (2014) - First game as a member of the Steel after being traded from Green Bay. Had a very good opening game with his new club; best game of any other Steel player. Olofsson just has the look of a pro. Everything is done smoothly, looks effortless, game just seems to come easy to him. Displayed excellent vision, made a number of really nice passes and set up numerous offensive chances. Creates space for himself well and makes plays. Very patient with the puck. Excellent skater, has a very smooth, fluid stride. Highly skilled. Played on the point for nearly all Chicago power plays. Very strong, had two huge hits, one a textbook hip check along the boards on a forecheck in the offensive zone. All around, very cerebral player, does all the little things right. Interested to see if his new surroundings spark his game. If this first game is any indication this could end up being a very good deal for Chicago.

CHI #2 Connor Yau D (2013) - Always one of the smarter players on the ice any time he is out there. Great decision maker, sees the ice and anticipates the play so well. Always made the good first pass to clear his zone, defensively sound and responsible. Got caught out of position one time but it was an aggressive mistake and was still able to recover on account of his speed and quick feet. Small in size but is deceptive strong and makes up for any lack in size with his intelligence and speed. Quick stick. Displayed some offensive upside with a couple of nice plays on his offensive blue line and setting up a great pass near the end of the game.

FINAL SCORE: 3-2 Chicago

SCOUTS NOTES:

Unfortunately, very questionable officiating took away from what was otherwise a very good game. Officiating directly affected the outcome, but taking that out of it, was a very evenly matched game. The chemistry of the Bradley-Piccinich-Connor line is as good as any line in the league. They are so good together and create so many plays. Very fun to watch. I also find Letunov to be a very intriguing prospect, and feel he could go higher in this draft than some project. The skill level and hockey sense are elite. Also interested to see how Olofsson fits in going forward and how his game is affected, or not, with his new address. The early returns are very positive. Came away very impressed with him in this contest.

Portland WinterHawks vs Everett Silvertips January 26 2014 (WHL)

EVT #10 C Sandhu Tyler (2014). Did not play.

EVT #89 C Nikolishin Ivan (2014). Played a good two way game, but seems to struggle and shut down against team with solid defenders.

EVT #12 W Leedahl Dawson (2014). His game to game is consistent. He brings energy and physical play to every game. What you see is what you are going to get with some offensive chipped in.

PORT #9 C De Leo Chase (2014). 1 goal. The energizer bunny just keeps going and going. Had high energy and aggression in all 3 zones. He was very good in tight showing some dazzling dangles to beat EVT defenders. I like how Chase just never seems to quite on any play. Well rounded game tonight.

PORT # 22 W Schoenborn Alex (2014). Alex brought high energy and tenacity on the forecheck, was very strong and dominate along the boards. EVT defender had a hard time knocking him off the puck. Battled for space in the scoring areas looking to pick up some garbage.

PORT #13 W Iverson Keegan (2014). 1 goal. Was driving the net and using his size to battle for time and space around the scoring areas. Was aggressive and physical around the corners and strong on the boards. EVT defenders had a tough time containing him. Best game I have seen Keegan play this year.

PORT #23 C Turgeon Dominic (2014). Always calm and poised, never seems to get rattled. Was strong in all game situation. Showed good offensive potential. Best two way player on the ice.

Final Portland 6-2

Jan. 28, 2014 - Dubuque Fighting Saints vs. Green Bay Gamblers (USHL)

DQ #9 Seamus Malone C (2014) -High end skill and playmaking ability on display, as always. Made a great play on his goal, which happened to be short-handed. Took possession of the puck and broke away with his speed through the neutral zone, dished a pass off to his teammate and then used his speed to evade his defender and found a soft spot of the ice to receive a pass back for a breakaway in which he made a nice forward-to-backhand move for a goal. The entire play was a perfect snapshot showcasing all of his skills; speed, intelligence, stickhandling. He's such a fluid skater, makes everything look effortless. Always went hard to the net and drives the net a lot when he has the puck. Fearless in that regard. On the other side of the puck, won the majority of his faceoffs and was defensively responsible and sound. Good two-way game.

DQ #28 Shane Eiserman C/LW (2014) - Had a slow start to the game. Wasn't very noticeable until the latter half of the second period and then became noticeable quick. Had a couple of very big hits and had a couple of really nice shots from the slot. Has a great shot, quick release, gets a lot on it. Battled hard low and along the boards, won a number of battles. Very strong in those areas. He has a big body and uses it well on both sides of the puck. Displayed excellent vision and hockey sense on a couple of offensive plays, one in particular when he gained offensive zone entry but had the wherewithal to recognize his linemates were all changing. He busted hard into the zone and gave the impression he was going to drive wide and take the puck to the corner, but made a tight turn on a dime and circled a few feet short of the top of the circle, towards the boards, and created all kinds of space for himself. By this time his linemates' replacements had entered the zone and he set up a great scoring chance for the late-coming defenseman, who had all the time the world because of the space Eiserman created. Was a beautiful play and illustrated not only his skill set but his intelligence and awareness.

DQ #8 Blake Hillman D (2014) - Smooth-skating defenseman had an excellent game. Did a little bit of everything. Always finishes his checks, rarely gets beat. Had two big hits, one a beautiful hip check along the boards on a forward trying to beat him wide just inside his defensive zone. Closed the gap and took the perfect angle on the hit, left the forward with no where to go but to the point of contact. Textbook. Always has good gaps and has the skating ability to step and be aggressive, close off passing lanes and leave offending player with few options with the puck. Was always in position defensively, very good defensive zone awareness. Offensively was very active. Jumped up into the rush a couple of times, and has a knack for getting open in the offensive zone. Made a great play at the point on his goal. Opened up the shooting lane with a nice, subtle little move with the puck and wisely took a nice wrist shot and put it right on target, finding the back of the net. Was a play where a lot of other players would have just tried for a slapshot, which in this case would have almost certainly lead to a blocked shot, if not a breakaway going the other way. Anticipated and read the play perfectly to pick off passes and jump the lanes all game.

DQ #7 Keegan Ford D (2014) - Doesn't have size on his side but has the smarts and speed to make up for it. Quick-footed, tenacious, plays tough and hard every shift. Despite his size he throws his weight around and finishes his checks. Got hit pretty hard a couple of times and just bounces right back up and sticks his nose in there. Doesn't get deterred. Tough defender. Was one-on-one with Schmaltz on a number of occasions and came out on top, didn't get beat or fooled by anything Schmaltz attempted.

DQ #31 Ben Johansson G (2012) - Big reason Dubuque came out on top in this game. Was phenomenal. Very large number of Green Bay's shots were of high quality. Numerous scoring chances in tight. Gave up few rebounds. Was very aggressive, made a lot of saves out past his crease. Very good on his angles, never lost his net. Came up big on a number of odd-man rushes. One of the stars of the game, in my book.

GB #9 Nick Schmaltz C (2014) - As always, one of the more fun players to watch on the ice. Was all over the ice. Had an assist on Green Bay's first goal in the second period. Showed great patience and great skill. Had possession of the puck for a good 15-20 seconds, kept circling around the offensive zone looking for a play to make, no one could get the puck away from him or even really catch him. Finally lulled Dubuque's defense to sleep and caught them watching, fired a pass over to Hurley for a great look and he buried it. Was a succession of plays and decisions few in this league are capable of. Beautiful play. Almost had a goal for himself earlier in the game strictly on his own accord. Took a defenseman wide and behind the net, almost stuffed the wraparound in. Drew a penalty strictly on account of his speed taking a defenseman to the outside again and beating him. Had a few other high-end offensive plays, toe-drags, etc. What's impressive is with all the chances he creates, he never once let it cost him or his team. No turnovers, no coughing up the puck, always came through to make a play. His compete level was high in this game, which is something that comes into question sometimes. Backchecked hard, worked hard in his own zone, was always moving. The complete package was on display this game.

GB #8 Dawson Cook F (2013) - Great two-way game. Played physical, hard, very involved every shift he was out there. Laid a couple of highlight-reel hits. Relishes the physical side of the game and takes advantage of his size. Smart player, plays well away from the puck. Played in all situations. Defensively sound and has good offensive ability. Just a solid game, all around. Very noticeable out there.

FINAL SCORE: 4-2 Dubuque

SCOUTS NOTES:

This game got off to a slow start. The first period was penalty-filled and didn't have much of a flow as a result. Malone's short-handed goal came in the latter stages of the period and was one of the few bits of action of note to that point of the game. From the second period on the game picked up and had a much better pace. Tightly contested. If not for Johansson coming up big, Green Bay could have easily walked away with the win in this one, though Dubuque had no shortage of offensive chances, themselves. Schmaltz had the kind of game that got him on the first round radar of the NHL draft. It was good to see his compete level high all game long.

Everett Silvertips VS Portland WinterHawks January 29 2014 (WHL)

EVT #10 C Sandhu Tyler (2014). Did not play. I project a possible 7th round pick if a team takes a chance on him. ECHL player at best unless he continues to develop his overall game

EVT #89 C Nikolishin Ivan (2014). Ivan continues to struggle to produce and offense against Port top defenders. I project Ivan to be late 5-6th round pick. Has potential to develop into a NHL player after some seasoning.

EVT #12 W Leedahl Dawson (2014). His game to game is consistent. He brings energy and physical play to every game. If someone takes a chances on Dawson he will be a Late 7th round pick. ECHL/AHL player at best unless he continues to develop his overall game

PORT #9 C De Leo Chase (2014). 1 goal and +2. Played a solid game in all 3 zones, showed some dirty mitts in tight and dazzled a few EVT defenders. I project Chase to be 2-3th round pick. Undersize player who plays a bigger game. Has the potential to develop into a NHL player after some seasoning in the minors.

PORT # 22 W Schoenborn Alex (2014). Alex brings high energy and tenacity on a consistent basis. Played a good all-around game. I project Alex to be 5-6th round pick. Only time will tell if he will develop into a NHL caliber player, I seem him as a top end forward in the minors with NHL call ups

PORT #13 W Iverson Keegan (2014). I like his size and physical play. Keegan has improved every game this season. He was strong all game. I project Keegan to be a 6th round pick. Keegan has the size but needs to work on his skating and overall tools of the trade. AHL caliber player with the possibility of call ups to the Show (NHL) if he improves the weak parts of his game.

PORT #23 C Turgeon Dominic (2014). 1goal tonight. Always calm and poised. I like how he never seems to be rattled. I project Dominic to be a 4th round pick. Good two way center who reminds me of Jarret Stoll. Will continued develop I see Dominic as a 3rd or 4th line NHL center.

Final Portland 8-1

Jan 31, 2013. Sherbrooke Phoenix vs Chicoutimi Saguenéens (QMJHL)

SHE #15 D, Deschamps, Jonathan (2013) In order to be good defensively, he really relies on his positioning. He knows he doesn't have the speed and the mobility to chase anybody, but he will make them pay if he has the opportunity to catch them. He was clearing his goalie's crease. He wanted to drop the gloves against overager Victor Provencher more than once in order to defend his teammates. His breakouts were bad.

SHE #32 D, Neill, Carl (2013) His starts were a bit slow compared to my last viewing. His first pass was effective as usual. He looked great on the powerplay. Was a physical force along the wall and compensated for his lack of footwork with sound positioning in his zone. Looked like he learned how to play in Chicoutimi.

SHE #97 D, Roy, Jérémy (2014) He had a bad game for Jérémy Roy. For any other defenseman in his age group, it would be a good one. He was somewhat overmatched against Laurent Dauphin's combination of skill and speed off the rush. Instead of following Dauphin, he was trying to get over him and that made Roy look like a fool on some occasions early in the first period. He was trying to play like Superman making odd decisions while rushing the puck. He looked great on the powerplay once again. He can circle the puck like few can and his slapshot is always dangerous and heavy.

SHE #28 C, Audette, Daniel (2013) I really like his anticipation. It looked like he knew where the puck was going. He showcased his superior agility and explosiveness once again. He lost some battles due to a lack of willingness. Like in previous viewings, he created scoring chances off the rush. If you give him too much room in the offensive zone, he can be deadly. He needs to cut towards the net on a regular basis to be more effective. He played way too much on the perimeter.

SHE #19 RW, Lundholm, Mitchell (2014) A big body, Lundholm lacks explosiveness. You don't see him that often. He has long strides but he needs to add muscles to his tall frame to be effective in the corners. He made some awful decisions with the puck.

CHI #28 D, Lyamkin, Nikita (2013) He was rarely beaten one-on-one, which wasn't the case early this year. He's improving and he communicates better with his teammates as well.

CHI #58 D, Allard, Frédéric (2015) Allard was outstanding. He's the steadiest defenseman on his team. He's not flashy but the decisions he makes with and without the puck are always good. He reads the play effectively and he positions himself properly to break up some plays in the defensive zone. He leaves very little space to opponents. His quick breakouts are on tape most of the time and even though he does not have a superior skillset like Jérémy Roy, his hockey IQ is great. He recorded two assists.

CHI #55 C, Roy, Nicolas (2014) Played a typical Nic Roy-type game. Excellent in the three zones, he was able to create scoring chances and cycle the puck. He liked to slow down the play when entering the offensive zone off the rush and he likes to cut towards the high slot. If often works out quite well.

CHI #26 LW, Bouchard, Jérémy (2014) For a young kid, he looked good on the penalty kill. Being the forward used on 3-on-5, he was able to keep the puck out of his box thanks to his hockey IQ. Looking forward to see his progression next year. He could be a good player if he improves his skating.

SCORE: CHI 4-3 OT

Northeastern vs. BC – Feb 10, 2014 (TD Garden – Beanpot Championship)

Northeastern Huskies –

#3 Josh Manson (D) – You can tell the Anaheim Ducks saw Manson as a project as that's what I exactly saw in the beginning too. At first you see a big-sized D-man with a physical presence. But then when you really watched he showed some good mobility for a 6'3" 205lbs. blue liner. He moved the puck pretty well and handled it adequately too. He threw a big hit in the 2nd period on BC's #24 Arnold just off the boards in the open-ice knocking the forward off his feet. He will play the body and could develop into a monster defensively to play against if he gets a more mean streak and sandpaper to his game. He plays hard, but for the NHL ranks could stand to be even nastier. In the last moments of the game he rushed the puck up ice eluding BC players and taking the puck down slot showing some good stick handling and did everything but the finish. He is a project still, but you like the potential. He grew on you as the game moved on. (Anaheim Ducks 6th Round – 2011)

#5 Matt Benning (D) – He played solid minutes all night for a freshman and was thrown into big situations as he was on the ice as Northeastern was down a goal late with the goalie pulled. Unfortunately, he made a rookie mistake in the neutral zone as puck was cleared out and he gathered at center ice. Instead of showing poise and making the right choice he panicked and quickly threw the puck back towards the offensive zone right on #13 Gaudreau's stick for an easy ENG in the neutral zone when he was the last man back. Overall, he game was decent on the night. He isn't a flashy type, but will play body effectively and move the puck. His skating is average right now but his game should grow in the NCAA ranks for a few years. (Boston Bruins 6th Round – 2012)

#6 Michael Gunn (D) – He is a tall D-man that plays a steady, no frills game. He is a decent skater and puck handler, but really will not give much on the offensive end. He is the steady stay-at-home defenseman that will play the body and move the puck up and out of the zone.

#8 Adam Reid (F) – You like his size, skating ability, and strength although there is nothing high-end here. He will play in all areas of the ice and create good net front presence but he is not a natural goal scorer. He could pan into a 4th liner at the next level, but will need to be quicker with his feet and puck decisions.

#14 Braden Pimm (F) – He is having a break-out season in his senior year although he looked average on the night. He plays on the top line for NU but did not really create a lot of scoring chances. You can see the offensive instincts but really did not do enough to "wow" for being Huskies leading scorer. In fact, I don't think he registered a shot on net. I would need to see more for his value.

#15 Kevin Roy (F) – He is on the smaller side for the NHL standard but comes with lots of skill and creativity. You could see BC defenders honed in on him to make life hard but he still managed to get a few scoring opportunities. In the 1st on the PP he received a pass just inside the blue line in stride and walked in and blasted one point blank, but #30 Demko was up to the task. In the 2nd period he made the score sheet and started the play to tie the game as he picked off the #28 Savage break-out attempt and went in all alone from the low circle on his off-wing. He got #30 Demko to move and tried going back short side but goalie made good pad save low. The rebound was kicked out in which #18 Stevens cleaned up on the backhand. He could stand to bulk up a bit especially since opponents' key on him, but the stick, skating, shooting, and offensive components and thoughts are already in good shape. (Anaheim Ducks 4th Round – 2012)

#18 John Stevens (F) – He scored Northeastern's only goal on the night as he looped back into offensive zone after recognizing the turnover created by teammate #15 Roy and skated into space to where the rebound then popped out and quickly released a backhander that beat the goalie's outstretched glove in the 2nd period. He is a good size kid at 6'2" who will continue to fill out as he develops at the college game. He can play in all three zones and will give honest effort. Stevens will chip in with points and at the other end not be a defensive liability.

#19 Mike Szmatula (F) – He was one of the better forwards for NU on the night as always dangerous when the puck was on his stick as shows good skating stride and puck skills, thoughts. He's a playmaker that makes things happen out on the ice. Most people think of #15 Roy as the leading scorer, but Szmatula is not too shabby either. Although he did not get on the score sheet he created opportunities and almost scored early in the 2nd period but BC D-man bailed the goalie out by deflecting the backhander wide. He produced good numbers in the USHL as rookie and is doing it again in the NCAA ranks as a freshman which is no surprise. Of course he was bypassed in the draft as playing in scarcely scouted league in draft year and then his size probably is a concern. He possesses a nice set of hands as took cross-ice pass in neutral zone in stride on his backhand like nothing where many would fail to handle the puck as good as he did. He is a free agent to definitely track and keep an eye on.

#23 Colton Saucerman (D) – He is a very choppy skater and that was exposed at times on the night with better and more skilled BC forwards. He definitely likes the physical game as threw a few big hits on the night, although don't think he is anything special.

#31 Clay Witt (G) – He might be one of those goalies that slipped through the draft cracks and will be a nice free agent pick up. He made big saves all night versus a very powerful Boston College club. The beauty of it, he has been doing it all season with his production. He was challenging shooters from the outside, being in good position, squaring to shooters, and limiting rebounds as well. He is definitely athletic and showed quickness as adapted a few times to make some highlight reel saves with his stick batting pucks out of mid-air that were labeled for goals. On one 3-on-2 he was playing shooter and the puck got re-directed to the far side and Witt quickly sticked away the puck. He made a good save on the break-a-way late in 1st period on #12 Hayes too. The quick reaction times came again in the 2nd period as a point shot got deflected and set up in the air over Witt, but the 'tender lunged back and whacked the puck out of harm. The 1st goal he was beat 5-hole as many engaged in on #13 Gaudreau with the puck on goal line and he then threw it out front and a quick #12 Hayes shot got the best of Witt. The GWG in 3rd period came of a re-direct that you cannot really blame Witt as shot/pass was going wide. Appeared Witt was trying to anticipate puck going wide as on right side of net but at last second was tipped through his 5-hole. After an ENG, the Huskies got sloppy and allowed a self-made break-a-way by #23 Brown who came in with determination and cleanly beat Witt over his glove, left shoulder for BC's 4th goal. He covers the net well and certainly gives NU a chance to win. An impressive performance even though on the losing side with 37 saves on 40 shots. He looked very determined and dialed in on the night.

#79 Cody Ferriero (F) – He looked average at best on the night. He didn't seem quick and was getting rubbed out of the play. At times it looked like he was frustrated as looked like relegated to 4th line duties but he did not do anything to impress. (San Jose Sharks 5th Round – 2010)

BC Eagles –

#3 Ian McCoshen (D) – Did not play; injured with concussion.

#5 Michael Matheson (D) – He is a very smooth skater and handles the puck well too. He was playing a physical game as well on the night as he delivered a few body checks at the blue line coming across ice. This was a game where I've seen Matheson make better puck decision from the backend. He seemed more poised and breaking the puck out or clearing puck to the right spots to alleviate pressure. A perfect example came late in game with face-off in defensive zone and opposing goalie pulled, the draw went into corner and Matheson quickly retrieved and confidently angled puck out of zone that led to the #13 Gaudreau ENG to secure the win. He was also on the ice for the 4th BC goal as he fired the puck again up the boards in which Northeastern D-man failed to keep in the zone which lead to #23 Brown goal. It was one of the more well-rounded games from Matheson at each end of the rink. He also managed to get pucks to the net. (Florida Panthers 1st Round – 2012)

#6 Steven Santini (D) – He is a D-man that continues to impress each time on the ice. He played solid minutes for a freshman in big time situations. He is very tough to beat 1-on-1 for opponents. He plays calm and collected and will not try to do too much as knows his game is more, shut-down defensive minded. He will make good outlet passes and get pucks to the net from the point or on an occasional rush. He really saw his ice time flourish in the 3rd period as he delivered by getting sticks in passing lanes, blocking shots, and bring a strong physical presence. The NJ Devils picked well on this player. (NJ Devils 2nd Round – 2013)

#7 Isaac MacLeod (D) – He is a big body player that uses his stick well to break up plays but could play with more grit and meanness with his size. On the flip side too he doesn't show any real offensive flair. He set-up the GWG in the 3rd period as he took pass from the corner at the point and made nice little stutter step with opponent pressuring a bit and was able get shot off that was redirected by #23 Brown for the goal out front. He might have been intentionally looking for a stick off the side of net. He is probably best to trend his game into a complete shut-down D-man in order to make the next level. (San Jose Sharks 5th Round – 2010)

#10 Danny Linell (D) – He is a smaller sized D-man that has played forward as well in his career at BC. He does some good things out there but sometimes his size and strength prohibit him from being effective. There were a few times he lost battles in the corners and actually took tripping penalty in 3rd period as faster skater exposed him to the outside.

#11 Chris Calnan (F) – He is a good sized forward that could potentially develop into the power forward type for the NHL as has good skating ability and decent puck skills, but right now his game seems a bit of a versatile, 4th liner winger. Looks like trying to adapt still to the NCAA pace as seemed get miss a few shift here and there on purpose by coach. (Chicago Blackhawks 3rd Round – 2012)

#12 Kevin Hayes (F) – He definitely has the pro-style frame and gets around the ice fairly well, although will need to keeping working on speed for the next level. He shows good puck possession utilizing his long reach as protects the puck well. He sees the ice pretty good as set-up line mate #24 Arnold in the second period with a quick pass from the boards out front but his teammate failed to convert. It seemed sometimes he tried to do a little too much, held the puck too long, and could have moved the puck more in the offensive zone to create more scoring chances. The part of his game is that he opens up space for teammates, if he could distribute a tad more he could be that much better. He made a nice read on the 1st goal as he intercepted a clear just outside offensive blue line then waited until line mates tagged up and slid a behind-the-back pass to #13 Gaudreau who had speed darting to the outside and then slipped a pass from the goal line off the side of the net that ended up hitting Hayes as he quickly fired shot 5-hole as defenders converged as he went to the net. He also recognized a scoring chance late in 1st period and took off out of the defensive zone and was hit with beautiful pass in stride up the middle by #13 Gaudreau for a break-a-way, but failed to finish. He should develop for the pro game and will spend a few seasons in AHL to hone skills. (Chicago Blackhawks 1st Round – 2010)

#13 John Gaudreau (F) – Each time he picks up the puck you can see something is going to happen for BC. Opponents definitely respect his game. He is not big in size, but plays Patrick Kane like with his stick skills and elusiveness. He made the 1st goal happen in the 1st period as he swung out of the zone to get back on-sides and then received #12 Hayes pass just inside the offensive blue line on his off-wing. He darted to the outside baiting the D-man with puck as he opened up his stride then quickly tucked it back to the outside and then fed a backhand pass in the slot that #12 Hayes cleaned up. On one breakout play on the wing he showed his creativity. He recognized the D-man pinching in and craftily angled his blade open with one-hand on stick and spun to the outside to get the puck and himself around the defender so that the play turned from possible turnover to an offensive opportunity the other way. In the 3rd period he showcased his quick stick and skating skills as he came down off-wing and gave the D-man on the 1-on-1 an inside/outside move that the D-man bit on, but he never did take the backhand shot instead opting to hold the puck on stick behind net to create opportunity. He also made great stretch pass in 3rd period to lead line mate #12 Hayes on a break-a-way up the middle. I have seen him a USA Hockey Select Camp and NJEC which he has always been deadly in the offensive sense. His game has definitely grown since Summer 2012 as he will engage physically more and smartly knows how to protect himself in the corners and along the walls when retrieving puck against bigger defenders. The beauty of his game is that he sees the ice well to elude checks and create constant scoring opportunity. You wish his size was more for the next level, but I don't hear anybody complaining about #88 on the Blackhawks for being under 6-feet. He just naturally finds a way to get on the score sheet every night. (Calgary Flames 4th Round – 2011)

#14 Adam Gilmour (F) – The freshman plays on the 4th line as the centerman with his lanky frame. He has some good stick skills and offensive thoughts. You can see he has the skill but at the same time lacks some confidence at the newer NCAA level in his 1st season. If he adds muscle and can develop that extra gear the future is bright. (Minnesota Wild 4th Round – 2012)

#19 Ryan Fitzgerald (F) – He plays a smart all-around game, but wasn't involved too much offensively in this game. You could see that his smaller frame needs to add muscle strength as when battling along the wall against bigger D-man he was out-powered. He made a good back check in the 3rd period as he nicely angled the puck carrier in the defensive zone by the hash marks taking his opponent to the ice legally. Overall, he is a smart, heads-up player. (Boston Bruins 4th Round – 2013)

#23 Patrick Brown (F) – The senior captain played a good game in his last Beanpot Championship. He played all 3 zones well as will forecheck, play the body, go into the corners, and shows a bit of offensive know-how as well. He potted two goals on the night with the 1st being the GWG on a redirect out front on a point shot by #7 MacLeod that looked to be going wide, intentionally or not. He managed to get his stick on puck even though he was battling with defender and falling to the ice. The second goal was even more impressive with under a minute left as he picked up the puck at center ice on a broken play and exploded into the offensive zone out racing two defenders and shelving a shot over the goalie's glove short side. He just showed pure determination on the play. He has not tallied a whole lot of points in his BC career but saving best year for last. Brown could develop into a 4th liner in the NHL, after all has bloodlines that certainly played in the big leagues.

#24 Bill Arnold (F) – He looks bigger than he is listed and plays a strong all-around game. He isn't that explosive and high-end skilled pivot, but rather a center that plays well at both ends of the rink. He will engage physically and also shows offensive instincts as feeds off line mates #13 Gaudreau and #12 Hayes very well. They are certainly one of the top lines in the NCAA. His game has polished up since the Summer of 2011 at the NJEC. The skating stride has improved and he excels because of a strong hockey IQ. He ended up receiving an assist on the #12 Hayes goal in 1st period as puck tipped off stick as he went to the net on the #12 Gaudreau pass. He also cleanly won a big face off late in game with Northeastern goalie pulled to help secure the win that lead to the ENG by #12 Gaudreau. (Calgary Flames 4th Round – 2010)

#26 Austin Cangelosi (F) – He is a smaller winger that plays hard and shows some good speed and offensive thoughts. He found the puck on the GWG by #23 Brown as he feed the puck from the corner out to #7 MacLeod at the point for the shot to pick up a secondary assist. He pressures on the forecheck hard to create havoc for D-men just like he quickly picked up puck on BC's 2nd goal. He also plays relentless on the PK.

#27 Quinn Smith (F) – He plays every shift with lots of energy and grit. He did not back down to the bigger players as would throw a hit to finish his checks.

#28 Scott Savage (D) – He played pretty steady through the first half of the game by keeping game simple with outlet passes and puck decisions. Then late in the 2nd period he received the puck in the defensive corner from #30 Demko and then forced a pass to centerman that was picked off by #15 Roy that lead to Northeastern's 1st goal. Then on first shift in the 3rd period, he badly misjudged a pass at center ice off the boards as he moved up instead of going back defensively and allowed a break-a-way chance for #17 Snydeman. After two questionable shifts his ice time seemed to dwindle for the rest of the game. But he did save his goalie early in 2nd period with his goalie out of position deflecting a #19 Szmatula shot attempt heading for the net. He is draft eligible again this year (2014) and had been playing himself into a mid-late round selection.

#30 Thatcher Demko (G) – He played technically solid all night. He uses his size and big equipment to his advantage as positions himself well to make the save. Sure he has a solid defense corp. in front of him although he mentally looked dialed in for a big game audience. He keeps things simple as squares to shooter, tracks pucks well, and keeps himself out of trouble as he limits rebounds. Just 5 minutes in the game he made a huge save on a 2-on-1 situation as he trusted D-man in taking passing lane and he confidently played the shooter making the save short-side. Later on in 1st period he made the initial save on a 3-on-2 play as the drop pass found the trailer. Although he did kick a rebound in the slot area he was fortunate to have a goal disallowed as players took net of the moorings as he was down on the play in the crease. It was one of the few plays on the night he misplayed but made the initial so you have to give him credit. He stood tall as well in the 1st period on PK situation as Northeastern was pressing hard. He made a great save on #15 Roy as he came down from high slot and blasted one but Demko stood tall and gobbled it up. The one goal allowed came off a turnover late in 2nd period as D-man made bad pass trying to go up center from the boards which Northeastern's #15 Roy picked off down low and cut across top off crease and firing forcing Demko to make a great low, left pad save. His momentum had him off the near post as he followed the initial shooter #15 Roy, but the rebound off the side of net was finished by #18 Stevens even though he attempted to save with his outstretched glove coming back the other way. He plays in one of the top NCAA conferences and seems to be gaining more comfort as the season has progressed. He is not overly athletic and show stopping, but successful on positioning, knowing angles of shooters, and composed mental game. If a comparison had to be made, he plays like Mike Smith of the Phoenix Coyotes. When tested he seems up to the task and reason why their is so much talk for 2014 NHL Draft.

Feb. 14, 2014 – Youngstown Phantoms vs. Muskegon Lumberjacks (USHL)

YO #7 Maxim Letunov C (2014) – Continues to impress more and more with each viewing. Aside from the obvious offensive skills, played a great game defensively. Good support for his defensemen down low in the defensive zone, in the slot, and in front of net. Willing to take hits to make passes to allow for breakouts. Made a couple of really nice plays at the offensive blue line keeping the puck in the zone and supporting his defenseman. Got sprung for a breakaway on one play where he read the defensemen were flat-flooted and he turned on the jets, received a nice pass and split the defensemen for a breakaway in which he was stopped with a nice save. Read the play and anticipated it beautifully. Very intelligent player and excellent awareness.

YO #12 JJ Piccinich RW (2014) – High motor and high compete level are always brought to the table when Piccinich is playing. Excellent game in the defensive zone. Very good away from the puck, always in position and responsible. Scored Youngstown's first goal on a nice shot in which he received a pass while streaking down his wing along the boards and fired a wrister top shelf from just inside the faceoff circle. He did so all in one motion, didn't lose a step. Great play all around.

YO #18 Kyle Connor LW (2015) – Connor's high-end skill was on display in all facets. Fastest skater on the ice, and coupled with his excellent puck handling skills was creating all sorts of space and offensive opportunities for himself and line mates. Has superior vision and playmaking ability. Set up the second goal with his speed, gaining offensive zone entry and cutting across the ice at the slot to the outside, pulling his defenseman toward him. This opened up the slot where he left a perfect drop pass to Kiefer Sherwood, who fired it home on a nice wrist shot.

YO #27 Luke Stork C (2013) – Strong, two-way forward had a solid game. He has pretty good speed and his feet are constantly moving. Very aggressive, hard forechecker, always finishes his hits and was physical, as is often the case, today. Gritty, sticks up for his teammates. Not great offensive skill but skates well and makes good decisions, takes care of the puck. Rarely makes mistakes, very dependable and stable.

YO #44 Kiefer Sherwood LW (2013) – Played a smart, hard game at both ends of the ice. Good speed and nice hands, played the point on the power play. Made good decisions and is a forward you can trust to play at the point because he can make a defensive play if the puck is brought back the other way. Not a liability. Scored Youngstown's second goal on a nice feed from Connor. Received the puck right between the circles in the slot and put a wrister top shelf.

YO #57 Steven Ruggiero D (2015) – Continues to be one of my favorite 2015-eligible players. Skates really well, especially for a kid of his size. Very mobile, and he's very confident handling the puck and skating up ice with it. Made a couple of very nice pinches, keeping offensive zone pressure alive for his team, and added two very nice keep-ins, as well. He has good offensive skill and upside and seems to be growing more and more confident utilizing that and picking his spots to make plays happen. Has a very good stick, and can make plays without having to use his body but certainly likes to be physical and finishes his checks.

MUS #6 Christian Wolanin D (2013) – One of the best players on the ice today and an ice-time leader. Played in all situations. I really like his game a lot. Big body, moves well, smooth skater, good stride, and has offensive skill. Carries the puck up the ice confidently, gains offensize zone entry well. Great poise with the puck. Made a great play springing Pooley for his goal. Read the defenseman drifting and placed a perfect pass right in front of the defenseman's feet to send Pooley in for a breakaway. Was a subtle play but displayed Wolanin's ability to read plays and his passing ability and skill level. Excellent game on both the power play and penalty kill. Sound defensive game, no mistakes. Was one-on-one with Connor breaking into his zone and took him out beautifully. Took a perfect angle on him and forced him into having no space and smothered him on the boards. Excellent, excellent game today.

MUS #11 Matt Iacopelli RW (2012) – Muskegon's leading scorer added another tally today on the power play and later got an assist, as well. Launched a few big shots. Has a heavy slap shot and also has a heavy wrister with a great release. Power play goal came on a one-timer slap shot from the point on a nice feed from Paulovic. Showed offensive creativity and hockey sense on his assist. Had the puck outside the top of the circle and wrist a low, hard shot along the ice wide of the net, but it deflected right to a teammate who was parked at the other side of the net for an easy tap-in.

MUS #20 Matej Paulovic LW (Dallas 149th Overall 2013) – Made a nice feed on Iacopelli's goal. High speed, hands to match. Won a few one-on-one battles with his stickhandling, speed, and body positioning. Strong, hard to take off the puck.

FINAL SCORE: 5-2 Muskegon

SCOUTS NOTES:

Youngstown had a tough time staying out of the penalty box in the first period and in net gave up a couple of softies and the game was essentially settled at that point. Game was more evenly matched the remaining two periods but the damage was done. Another solid game from Joseph Cecconi (D 2015) for Muskegon. Good decisions, no mistakes, just a solid game. Has some offensive upside but didn't do much today. Defensive effort was worth noting, however.

Feb 15, 2014. Rouyn-Noranda Huskies vs Chicoutimi Saguenéens (QMJHL)

ROU #5 LD, Lauzon, Jérémy (2015) His head is always up and that helps him make the right decisions on the breakout. His man-to-man coverage is pretty good for a 16-year-old defenseman. His shot from the point is pretty hard and he likes to join the rush when the opportunity is there. He also moves his upper body a lot in order to deceive players on the forecheck. He didn't look out of place while playing on the second pairing against the Sags.

ROU #6 RD, Myers, Philippe (2015) Myers really improved his footwork. He still lacks quickness, but he used his long reach adequately to cover that weakness. He looked confident with the puck as he did things with the puck he wouldn't normally do. He rushed the puck past the red line and his breakouts were OK.

ROU #20 LW, Nantel, Julien (2014) He was able to rush the puck a bit but he's not overly creative when the play is installed in the offensive zone. Nantel never turned the puck over and he was aware of his play without the puck as well. He constantly took shots while cutting to the middle of the attacking zone off the rush, which was something I wanted to see him do in my last viewing. He was great on the forecheck again. He played like a third liner all game long and he played on the second unit on the powerplay. Formed a great duo with Perron on the penalty kill because of his anticipation.

ROU #27 RW, Perron, Francis (2014) Perron's main quality is his ability to control the puck. His dangles are quite effective as they often led to scoring chances. He played on the point during powerplays and he was really good. It was a beauty to see him getting rid of the opposition, circling the puck like crazy and taking one-timer shots. He's an East-West style of player. He played well in his zone. He played on the second line and he was on the first powerplay unit. He was a threat on the penalty kill with Nantel because of his hockey sense. I really liked his game and thought he was better than Nantel.

CHI #30 G, Billia, Julio (2014) Billia was stellar in this game. He looked like the same guy we saw at the World U-17 last year. He was sharp and he showcased his great reflexes all game long. He made 46 saves, many of which were outstanding. He regularly stopped 2-on-1's, breakaways, etc. Julio showed awareness of his lack of size by getting out and cutting down angles effectively. Rouyn-Noranda forwards tried to beat him with high shots but he displayed his great upper net coverage.

FINAL SCORE: 2-1 ROU

Sherbrooke Phoenix vs Blainville-Boisbriand Armada, QMJHL, February 15th 2014

Sherbrooke

#15 Jonathan Deschamps D (2014): The team captain played his usual game with some good defending in his zone and good battles in the corners. Had some problems with the speed of the Armada forwards off the rush. Almost scored a goal following up on a rush where his shot either touched the cross bar or Marcoux's pad. Overall, not a lot of showings with the puck in this game.

#18 Julien Bahl D (2014): Plays at even strength with Jérémy Roy, his former partner from their midget days. Not very noticeable in this game as he played a safe game in his own zone and made sure to always come back when Roy rushed the puck, in case of a turnover. Good active stick on the PK, broke a couples of passes in front of the net with it. Got caught with a man behind him, which led to breakaway, but he did a nice job coming back without taking a penalty to enable Jevpalovs to take a quality shot.

#28 Daniel Audette C (2014): This was one of my best viewings of Audette in the last two years. He did a terrific job distributing the puck all night long. Scored two goals tonight, both on the backhand. For both goals, Audette showed some great speed and quick hands. Made a nice saucer pass to Jérémy Roy in the slot from the half-wall position on the power play. He is dangerous when he gets his feet moving in the neutral zone and can generate real good speed attacking opposing defensemen on the rush. On the power play, he plays on the half-wall and distributes the puck from there. Liked his effort all night, as he worked hard and provoked some penalties by keeping his feet moving. Good compete level.

#32 Carl Neill D (2014): Played in every situation of the game, including the top power play unit with Jérémy Roy. Has a big shot from the point but I didn't see that from him tonight, as he was used more as a puck distributor on the power play. His mobility and footwork need work, and the same goes for his decision-making.

#97 Jérémy Roy D (2015): Sherbrooke's top defenseman logged a lot of ice time for this young team. Not shy to join or lead the rush, and is a good skater with impressive lateral agility. Poised with the puck and never seemed to panic with it. Makes quick decisions, and his passes are always crisp and accurate. Scored a nice goal getting open in the slot on the power play and re-directing a great pass by Daniel Audette behind the Armada goaltender Etienne Marcoux.

Blainville-Boisbriand

#8 Emil Aronsson C (2014): Didn't see many plays in the offensive zone out of him today. Good game away from the puck, as he took care of things in his own zone and always came back deep to help his defensemen out. Doesn't own a particularly strong shot, his skating is fine rather than a weakness and does not have a strong point (presence?) either.

#71 Nikita Jevpalovs C (2014) Jevpalovs got a hat trick in this game. His first goal came from a rebound in front of the net, the second came from a wrist shot from the point and the third was into an empty net. I love his shot and he likes to use it whenever he can. He is a good player on the power play and is being used on the point on the first power play unit. Love his work ethic as well, as he started the game with a strong forechecking shift where he showed some nice speed.

#77 Guillaume Beaudoin D (2014): The rookie defenseman was paired once again with Daniel Walcott tonight, and showed some good stuff in a couple of rushes but overall he was quiet most of the night. Made some good first passes when he was not pressured into them. Good skater who, when he decides to rush the puck, is rather effective at it.

#85 Daniel Walcott D (2014): Had a tough first period being matched versus Daniel Audette tonight. He got beaten on the opening goal of the game, as he was not able to contain the speedy forward from Sherbrooke. Was also stripped of the puck by Audette, which led to him taking a penalty. Was caught being overaggressive at times in the neutral zone which led to odd-man rushes, such as on the 4th goal by Sherbrooke. Showed once again his superb skating ability whether it's in rushing the puck in the offensive zone or with his lateral mobility on the blueline.

February 15, 2014 – Peterborough Petes at Barrie Colts (OHL)

PET #10 RC Cornel, Eric (2014) – Eric was most noted in this game for strong passing ability. Especially early on in the game Cornel was able to utilize his passing ability to create chances. He struggled handling the puck but was consistent moving the puck well to teammates.

PET #20 LW Ritchie, Nick (2014) - Ritchie did a good job opening himself up for shooting opportunities. He won a ton of battles along the wall and punished opponents regularly. He faced top prospect Aaron Ekblad and dominated him every single shift all game long. He displayed excellent puck moving ability on a few occasions tonight. Nick was willing to sacrifice the body to block shots for his team.

BAR #5 RD Ekblad, Aaron (2014) - Tonight's game started out strong for Ekblad. He had some power play time and displayed his outstanding shot. He gets so much power behind it, it's hard to see. He also has pretty effective accuracy on it. He however had a mental lapse on the power play when the opposing player got out of the box, he didn't play back to cover the potential pass and nearly turned into a breakaway chance against his team. He holds the offensive line well when there is pressure to clear. He began getting frustrated and started losing battles against Nick Ritchie on a regular basis tonight. At one point Matt McCartney gave Ekblad a face wash at which point Ekblad complained to the officials quite heatedly about the lack of a penalty call on this play. This held significance a few shifts later as Ekblad is called for a bit of a weak interference call at which point he verbally unloaded on the official turning a 2 minute penalty into a 4 minute penalty. He was bale to make up for this by selling a hit later on to draw a power play. Overall a frustrating game for Ekblad who showed strong offensive attributes but struggled both defensively, down low and also with his temper.

BAR #21 LW Lemieux, Brendan (2014) - Brendan showed his grit in this game jumping in early on to defend his teammate. He showed a desire to get into every post whistle scrum he could and got every shot he could on his opponent every chance he got. He was pretty effective getting under the skin of the opposition but playing on the edge caught up to him later on when he took a very undisciplined penalty in the offensive zone after the puck left the zone negating his team's power play. He showed his value up 2-1 in the final seconds of the game blocking a shot to preserve the lead.

BAR #26 LW Mangiapane, Andrew (2015) - Mangiapane had an excellent game. He was capable of forcing turnovers all night and showed a great non stop effort. At one point he kept the play going in the offensive zone which lead to Barrie's first goal of the game and an assist for Mangiapane. He consistently made intelligent decisions with the puck all game long and made good passes under pressure. He reads plays extremely well and shows excellent positioning without the puck. Despite his size he's willing to play physical and landed a few solid checks. He struggled in battles along the wall against bigger and stronger defenders. In the final minute Mangiapane was used with his team up 2-1 playing a key defensive role. He made a great play to strip the puck of the opposition and just missed an empty net goal.

BAR #29 G Blackwood, Mackenzie (2015) - Mackenzie had a great game tonight against Peterborough. He made multiple very strong glove saves. He displays good lower body movement for such a big goalie and was strong on the poke check. His overall reaction time is also good.

Scouts notes: A tight checking game between two teams battling each other for playoff positioning in the Eastern Conference. Barrie was able to jump out to a 2-0 lead with goals scored by Andreas Athanasiou (Detroit) and a good second effort by Kevin Labanc (2014). Peterborough was able to get one back. Michael Clarke (Colorado) would score late in the second to make it a one goal game but an excellent defensive stand by the Colts in the final minute helped them escape with a very valuable 2-1 victory.

Feb. 16, 2014 – Tri-City Storm vs. Chicago Steel (USHL)

TC #44 Chris Wilkie LW (2014) - Displayed good offensive instincts and a nose for the net. Created a lot of scoring chances for himself and teammates in the offensive zone. He has good hands and that was evident with a few crafty passes in tight below the face-off dots in the offensive and defensive zones, one being a beautiful backhand saucer pass springing a teammate in alone for a quality scoring chance. Also made a really nice wrap around attempt for what almost resulted in a goal. Read the goaltender overcommitting and tried to beat him to the other side. His skating left a little bit to be desired. Ok speed, kind of an upright skater, not overly great foot speed. Has the intelligence and awareness to make up for it and still creates a lot of offensive opportunities.

TC #11 Austin Poganski RW (2014) - Overall a rather mediocre game. Austin's a strong straight-line skater. He generates a lot of power in his stride and has good speed which he utilizes well on the forecheck and in finishing checks. That straight line speed along with his good size equals a lot of heavy hits and he plays a good physical game. Did not do a whole lot to be noticeable in this game other than that. Had a long stretch in the 2nd period where he did not see the ice but remained on the bench. I never noticed any medical attention received. Got back to a regular shift in the 3rd period. He seemed to be slower laterally and in tight spaces where he wasn't skating straight in open ice. Didn't create much with the puck in one-on-one situations. Always worked hard and I didn't see a lack of effort, just not a lot of production and looked very average.

TC #6 Kevin Kerr LD (2014) – Strong game. Probably TC's best player. Really like his patience with the puck at all areas of the ice. Excellent at the point on the power play. Had a number of nice keep-ins, and is very calm and cool with the puck at the offensive blue line. Made nice moves to evade defenders and open passing and shooting lanes at the point. Very quick feet and quick hands. Solid defensively, always had good gaps. Did get beat to the outside one time, giving up a quality scoring chance but was never beat anywhere on the ice the rest of the game. Very aggressive on the puck, steps up on offending players in the offensive zone well. Strong, intelligent game. Steady as they come.

TC #41 Hayden Lavigne G (2014) – Pulled after the third goal given up in the 1st period. Didn't really have much of a chance on goal number one; made a nice save and the rebound went right to an undefended Steel player for a goal. The second goal was a softie. Very stoppable low stick-side wrist shot from the point, caught a piece with the tip of his pad but managed to get past him for a goal. Third goal he had no chance at; cross-ice pass on the power play for a one-timer. Bang-bang play. Team wasn't doing very well in front of him but just didn't look settled or confident from the outset.

CHI #20 Artem Artemov LW (2015) – Artemov continues to impress in my viewings this season. He's one of those players that just does everything well. He has great patience with the puck and that especially shows when he's on the power play. On one play he made a really nice move to draw the defending forward over toward him and the boards and then placed a perfect pass through the forward's legs to his defenseman the point, who proceeded to be able to walk in a few steps and get a high quality shot on net. On another occasion he wound up on the point for the power play, made a great keep-in and then made a beautiful flip-pass to himself over a defender's stick to open up space down on the half-board to start a new setup. As always, he was as good defensively as he was offensively. Very responsible, always backchecked hard, high compete level at both ends of the ice. Played in all situations. Very intelligent, great hockey sense. Always seems to be a highlight player in every viewing.

CHI #23 Robby Jackson LW (2015) – Jackson was his usual self; high motor, aggressive, feet constantly moving. Always a high intensity player with a maximum effort and compete level. Was strong along the boards, wins battles way more than he loses them. Created some good opportunities offensively with his speed and quick feet, two of his strong suits. His size is still somewhat of a concern but his speed and hockey sense can go a long ways toward balancing that out. He's also very strong and solid on his feet and like many games, he wasn't knocked around and taken off the puck very easily and can be physical in his own right. Always count on a consistent effort and game from him.

CHI #17 Fredrik Olofsson RW (2014) – Olofsson continues to be a very intriguing prospect for me. I have had increased viewings of him since his trade to Chicago and while he has not lit up the score sheet I've been very impressed with his play. He does so many things well and everything he does looks to come with such ease and is so smooth. He's always very cool and collected and never seems rattled, stressed, or hurried in anything he does. He is as good as anyone I've seen at using his body to protect the puck, be it while he has possession, in anticipation of receiving it, or battling for it when it's loose. As always, he was very strong on the puck along the boards and was very difficult to remove from the puck. He scored a power play goal in this game where he found a soft area of the ice and fired a nice cross-ice pass from Ernsting past Lavigne. The play displayed his excellent hockey sense and awareness. He's a very cerebral player and is great at creating plays and space for not only himself but his teammates and is always in the right place. He was used on the point for the power play as is often the case, and he's very effective there. He's also strong defensively in the event that the play comes the other way on the power play and even during even strength play he's always in the right position and plays a very good two-way game. He saw quite a bit of penalty kill time, as well. Just a very slick, smooth, professional-looking player in everything he does. Look forward to seeing more of him.

CHI #31 Chris Nell G (2012) – Yet another strong game from Chris. He has been a big reason behind the Steel's resurgence after an 0-10 start to the season. He played his angles well and was very aggressive, coming out past the crease to challenge shooters often. Looked very confident and cool. Got run into hard a couple of times by Storm players and it didn't rattle his game at all. He had excellent rebound control and was especially strong when down on the ice for scrambles in front of his net. He's decent athletically as far as lateral movement when down and getting up from being down, but not great. Had a strong glove. Tri-City had a high number of high quality chances, not a lot of cheapies in the shot totals. Got beat at the five-hole on a breakaway for the first goal.

CHI #15 Mason Bergh C (2013) – Speedy forward had an excellent game and was one of the more noticeable players on the ice. Bergh was coming off a hot stretch in which he had five points his previous two games over the weekend. He added a goal to his weekend tally in this one. Bergh was very involved, be it blocking shots, creating scoring chances, checking; was all over the ice. Has exceptional speed and good hands to match. Was creating all sorts of havoc in the offensive zone. Does a very good job of carrying the puck through the neutral zone and gaining offensive zone entry. Saw the ice very well and has very good awareness all-around. Excellent game and will be someone to watch going forward the rest of the season.

FINAL SCORE: 4-2 Chicago

SCOUTS NOTES:

The Steel's climb up the standings after an 0-10 start has been very interesting to watch and to call it unexpected would be an understatement. They're better than an 0-10 team but their climb out of that hole has been impressive. As of the conclusion of this game, they are one point out of the playoffs, with them continuing to play very good hockey. It's made for much better viewings all around for both them and their opponent that given game. For Tri-City, defenseman Tory Dello (2015) and forward Nolan Aibel (2015)

February 18th, 2014 Dubuque Fighting Saints vs Lincoln Stars

DBQ #9 Malone, Seamus C (2014) – Scored a tap in goal at the end of the second period to tie the game. Good game overall for Malone. Very talented offensive player. Has a great sense of where his teammates are on the ice and how to find them. Seemed to shy away from contact and stay away from the dirty areas against the physical Lincoln Stars.

DBQ #24 Kuhlman, Karson RW/C (2014) – Showcased his speed multiple times in this game. Certainly not afraid to battle in the corners as a 5'10" forward. Gets to the dirty areas and works hard. High compete level. Picked up a secondary assist on Seamus Malone's second period goal. Seems to lack elite vision.

DBQ #28 Eiserman, Shane LW (2014) – Uses his size well. Projects very well as a two-way forward at the next level. This was not his best showing. Dubuque fell apart in the third period and

Eiserman looked lost late in the game. Showcased his skating ability – one of the best skaters in the league. Developing his offensive game to compliment his physical game would only serve to benefit him in the future.

LIN #4 Daniel Willett LD (2014) – Showed off his puck moving abilities in the third period of the 6-3 victory. Started the breakout a couple of times with a nice stretch pass as the Fighting Saints had a complete defensive breakdown late in the game. Willett has a long, uphill battle to make it to the next level. His size limits him in his own end and he cannot be relied upon to clear out the crease. He is a very one-dimensional player, might be better suited as a forward at the next level.

LIN #13 Keegan Ward RW (2015) – The youngest player on the roster only got a couple of shifts until late in the game when the Stars had a 2-0 lead. Has a fiery temper, cares a lot about the game whether he's in the stands, on the bench, or on the ice. Aggressiveness leads to mistakes often. As he is coached up at the USHL level I expect him to blossom into a nice energy player for the Stars. Still has a lot of work to do.

Scouts notes: The first two periods were full of great hockey as Dubuque and Lincoln traded goals back and forth. Dubuque went into the second period with a 3-2 lead. In the third period Lincoln scored four straight goals to win the game 6-3. Stars goalie Michael Bitzer played absolutely great, turning away 34 of 37 shots he faced.

Feb. 21, 2014 – Omaha Lancers vs. Dubuque Fighting Saints (USHL)

OMA #18 Anthony Angello RC (2014) – Angello had no shortage of quality chances, he just couldn't capitalize and finish. He was stopped on a breakaway and was stopped a couple of times in tight on the power play. He had a smart game, he finds the open ice really well and uses his speed to exploit holes in coverage, which is how he got his breakaway. Excellent speed, quick feet, and crafty hands. Unfortunately no payoff tonight. Got sucked into taking a bad penalty retaliating on Keegan Ford.

OMA #1 Hayden Hawkey G (2013) – Excellent game in a 22 save shutout. Not a high volume of shots but many were quality chances for Dubuque's high-powered offense. Plays with great poise, never seems rattled. Played a really strong game down low on the ice, doesn't give up his net at all. Good positioning and angles. Came up big when he needed to and given Reich's strong game in the other net only allowing one goal, Omaha needed it.

DBQ #7 Keegan Ford LD (2014) – Solid all around game for Keegan. Played chippy and physical as usual. Took a bad penalty against Angello but was able to goad him into retaliating so it evened up. Had good speed and pace to his game, is a quick and shifty skater. He jumped into the rush a few times, seems to be growing more confident offensively and handling the puck. Was aggressive on puck carriers and in puck and board battles. Got off a couple nice wrist shots. Had a few shifts on the PK. He's really good at getting his shots through to the net. Knows well went to shoot or when to dish it off down low and avoid a shot block. Like his game a lot.

DBQ #8 Blake Hillman LD (2014) – More of the same for Hillman, yet another strong game. His game is very predictable, and that is meant as a compliment. You always get the same effort out of him night in and night out, and even on nights where he maybe just doesn't have "it", you still get a maximum effort and a mistake-free game. He was skating well tonight and handling the puck exceptionally well. He's real smooth. Had a strong game on the point keeping the puck in and play alive during offensive possessions. He has a lot of poise to his game at all times, just always cool and collected. Played his position well, gave up no space to puck carriers and finished his checks. Excellent two-way game.

DBQ #9 Seamus Malone LC (2014) – Seamus didn't have his best game but it wasn't awful. Effort was good and he was skating well, just seemed to be fighting the puck a bit. He was missing passes and his pass receipts weren't always overly smooth. Puck left his stick a couple of times uncontested. He had a bad turnover the lead to a goal against. Uncharacteristic unforced puck handling errors by Malone. Still had a solid overall effort. Took hits to make plays, was finishing checks and engaging physically. He's a small body but he's fearless. Played scrappy and agitates the opposition. He did manage one really nice offensive play stick handling through a defenseman for a quality chance. Defensively, caused a couple turnovers, one on the backcheck where he had a textbook pick-pocket steal of the puck and started a rush back the other way.

DBQ #24 Karson Kuhlman RW (2014) – High-energy, high-motor game from Karson. Saved an icing outskating the trailing defenseman that lead to a good offensive possession. Gained the offensive zone well on entries with control of the puck. Protected the puck well and won battles stealing the puck from opposing players. Aggressive on the puck and fights hard for it. Good, active stick. Skates well and has some good offensive skill and upside to his game.

DBQ #28 Shane Eiserman LW (2014) – I don't know what the official hit stats were but based on watching the game, no one was throwing their body around more than Eiserman. Numerous heavy hits, very physical game. If you touch the puck and he can legally do so, he's putting a body on you hard. Highlight reel hit on Angello. Takes hits to make plays, blocks shots. Made good decisions with the puck in all situations, smart player. Good hockey sense. Took the puck hard to the net a few times, likes to bull his way into traffic but also has the hands to finesse his way around traffic. Sees the ice well and looks really comfortable handling the puck.

DBQ #1 Kevin Reich G (2014) – Tough night when you only give up one goal on 27 shots and still come out with a loss. Reich had a really strong game, but Hawkey outdueled him. He faced a lot of high quality chances and stopped almost all of them but it wasn't enough. He's really quick and athletic, gets up and down quick and smooth. Strong down low when protecting the bottom half of the net, doesn't drop down too soon. Maintains his positioning in net. He deserved better in this one.

FINAL: 1-0 Omaha

SCOUTS NOTES:

This game got off to a sluggish start but picked up quickly. Dubuque with the better of the chances as the 1st Period wore on but it evened out after that. The game took on a nasty tone as it went along. Very chippy, a lot of altercations and shots after the play was stopped and away from the puck. A true goaltenders duel and Hawkey came out on top. First time Dubuque had been shut out at home since 2012.

Feb. 22, 2014 – Muskegon Lumberjacks vs. Chicago Steel (USHL)

MUS #4 Joe Cecconi RD (2015) – Notched an assist midway through the 3rd Period and registered three shots on goal. Had a solid game, strong defensively. Continue to be impressed with his poise and calm. Never gets rattled, plays like seasoned vet. Had a couple of nice hits and had a strong game overall.

MUS #6 Christian Wolanin LD (2013) – Decent game for Wolanin but not great. Had a couple of lapses in the defensive zone, uncharacteristic of him. Skated well and moved the puck well, created some decent offensive chances. Three shots on goals. Fought Tischke in a decent tilt. Lapses aside, like his skating and ability to move the puck up ice. Really comfortable and smooth with the puck. Good feet and overall speed.

MUS #11 Matt Iacopelli RW (2011) – Scored the then tying goal for Muskegon on a nice shot. Had a game-high nine shots on goal. Par for the course for Matt, he loves to shoot the puck and with the shot he has, why not? It's among the best in the USHL. Lightning-quick on the release and tons of velocity. Really accurate. Had a decent game aside from the offense. OK on defense, decent compete level overall but could be better.

MUS #29 Eric Schierhorn G (2014) – Not Schierhorn's greatest game but he didn't have much help in front of him. Let in a couple he'd have liked to have back. Rebounds were an issue which is not usually the case for him. He did make some big saves, too, though. Chicago had a lot of wide open looks and good chances in tight. Overall a game to just move on from and on to the next one.

CHI #17 Fredrik Olofsson RW (2014) – His nice two-goal night was overshadowed a bit by Jackson's monster game. Fed the puck to Ernsting for an odd-man break leading to Jackson's third goal. Strong game on the puck, as always. Very creative, opened up a lot of space, had some excellent passes. Great overall awareness and hockey sense. Very good defensive game. First goal was Chicago's third goal in as many minutes at that time and basically blew the game wide open.

CHI #20 Artem Artemov LW (2015) – Strong two-way game. Created the two-on-one that lead to Jackson's second goal. Excellent vision and awareness. Very good hockey sense and had a physical game. Really like how hard he works on both sides of the puck. Really smart player.

CHI #23 Robby Jackson LW (2015) – Jackson had quite the game, getting a hat-trick and adding two assists. All three goals came on odd-man breaks. The first he received a pass on a two-on-one and made a nice deke to the backhand for his first goal. The second came on another two-on-one which Artemov started with a nice stretch pass. Jackson was going hard to the net and one-timed a cross-ice pass from Bergh. His third goal displayed his excellent patience with the puck, as he took a pass on a two-on-one and instead of shooting right away, he held on to the puck for a second and waited for Scheirhorn to commit and then went backhand-forehand and put it past him. Was an excellent display of patience, vision, and stick handling. Jackson never stops moving and these goals were a result of that hard work and willingness to go to the net hard.

CHI #28 Alec Vanko RD (2012) – Mistake-free defensively. Made good decisions with the puck, good outlet passes. Skated the puck out of trouble well and had some good neutral zone carries. Moves really well, good agility. Physical. Made a nice play to Olofsson for one of his goals. Like his size, speed, skill combo, and plays a smart defensive game.

FINAL: 7-3 Chicago

SCOUTS NOTES:

Jackson, Olofsson and Ernsting were on fire together tonight. Tons of chemistry and a lot of really good passing and offensive creativity. Muskegon mounted a brief comeback until three straight Chicago goals blew the doors of the game open and they never looked back. Nell outplayed Schierhorn, stopping 41 of 44 shots.

Feb. 22, 2014 – USNTDP U18 vs. Indiana Ice (USHL)

US #2 Jack Dougherty RD (2014) – Solid game, handled the puck well. Increased poise and confidence in his puck handling ability. Made good decisions and played a smart game. Excelled under pressure. Got some good looks on the power play.

US #6 Ryan Collins RD (2014) – Collins had a strong defensive game. Maintained good gaps and stepped up on puck carriers well. Good angles. Continue to be impressed with his smooth-skating nature for such a big, lanky body. Solid agility and good foot speed. Doesn't look awkward or gangly at all like some kids do who are so tall at such a young age. Has good control of his body and plays an intelligent, calm game.

US #7 Anders Bjork LW (2014) – Bjork got rewarded for his hard work and willingness to pay the price in front of the net by getting a nice deflection goal on the power play off of Jack Glover's stick. Bjork isn't afraid of the dirty areas and is willing to work hard and pay the price for goals such as that. Carried the puck well tonight, displaying his high end speed and agility. Couple good rushes through the neutral zone. Strong on the forecheck, attacks the puck. He plays such a smart, fluid game, no mistakes.

US #8 Jack Glover RD (2014) – Assisted on Bjork's power play goal with a nice, low wrist shot on net. Showed his offensive awareness, skating and puck skills on the play. He got the puck along the boards and smoothly pulled it toward the middle of the blue line and opened up the entire shooting lane, snapped off a quick wrister that made it through traffic and on net. Good offensive instincts and decision making. Still prone to bad turnovers in his own end and in the neutral zone. The decision making process changes once he crosses that offensive blue line and back into the neutral zone. Needs to increase his awareness and get more confident handling the puck in those zones.

US #11 Jack Eichel RC (2015) – Had a nice set up on Milano's goal. Drove the puck wide on defensemen a couple of times and beat them for quality scoring chances. It's fun to watch him shift into the top gear when he needs to in those situations. It's so smooth and understated when he does it but you can see his speed increase. You can't teach that kind of skating ability. Used that speed and burst ability on the defensive side of the puck causing turnovers and disrupted passing lanes on the forecheck. One such turnover lead to a penalty drawn on the player he took the puck from. Stick handles with such ease, puck on a string. Great length and strong stride, he is able to beat you in so many ways and with what looks like such little effort, but there's never a lack of effort or compete in his game. Notched an empty-netter late for good measure.

US #16 Johnathan MacLeod RD (2014) – Played a solid, no nonsense, stay at home defensive game, though he did notch a secondary helper on the Eichel empty-netter on, naturally, a good outlet pass from his zone. Solid with the puck, protects it well and never takes any unnecessary chances. Good passes and good outlets. Made a couple really nice stretch passes springing forwards for breaks. Took a checking from behind penalty that was bad but the penalty was successfully killed.

US #17 Alex Tuch RW (2014) – Had a nice goal on a wrap-around where he beat the defenseman behind the net, muscled his way to the front of the net and put the puck five-hole. Total power move, and the type of goal that garners Tuch the attention he gets. He is a rare combination of brute force with finesse capabilities. Battled hard for the puck in all zones and offered good support for line mates. Sets up a lot of scoring opportunities taking the body and battling for loose pucks and corner battles.

US #19 Dylan Larkin LC (2014) – Got the secondary assist on the Bjork goal, feeding a nice pass to an open Glover. Normally very aware and sure handed with the puck, he left a bad, errant drop pass in the defensive zone the Indiana capitalized on for their lone goal. Uncharacteristic mistake for Larkin. Still had a good game otherwise. Always skating hard, full effort, driving the net hard. Showed off his speed driving the puck wide entering the offensive zone and beating defensemen. He plays such a well-rounded game, rarely makes mistakes. He can do it all.

US #27 Sonny Milano LW (2014) – Notching a goal and two assists, Milano had quite a good for himself. He dished the puck off to Tuch on his goal and head-manned a feed to Eichel on his empty netter. Had a highlight-reel, top shelf-clanking one-timer on a nice dish from Eichel early in the 2nd Period. He put the puck about the only place it had room to go. Truly elite shooting ability and offensive skill in general.

US #5 Brandon Fortunato LD (2014) – Fortunato's play continues to impress. He is such a cerebral player. Sees the ice so well and is flawless in his decision making. Tonight was no different. He reads the play as well as anyone defenseman in this league, excellent anticipation and with his explosive quickness he jumps passing lanes and causes turnovers at will. Super shifty and quick, he is an escape artist with the puck. So many times he is under pressure and you think he's going to get stopped, yet his slips out of it somehow and finds open ice and takes off. Skilled passer and just rock solid in every facet of the game. It's easy to point to his size immediately but he plays above it and quite frankly, rarely has it caused him an issue at this level.

US #29 Edwin Minney G (2014) – Had a strong game playing the puck. He handles the puck exceptionally well and makes life on his defensemen much easier as a result of it. He also made a couple of nice outlet passes to forwards up ice, having the heads up awareness to see Indiana making line changes and trying to get a jump on the offensive attack. Gave up one only goal on 35 shots, many of which were in tight and of high quality. His play covered up for a lot of sloppy play by his own team and the ice being titled quite a bit in Indiana's favor. Great athleticism and strength, and he was sound in his positioning and angles.

IND #4 Ryan Mantha RD (2014) – Mantha wasn't overly noticeable other than looking sluggish and slow. Wasn't skating well and didn't look very mobile. He didn't make any glaring mistakes or play a bad game, really, other than getting outskating to some pucks and beat one-on-one a couple of times, but didn't do much positive, either. He was kind of just there, very pedestrian and slow looking.

IND #8 Joshua Jacobs RD (2014) – Jacobs had a really strong game on both sides of the puck. He always bring a mean, physical element to his game and tonight was no different. Had a couple of heavy hits. Had a strong game in his own zone, made good first passes and outlet plays, mistake-free and smart. Played a 2-on-1 with Milano and Eichel perfectly, taking a perfect angle that suffocated the puck carrier's options but also prevented any kind of passing lane to the open man. Handled the puck really well. He's really comfortable and poised with the puck, handles it through traffic in the defensive zone and neutral zone well. Jumped up into the rush a few times. He really likes to be involved offensively. Got off a couple of nasty slap shots. His shot his heavy and he gets it off quickly. Really solid all around game for Jacobs.

FINAL: 4-1 USNTDP

SCOUTS NOTES:

Deceiving final score, as Indiana was actually the better team and carried a lot of the play. The US had a really sloppy game overall. They took a lot of penalties, including four straight in the 2nd Period which included a long two-man advantage for Indiana that was successfully killed. A combination of a strong performance by Minney and the US capitalizing on their high quality chances and a power play tally allowed US to "escape" this one with a 4-1 victory.

Kootenay Ice vs Spokane Chiefs February 22 2014 WHL (Regular Season)

KTN #14 W Deschenean Jaedon (2014) Jaedon finds the scoring areas and shows a good touch in the paint. He showed his creativity and hockey sense tonight with a few dazzling passes. Not overly big but his size allows him to slip checks which makes him hard to hit. He compliments Reinhart very well.

KTN #23 C Reinhart Sam (2014) 1 Assist tonight. Sam shows a high level of Hockey IQ and vision, he was setting up his line mates most of the game. Sam was thinking the game a few steps a head of his teammates which tend to make his game slow down to their level. Sam is a very dynamic offensive player.

KTN #24 D Valiev Rinat (2014) 1 Assist tonight. Good defender who has a decent 1on1 game. Likes to compete and battle and always seems to come away with the puck. Makes a good first outlet pass thats crisp and hard.

KTN #12 C Philp Luke (2014) 1 Assist tonight. Had a good two way game. I like his creativity and willingness to try things to set up scoring chances. Likes to battle and showed great work ethic away from the puck. Has the ability to slip in the scoring areas unnoticed.

SPO # 32 D Bobyk Colton (2014) Played a good defensive game. Made a couple good outlet passes and was jumping into the rush.

SPO #17 W Holmberg Mitch (Free Agent) 3goals tonight. This is way he leads the WHL, Mitch will reach 60 goals this season. A pure goal scorer. The puck just seems to find his stick in all situation.

Portland WinterHawks vs Everett Silvertips February 23, 2014 (WHL)

EVT #10 C Sandhu Tyler (2014) Did not play

EVT #89 C Nikolishin Ivan (2014) Started out a little sluggish but his play improved over the course of the game. Started off the third showing his hands with a dirty dangle and then split the Portland D just inside the blue and finish with a nice gino for Everetts lone goal of the game. Becoming more impressed with his level of hockey IQ. Needs to add muscle to his frame.

EVT #12 W Leedhal Dawson (2014) Had a couple door step scoring chances but couldnt finish. Played aggressive on the forecheck which looked to frustrate Portlands top d-pairing. Had a solid hit on 1st rounder Dumba and knocked him off his wheels. Dawson was seeing lots of ice time in all situations.

EVT #38 D Davis Kevin (2015) I like this kid, plays a solid defensive game, does not make many mistakes. Moves the puck well, if he has no pass option he will skate out of the zone. Plays physical at times and does not seem to get hit all that much, put himself in good position to make the play.

PORT #9 C De Leo Chase (2014) Mighty mouse showed some good offensive flash, every shift he is making something happen. I liked his compete level in the faceoff circle, always looking to win the draw.

PORT #13 W Iverson Keegan (2014) Was using his big frame tonight with good puck protection and was showing good compete level winning the puck battles. Would still like to see him muscle his way into the scoring areas more often.

PORT #22 W Schoenborn Alex (2014) Played a strong game on the wing using his size to create space and chances. I liked his defensive game tonight very responsible and played a 200ft game.

PORT #23 C Turgeon Dominic (2014) Was 75% on the draw tonight giving his team puck possession. I like how he competes in the circles, always looks determined to win the draw. Always seems to play a two way game and do the little things that wins games. Plays with heart.

Prince Albert Raiders vs Everett Silvertips WHL February 26, 2014 (Regular Season)

EVT #10 W Sandhu Tyler (2014) Did not play

EVT #89 C Nikolishin Ivan (2014) Was a spark plug for 3 periods. Tried to force the pass early in the first and caused a couple turn overs but settled down later on. In the second working the top of the circle he delivered a hard laser pass crossed ice through traffic to set up a PP goal. He added another assist later in the game. Was shifty and hard to hit tonight. Was involved in the play every shift.

EVT #12 W Leedhal Dawson (2014) Lots of playing time in all situations tonight. Was involved in the PP and had a couple scoring chances in the paint. Was aggressive on the forecheck and brought energy. Kids competes every game.

PA #19 W Gardiner Reid (2014) Was involved every shift. Good compete level battling for pucks along the boards. Liked his ability to slip checks and create offense. Like to drive the net and look for rebounds. Seems to make the right play in most game situations. Skating needs to improve.

PA #29 C Draisaitl Leon (2014) Seemed very sluggish throughout the 1st period. His game picked up in the second and showed some flashes of offense and possesses a nice set of hands. Strong kid who is hard to knock off the puck. Seems to win any 1 on 1 puck battle with his size and strength with a high compete level. Not overly fast skater, but when the train gains speed look out. Was little lazy on the back check coming into his defensive zone. Needs to add some quickness and speed to his game.

Tri City Americans vs Everett Silvertips February 28 2014 (WHL)

EVT #10 C Sandhu Tyler (2014) Did not play

EVT #89 C Nikolishin Ivan (2014) Played an effective 200ft game. Was physical in the corners and strong winning the 1 on 1 battles. Slipped a couple check and set up two good scoring chances. Was committed on the back end and played a solid defensive game.

EVT #12 W Leedahl Dawson (2014). Nothing more than crash and bang, hitting everything that moves. His game never really changes, his play is mostly consistent every night. You get what you see, a hard working player who brings energy. Seeing more PP and PK time and was very effective on the PK.

TRI #22 W Vickerman Taylor (2014.) Did not play

TRI #23 C Gutierrez Justin (2014) Tall lanky center who is a decent skater. Not very aggressive or physical. Had a couple decent shifts with good scoring chances but couldn't finish. Needs to use his size to drive the net and fight for space in the scoring areas. Needs to get aggressive and compete on the 1 on 1 puck battles.

TRI #2 D Thrower Josh (2014). Physical defenders who loves to hit and punish. Was patient with the puck, if he did not have a passing outlet coming out of the zone he would rush the puck. Made smart pinches in the offensive zone and played tough in the paint. He boxes out the forward very well.

Kamloops Blazers vs Calgary Hitmen WHL Regular Season, February 28, 2014

Cal #18, Virtanen, Jake (2014) – Virtanen had a game to forget. While he had a few opportunities to score using his tremendous speed to drive to the outside, Virtanen was unable to generate solid chances due to his inability to see the ice. Virtanen chose to shoot often from the outside instead of finding teammate in better shooting position. When he did shoot, he had an apparent allergy against shooting for rebounds and instead tried to score glove-hand over and over on Blazers netminder Bolton Pouliot. In transition, Virtanen had some nice jump and was dangerous through the neutral zone in creating odd-man rushes. The downside to that Virtanen tried to do too much himself and often tried stickhandling through 3 or 4 players often getting past the first couple players before being stymied and trapping his linemates deep. To cap off to poor showing, Virtanen actually batted a puck into his own net in an unforced error where he attempted to clear a puck from out of the air while in his own crease. Virtanen has strung together numerous games in similar fashion that create questions regarding how he projects at the pro level. He has a knack for goal-scoring at this level and is as talented as any player in the draft, but his offensive ceiling will be completely related to his ability (or inability) to increase his poor vision with the puck.

Cal #21, Draude, Terrell (2015) – Draude has been making the most out of his ice time and earned some minutes on the 3rd line tonight. His skating is starting to improve and he is hard to move due to the 16 year-old's already large frame. Draude effectively uses his size. His first step still requires work, but progress is being made.

Cal #27, Thomas, Ben (2014) – Real steady defensive play on the night. While he projects as a defense-first player that can handle the puck, Thomas showed a bit of offensive skill and instinct by having some good timing on when to pinch. At one point, he made a very accurate pass through traffic to set up Virtanen nicely on a give and go play.

Cal #32, Sanheim, Travis (2014) – While Sanheim doesn't have the prettiest stride, he does get where he's going in a hurry. He has long strides and is able to cover a lot of distance quickly. This was useful in allowing him to jump into the play offensively and still being back to defend while in transition. Sanheim made numerous seemingly small plays that led to the Hitmen maintaining possession of the puck and generating scoring chances. These pinches and successful loose puck battles were effective and timely as they often prevented the Blazers from getting a line change after spending time stuck in their own end. Sanheim has intriguing upside with a blooming offensive game, but he is still raw and this is particularly noticeable at times with his positioning.

Kam #15, Shirley, Collin (2014) – Shirley hasn't seemed to have found his game offensively since being traded to the Blazers earlier this season. Even when he's not scoring, Shirley has some value as a big bodied centerman with size and a willingness to hit everything in sight. His hands were just average on the night. He consistently gave a full effort. With his compete level and upside, Shirley could be worth a look late in the upcoming draft.

Kam #24, Rehill, Ryan (2014) – Wore an 'A' for the young Blazers squad. Rehill already possesses NHL size, but his mobility and skill level are concerns. His pivots and general skating abilities are lacking. Rehill played a very simple game, but the question is whether he can play a more advanced game and just opted to play overly simplistic, or whether he's limited by a low skill level. He often was able to clear the zone, but he seemed to have more success in shooting it off the boards or glass than to a teammate to have his team retain possession of the puck.

Kam #27, Connolly, Josh (2014) – Connolly was passed over in last year's NHL draft, but has broked out in a big way this year. A small defender, Connolly has very good puck-moving skills. He defended against the rush well, but was not strong enough to win battles against the boards. His pivots were good and he has the abilities to run the powerplay. NHL teams will like offensive upside, but he is a work in progress. The skill is readily apparent, but the question is whether he can consistently play at a high level. His effort level seemed to vary shift-to-shift and game to game.

Kam #29, Harlacher, Edson (2014) – The big Swiss defenseman really looked sluggish on the night. He has strength, but he was late getting to loose pucks and seemed uncomfortable in certain defensive situations. Turned over the puck under pressure.

Game Notes: Over 14,000 fans took in a surprisingly close game through two periods in a matchup pitting one of the league's top teams in Calgary versus the Western Conference basement-dwelling Kamloops Blazers. Despite Calgary heavily outchancing the lowly Blazers, the game was 1-1 until late in the 2nd period. Calgary finally opened things up in the 3rd and walked away with a 5-1 win.

Feb. 28, 2014 – Omaha Lancers vs. Green Bay Gamblers (USHL)

OMA #1 Hayden Hawkey G (2013) – Excellent performance by Hawkey, stopping 38 of 39 shots on the night. The shots were not only significant in quantity but also quality. Hawkey had three breakaway saves in this game, and made a number of other spectacular saves on great chances for Green Bay. The one goal he did give up was while Omaha was on the penalty kill and came on a rebound that he had no chance at saving. Otherwise stellar performance. His blocker and glove are both exceptionally quick, as is his lateral movement. He made a post-to-post save and a cross-ice one-timer play that was simply phenomenal. I thought it was going to be a sure goal. Excellent rebound control.

OMA #18 Anthony Angello RC (2014) – Angello did some nice things and some not so nice things. He had a strong defensive game, which included a monster open ice hit. He has a knack for those, he lines guys up well in open ice. He has great length and caused a lot of turnovers with his speed, reach, and active stick. He was skating well and handled the puck skillfully as usual, but only did so on his defensive side of the red line. Didn't generate much offensively at all and was held without a single shot on goal. He also caused a bad turnover near the offensive blue line trying to skate into the zone 1-on-3, coughed the puck up, and a breakaway went the other way in which Hawkey stopped and bailed him out. Inconsistent effort overall.

OMA #21 Ryan Tait RC (2014) – High speed; always the first thing to comes to mind when watching Tait. Top speed is excellent and he gets there quickly, quick feet. His hands much his feet, and he loses no speed when handling the puck. Managed three shots on goal and was creating some chances in the offensive zone but as a team Omaha was rather flat offensively. Always a top notch effort and compete level out of Tait, and even on a night where not much was happening offensively he was still flying around and doing his job on the other side of the puck and gave maximum effort.

GB #9 Nick Schmaltz RW/C (2014) – Took shifts at both center and wing tonight. Despite being held off the score sheet had a really good night with the puck. Excellent movement and set ups on the power play. Displayed his patented poise and patience with the puck all night. The puck is on a string when in his possession. He is so hard to take the puck away from, between his world class hands, his speeds, and shiftiness and ability to protect the puck with his body while spinning and changing directions. He keeps defenders on their heels and guessing. He created a couple of breakaways with really nice passes, displaying his second-to-none vision and awareness. He knows where everybody on the ice is at all times, and that combined with his patience with the puck are a lethal combination offensively. He also uses his quickness to cause turnovers, which he did a few times tonight. Effort level is a question mark with Schmaltz sometimes but his effort was excellent tonight.

GB #10 Connor Hurley LW (2013 BUF 38th Overall) – Manning the point on the power play, Hurley is a slick skating offensive wizard with the puck. So crafty and quick with the puck, he is ideal on the point running a power play. He has a top notch slap and wrist shot, and with his mobility and hands he does a great job and moving around to open up lanes while on the point. Both on the power play and 5 on 5 he is really sneaky, and is adept at finding the soft areas of the ice for open looks at the net. Excellent poise and is really strong with maintaining possession and control of the puck on zone entries. Strong defensive effort tonight, as well. Backchecked hard, covers his guy in the defensive zone. Makes smart plays with the puck in his own zone. Fun player to watch.

FINAL: 4-1 Omaha

SCOUTS NOTES:

Very much a back and forth affair as far as who carried the play when. It was mostly all Omaha in the 1st Period, then Green Bay evening things out the rest of the game. Strong power plays on both sides. Hawkey had a huge game for Omaha and was a major reason for the final score. Green Bay was buzzing with chances most of the night and had a ton of high quality chances, including the already mentioned three breakaways, all stopped by Hawkey. Fairly chippy game. A lot of penalties.

Chicoutimi Sagueneens vs Blainville-Boisbriand Armada (QMJHL) March 2nd 2014

Chicoutimi

#26 Jeremy Bouchard LW (2015): Some real good feet, always in movement and is first on puck often. Strong work on the PK for a 16 year old rookie. Lacks strength at the moment to be more effective in battles along the wall.

#28 Nikita Lyamkin D (2014): Tall, lanky defenseman with some good feet and mobility. Struggled defensively today, as he played the puck instead of the man in one-on-one confrontations and was burned on a couple of occasions. Turned the puck over while carrying it from his zone, or forgot to cover a player behind him which led to the Armada's 1st goal. Played on the Saguenéens' 2nd power play unit. With his size, I would like to see him play with more grit in his zone, as he's too easy to play against.

#30 Julio Billia G (2014): Love his quickness in his crease; he has terrific feet and covers the lower part of the net well. Good lateral movement, but doesn't get much help in front of him from his defensemen. Can't blame him for any of the goals tonight. His lack of size hurts him and he needs to stay on his feet longer because of it.

#55 Nicolas Roy C/Rw (2015): Strong positional game with and without the puck. Already plays a big role for the Sags on the PK. Showed good vision, but couldn't get much going offensively for his team. His skating is still rough, but he showed good puck protection, using his big frame well.

#58 Frederic Allard D (2016): Moved the puck well, tried a stretch pass at the beginning of the 2nd period that was tipped by an Armada player, but the puck found its target anyway which led to the Saguenéens' lone goal of the game. Makes quick decisions with the puck and has good footwork. Needs more strength, because it's tough for him to compete defensively against bigger, stronger forwards.

Blainville-Boisbriand Armada

#25 Joseph Strong LW (2014): Played on the 4th line for the Armada, and was used as an enforcer-type player. He did not receive very much ice time and looked slow compared to his teammates, as his team is full of quick forwards. Threw some good hits in the game.

#71 Nikita Jevpalovs C (2014): Had a real good scoring chance early in the first period, taking a shot from the slot, but after that, he was quiet on the offensive front. Worked hard at both ends of the ice, finished his checks on the forecheck, and played as the point on the Armada's first power play unit with Walcott.

#77 Guillaume Beaudoin D (2014): Held the blueline well and made some good pinches. Showed nice smarts, never getting caught while pinching deep in the offensive zone. Good first pass out of his zone and always had his head up. Moved well, and had a strong game along the wall.

#85 Daniel Walcott D (2014): Typical game from Walcott. He had a strong transition game with some good sequences, rushing the puck with his great speed. Showed nice patience with the puck, will wait an extra second to make a play and he's also willing to take a hit to make a play. Very strong one-on-one, plays the man well.

#92 Marcus Hinds Rw (2014): Energetic first period from Hinds, who used his speed well and was involved physically. Scored the Armada's first goal on a two-on-one after a turnover in the neutral zone, with a nice finish using a quick one-timer. A threat on the PK, as he has great anticipation and a good stick. Create a few scoring chances while down a man.

Mar. 3, 2014 – Sioux Falls Stampede vs. Sioux City Musketeers (USHL)

SF #8 Joshua Jacobs LW/C (2014) – Sioux Falls' best player, Joshua had a strong game in all facets. He was a big physical presence at all times. He hits a lot and bounces off of hits, it's really hard to knock him off of the puck. He drove the net hard and was nasty to deal with in the offensive corners and down low in the offensive zone and around the net. He's so strong and such a good skater he's really a lot to handle when he has the puck. He imposes his will en route to the net. He isn't all brawn, has really good hands, too. Made a great move on Pionk to spring himself alone for a quality chance, which doesn't happen to Pionk often. Took the puck wide on defensemen and drove to the net for a couple of chances. High end speed, especially for a bigger body. On one such drive he made a really nice toe-drag behind him, using his body to shield the puck from the defender and pull it away from Hayton's ability to poke check him and got a great shot on net in which Hayton stopped. Notched a short-handed goal in which he snapped a rocket top-shelf on the short side. Was a beautiful goal. Great mix of power and finesse.

SC #5 Neal Pionk RD (2013) – Real physical, edgy game tonight, which is more or less typical for Pionk. Two really big open ice hits. Tenacious on the puck in his own zone, refuses to get beat. Strong defensive zone play other than the one play he got beat by Joshua. Jumped into the offensive rush, handles the puck well and with confidence. Lead a good rush where he took the defenseman wide and made a nifty stick handling move to the front of the net for a shot on goal. Strong game other than the one gaffe on the Joshua play.

SC #43 Waltteri Hopponen RW (2014) – Playing his off-wing, had a strong game in all three zones. Hard on the forecheck, aggressive in and around the net, and equal effort on defense, it was the typical two-way game you expect out of Hopponen. Worked the puck well on the power play, heads up, smart passes to create better power play looks, especially up to the point men. He's a really smart player, example being a play in the offensive zone where he was around the half board and received a pass from a line mate who was in the corner. There was a defending player within a stick length of Hopponen. Instead of catching the pass and having that defender on him and pinning him to the boards immediately and risking a loss of possession, Hopponen faked that he was going to catch the pass but let it go right on by to his defenseman behind on the point. The defender took Hopponen as if he has the puck and it opened up a wide open shooting lane for his defenseman to walk a few steps in and take a really good, completely uncontested shot on net. Was an excellent display of IQ and overall awareness. It's the kind of play Hopponen makes regularly. Also made a lot of things happen with his wheels and hands, driving the puck wide around defensemen and creating plays to the net. He has really good speed and is equally agile.

SC #27 Kyle Hayton G (2012) – Not much of a chance on any of the goals against, especially the third goal which was a beautiful cross-ice one-timer on a 2-1 top shelf that no one in the world could have stopped. He made two huge saves on similar plays a that third goal, going post to post and somehow managing to stop the one-timer. Great athleticism and strength.

FINAL: 3-2 Sioux Falls

SCOUTS NOTES:

Great pace to this game, lots of back and forth action with the teams trading chances. Few whistles and a lot of flow to the game. Sioux City put 40 shots on a goal but there were quite a few from the perimeter that weren't overly tough stops for Sioux Falls' Brey. Sioux City forward Jared Thomas (2012) was out of the lineup.

March 4th, 2014 Sioux City Musketeers vs Lincoln Stars

SC #4 Olson, Jacob D (2015) – Played limited minutes. This game at Lincoln was one of the two he played for Sioux City as they borrowed him from Hill-Murray High School. Would be unfair to judge him at this level in two games played in the USHL. Showed potential and will progress as he makes the jump to the USHL full time next year. 6'3" 210 frame as a 17 year old.

SC #5 Pionk, Neal RD (2013 UD) – Pionk played well this evening. Showed off his puck moving skills throughout the game. Picked up an assist on the powerplay in the second period. Did a good job quarterbacking the second power play unit. Sees the ice well. Could use to improve his game in his own zone, looks lost in the defensive zone at times. Offensive skill set is there, just needs to develop his defensive game.

LIN #13 Ward, Keegan RW (2015) – Ward is the manliest 17 year old I have ever seen. He has struggled to get into the Stars' veteran lineup all season, but the physical forward got into the lineup tonight vs. Sioux City. Offensively, Ward is still discovering himself at the USHL level. He plays the game with a reckless abandon hitting everything that moves and not backing down from any fight, which is interesting to see as a guy who is a couple years younger than most of the guys he's playing. Ward got into a fight in the second period and fought again when the game devolved into a brawl in the third period. Ward is a very raw player but I see some potential there. He is hands down the most competitive player on the ice at any given time. As he gets more regular playing time in 2014-15 with the Stars I see him developing into a player that brings a lot of energy with his physical game but can also chip in a goal here and there. His development will be something to keep an eye on.

Scout's notes: This was a great hockey game through the first two periods with some nice back and forth action, but Sioux City entered the third period with a 3-0 lead. Lincoln scored a couple minutes into the third, but never found the footing to come back. With seven minutes left in the game, Lincoln coach Jimmy McGroarty was thrown out for abuse of officials and then with four minutes remaining there was a large brawl that saw multiple fights and ejections.

Kelowna Rockets vs Everett Silvertips March 4th 2014 (WHL)

EVT #10 C Sandhu Tyler (2014). Did not play

EVT #89 C Nikolishin Ivan (2014) Ivan Received a nice cross ice feed coming out of the defensive zone , slip a check at the blue line and slowed up creating a 1 on 1 and showed good patients waiting for the lead man driving the net then delivered a nice crisp pass for Everett first goal. Ivan showed a good compete level and battled hard all game

EVT #12 W Leedahl Dawson (2014).   Dawson seen significant ice time in all situations. On the power play he was causing havoc in the Kelowna paint. In the second delivered a good defensive hit to cause a turn over and gain puck possession made a slick pass to his teammate who put the biscuit in the net. Dawson was aggressive on the forecheck and along the boards winning the puck battles. Show good confidence and poise killing penalties.

EVT #38 D Davis Kevin (2015) I like this kids game, His style of play is like a chameleon and that he will adjust his game to adapt to the current flow of the game. Makes very limited mistakes coming out of his own zone, will give a hard flat pass to the tape or use his wheels and if there is no other option he puts it off the glass. Not very offensive but has a good Defensive hockey awareness.

EVT #8 W Bajkov Patrick (2015) Another gamer who is starting to show his poise and offensive caliber. He's young and still makes a few mistake but has shown he can recover. The last few games he has had a very high compete level and tonight he was aggressive in all 3 zones.

EVT #17 C Fonteyne Matt (2015) Matt is another gamer who is showing his hockey potential. I like how he uses his quick feet to win battles or put himself in good scoring areas. Matt made a good defensive hit that lead to a Everett goal and was rewarded with an assist on the play.

KEL #14 C Chartier Rourke (2014). . Rourke showed good speed and poise. The kid is just relentless on the forecheck always putting pressure on the puck carry and very determined to winning the small battles along the boards. He is a very a shifty player who is hard to hit down low or open ice and has this uncanny ability to sneak into the scoring areas untouched. The puck seems to be glued to his tape at times. Played a solid game in all 3 zones.

KEL #23 W Kirkland Justin (2014). Good size player who played physical at times. I was not impressed with his play for much of the first and he went pretty much unnoticed until the third where his game seemed to elevate to another level. He's hard to knock off the puck when he uses his size to his advantage and showed his ability to use his size and find his way to the scoring area in the 3rd period and was rewarded with a nice goal.

KEL #24 C Baillie Tyson (2014). Did not play

KEL #3 D Stadel Riley (2014) Very calm and poised when carry the puck and his game does not seem falter under pressure. He moved the puck out of the zone well for 3 periods of play. What i like about

Mar. 6, 2014 – Indiana Ice vs. Waterloo Black Hawks (USHL)

IND #4 Ryan Mantha RD (2014) – Foot speed continues to be an issue for Mantha. His first step is slow, and overall his skating ability needs work. He is very upright. He is a big body but isn't overly physical and not as strong on his feet as you would like for a bigger body. Opponents numerous times were able to get leverage and body positioning on him. I would go so far as to say he's a bit soft. Just looks awkward and not very in control of his body. Had a really bad turnover in his own zone but to his credit was able to recover, using his long reach to poke check the puck away.

IND #8 Joshua Jacobs RD (2014) – Typical mix of physical defensively play and offensive flair. Plays with a mean streak, throws his body around any chance he gets. Strong defensive zone play, though he did have some decision-making gaffes. He can freeze up and cough up the puck. Was able to recover and take the puck back. His speed and quickness allow him to recover from mistakes, but that could cost him more at the next level. Had a lot of shot attempts. He has a good slap shot but it seems like he could put more on it if he wanted to. He's a big body and strong, would be well served to put more strength into his slap shot, though he does get it off quickly and it still has solid velocity. Handled the puck well, very comfortably. Made a couple of really nice stretch passes up the ice. He has good offensive instincts. Wisely opted for the quick wrist shot over the longer-taking slap shot in a couple of situations to avoid shot blocks and better have a chance hitting the net.

IND #91 Mitch Hults LW/C (2013) – Big body with wheels, Hults was a big physical presence in this game. If you touch the puck you were his man, he hit you. Plain and simple. Makes you pay the price for having the puck. Has good offensive skill, too, nice hands. Quick feet. Worked really well on the cycle in the offensive zone, can move quick and handle the puck well, excellent at protecting it with his body and length. Drives hard to the net with and without the puck. High compete level.

WAT #22 Tyler Sheehy RC (2014) – Assisted on the first Waterloo goal by carrying the puck up the ice with speed, gaining zone entry with control and taking the puck down the corner. Made a curl to create space and fed the point the puck from the goal line, where it was subsequently put in the back of the net. Good speed and very shifty. Really patient with the puck, which came in handy on the Waterloo power play. Works the puck down low really well, good vision. Scored a power play goal of his on a tough angle shot from the goal line that snuck its way in short side on Pawloski. Heads up passer and playmaker, finds his line mates well in the offensive zone. Has a nose for the net.

WAT #62 Brandon Montour RD (2012) – Notched a couple of quality shots on goal from the point and had a good overall game. Really skilled with the puck, super poised. Excellent skater and moves the puck up the ice really well. Does everything very smoothly and effortlessly. Strong defensive game, mistake-free. Smart, simple plays in his own zone. Didn't make the score sheet but high end offensive skill, has the puck on his stick a lot and is very comfortable with that.

FINAL: 5-2 Waterloo

SCOUTS NOTES:

Sloppy game by Indiana. They took two too-many-men penalties and Indiana coach Jeff Brown took an unsportsmanlike conduct penalty for his reaction to the second one called. Waterloo took advantage of their power play opportunities and were really good as a team with the man advantage. Waterloo carried the play for most of the game and added an empty-netter for the fifth goal. Indiana defenseman Aidan Muir (2013 EDM 213th Overall) left the game after blocking a shot and never returned, leaving Indiana shorthanded on their defensive corps. Waterloo was also without defenseman Mark Friedman (2014), who was scratched due to injury.

Swift Current Broncos vs Red Deer Rebels WHL, March 7, 2014

SC #6, Honka, Julius - high skill, very good speed. Soft hands on partial breakaway to nearly score while obstructed. Exceptional pivots and mobility. Can handle puck well while on his edges. Wasn't afraid to chase the puck deep in offensive zone. Good offensive instincts. Was able to skate the puck out of trouble. Played the body in own zone. Only question is size as he is quite small for his position.

SC #3, Harris, Jordan - Harris made a couple good plays along the boards to keep Red Deer on the defense, but had some struggles with puck. While he has decent size, he didn't use it well. Gap control wasn't good and his own zone play was too passive.

RD #16, Pawlenchuk, Grayson - Excellent 200 ft game. Great defensive zone awareness. Very responsible player everywhere on the ice. Stuck very close to his check at all times. Protects puck well. Good possession player. Played LW. Had an assist on a shot that would have gone in outright but hit a teammate in the crease along the way.

RD #25, Musil, Adam - Showing good improvement from earlier this season. Own zone support was overall decent and he did well to support the puck along wall. First step could improve. Good speed, long stride. Scored on a rebound.

RD #4, Fleury, Haydn - Calm and very composed with the puck. Good grit in board battles and would not allow anyone to take liberties against him. Excellent skater. Can skate puck out of trouble. Often skated the puck into the offensive zone and then was content to get back to his position. Strong in defending the rush. Constantly had the puck moving the right direction and finished the night a game-best +3.

RD #9, Bleackley, Conner - Had a quiet game by his standards. Very good hands and strong moves on rush. Able to handle puck in traffic and constantly challenged defenders. Strong skater. Didn't use teammates as well as he's shown in the past. Scored when his original shot was blocked by a defender and came right back to him.

SC #15, Gawdin, Glenn - RW. Strong offensive zone instincts, but didn't play North/South enough in neutral zone. Didn't always provide his defensemen an option when breaking out of their end. Had a nice play to draw a defender to him before dropping a pass to the trailer for a good chance.

SC #5, Martin, Brycen - Just average size for his position. Looked tentative both with and without puck. Gave up too big of a gap on the rush and played too deep in his end allowing shooters space in the slot. Average hands. Didn't display much grit. Passing was decent, but seemed to struggle even though he was playing sheltered minutes.

SC #4, Lernout, Brett - Great size and moves very well for a big man. Good mobility. Played more minutes (and tougher ones) than Martin tonight. Was a willing fighter against Doetzel and held his own. Decent toughness. First pass was rough at times, but he wasn't a liability with it either. Reminded me of Kenton Helgeson in his draft year. Lernout could be in the mix as a late round NHL selection this year.

Game Notes: Swift Current heavily outshot the Rebels, but strong goaltending by Red Deer's Bartosak combined with opportune scoring led to a convincing Red Deer win. Heatherington looked particularly sharp for Swift Current as the veteran defender dominated in his own zone, showed excellent footwork and even jumped into the play offensively.

Mar. 7 2014 – Muskegon Lumberjacks vs. Tri-City Storm (USHL)

MUS #4 Joe Cecconi RD (2015) – Other that one turnover blunder, Cecconi had a really solid, smart game. Good hockey sense, makes good passes and simple plays, but has the wheels and confidence in his hands to skate with the puck up ice. Very mobile and quick-footed, Cecconi has nice offensive skill and is likely capable of more point production going forward as he develops.

MUS #6 Christian Wolanin LD (2013) – Displayed his rocket slap shot on a power play tally from the point tonight. Laser beam from the middle of the ice and picked the top corner. He also hit the post two other times during the game. He has a really good shot and is good at getting it on net and through traffic. Him and Iacopelli as a point tandem on the power play is a really, really good combination. Both are mobile with good hands and rockets for shots. Carried the puck up ice a lot, extremely confident handling the puck. Weaves through traffic smoothly and without panic. Very poised with the puck. Likes to head-man to forwards and spring into the open ice for a return pass and break into the offensive zone. Really explosive first step and gets to top gear quickly. Strong game along the offensive blue line. Slick feet and hands. Strong defensively, keeps tight gaps and has the skating ability to make up for the odd miscue and recover.

MUS #11 Matt Iacopelli LW (2012) – As mentioned, excellent point weapon on the power play in tandem with Wolanin. They have good chemistry, move the puck well, and both have canons for shots. Rang a wrist shot off the corner pipe, completely beating Johansson. Unreal release. World class wrist shot, probably the best in the USHL. Great offensive skill. Stronger effort in the offensive zone than the other two zones. Effort level definitely in question much of the time. Even in the offensive zone is guilty of floating and sitting back a bit, letting teammates do more of the dirty work, but when motivated is a good forechecker and big body, throws high weight around. With his size and skill he can pull off really nice power moves with the puck, overwhelming defenders. Stopped on a breakaway chance. He has a lot of skill, but he is lacking in hockey sense.

MUS #29 Eric Schierhorn G (2014) – Solid game with a big breakaway save at a crucial time. He made a lot of stops in tight. Not much of a chance on the second and third goals, just nice plays. Ended up 29 saves on 32 shots.

TC #6 Kevin Kerr LD (2014) – Other than a bad backhand pass for a turnover in his own zone, Kerr had a rock solid game. Very sure-handed and smart, he makes good decisions with the puck and is really sound in his own zone. Shifty skater with good hands, he created two good offensive opportunities for himself with his quick feet and ability to read the play and exploit a slight hole in defensive coverage. Finishes his checks, takes good angles on puck carriers and wins a lot of his battles. Really nice defenseman.

TC #11 Austin Poganski RW (2014) – Plays the game like a runaway locomotive. He's always at top speed and with his straight line speed and size combined, is a very heavy hitter. Explosive, strong stride. Really good game on the penalty kill; very aggressive and active. Strong boards battles freezing the puck and killing valuable power play time for the other team. Forechecks hard and broke up what would've been an odd-man break on one play because of his hustle. Always a high effort level. Had some good looks on the power play. Tallied an assist on the third goal with a hard hit on an opposing puck carrier in which he took the puck away and dished it to a teammate who then set up the goal. Whole play was started by his forecheck and hit on the puck carrier. He's a really good north-south skater but needs to work on his lateral mobility and foot speed a bit. The effort is there but sometimes he's a half step slow to pucks and puck carriers when in tight in stop-and-start situations or when having to change directions quickly.

TC #44 Chris Wilkie RW (2014) – Utilized on the point on the power play, Chris is a really good fit there. Great offensive skill and instincts, strong with the puck along the blue line. He also did a really good job protecting the puck in traffic. Very hard to knock off the puck or steal it from. Great hands and good length, took hits to make plays. Carried the puck well through traffic, no panic. Can have an inconsistent effort level but he was on tonight.

TC #30 Jacob Johansson G (2011) – If not for the veteran Swedish goaltender, the Storm could have blown out of the water in this game. I lost count as to how many breakaway and semi-breakaways he stopped, and that's not taking into account the high volume of chances Muskegon had from the hash-marks in. The only goal he really had any kind of chance on was the fourth goal given up to Paulovic, which was a sneaky shot to the low blocker side. Given the number of shots he faced there were few playable rebounds but unfortunately one was capitalized on for a goal. Really strong game and deserved better.

FINAL: 4-3 Muskegon

SCOUTS NOTES:

The game was rather uneventful in the first period, with not much happening offensively for either team, but the game opened up drastically in the second. Tri-City carried the play early but Muskegon turned the tide shortly thereafter and never looked back. Score could have a lot worse for Tri-City if not for Johansson.

Mar. 8, 2014 – Sioux Falls Stampede vs. Dubuque Fighting Saints (USHL)

SF #8 Dakota Joshua LC (2014) – Joshua didn't generate a ton offensively but had a handful of decent chances; two on the power play and one at even-strength of note. He was denied by Reich on all three. His lack of offensive opportunities wasn't for a lack of effort, was just kind of one of those nights for Sioux Falls as a whole. Still had a high compete level, played physical, tended to his defensive responsibilities.

DBQ #7 Keegan Ford LD (2014) – Notched secondary assists on the second and third goals, Ford had a nice game at both ends. Chipped in offensively and his usual scrappy, physical agitating game on defense. Got time on both the power play and penalty kill. Had some nice pinches, keeping plays alive. Skillful at getting under the opponents skin. Walks that fine line.

DBQ #8 Blake Hillman LD (2014) – Solid game moving the puck and keeping things simple. Not a lot of offensive opportunities other than a couple of shot attempts. Mistake-free in his own zone, good neutral zone play both ways. Not a bad game at all, just solid and unspectacular. Good job handling and moving the puck.

DBQ #9 Seamus Malone LC (2014) – Effective game offensively but held off the score sheet. Made a lot of really good, crafty passes. His vision and awareness are really good, seems to always know where everyone is on the ice at all times. A couple of risky but successful no-look passes. Plays a scrappy, abrasive game and isn't afraid of anyone despite his size. Real good game on special teams, good effort.

DBQ #24 Karson Kuhlman RW/C (2014) – Big game tonight for Kuhlman. Had an excellent goal. He sped wide and got the angle on the defenseman and then did a great job of not only cutting to the net but he made a really nice toe-drag to bring the puck and his body centered to the net and protected from both the defenseman and goaltender and fired it right through the stacked pads five-hole on Brey. Total power move and nice mix of speed, power, and finesse. Kuhlman's an excellent skater with a nice, smooth, effortless stride. Had a strong game on the penalty kill, as well. Broke up some plays and applied good pressure, forcing errors and denying plays. Strong game.

DBQ #27 Dylan Gambrell C (2014) – Got rewarded for going hard to the net tallying a backhand one-timer on the power play. Always skates hard, plays with a lot of intensity. Good puck carrier, had the puck on his stick a lot in this game, looked really comfortable and calm. No rush or panic. Gets a little too intense sometimes. Took two bad battles in a row in the 3rd Period. Needs to control his emotions better. Good defensively and contributed to Dubuque's strong penalty kill as a team this game. Aggressive and hard on the puck, forces oppositions' hand.

DBQ #28 Shane Eiserman LW (2014) – Eiserman had a solid defensive game but generated little in the way of offense. You don't expect points every game but Eiserman needs to find better consistency to his game, especially offensively. Too talented to be devoid of offensive opportunities as often as he is. As stated, still had a solid game defensively and good effort on that end.

DBQ #1 Kevin Reich G (2014) – Reich gave up one goal on 26 shots in a solid effort. Stopped Joshua point-blank with a nice save and was a difference maker on Sioux Falls' first power play, which in hindsight really might have changed the outcome of the game. Quick legs and really athletic. The lone blemish was his goal against. Shot was a low wrister to the blocker side from the faceoff dot he should have had.

FINAL: 6-1 Dubuque

SCOUTS NOTES:

Dubuque carried the play for most of the game, but Reich denying Sioux Falls on that first power play really changed the tide of the game given the score at the time and how things played out from there. The game turned chippy in the 2nd Period, with two fights and a lot of altercations and shots after the whistles and behind the play. Very physical game.

Victoriaville Tigres vs Drummondville Voltigeurs (QMJHL), March 9th 2014

Victoriaville

#27 Gabriel Gagne RW (2015): Showed good puck protection during this game. It's tough to take the puck away from him when he's using his big frame to protect it. Makes nice use of his long reach. Got his nose dirty in front of the net, with a couple of scoring chances in close. Good on the cycling. His skating is average, but he has long strides that make him look faster.

Drummondville

#11 Joey Ratelle RW (2014): Had a target on his back all game long, was hit hard often but didn't back down and continued to battle hard all game long. Had the main assist on the game-winning goal after his pass was tipped in mid-air by Jérôme Verrier behind the Victoriaville goaltender. Had a tougher time getting positioned in front of the net on the power play like he usually does, mainly because of the size of the Victoriaville defense.

#19 Cameron Askew RW (2015): The 16 year old rookie didn't see much ice today, and his ice time only seems to be diminishing with the playoffs coming up as his coach is looking to put more trust in his veterans than rookies.

#95 Georgs Golovkovs C/W (2014): Showed some good skills with the puck, possesses a good wrist shot but passed on opportunities to shoot on the power play. Was challenged physically in this game, got hurt late in the third period after a collision deep in the offensive zone. Lacked creativity with the puck at times.

#6 Julien Carignan-Labbé D (2015): Played a regular shift at even-strength most of the game. Props to him for stepping up big-time and fighting Tommy Veilleux after he hurt one of his teammates after a big hit. Not many 16 year olds in the league would have done that. Good battle level along the wall; he showed that he's a strong player for his age. Puck movement was just okay from him—he won't ever be known as a puck-moving defenseman but he was decent in this area.

#15 Nikolas Brouillard D (2014): The first period was average for him, as he took some risks and got caught a couple of times. He was much better in the 2nd and 3rd periods. Made a great end-to-end rush to set up the second Drummondville goal. Used his speed well while carrying the puck and almost scored the game-winning goal on a breakaway after jumping on a loose puck in the neutral zone. Was involved physically in the game and battled hard, but was just not good enough or strong enough physically versus the big, physical forwards Victoriaville has.

#55 Sergei Boikov D (2014): I love how he competes, as he doesn't back down from the physical game and will get his nose dirty out there. Got hit hard all night and always seems to put himself in a bad position to get hit hard, something I have noticed all year long. His puckhandling and decision making were average, as he is not a natural puck moving defenseman. His shot lacked accuracy and he needs to put more power behind it. Made a bad read on Victoriaville's 1st goal, was too aggressive on the puck carrier on a three-on-two and put himself out of position.

Lethbridge Hurricanes vs Calgary Hitmen, March 11, 2014 (WHL)

Leth #16, Duke, Reid (2014) - shifty more than fast, Duke has very good hands and can control the puck with good speed. Defensively, he had an active stick, but was otherwise passive when in shooting lanes where he gave defenders far too much space. Did well to find open ice. Created some good scoring chances both for himself and teammates. Typically had the puck moving the right way, albeit in mostly soft minutes tonight. Compete level was better tonight than in some pre-

vious viewings this year. Not overly big, but finished his checks.
Leth #10, Khenkel, Kris (2014) - DNP
Leth #11, Cooper, Taylor (2014) - Average size. Skated well and thinks the game well. Above average talent, but didn't overly excel in any one area.
Leth #31, Skinner, Stuart (2016) - 1st career start. Some nerves early and allowed a terrible goal on the first shot attempt. Seemed to regain composure after giving up goals on first two shots faced, but was expending too much energy and was fighting the puck. Very good size frame with good athleticism to go with it. Strong glove hand. Eventually settled in and finished strong with 39 saves over 44 shots on the night.
Cal #32, Sanheim, Travis (2014) - Poor handling of bouncing puck led to a Tyler Wong breakaway goal. Good tendencies to jump into the play offensively. Shoot-first mentality. Didn't play with much grit.
Cal #27, Thomas, Ben (2014) - Steady defensive play to support back end while Sanheim jumps into play. Smart player.
Cal #18, Virtanen, Jake (2014) - used his speed to drive wide. Used his slapshot effectively and had a goal on the night. Handled the puck very well through traffic. Showed good positioning when defending the neutral zone.

Game notes: After a wild start resulted in 4 goals over the game's first 6 shots, the teams settled down with the Hitmen pulling out a 5-3 win. The ice was tilted in the Hitmen's favour for much of the last two periods. Riley Sheen had a good game for the visitors as he potted a couple of well-earned goals.

Val d'Or Foreurs vs Blainville-Boisbriand Armada (QMJHL), March 14th 2014

Val d'Or

#9 Anthony Richard C/LW (2015): Showed good hustle and energy during this game; he skates well and knows how to get open in the neutral zone. Had 2-3 breakaways in the 3rd period, getting in behind the Armada defense. He sees the ice well; I saw him make some nice passes to his two linemates. He may be undersized and lack strength, but he still demonstrates a good compete level, gets his nose into traffic and has a good wrist shot.

#12 Julien Gauthier Rw (2016): Played on the Foreurs' 3rd line during this game, a big-sized winger who moves pretty well with that frame. Did a real good job protecting the puck along the wall on the Foreurs' 4th goal, coming from behind the net with the puck. In his limited ice time on the power play, he was used to screen the goalie in front of the net. One of the youngest players in the league.

#16 Nicolas Aube-Kubel Rw (2014): Played on Val-d'Or's 2nd line with Richard and Beauregard and played on the 2nd power play unit. Showed some good speed, was able to beat defensemen wide, and has real quick, soft hands. He also has a quick release on his shot, which more often than not was a wrist shot. Lacks strength in battles for pucks along the wall, but defensively, he did a decent job tonight.

#26 Olivier Galipeau D (2015): Didn't see a whole lot out of him. He has decent mobility and is a smart defender in his zone. A very capable physical player, but was little quiet in that area today, though he did show a good active stick in his zone.

Blainville-Boisbriand

#8 Emil Aronsson C (2014): Showed again tonight that he's a very smart player away from the puck who understands the game well in his zone. Always takes a defenseman's position when one is pinching, and is the first one back defensively to help out. Battles hard along the wall for the puck and shows a good compete level. Didn't see much offensively out of him, he did have a couple of good scoring chances but was late to get to the puck in near the net.

#77 Guillaume Beaudoin D (2014): Beaudoin played with veteran Aaron Hoyles tonight, showing decent mobility and that he is not afraid to rush the puck when he had no option for passes. Makes good decisions with the puck, with decent mobility and footwork as well.

#85 Daniel Walcott D (2014): Always aggressive on the puck carrier in the defensive zone, never leaves them with much time to make plays. Was matched up versus the Anthony Mantha line with Nathanael Halbert, and they played hard against them, but Armada was no match for the Foreurs tonight. In the neutral zone, he was caught being too aggressive, resulting in odd man rushes. Had trouble with the puck on the power play, as many of his passes were easy to read for the Foreurs and they were able to break those plays.

Mar. 14, 2014 – Sioux City Musketeers vs. Waterloo Black Hawks (USHL)

SC #5 Neal Pionk RD (2013) – Physical, aggressive, chippy game. Always plays with a bit of a mean streak. Had some good shots on goal, good decisions to go with wrist shots over slap shots given the pressure on him and available lanes. Very smart player, great hockey sense. Aggressive on the puck, active stick, tenacious defender. Bailed teammate Hopponen out on a bad turnover, was able to get back and stop what would've been a lone break for the Black Hawks player.

SC #10 Jared Thomas LC (2012) – Thomas is has pretty dynamic offensive skilled. He created a lot of offensive plays, be it getting shots himself or setting up teammates. Excellent playmaking ability. Uses his size and length well to protect the puck. He uses his teammates well, lot of give-and-go plays and good cycling. Drove the net with the puck effectively, tough to defend. Notched an assist on the power play with a nice dish to Hawkins for a one-time blast. Scored a rebound goal from a point shot on a delayed penalty he drew beating the Black Hawk one-on-one and forcing him to take a penalty to slow him down. For his third point of the night he chipped the puck over to Mueller who then got the primary assist on the goal. Good length and skating ability. Good effort level tonight but overall needs better consistent effort in games.

SC #43 Waltteri Hopponen LW (2014) – Had a bit of a rough game overall. Terrible turnover in the defensive zone that Pionk bailed him out on. He didn't see the ice again for quite a few shifts after that. Play picked up a little bit when he got back into the game but overall rather invisible and didn't generate much offensively. He did have a nice shot in the shootout but hit the crossbar

WAT #22 Tyler Sheehy RC (2014) – Strong game on the boards, especially on the power play. High compete level. Won most of his faceoffs. Walked in uncontested from the goal line on the power play for a goal, assisted on two others. Showed his great compete level and hustle by outskating a defenseman to save icing at the end of a shift. Strong two-way game.

WAT #51 Mark Friedman RD (2014) – First game back after an absence due to injury. Tallied a power play goal on a wrist shot from the dot, soft goal but put the puck on net. Quick feet and nice speed. Really good stick, had a lot of effective poke checks. He was a shot-blocking machine in this game. Always willing to lay out but had a few really big ones tonight. Played a physical game, had a really nice open ice hit. Packs some punch in his checks. Smart, simple game in his own end, makes good decisions. Solid first game back.

WAT #12 Zach Sanford LW (2013 WSH 61st Overall) – Big body, great length. Nice, smooth, pro caliber stride with quick feet and good lateral movement. Excellent on the power play, good hands and decision making. Skates hard at both ends. Got an assist on the fourth goal. Was denied in the shootout. Really good looking prospect for Washington.

WAT #62 Brandon Montour RD (2012) – Good offensive effort once again. Notched an assist and registered four shots on goal. Great offensive skill, has a knack for getting shots through to the net. Good instincts and great puck handling ability. Good on the defensive end, doesn't give up defense for offense, balances both well and knows how to pick his spots.

FINAL: 5-4 Sioux City (SO)

SCOUTS NOTES:

This was a penalty fest for Sioux City, taking four consecutive penalties in the 1st Period and giving up goals on three of them. Usually not a recipe for a win yet Sioux City pulled this one out, somehow. They got two quick goals to start the 2nd Period and were right back in it. Unpredictable, entertaining game. Continue to be impressed with Montour's game.

Mar. 15, 2014 – USNTDP U18 vs. Cedar Rapids Rough Riders (USHL)

US #1 Blake Weyrick G (2014) – Fought off a late Cedar Rapids surge in the 1st Period. Gave up a weak first goal but was solid the rest of the way. Really quick legs. Strong down low, held his ground while on the ice trying to freeze the puck on some scrambles.

US #2 Jack Dougherty RD (2014) – Solid game skating and moving the puck. Speed and quickness are ok but but he plays a really smart game and has good anticipation, reads plays really well. Good passer. Good gaps on attacking players, stepped up well. Heavy slap shot and has a good wrist shot, too. Gets the puck on net a lot. Good mobility and smarts along the offensive blue line.

US #5 Brandon Fortunato LD (2014) – Smooth, smart, crafty game as usual for Fortunato. High hockey IQ and awareness, real good speed and super quick feet. Hits the holes quickly carrying the puck and is very elusive. Good movement on the power play.

US #6 Ryan Collins RD (2014) – Strong game in his own end, good outlet passes and smart decisions. Real physical, always finishes his checks. Really solid stay-at-home type game, no mistakes.

US #9 Shane Gersich LC (2014) – Caused a couple of turnovers for a good chances. Drew a penalty with hard work on the puck on one play but all in all kind of a pedestrian game for Gersich. Other than these couple of instances he didn't do much. Would like to see more consistency to his game, capable of much more than that.

US #11 Jack Eichel RC (2015) – Uncharacteristic off-game for Eichel defensively. It wasn't awful but was a little sloppy on that side of the puck and was on the ice for two goals against. Still skated really well, such a great skater. So fluid and smooth but powerful at the same time. Unparalleled stick handling ability. Puck on a string. Dominating with the puck in the offensive zone, could probably cycle around on his own at will if he really wanted to. Was held off the score sheet but generated good chances for himself and line mates.

US #16 Johnathan MacLeod RD (2014) – Solid defensive game, save for the one time he got caught looking and playing the puck instead of the man and got walked. Rare miscue for MacLeod. Great length, hard to get around. Takes good angles and is aggressive stepping up. Very physical. Good stick, efficient poke checker.

US #17 Alex Tuch RW (2014) – Physical game, had a couple of really big hits in his defensive zone, one in front of net on a scramble for the puck. He got a penalty call on the play but it shouldn't have been. Was a bang-bang play and he cleanly shouldered the player immediately after they lost the puck. Strong synergy with his line mates. Can't be said enough how much chemistry that line has and how well they work together. Hard on the forecheck and had some good physical play there, as well. Registered five shots on goal, generated some good offensive chances but didn't crack the score sheet.

US #36 Colin White RW (2015) – Big, bruising body. Strong on his skates and really good speed. He dominates the boards and the tough areas. He's a bear to play against and defend, so strong and has some mean in him. Sometimes that gets the best of him and he takes unnecessary penalties which he did in this game. Great awareness and hockey sense. Back to his skating, he's actually really shifty and nimble for such a big body and young kid, really impressive. He can beat players one-on-one with the puck. Good set of hands and nice touch. Great combination of size and speed.

US #55 Noah Hanifin LD (2015) – Rare mix of size, speed, offensive skill, hockey IQ, and overall maturity. Hanifin's game is so mature and polished for a young defenseman. Skates like that wind with great power, very mobile and agile, high end offensive skill, his dominance with the puck is bested only by his teammate Jack Eichel. He can take over a game. Great poise, excellent decision making and a great playmaker and passer in general. Very good vision and awareness. Made a great pass to Larkin on his goal to set him up. Great offensive instincts. Had a really nice fake slap shot-behind the back pass to spring a forward for a great chance. Picked up another assist on yet another fake-slap shot-pass to Belpedio for a one-time goal. It's incredible to see such a polished, pro-style game already from such a young player, let alone a defenseman.

US #19 Dylan Larkin LC (2014) – Larkin had some great power moves with the puck tonight. On one he had the puck behind the net, used his body to shield the puck and pulled out in front of the net for a chance all alone that was stopped. Drives the net hard and has excellent speed to the outside with the brawn and skill to drive to the net. Was set up on a beautiful cross-ice pass from Hanifin for a one-timer that found the twine. Great game defensively, good support for his defensemen and wingers. Physical and finishes his checks. Yet another excellent two-way game from Larkin.

US #22 Jared Fiegl LW (2014) – Physical and aggressive, Fiegl is a banger. Really likes to initiate contact. Occasionally crosses the line and takes penalties. Took one such penalty tonight on an elbowing call that just as easily could've been interference. Handles the puck well in tight and in traffic. Strong, powerful stride. Good defensive forward who always has a good compete level.

US #27 Sonny Milano LW (2014) – Milano didn't generate much offensively individually, which is a rarity. His line as a whole did well but he didn't get many sniffs at the net. Effort level was okay, but could have been better. There seemed to be some let up to his game, little bit of coasting.

US #36 Auston Matthews LC (2016) – With a game high seven shots on goals, Matthews was quite engaged offensively. Quick hand and lightning quick release, high end offensive skill. Has a nose for the net. Strong skater with great hockey sense. Big body and physical. Plays hard at both ends.

CR #9 Ivan Provorov LD (2015) – Phenomenal skater. Strong, wide base with quick feet, extremely shifty and can change directions on a dime and his hands are as skilled as his legs. Really smooth with the puck and an excellent passer. Very good vision. High end skill. Decision making seems good and he has a good sense of the ice and where everyone is at. Really skilled hands and feet.

CR# 35 Danny Tirone G (2012) – Tirone was literally about the only reason this was even a game for Cedar Rapids, as the US dominated the play from puck drop to end buzzer. He faced a barrage of quality chances and fought them off and kept his team in the game. Really good rebound control, seemed to smother everything. Very athletic, made a lot of saves post-to-post. Was very aggressive and was challenging the US' talented shooters. Phenomenal effort by Tirone.

FINAL: 4-3 Cedar Rapids (SO)

SCOUTS NOTES:

Despite the score, this game was thoroughly dominated by the US, outshooting Cedar Rapids by more than double, and many of those were of high quality. Cedar Rapids pulled their goal with over two minutes left and they were able to get two goals with the extra attacker, completely stunning the US, and wound up taking the game in a shootout.

OHL Playoffs: Sudbury vs Barrie – Game 1, March 20, 2014

BAR- #5 D Aaron Ekblad (2014) – Ekblad was one of the best players on the ice in this night. He read plays quickly and made smart decisions with the puck even when pressured. He missed a few outlet passes and that's something he'll need to continue to improve on. He always made smart, simple plays with the puck and didn't do anything that would get him in trouble. He closed his gaps well and kept his stick active, which made him extremely tough to get around. He was a beast on the boards finishing his checks and winning a ton of battles for loose pucks. He also was a staple on the penalty kill and at the end of one shift well over a minute; Ekblad used the last bit of energy he had to sprawl in front of a slap shot that clearly stung him. Offensively, he was able to use his big shot a couple times and when pressured he smartly put quick wrist shots on net that always seemed to get through.

BAR - #21 LW Brendan Lemieux (2014) – Lemieux was up to his typical tricks in this one. He was starting scrums after the whistle, snowing the goaltender, and making life very difficult on Sudbury. His net front presence was impressive, especially on the power play. He won a few races for loose pucks due to his improved skating ability. He was very tough to knock off the puck and showed some creativity when he had it. At the end of a shift when Lemieux was going off he happened to knock a stick out of a Sudbury player's hand. Lemieux made no effort to get out of the way, as he ended up stepping on it and discretely kicking it towards the Colts bench. He also got away with a cross check to a Sudbury defenseman's face after a whistle. Towards the end of the game he did take a minor, though, as he said something to the ref going off and was given two for unsportsman-like. Otherwise he played a strong two-way game with no glaring mistakes.

BAR - # 26 RW Andrew Mangiapane (2014) – Mangiapane doesn't get much hype, but he's a good player and played a real solid game against the Wolves. Despite his small stature, he was not afraid to initiate contact and seems to embrace it. He's relentless on the puck and his non-stop motor gives a lot of people problems, even players with immense size advantage. He was very shifty with the puck on his stick and was tough to contain, as he always seemed to find a way through small gaps or holes in the defense. He sees the ice well and made some very nice passes on the powerplay coming off the half-wall. He took a regular shift on the penalty kill playing with Andreas Athanasiou and seemed to fit like a glove there. He took care of his defensive assignments but when he had the puck he wasn't afraid to try and create some offense. On several occasions he grabbed the puck in the defensive zone and carried it out of trouble. He showed good puck skills, as he was able to stickhandle around defenders.

BAR - #22 C/W Andreas Athanasiou (Red Wings) – Athanasiou wasn't dominant offensively, but he played a solid game in front of Kris Draper and some Red Wings brass. He displayed his elite skating ability a few different times and was able to gain top speed in just a couple strides. He received several bad passes that he was able to easily corral and turn into scoring chances. Athanasiou showed the ability to create his own shot as his shiftiness, stickhandling ability and speed allowed him to change the lane or get around defenders and give him an extra second or two to get a shot off. He won several battles for loose pucks and looked good taking a regular shift on the penalty kill. He anticipates the play well.

BAR - #12 RW Kevin LeBanc (2014) – LeBanc played one of the best games I've seen from him all season. He was used on the first powerplay unit in the slot as a double screen (Lemieux was in front of the goaltender). He showed confidence and good stickhandling ability when he was able to dance around a couple defenders before carrying the puck into the high slot and dropping it for Justin Scott, who was able to finish the play off with a goal. He took a regular shift on the penalty kill and did well, making nice plays to get the puck out several different occasions. He makes smart reads with the puck and doesn't rush things, allowing plays to develop before making a decision with the puck. He was hard on the forecheck all game long and was all over the puck. He's a north-south player, but he can make skill plays with the puck and fits in well with high-end players. He finished the game with a goal and an assist.

BAR #27 C Cordell James (2014) – James played a good north-south game. He was strong on the puck and played his role to a tee. He got pucks in deep, and finished his checks every time he could. Despite not seeing much even strength ice due to playing on the 4th line, he was used on the penalty kill. He sealed players off when he could, wasn't afraid to crash the net and had a couple nice chances.

BAR #29 G Mackenzie Blackwood (2015) – Blackwood made his first career playoff start and didn't look nervous at all. He was eased into the game early, facing only four shots in the first. That said, his workload picked up significantly in the final two frames and he was able to hold the fort nicely. His rebound control was good for the most part, though he wasn't able to control one late that led directly to Sudbury's 2nd goal. His positioning was good and he was almost always square to the shooters. He's still growing into his big frame and learning to play big, but I thought he handled himself well considering how young and inexperienced he is.

SDY #27 RW Matt Schmalz (2014) – Schmalz was very disappointing in this game. He played a limited role and didn't see much ice, though when he was out there he failed to do much of anything. He was a step too late on more than one occasion, and it looked like the pace of the game was too fast for him. He wasn't able to close gaps quick enough to finish his checks, and he didn't create much offensively when he did have the puck. His shifts were few and far between.

SDY #14 RW Nick Baptiste (Sabres) – Baptiste was pretty quiet in this game. He was bottled up well by Aaron Ekblad several times and didn't have any opportunity to reach his top end speed. He was creative on the powerplay when he was given time with the puck and had a few chances when up a man, but at even strength he was pretty ineffective.

SDY #22 D Trevor Carrick (Hurricanes) – Carrick was real physical in this game. He was aggressive and threw his body around whenever he could. He was tough along the boards, and at times he took things a step too far. After killing a penalty, Carrick decided to hit Hooey then throw him down on the ice, which gave Barrie another powerplay. Offensively he was good holding the zone as he kept several pucks in that probably should have gotten by. He also had an assist. At no point was he given enough time or space to utilize his big shot, though.

Scout's notes: Zach Hall played a real solid game. He was quick, agile and very creative with the puck. He danced around defenders on several occasions and scored on a blast, which turned out to be the game-winning goal. Nathan Pancel scored a pair, and was all over the puck all game long. He wasn't afraid to mix it up in the corners or crash the net. Radek Faksa was OK defensively but very ineffective offensively. He was involved in several scrums, including a couple with Ekblad.

Moncton Wildcats vs Blainville-Boisbriand Armada (QMJHL) March 21st 2014

Moncton

#2 Adam Holwell D (2015): Played a regular shift and even got some power play time, showing good poise with the puck in the offensive zone, holding onto it an extra second to make a play. I liked his gap control, as he eliminated space quickly for opposing forwards to make plays. However, his mobility and footwork still need work.

#8 Connor Garland Rw (2014): Great game from Garland, who scored a beauty of a goal outwaiting an Armada defenseman and then beat Marcoux with a great backhand shot, coming from the point untouched. Played the point on the power play, and showed nice vision all night. Made a superb pass to Barbashev on the Christophe Lalonde goal; a great, cross-ice tape-to-tape pass. Loved that he always kept his feet moving, and he may not be the best skater but he is always in movement. He worked hard defensively and made some nice plays in the neutral zone, breaking plays out. Does need to get stronger, as he is easy to knock off when he protects the puck.

#11 Mathieu Olivier RW (2015): Didn't see him a lot, but I noticed him mostly when he was protecting the puck in corners. On one play, he won a puck battle in the corner and drove the net hard, which led to a quality scoring chance for the Wildcats.

#21 Vladimir Tkachev LW (2014): He's a little wizard with the puck on his stick, and likes to come back his zone and rush the puck from there. A fluid skater who showed that he can change directions easily, making him tough to handle one-on-one. Not big, but he's not afraid, and will finish his hits. His two goals tonight were scored while standing in front or at the side of the net. The first one came from a rebound and the second (the OT winner) was from a great feed from Barbashev for an easy tap-in. A fun player to watch, as he is very entertaining with the puck. However, he lacks strength, a factor that can hurt him in battles for puck.

#22 Ivan Barbashev C (2014): Barbashev showed tonight why he's one of the most complete players from his draft class. Very strong game without the puck, broke up plays in the neutral zone and always backchecked hard. Engaged physically all game long and love to hit. Made two remarkable passes that led to two goals for the Wildcats, and showed nice vision finding those teammates in front of the net. His goal came from a juicy rebound by Marcoux at the side of the net. On the OT winner, not only did he show nice vision, but he also had great patience with the puck, waiting an extra second before finding Tkatchev with an open net to shoot at.

Blainville-Boisbriand

#5 Nathanael Halbert D (2014): Strong game from Halbert tonight, who did a nice job covering Tkatchev on one sequence, giving him no space to make plays and staying with him the whole shift. Very steady in his own zone, making simple outlet passes from his zone. He had a strong positional game in his own zone, with a good stick as well, breaking up passes in front of his net in PK situations.

#8 Emil Aronsson C (2014): Got hit hard in the first period while skating with his head down, which looked like a head shot from my point of view. Don't think he saw one shift after that hit.

#71 Nikita Jevpalovs C/W (2014): Tonight was a good game from the Latvian forward, who scored three goals, including the last one with 35 seconds left in the 3rd period to send the game to overtime. Every goal was scored with a one-timer from the left faceoff circle, two were on the power play and the last one came with an extra attacker. Jevpalovs loves to shoot the puck, and if he has space in the offensive zone, he can be lethal with his one timer. Showed nice puck protection, using his size as a shield and also changing directions quickly.

#77 Guillaume Beaudoin D (2014): Started the game with a fight against Will Smith, and was also physical in front of his net. Beaudoin is a good competitor. However, he did get caught flat-footed in the neutral zone being too aggressive on the puck carrier, and also fumbled the puck in the offensive zone which led to the Wildcats' 5th goal of the game, when the Armada had the momentum in this period. Showed some good acceleration carrying the puck from his zone, can get away from forecheckers easily with that acceleration.

#85 Daniel Walcott D (2014): Another good game from Walcott who, with just a fluid skating stride, is tough to handle when he rushes the puck, as Moncton doesn't have the most mobile defense corps. Moved exceptionally well laterally and loves to do so while on the power play to make the opposing PK unit move. Was physical in the game, threw a big hit deep in the offensive zone which shook up Garrett Johnston. Showed great patience and vision with the puck on Jevpalovs' 2nd goal of the game, as he was about to shoot and saw his teammate wide open, making a perfect pass for the Armada's 3rd goal.

#92 Marcus Hinds Rw (2014): A solid effort from Hinds, who was one of the most consistent forwards for the Armada tonight. His goal came from a nice tip in front of the net. Good, powerful strides help him beat defensemen on the outside and he is not shy to take the puck to the net. A great penalty killer who did a great job on a 5-on-3 opportunity in the game.

Mar. 22, 2014 – USNTDP U18 vs. Chicago Steel (USHL)

US #11 Jack Eichel RC (2015) – Dominating offensive effort…again. Seems like he can just keep the puck on his stick all game at will and never lose it. Can weave and dangle in and out of traffic with ease. Eyes in the back of his head playmaking ability. Tied for a team high four shots on goal and had an assist on a sly little pass to Hitchcock on his beautiful backhand goal. Strong defensive play, good work on the penalty kill. It continues to impress how a player of his caliber with the attention he gets remains grounded and plays such a good team game with such maximum effort on a nightly basis.

US #17 Alex Tuch RW (2014) – Notched a secondary assist on Hanifin's power play tally. Strong game on the boards and in the corners, which basically is what you could consider his office. Not afraid to do the dirty work. Physical game, had some solid hits. Took a high-sticking penalty but it was just a hockey play. His temper and emotion can get the best of him so it's something to keep an eye on but he kept it in check tonight and channeled it properly. Such a good skater for such a big, thick body. Really agile and has that first quick step to get to top speed in a snap. Such an enticing mix of skills and size.

US #27 Sonny Milano LW (2014) – Milano had a solid 1st Period but his night was cut short by an injury early into the 2nd Period. He took a bad kneeing penalty from John Schilling and left the game and was helped off the ice with assistance. It was a blatant knee and Schilling was penalized accordingly for it. Milano had a good 1st Period, displaying his vast array of skills and talent. He was seeing the ice really well, making nice heads up passes. Really poised and calm with the puck, hates to give up possession of it and fights hard for it. Really elusive and difficult to remove from the puck. Hopefully for the sake of Milano and Team USA the injury isn't serious but at a stop in play soon after his injury he was escorted off the ice and was later seen in street clothes walking in crutches.

US #9 Shane Gersich LC (2014) – Solid effort and compete level but didn't generate much in the way of offense or really stand out all that much in this game other than one breakaway he was stopped on that was set up nicely by a Collins pass. That seems to be a prevailing issue with Gersich's game; consistency, or a lack thereof. He's far too talented to have as many nights as he does where he's so unnoticeable. The nights where he is prove that. He really needs to find better consistency to his game, because when he's on he's on. He's a talented and skilled player and is capable of much more than he shows some nights.

US #5 Brandon Fortunato LD (2014) – Really good game all around. He's so sure-handed with the puck and confident with it, especially in his own zone and into the neutral zone. His skating ability is remarkable, and he's so quick in transition and in short bursts. Such a snappy first step. Changes directions on a dime and his elusiveness is such a huge factor in his ability to slip out of trouble and lead to breakouts that other players simply aren't capable of. Oozes hockey sense and reads the ice so, so well. Even when he does take contact he takes it well, never shies away and always takes hits to make plays. Even with his size he rarely gets hit hard and knocked down. Dynamic player.

US #16 Johnathan MacLeod RD (2014) – Had a particularly high level of snarl to his game tonight. He's always physical and mean but he was especially chirpy and engaging in this one. Really solid, smart game in his own end. He's really dependable in his own zone. He makes the simple play and good first pass and is no-nonsense with the puck there. Sees the ice well, generates a lot of nice passes and they're always tape to tape with a lot of zip.

US #21 Ryan Hitchcock LW (2014) - Excellent game. Flying all over the ice. Created a lot of turnovers and was just pain in the butt for the Steel all night. Scored a goal-scorer's goal; really, really nice backhander top shelf in very tight of the net. Was the only place that puck could go and he put it there. High talent goal. Really quick hands and operates the puck well in tight. Very shifty skater, quick first step and very mobile. Like his game a lot.

US #7 Anders Bjork RW (2014) – Bjork had a good two-way game, which is more or less the norm for him. It's rare he has an off night, it seems. Always a consistent effort and you know what to expect from him. Seemed to have an extra spring in his step tonight. He's always an excellent skater but he was really getting around. Really strong game on the boards, won a lot of battles. He's got an excellent compete level, hates to lose. Had a couple good shots on goal, set up a few others. Just another solid two-way game from Bjork.

US #6 Ryan Collins RD (2014) – Bit of an up and down game for Collins. Had a really nice stretch pass to spring Gersich on a breakaway. Just seemed indecisive tonight. Was fighting the puck a bit and seemed to second-guess himself and hang on to the puck too long which resulted in a couple of turnovers and mucking up the transition game for the US. Uncharacteristic for Collins, who's usually a solid decision maker and very sure of himself with the puck.

US# 1 Blake Weyrick G (2014) – Played well enough for his team to win. Had a solid game, but not spectacular. Faced two breakaways, stopped one and got beat on the other. Second goal was a rebound all alone, no chance at it. Weyrick had a few gaffes trying to play the puck. It's not a strong suit of his yet he continued to do it and at poor times, making poor decisions with the puck and coughing it up to the opposition.

US #55 Noah Hanifin LD (2015) – Had three assists and a beast of a game. Does everything so smoothly and with such ease and poise. No panic to his game whatsoever in any situation. Great speed and highly mobile, quick first step. Powerful, explosive stride. Really strong on his feet. High hockey IQ and anticipation, caused all kinds of turnovers jumping the passing lanes and stealing the puck from opposing puck carriers. Rocket of a shot. Rushed the puck a lot in this game and is dominant with the puck. Really hard to defend when he has a full head of steam. Great hands and really creative with the puck. Excellent vision and playmaking ability. Stunning how dominating his game is already at his age. Very polished and mature. Hard to find anything negative about his game.

US #36 Colin White RW (2015) – High motor and high compete level. White is a bull in a china shop. Hits everything he sees, tenacious on the forecheck. His skating ability is very impressive. Powerful stride, quick feet and very agile. Had a really strong game, was around the puck a lot. Very physical.

CHI #20 Artem Artemov LW (2015) – Great effort every shift, always a good compete level and battle from Artemov. Aggressive forechecker and backchecker. Caused a lot of turnovers, a couple with sneaky pick-pockets on the backcheck. Created a lot of offensive chances, really good playmaker. Assisted on Chicago's second goal with a really nice passing play through a couple sets of US legs. Really impressed with his vision, he's an excellent passer and is really adept at finding open teammates in situations that don't seem possible at ice level. Played a strong two-way game.

CHI #23 Robby Jackson LW (2015) – His feet never stop moving. High speed and high motor. Really strong defensive game. He's a turnover machine, has really good closing speed. Had some good plays and good looks on the power play and had a grade A scoring chance snuffed by Weyrick. Gritty, in your face type player. Plays with no fear and plays with a lot scrap. Had a couple turnovers of his own. Has a tendency to try and stick handle through too many people and carry the load on his own. His hands are really good and he's really shifty but he still tries to do it too much and sometimes in really bad areas, at the blue lines in particular. He needs to learn to be safer and protect the puck better, but the confidence and comfort with the puck is a good thing.

CHI #17 Fredrik Olofsson RW (2014) – Olofsson was on the ice for three goals against but none of the goals were his responsibility. He had his defensive assignments covered all game wrong and that's something impressive about his game. Really like seeing how his two-way game has evolved since the start of the season, in particular since coming to Chicago. The transformation in his game since the trade had been remarkable. Only got one shot on goal but had a couple of other attempts and set up some others. Excellent playmaking ability. Such great hockey sense and poise. Plays a pro style game, just really calm, fluid, completely devoid of panic. Made lots of subtle little smart plays and does every game multiple times a game. Just a really smart, skilled player that continues to impress. Like his game a lot.

CHI #28 Alec Vanko RD (2012) – Vanko's game has really come on the the second half of this season. Plays a rock solid defensive game but has some offensive skill and upside. Sees the ice really well, which was evident on his stretch homerun pass to Smith on Chicago's first goal. Vanko was about 10-15 feet inside his own blue line and laced a rocket of a pass through traffic all to the far blue line and his Smith right in stride for a breakaway. Beautiful play. Has nice hands and handles the puck well. Shifty feet and good mobility. Had a really strong defensive game. Maintained good gaps and closes on his man really well. Shuts down zone entry options and has good angles. Good size and uses it. Very physical, finishes his checks. Late-bloomer whose game has really come on this season.

FINAL: 5-2 USNTDP

SCOUTS NOTES:

Good pace to the game overall. US carried the play for the most part. They were really dominant offensively. Overmatched Chicago quite a bit in the offensive zone on the cycle. Unfortunate hit on Milano. Hopefully it isn't serious and doesn't affect the rest of his season, especially with the World U18 tournament right around the corner.

Sudbury Wolves vs Barrie Colts – Game 5, March 28, 2014

BAR #21 LW Brendan Lemieux (2014) – Lemieux scored an early goal in the 1st period on an excellent shot from the slot. He was able to get a shot off in a hurry, and he ripped it past Palazzese showing off his good release. He was strong on the puck, and good along the boards. He made a nice play coming from behind the net that led to a Fawcett goal to make it 2-0. Lemieux was good in front of the net and made it difficult on Palazzese to see past him. He drew a call in that area as Trevor Carrick got a little carried away trying to clear the crease. He did take two minors in this game, but one was a soft call where he was pushed into the goaltender. He also drew two calls to help offset it. He went toe-to-toe with Carrick all game and won the majority of the battles. Lemieux finished his checks consistently and overall played a very strong game.

BAR #26 RW Andrew Mangiapane (2014) – Mangiapane played another solid game. He was good on the powerplay, and displayed nice vision while up a man, setting up several quality chances for his teammates. He rotated between the point and the halfwall, and was effective in that role, as he picked up a primary assist. He also made a nice cros- ice feed to Johnny Laser early in the 3rd on what was Barrie's 6th goal. He was able to win his fair share of puck battles, and actually knocked players off the puck at times. Bigger players do not intimidate him, which helps him remain effective despite his size. He showed some creativity with the puck, as he was able to dance around defenders, even in small spaces.

BAR #12 RW Kevin LaBanc (2014) – LaBanc has really had a coming out party in the playoffs thus far. He's been effective at even strength, on the powerplay and while killing penalties. He was good in his own zone and consistently went in the shooting lanes to block shots. He was strong on the forecheck and always on the puck. He didn't show any hesitation to go to the dirty areas, either. He made a couple nice defensive plays in his own zone by using his active sticks to break up plays. He scored on an absolute snipe going bardown, and also scored another goal on a 2-on-1. LaBanc could have had a hat trick as he hit the post hard in the 2nd period.

BAR #27 C Cordell James (2014) – James played a solid game once again. He was good on the forecheck, and was a regular on the penalty kill. He broke up a couple plays in his own zone and consistently was able to get pucks out. James knocked a couple defensemen off the puck, and created a couple scoring chances off late. His game was cut a period short, though, as he stepped in for Mac Clutsam in a fight to end the 2nd. James went toe-to-toe with 19-year-old Brody Silk and more than held his own, which was appreciated by his teammates. He was given 2, 5 and 10 for his efforts and didn't play in the 3rd as a result.

BAR #22 LW/C Andreas Athanasiou – Athanasiou was electric once again. He was creating all game long, and was awfully dangerous on the rush. He used his speed to blow by defenders regularly and generate scoring chances. He scored two goals, one on a snipe from the slot area and another on a breakaway where he duck Palazesse out of his crease. In the offensive zone he was able to lose defenders with his quick stops, starts and cuts. Like Lemieux, he didn't play in the final 10-

15 minutes.

BAR #27 RW Matt Schmalz (2014) – Schmalz was completely ineffective once again. He didn't play in the 1st, saw limited action in the 2nd and played regularly in the 3rd once the game was well out of reach. He was too slow to get in on the forecheck, and didn't do much with the puck when he had it on his stick. The highlight of his game was probably leveling Kevin LaBanc into the boards after he scored to make it 7-0.

BAR #22 D Trevor Carrick (Hurricanes) – Carrick failed to impress me once again. He wasn't able to get a good shot off at any point, and put several pucks into shin-pads. He was caught pinching a couple times and didn't have the best game defensively. Carrick was worked off the puck a couple times by smaller players (LaBanc, Mangiapane, etc.). He was also slow getting off at one point, which led to a too many men call. On top of that, he took a bad penalty while already shorthanded getting overly aggressive with Lemieux.

Scout notes: Aaron Ekblad (knee) and Mitch Theoret did not play...Despite that, Sudbury came out slow and never really got going and this game...Zach Hall injured his ankle, left the game and did not return...Like most of the series, Baptiste did next to nothing in this game until it was well out of reach.

Mar. 29, 2014 – Omaha Lancers vs. USNTDP U18 (USHL)

OMA #18 Anthony Angello RC (2014) – Essentially invisible this game. Hardly noticeable at all. Generating next to nothing offensively for himself or teammates. Probably the most pedestrian he's looked in viewings all season. Needs to find some kind of consistency to his game. Big body with wheels and a lot of skill. He should never be invisible, even on an off night.

OMA #21 Ryan Tait RW (2014) – Kid can flat out fly. Was buzzing all over the ice tonight. High end speed and has pretty quick hands, too. Notched a power play tally on a really nice speed move where he burned the defenseman wide and while crossing over on his drive to the net took a really quick wrist shot in stride and completely fooled Minney and hit the back of the net. It wasn't a hard shot but between the release and how he didn't break stride at all when taking it I think it just caught Minney by total surprise. Also added an assist later when he chipped a rebound over to Snuggerud, who then dished to the goal scorer. Camps out in front and goes to the tough areas, no fear. Took hits to make plays. Really like his game.

OMA #1 Hayden Hawkey G (2013) - Gave up a softie to Larkin on a bad angle backhander but that was the lone blemish on an otherwise stellar day. Hawkey stopped an Eichel breakaway, two other Larkin opportunties all alone, a two-on-0, along with stoning Hitchcock when he had a chance uncontested. Unfortunately all three aforementioned US players got their revenge in the SO, each scoring on their opportunities. Other than the Larkin backhander, he had no chance on any goals. The score would've been more lopsided if not for Hawkey, and he's really the reason Omaha it even went to overtime and a shootout at all. Superb rebound control, big-time/big-moment stops, he did it all. Really poised and calm. Never got rattled, never showed any emotion, cool as a cucumber. Really strong performance.

US #2 Jack Doughery RD (2014) - Solid game. Not great, not bad, just solid. Mistake-free, dependable. Moved the puck well and made good decisions, smart game. Kept it simple. Good outlets and defended the defensive zone well. Didn't generate much offensively. Had a couple of shot attempts but no shots on goal.

US #5 Brandon Fortunato LD (2014) - Strong skating and puck handling game. Was all over the ice, had his puck on the stick a lot and was excellent with it. Had a number of rushes up the ice and into the neutral zone, with one leading to a goal. He made a really nice play to gain zone entry, bought some time, and then dished the puck off to an open Tuch who then combined with Milano to set up an Eichel goal. Top notch speed. Such a great skater. Super shifty and can stop, weave, change direction on a dime. So hard to attack and defend against when he has the puck. See the ice and reads the play so well. Picked up the puck in his corner and took a look up the ice and saw there was a seam right through three opposing players and he just turned on the afterburners and exploded in a straight line up the ice through the gap and out of his own zone, leading a rush that ended with a solid offensive zone possession.

US #6 Ryan Collins RD (2014) - Had an okay game but seemed a bit off in the head. Had some issues with defensive awareness and allowing opposing forwards to be open and being unaware of their presence. One time what should have been a two-on-two ended up essentially a two-on-one because he drifted over too far towards his partner who already has the puck carrier covered almost as if he wasn't aware of the trailing forward. The lack of awareness happpen from time to time and he needs to improve on that and maintain his focus.

US #7 Anders Bjork LW (2014) - Top notch effort from Bjork, which is basically the norm from him. Always a hard worker but is smart and skilled, to boot. Strong board work with and without the puck. Made a couple of really nice cross-ice passes from the offensive half-board to open point men for good looks. Displayed not only his skill but his excellent vision and hockey sense on a really nice no-look tip pass to a streaking teammate which created an odd-man break. The pass to Bjork was a rocket but he knew exactly where his other teammate was and redirected the pass at the perfect angle to tip to his teammates stick and send them on a break, all without even looking at that player. Beautiful play. Strong game defensively, was a turnover-causing machine. Aggressive forechecker and pokechecker. Excellent hands and patience with the puck. Always a smooth operator, no panic.

US #8 Jack Glover RD (2014) - Didn't get a lot of playing time in the 1st Period. Questionable decision making. Hesitant with the puck. He backs off from the offensive zone too early too often. Not a close enough gap and doesn't put enough pressure and resistance to opposing forwards attempting to break out of their zone. Makes it tougher for his forwards to backcheck. Handled the puck decent in the offensive zone, but all in all unimpressive game overall.

US #9 Shane Gersich LW (2014) - Paid the price in front of the net to earn the first goal of the game. Took a hit in front of the net to get a rebound shot off that found the back of the net. Solid game in front and in the corners but seemed to get outmuscled and outmaneuvered for body positioning a lot. Okay game but nothing special.

US #10 Joe Wegwerth LW (2014) - Good defensive effort. Blocked a lot of shots. Forechecked hard, got a couple steals and disrupted plays. Not much on the offensive side of the puck but skated hard and was a difference maker defensively. Skated well, decent speed. Physical game.

US #11 Jack Eichel RD (2015) - Scored a goal on kind of a flukey play but was in the proper position so made his own luck on the play, so to speak. A Tuch shot bounced off the glass and came right back in front of the net. Eichel appeared to be the only who saw the puck come backa and he tucked it home without much of an attempt from Hawkey, who had no idea where the puck was until it had gone past him. Coughed the puck up at the offensive blue line on more than one occasion, which is rather uncharacteristic. Made up for it by causing a turnover of his own deep in the defensive zone and after stealing the puck, dished it off to Milano for a quick-strike goal. Really nice play. Strong game all around other than the couple of turnovers. Great handling the puck as always and doing what he does game in and game out.

US# 17 Alex Tuch RW (2014) - Was all over the ice, causing havoc everywhere he went. Physical game, hard on the forecheck and hard on the puck carrier in all areas of the ice. Had a couple of really nice finesse plays, one being a nifty tip pass to Milano for a high quality chance. Had a couple of quality shots, one leading to the Eichel goal.

US #19 Dylan Larkin LC (2014) - Registered a game-high eight shots on goals. Larkin was all over the ice. Had the puck on his stick all night and was creating plays like a man possessed. Notched a goal in the 3rd Period on a top shelf, tough angle shot, as well as getting the game-winner in the shootout. Larkin's alwasy got speed but he seemed to have an extra jump in his step tonight. Had some really nice power moves to the net with the puck. He is really good and smart about following his own shots to the net for rebounds. He follows them hard, probably does it better than anyone else. Really aware of it and likes to get that jump on defensemen. Best player of the game.

US #21 Ryan Hitchcock LW (2014) - Really like Hitchcock's game of late. Seems to always be invovled in the play and be around the puck a lot. High speed, high motor, never quits. Tenacious on the puck and high energy all the time. Great hockey sense, good vision. Smart player with the puck. Really likes to come into the offensive zone at full speed and back the defensemen off and then make a tight curl and look for the trailers coming into the zone for an open look. Has a real nose for the net and loves to mix it up and in the tough areas. Had quite a few scoring opportunities tonight but was stopped by Hawkey, though he returned the favor by scoring in the shootout.

US #22 Jared Fiegl LC (2014) - Strong defensive game, especially on the penalty kill. Good shot blocker. Finshed his checks any chance he got. Makes you pay for having the puck. Really physical. Big body, moves pretty well. Not much in the way of offense tonight but a strong defensive contributor.

US #27 Sonny Milano LW (2014) - Had a nice one-timer goal on an Eichel feed after Eichel stole the puck from a defenseman. Bang-bang play. Skated really well tonight, even more springy and shifty than normal. Good to see after injuring his knee last week. Had some spunk tonight, was especially physical and going out of his way to hit and finish checks. Had a good game driving outside on defenseman wide. Uses his edges really well. Strong for a smaller player, really hard to take off the puck. Excellent game. Trailed only Larkin in shots on goal with seven.

US #29 Edwin Minney G (2014) - Gave up kind of a weak first goal to Tait. Seemed to get handcuffed with the shot, as Tait fired it off really quickly mid-stride as he was cutting to the net. Second goal was a redirect he had no chance on and the third was a bang-bang rebound goal all alone. Stopped five out of seven shooters in the shootout. Made the big saves on plays in tight all game long, strong down low. Didn't give shooters much to shoot at.

US #24 Auston Matthews RW (2016) - Playing on his off-wing. notched an assist on the Gersich goal. Took a bad angle shot that left a funky rebound that was pounded home. Skated well, like his speed and agility for a big body. Strong defensive effort, good compete level. Kept his feet moving and was always active in the play.

US #55 Noah Hanifin LD (2015) - After a quiet 1st Period, his play picked up the remainder of the game to his usual dominant levels. Had a few really great passes. He sees the ice so well and can seemingly hit guys on the tape at will, no matter the traffic in between. Conversely, he's a nightmare to try and complete passes against defensively. Jumps the lanes and disrpupts more passes than anybody. Speaks to his hockey smarts and ability to read plays and anticipate the action, as well as his excellent foot speed, mobility, and transition ability. Dominant 2nd and 3rd Period. Say it every time he's viewed; incredibly polished and mature game.

US #36 Colin White RW (2015) - Turnover machine. Kid just creates havoc in the offensive zone on the forecheck. Tenacious, aggressive, man on a mission. Heavy hits, loves to bang and crash. Had complete ownership of the boards and corners where he was involved. Physically dominating player with a refuse-to-lose will.

FINAL: 5-4 USNTDP (SO)

SCOUTS NOTES:

The US dominated the first two periods, but in the 3rd Period the play evened out much more until the US surged in the closing moments. Continue to be impressed with the progression of Hitchcock's game, and the youngsters like Hanifin, White, *and Matthews have fit seamlessly with the U18 squad and are playing excellent hockey.*

Moncton Wildcats vs Blainville-Boisbriand, March 30th 2014 (QMJHL playoff)

Moncton

#8 Conor Garland W (2014): Liked his game today. Garland worked hard and got his nose dirty all game long. A fearless player that gets outmuscled a ton and doesn't win many one-on-one battles, but his motor never stopped working. Made a great pass to Klebanskyj on Moncton's 1st goal, sees the ice well and showed strong playmaking skills tonight. He was arguably the most dangerous forward offensively for the Wildcats. However, his speed is just average.

#11 Mathieu Olivier W (2015): Didn't get many opportunities offensively, but I liked his intensity and physical game, as he was often involved along the boards. Made a great play on Moncton's 1st goal, winning a race for the puck and sending it back to Garland who made the pass to Klebanskyj at the side of the net for the goal. Played his grinder role well tonight.

#21 Vladimir Tkachev W (2014): A little bit too fancy with the puck tonight, turned the puck over trying to beat guys with unnecessary stickhandling or doing an extra move instead of shooting the puck. Liked his compete level, as he doesn't back down from physical contact even if he's undersized. Scored the 2nd Moncton goal after jumping on a rebound at the side of the net. Shot is average, but his hands are super quick.

#22 Ivan Barbashev C (2014): Played a strong physical game, was tough along the wall and threw some good hits, though he was on the receiving end of some as well. Was strong on his skates, and rushed the puck in the offensive zone many times tonight. In the first half of the game I thought he was trying too much with the puck on the power play and lost it too easily. Played his typical, strong two-way game and always came back in his zone to support his defense. Had some good physical battles versus Daniel Walcott in the 2nd & 3rd periods.

Blainville-Boisbriand

#5 Nathanael Halbert D (2014): Superb game from Halbert, who played hard along the wall and was tough to beat one on one. Matched up with Walcott against Moncton's top line of Barbashev-Caissy-Tkatchev, and did a great job of it during the game. Used his stick well and didn't provide much room for that line to create things offensively. Didn't see much offensively out of him, other than a great rush late in the game where he tried to beat a Moncton defenseman on the outside. Overall, he took care of things in his zone and let the more offensive Walcott take care of the offense.

#71 Nikita Jevpalovs C/W (2014): Scored the 4th Armada goal after he got hit hard at center ice and missed a couple of shifts. On his goal, his line did a terrific job pinning down the Moncton defense in their zone and cycling the puck. He's dangerous when he has the puck in the offensive zone; he has a quick release on his shot and loves to use it like he did tonight. Not a speedster, but he does go in the tougher areas of the ice. Liked his puck protection along the wall, he's a strong player who showed some real good stickhandling abilities in this game.

#77 Guillaume Beaudoin D (2014): Made good reads jumping into the play offensively, while remaining steady in own zone. Not flashy, but I like his decision-making with the puck, and he has decent mobility and footwork as well.

#85 Daniel Walcott D (2014): Paired with Halbert against Moncton's top line. A strong skater that is tough to knock down. He made good decisions with the puck all the time in the offensive zone, whether it's jumping into the play or finding his teammates. Scored the 3rd goal for his team after jumping into the play and following up on it, jumping on a rebound in front of the net. Hard to play against, and is quick to react in defensive situations to cut off spaces for opposing players to manoeuvre. Loved his battles versus Barbashev.

#92 Marcus Hinds RW (2014): Strong work along the wall protecting the puck, used his size well to shield opponents from it. A powerful skater who made some nice rushes using his outside speed. Does a good job on the forecheck with that good speed, and made some smart plays with the puck and some good passes as well.

Mar. 30, 2014 – Waterloo Black Hawks vs. Green Bay Gamblers (USHL)

WAT #9 Lawton Courtnall LW (2014) - Slick skater with a smooth stride and quick hands. Nice looking player. Plays a smart game, handles the puck well. Good hockey sense and decision making.

WAT #22 Tyler Sheehy RC (2014) - Strong game from Sheehy in all three zones. Both of his goals were the result of hard forechecking and him causing turnovers. His first goal came on a wrister from the hashmarks after picking off a cross-ice pass attempt in the slot. The second was a beautiful play in which he caught Schmaltz sleeping with the puck as he was skating behind the net on the power play. Sheehy all in one motion picked Schmaltz's pocket and made one stick handle to complete the wrap-around and tucked it home five-hole. Hackett didn't even know what happened it was such a quick play.

WAT #62 Brandon Montour RD (2012) - Montour had four or five really strong pinches. Really smart and knows when to pinch and not. His size, speed, and anticipation allow to really get in and pressure the play along the boards. Excellent release on his wrist shot, especially for a defenseman. Had one get blocked that sprung the blocker on a breakaway the other way but Montour used his excellent speed to recover and catch the player and squash the entire play. Got his one assist moving the puck up ice through the neutral zone and making one nice move to evade an attacker and then dished the puck off. Other came on a quick wrister he put on net and the rebound found the back of the net. Was a really smart play to take a wrist shot over a slap shot, slap shot would've been blocked. Great awareness. Slap shot is a howitzer but good intelligence and restraint in making the smart play to the net and it paid off. Great passer in all three zones. Blocks shots. Excellent decisions with the puck in all three zones. Plays strong in his own end. Great two-way game.

WAT #12 Zach Sanford LW/C (2013 WSH 61st Overall) - Great length, smooth, long, powerful stride and quick feet. Ton of poise, so good with the puck. Strong in his own zone, had two or three really heads up outlet passes.

GB #8 Dawson Cook LW (2013) - Aggressive on the forecheck and really strong defensively, had a good two-way game. Physical and chippy but plays smart, doesn't take penalties. Had a few offensive looks. Good passes, solid playmaking ability. Has really good chemistry with Schmaltz.

GB #9 Nick Schmaltz RW/C (2014) - Had shifts at both center and wing. As always, had the puck on a string. Such an incredible stick handler and so creative. Really hard taking the puck away from him. He was able to circle the entire offensive zone with the puck a few times. Has the ability to just circle around until he can find an open shot or open teammate. Sometimes will hang on to it too long and cough it up, but it worked tonight. I like his willingness to take the puck to the middle of the ice. Had a strong game on the boards. Highlight reel assist on the Weis goal. He brought the puck into the zone and curled just above the top of the circle toward the boards on his back hand. He drew a defenseman, forward, and got the other defenseman to drift to him, bought a couple of seconds and then saucered a perfect back hand pass over all their sticks to a streaking Weis he went in all alone for the goal. Great example of the space he creates for his line mates and his ability to find them. He did get caught being lazy and lackadaisical with the puck on the Sheehy goal. Was being real casual with the puck behind his own net and wasn't aware Sheehy was streaking toward him from behind and he completely pick-pocketed him and wrapped the puck for a goal. Really bad play and the kind of effort, or lack thereof, that drives you nuts about Schmatlz after doing other things so well in the same game or even same shift.

GB #10 Connor Hurley LC (2013 BUF 38th Overall) - Had the puck a ton in the offensive zone. Great hands and excellent control and comfort with the puck. Not afraid to drive the net but has the vision to peel back and find open teammates. Great vision and playmaking ability. Excellent skater and good defense game. Played the point on the power play which is the norm. Also had an exceptional hit on an opposing defenseman at the defensive blue line. He released the puck and Hurley skated through him and tossed him to the ice. Shoveled in a rebound goal in the final seconds of the game. Really fun player to watch. Plays well at both ends and is electric.

FINAL: 4-3 Waterloo

SCOUTS NOTES:

Back and forth affair with both teams trading times of carrying the play but all in all pretty evenly matched. Green Bay got a bit sloppy as the game progressed and allowed Waterloo to take over a bit. Continue to be impressed with Montour. His fingerprints are all over every game he's in.

Apr. 2, 2014 – Youngstown Phantoms vs. Chicago Steel (USHL)

YOU #12 J.J. Piccinich RW (2014) - Typical high energy, high motor game. Strong defensively, smart in his end. Good outs. Finished his checks. Aggressive on the forecheck and backcheck. Took hits to make plays.

YOU #7 Maxim Letunov LC (2014) - Really strong game in all areas. Good length, really good hands. Creates a lot of opportunities. Drew a penalty dangling a defenseman and getting pulled down in desperation to stop a scoring chance. Really deceptive speed. His lanky build and stride make it look he's not moving very quickly but he is, and he can explode with that quick step to hit the next gear and walk right around you. Carried the puck through traffic well. Good defensive support and while not lanky and thin, doesn't shy away from the physical game. Finished all of his checks, took hits to make plays, plays without fear.

YOU #18 Kyle Connor LC (2015) - Assisted on a power play tally. Excellent playmaking ability. He sees the ice so well and has such great hands and offensive instincts. World class offensive skill. Usually not afraid of contact but was shying away from hits a couple of times tonight. I'm not sure if he's fighting an injury of some kind or what but that's uncharacteristic of him.

YOU #44 Kiefer Sherwood RW/C (2013) - Notched a power play goal on a nice shot. Created a couple of other chances for himself, one on a really nice pass to himself. He chipped the puck with the just right amount of force past the Chicago defenseman and beat him to the puck behind him. Good burst of speed. Also got the secondary assist on the same goal Connor assisted on. Had a couple solid hits and played a good two-way game.

CHI #20 Artem Artemov LW (2015) - A rare off night as far as offensive opportunites and production but, as always, a maximum effort and strong defensive game. Broke up a lot of passes and did a good job of clogging the passing lanes. Backchecked and forechecked hard. Good game, just one of those nights offensively. Didn't get much going.

CHI #23 Robby Jackson LC (2015) - Was all over the ice as he often is. So speedy and shifty, strong skater and really quick feet. Plays hard at both ends. Protected the puck well and made good decisions. Really smart player, excellent hockey sense and awareness. Love how elusive he is with the puck. He's really tough to get a clean check on. Very slippery but also really strong, doesn't get knocked around. Always plays with an edge, fearless. Dropped the gloves and got the better of his foe. Love his game.

CHI #17 Fredrik Olofsson LW (2015) - Set up two goals and could've had even more helpers with some more finish from teammates. Saw the ice really well, excellent playmaking ability. Great vision and high hockey IQ. He plays with such poise and is just a calming influence when on the ice. He seems to slow the game down. Made really smart, talented plays pulling up just inside the blue lines and finding late attackers. One time it was on a line change and he not only was aware of the change, but was able to kill enough seconds to allow for them to get into the zone and dished it off for a good chance. Great feet, both as a skater and catching the puck. Was streaking down the neutral zone boards and caught a pass in his feet and kicked it up to his stick all without losing any speed and hardly breaking stride. High end offensive talent and great hockey sense. Creates so many offensive chances with his forechecking and aggressive pursuit of puck carriers. Has been a force since coming to Chicago from Green Bay. Plays a pro style game already.

CHI #28 Alec Vanko LD (2012) - Didn't get on the score sheet at all but had a nice game offensively no less. Snuck in the backdoor for a couple of what would have been great chances had the pucks been on the tape and allowed him an opportunity to shoot. Crafty veteran player with a really good head on his shoulders, plays smart. Excellent decisions, protects the puck. Sound defensive game, maintains good gaps and is just rock solid defensively with quiet, sneaky good offensive skill. Handles the puck really well and has a lot of confidence.

FINAL: 5-2 Chicago

SCOUTS NOTES: Excellent game by Chicago as a team, and some very good individual efforts. Continue to love Olofsson's rise since coming to Chicago. Love every part of his game and how he carries himself.

North Bay Battalion vs Barrie Colts – Game 3, April 8 2014

BAR #5 D Aaron Ekblad (2014) – Ekblad had a mediocre game by his standards. He had a couple nice rushes with the puck, and used his active stick to break up several chances, but overall he wasn't as good as I'm accustomed to seeing. There were a couple times where his mishandled the puck in the defensive zone and it resulted in a couple turnovers and some scoring chances against. He also missed a few breakout passes, though he was as good or better in that regard than normal. He was physical along the wall when he could be, and got into it pretty good with Ben Thomson on several occasions. He had a couple bombs on the PP that he wasn't able to convert, but was still a big threat.

BAR #21 LW Brendan Lemieux (2014) – Lemieux also had a mediocre game by his standards. He wasn't able to agitate and get under the skin of North Bay players as much as he usually does. He also had trouble getting the puck out of his zone a couple times in the 1st period, which led to some scoring chances against. As the game went on he started to settle in. He was good in front of the net, especially on the powerplay, and had a couple nice scoring chances in front on deflections. He also made a couple heady passes in the offensive zone that led to quality scoring opportunities. He played much better in the final 40, though he was called for a penalty. He jumped into a scrum to pull a North Bay player away and was given the lone minor. It was a pretty soft call and, luckily for Lemieux, did not cost the Colts.

BAR #12 LW Kevin LaBanc (2014) – LaBanc continues to impress me as this Colts playoff run continues. He used his speed, and displayed good hands while dancing around defenders on several occasions. He won a battle against Kyle Wood on the powerplay that led directly to 2-3 good chances. LaBanc had a couple nice give-and-go plays, and was dangerous in the slot area. He also showed off nice vision hitting a few streaking players with cross-ice passes in the offensive zone.

BAR #27 C Cordell James (2014) – He played a very solid two-way game. He was very effective on the forecheck, and won a couple battles for loose pucks that led to scoring chances in the net mouth area. He used his stick to break up plays while killing penalties, and always covered his man in the defensive zone. James isn't fancy, and won't wow you, but he plays his ass off every night and you always know what you're going to get.

BAR #26 LW Andrew Mangiapane (2014) – Mangiapane played a very solid game. He used his speed, and shiftiness to step around Wood and beat him wide with speed. He assisted on Jake Dotchin's 1st period goal, and was smart with the puck, keeping it simple rather than forcing plays that weren't there. As usual, he wasn't intimidated by bigger bodies, and was more than willing to battle for pucks in the corner despite his size. Mangiapane had a couple nice shifts on the penalty kill with Andreas Athanasiou, and was able to get pucks out whenever he had the opportunity.

BAR #28 W/C Zach Hall (OA) – Hall really impressed me with his game tonight. He's playing with a pretty bad ankle injury, and still managed to make a positive impact almost every shift. He was creative with the puck, finished his checks and back checked hard whenever necessary. Hall really put his ankle to work, and at times looked like he was playing in pain but continued to persevere. He scored a beautiful shorthanded goal as he undressed Jake Smith alone in front before potting his 5th goal in six playoff games this season.

NBY #18 C Mike Amadio (2014) – I thought Amadio played a solid two-way game. He made smart decisions, and rarely put the puck somewhere it'd put his team in trouble. At one point he turned it over and lost the puck to LaBanc, but he back checked hard and pick pocketed the puck before LaBanc was able to get a shot off. Amadio took a huge hit from Jake Dotchin, got up and made a play. He didn't look to retaliate, but rather to make a play that can help his team. Amadio was strong on the puck, and was good protecting it along the boards. He also displayed his nice release on a couple different occasions.

NBY #3 D Kyle Wood (2014) – Wood was beaten by speed a couple times, but he played a pretty solid game. He was physical in the corners, and did a good job separating Colts forwards from the puck to prevent any chances. He anticipated the game well, and picked off a couple passes as he moved in position to take them before they were even made. Wood also made a great defensive play preventing the Colts from even getting a shot attempt on a 2-on-1, as he broke up a centering pass, and erased what looked like a play that could have led to a goal. He was pretty safe with the puck, but at one point forced a bad pass and turned it over in the defensive zone as he tried to avoid a big hit.

NBY #1 G Jake Smith (2014) – Smith was excellent in this game and was the only reason it was close. He probably made 10 quality glove saves and was very calm in the crease. He rarely left a rebound, and when he did he recovered to make the 2nd and 3rd save. Smith stood on his head all game long and made several Grade A saves in the final 40 to give the Battalion a chance to get back in it. He may not have the size, but he's pretty athletic, positionally sound and never gives up on a play.

Notes: The Colts' 4th line played more in this game than any other to date...they were effective on the forecheck and had some good shifts when out against the Battalion's top defense pairing...Blujus and McIvor both played solid defensive games... they were real physical...Ben Thomson took a bad penalty late in the 3rd when the Battalion were still trailing 2-0...Thomson got into it pretty good with Ekblad a few times, and was very tough to move in front of the net...Barclay Goodrow was pretty quiet as he didn't generate much offensively...2014 draft eligible Zach Bratina was scratched...C.J. Garcia looked good while playing a regular shift with Liam Maaskant.

North Bay Battalion vs Barrie Colts – Game 4, April 10, 2014

BAR #5 D Aaron Ekblad (2014) – Ekblad got off to a slow start once again. He was tied up in front of his net by a Battalion forward, couldn't get free, and allowed Michael Amadio to walk in and score as a result. The Colts fell behind 3-0 pretty early and after that it seemed like he was trying to do too much. He made some good plays, but other times he tried to force passes or shots that weren't there. After the first, he really settled down. He was physical, good clearing the net on the penalty kill, and made some good plays with his stick defensively. He consistently knocked players off the puck, and had some nice rushes with it as well. Ekblad was good with zone entrances, too, as he safely carried the puck over the line and set up plays regularly. He had some nice blocks on the penalty kill, and skated the puck out of trouble whenever he needed to. Ekblad also showed leadership late in the game. Andrew Mangiapane found himself in a scrum with a much bigger player (didn't see who) and Ekblad skated over, brushed Mangiapane and confronted the Battalion player. Ekblad was also hit from behind at one point, and when Colts players went to retaliate Ekblad got up and sent them off so the Colts would get a powerplay.

BAR #21 LW Brendan Lemieux (2014) – For my money Brendan Lemieux was the best player on the ice. He had a hat trick and was instrumental in the Colts coming back from 3-0 and 4-1 down. He created havoc in front on the powerplay as he was screening Smith, and scored a pair of goals off deflections there. He blew his coverage on the Battalion's 3rd goal, but more than made up for it with his hat trick. He also played well defensively, besides that mishap. As usual, he finished his checks and was involved after the whistle. Lemieux took a blindside hit but was able to bounce up and continue playing. He had a couple quality chances while short handed, and displayed his good shot when he ripped an absolute laser bardown in the slot on the powerplay. He wasn't perfect, but he played an excellent game, and once again came through for Barrie when they needed him most.

BAR #26 LW Andrew Mangiapane (2014) – Mangiapane showed off his nice hands on a couple of occasions in this game. No time more so then when he was tripped up in the neutral zone and stickhandled around a couple North Bay players from his knees before passing it off to another player. He was shifty, and tough to contain in the corners, and won his fair share of battles against bigger players once again. Mangiapane played the point on the 2nd powerplay unit and looked relatively good in that role. Playing there allowed him to use his nice vision and playmaking ability. He also played regularly on the PK, and had a couple nice backchecks where he pick pocketed a Battalion player before clearing the zone.

BAR #12 LW Kevin LaBanc (2014) – He wasn't as impressive as he's been most nights during this playoff run, but he was effective once again. LaBanc won several battles along the boards, and used his speed to get around defenders on a couple different occasions. He also had a nice stick check where he poked it off a Battalion player, recovered the puck, and eventually recorded an assist on Tyson Fawcett's 3rd period goal.

BAR #27 C Cordell James (2014) – James didn't play much in the 1st as the Colts spent a good amount of time on the powerplay. He was used more frequently as the game went on, especially in the 3rd when Barrie couldn't stay out of the box. As usual, James played his game to a tee. He was able to get pucks out, finish his checks, and took care of his defensive responsibilities. There's not much flash in his game, but he knows his role and sticks to it.

NBY #18 C Michael Amadio (2014) – Amadio played a strong game, and was particularly good early on. He was able to make Barrie pay when he had time and space by finishing a play off in the slot with a goal. He was also able to regularly draw multiple defenders to him, before finding the open man to create a chance. Amadio was always the first forward back into his own zone, and was consistently there to help his defensemen out whenever necessary. He displayed nice vision and patience, waiting for lanes to open up before exploiting them.

NBY #3 D Kyle Wood (2014) – Wood played a real solid game on the backend for North Bay. He was sound defensively, especially in the 1st, and was good separating Colts players from the puck. Wood was steady defensively, but when seams opened up he wasn't afraid to exploit them. He jumped into the play early in the 2nd and sniped one over Blackwood, which gave the Battalion a 4-1 lead at the time. He played a regular shift on the penalty kill, and was the first defenseman used during a 5-on-3 kill. Wood also showed poise on the backend, as he was pressured hard a couple different occasions but managed to make a smart play with the puck and get it out rather than turning it over. He's not flashy, but he's effective.

NBY #1 G Jake Smith (2014) – Smith started the game off well, making a few big saves for North Bay before they exploded offensively and got him a few goals of support. He was gobbling up rebounds, and made a few flashy saves with his glove. The wheels fell off in the final 40, though, as North Bay took penalty after penalty, and eventually the Colts started to take advantage of that. He allowed seven goals, though four of them were on the powerplay.

Notes: Ben Thomson played an effective game...he had a goal, an assist and wanted to drop the gloves on two occasions, both times the refs came in...Mackenzie Blackwood was pulled for Daniel Gibl, who was good in relief...Zach Hall played an excellent game and was able to generate consistent offense...He had a goal and two assists...Barclay Goodrow took Aaron Ekblad inside out a couple times, and finished the game with a goal...Jake Dotchin played a good two-way game and pummeled Brett McKenzie pretty good in a fight.

North Bay Battalion vs Barrie Colts – Game 6, April 13, 2014

BAR #5 D Aaron Ekblad (2014) – Ekblad was not at all impressive in this game. He turned the puck over several times in his own zone, and looked quite shaky at times. He was burned wide with speed on several occasions. Ekblad also left his man (Ben Thomson) wide open on the 2nd goal, which happened to be the difference in this game. He did make a couple nice plays in the defensive zone with an active stick, and his outlet passes were OK, but it certainly wasn't his best showing. Ekblad also scored late in the 3rd on a blast from the point, but it was too little, too late from the Colts captain.

BAR #26 LW Andrew Mangiapane (2014) – Like most Colts, Mangiapane had a pretty quiet game. Due to North Bay's structured trap-like system, he rarely had space in open ice or in the offensive zone to make a play with the puck. He continued to show that he won't back down against bigger players, though, as he was involved in a few scrums and had a couple big hits on players much bigger than he was.

BAR #1 LW Brendan Lemieux (2014) – Lemieux was OK, not great in this game. He protected the puck well down low at times, and had some nice scoring chances. That said, there were a couple hiccups in the defensive zone, and offensively he couldn't capitalize on any of the few chances he had. He had a couple nice stops and starts, and showed his improved skating.

BAR #12 LW Kevin LaBanc (2014) – LaBanc was one of the few Colts forwards I felt made in impact in this game. He won races for loose pucks, battled in the corners, and had several chances in and around the net front area. He displayed good speed on a few occasions, and made some nice passes in the offensive zone that led to chances.

BAR #27 C Cordell James (2014) – James was used sparingly, but he was mostly effective when he saw ice. As usual, he kept his game simple – got in on the forecheck, used his body and battled along the wall. He had a couple nice chances as a result to strong play on the boards, and was good in his own zone as well. James always stayed with his man.

NBY #18 C Mike Amadio (2014) – Amadio was pretty quiet compared to past viewings, but he wasn't bad at all. He took care of business in the defensive zone, and always backchecked hard. He also made a smart pass to a Battalion player streaking towards the net, which led to the Colts taking a penalty. He also had a couple nice chances near the slot where he was able to get shots off quick because of his release.

NBY #3 D Kyle Wood (2014) – Wood played a sound defensive game and you didn't notice him much, which is good considering his style of play. He had an active stick in the defensive zone, and was physical along the boards when he needed to be. He did have a hiccup in the 1st, though, as after pick pocketing the puck from Mangiapane, he turned it over and it led to Hooey's goal. Wood was positionally sound on the penalty kill, and overall played a pretty solid game.

NBY #1 G Jake Smith (2014) – Smith definitely had help from his teammates clearing rebounds and getting the puck out of trouble, but he was excellent in this game. He made several big saves including a sprawling save when it looked like he was down and out. The Colts were the much better team in the 1st period, but Smith weathered the storm and had the game tied up entering the 2nd. Smith wasn't tested much in the 3rd, but he did his job in the first two periods keeping the Battalion in it and giving them a chance to win.

Notes: Barclay Goodrow had three minor penalties in the 1st period...Ben Thomson scored a pair of goals including a shorthanded breakaway goal, which was the game winner...Nick Paul was excellent, playing in all situations, scoring a goal and assisting on Thomson's 1st goal...Andreas Athanasiou tried to do too much and made a negative impact as a result.

April 17th, 2014 – Slovakia vs Russia (World U18)

RUS #10 – Nikita Lyamkin – Had a decent game but still has the glaring weakness of being weak in any sort of physical battle.

RUS #28 – Nazarkin, Yevgeni – Played a poised confident game today. Did make some mental mistakes reading plays poorly. Bad pinch and some crazy passes including a 6 footer in mid air that was totally unnecessary.

RUS #14 – Vovchenko – Went to net and showed some dynamic plays today.

RUS #16 - Vladislav Kamenev – Good size, good feet. Showe some smarts and natural instincts. Showed off a decent slapper and a one-timer from the slot.

RUS #7 – Yevgeni Svechnikov – Bad turnover at the top of slot in his own zone. Quick release. Quick hands. Shifty. Looked like a great skater. He was one of the best players on the ice today.

RUS #25 – Alex Protapovich – Showed some smarts. Good down low. Physical player. Skating not as good as a few of his forward teammates.

RUS #19 – Radel Fazleyev – Played smart. Good skater overall, quick. Decent wrist shot.

RUS #26 – Korshkov Yegor – Showed some poise with the puck. Looked smooth and shifty for a big kid. Flashed a nice toe drag.

RUS #12 - Pavel Kraskovski – Liked him. Worked his butt off. Not a ton of skill but played his role very well. Finished every check.

SVK #10 – Erik Cernak -Decent game today. Played better than the last time I saw him. Skating was smooth. Closed gaps and won battles.

SVK - #24 Radovan Bondra – Big kid who plays big. Was all around the puck and got involved in play.Was great on PK.Showed pretty quick feet for a big kid.

SVK - #28 – Kristian Pospisil – Scored a short-handed goal on a 2 on 1. Controlled the puck. Worked hard.

Scouts Notes: Several Russians had good games but the Slovaks gave them all they could handle by playing a very physical game.

April 19th, 2014 - Finland vs Switzerland (World U18)

FIN - #3 Miro Keskitalo - Positioned well in Dzone. Battles hard, is a real gamer. High compete level. Feet looked ok. Showed off a nice one-timer. Blaocked shots.

FIN - #24 Kasperi Kapanen -Speed was displayed on an impressive end to end rush, blew buy defenders. Let go a couple of laser shots.

FIN - #20 Teemu Lamsa - A bit of a knock kneed skater, ugly first few steps.

FIN - #26 Mikko Rantanen, - One of the best players on the ice. High work ethic, didn't see him lose a battle al game long. Worked hard in dirty areas and made good decisions with the puck coming out of the corners. He made good decisions with the puck on the powerplay. High end player.

FIN - #28 Juho Lammikko - Beat defender wide with speed and got a good shot away off the rush. Got better as game went on.

FIN - #10 Sebastian Aho - Scored on a slick wrap around play. Turned over a lot of pucks in the first period but played better after that. Has some skill.

SUI - #30 Gauthier Descloux - Not a huge kid but he battled hard and kept his team in it. Was square to shooters and showed good recovery ability to stop 2nd chances. He was quick in all facets.

SUI - #25 Roger Karrer - Played a physical game. Logged a lot of minutes. Made some poor plays under pressure. Decent Dzone awareness.

SUI - #9 Kevin Fiala - Unreal rush topped off a solid game. Made a slick backhand pass to the slot after a dangle to buy time. Good feet, quicker than you think he will be. Uses shifttiness to buy time. Quick hands. Cheated defensively a couple times.

SUI -#27 Noah Rod - Really liked this kid. He was good on P.K and plated smart effective hockey each shift. He was a productive player who created space for his skilled linemates. Will watch him closely.

Scouts Notes: Fiala, Kapanan and Descloux stole the show. Fiala and Kapanan showed why they should both be first rounders. Descloux made a name for himself as did Rod.

April 22, 2014, Finland vs. USA (U-18)

FIN # 25, F, Saarela, Aleksi – Saarela showed good speed through the neutral zone, and was able to find holes in the opposing defense. He took a pass from Kekitalo in the 2nd period, split two defenders and made a power move towards the net before beating Ndeljkovic for Finland's 2nd goal of the game. It was an excellent play from Saarela, and his ability to make a play with the puck at a high speed while having defenders all over him was impressive.

FIN # 16, F, Kalapudas, Antti – Kalapudas did a good job of attacking opposing players with the puck, and not allowing them time to get set and make a play. He was good when pushing the puck north south and keeping the game simple. At times he'd turn the puck over when trying to be fancy and step around defenders with toe drags or other high skill plays.

FIN # 24, F, Kapanen, Kasperi – Kapanen showed good speed and vision throughout this game. He was able to gain the line with speed, slow the game down and hit trailing teammates with passes on the tape. He made a nice cross-ice feed off the rush to an open man, but the shot attempt was fanned on and nothing came of it. Kapanen also made a nice play gaining the line with speed, avoiding a couple stick checks and dishing it over to Joel Kirivanta who made no mistake going shelf and giving Finland a 3-2 lead.

FIN # 19, F, Makinen, Miro – Makinen was able to read and react quickly, and showed good speed while killing penalties. He's a good skater going north south, and his ability to close on defenders in a hurry led to some turnovers. He was relentless attacking puck carriers, and displayed a non-stop motor.

FIN # 28, F Lamikko, Juho – Lamikko did a nice job carrying the puck up ice and into the offensive zone. He made smart plays with the puck, kept it simple and put pucks on net when he could. He assisted on the 1st goal by just throwing a puck towards the goal. Lamikko did a good job finding open space in front; as he slipped away from his man and was left wide open for a great chance on the doorstep. He had several quality chances in this game, but seemed snake bitten and couldn't find a way to get one to go.

FIN # 3, D, Keskitalo, Miro – Keskitalo showed a willingness to get in the shooting lanes early, as on his first shift he blocked a shot. He did a good job of eluding forechecks, and making good outlets to start the rush. Keskitalo made a nice read jumping into the play, driving the net and scoring the 1st goal of the game. Kekitalo was calm with the puck under pressure, and was able to regularly elude oncoming forecheckers. He made an exceptional pass to Saarela to send him through two defenders, which led to their 2nd goal.

FIN # 1, G, Kahkonen, Kaapo – Kahkonen did a nice job of keeping the Finns in this game. Early on USA was the much better team, but Kahkonen held down the fort. He showed off good athleticism stretching out to make some high-end saves, and he did a nice job of keeping on the post even with opposing players whacking at him on the doorstep. Kahkonen also did a nice job of tracking the puck, staying square to the shooter and making sure he was in position to make a play. Kahkonen allowed a goal in the final minute of all three periods, and looked surprised when Eichel threw a puck on net late in the 3rd.

USA # 11, F, Eichel, Jack – Eichel showed good skill coming off the wall, a willingness to go to the dirty areas, and drive the net. He was good protecting the puck, and put pucks on net every opportunity he had. Eichel misplayed the puck attempting to make a pass to a defenseman on the powerplay - which led to a turnover – but nothing came of it. Eichel did a great job of stickhandling around a couple defenders before throwing a puck on net from beside the crease late, which bounced off the goaltender's foot and in.

USA # 17, F, Tuch, Alex – Tuch took a bad holding penalty in the offensive zone right after the Americans drew a powerplay. Tuch showed good hands dragging the puck around a defender before getting a good shot off in the scoring area.

USA # 25, F, Conner, Kyle – Connor had some very good shifts cycling the puck, and drew a penalty behind the goal while doing so. His line generated scoring chances almost every time he was on the ice, as they were consistent threats on a shift-to-shift basis. Conner was in the right place at the right time and buried a rebound on the doorstep with less than a second to play in the 2nd period. He only finished the game with two shots, but he probably put 5+ pucks towards the goal throughout the game.

USA # 27, F, Milano, Frank – It seemed like every time he touched the ice surface he made something happen. He finished the game with an assist and two shots, but the stat line was deceiving. He consistently gained the opposing line with speed, and he was very creative with the puck. He cycled well, protected the puck well and created chances almost every shift. He was very shifty with the puck, and when nothing was there he'd simply cycle the puck around the boards to a teammate, or put the puck in a place where it wouldn't hurt his team.

USA # 7, F, Bjork, Anders – Bjork was one of the best players on the ice in this game. Almost every shift he was generating scoring chances, and he scored USA's 2nd goal of the game on an absolute rip from the slot. Bjork threw everything he could on net, and finished the game tied for a game-high with six shots.

USA # 19, F, Larkin, Dylan – He was confident carrying the puck ice, and was able to generate good speed through the neutral zone. This forced defenders to back off, and allowed Larkin to gain the offensive zone line with possession of the puck. Larkin also had a couple nice plays on the backcheck, and was able to force some turnovers as a result. He wasn't afraid to drive the net, and had some good chances in tight. He showed good speed breaking away from a defender and getting a mini-breakaway, which led to a powerplay the team capitalized on immediately.

USA # 21, F, Hitchcock, Ryan – Hitchcock turned it over early in the neutral zone doing too much, but Finland didn't capitalize. He was good along the boards on the cycle, and created a couple chances that way. Hitchcock also assisted on Bjork's goal early in the 1st period.

USA # 20, D, Hanifin, Noah – Hanifin moved the puck well up ice, made good outlets and wasn't afraid to carry the puck when he had to. He was sound defensively, as his positioning was good, and he used his stick well to break up plays. He also simply rubbed opposing players off the puck at times. He made a nice play up a man just throwing the puck in front. Luckily for him it hit someone in front and found its way into Finland's net, which tied the game for USA with three seconds remaining in the 1st.

USA # 5, D, Fortunato, Brandon – Fortunato did a nice job holding the line in the offensive zone. He kept several clearing attempts in the zone, which allowed his team to reset and create offense. Fortunato walked the line with composure, and did a good job of putting the puck in good places. He was smart with the puck, as he kept pucks low, got them through and shot for deflections.

USA # 16, D, MacLeod, John – He did a good job of finishing players off, and laying the body whenever he could. MacLeod rubbed opposing players of the puck on several occasions, and helped his team turn play up ice.

USA # 30, G, Nedeljkovic, Alexander – He didn't face a lot of rubber, and was kind of shaky when called upon. On the 1st goal he gave up it didn't look to be a dangerous shot, he lost track of the puck, didn't know where it was and by the time he realized he didn't have it, it was in the back of his net. At times his rebound control wasn't good, but he used his speed and athleticism to get back in position and find ways to stop the 2nd and 3rd shots.

Apr. 25, 2014 – Sioux City Musketeers vs. Waterloo Black Hawks (USHL)

SC #10 Jared Thomas LC (2012) – Assisted on the first goal in which he brought the puck in the zone with a good entry with control. Really good offensive skill. Handles the puck well and does a good job protecting it. Quick hands and mobile on his feet. Good size and really strong. Okay defensive game but could've been better. Questionable compete level at times but really good offensive skill and instincts.

WAT #12 Zach Stanford LW/C (2013 WSH 61st Overall) – Excellent game at both ends. Such a smooth, long, powerful stride and with the quick feet and mobility he is such a tough player to defend, especially with his size added into the mix. Great hockey sense. Assisted on the first goal, took a good shot from the slot that Hayton stopped and the rebound was put in.

WAT #22 Tyler Sheehy RC (2014) – Tallied a goal with the extra attacker. Gritty, pesky, two-way game. Strong at both ends. Not afraid of the tough areas, likes to camp out in front of the net. Speedy, shifty skater. Played a physical game. Not afraid to engage. Creative with the puck down low and in tight in traffic.

WAT #51 Mark Friedman RD (2014) – Rough game defensively for Friedman. Got completely walked by Olson on his goal. Was a nice move by Olson on the toe-drag but a play that should've been defended. Got caught looking at the puck and was flat-footed. He slammed his stick on the crossbar in frustration afterward. Rare miscue for Friedman. Seemed to be fighting the puck a bit all night and not as sharp with his decision making as usual. Did get an assist on the first goal along with Sanford.

WAT #61 Brandon Montour RD (2012) – His howitzer of a shot resulted in two assists tonight, both coming off of rebounds. His shot is heavy and gets off quick. Hayton fought both off but wasn't able to corral the rebound either time. Absolute rocket. Skated well. He has really good mobility and good wheels to go along with his slick hands and good offensive instincts. Created open shooting lanes and finds the soft spots in coverage. Extreme confidence handling the puck, made good decisions.

FINAL: 3-2 Waterloo

SCOUTS NOTES:

This was Game 1 of the series between these two excellent teams. Sioux City was without the services of Neal Pionk and Waltteri Hopponen. Very much a back and forth affair overall and very evenly matched. Brandon Montour continues to be on a tear offensively. Really impressive offensive skill and puck handling ability. With his size and offensive skill set he is a lot of fun to watch. Very creative and dangerous in the offensive zone.

April 25, 2014 – Portland Winterhawks at Kelowna Rockets (WHL)

WHL Western Conference Finals – Game #5

POR #7 LW Bittner, Paul (2015) - Paul played a good game from start to finish opening the game by forcing a turnover and turning it into an immediate scoring chance. He does an excellent job of reading the play and reacting which was giving him the inside track on Kelowna players all night. He cycled the puck then drove the net receiving a pass and turning it into a scoring chance. He displays good patience with the puck and doesn't panic and lets the play open up for him. He jumped up in the play and got a partial breakaway and scoring chance utilizing his powerful shot. While he didn't finish on any of his chances, his intelligent positioning, hockey sense and skilled helped open him up for several chances.

POR #23 LC Turgeon, Domenic (2014) - Turgeon generates decent speed when driving down the wing with the puck. He scored the opening goal of the game when he unleashed a hard shot creating a rebound that went off a Kelowna defender then into the net. He was a key defensive option for the Winterhawks playing big penalty kill situations including being the only forward on a big 5 on 3 kill. He struggled in the face-off circle finishing around 30%.

POR #28 LW Leipsic, Brendan (Nashville) - Brendan was noticeable scoring Portland's second goal of the game with a powerful one timer. He then walked in off the side wall and wound up for a slap shot scoring Portland's 5th goal of the game. Later in the third period Leipsic would be ejected for spearing an unsuspecting Kelowna player receiving 5 and a game after the game was virtually over and could have put himself out of the line-up to open the WHL Championship due to his lack of discipline which was on display throughout this series.

KEL #3 LD Stadel, Riley (2014) - Riley showed good speed rushing the puck up ice getting consistent shifts on the second power play. His decision making in regards to passing the puck off on the rush was very hit or miss. Unfortunately Portland's first goal of the game went off his skate and in while he was defending a forward in the slot. Riley sometimes tries to force passes in the defensive zone that aren't there.

KEL #10 RC Merkley, Nick (2015) - Nick was much quieter tonight overall, but picked up his play a little in the second making a great pass to create a big scoring chance in the shot. He also has a powerful shot.

KEL #14 LC Chartier, Rourke (2014) - Rourke constantly challenges defenders one on one winning some of these match-up's. One of which turned into a scoring chance when made a great play with his stick at the high point on the penalty kill to steal the puck then beat the defender one on one. Took a penalty trying to poke at the puck and got his stick caught in Pouliot's skates. Rourke got ice in all game situations and was the only forward used on a 4 on 3 penalty kill. Rourke was slightly over 50% in the face-off circle.

KEL #23 LW Kirkland, Justin (2014) - Justin was constantly noticeable finishing his checks and asserting himself along the wall. He is a good skater for a player of his size. Despite going down three goals in the third period, Justin was one of the hardest working players on the ice, continuing to battle and force turnovers. He showed good hands in the slot to pick up the puck in the slot and backhand it in on a tight angle on what would be the last goal of the season for Kelowna.

KEL #24 RC Baillie, Tyson (2014) - After a bit of a quiet game in Game #4 two days ago, Tyson really put together a solid game. He provided an excellent forecheck with decent skating ability to win races to pucks and physical battles for pucks. He kept the play going in the offensive zone winning battles and got the puck out of the defensive zone beating opposing forwards along the wall. He scored an outstanding goal batting the puck out of mid air while falling to the right of the Portland goal to open the scoring for Kelowna. Tyson was very good in the face-off circle winning approximately 70% of his face-off's

Scouts Notes: Both teams came out very competitive with the Portland Winterhawks leading the Kelowna Rockets 3-1 in this series. Portland got the edge early on and scored 3 quick goals late in the first period and early in the second period to take a 3-0 lead. Kelowna did an admirable job taking the momentum back and scoring twice to make it a 3-2 game going into the intermission. Heading into the third the Rockets seemed to have all the momentum, but for the second straight period, the Winterhawks scored in the first minute of the period and followed up with two more consecutive goals to secure what would end up being a 7-3 victory and yet another Western Conference Championship. Portland got support by several of their top players. Taylor Leier (Philadelphia) picked up a loose puck in the slot and scored Portland's third goal. He then made a solid pass to set up Portland's sixth goal. Olivier Bjorkstrand (Columbus) Made an excellent pass early in the third period to set up the game winning goal. Also, Nic Petan (Winnipeg) wasn't as big of a game-breaker tonight as he was earlier in this series, but he made a simply outstanding cross ice pass which set up Portland's second goal of the game.

April 26, 2014 – Medicine Hat Tigers at Edmonton Oil Kings (WHL)

WHL Eastern Conference Finals – Game #5

MH #11 RC Owre, Steven (2014) - Steven did a good job showing his bottom six potential at the next level. He provided a relentless backcheck all game long and plays a full 200 foot game. He gets into opponents faces and finishes checks. He competes along the wall and wins battles against bigger players. He is a good skater which helps him force more turnovers on the forecheck along with winning battles on the dump and chase. While his game is largely focused on a hard working two-way game, he did show some flashes of decent hands in the offensive zone.

MH #17 LW Penner, Blake (2014) - Blake played top unit penalty kill and was very effective getting in lanes and pressuring the points. He isn't a great skater but gets to where he's going effectively enough. In open ice he is all over the puck carrier. Blake was involved in a few offensive rushes but wasn't very dangerous in the offensive zone.

MH #21 RW Butcher, Chad (2014) - Chad was noticeable providing good defensive zone pressure in 5 on 5 situations. He was also willing to block shots.

EDM #24 RD Irving, Aaron (2014) - The first period was not kind to Irving tonight. He was most notable on two occasions making a bad D to D pass on the power play which nearly resulted in a short handed opportunity. Then in the final shift of the period he got too casual just lightly back-handing the puck off the boards, going directly to a Medicine Hat player who turned it into a scoring chance putting it off the post. He picked up his game the final forty minutes, but despite the improved play he still served up over a half dozen turnovers in his own zone the rest of the game with bad puck decisions in his own zone. Aaron's puck moving ability seemed to improve the further he got from his net and made one amazing pass as the "tac" in a tic-tac-toe play resulting in a goal on the power play. He has a hard shot from the point and while he loves to shoot the puck, he only utilized his shot when the lane was available. He made a great play coming off the bench to break up an odd man scoring chance. He displays average skating ability. Aaron commonly wasn't choosing the smart option with the puck when he had multiple options available to him. He consistently staggers appropriately, and usually doesn't try to force things at the offensive line and will get into defensive positioning preparing for the rush if the opposition appears they will be able to get out of the zone.

EDM #37 RD Mayo, Dysin (2014) - Dysin was used on the Oil Kings' top power play unit and moved the puck very well and likes to sneak in off the point and get into an open lane. He generally made the smart play with the puck on the power play all game long but made one notable mistake where he telegraphed his pass and was intercepted for a partial break short handed. Dysin is capable of rushing the puck up the ice and is a good skater with smooth direction changes. He didn't force the puck rushing game and was willing to make the safe play instead of forcing it. He has decent defensive zone positioning and gets into passing lanes effectively. He is aggressive below the goal line towards the puck carrier but can be a little too aggressive on the puck carrier at times losing his defensive positioning. He made a smart play in his own zone reading a play and jumping up to intercept a pass, turning it into a 3 on 1 rush for his team.

EDM #39 LC Pollock, Brett (2014) - Pollock got off to a bit of a slow start but he sure had a strong second half of the game. He displayed excellent vision and passing ability, maybe the most notable was a picture perfect cross ice pass from the side wall of the offensive zone through the slot to the far face-off dot in the zone initiating a tic-tac-toe goal that opened to scoring for Edmonton. He also has quick feet and is a good skater with a strong top speed, especially for a 6'2" forward. He did an outstanding job taking the puck from the corner, protecting it while driving the net, getting his shot off, then batting the puck out of mid air on the rebound to score Edmonton's second goal of the game. Brett then went to the net late in the third and banged home a rebound in the slot to give Edmonton a 4-3 lead and score the eventual Eastern Conference Championship winning goal. He delivered a few decent hits but is not very physical whatsoever for a forward of his size. He was also too casual on the backcheck and needs to improve his effort away from the offensive zone, however he easily the most impactful player in the offensive zone on either team in this critical playoff game.

Scouts Notes: A very tightly contested game by both teams, Medicine Hat was able to maintain the lead for the majority of the first half of the game despite being heavily out shot and out chanced. The Oil Kings were able to come back and take a 3-2 lead into the second intermission. Medicine Hat was able to tie the game but Brett Pollock (2014) scored with just over 5 minutes left. Then an extremely soft/questionable penalty call against Medicine Hat with 2 minutes left sealed the deal and will see the Edmonton Oil Kings advancing to the WHL Championship.

CREDITS

CREDITS

I want to thank all the people who helped put this book together. Thank you to all our NHL Draft Scouts: Ryan Yessie, Jérôme Bérubé, Kevin Thacker, Scott McDougall, Ron Berman, Jean Francois Dore, Sean White, Russ Bitely and Robert Blaine. I appreciate the countless hours in the rinks and the effort put in writing reports. The effort this year was fantastic.

Once again this year we travelled to rinks across Canada, USA and Europe. Our goal is to mirror what NHL scouting staffs do, albeit with a much smaller travel budget. In essence we try to act as though we are a 31st NHL team. With scouts based in numerous locations, we are able to scout hundreds of prospects. I travelled to Finland to attend the World under 18 Championship again this year. It's always one of my favorite events of the season. We also made our regular trips to all the other large events that take place during the scouting season.

As I write this, I just completed attending the 2014 NHL Combine in Toronto. It's an event I have attended for years and when we publish after the combine, we are able to include information from combine in our book.

I also want acknowledge the contributions of Kathy Kocur, Michelle Sturino, Steve Fitzsimmons, Justin Schrieber and our intern Todd Cordell. More hard work that is very much appreciated.

A shout out to those who prefer to remain behind the scenes but helped us with editing and all the other little details that are necessary to get through the season and put a book like this together.

Thanks to media staff from around the NHL, CHL, the USHL and to Hockey Canada who help us out and are a pleasure to deal with.

Mark Edwards
Founder & Director of Scouting

www.ingramcontent.com/pod-product-compliance
Lightning Source LLC
Chambersburg PA
CBHW062124160426
43191CB00013B/2191